ENGLISH NONCONFORMIST POETRY, 1660–1700

Edited by
George Southcombe

Volume 2

PICKERING & CHATTO
2012

Published by Pickering & Chatto (Publishers) Limited
21 Bloomsbury Way, London WC1A 2TH

2252 Ridge Road, Brookfield, Vermont 05036-9704, USA

www.pickeringchatto.com

BRITISH LIBRARY CATALOGUING IN PUBLICATION DATA

English nonconformist poetry, 1660–1700.
1. Religious poetry, English – Early modern, 1500–1700. 2. Political poetry,
English – Early modern, 1500–1700.
I. Southcombe, George.
821.4'08-dc22

ISBN-13: 9781851969654

Typeset by Pickering & Chatto (Publishers) Limited
Printed and bound in the United Kingdom by the MPG Books Group

CONTENTS

BENJAMIN KEACH, *WAR WITH THE DEVIL* (1673)

Date

First published 1673; licensed 24 November 1673 by Roger L'Estrange.[1]

Copy Text

K103 Benjamin Keach, *War with the devil: or The young mans conflict with the powers of darkness* (London: Benjamin Harris, 1673), pp. 15–195. Octavo.[2] This edition exists in two states, with minor differences. Beinecke Library classmark IJ K191 674 has catchword 'Of' on p. 19, Bodleian Library classmark Vet. A3 f.1915 has no catchword. The primary text used here is the Bodleian copy, noted as K103; the Beinecke copy is noted as K103 Beinecke.

Variants

The variants collated are: K103aA Benjamin Keach, *War with the devil: or, The young mans conflict with the powers of darkness* (London: Benjamin Harris, 1674); K103A Benjamin Keach, *War with the devil: or, The young mans conflict with the powers of darkness* (London: Benjamin Harris, 1675); K104 Benjamin Keach, *War with the devil: or The young mans conflict with the powers of darkness* (London: Benjamin Harris, 1676); K104 (ESTC R229873) Benjamin Keach, *War with the devil: or The young mans conflict with the powers of darkness* (London: Benjamin Harris, 1676) [the copy consulted, Congregational Library 35.3.32, is missing the title page, introductory matter and first ten and last two leaves of the text; according to the ESTC this edition ends the text on p. 206 before the Apostate's final reply]; K104A Benjamin Keach, *War with the devil: or, The young mans conflict with the powers of darkness* (London: Benjamin Harris, 1678); K104AB Benjamin Keach, *War with the Devil: or, The young mans conflict with the powers of darkness* (London: Benjamin Harris, 1680); K105 Benjamin Keach, *War with the devil: or, The young mans conflict with the powers of darkness* (London: Benjamin Harris, 1683);K106 Benjamin Keach, *War with the devil: or, the young mans conflict with the powers of darkness* (London: Benjamin Harris, 1684); K106A Benjamin Keach, *War with the devil: or, The young mans conflict with the powers of darkness* (London: S. Harris, 1691); Opie1 *Benjamin Keach, War with the devil: or the young mans conflict with the powers of darkness* (London: Benjamin Harris, 1695); K106B *Benjamin Keach, War with the devil or, The young man's confllict with the powers of darkness* (London: Benj. Harris, 1700); K107 Benjamin Keach, *War with the devil: or, The young man's conflict with the powers of darkness* (Belfast: Patrick Neill and Company, 1700).

Context

Benjamin Keach's *War with the Devil* was first published in 1673, and it was phenomenally popular (the bookseller John Dunton later opined that he thought it would 'sell to the end of Time.').[3] A verse preface signed E.B. defends poetry against the charge that it is necessarily prophane and thus vindicates Keach's use of the medium:

> Though some there be that Poetry abuse,
> Must we therefore not the same method use?
> Yes sure, for of Science it is the best,
> And doth deserve more Honour than the rest:
> For 'tis no Humane knowledge, gain'd by Art,
> But rather 'tis inspir'd into the heart
> By Divine means, for true Divinity
> Hath with this Science great Affinity[4]

Keach thus sought to harness poetry, which was certainly used for some prophane purposes in Restoration England, for godly ends. In particular, he 'intended' his work for 'the Instruction of the Younger-sort.'[5] Keach's poem details the travails of a young man and ultimately his religious conversion. The poem makes it clear that, in fact, the youth is on the cusp of manhood, and in some later editions of *War with the Devil* he is depicted on the frontispiece as sixteen years old.[6]

Keach, having examined the troubles that might beset the young, included as an appendix to the poem a dialogue between an aged apostate and a young professor. As Keeble argues, in this dialogue Keach sought to demonstrate 'the tenacity required of the saint: he must be not merely bold in undertaking his pilgrimage and watchful in pursuing it but also resolutely determined to complete it.'[7]

Finally, it should be noted, given Keach's fame for his contribution to this area, that most later variants of *War with the Devil* include a series of hymns (see below, p. 129).[8]

Sources

Keach appears to have drawn on both AV and the Geneva Bible in his poem. When it appears that he used the Geneva Bible this has been indicated in the notes. The poem contains a large series of borrowings from the *Emblemes* of

Francis Quarles (1592–1644), which were first published in 1635. Quarles's work was enduringly popular, and given that Keach at times reproduced his words almost verbatim, early readers may well have been aware of these borrowings. However, Keach interwove Quarles's words with his own theological, pastoral and educational preoccupations, giving them a distinctive Particular Baptist meaning. In the appendix containing the dialogue between the apostate and the young professor, Keach turned to the history and martyrology of the true Church. At one point in his account of the Waldensians he specifically cited the work of Samuel Morland.[9] However, even in writing about this group not all of his details are taken from a single sources, and it seems clear that he amalgamated and versified a number of different accounts of the sufferings of the true Church through the ages.

Notes

1. E. Arber (ed.), *The Term Catalogues, 1668–1709* 3 vols (London: Edward Arber, 1903–6), vol. 1, p. 147.

2. This edition was to be sold by Robert Clavell in Little Britain for 1s 6d: Arber (ed.), *The Term Catalogues, 1668–1709*, vol. 1, p. 147.

3. J. Dunton, *The Life and Errors of John Dunton* (London: S. Malthus, 1705), p. 732 (this is the page number given; it is incorrect but Dunton's pagination is so erratic that it is still the most helpful reference to provide: it follows pp. 241–36 (*sic*) and comes before p. 238 (which is appearing for a second time)).

4. Benjamin Keach, *War with the Devil* (London: Benjamin Harris, 1673), sig. A3r. See also the comments of N.H. Keeble, *The Literary Culture of Nonconformity in Later Seventeenth-Century England* (Leicester: Leicester University Press, 1987), p. 186.

5. Keach, *War with the Devil*, titlepage.

6. S. Achinstein, *Literature and Dissent in Milton's England* (Cambridge: Cambridge University Press, 2003), p. 20.

7. Keeble, *The Literary Culture of Nonconformity*, p. 275.

8. see also the comments of J. R. Watson, *The English Hymn: A Critical and Historical Study* (Oxford: Clarendon Press, 1997), pp. 110–14.

9. S. Morland, *The History of the Evangelical Churches of the Valleys of Piemont* (London: Adoniram Byfield, 1658); see Keach, *War with the Devil*, pp. 98–9, below.

War with the Devil:
OR THE
Young Mans Conflict
WITH THE
Powers of Darkness.

In a Dialogue,
Discovering the corruption and vanity of Youth, the horrible nature
of Sin, and deplorable condition of fallen Man.
Also, a Definition, Power, and Rule of Conscience, and the Nature of
true Conversion.

To which is added,
An Appendix, containing a Dialogue between an Old Apostate, and
a Young Professor.

Worthy the Perusal of all, but chiefly intended for the Instruction of
the Younger-sort.[a]

By *B. K.*[b]

Psal.119.v.9. *Wherewithall shall a Young-man cleanse his way?*
By taking heed thereto according to thy Word.

Licensed, and Entred according to Order.

London, Printed for *Benjamin Harris*, and are to be sold at the Sign
of the Stationers-Armes in *Bell-Alley* in *Coleman-street*.
Anno Dom. 1673.[c]

Youth in his Unconverted State.

Youth.

The *Naturalists* most aptly do compare
My age unto the Spring, whose beauty's rare,
When *Sol* enters into[a] the golden Sign
Which is call'd *Aries*, his glorious shine
And splendent[b] rays do cause the Earth to spring,
And Trees to bud, and quickens[c] every thing.
All Plants and Herbs and Flowers then do flourish,
The grass doth sprout, the tender lambs to nourish
Those things in Winter that seem'd to be dead,
Do now rise up and briskly shew their head,
And do obtain a glorious[d] Resurrection
By *Sol's*[e] hot beams, and powerful Reflection.
How in the pleasant fruitful Month of *May*,
Are Meadows clad with Flowers rich and gay:
And all Earth's Globe adorn'd in garments[f] green,
Mix'd with rare yellow, crown'd like to a Queen
The Primrose, Cowslip, and the Violet,
Are curiously with other Flowers set.
And chirping Birds with their melodious sounds
Delight mans heart, whose pleasure now abounds.
The Winter's past, with stormy Snow and Rain,
And long 'twil be e'er such things come again;
Nought now save[g] joy and sweet delights appear,
Whilst doth abide the Spring-time of the year.[1]
    Thus 'tis with me who am now in my prime,
In merriment and joy I spend my time:
And, like as Birds do in the lovely Spring,
I so rejoyce with my Consorts and Sing,
And spend my days in sweet pastime and mirth,
And nought shall grieve or trouble me on Earth;
I am resolv'd to search the world about,
But I will suck the sweetness of it out.[2]
No stone I'le leave unturn'd, that I may find
Content and joy unto my craving mind:
No sorrow shall, whilst I do live, come near me,
Nor shall the Preacher with his Fancies fear me:[3]
At Cards & Dice, and such brave Games I'le play,[4]
And like a Courtier[5] deck my self most gay,

With Periwig, and Muff, and such fine things,
With Sword and Belt, Goloshoos,[6] and gold-Rings:
Where Bulls & Bears they bait,[7] and Cocks do fight[8]
I do resort with speed, There's my delight.
To drink, and sport amongst[a] the jovial crew,
I do resolve, what ever[b] doth ensue;
And court fair Ladies that I also love;[9]
And of all things do very well approve:
Which tend my sensual part to satisfie,
From whence comes all my choice felicity.[10]
What e're mine Ears do hear, and[c] Eyes behold,
Or Heart desire, if so that all my Gold
And Silver can for me those things procure,
I'le spare no cost nor pains you may be sure,
Thus is my Life made very sweet to me,
Whilst others hurri'd are in miserie,
Whose minds with strange conceits troubled remain
Thinking by losing all, that way to gain.
Such Ridles I can't learn, I must them leave,
What's seen and felt, I am resolv'd to have;
Let ev'ry man his mind and fancy fill,
My Lust I'le satisfie, and have my Will.[11]
Who dares controul me in my present way,
Or vex my mind i'th' least, or me gain-say?
What state of life can equal this of mine?
Youths galantry so bravely here doth shine.

Conscience.

Controul you, Sir! in truth and that dare I,
For your contempt of my Authority.
You tread on me without the least regard,
As if I worthy was[d] not to be heard;
You strive to stifle me, and therefore I
Am forc'd aloud *Murder* with speed to cry:
I can't forbear but must[e] cry out amain,
Such is the wrong which from you I sustain.

Youth.

What are you, Sir, you dare to be so bold?
I scorn by any he, to be controul'd.
E're I have done with you, I'le make you know,
You shall your Power and Commission show.

Conscience.

Be not so hot, and you shall know my Name,
And also know[f] from whence my Power came.

I'am no Usurper, yet I do Command
You for to stop and make a present stand.
Your Pleasures you must leave and Vitious life,
Else there will grow a very bitter strife
'Tween you and I, as will appear anon,
If from these Courses you don't quickly turn.
For all your courage which you seem to take,
The news I bring is^a enough to make you quake.

Youth.

Who e're thou art, I'le make you by and by,
Confess you have accus'd me wrongfully.
From Murder I am cleer in thought and deed,
Thus to be charg'd, doth cause my heart to bleed;
Pray let me crave your Name if you are free,
If you provoke me, worse 'twill quickly be;
You seek occasion, and are quarrelsome,
And therefore 'tis I do suppose you'r come.
But if your Name you don't declare to me,
I am resolv'd to be reveng'd on thee.

Conscience.

What violence (alas!) can you do more,
Than that which you have done to me before?
Forbear your threats, be still and hold your hand,
And quickly you shall know and understand,
My Name, my Power, and place of Residence,
Which may to you prove of great consequence.
I am a Servant to a Mighty King,
Who Rules and Reigns and Governs every thing,
Who keeps one Court above, and here be-low
Another he doth keep, as you shall know.
O're this inferiour Court placed am I,[12]
To Act and do as his great Deputy.
I truly Judge according to my Light,
Yea, and impartially do each man right.
Those I condemn who vile and guilty are,[13]
And justifie the Holy and Sincere.
I order'd am to watch continually
O're all your Actions with a wary eye:
And I have found how you here^b of late time,
Committed have many a horrid^c Crime
Of Murder, Treason and like Villany
Against the Crown and glorious Dignity
Of that great Prince from whence you have your breath,
Who's King & Ruler over all the Earth.
I am his Judge, Attourney-General,
And have Commission also you to call

Unto the Bar, and make you to confess
Your horrid crimes, and fearful guiltiness.
A black Indictment I have drawn in truth,
Against thy self thou miserable Youth;
Thy Pride I shall abate, thy Pleasures[a] mar,
And bring thee to confess with tears at Bar,
Thy Sports and Games and youthful Lust to be,
Nought else but Sin and cursed Vanity.[14]
And for to put thee also out of doubt,
My Name is *Conscience*, which you bear about,
No other than th'[b] accusing faculty,
Of that dear Soul which in thy Brest doth lie:
I by that Rule mens thoughts and ways compare,
By which their inward parts enlightn'd are;
And as they do accord, or disagree,
I do Accuse or Cleer immediatelie.[15]
According to your Light you do not live,
But violate that Rule which God doth give
To you, to square your life and actions by,
From hence[c] comes in your wo and misery.

Youth.

Conscience art thou! why did'st not speak e're now?
To mind what thou dost say I can't tell how.
Thou melancholly fancy, fly from me,
My Pleasures[d] I'le not leave in spite of thee.
Other brave Guests, you see, to me are come,
And in my house for thee there is no Room.
Dost think I will be check'd by silly thought,
And into snares my foolish fancy brought?
Is't you which cry[e] out *Murder*, only you?
A Fig (alas!) for all that you can do.
For though against me you do Prate and Preach,
Your very neck I am resolv'd to stretch.
I'le swear, carrouse, and whore, say[f] what you will,
Till I have stifled you, and made[g] you still.
I'le clip your wings, and make you see at length,
I do know how to spoil you of your strength.
When you do speak, I will not lend an ear:
I'le make (in truth) as if I did not hear.
If you speak loud when I am all alone.
I will rise up, and straightway will be gone
To the brave Boys, who toss the Pot about,[16]
And that's the way to wear your patience out.
I'le go to Plays, and Games, and Dancings too,
And e're a while I shall be rid of you.

Conscience.

Thou stubborn foolish youth, be not so rash,
Lest ere you be aware you feel my lash.
I have a sting, a whip, yea and can bite,
Before you shall o'recome, I'le stoutly fight:
I'le gripe you sore, and make you howl anon,
If you resolve in sin still to go on.
I have o'recome strong hearts and made them yield,
And so shall you before I quit the field.[17]
Go where you will, be sure I'le soon come after,
And into sorrow will I turn your laughter.
'Twill prove hard work for you to shake me off,
Though you at me do seem to jear and scoff,
As if o're you I had no Jurisdiction,
Or was a Dream, a Fancy, or some Fiction:
For all your Wrath, I must you yet disturb;
Though you offended are, I can't but curb
And snib[18] [a] you daily, as I oft have done,
Till you repent and from lewd courses turn:
For, till the Cause[b] be taken quite away,
Th' Effect will follow what ere you do or say:[c]
Unless your Light wholly extinguish'd be,
If sin remains, disturbance you will see.[19]
Therefore I do beseech you soberly,
For to subject[d] to my Authority;
Obey my voice, I prithee make a trial,
Before you give another flat denial.
If more sweet comfort I don't yield to you,
Than all which doth from sinful actions flow.
Then me reject: but otherwise, my Friend,
My Checks receive, and to my Motions bend.
Get peace within whatever thou dost do,
And let vain Pleasures and Corruptions go;
That will be better for thy Soul at last,
Than Gold or Silver, or what else thou hast.[20]
And since we are alone, let thee and I
More Mildly talk about Supremacy.
Is't best for you that Pride and Folly reign,
Which nought doth bring save sorrow shame and pain,
And Conscience to reject, who perfectlie
From guilt and bondage strives[e] to set you free?
Have not these Lusts by which thou now art led,
Brought many men[f] unto a peice of bread?
What brave Estates have some consum'd thereby,
And now are forc'd in Barns on[g] Straw to lye?
How has the Wife been ruin'd with the Child,
Besides poor Conscience grievously turmoyl'd?

Nay, once again, give ear, I prithee hark;
Hant[a] many a brave and curious Spark[21]
Been brought in stinking Prisons there to lye,
For yielding to their Lust and Vanity?
How many swing at *Tyburn*[22] every year,
For stabbing Conscience without care or fear?
And some also out of their Wits do run,
And by that means are utterly undone:
Sometimes men stifle[b] me, I cannot speak,
And then they sport and play and merry make,
Resolving that I shall not gripe them more;
But quickly then a fresh I make them roar.
Some of them I do drive into despair,
When in their face I do begin to stare;
No rest nor peace at all their Souls can find,
I so disturb and still perplex their mind.
What say you now, young-man, will you submit?
Weigh well the danger and the benefit.
The danger on the one hand will be great,
If me you do oppose and ill intreat.
Sweet profit comes, you see, on th' other hand,
To such who subject are to my[c] Command.
What dost thou say, Shall I embraced be?
Or, wilt thou follow still thy Vanitie?

Youth.

   Was ever young-man thus perplex'd as I,
Who flourished in sweet prosperity?
Where e're I go, *Conscience* dogs me about,
No quiet I can have in doors nor[d] out.
Conscience, what is the cause you make such strife,
I can't injoy the comforts of my life?
I am so grip'd and pinch'd in my brest,
I know not where to go, nor where to rest.

Conscience.

   'Cause you have wronged and offended me,
Loving vain Pleasures and Iniquitie.
The Light you have, you walk not up unto,
You know 'tis evil which you daily do.
My witness I must bear continually
For the great God, whose glorious Majesty
Did in thy Soul give me so high a place,
As for to stop you in your sinful race;
I must reprove, accuse, and you condemn,
Whilst you by sin his Sov'raignty contemn:
I can't betray my tryst,[e] nor hold my peace,

Till I am stabbed, sear'd,[a] or Light doth cease;
Till you your life amend, and sins forsake,
I shall pursue you, though your heart doth ake.

Youth.

How bold and malipert is *Conscience* grown;
Though I upon this Fellow daily frown
And his Advice reject, yet still doth he
Knock at my door, as if he'd weary me.
Conscience I'le have you know in truth that I
A Person am of some Authority
Are you so saucy as to curb and chide
Such a brave Spark, who can't your ways a bide?
Tis much below my Birth and Parentage,
As[b] it agrees not with my Present Age;
For to give Place to you, or to regard
Those things from you I have so often heard.

Conscience.

Alas, Proud flesh, dost think they[c] self too high
To be subject to such a one as I?
Thy betters I continually gain-say,
If they my Motions don't with care obey.
My Power's great, and my Commission large,
There's scarce a man but I with Folly charge.
The King and Peasant are alike to me,
I favour none of high or low degree:
If they offend, I in their faces fly,
Without regard or fear of standers-by.

Youth.

   Speak not another word, don't you perceive
There's scarce a Man or Woman will believe
What you do say, you're grown so out of date,
Be silent then and longer do not prate.
I'th' Country your credit is but small,
There's few cares[d] for your company at all:
The Husband-man the Land-mark can't remove,[23]
But you straightway him bitterly reprove;
Nor Plow a little of his Neighbors Land,
But you command him presently to stand.
There's not a man can go i'th' least awry,
But out against him fiercely you do fly.
The People therefore now so weary are,
They've thrust you out almost of ev'ry Shire;
And in the City you so hated be,
There's very few do[e] care a rush for thee:
For if they should believe what you do say,
Their Pride and Bravery would soon decay;

Their swearing, cheating, and their drunkenness,
Would vanish quite away, or grow much less.
Our craft of Profit, and our pleasure too
Would soon go down and ruin'd be by you.
The Whores[a] and Bawds, with the Play-houses then
Would be contemned by all sorts of men.
You strive to spoil us of our sweet delight,
Our Pleasures you oppose with all your might.
The Fabrick of our Joy you would pull down,
And make our Youth just like a Country Clown.[24]
We half Phanaticks[25] should be made ('tis clear)
If unto thee we once inclined were.
But this amongst the rest doth chear my heart,
There's very few in *London* take thy part.
Here and there one, which we nick-names[b] do give,
Who hated are, and judg'd not fit to live.[26]
'Tis out of fashion grown, I daily see
Conscience for to regard i'th' least degree.
He that can't whore and swear without controul,
We do account to be a timerous Fool.
Therefore though you so desperately do fall
Upon poor me, yet I do hope I shal
Get loose from you, and then I'le tear the ground,
And in all joy and pleasure will abound.

Conscience.

Ah! poor deceived Soul! dost thou not know,
That most of all mankind i'th' broad-way go?[27]
What though they do most wickedly abuse me?
Wilt thou also in the like manner use me?
What though they will of me no warning take,
'Till they drop down into the *Stygian* Lake?[28]
Wilt thou be-friend the cursed Serpent so,[29]
As to go on till comes[c] thy overthrow?
What though I am in no request by them?
Don't they likewise Gods holy Word contemn?
Don't they the Gospel cast quite out of sight,
Lest from their Pleasures it should them affright?
What though my friends are tost about and hurl'd
Their inward peace is more than all the World
Can give to them, or from them take away,
Whilst they with diligence do[d] me obey;
As I enlightned am by God's Precepts,
Which is[e] a guide, and Lanthorn to my steps.[30]
O come proud heart, and longer don't contend,
But leave thy Lust, and to my Scepter bend:
For I'le not leave thee, but with all my pow'r
I'le follow thee unto thy dying hour.

Youth.

Into some private place then I will fly,
Where I may hide my self, and secretly
There I'le enjoy my self in spite of thee,
And thou shalt not i'th' least know where I be.

Conscience.

Nay, foolish Youth, how can that thing be done,
From *Conscience* it is in vain to run.
No secret place can you find out or spy
To hide you[a] self from me, such is mine eye,
I see i'th'[b] Dark as well as in the Light,
No doors nor walls will keep thee from my sight.
Where e're thou art or go'st, am I not near,
Thy Soul with horrid guilt to scar[c] and fear?
Could *Cain* or *Judas* get out of my reach,[31]
When once between us there was the like breach?
Did I not follow them unto the end,
And made them know what 'twas for to offend
My Glorious Prince, and me his true Viceroy,
Vengeance doth follow them who US annoy.
My Counsel then I prithee take with speed,
For that's the way alone for to be freed
From Vengeance here, and Wrath also to come
When thou dost die, and at the day of Doom.

Youth.

What! can't I fly from thee, nor the[d] subdue?
Then I intreat thee, *Conscience*, don't pursue
Nor follow me so close, forbear a while,
Don't yet my beauty, nor my Pleasures spoil.
This is my Spring and Flower of my Age,
Oh! pity me, and still[e] thy bitter rage:
Don't crop the tender bud, it is too green;
Oh! let me have those days others have seen.
Forbear thy hand, till my wild Oats are sown;
They must be ripe also before they'r mown.
Thou hast forborn with some for a long time
That which I ask of thee is but the prime
Of those good days which God bestows on me,
Oh! that it might but[f] once obtained be!
'Tis time enough for to adhere to thee,
After I've spent my time in Gallantrie,
In earths sweet joys, & such transcendent pleasures
Which young-men do esteem the chiefest treasures.[32]

Conscience.

After all violence and outrage great
Done to poor *Conscience*, you begin to treat;[a]
Thinking for to prevail by flattery,
But that in truth I utterly defy,
'Tis quite against my nature; you must know
Unto vile Lust fond pity for to show;
God has not given such such a dispensation
For me to wink at your abomination:
If God doth once but blow your Candle out,
I shall be quiet then you need not doubt;
(But wo to you as ever you were born,
If God doth once his Light to Darkness turn.)[33]
But while in you remains that legal Light,[34]
Your sins I can't endure in my sight.
No liberty God, I am[b] sure, will give
To any one in horrid sin to live;
Nor will he give allowance for a day:
'Tis very dangerous for to delay
The work of thy Repentance for an hour.
What thy hand finds to do, do with thy pow'r.[35]
If me you don't believe, I prithee, Youth,
For to resolve thy self, go to Gods Truth.

Youth.

Well! since that you no comfort do afford,
I will enquire of God's most Holy Word:
So far I will your Counsel take, for I
Am sorely troubled, whither shall I fly?[36]
I will make tryal, I resolve to see,
Whether the[c] *Truth* and *Conscience* do agree.
The lip of Truth can't lye, though Conscience may:
When that misguided is, it[d] leads astray.[37]
If *Truth* and *Conscience* speak the self-same thing,
'Twill some amazement to my Spirit bring.
That now I ask for, and earnestly crave,
Is some short time in sin longer to have.
Conscience denies it me: *Truth*, what say you?
Oh! that you would a little favour shew
To a poor Lad, alas! I am but young,
Like to a Flower which is lately sprung
Out of the ground, and *Conscience* day and night,
Strives for to tread me down with all his might:
Or, as the Frost the tender bud doth spoil;
So has he striven to do a great while.
Must I reform, and all my sins forsake?
Some fitter season then O let me take.
For all things there's a time under the Sun,[38]
And when I older am, I will return.

Truth.

Nay, hold, vain *Youth*, you are mistaken now,
No time to sin God doth to thee allow.
If I may speak, attend, and you shall hear,
I with poor *Conscience* must my[a] witness bear,
I am his guide, his rule, 'tis by my Light
He acts and dos, and speaks the thing that's right.
You are undone, if you don't speedily
Leave all your sins, and cursed vanity.
Art thou too young thy evil wayes to leave
And yet hast thou a precious Soul to save?
Art thou too young to leave iniquity,
When old enough in Hell for sin to ly?
Some fitter season (Youth) dost think to find?
The Devil doth dart that into thy mind.
No time so fit as when the Lord doth call:
Those who rebellious are, they one day shall
Smart bitterly for their most horrid evil
In yielding to, and siding with the Devil.
But once again, I[b] prithee heark to me;
Don't God, whilst thou art young, call unto thee?
Remember thy Creator therefore now,[39]
And unto him with speed see you do bow.
The first ripe Fruit of old, God did desire:[40]
And so of thee likewise he doth require,
That thou to him a Sacrifice shouldst[c] give
Of thy best days, and learn betimes to live
Unto the Praise of his most Holy Name,
And not by Sin so[d] to prophane the same.
This is (Young-man) also thy choosing time,
Whilst thou therefore dost flourish in thy prime,
Place thou thy heart upon the Lord above,
And with Christ Jesus also fall in love.
Did not *Jehovah* give to thee thy breath,
And also place thee here upon the Earth,
And many precious Blessings give to thee,
That thou to him alone shouldst subject be?[41]
God out of Bowels sent his precious Son,
Thy Soul from evil ways with speed to turn;
Who for thy sake was nailed to the Tree,
To free thy Soul from Hell and miserie.
And whilst in sin (vile wretch) thou dost remain,
Thou dost as 'twere him Crucifie again:
Thy sins also (O young-man God doth hate
His Soul doth loath and them abominate.
Nought is more odious in his blessed sight,
Than those base lusts in which thou tak'st delight.

And wilt thou not, Oh young-man! be deterr'd
From thy vain ways? what, is thy heart so hard!
Shall nothing move thy Soul for to repent,
Nor work Convictions in thee to relent?
Give ear to *Truth*, Truth never spoke a lie,
And fly from sin and youthful Vanity.[42]
Those that do seek God's Kingdom first of all,
     And do obey God's sweet and gracious Call,
They shall find Christ, and ly too in his brest,
And reap the comfort of Internal[a] rest.
But if thou should'st this golden time neglect,
And all good motions utterly reject,
And slight the day of this thy Visitation;
That will to God be such a Provocation,
That he'l not wait upon thee any more,
Nor never knock hereafter at thy door.[43]
Whilst[b] tearms of peace God doth therefore afford
Subject[c] to him, lest he doth draw[d] his Sword.
If once to anger him you do provoke,
He'l break your bones, and wound you with his stroke:
Who can before his indignation stand,
Or, bear the weight of his revengeful hand?
How darest thou a War with him maintain,
And say o're thee Christ Jesus shall not Reign.
Wilt thou combine with his vile Enemy,
And yet presume on his sweet clemency?
Wilt thou, vile[e] Traytor like, contrive the death
Of that great King, from whom thou hast thy breath,
Wilt thou cast dirt upon the Holy One,
And keep Christ Jesus from his rightly[f] Throne?
Is't not his Right thy Conscience for to sway?
Ought he not there to Reign, and thou Obey?
Dar'st thou resist his dread and[g] Soveraign Pow'r?
Yea, or hold parley with him for an hour,
To gratifie the Devil, who thereby
Renews his strength, yea and doth fortifie
Himself in thee, and makes his Kingdom strong,
By tempting thee to sin whilst thou art young?
The Blackamoor as soon[h] may change his skin,
As thou mayst leave and turn away from sin,
When once a habit and a[i] custome's tak'n,
Then sinful ways are hard to be forsak'n.[44]
Dar'st thou, vile wretch, Christ's Government oppose,
And with the Devil and corruption close?
Hadst rather that the Devil reign o're thee,
Than unto God Almighty subject be?
Which will be best, dost think for thee i'th' end,

The Lord to please, and Satan to offend?
Or Satan for to please, and so thereby
Declare thy self *JEHOVAH'S* Enemy?
For those who live in sin, 'tis very clear,
They Enemies to *GOD* and *JESUS* are.
And wilt thou yield unto the Devil still,
And greedily also his will fulfil?
Dost think, *vain youth*, he'l prove to thee a freind,
That thou dost so his cursed waies commend?
Has Sin, which is his odious excrement,
So sweet a smell, yea and a[a] fragrant scent?
Shall that which is the superfluity
Of naughtiness, be precious in thine eye?
And dost thou value Christ and all he hath,
Not worth vain pleasures here upon the Earth
Shall he esteemed be by thee (vile dust!)
Not worth the pleasures of a cursed Lust?
Is there more good in sinful Vanity,
Than is in all the glorious Trinity?
That which men think is best, that will they chuse
Things of small value 'tis they do refuse.
What thoughts hast thou of Christ then, sinful Soul,
That thou his Messengers dost thus controul
And dost to him also turn a deaf[b] ear,
His knocks, his calls, and wooings wilt not hear;
Nor him regard, though he stands at thy[c] door
With Myrrh and Frankinscense, yea and all store
Of rare Fruit, and chief Spice, as *Cinnamon,*
Aloes, Spikenard, Camphire and *Saffron;*[45]
All precious things (poor Soul!) of Heaven above
He has with him, yet nothing will thee move
To ope[d] the door: for all his calls and knocks,
Thou let's[e] him stand until his precious locks
Are wet with dew and drops of the long night.[46]
Thus thou dost him despise, reject and slight,
And rather keep'st thy Lust and Pleasure still,
Than that Christ should thy Soul with heaven fill.
Though he ten thousand Worlds doth yet excel,
And makes that heart where he in truth doth dwel
To be a Heaven here upon the Earth,
Filling the Soul with precious joy and mirth;
Which makes gray-headed Winter like a Spring,
And Youths like to[f] Cœlestial Angels sing;
The Soul he doth so greatly elevate,
That it disdains and doth abominate
All sensual pleasures in comparison
Of Jesus Christ his dear and only One.
Let me perswade thee for to taste and try

How good Christ is, for then assuredly
Thou wilt admire him, yea and praise the Lord
That ever he did to thy Soul afford
Such a dear Saviour, and such good Advice
To lead thy Soul into sweet Paradice.
For none do know the nature of that peace,
That inward joy the which shall never cease,
But he himself who doth the same possess,
Oh! taste and see, for then you will confess
No Pen can it express, no Tongue declare,[47]
It's Nature's such (Oh young-man!) 'tis so rare,
Christ is the *Summum bonum*,[48] it is He
In whom alone is true felicitie.
Such is the nature of man's panting brest,
There's nought on earth can give him perfect rest.[49]
'Tis not in Honour, that is vanity:[50]
For such, like Beast's, and other Mortals, die.
Kingdoms and Crowns they tottering do stand,
The Servant may the Master soon Command.
Belshazzar, who upon the Throne did sit,
His knees against each other soon did hit.
How was he scar'd when the hand-writing came,
And wrote upon the Wall, ev'n the same
That afterwards befel, his End being come,
Then straitway followed his final Doom.[51] [a]
Great men oft-times are filled with great fear,
Being perplext they know not how to stear.
Tall Cedars fall, when little shrubs abide,
Though winds do blow, and strangely turn the tide.
For man in Honour lives but a short space,
He dies like to the Beasts, so ends his race.[52]
Where's *Nimrod* now, that mighty Man of old,[53]
And where's the Glory of the Head of Gold?[54]
Great Monarchs now are moulder'd quite away,
Who did on Earth the golden Scepter sway,
In highest place of Humane Government;
None ever found therein solid content.
Of *Alexander* 'tis declar'd by some,
How he sate down when he had overcome
The Eastern-World, and did weep very sore,
Because there was one World, and was no more
For him to Conquer.[55] Thus also 'tis still,
This World's not big enough man's soul to fill.
Riches and Wealth also can't satisfie
That precious Soul which in thy brest doth lie.
If store of Gold and Silver thou should'st gain,
'Twould but increase thy sorrow, grief and pain.
Riches, O young man, they are empty things,

And fly most swift away with Eagles wings.[56]
When riches thou dost heap, thou heap'st up sorrow[57]
They'r thine to day, alas! but gone to morrow.[58]
Fires may come and all[a] thy treasures burn,
Or Thieves steal[b] it, as they have often[c] done.
He that has[d] thousands by the year, this night
May be as poor as *Job*[59] before 'tis light.
And as for Pleasure which thy Age doth prize,
Why should that seem so lovely in thine eyes?
'Tis but a moment they with thee will last;
And sadness comes also when they are past.
The Bruit his pleasures[e] hath as well as thee,
Man's chiefest good therefore can't pleasures[f] be.
And whilst thou striv'st thy evil Lust to please,
Thy raging conscience (youth) who shall appease?
With this sweet meat I tell thee also Friend,
Thou shalt have sour sawce besure i'th'end.[60] [g]
And as for Beauty, that also is vain,
Unless thou can'st the inward Beauty gain.
What's outward Beauty save[h] an evil snare,[61]
By which vain ones oft-times deceived are:
And on a sudden draw[i] into temptation,
For to commit most vile abomination.
That Beauty which mans carnal heart doth prize,
Renders not lovely in *Jehovah*'s eyes:
Though deck'd with jewels, rings, & brave attire,
The glorious King their Beauty don't desire;
His heart's not taken with't, but contrar'wise[j]
The Beauty of vain ones he doth despise.
Though very fair, yet if defil'd with sin,
They like unto Sepulchres are within;
Loathsome and vile i'th sight of God are they,
And soon their seeming Beauty will decay.
It fades and withers, and away doth pass,
Just like unto the flower of the grass.
The curled Locks,[62] yea and the spotted Face,[63]
God e're a while will bring into disgrace.
Those Ladies which excel all others do,
Must feed the worms within a day or two,
Death & the grave will spoil their beauty quite,
And none in them shall never[k] more delight.
As for thy Age in youthful daies we see,
Youth minds nought else save cursed vanity.
Soon may thy[l] Spring also meet with a blast,
And all thy glory not an hour last.
The flower in the Spring which is so gay,
Soon doth[m] it fade and wither quite away.

Nothing on earth can'st thou find out or spy,[a]
That will content thee long, or satisfie
That soul of thine, if still you search about
Till you do find the rarest Science out.
For if on Learning once you place[b] your mind,
Much vanity in that also you'l find.
For Humane Knowledge and Philosophy,
Can't bring thy soul into sweet Unity
With God above, and Jesus Christ his Son,
In whom, poor youth, is happiness alone.
Dote not on Honour then, nor yet Treasure,
Nor Beauty,[c] Learning, Youth, nor[d] Pleasue;[e]
All is but Vanity that's here below,
Truth and Experience both the same do show.
Come, look to Heav'n, seek thou for higher joys,
Let Swine take Husks,[64] & Fools these empty toyes,[65] [66]
Come taste of Christ, poor Soul, and then you will
Of joys Cœlestial receive your fill.
If thou dost drink but of the Crystal Springs,
These outward joys thou't see are striking[f] things.
If Heavens sweetness once thou hadst[g] but caught,
Thou wouldst account Earth's best enjoyments naught[67]
Honor & riches too Christ has great store,
And at's *Right hand pleasures for evermore.*[68]
Dost think that he who makes man's life so sweet,
Whilst he with grievous troubles here doth meet,
And in believing hath such sweetness placed,
Though[h] his own Image greatly is defaced,
Can't give to him much greater Consolation,
When all the sowr's[i] vanisht of temptation.
If with the bitter, Saints such sweetness gain,
What shall they have when they in Glory reign?

Youth.

   Be silent *Truth*, leave off, for I can't bear
Your whyning strains, nor will I longer hear
Such melancholy whymsies, they'r such stuff
Which suits not with my Age, I have enough
Of it already, and also of you,
Sith ye my Intrests[j] strive to overthrow.
When I Appeal'd to you, I was perplext,
And with sad melancholly sorely vext:
But since I do perceive the Storm is o're,
You I don't think to trouble any more.
Long-winded-Sermons, Sir, I do not love,
Nor of your Doctrine in the least approve.
No liberty to me I see you'l give,

In sweet delights[a] and pleasures for to live.
I don't intend Phanatick yet to turn,
Nor after such distracted People run.
An easier way to Heaven I do know,
And therefore, Sir, Farewel, farewel to you.
My Pride,[b] my Sports, and my old Company
I will enjoy, and all my bravery
I will hold fast, yea, and also[c] fulfil
My fleshly[d] mind,[69] say Preachers what they will.

Conscience.

Ah Youth, ah Youth, is't so in very deed!
Wilt thou no more unto God's truth give heed.
'Twas but my mouth to stop, I now do find
That unto Truth you seemingly inclin'd.
But this, Oh Soul, I must assure to thee,
What thou hast heard, has much enlightned me.
And my Commission too it doth renew,
As will appear by what doth next ensue:
Have you from God been called thus upon,
And shall your heart be hearden'd like a stone.
You can't plead ignorance, Oh Youth, 'tis so,
You plainly now have heard what you should[e] do.
Your sin will be with[f] grievous Aggravation,
If quickly you don't make a Recantation.
Your sin will now be of a[g] scarlet-dye,[70]
And many stripes prepared I espy,
With which you must be beat, because that you
Your Master's Will so perfectly do know.[71]
But for to do the same you still refuse,
And your poor Conscience wickedly abuse,
You'l shew your self a cursed Rebel now,
If unto Christ with speed you do not bow.
Wilt thou thy sins retain, when thou dost hear
How much against the Living God they are,
Wilt thou cast dirt into his blessed face,
Oh! tremble Soul, and dread thy present case.[72]

Youth.

Now my good daies, I see, they will be gone,
My inward thoughts will ne're let me alone.
Ah! that I could but sin without controul,
And Conscience would no more disturb my soul!
His bitter gripes much longer I can't bear;
He's grown so strong, that little hope is there;
But he'l prevail; such conflicts do I feel,
My Courage now and Resolutions reel;
But yet I am resolv'd once more to try,

And struggle will[a] to get the mastery.
I cowardly will not acquit the Field
Nor at the second summons will I yield:
I'll make once more another stout assay,[b]
E're unto Conscience I will yield the day:
Ah! how can I my sweet delights forsake,
Without resistance to the last I make?
Conscience, although I sinful am, I[c] see
There's many thousand sinners worse than me:
There's none can live and from all sin be clear,
That I from *Truth* did very lately hear.
My heart is good, though it is true, that I
Am o're-come through humane infirmity.[d]

Conscience.

O cursed wretch! dar'st thou thy heart commend?
Come tremble Soul, and it to pieces rend.
Don't I most clearly in thy heart behold
Most horrid lust, 'twould shame thee were it told?
All rottenness and filth[e] I do[f] espy
In that base heart of thine, to lurk and lie.
There thou dost breed Vipers and Cockatrice;[g]
The spawn[h] of every Sin and evil Vice
Like a Sepulchre, Soul, thou art within,
Nought's there but stink and putrifying sin.[73]
Out from thy heart all evil doth ascend,
And yet wilt thou thy filthy heart commend?
And dost thou think thy state good for to be,
'Cause thou dost find many as bad as thee?
You are so nought, if you from sin don't turn,
You must for sin in Hell for ever burn
Except ye do repent, *Truth* tells you plain,
You perish must, and fry in bitter pain.[i]

Youth.

  Well, say no more, if this be so, I must
Go unto *Truth* again, or I shall burst;
My heart will break I clearly do discern,
I therefore now must yield, and also learn
What's my Estate, my Nature. Oh![j] that I'd know.
Come, *Truth*, I pray will you this favour show,
As to explain this thing to me more clear,
For *Conscience* doth my Soul with horrour scare,
Is he i'th' right, Oh *Truth*! or is he wrong?
I find Convictions in me very strong.
What is my state? declare it unto me,
And set also my[k] soul at liberty.

Truth.

What *Conscience* speaks, O young-man, it is[a] right,
And vain it is with him longer[b] to fight:
Conscience against thee doth his[c] Witness bear,
And dreadful danger also doth declare.
Those he condemns by Light receiv'd from me,
Th'Eternal God condemns assuredlie.
And God is greater than thy Heart, Oh Soul!
Who can enough thy grievous state condole?
If *Conscience* doth[d] its[e] Testimony give,
That you in sin and cursed waies do live,
And that thou art an unconverted wretch:
If 'tis from hence, between you there's a breach.
If this[f] be so, as it you can't deny,
What would you do if you this night should dy?
If in this state this life you do depart,
Undone for evermore, Young-man thou art,
As sure as is the mighty God in Heaven,
Against thy Soul the Sentence will be given.
Conscience his Power did from God receive;
And if you don't obey and him believe,
But[g] do reject his Motions, 'tis all one
As if Christ Jesus you did tread upon:
Whilst he doth Rule by Laws that are Divine,
'Tis Treason him to stab[h] or undermine.
And once again to shew thee thy estate,
Thou being, Young-man, not regenerate.
No God nor Christ have you, 'tis even so,
And this indeeds the sum of all your wo.
In God no Interest (Youth) hast thou at all,
He's quite departed ever since the Fall,
And is become thy[i] dreadful Enemy,
His angry face is set most veh'mently,
Against thy Soul, and that's a fearful thing,[74]
Enough thy Pride with Vengeance down to bring
Each Attribute against thy Soul is set,
And all of them also together met;
To make thee every way most miserable,
Which wrath for to withstand, what man is able?
He'l suddenly thy Soul to peices tear,
And his eternal Vengeance make thee bear
His wrath it will upon thy Soul remain,
'Till you by Faith are truly born again.

Youth.

This Doctrine which to me you do[j] declare,
It 'tis[k] enough to drive one to despair;

If it be so, I grant I am undone,
But God is gracious and has[a] sent his Son:
He's full of bowels,[75] therefore hope do I,
He'l not on me his Justice magnifie.[76]

Truth.

'Tis true God's gracious, yet he will not clear
Those guilty Souls who don't his Justice fear
He's very gracious, yet he's full of[b] ire,
And is to such like a consuming fire.[77]
He sent his Son, 'tis true, for Souls to dy,
But many miss and falsely do apply
His precious blood; therefore my Counsel take,
Don't you to[c] soon an Application make
Of Gods sweet Grace, nor yet of Christ's dear Blood,
Until by you the Gospel's understood.
Those who are whole need no Physician have,
The sick and wounded Soul Christ came to save.[78]
What dost thou judg thy present state to be,
How dos it stand, and is it now with thee?

Youth.

I am a Sinner, and my heart doth bleed,
My sin-sick-Soul[79] doth a sweet Saviour need,
My Conscience tells that I am most vile,
And grievously for sin doth me turmoile.

Truth.

No Saviour you can have unless you do,
Resove[d] to leave your sins, and let them go:
Nor for your Wounds is there a help be sure,
Till Causes be removed which do procure,
And bring on you that pain and bitter smart
Which you cry out of in your inward part.[e]

Youth.

My trembling Soul's amaz'd and fill'd with fear,
Another way, Oh *Truth*! I now will[f] stear;
I must forsake all evil ways, for I
Do see the danger and the misery
Which doth attend the way that I am in,
Whilst I do keep and hug my cursed Sin.
There's scarce a night which passeth o're my head,
But dread I do the making of my Bed;
(E're Morning comes) in the sad depths of Hell.
My Conscience therefore now does me compel,
To bid adieu to all sweet joy and pleasure,
And unto all unlawful gain and treasure.[g]

In sports and games I'le take no more delight,
But contrariwise[a] I'le pray both day and night.
Conscience has overcome me with his gripes,
Truth follows him so with his threatn'd stripes.
The Wall's broke down, the old-man[80] runs away,
And *Conscience* follows close to cut and slay:
And threatens too no Quarter he will give,
And seems before him every thing to drive.
Lust forced is in corners now to fly,[81]
Where it doth hide it self close[b] secretly,
And watcheth also, thinking for to get
An opportunity once more to set
And fall on *Conscience*, which it doth disdain
'Cause *Conscience* says Corruption must be slain.
I side with him because I would have peace,
But still 'tis doubtful when these Wars will cease.

Devil.

What pity is't thy Sun should set so soon,
Or should be clouded thus before 'tis noon:
No sooner risen in thy Horizon,
And sweetly shines, but presently is gone.
Shall Winter come before the Spring is[c] past,
And all its fruit be spoyl'd with one sad blast?
Shall that brave flower which doth seem so gay,
So quickly fade and wither quite away?
What pity 'tis that one so young as thee
Should thus be brought into Captivity.
Heark not to Conscience, *for I dare maintain,*
'Tis better for to hug thy sins again.
Thy Conscience, Youth, thou hast too lately found,
Doth but amaze and give thy Soul a wound.
Consider well, advise, and thou shalt see,
My ways are best, come hearken unto me:
I'le give thee[d] Honour, Pleasure, Wealth, and things[82]
Which prized are by Noble Men and Kings.
Let not this Make-bate[83] [e] with one angry frown,
Throw all thy Glory and thy Pleasures[f] down.
Let not strange thoughts distress thy troubled mind;
What satisfaction canst thou have or find,
But that which floweth from this World alone,
'Tis I must raise thee to the sublime thrown.[g]
The Hell thou fearest, may be but a story,
And heaven also but a feigned Glory.
If this don't startle thee, then speedily
I will stir up some other Enemy:
Old-man rouze up, I charge you to awake,
And swiftly too, your life lies at the stake.

And Mistris Heart, stir up your wilful Will,
Is this a season for him to sit still?
If unto Truth *and* Conscience *he gives place,*
Our Intrest will you'l see go down apace.
Judgment is gone already and doth yield,
And Courage too I fear will quit the field.
Some sins are slain, and in their blood do[a] *ly,*
And others into Holes are forc'd to fly.
As for Affection he doth hold his own,
Though Conscience *doth upon him sadly frown:*
Remembrance will unto him tray'trous prove,
If I his thoughts from Sermons can[b] *remove.*
I'le make his Mind run after things below,
And raise up trouble which he did not know.
And he'l forget what he did lately hear,
And cease will then his former thoughts and fear.
If I can please his sensual appetite,
There is no fear of any sudden flight;
His breast is Tinder,[c] *apt to entertain*
The sparks of Lust which long he can't restrain.
I'le blow them up and kindle them anew,
And to Convictions soon he'l bid adieu.
New objects I'le present unto his sight,
In which I'am sure he can't but take delight.
I have such hold of him, there is no doubt
But I once more shall turn him quite about:
His old Companions *also I'll provoke,*
At's door again to give another knock;[d]
Their strong inticements hardly he'll withstand,
They can (you'll[e] *see) his Spirit soon command.*

Youth's old Companions.

How do you, Sir? what is the cause that we
Can't here of late injoy your Company?
It seems to us as if you were grown strange,
As if in youth there were some sudden change.

Youth.

I have not had the opportunity,
Besides on me there do's some burden lie,
Which doth press down my Spirits very sore,
And makes me seldom to go forth o'th'[f] door.

Companions.

I warr'nt you, Sirs, 'tis sin afflicts his soul,
And he's just going now[g] to[h] turn fool.
Come, come away, to Age such grief belongs,
To youth, brave mirth & sweet melodious songs.

Come drive these thoughts away with Pipe & Pot.
Sing and Carouse till they are quite forgot.
The lovely strains of the[a] well-tuned Lute,
Where Playes they Act,[84] do with our Nature sute.
Come, go with us upon a brave Design,
The which will chear that drooping heart of thine.
Come generous Soul, let thy ambitious eye,
Such foolish fancies and vain dreams defie.
Shall thy Heroick Spirit thus give place,
To silly dotage to thy great disgrace?

Uicinus.[85]

The young-man yields, being possess'd with fears
They would reproach him else with scoffs and jears.
But afterwards[b] his head begins to ake,
And *Conscience* then afresh begins to wake,
And stings him after such a bitter sort,
It puts a period to his jovial sport.
The thoughts of death, which sickness doth presage,
Doth trouble him, he cannot bear the rage,
And inward gripes of his inlighten'd brest,
And therefore now again he thinks 'tis best
To heark to *Conscience*, whom he did refuse,
And grievously did many times abuse.

Conscience.

Go mourn, thou wretch, for sad is thy condition,
Pour forth amain the water of Contrition.
Wilt thou appear to men godly to be,
When all is nothing but Hypocrisie?
Wilt thou to *Truth* so often lend an ear,
And yet to *Satan* also thus adhere?
You were[c] as good have kept your former station,
As thus to yield afresh unto temptation:
Go unto *Truth*, if God give space and room,
Before I do pronounce your final doom.

Truth.

Come, come, Young-man, don't thy convictions loose,[d]
But cherish them, and timely also choose
The one thing needful, which alone is good,
That God may wash thy Soul in Christ his blood.[86]
Thy Soul is precious, 'tis of greater worth
Than all the things that are upon the Earth.
For if that the whole World you now could gain,
And all[e] the pleasures of it could obtain;
And in exchange your Soul should lose thereby,
What would your profit be when you do[f] dy?

When once thy Soul is lost, thou losest all:
Oh! that will be a very dismal fall!
Dost thou not know what I of Hell declare,
Of th' hideous howlings of the Damned there?
How canst thou with devouring fire dwell?[87]
Or, lie with Devils in the lowest Hell?[88]
Those who do in their natural state remain,
Must live for ever in that restless pain.
All Fornicators, Drunkards, and the Liar,
Must have their Portion in that Lake of Fire,
With Thieves, Revilers, and Extortioners,
And such who are most vile Idolaters:
The Proud, the Swearer, and the Covetous,
God doth pronounce on them the self-same curse.[89]
And those who live in vile Hypocrisie,[90]
Or do backslide into Apostasie;
Let such unto my present words give heed,
Their pain and torment shall all men's exceed,
What wilt thou do, or whither canst thou fly,[a]
Where canst thou hide from the great Majesty?
Who tries the reins, and searches every heart.[91]
Conscience declares that thou most guilty art.
Condemned Soul! thou knowst that this is so,
And this moreover which I plainly show,
Will come to pass, as sure as God's above.
If from all sin with speed you don't remove;
As sure as you do live when[b] e're you die,
To hell you go to all Eternity:
Except Repentance in your soul be wrought,
With vengeance thither you'll at last be brought.
You are the man for whom God did prepare,
That dreadful Tophet[92] where the Damned are,
The which is made exceeding large and deep,
The Damned in that doleful place to keep.
Oh! call to mind what *Conscience* doth this day
Charge you withal before you'r swept away;
Lest you from him do hear no more at all,
Till you into those scorching flames do fall.
What mercy is't that *Conscience* strives[c] so long,
And his Convictions still in you are strong!
Oh! fear lest sin do sear your Conscience quite,[d]
And God also put out your Candle-light;[93]
And give you up unto a heart of stone,[94]
As he in Wrath has served many one.[e]
Then to repent it will be much too late,
Such is the danger of a lapsed state.
Young-man[f] take heed you don't this work delay,

And put it off unto another day.
Your own Experience may discover this,
Man's Life a bubble[95] and a vapour is.
Alas! thy daies on Earth will be but few,
They fly away like to the morning dew;
Like as the cloud and shadow swiftly flies,
Or, dew doth pass as soon as Sun[a] doth rise:
So fly thy daies, thy golden months and years,
Much like the blossom that[b] most gay appears,
And on a sudden fades and do's decay;[96]
So Youth oft-times doth wither quite away.
Thy Age thou dost unto the Spring compare,
And to the flowers which appear so rare.
From hence, O young-man, learn Instruction[c] now,
Don't thy Experience daily teach thee how,
The Flower withers and hangs down its head?
Which curiously of late so flourished.
The Meadow's clad in glorious array,
But's soon cut down, and turned all to Hay.[97]
Like *Jonah*'s Gourd which sprang up in a[d] night,
And perished as soon as it was light.
Or like a Post which quickly[e] passeth by,
Or Weaver's Shuttle which he maketh fly.
Or as a Ship when she is under sail,
Doth run most swift when she has a full gale.
So are thy daies, they in like manner fly.
How many little Graves maist thou espy?
Come measure now thy daies, & see their length,
Number them not by years, by helth nor[f] strength.
All these uncertain rules you must refuse,
Though that's the way which most of men do use.
They think to live till they Old-aged are,
'Cause their Progenitors long-lived were.
That Rule from *Truth* you see doth greatly vary,
And with[g] Experience shews the[h] contrary.
You hear the things which you should reckon by,
Things swift in motion, gone most speedily.[98]
Thy life's uncertain, Youth, 'tis but a blast,
Thy Sand is little, long it will not last.
Thy house though new, yet it is very old,
Gone to decay, and turning to the mould.
You'r born to die, and dead also you were,
Before you liv'd or breathed in[i] the Air.
And die you must, before that live you do,
Except you die to live as I do show.
Thy dreadful ruine, Soul, is very nigh,
Unless thy Tears prevent it speedily.
What is thy purpose now, what's in thy mind?
Which way dost think to take, how art inclin'd?

Youth.

Thy ways, Oh *Truth*, I am resolv'd to run,
And never more will I to Folly turn.
I tremble at the thoughts of Death and Hell,
My Soul is wounded, and my wounds do swell.
My Pains increase, therefore my purpose now[a]
Is far more strict to be, and for to bow
Unto Christ Jesus, that I may obtain
Some healing Med'cine to remove my pain.
No rest can I, save in my Duty find,[99]
I unto Prayer am very[b] much inclin'd.
God will, I hope, these latter sins forgive,
Since I more godly do intend to live:
And do[c] resolve to watch and take such care,
That Satan shall no more my Soul insnare.

Uicinus.

He from this day becomes a great Professor,[100]
Though far from being yet a true possessor.
Christ he has got into his mouth and head,
But[d] not internally rais'd from the dead.
But in old Adam still does he remain,
Not knowing what 'tis to be born again.[101]
When Satan sees it is in vain to strive,
The Soul into its former state to drive.
But that it will forsake gross[e] wickedness.
And will also the Truths of Christ profess,
He yields thereto resolving secretly,
To blind its eyes in close Hypocrisie.
And so appears under a new disguise,
Most subtilly the[f] Soul for to surprise.
Perswading him the War which he doth find,
Daily to be within his troubled mind,
Is saving Grace against iniquity,
Which has prevail'd and got the victory;
When it is common Grace (we do so call)
And not the Grace that's supernatural.
He takes the work of[g] legal Reformation,
For th' only work of true Regeneration:[102]
Here he doth rest and seem to be at ease,
When all is done his Conscience to appease.
But i'll give place to this Religious Youth,
To hear discourse between him and the Truth.

Youth.

Oh! happy I, and blessed be the day,
That unto *Truth* and *Conscience* I gave way.
I would not be in my old state again,

If I thereby some thousands might obtain.
From Wrath and Hell my soul is now set free,
For I don't doubt but I Converted be.
The Word with power so to me was brought,
A glorious change within my Soul is wrought.

Truth.

Young-man take heed lest you mistaken are,
Conversion's hard, it is a work so rare,
That very few that narrow passage enter,[103]
Though far that way there's thousands do adventer,
Yet miss the mark for all their inward strife,
They fall far short of the new-Creature-life,
Come, let me hear your Grounds of[a] evidence,
For I don't like your seeming confidence.
I doubt[104] I shall find you under God's curse,
And still your Case as bad, if not much worse,
Than 'twas when you did no Profession make,
But did your swings in[b] all Prophaneness take.
The *Pharisee* was a Religious man,
Yet nearer Heaven was the *Publican*.[105]
If short of Christ you fix or fasten do,
'Twill be your ruine and your overthrow.

Youth.

What do you mean, this Doctrine's too severe,
For all might see that I converted were.
But if my Grounds you are resolv'd to weigh,
You shall forthwith hear what I have to say;
And the first Ground which I resolve to bring,
For to evince, to clear, and prove the thing,
Is from Convictions which I have of Sin,
Which once I hugged and delighted in.

Truth.

Alas poor Soul! this Reason soon will fly,
For most do see their vile iniquity.
They are convinced by their inward light,
That Sin is odious in *Jehovah*'s sight.
But yet vile Sinners are nevertheless,
And don't one dram of saving Grace possess.
King *Pharaoh*, *Esau*, yea, and *Judas* too,[106]
They were convinced of their sins (you know:)
That they were Saints, there's no man doth believe,
For all those three the Devil did deceive.
As he beguiled them, he may likewise
With cunning Stratagems your Soul surprise.
Nay, and he has, so far as I can judge,

Unless you do some better Reason urge
To prove Conversion in your Soul is wrought,
I do declare your state is very nought.
How many men under Convictions lie,
Yet never born again until they die?
What hast thou else to say and to produce,
Sith[a] slight Convictions are of little use?

Youth.

I do not only see my Sin, but I
Do mourn and grieve for sin continually.
And those which so do mourn they blessed are,
Don't you also the self-same thing declare?

Truth.

Nay hold a little, thou may'st weep amain,
And yet in thee may many evils reign.
Thou[b] mayest mourn for sin, as many do
Because of shame, of bitter pain, and wo,
Which now it brings and leads unto i'th' end,
And not because thereby you do offend
The Living God, and wound your Saviour, who
Did for your sake such torment undergo.
Mourn more for th'evil which doth come thereby
Than for the evil which in it[c] doth ly.
This ground is weak, for *Esau* it appears,
Did mourn and weep, and let fall bitter tears:
And yet you know that *Esau* was prophane,
And far was he from being born again.[107]

Youth.

But I go further yet, I do confess,
My horrid evils and my guiltiness.
If I confess my sins, as I have done,
God he is just, and is the Faithful One;
Who will my sins forgive and pardon quite,
And blot them out of his own precious sight.
This being so, what cause then can you see,
But that I'm[d] turn'd from my iniquity?

Truth.

This will not do, 'tis not a certain ground:
Some do confess their sins whose heart's unsound.
When *Pharaoh* saw the Judgment of the[e] hail,
His heart began then greatly for to fail.
I've sin'd this time, the Lord is just, said he,
I, and my People (also) wicked be.[108]
Though *Pharaoh*, *Saul*,[109] and *Judas* each of them

God did reject and utterly condemn;
Yet these, when under wrath, are forc'd to cry,
Lord, we have sin'd; their Conscience so did fly
Into their faces, that it made them quake,
And unto God Confession straight to make.
Confession may be made also in part,
And not of ev'ry sin that's in the heart.
Men may confess their sin, and their great guilt,
Who the dire nature of it never felt.
Confess their sins in their extremity,
When Conscience pinches them most bitterly.
Confess their sins which they committed have,
Yet don't intend those cursed sins to leave.

Youth.

But I confess, and also do forsake,
My state therefore, 'tis clear, you do mistake;
Those who confess and do their sins forgo,
God will to them his precious Mercy show.
Therefore don't trouble me, 'tis very plain,
I for my part am truly born again.

Truth.

In this also you may deceived be,
Men may forsake all gross iniquitie;
Yet in their souls may[a] some sweet morsel[b] lie,
Which they may hug and keep close secretly.
They may sin leave, but not as it is sin,
Which has too often manifested bin.
If the least sin thou didst forsake aright,
All sin would then be odious in thy sight.
Judgment and Reason may your sins oppose,
And utterly refuse with them to close;
Yet may thy will and thy affections joyn,
To favour still and love those sins of thine.
If sin's not out of thy affection cast,
Thou wilt appear an Hypocrite at last.
If sin's i'th' will and in th'affections found,
'Tis a true sign thy heart is quite unsound.
Like to the Seaman, some Professors do,
Who over-bord some Goods are forc'd to throw,
When they do meet with storms & with[c] bad weather
Lest all their goods & ship do sink together.
When in the soul great storms and tempests[d] rise,
The Devil then may subtilly advise
The soul to throw some of its sins away,
To make a Calm, that so thereby he may
Perswade the soul the danger is quite gone,

And that the work in him is fully done.
'Tis not enough therefore some sins to leave,
But every sin you must[a] resolve to heave
And cast o're-board, yea and that willingly,
Or else you sink to all Eternity.
Not by constraint as *Conscience* doth compel,
As some are forc'd to do, who like it well;
Who leave the Act, but love to it retain:
Such leave their sins, and yet their sins remain.

Youth.

    These are hard sayings which you do relate,
And I indeed should question my estate;
Wer't not for other grounds and reasons clear,
By which I know that I converted were.
Sir! there's in me a very glorious change,
Most men admire it, and think[b] it strange,
That one who lately did both scoff and jear
Those men and people, which I now do hear;
And follow'd Vice and ev'ry vanity,
Should on a sudden thus reformed be:
And utterly my self also deny,
Of my sweet joys, and former Company.

Truth.

    From outward filthiness a man may turn,
And not be chang'd in heart when he has done.[110]
A legal change I grant he may be under,
Yet may not Soul and Self be cut asunder.
An outward change in men there may be wrought
And yet their hearts within be very nought.
The Swine that wallows in the mire now,
May washed be, but still remains a Sow.
Persons may cleanse the out-side of the Cup,
And Dogs may spew their nasty Vomit up;
But yet do keep their beastly Nature still,
And e're a while they manifest it will.[111]
Many Professors fall away and dy,
For want of being changed thorowly.
The *Pharisee* was chang'd, he did appear
As if indeed a precious Saint he were;
And differ'd quite from the poor *Publican*,
And thought himself a far more happy man.
But all this was in shew, and not in heart,
And therefore had in Christ no share nor part.
Except your Righteousness doth his excel,
You in no wise shall in God's Kingdom dwell.[112]
'Tis a false change, and cannot be a true,

Unless in you[a] all things are wholly new.
Old *Herod* will reform in many things,
When once he finds his Conscience bites & stings;
To hear *John Baptist* also was he led,
Yet afterwards depriv'd him of his Head.
So far this seeming-Saint was turn'd aside,
That he also your Saviour did deride;
And with his Men of War set him at nought,
Whil'st Accusations they against him sought.[113]
Simon the Sorcerer, also you read,
Was changed so, he gave great care and heed.
To *Philip's* Preachings; yea, and suddenly
He leaves his Witch-crafts and his Sorcery;
And yet a cursed Caitife[114] [b] all the while,
Like a Sepulchre painted, inward vile.[115] [116]
Another man in show 'tis like thou art,
Yet not made new, and changed in thy heart.
Men in thy Life may no great blemish spy,
Yet in thy brest much rottenness may ly.
Towards[c] all men thy Conscience may be clear,
Conscience so far may for thee witness bear,
That you in Morals it do not offend,
Yet unto God it may not you commend:
But contrar'wise[d] it in your face may fly,
And you condemn for sin continually.
For secret evils which it's privy too,
Which none knows of, save God and only you.[e]
Threrefore, Oh! Young-man, if you look about,
Of your Conversion you have cause to doubt.
Satan so greatly may your heart deceive,
That one[f] dram of Grace your Soul may have
Which saving is, and of the purest kind,
For that, alas! there's very few do find.

Youth.

But I am call'd of God, and do obey
The Voice of *Truth* and *Conscience* every day.
God's called Ones I'm sure you can't deny,
But they are such whom he doth Justifie:
Therefore 'tis clear and very evident,
That Grace alone hath made me penitent.
My heart is sound, my Graces true also,
My Confidence there's none shall overthrow.

Truth.

Thou seem'st too confident, 'tis a bad sign;
For Fears attend where saving Grace doth shine.
I tell thee, Youth, that many called be;

But few are chosen from Eternity.
Judas was call'd, and did obey in part,
And yet was he[a] a Devil in his heart.
There is an outward, and an[b] inward Call,
The latter only is effectual.[117]
Therefore you must produce some better ground,
For this don't prove that your Conversions sound;
But that thou mayst stick fast still in the birth,
Or prove Abortive when thou art brought forth.
'Tis rare, Oh Youth! for to be born anew,
And hard to find out when the work is true.

Youth.

    Though it be so, what cause have I to fear,
When that my Evidences are so clear?
I do believe, and trust in God through Faith,
And he which so doth do, the witness hath
Within himself, and shall assuredly
Be saved also when he comes to dy.

Truth.

    Thou mayst believe as most of People do,
And yet to Hell at last thy Soul may go.
The Faith of Credence[118] it is like you have,
Which cannot quicken, purifie or save.
Some *Jews* believ'd in Christ you also find,
Yet to their Lusts their hearts were then inclin'd,
And out of Satans Kingdom were not freed,[119]
Nor made Disciples of the Lord indeed.
Simon the Sorcerer, he did believe;
Yet did his Soul no saving Grace receive:
But was a Child of Satan ne're the less,
And still was in the Gall of bitterness.[120]
The stony ground with joy receiv'd the seed,
And for a time brought forth, as you may read;
And yet their hearts they were but hearts of stone,
Their Faith was temporary, soon 'twas gone.[121]
The *Devils do believe* as well as you,
Yea, and confess that Jesus they do know;
They tremble also,[122] which some men can't say,
They ever did unto this present day.
Such Faith as Devils have, most men obtain,
Which serves for nought, save to augment their pain.
If on a Death-bed *Conscience* do awake,
'Twill cause them then to tremble and to quake,
And roar like Devils when they do espy
The dreadful wrath of that great Majesty,
Whom they offended, and against their Light

And knowledge too, most wickedly did slight.
This Faith will serve their grief to aggravate,
But not to help them out of that estate.
'Tis easie to believe that Christ did dy;
But hard his blood in Truth[a] for to apply.[123]
Men may raise up the dead to life again,
As easie as true saving Faith obtain
By their own Power, and inherit[b] skill,
Nought doth oppose it more than mans own will;
Until Almighty Power makes it bend,
'Twill not to Grace, nor Jesus condescend.
That Pow'r which rais'd up Jesus from the dead,
Works Faith in Saints, whereby they'r quickened:
The Faith of Credence, and Historical,[124]
Is easie had, I ne're deny it shall:
But precious Faith, the Faith of Gods Elect,
As 'tis a Grace, and gloriously bedeckt
With other Graces, so, 'twill never grow
But in the honest heart, where God doth sow
The blessed Seed, which, like a Garden pure,
Doth yield its fruit[c] to th' last, you may be sure.[125]
And when this Faith is wrought in any Soul,
It throws down self, and wholly then doth rowl
On Jesus Christ, as its beloved one,
On whom it rests, and doth depend alone.
If God hath wrought this precious Grace in thee,
Sin thou dost hate, yea all iniquity;
And Lust doth not predominate and reign,
If thou by Faith art truly born again.
Christ thou exalt'st[d] as he is Priest and King,
And as thy[e] Prophet too in every thing:[126]
He does in thee wholly the Scepter sway,
And thou art govern'd by him every day.
Sin can't prevail, such is thy happy case,
If thou hast got this rare victorious Grace:
It purges and doth purifie thy heart,
Wholly renewing thee in every part.
Men by its fruits true Faith do come[f] to know,
And by their works the same do also show,[127]
What Faith is thine? what thinks[g] thou now of it?
I greatly fear 'twill prove a counterfeit.
Examine thy Estate, and take good heed
To close with Jesus Christ, and that with speed.
For as th' Body without the Spirit's dead;
The same of Faith you know is also sed.
Without Obedience doth thy Faith attend?
Yet for all this you'l perish in the end,

Youth.

I am obedient, and am free to joyn
In fellowship with Saints, such Faith[a] is mine:
I willing am to do, as to believe;
The Devil can't therefore my Soul deceive.
For I have clos'd with Christ already so,
That none my Faith shall ever overthrow.
The many Prayers I make both day and night,
Do doubtless prove that my Conversion's right.

Truth.

I tell thee, Soul, men may do more than this,
And yet they may of true Conversion miss.
God's Ordinances many do obey,
And Members of Gods holy Church are they.
And of its Priviledges seem to share,
As if that they truly Converted were.
They may discourse and seem to be devout,
And may not be descerned nor found out.
They with the Flock may walk, lie down and feed,
And so remain till many years succeed:
Nay, not discovered be until they stand
Amongst[b] the Goats at Jesus Christs left hand.[128]
The foolish Virgins joyn'd themselves with wise,
And for to meet the Bridegroom did arise:
But e're the Bridegroom came their case was sad,
For they nought else save empty Vessels had.
A bare Profession, and a meer out-side,
And did no Oyl, no[c] saving Grace provide,[129] [d]
Many great Preachers and Disputers too
Christ will not own, nor any favour show;
Though in his Name they mighty works have done,
He'l say to them, *Ye wicked ones, be gone,*
I know you not, therefore begone from me
All you vile workers of Iniquity.[130]
You say oft-times you seek the Lord in Prayer.
That you may do, and let fall many a tear,
And yet not be in a converted state:
For many seek with tears when 'tis too late.
Others, like Seamen, in a Storm do cry,
When *Conscience* doth rebuke them bitterly.
And some under Afflictions[e] cry and howl,
And grievously their state do then condoul.
Then Promises and Resolutions make,
That they such Courses will no longer take:
But when the storm and the affliction's o're,
They are as bad, nay worser than before.
Some Pray in Form, and others Pray by Art,[131]

And some to mend the badness of their Heart;
Their hearts are wounded, and then speedily
Their Prayers to heal it they do straight apply.
They Sin i'th' day, and Pray when it is night;
They Sin again, but Pray'r doth heal it quite.
They think 'tis well if Tears they can let fall,
Their Prayers and Tears[a] they think will cure all.
And so that way poor *Conscience* they beguile,
They silence him; yet sinners all the while.
Their Prayers, alas! can't wash their filth away,[132]
Though they do nothing else both night and day.
'Tis on their Prayers they rest, and do depend,
Which like a broken staff will fail[b] i'th' end.
A Saint in Prayer, no rest nor ease can gain,
Unless Christs blood thereby he doth obtain:
And Grace also his sins to mortify,
For Christ, as well as Pardon, he doth cry.
But contrar'wise[c] it is with most of men,
They cry for Pardon, but do also then
In their vile hearts regard iniquity;
And for this cause God doth their suit deny.
Their Prayers are to God abomination,
Whilst they do hide and cover their transgression.
Some out of Custom do perform their Prayer,
Not out of Conscience, or from godly care.
And others also for vain glory sake,
Like *Pharisees*, they many Prayers make.
In sight of men, in Publick such will pray,
But in the Closet little have to say.
And some to God also seem to draw near,
Yet not in love, nor out of filial fear,
They with their mouths & tongues much kindnes show,
When as their hearts are fixt on things below.
'Tis for the heart when Christ[d] chiefly call,
And reason 'tis that he should have it all.
For he the same did buy and purchase dear,
Yet Satan has the chief possession there.
God at the door, and in the porch doth stand,
While Satan may the bravest room command.
They'll ope to him, and keep *Jehovah* out,
And yet in Pray'r they seem to be devout.
There's some will pray, and up this Duty keep,
When th' Soul is quite,[e] and th' Body neer asleep.
Whoever praies, and praies not fervently,
In Faith, in Truth, and in Sincerity;
Their Pray'rs are sin, and them God will not hear,
Nor mind their cry when they to him draw near.

'Tis not enough a Duty for to know,
But how also each Duty you should do:
For men may Pray, Read, Hear, and Meditate,
And yet be in an unconverted state.
They outwardly may many Truths profess,
But not in heart the pow'r of them possess.
The Law i'th' Letter keep, yea, have the shell,
Yet feeds on husks, and want the true kernel,
The Young-man which to Jesus Christ did run,
He many things as well as you had[a] done,
And yet fell short, as you may plainly see,
Of the chief part of true Christianity.[133]
What say ye[b] now, O Youth, do you not fear,
That you by Satan much deceived are.
Have you no *Dalila* which secretly
Doth in your heart, or in your bosom ly?[134]
Don't you to sin some secret love retain?
If it be so, you are not born again.
Conscience I fear, and Gods restraining Grace
Has only stopt you in your former race.
Like to a Dog that's kept up by a Chain,
So *Conscience* dos from sin oft-times restrain.
But if the Chain should slip, then loose he goes,
And presently his churlish nature shows.
To your own Righteousness do you not trust?
I fear you do, come speak, or *Conscience* must.
Don't you conclude God is oblig'd to you,
Since you have let so many evils go?
And are so holy here of late become,
Are not your duties set up in the room
And place of Christ? Oh! see you do not make
A Saviour of your own (for Jesus sake)
Did ever Sin, sinful to you appear?
And, as 'tis sin, to it great hatred bear:
Would you not sin, were there no Hell of Pain,
Because you know the Lord doth it disdain?
Rather, is't not from[c] fear of punishment,
That you of late seem thus for to relent?
Or, doth there not some carnal base design
Move thee so far unto God's Truth to joyn?
Is not thy end to get a Name thereby?
Or only done, *Conscience* to satisfy?
Or done to free thee from reproach and shame,
Which sin doth bring upon a Person's Name?
Hast not it done, and wisely cast about
This way, for to prevent a bankerout?[135]
Or done for to augment thy outward store,

To save thy stock, and add unto it more?
For Rietous Living which attends thy Age,
Consumes apace, and Want it doth presage.
Come speak, O Youth, and be thou not unfree
To let me understand how 'tis with thee.
Come, call to mind what thou hast heard of late,
And thereby judge of this thy present state.

Youth.

    I do not see but my Condition's good,
I have such hope[a] & faith in Christ's dear blood:
Though many imperfections I do see;
Yet God is gracious, and will pardon me.
For many failings there is[b] in the best:
What is amiss, I'le mend, and so do rest.

Truth.

    Thy Hope will fail like to the Spider's webb,
Thy flood of Confidence will have its ebb.[136]
If thou prove guilty of those things which I,
Did unto thee so lately signifie.
Thy spots will not be like the spots of those,
Which God for Children to himself hath chose.[137]
And since you are so loth for to be tri'd,
And lest you should also some evils hide;
To *Conscience* I'll appeal, you have done wrong,
To stop his mouth, and hinder him so long:
He's so inlightened now he can declare,
As much as we at present need to hear.
He'll speak the truth, and his opinion show,
And nothing will he hide which he doth know.
If unto him you will attend with care,
Of other witnesses no need is there.
If he, O Young-man, be but on your side,
And is your Friend, you need none else provide.
But if against you, and do prove your Foe,
With vengeance then be sure down you will go.
But if you will not hear what he shall say,
He'll make you tremble in the Judgment-day.

    Conscience, I do i'th' Name of the great King,
Require you your[c] Evidence to bring
Against this man, accuse, or set him free,
According as you find his state to be:
Stand up for Christ your dread & Soverain Lord,
And judge for him as he doth Light afford.
Be not deceiv'd by Lust, a Bribe to take,
But judge by Law; Christ's honour lies at stake.

For to speak home and loud have you forgot?
Is he converted now, or is he not?
What do you say? your Testimony give:
Is all sin dead, or doth there any live?
Is he new born, and chang'd in every part?
Or is't in shew only, and not in heart?

Conscience.

Sir, say no more, I am at your Command,
And you shall hear how things at present stand.
He hath, *O Truth*, almost deceived me
By's late pretences unto Sanctity:
But having now afresh receiv'd more light,
I must declare he is[a] an Hypocrite.
He's not renew'd or truly born again,
Which I to you shall clearly now explain.
For, first of all, his Faculty, call'd Will,
That is perverse and very wicked still;
Though I stir up to[b] good every hour,
Will doth oppose it with his greatest pow'r.
He'll never pray in private day nor night;
But I must force him to't with all my might.
The old Man is not slain I do espy,
But has much favour shown him secretly.
Though I do force him into holes to run,
Yet he doth nourish him when all is done.
His Love and his Affections are for sin,
And so in truth they ever yet have bin.
He's troubl'd more at sin because of guilt,
Than at the *Odium* of its cursed filt.[c]
When he's abroad amongst Religious men,
Precise[138] and Zealous he is always then:
But when amongst such who ungodly be,
He suits himself to their vile company.
Some sins are left which men condemn as gross,
Yet one he keeps, and hugs it very close:
Lust doth bear rule and much predominate,[d]
And he on it doth love to ruminate.
'Tis shame and[e] outward fear doth him restrain,
Or else the act he would commit again.
If he from outward blots can keep his Name,
That Saints can't him accuse nor ustly blame,
He's satisfied, and very well content,
Though to his Peace I never gave consent.
Peace he oft-times doth speak unto his Soul,
And scarce will suffer me him to controul.
When I sometimes do catch him in a ly,
And do reprove him for Hypocrisy:

To stop my mouth he vows he will with speed
Amend what is amiss, and take more heed.
And more then this of him I could relate,
And shew how you have hit his present state:
But that he will not suffer me to speak,
He blinds my[a] eyes, that so I might not rake
Into his heart and life, lest he thereby
Meets[b] with great shame for his iniquity.

Truth.

    Conscience, forbear, you need not to inlarge;
If you do lay these things unto his charge.
He is undone, alas! his precious Soul
Is under wrath, who can enough condole
His sad estate! the Gospel he'l profess,
But still remains i'th' gall[c] of bitterness.
Is this the Saint which[d] seemed so precise,
And did appear God's Statutes much to prize?
A Saint in shew, a Devil in his heart,
And must with Devils also have his part.
The[e] day is coming, and is very near,
When Hypocrites shall be surpriz'd with fear;
The everlasting burning fiery Lake,
Is made more hot on purpose for their sake.[139] [f]
But since you are not sear'd,[g] nor I yet gone,
Before we leave him quite, do you go on:
Let us pursue him still, for who doth know
What God may yet upon his Spirit do?
If God grant him one dram of saving Grace,[140]
That will yet do, though 'tis a doubtful case.
Whether or no God will his Grace afford
To such as he who thus offend[h] the Lord.
For such whom Satan doth this way deceive,
'Tis hard to bring truly for[i] to believe,
He never was convinced thorowly,
Of Sin, and of his nat'ral misery.
His lost estate he truly never saw,
Nor what it is for to transgress Gods Law.
How he's undone thereby he never knew,
Nor what for sin original is due.
And as he did for sin ne're kindly bleed;
So of a Christ he never saw the need.
Th' absolute want and great necessity
Of Jesus Christ, he never did espy:
But on false bottoms he has built 'tis clear;[141]
I do conjure you therefore to declare
Him utterly unclean from top to toe,
And let him understand you are his Foe.

The Plague is in his head, and no place free,
But in his heart it rages vehementlie.
Lance him unto the quick, and make him feel,
Lay on such blows which[a] may cause him to reel.[142]

Conscience.

Come, come, O Young-man, listen unto me,
I will no longer thus deceived be.
I from Gods Word Commission have anew,
To tell thee what is like to[b] ensue;
For all thy hopes and seeming goodly show,
Thou art a wretched Sinner thou dost[c] know.
Think'st thou on *Conscience* to commit a Rape,
And yet Gods dreadful vengeance to escape?
Dar'st thou again under a new disguise,
Encounter with thy[d] former Enemies?
You are the same I am[e] sure although you have
Changed your Coat, poor Mortals to deceive.
Ungodly wretch! dost thou not dread my Name,
Who'm come once more against thee to proclaim
A second War, and to declare also,
God's still thy Enemy and bitter Foe.
His Sword is whet, his Bow he'l also bend
To cut down those that do, like thee offend.[143]
Nought he hates more than vile Hypocrisy,
And from his Presence, Youth, thou canst not fly.[144]

Youth.

Conscience, be still, though a[f] sinner be,
There's none doth know it now save only thee.

Conscience.

Deceived Soul! doth none know it but I?
Where's the great God, is he not[g] also nigh?
Dost think, vain Youth, the interposing cloud,
From God's all-searching eye can be a shroud?
Or dost thou think God s Seat is so on high,
That he cannot thy inward thoughts espy?[145]
None know't but me! know'st thou not who I am?
Have I not pow'r for to accuse, and damn?
Should I be still, it would be a sad day,
Unless thy sins were purged clean away.
And whilst I speak, and thou dost[h] stop thine ear,
Nothing but War and Tumults thou wilt hear.
I'le never side with thee, nor take thy part,
Whilst horrid guilt remains in thy base heart.
Nor would I mind thy flattery or frown,
Wert thou the highest Prince of great'st Renown.

That ever did on Earth a Scepter sway,
Before thy face I would thy evils lay.
At th' smallest[a] sin before[b] I can't connive;
And therefore with me 'tis in vain to strive.
For where I am an Enemy indeed,
I'le plague that heart until I make it bleed.
A close and secret Foe, Young-man, am I
Who am also with thee continually.
What e're you think or speak, yea, act or do,
Of it (poor Soul) I very well do know:
Thy secret Lust, and what is done i'th' night,
Which thou ashamed art should come to light.[146]
I then am nigh, and know it very well,
And more than this I am resolv'd to tell;
I unto thee shall prove an Enemy,
When thou are brought into Adversity;
When death and sickness comes, then thou shalt see,
How thou with horrour shalt amazed be.
Then my black Bill against thee will be large,
For then against thee I will bring a Charge,[147]
Which will make thy sad face like Ashes look,
And wound thy Soul as if a knif was struck
Into thy very heart, and make thee mourn,
And curse the day that ever thou wast[c] born.
I'le make thee understand (clearly) i'th' end,
What 'tis (vile wretch) poor *Conscience* to offend.
Hark once again, for I have more to say;
When this life's ended, there's another day.
Look now about thee, Youth, for there's to come
The black, the dark, and[d] dreadful day of Doom.
When thou dost die, I'le bite and sting thy Soul,
Whilst that in flames doth burn and doth condole
Its damned state for yielding unto sin,
Which has alone the ruine of it bin.
And also when i'th' Judgment Day you stand
Amongst the Goats at Jesus Christ's left hand,
Thy dreadful state and tryal for to hear,
Then I against thee straitway must appear;
Yea, and shall speak more plain[e] than now I can,
Because I'm clouded by the Fall of Man;
And am by Satan oftentimes misled,
And utterly unable rendered,
A true and right decision for to make,
He so beguiles me that I do mistake,
And a wrong Judgment oftentimes[f] retain,
Till *Truth* me[g] into th'[h] right again.[148]
But Satan then shall no more power have,
The heart of any man for to deceive.

I in that Day shall you provoke and urge,
For to confess with shame before the Judge,
Thy evil Lust and close Hypocrisie,
Unto thy own Eternal miserie.
I shall accuse thee so in that great Day,
Thou shalt not have one word (young-man) to say,
Thy inward parts so opened then shall be,
That nothing shall be hid i'th' least from me,
And I before the dreadful[a] Judge shall show,
All secret things that ever you did do;
And in your face so fiercely also fly,
That you with horror shall be forc'd to cry,
Guilty, guilty, O Lord! then thou must hear
The dreadful Sentence, which no one can bear;
Go, go, ye Cursed![149] that's a word of ire,
And you must go[b] into Eternal fire,
Where Hypocrites and Unbelievers lie,
Broyling in pain to all Eternitie.
And as the fire evermore will burn,
And thou from thence shalt never more return:
So I also shall then afflict thy Soul,
Whilst thou in scalding Sulphur flames dost roul.[150]
I like a Worm, or Serpent, then will bite,
And gnaw thy Soul, thou cursed Hypocrite.
Those inward stings which always thou wilt find,
Or cruel gnawings in thy[c] tortur'd mind.
Will then increase and aggravate thy wo,
In such a sort there is no tongue can show.
You then will think how you did me abuse,
And my good Counsel utterly refuse.
And how you labour'd to put out[d] my Light,
Who in God's paths would lead your feet aright.[151]
Your base delays and put-offs you'l repent,
And that your time so foolishly was spent:
And how[e] for love which unto Lust you bore,
Should lose your Soul, and that for evermore.
To think how near you were unto Salvation,
Will prove another grievous aggravation:
To bid so fair for Heaven, yet to miss,
What greater trouble can there be than this?
To see the Ship i'th' mouth o'th' Haven[f] lost,
That doth, ye know, perplex the Merchant most.
I'le tell you also how you wilfully
Brought on your self that dreadful misery:
And how I did oft-times to you declare,
The bitter torments which you then must bear:
And what your Pride and Lust would bring you to,
If you did not resolve to let them go.

Ah! thou wilt see how thou art quite undone,
And how all hopes for evermore are gone.
Thoughts of those golden Seasons once you had.
Which you did lose,ᵃ will then be very sad.
Thou might'st, hadst thou improv'd the means of Grace,[152]
Beheld with Saints God's reconciled face.[153]
And enter'd Paradise, where Angels sing
Anthems of Joy to the Eternal King:
Andᵇ might'st have sung to him melodious Psalms,
With those whose hands shall bear triumphant Palms;
Who with Eternal Love shall ravish'd be,
Raigning with Christ to all Eternitie.[154]
Heaven is a place whose glory doth excel;
The thousandᶜ part of it no tongueᵈ can tell.
Man's heart (*Truth says*) cannot i'th' least conceive
What those shall have who truly believe.ᵉ
Who would lose Christ and his Immortal treasure?
For one base Lust and moments time of pleasure?
But if what's said of Heav'n will not invite thee,
Then let Hell torments with black vengeance fright thee
And make thee yield to Truth without delays,
Before God puts a period to thy days.
As Eye can neither see, nor Tongue express
The Glory which God's Saints in Heav'n possess:
So there's no man which can conceive the wo,
That Souls shut up in Hell do undergo.
If men could number all the Stars of Heaven,
Or count the Dust which with the wind is driven;
Or tell the drops of waterᶠ in the Seas,
Or count the Sands; then mayᵍ a man with ease
Declare the nature of that dreadful pain,
Which damned Souls for ever mustʰ sustain.
But stars, nor dust, nor drops, nor sands can be
Number'd by any man, neither can he
Express the nature of God's dreadful ire,
Which Souls lie under in Eternal fire.
In Hell all's Darkness, not one beam of Light:
What's greater sorrow thanⁱ Eternal Night?
In Hell all's Death, and yet there is no dying,
Nought there is heard but a most hideous crying.
Their pains end not, from it there's no exemption,
Their cries admit no help, there's no redemption,
Nor none to pity them, nor hear their groans,
Whilst they do make their lamentable moans.
The Lord who dy'd will then rejoyce to see,
Vengeance pour'd forth upon those Souls that be
Vessels of Wrath,[155] who for rejecting Grace
Must have their portion in that doleful place.[156]

No Earthly pain or torment can declare
The woful Anguish which the Damned bear:
For if those Plagues could be defin'd by men,
Infinite Punishment 'twould not be then.
Infinite Wrath it is to satisfie;
And God, be sure, will Justice magnifie.
Didst thou but hear the groans and hideous cry
Of Souls condemned to Eternity,
How would it scare, and cause thy Heart to ake,
And every limb of thee^a tremble and quake![157]
Think, think on this, before the time doth come
That God doth pass on thee thy final Doom.

Truth.

What say'st thou now? how can'st thou sleep in peace
Until these inward gripes of *Conscience* cease?
How can'st thou think i'th' least thy state is good,^b
When *Conscience* swells and makes so great a flood?
Or raises storms and tempests in thy brest?
Because of sin he will not let thee rest.
Come, make a search, *Conscience* is not misled,
The very Truth before you he has spred.
What will you do at Death and Judgment Day,
If *Conscience* thus you slight and disobey?
Make peace with God, for worser are his cries,
Than if ten thousand witnesses should rise
Against thy soul? 'twill be a dreadful thing
To have thy Conscience then to bite and sting.

Youth.

Some comfort, *Truth*, alas my Soul doth melt?
Such gripes as these what man has ever felt?
I have some doubt my state is very nought,
And that Conversion is not truly wrought.
My heart condemns me, and doth me reprove.
'Tis thou alone which can^c my grief remove.

Truth.

Before you have a Plaister for your sore,
Your wound must yet be search'd a little more:
If slightly heal'd only for present ease,
The Remedy's as bad as the Disease.
Dost know what time thou didst this wound receive?
'Tis worser far, I fear, than you believe:
'Tis deepe, it stinks, yea, and 'tis venomous,[158] [159]
And doth expose thee to God's dreadful Curse.
The sting or dart sticks fast too in^d thy Liver,^e
Which doth thy smart^f and bitter pains procure.

Thy state is bad, thou hast thy mortal wound,[160]
No Limb, or any part of thee, is sound.
If thou couldst live, and never more offend,
Yet by the Law thy Soul is quite condemn'd.
If from all actual sin you should be clear,
Yet by the Law you still most guilty are
Of former Crimes, Treason and Felony,
And Justice doth aloud for Vengeance cry,
Nor will she Pardon or[a] Reprieve give forth
To any Sinner living on the Earth.
Against thee too the Sentence is forth gone,
And th' Day of Execution doth draw on;
Nought is between thee and Eternal Death,
But some short hours of uncertain breath.
Sin is so vile, and Justice so severe,
That in the least 'twould not *Christ Jesus* spare;
But Justice he must[b] fully satisfie,
Who came to be man's blest Security.
And since in Christ thou hast no share nor part,
See what a self-condemned Soul thou art.[161] [162]

Youth.

O cursed Sin! is this my sad condition?
Truth I believe has[c] made a right decision.
I have my Soul deceived all along,
Though in my heart Convictions oft were strong.
Oh! horrid Lust, and base deceitful Devil,
Is this the fruit of your sweet-pleasing evil?[163]
And thou false World, what art thou now to me?
For I, alas! am ruined by thee.[164]
O whither[d] shall I fly? what path untrod?
For to escape th' incensed wrath of God?
Will none for me some secret place provide,
Where I from flaming Vengeance close may hide?

Truth.

Vain is all this, for none can find a place
To hide from God (such is thy better[e] case)
If to the ends of all the Earth you fly,
Vengeance will you pursue with *Hue*[f] *and Cry*.[165]
If you should take a sudden hasty flight,
To seek some shelter in the shades of Night;
'Twould also fail thee, though it should be done:
For unto God Darkness and Light is one.
Or, if thou couldst some solid Rock espy,
To hide thee from God's dreadful Majesty.
Can Rocks, dost think, prevent, yea, or restrain
The stroke of Justice, and not fly in twain?

There is no Sea, nor Shade, nor Rock, nor Cave,
Which can from Vengeance shelter thee or save.
The Sea would part, the hardest Rock will[a] split:
Where Justice aims, her fiery Darts must hit.
Canst thou escape, alas! what place is there
To hide from him who's present ev'ry where?[166]

Youth.

Oh *Truth*! what shall I do, how can I stand,
Or bear these tortures of God's heavy hand?[167]
My Spirit may Infirmities sustain,
But who can bear this inward cutting pain.
Is there no help, no Salve to heal my Wound;
What, no Physitian[168] for me to be found!
Will Tears nor Prayers no help at all afford,[169]
Watchings, Fastings, nor Hearing of the Word?[170]
Or if that I could live and sin no more,
O what is sin, and what's my Gangrene sore!
O what's the nature of iniquity,
If nought my Soul can cleanse or purifie?
Rivers of Oyl, much Gold, or Earthly Wealth[171]
Will not redeem my Soul, nor purchase health.
Ah! I am lost! the cause is truly so,
I am undone, and know not what to do!
Have you no word of Comfort now for me?
Oh! must I die in this extremitie?

Truth.

Dost find thy self sick at the very heart?
And doth my searchings make thy Wounds to smart?
Doth sin, as sin, upon thy Spirit ly?
And doth its weight and burden make thee cry?
Dost know thy wound is Epidemical?[172]
And that for thee there is no help at all
By Law nor Levite?[173] dost thou see thy loss,
And thy own Righteousness to be but dross?

Youth.

I know not what to say, I am in doubt
Some Sin is hid, which yet I can't find out.
My heart is deep and very traiterous;
Every day I find it worse and worse.
I grieve for sin, and yet I am in dread
That I in sin am greatly hardened.
Yet this, O *Truth*, I hope is wrought in me,
Sin I do hate as 'tis inquitie.
I would not Christ offend nor grieve[b] again,
Were there no Hell or place of future pain:

O that e're I against the Lord should sin,
Who has to me so good and gracious bin.
Against the Lord, against the Lord alone,
Have I this horrid evil often done.
Oh! I do see that I in sin am dead,
And my iniquity's gone o're my head,
As a great burden which I cannot bear,
Oh! that I might but of a Saviour hear.
All my own Righteousness I prize no more,
Than stinking refuge[a] of a Common-shore.[174]

Truth

Come Youth, chear up, if this be so indeed,
I tell thee then Christ for thy Soul did bleed.
Glad tydings now I unto thee do bring,
There's Mercy for thee in the Heav'nly King.
Christ to appease God's Wrath did hither come,
And I am sent by him to call thee home.[175]
Rise up, rise up, his blood for to apply,
And thou shalt soon be healed perfectly.

Youth.

Ah! could I but believe what thou dost say
Unto my Soul, 'twould be a joyful day.
Alas! on me a mighty burden lies,
I cannot stir, nor power have to rise.
Can Lazarus, who in the Grave doth ly,
Death's cruel Fetters and strong Bands unty?
Can he awake? what pow'r has he to strive,
When dead, and stinks? alas! he can't revive,[176]
Although dead but four days:[b] then how[c] shall I,
Who have lay'n dead in my iniquity
Ever since *Adam* (as it plain appears)
Which is indeed above five thousand years?
Jehovah which at first my heart did make,
Must by his Pow'r it into pieces take;
That so he may create my[d] heart a-new,
E're good from Christ doth to my Soul accrue,
'Tis he must give me pow'r to will and do,
And raise up[e] e're I can creep or go.

Truth.

Though that be true, yet harken unto me,
And take the Counsel which I'le give to thee?
And thou shalt find, as sure as God's above,
He will thy Fears and all thy Doubts remove,
And raise thee up out of the empty Pit,[177]
And on a Rock also still set thy feet.[178]

First thing of all which to you I commend,
Be sure you don't your Conscience more offend,
Do not grieve that, but alwayes take great care
In every thing to prove your self sincere.
He that in Morals walks not faithfully,
No marvel 'tis if Christ do pass him by.
In ev'ry Nation those accepted[a] are,
Who walk uprightly, and the Lord do fear!
Those who do follow on to know the Lord,
He will to them his saving help afford.
I do exhort you in the second place,
For to attend upon all means of grace.
Do not neglect to hear God's blessed Word,
But prize each season which the precious Lord
Is pleas'd in mercy on you to bestow,
For unto you thereby much good will flow.
My third advice, make use of speedily,
Lift up your voice, unto the Lord on high!
Pour forth your Soul to him both night and day,
And you'l prevail, though he at first say nay.
Though you at first may with repulses meet.
Your Soul yet prostrate at *Jehovah's* feet.
He's full of bowels, long he can't refrain
E're he comes forth to ease you of your pain.
Thy prayers, and tears, and spiritual contrition,
Will move his heart to send thee a Physician,
Who will apply a Plaister to thy Wound,
Which will hereafter ever make thee sound.
Christ's blood will heal, 'twill cleanse and purify,
If now the same by Faith you do apply.
Such grief is thine, no Med'cine will do good,
Nor heal thy Soul but thy dear Saviour's blood.
The good *Samaritan* will cast a look,
Though thou of Priest and Levite art forsook?
Into thy Wounds he'l pour[b] in Oyl and Wine,
The which will heal that bleeding Soul of thine. [179]
O Cry to God, my sister *Grace* to send,
'Tis she at last will prove thy special Friend.
If God is pleased but to send her down,
Thy head with Glory she will straightway crown.
But here I'le advertise thee first of all,
Be sure you do for the right Sister call:
For there are two, and both of one Sirname,
The one is lovely fair, the other lame.
The one is common, th' other chaste and pure,
And will be true to thee thou mayst be sure.
The one will dwell where Sin predominates,[c]

The other loaths, and bitterly it hates,
And makes a thorow-change where she doth dwel,
And will all filth out of that heart expel,
Where she doth take up here[a] sure resting-place;
Rare is the nature of true saving Grace.
Thy stubborn will she'l make for to submit,
And thy Affection's change as she thinks fit.
Thy heart she can new-mould, & make it soft,
And will bring down each high & sinful thought.
The old-man she will into pieces tare,
She'l cut and kill, and nothing will she spare,
That's opposite unto the Prince of Light,
She'l put the Devil to[b] a speedy flight;
She'l make him leave his strongest Hold, and run
And quite forsake his former Garison.
She'l take no pity on the Old-man's Age,
She'l pay him off for all his wrath and Rage,
And cursed Malice, Pride, and every Sin,
Which a-long-time[c] he has the Author bin.
'Tis she can work upon the Covetous,
And change his heart to keep an open-house,
To give and to distribute of his store,
To th' cloathing and refreshing of the Poor.
'Tis she brings down the proud and lofty mind,
Which naturally was to that vice inclin'd.
'Tis she can tame the wild strong-headed Youth.
And make the Liar always tell the truth.
'Tis she which makes the froward very meek,
And the revengeful not revenge to seek.
'Tis she which quenches young-men's lustful fire,
And makes them to disdain that base desire.
'Tis she will make thy[d] Soul for to defie
Each *Dalila*, and all Hypocrisie.
She's like to Oyl and Wine, and will give peace
And inward joy, which never more shall cease.
'Tis she must put Christ's blessed Robes on thee,
And bring thy Soul out of Captivitie.[180]
'Tis she must thee adorn and beautifie,
And make thee lovely in Christ Jesus eye.
Oh! she'l inflame thy[e] Soul with[f] precious love
To Christ alone, which none shall ne're[g] remove.
'Tis she which ties that conjugal blest knot,
Which can't be broke, or ever be[h] forgot.
'Tis she that makes Christ and the Saints but one,
And makes them of his very flesh and bone.
'Tis she will help thee in this time of need,
Yea, a Disciple will thee make[i] indeed.

And this to thee also I[a] must declare,
Thou of this *Grace* shalt have a part and share.
Since 'twas for thee thy precious Lord did dy,
He can't thy Soul of saving Grace deny.
Give him no rest, 'till more he doth give forth,
For to compleat in thee the second Birth.
Be earnest with him, strive to hold him fast,
And thou, like *Jacob*, wilt prevail at last.[181]
Though he at first may seem to stop his ear,
Yet importunity will make him hear.
Thy time I'm sure it is the time of love,
And thy deep wounds will make him from above
To pity thee, and for to cast an eye,
As thou polluted in thy blood dost[b] lie;[182]
What e're is needful to thee he will give,
And raise thee up to life, and make thee live;
Yea, manifest to thee such consolation,
As for to cloath thee with his own Salvation.
Come, make a tryal, and do not despair,
Look up to Heaven, Soul, thy help is there.

Youth.
Thy Counsel I resolve to take with speed.
If 'twas for me Christ on the Cross did bleed;
I will send up a sigh, a bitter groan,
And earnestly implore his gracious Throne.
Most Holy God, who dwellest in the Light!
Ah! what am I before thee in thy sight?
Wilt thou attend, or listen to my Cry?
Thou knowest my grief, and where my pain doth lie.
Canst thou not ease[c] my deeply wounded Soul,
Who in my blood am forc'd to lie and roul?
Is there no Balm in Gilead, *is there none?*[183]
Into dark silence then, Lord, I'le begone.
Where are thy Bowels, is thy Mercy fled?
Lord, think upon the blood Christ Jesus shed,
If thou can't heal my Soul of all its grief,
Then let me perish without all relief.
Why were thy sides pierced,[d] Lord Jesus, why?
Didst suffer for thy[e] own Iniquity?
There was no sin, I'm sure, nor guilt in thee
That caus'd thy pains; didst thou not die for me?
Didst thou not Justice fully satisfie,
And pay the debt? Must I in Prison lie,
When Restitution's made i'th[f] highest degree?[184]
Oh! come and set my Soul at libertie.
Knock off these bolts and chains, and bring me forth
Out of this Pit, deep Mire, and bands of Death.

Lord, must I bleed? did I not bleed before
In thy sad Wound?ᵃ can Justice challenge more?
O! shall my heart-strings break? my Soul doth groan:
I languish, Lord, whilst thou stand'st looking on.
Lord, dost thou hear the Ravens when they cry?[185]
And wilt thou not my present wants supply?
Wilt thou the door of Mercy ne're unlock?
Lord, open unto me, now I do knock.[186]
O Son of David, *help; think on thy Word,*
And unto me some Mercy, Lord, afford.

Jesus.

What voice is this? who is't that makes this cry?
What sinful Wretch is in extremity,
That thus implores for help, and follows me;
That takes no nay, although I silent be?

Youth.

Lord, 'tis a poor dejected piece of Earth,
That is undone, and sighs for a new-birth.

Jesus.

Was I not sent only toᵇ Jacob's *race?*
How com'st thou then to have so bold a face
To importune me, when ye know full well
You are not of the stock of Israel?
Come you not of the cursed Gentile *seed?*
Begone from me, and further don't proceed.[187]

Youth.

Ah! help, dear Lord, and some compassion show,
For to whom else, or whither can I go?

Jesus.

Is't meet that I should give to Dogs that bread,
With which the Children should be nourished?

Youth.

True, Lord, that I do grant, and ever shall:
Yet may the Dogs eat up those Crums which fall
From their own Master's Table: though a whelp,
Lord, look on me, O precious Saviour, help.

Jesus.

What ailest thou, poor Soul, what's thy condition,
Which makes thee shed these tears of sad contrition?

Youth.

My grief, my pain, and great extremitie,
Lord, thou dost know, and all my wants dost see.
Ah! I have sin'd, and am so vile and base,

I hate my self, and loath my present case.
I am a lump of filth, wholly unclean,
A viler Creature there has never been.
I languish, Lord, my wounds they are not small;
And I have wounded thee, that's worst of all.

Jesus.

Come, cease thy grief, what is't thou dost desire?[188]
My Soul doth melt, my heart is set on fire;
My bowels yearn,[189] *I longer can't refrain*
From tears, as well as thee, I am in pain:
Thy wounds afflict me, and thy bitter cry
Doth pierce my heart, I know thy misery.
What is it, Soul? speak forth thy mind to me;
What dost thou crave, or shall I do for thee?
Come, ope[a] *thy heart to me, for I am nigh*
Thy suit to grant, thy wants for to supply.

Youth.

'Tis not for Riches, nor for Pleasures here,
Nor Honours, which by men so prized are,
Nor length of days, Lord do I seek or crave,
'Tis something else my Soul doth long to have.
The Earth's a blast, and all this[b] World's a bubble:[190]
There's nothing in't can ease me of my trouble.
Such is my state, nought but thy hand[c] can save,
'Tis thou must raise dead *Laz'rus* from the grave.
Knock off these bolts, and set thy Prisoner free,
And give thy Grace (Lord Jesus) unto me.
My fainting Spirit comfort and refresh,
O Spare my Soul, but crucifie the flesh;
Compleat thy Work (Lord Jesus) on my heart,
And thy own Righteousness to me impart.
There's nought I see will do me any good,
Save the dear Merit of thy precious blood.
My bleeding Soul will faint away and dy,
If thou dost not thy blood with speed apply.
How has my panting breast sent many groan,[d]
With bitter tears, up to thy gracious Throne,
For one sweet look and aspect of thine eye?
There's nothing else which[e] will me satisfie:
Oh! manifest thy Love unto my Soul,
For that will cure me, and make[f] me whole.
My gasping[g] Soul's dissolv'd into tears,[191]
Whilst[h] pleas'd with hopes, and yet possess'd with fears:
My great request, alas! is only this,
Come seal thy Love to me with a sweet kiss:
For nought is there in[i] Earth, nor Heaven above,
Which I esteem or Value like thy Love.

A Promise grant, some word to lie upon,
Before my life and little hopes are gone.
My Soul's afraid, and trembles thou dost see,
Before[a] I know how I unworthy be:
Ah! I have made thee bleed, I am so vile;
Thy frowns[b] I do deserve, but not one smile.
How did I grieve and put thy Soul to[c] pain!
The thoughts of it doth cut my heart in twain.
Thy Messengers, how did my Soul refuse!
And my poor Conscience wickedly abuse:
Who did receive Commission from above,
Either to clear, or sharply to reprove.
I unto *Truth* oft-times turn'd a deaf ear,
And unto *Satan* rather did adhere.[d]
I slighted thee, and sin I did embrace,[e]
Which shames me greatly to look in thy face.[f]
If thou shouldst pardon such a one as I,
And save my Soul to all Eternity,
And me imbrace in a contract of love,
And all thy wrath for ever quite remove:
It would be Grace and Love beyond degree,
And such which never can expressed be.
O, wilt thou speak again! dear Saviour do,
A Promise, Lord, or I'le not let thee go.

Jesus.

What Faith hast thou, poor Soul, canst thou believe,
And stedfastly my benefits receive?
Dost think that I have pow'r and a heart
To save, to help, and[g] free thee from thy smart?

Youth.

　　My Faith, alas! is weak, O send relief!
Lord, I believe, O help my unbelief![192]
That precious Voice which I did lately hear,
Will soon remove my doubts, and all my fear.
If Love as well as pity thou dost show,
'Twill give me joy, and take away my wo.
But thou may'st, Lord, my Soul commiserate,
And yet may I[h] be in a dying state.
Over *Jerusalem* thou didst lament,[193]
Who had no saving Grace for to repent.
Is there in thee such bowels of compassion,
As to bestow thy self and thy Salvation
On such a Worm as I,[194] whose wounded brest,
Is heavy loaded, and would fain have rest?[195]
O help, dear Lord; my fainting Soul will dy,
Without an answer from the[i] speedily.

Jesus.

Look up to[a] me, and see my Love descending,
'Tis from Eternity, and has no ending.
Canst thou have more, dear[b] Soul! thou hast my heart;
What e're is mine, to thee I will impart.
Thy scarlet-sins are washed quite away,
Not one of them unto thy charge I'le lay.
Pull up thy drooping heart, be of good chear,
Thy sins, though ne're so great, forgiven are.[196]
I able am to save to th' uttermost,
All those who do in me put[c] all their trust.
Those which do[d] come to me, I in no wise
Will cast them out, therefore lift up thine eyes:
Behold my hands and feet, and do not doubt,
For I have washt and cleans'd thy Soul throughout.
Thy debts I ve[e] paid, and quitted the old score;
Thy former faults I'le ne're remember more.
Enter the Royal Fort, thou hast obtain'd
Th' fountain[f] of pleasure, holy love unstain'd:[g]
Take up thy lodging in Eternal Love.
What's here below? thy treasure is above.[197]
Chear up, poor heart, I tell thee thou art mine,
My blood was shed to save that Soul of thine:[198]
With endless joys thy Soul I'le satisfie,
And in my Bosom ever shalt thou lie.
In my enfolded Arms I now do take thee,[h]
And do engage I never will forsake thee.[i]
I'th' fire and in the water[j] I'le be neer,
And help thee through all grief and troubles here:
Yea, I'le be with thee always to the end,
And Death at last I'le cause to be thy Friend;
And make its passage also unto thee,
Only an entrance to felicitie.
Rivers of Pleasures thou shalt have to th' brim,[199]
Wherein the Prophets and Apostles swim:[k]
And with great Glory thou shalt crowned be,
And on the Throne sit down also[l] with me.
World, Death, nor Devil ever[m] shall remove
My heart from thee; for those I truly love,
I love to th' end: Ah! Soul 'tis thou shalt lie,
In my own Arms to all Eternitie.

Youth.

Darkness is gone, day-light begins to spring;
Heavens melody I find is[n] the sweetest thing.
The Sun is risen now, it is broke forth,
And gloriously inlightens my dark earth.

My Soul is ravish'd with this joyful sight,
Yea, and dissolv'd with love and true delight:
My heart is melted with Cœlestial fire,
And has obtain'd at length it's own desire.
My frozen Soul must needs run down amain,
Which such hot beams from *Jesus* doth obtain:
The door is open'd, Christ has giv'n a knock
Has made it fly, and hath dissolv'd the rock.[200]
My heart which was so hard is made to yield,
Christ has o'recome me now and wone the field.
The War is ceas'd between the Lord and I,
A Peace is made to all Eternity.
What joy is this! Ah, 'tis beyond measure,[a]
There's nothing like to inward joy and pleasure.
As was my burden, so I find my rest,
O that was great! and this can't be exprest.
What heart can taste of these transcendent joys,
And not account Earth's pleasures empty toys![201]
Such is the nature of a second birth,
Makes Heav'n on Earth, turns sorrow into mirth.[202] [b]
Once was I blind, senseless, bewitch'd, nay, mad;
I thought in Christ no comfort could be had.
Religion was, I thought, a foolish thing,
Which could no pleasure nor no profit bring.
I thought Professors greatly were misled,
When I beheld what things they suffered:
But I am now convinc'd of my mistake,
For I my self could, for Christ Jesus sake,
Any derision or affliction bear,
Such inward peace in him, and joy[c] is there.
"What man would not all earthly glory slight,
"For one small dram, or taste of such delight?
To have Christ's Love, and in his bosom lie,
Yields true content, and sweet felicitie.
Ah happy I, I live! my Soul's involv'd
In secret raptures, sighs to be dissolv'd,[203]
And be with Christ my home and resting-place,
For to injoy and see him face to face.[204]
And in the int'rim, Lord, whilst here I stay,
I faithfully will do what thou dost say.
And help me, Lord, thy praise for to declare
To[d] all precious Children far and near.
O help me to lift up my voice on high!
Let joyfull *Hallelujahs* pierce the sky,
And eccho back again, resound on Earth,
Since thou hast wrought in me the second birth:
Let me with the Cœlestial Angels sing,
And make thy Praises round the World to ring!

Thou'st brought my Soul out of the th' lowest Pit,
And in the paths[a] of *Sion* set my feet![205]
Thou hast from Darkness brought me into Light,
And to mine eyes thou[b] hast restored sight![206]
Nay, hast my Soul sav'd from Eternal death,
And shall not I thy praises, Lord, sing forth?[c]
O let my tongue, my heart, and life make known
The favour, Lord, which to me thou hast shown!
Let me aloft, by thy blest[d] Grace, aspire
To sound thy praise with the Cœlestial Quire!
With swift wing'd *Cherubims*, Lord, let me joyn,
To magnifie that glorious Name of thine.[207] [e]
Let not remainers[f] of the flesh disturb
My precious peace, that's new: O do thou curb,
Yea, kill and crucifie each evil thought,
With vengeance let those Rebels down be brought.[208]
And let me on the Earth live all my days
Unto thy Glory and transcendent praise.
And then, great God, when these short days are o're
With *Seraphims* I'le sing for evermore.[209]

Truth.

What Melody and Triumph do I hear?
Whose voice is this that soundeth in mine ear?
What Eagle-ey'd Soul's this that soars on high,
That with swift-wings[g] aloft doth mount and fly;
And in Eternal Love seems to lie down,
Adorn'd with Grace, and ravish'd with the Crown
Of inward Peace? that taketh up its rest
At Jesus Christ's sweet satisfying breast,
And breaketh[h] forth in raptures, can't express,
As he would do, his humble thankfulness?[210]

Youth.

'Tis I, blest *Truth*, the Conquest now is wone,
Grace has prevail'd, I am the conquer'd one:
My grief is turn'd to joy, yea and my night
Is also chang'd into Eternal Light.
Thy power's[i] great, when *Grace* doth work with thee,
Ye[j] soon do then obtain the victorie.
Blest be the day that ever thou wast[k] sent,
To change my heart, and move me to repent!
Dear love to thee, O *Truth*, I shall retain
So long as I upon the Earth remain.
I'le keep thee close, and hide thee in my heart,
For thou more precious than rich Jewels art.
I'le lose[l] my All before I'le part with thee,
So much I love and prize thy companie.

Though Satan stir up foes never so cruel,
Devils nor Men shall[a] rob me of this[b] Jewel.
I am resolv'd a thousand deaths to dy,
Before I will God's blessed Truth deny.
Though of Deceivers there's a multitude,
Yet none of them shall my poor Soul delude.
Though they do thee reproach, slight and contemn
I by Exper'ence can refute all them,
Who say thy words nought but dead letters are,
Which men may burn, or into pieces tare:
The out-side of the Book they only see,
Who thus do speak reproachfully of thee:
For did they but thy inward power know,
They'd never speak, as oftentimes they do:
But soon they would God's written Word extol,
Above that Light which they cry up in all.
The Light which *Conscience* unto me doth give,
I'le always own as long as I do live,
But from God's Word doth its chief light[c] descend,
Therefore the Holy Scriptures I'le commend:[d]
For had we not God's Word to light our hearts,
The Heathens which[e] do live in Forraign parts,
Who never heard of Christ, might understand
As much as any do[f] in this our Land:
Alas! we should have been unto this day,
In all respects as Ignorant as they.[211]
But I'le forbear, because I must with speed
Attend upon God's Truth with care and heed,
To hear what he will say; O *Truth* wilt thou
Concerning me shew[g] forth thy Judgment[h] now?
I do intreat thee prove me thorowly,
For still I do retain a jealousie.
Over my heart, because that[i] I have seen
How I deceived oftentimes have been.

Truth.

Conscience, to thee I must[j] once more descend,
The Controversie thou alone must end:
How is it with him now? what dost thou say?
Hast any thing unto his Charge to lay?
Remember what I formerly have shown,
And let thy present thoughts with speed[k] be known.

Conscience.

I always ready am Judgment to give,
According to the Light I do receive,[l]
And never was more free than now am I

My thoughts to shew; your suit I can't deny.
O Sir! the case is chang'd! I am his Friend,
His sweet Condition I must needs commend.
Grace has subdu'd corruption in his heart,
That he's made clean, and wash'd in every part.
My testimony you may take for truth,
He's now become a very humble Youth;
He's truly Godly, Faithful, and Sincere,
I do for him, and shall my witness bear:
All kind of Evil doth his Soul defie,
And[a] hates above all things Hypocrisie:
Will and Affections now are changed quite,
That in the Lord alone is his delight.
There's no Commands of Christ,[b] not any one
That he's convinc'd of, but he has done:
He faithfully also the Lord obeys,
Without excuses, put-offs, or delays.
He grieveth most for sins that secret are,
Which unto men do not i'th' least appear.
He's more in substance than he is in show,
When high'st in joy, his heart is very low.
All his own Righteousness he doth disown,
And does rely on Jesus Christ alone.
Christ is become so precious in his sight,
He's first with him i'th' morn, and last at night.
He willingly has taken up the Cross,
And doth account what e're is his[c] but dross;
And parts with it most freely, Christ to gain,
Since he hath found Earth's best injoyments[d] vain.[212]
Christ he exalts as King i'th' highest degree,
And gives each Office its full dignitie.
He uses me also most tenderly,
Because he knows that my Authority
Is from a bove, it is for Jesus sake
He sides with me, and doth resolve to take
My part alwayes, what ere he doth sustain,
He'l rather suffer than wound me again.[e][f]
Christ has in me set up his blessed Throne,
And over me no other King[g] he'l own:
Christ must alone in me the Scepter sway,
And he will die before he'l give a way[h]
Christ's Right and Soveraignty in his dear Soul,
He is resolv'd to suffer no controul,
In things alone which to me appertain,
Fear least[i] thereby Christ's Glory he should stain.[213]

Truth.

Oh! happy young-man! blessed from above,
Blessed with Grace, and ravisht with the love,
Of thy Eternal Lord, in whose sweet breast
Thou now dost lie, and evermore shalt rest.
Thy Honor's lasting, now it can't decay,
Thy Tresure's sure, Thieves can't[a] steal't[b] away:
Thy Pleasures are beyond thought or conceit,
And thy rare Beauty is without deceit.
Thy Strength, thy Wisdom, nor thy Youth shall fade,
Nor canst thou die, thou art immortal made.
Eternal Life is given unto thee,
And thou shalt reign to all Eternitie.

Uicinus.

There's none on Earth is able to express,
The inward peace this Young-man doth possess;
Whilst to his joy, he clearly doth espy
This blessed Concord, and rare Harmony:
Conscience and *Truth* most sweetly do agree,
He's free'd from Bondage and Captivitie.
Christ's Spirit doth with *Conscience* witness bear,
He's born of God, and is become an Heir
(With his dear Saviour) of Eternal bliss:
What Consolation can there be like this?
But whilst thus fill'd with joy and true delight,
The Devil falls[c] on him with all his[d] might;
With strong assaults, his Faith for to destroy,
Which much abates, and mitigates his joy:
But Satan failing in his Enterprize,
In one respect, another way he tries;
And with malicious threats, he breaketh forth,
Spiting his venome and his hellish wrath:[e]
Which in some measure may to you appear,
By what immediately doth follow here.

Devil.

Heark, heark, thou cursed wretch, vengeance is mine,
And I'le repay't upon[f] that Soul of thine;[214]
In dreadful wrath I will contend with thee,
If thou wilt not again submit to me.
Will not my shining Glory thee invite,
Nor all my Agents[g] thy Soul affright,
To leave those cursed ways in which you go?
Then I'le some way contrive your overthrow.
Though out of your Dominions I am beat,
And forced am at present to Retreat;
Yet I'le return like to[h] a Lion strong,
And break thy bones in pieces ere't be long.[215]

Youth.

Father of Lyes,[216] dost think I dread thy frown,
'Tis past thy skill to throw my Glory down;
Thy head is broke,[217] thou art a beaten Foe,
And chained up; alas! thou canst not do
According to thy wrath and cursed[a] spight,
Christ's Power is mine, who stronger is in Might;
Me he'l not leave, though tempted am by thee,
Yet he knows how to help and succour me.
What matter is't although thou art inraged,
When the great Pow'r of Heaven is ingaged
To side with me always, and take[b] my part:
Though thou a Lion and a Serpent art,
Yet mayst as soon the Lord of Life o'recome,
As to produce or work my final Doom,
So long as I do for his Glory stand,
And am obedient to his blest[c] Command.

Devil.

But I have so much craft and subtilty,[218]
That I can make the Lord thine Enemy;
Though thou dost think he is become thy Friend,
I'le by temptation move thee to offend
Him ere't be long; and soon you will espy
In's anger you he'l cast off utterly:
And then I'le tear and rend you[d] *as I list,*
And you shall have no power to resist.

Youth.

God has bestow'd on me his precious Grace,
That I abhor the thoughts of[e] giving place
To thee, O Satan, though thou dost intice;
God will preserve my Soul from deadly vice:
But if through weakness him I should offend,
In bowels he'l to me his Pardon send.
Christ is my Advocate; God will pass by
All sins of Weakness and Infirmity.
Although he use the Rod, his precious Love
I'm sure from me he never will remove.

Devil.

Your hopes will fail, alas! black clouds will hide
Your glorious Sun, your steps will quickly slide:
Your morning's bright, but soon 'twill over-cast,[f]
And all your joy will scarce a moment last.
Though Truth *doth now thy present state commend,*
Yet you will[g] *find the Proverb true i'th' end.*
That the young Saint will an old Devil be:[219]
You'l die and perish in Apostasie.

Youth.

'Cause thou hast lost thy former happy state,[220]
With malice thou stir'st up thy bitter hate
Against my Soul, thou show'st thy wicked spite,[221]
But thy vile teeth are broke, thou canst not bite.
Thou dost on me cast forth an env'ous frown,
Because thou hast for ever lost thy Crown.
Because thy morning's turned into night,
Dost think thou shalt my Soul amaze and fright
With such insnaring[a] thoughts? I thee defie,
Nothing can break that blessed Band and Tie,
Or Covenant which Christ with me has made,
My standing's firm, my Crown can never fade.
He that has in my Soul this work begun,
Will finish it I'm sure e're he has done.
There's ne're a Lamb or Sheep of his dear fold,
But he will keep, he has of them such hold,
That in the midst of danger they shall stand,
And none shall pluck them out of his strong hand:[222]
They by[b] his Pow'r are kept in ev'ry Nation,
'Till they'r[c] safely brought unto Salvation.
Upon the Rock of Ages I am placed,
And my foundation never can be raz'd.[223] [d] [e]
Though the Mountains should[f] depart, and Hills remove,
Yet[g] Christ will never change in his dear Love.
Nor cause his Covenant of lasting[h] peace
To be remov'd, nor his sweet Mercy cease.[224]
The *Truth* and *Conscience* both joyntly agree,[i]
That the[j] new-birth is truly wrought in me.
Th' Immortal seed I'm sure must needs bring forth
A Babe Immortal; my Heavenly[k] birth
Doth shew to all, and clearly signifie,
I cannot perish in Apostacy.
The Head and Members of one Nature are,
Or else Christ's Body a strange Monster were.[225]
As sure as He's in Heaven, so shall I,[l]
And reign with him to all Eternity.

Devil.

My words I see no place at all can find
Within the Center of thy evil mind:
I'll leave thee therefore with my dreadful Curse,
VVhich is as bad as Hell, nay, it is worse
Than all the Plagues of the infernal Lake;
And let all[m] those who love me, vengeance take
Vpon so vile a wretch: and though I do
Forsake thee now, within a day or two
I'll come again, and will thy Soul torment,
Vnless that speedily thou dost repent.[n]

Youth.

O Lord, I praise thee for that glorious Pow'r,
Which helpt my Soul in such a needful hour
Of strong assaults from the vile wicked one;
Thou help'st me to resist him, and he's gone.
Therefore, dear God, be pleased to inflame
My heart with Grace to magnifie thy Name:
And when he comes again, O then be near,
And let thy *Truth* also for me appear:
Though I am young and weak, I shall thereby
Not fear the assaults of any Enemy.
Come, speak, O *Truth*, wilt still[a] be on my side?
'Tis in thy strength I[b] very much confide.
Though I am feeble, thou art mighty[c] strong;
And whilst for me, there's none can do me wrong.

Truth.

I will, dear Soul, support thee whilst on Earth,
And save thee from the rage of Hell and Death:
I will assist thee by my[d] mighty Arm,
And keep thee day and night from hurt and harm;
And with my glitt'ring Sword cut down and slay
All cursed Enemies who thee gain-say.

Grace.

If *Truth* should fail, I will thy wants supply,
Thou need'st not doubt of my sufficiency.
Light I will be in Darkness, Joy in Grief,
And when in Trouble great, I'll bring Relief.
If alwaies thou dost on my Arm[e] rely,
The *Devil* will be forc'd with speed[f] to fly.
Never on me did any Soul depend,
But they obtain'd Deliv'rance in the end.
I'll help thy Soul through all its Christian strife,
And bring thee safe to Everlasting Life.

Conscience.

I'll be the *third* that will lend thee an hand,
We'll all combine to make a triple band.
A threefold Cord can't easily broken be,[226]
I'le be a Friend in thine[g] Adversitie.
There's not a Foe on Earth thou needst to fear,
So long as I for thee my witness bear,
That thou in Truth dost walk before the Lord,
And that thy ways do with his Word accord;
The evil Foe will[h] be ashamed quite,
Whilst faithfully thou walk'st up to thy Light;
And Satan never can get any ground,
Whilst I declare thy heart is[i] truly sound.
Chear[j] up, poor Soul, I'le feast thee constantly,

And plead for thee before the Enemy.
My sweetest Wine also I'le keep to th' end,
At death I will thy Soul with that befriend.
God's Word that is thy ground in every thing,
His Glory is thy aim, from thence doth spring
All service thou dost do[a] towards the Lord,
His Spirit therefore to thee he'l afford,
That doth bear witness for thee, so do I,
And will also when thou dost come to dy.[b]

AN APPENDIX
Containing a Dialogue between an old
Apostate, and young **Professor**.

Apostate.

HOw many straights and crosses have I met,
Since I my self to seek for *Canaan* set?
Red-Seas and Wildernesses lye between
Why venture I for what I ne'r have seen?[227]
Why can I not here where I am[c] Remain?
Or to my old delights turn back again.
My head has been perplext with cares and fears,
Since to these Preachers I inclin'd mine ears.
They were but fancies that disturb'd[d] my mind,
I sought for something which I could not find.
Would God in *Egypt* I had still remain'd,[e]
For there's no *Canaan* likely to be gain'd.
Conscience be silent, don't disturb me more
Upon such things, I will no longer pore,
For back to *Egypt* I will now retire
Where I shall have things to my hearts desire.

Devil.

Pursue thy purpose, thou shalt understand,
What ere I have shall be at thy command:
My Kingdoms great, this world is wholly mine,
Bow down to me, and all shall then be thine.
Afraid I was I should have lost the[f] quite,
There's nought like that which here's now in thy sight.
Behold the Bags of Gold which thou shalt have,
Honours on earth, riches and pleasures brave,
When others forc'd in Prison are to lie;
Thou shalt enjoy thy precious liberty.
When Kings and Princes do upon them frown,
Thou shalt be held in honour and renown.[228]

Thou hast much goods laid up for many years,
And long shalt live free from all cares and fears.[229]
Thy Seed establish'd too shall be on Earth,[230]
And thou shalt spend thy days in joy and mirth:
Thoughts of Religion utterly disdain,
Nor think of God, or Jesus Christ again.
Phanatick fables never more regard,
The pains of Hell of[a] which thou oft hast heard,
Are nought save fictions of their crasy[b] head.
With fear of nothing are they frightned.
That mad men like, they do[c] tread under feet
Those lovely joys which wise men find most sweet.
Religion's nought but a devised thing,
Which up at first some crafty head did[d] bring
To awe the minds of fools, who wanting wit,
Take that for gold that's a mear counterfeit.
The truth of th'Scripture thou hast cause to doubt,
For divers places thou may'st soon find out
Which inconsistent to each other be,
Of what it speaks there is no certaintie.
Conclude in Truth there is no God at all,
Why should'st thou be so foolish as to call
On him, whom thou did'st never see or know,
Unless it's thus; because that most[e] do so.[231]
Let melancholly fancies now therefore,
Ne'r vex thy mind, nor grieve thee any more.
Enjoy thy self on Earth, and heap up Gold,
No good like that which purse and[f] bags do hold.
Come eat and drink, tomorrow thou must die,[232]
And afterwards[g] there's no Eternity
As some suppose, for thou i'th grave shalt rot,
And as the Beast be utterly forgot:
But since you know it is reproach to them,
Who all[h] Religion utterly contemn.
Thou mayest Religious also seem to be,
For there is one that's[i] very fit for thee.
Mellodious sounds, sweet mirth, and Musick rare,
Do much affect the heart, and charm the ear.
No worship on the Earth doth[j] suit so well
With flesh or[k] blood, or doth for ease excel,
Or with man's interest doth so well agree,
Like what's maintain'd in famous *Italy*.
That that's the worship which for thee I pick,[l]
I'm not against thy turning Catholick.
If there's a Heaven, of[m] this thou need'st not doubt,
An easier way for thee I can't find out.
The way's so broad, whole Nations walk therein,

And persons of all sorts, no let is sin.
Wer't thou at *Rome*, thou'lt hear melodious sounds,
Sweet joys[a] and mirth on every side abounds:
Fine boys and men ravishing notes do sing
Whil'st Organs play in Consort, and Bells ring;
In that brave way thou't have thy liberty
To do such things as others do deny.
Thou mayst be mad, carouse, and domineer,
Strict *Roman Catholicks* such things can bear.
If thou dost swear, drink healths, yea, or should'st curse,
There's few i'th' Church would[b] like the e're the worse.
Or if thou should'st some curious *Lady* spy,
Or view some pretty Maid with wanton eye,
To court or play with her[c] thou needst not fear,
For venial sins alas all such things are;[d]
And one great help and remedy thou't have,
Which from all grief and danger will thee save.
If it fall out by chance at any time
Thou should'st commit some great and hainous crime,
There is straight-way the blessed Absolution,
A present help, and yet no superstition.
For a small sum of mony soon is had
A pardon for all sins, though ne'r so bad.
His Holiness for a few shillings can
Murder and Perjury forgive to man;
Nay unto thee can grant a Dispensation
To kill and murder any in a Nation;
Who us and th' holy Church hate and oppose,[233]
Come trouble not thy self, but straight-way close
With this fam'd *Church*, to whom such powers given
To ope[e] and shut with ease the Gates of Heaven.
And make that sin to day which[f] ne'r was sin,
And that lawful, which lawful ne'r hath[g] bin.
Come buy thee[h] Beads[234] and Crucifix also,
And as the Church believes,[i] believe thou too.
For this I hope to see o're[j] a few days,
Some thousands more cleaving to those[k] old ways,
And thou wilt not such advantage[l] gain,
As now thou may'st with ease I am sure[m] obtain.
And since in kindness and affection dear,
I've shew'd thee how to be preferred here.
And do engage thy faithful friend to be:
There's some small thing I'd[n] have thee do for me.
Speak evil of the way thou late wast in,
Believe[o] them all, and charge them too with sin.
Their faults lay ope,[p] let nought at all be hid,
Revile, reproach, and slander in my stead:
Shew how they differ, that they can't agree,

There's little love and want of Charitie.[235]
Of *Canaan* Land raise thou an ill report,
To turn them back who are a going[a] for't.
One thing at present I would have thee do,
There is a friend of mine which thou dost know,
Who hath a Son which is indeed his Heir,
That to these foolish Notions doth adhere.
If he should visit thee, with speed do thou
Treat with the peevish youth, I'le teach thee how
To controvert the cause, my place supply,
And do what I could not do formerly.
His forward zeal will do my kingdom wrong,
Cause[b] others also in that way to[c] throng.
And you shall also some derision bear
Through his hot zeal, if that you ha'nt a care.

Uicinus.

The thoughts which Satan darts into his mind,
He closeth with, and fully is inclin'd
His Councel for to take, what e're become
Of his poor Soul at the great day of Doom.
An Atheist he's become in heart and life,
And hath abandon'd all his Christian strife.
He's ready now, and fit for any evil,
An Instrument prepared for the Devil.
But since the Gentleman and he are met,
I will give way, and hearken how they treat
About this youth, that has of late begun,
Resolvedly to Heaven for to run.
You'l hear how this Apostate will ingage,
To turn him from his blessed Pilgrimage.

Apostate.

What my old Friend *E. R.* Sir, I am glad
To see you once again, yet I am sad,
And grieved sore, to see you look so ill,
What evil Sir, I pray, has you befel?
    What is the cause of this your present grief?
If I can give, or help you to relief,
Or comfort you i'th' least, I willing am,
And shall[d] rejoyce, also I[e] hither came.

Gent.

Ah Sir, my Son, my Heir, doth grive my mind,
He from whom I most[f] comfort hop'd to find,
Contrariwise will[g] prove a plague to me,
Unless he can with speed recovered be.
He'll be a Preacher I do think e're long,

He's such a Bookish-fool, and so headstrong,
That I have little hopes he'll e're be good;
Here's cause of grief, if rightly understood.
He is become such a vile[a] Heretick,
That *Rome*'s good Church,[b] and the true Catholick,
Most vilely, I perceive, he doth disdain,
And doth, forsooth, tell me he's born again.
I do beseech ye[c] Sir, do what you can,
If you can't change his mind, there's not a man
I think, in truth, that ever prevail will;[d]
O arm your self therefore, and try your skill;[e]
If you can turn him from these waies, then I
Shall be ingag'd to you until I die.
You were deceiv'd your self some time ago,
And therefore now more able are to show
The vanity of these devised waies,
And Bookish-fables of these silly daies.
Having the Scripture in our Mother-tongue
Has been the ruine of us all along:
For, since men did our holy Church forsake,
And up new notions of[f] Religion take,
Nought but confusion in the World we see,
And otherwise, in truth, 'twill never be
Until their Books i'th' fire all do burn,
And they unto the Ancient Church to[g] turn.

Apostate.

I am good Sir of that opinion too,
And sorry am to hear what now you do
Relate to me, and will also in truth
Do what I can to turn that silly youth;
For I can shew, and make him understand
The danger that attends on ev'ry hand.
The hopes of unseen things will him deceive,
And Faith's but a meer fancy I believe:
That's the chief good which man doth here enjoy,
And that's he evil which doth him annoy,
Or doth deprive him of this[h] joy and bliss,
None but Phanaticks will deny me this;
Who boast of that they never did possess;
They lie alas, and are (in truth) no less
Than frantick fools, for I could never see
Of what they speak, there's any certainty.
I will therefore endeavour out of love,
Your Son from these delusions to remove:
And since I do perceive he's neer at hand,
I'le take my leave,
　　　　　Your Servant to Command.

THE PROLOGUE.

ATtend kind Friend, read with a serious eye,
And thou shalt a sharp Conflict soon espy
Between a man quite void of godly fear,
And a dear youth most holy and sincere.
The one affirms all godliness is vain,
The other counts it for the greatest gain.
Mark thou the end of both, and thou shalt see
What's best to chuse, Grace or Iniquitie.

Apostate.

Well met, good Sir, from whence pray did you come

Professor.

I am a stranger, and am Trav'ling home.

Apostate.

Are you a stranger in this Country,

Professor.

Yea, as were all our Fathers formerly.

Apostate.

But from whence came ye, let's confer together.

Professor.

From *Egypt* Sir, **Apos.** I am Trav'ling thither.

Apostate.

    What is your business Sir, that thus in pain
You strive against the wind with might and main?
E're further you do go, sit down, account,
See whether that you run for will surmount
The labour great, and loss you will sustain,
Before the price[a] in Truth ye do obtain.
What place is it to which you think to go,
That to advise you I may fully know?
For good instruction to you I'le afford,
When I this thing from you have plainly heard.

Professor.

    I am for *Canaan*, that most Holy Land,
I'le travel thither, as God doth command,
Whose worth and value I do know full well,
For Riches it doth far all things excel.
And though all things I lose e're I come there,
'Twil all my losses I am sure repaire.
The worth of that therefore for which I run,
I did account before I first begun.

Apostate.

Know you of certain, the place is so rare,
You may mistake, for you were never there.

Professor.

Ah Sir, of it I have a glorious sight,
Which doth my Soul transcendently[a] delight,
Although in person there I ne'r have been,
Yet I most plain sweet *Canaan* oft have seen:
Besides, I lately spoke with a dear friend,
Who did the other day from thence descend;
And unto me it's glory he did show,
It's precious worth from thence[b] I came to know:
Some of its fruit[c] also to me he gave,
Which makes me long till I possession have.

Apostate.

Is't not the fancy of thy crasy-head,
I have likewise of such a *Canaan* read;
It may be so, or so it may not be,
It ne'r seem'd real truly[d] unto me.
Who would for things which so uncertain are,
Such losses suffer, and such labor bare.
A Bird i'th' hand's worth two i'th' bush, ye know,
This Zeal (*poor Lad*) will work thy overthrow.

Professor.

You vainly talk, and live by sight and sence,
I walk by faith, which is the evidence
Of things not seen, hear[e] with an outward eye,
What thou see'st not I clearly do espy.
'Tis not the fancy of a crasy-brain,
For *Moses* that it's glory he might gain.
All *Egypts* Treasures quickly did forgo,
Was that the way unto his overthrow?
No, no, dear Sir, he saw it was the way
To peace and honour in another day:
The glory real did his Soul behold,
To be so great, that never can be told.[236]
If thou hadst drunk but of its glorious springs,
Thou would'st it prise above all earthly things.
If thou hadst tasted but of *Canaans* hony,
Thou wouldst esteemd[f] it more than bags of mony[237]
Although I make, alas, a poor profession,
Yet I have now something in my possession.
Lock'd up most safe within[g] my refreshed brest,
More rare than Pearls within a golden Chest.[h]
True peace of *Conscience* that through grace I have,

Which passeth all mens knowledge to conceive,
I would of it not be depriv'd[a] again,
If that I might ten thousand worlds obtain.

Apostate.

Tush, silly Fool, kick Conscience quite away,
Ne'r mind his motions, nor what he doth say.
I stifil'd him, and that a good while since,
And took revenge for his proud Insolence.
His gasping groans I no ways did regard,
But let my heart against him grow so hard,
That I do judge I have his business done.
He's dead in truth, and to dark silence gone;
That now I can, without the least controul,
Have any pleasures which[b] delight my Soul.

Professor.

Ah Sir, go on, if that's the choice ye[c] make,
I never will such cursed Councel take.
Who ever doth his Conscience so abuse,
Doth his dear Maker in like manner use.
And though in your[d] poor *Conscience* now lies slain,
I'th' Judgment day will[e] revive again.
And then against you his sad witness bare,[f]
And in your face most gastfully will stare,
You'l have the worst at last, I grieve to see
You hardned thus in your Iniquitie.

Apostate.

My sorrow's gone, but thine alas will double,
Concerning me, thy self do thou not trouble.
The storms and blustering winds are over-past,
And very safe I am arriv'd at last.
In that same Port where Princes do delight
For to repose, and harbour day and night.[238]
Tost'd[g] I have been upon the boysterous Seas,
And 'till of late ne're could find rest nor ease.
But now am[h] safely landed, and with good
Shall satiated[i] be, whilst thou art toss'd i'th flood.
Thou shalt poor youth with dreadful storms be hurl'd,
Whilst I shall find a very quiet world.
All thy best days are gone, and plung'd thoul't be
Into sad Gulphs of woful miserie.
Unless thou dost recant, & stop thy course,
Thou'lt see things with thee will grow worse and worse
Those fools who do their nicer Conscience mind,
E're long they shall but little friendship[j] find.

Youth.

Sir, Storm and Tempest[a] do I know attend,
Those who resolve poor Conscience[b] to befriend.
Paul's portion 'twas, who from his very youth,
Had kept good Conscience, and obey'd the truth.
He met with blustering winds, was toss'd about,[239]
Yet did bear up for *Canaan* most devout,
'Till he at last the glorious Voyage made,
Getting the Crown which ne'r away shall fade.[240]
All those who sayl'd this way, have all along,
Met with great opposition[c] and much wrong
From Pyrate[d] Spoylers, and Usurpers, who
Contrived have the Righteous to undo.[241]
This terrefies me not, because that I
Know 'tis the way to true Felicitie.
The gold and precious things the Merchant gains,
Doe quit his cost,[e] and recompence his pains.
The Riches which he brings at his return,
Makes him great dangers oftentimes to run.
So hopes of joys, the which Cælestial are,
Makes me no labour nor no cost to spare.
You are for present things, I further see,
You are for Earth, but Heaven is for me.
You are for pleasures, and for bags of Gold,
I am for that which *Moses* did behold.
You are for ease, what ever it doth cost,
And honours here, though Soul for it be lost.
Who makes the wisest choice, let him declare,
Let Death and Judgment shew who wise men are.
My purpose I'e pursue what ere I meet,
My portion's great,[242] my peace, no[f] counterfit.
Heaven is my port, there's such a place I'm sure,
Nought shall intice me nor my soul alure.
To lose[g] my hold I'le keep firm in my station,
Though in my way I meet with tribulation.
Yet I most safe shall there at last arive,
No men nor Devils ever shall deprive
My soul of that eternal dwelling place,
Such confidence I have obtain'd through grace.

Apostate.

If I should grant things which so doubtful are,
That there's a *Canaan* or a Heaven where:
Sweet joys abound beyond whats here below
Yet hard it is for any man to know
The ready way unto that seeming place,
Consider this, Oh 'tis a weighty case!
For there's[h] so many ways and voices be,

How thou shouldst[a] find the way[b] I do not see.
Thou art a stranger too thou toldst, be[c] plain,
Come come young man, turn with me back again.

Youth.

Nothing (dear Sir) more certain is then this,
That there's a heaven or[d] eternal Bliss.
The Heathens could by nature[e] light espy,
Mans chiefest good or best felicity.[243]
Must needs excel the highest enjoyments here,
And shall this doubtful unto those appear.
Who have Gods works (most dreadfully made known)
Yea and his word which very few or non
Who live in any land the like have had,
Shall such turn Atheists, this is very sad.
Is not Jehovah every where made known
By fearful[f] Judgments, which are dayly shown,
And why think you I can't the true way find,
Seeing Jesus has in writing left his mind[g]
In plain Caracters, which whilst I observe,
I from the truth am sure no ways can[h] swarve.
He came from thence himself the other day,
And gave directions how to find the way.
This writings firm, 'tis signed with his blood,
That the old dragon with his mighty flood,
Of superstition, and persecuting fire,
Could not it spoil nor gain his curst desire.[244]
The holy Scripture God to us have[i] given,
To guide our souls in the right way to heaven.
Though Satan has made opposition strong,
Yet still we have it in our mother tongue.
And by this means, most plain I come to[j] know,
The very foot steps where the flock did go.

Apostate.

Though you of Scripture seem to make your boast,
Your hopes of this will suddenly be lost.
For you much longer it, an't like to have,[k]
Your souls and others thus for to deceive.
For holy Church[245] once more will quite destroy
This *English* God, which they seem to enjoy.
Thou art unlearn'd, the Scriptures dost[l] not know,
But wresteth[m] them unto thy overthrow.

Youth.

They are unlearn'd, whom God has[n] never taught,
But have in Popish darkness up been brought.
They are unlearn'd, who never had the Spirit,

Who think they can by Works salvation[a] merit.
They are unlearn'd, who foolishly deny
The Spirits Teachings and Authority.[246]
For to excell all humane Arts and Science,
And on man's teaching wholly have reliance.
They are unlearn'd, or very poorly read,
That teach Christ Jesus is a peice of Bread,
Which Rats and Mice may eat, and vomit up,
And do deny the Layety the Cup.
For those for whom Christ did his Body break,
He of the Cup bad[b] them all partake.
They are unlearn'd, who think that Purgatory,
To[c] be ought else than a meer fained Story.
They are unlearn'd, whose Doctrine doth declare
The Church two heads, doth on its[d] shoulders bare.[e]
That Woman which hath any Husbands[f] more
Than only one, is a notorious Whore.[247]
That man's unlearn'd, who learned never hath
The A B C of the True Christian Faith.
That man I grant is wholly yet unlearn'd,
Who never knew himself, nor yet discern'd
The cursed nature of his hanious sin,
Nor what estate by nature he is in.[248]
That man's unlearn'd who never went to school,
To learn for[g] Christ how to become a fool.[249]
That man's unlearn'd, yea and a very sot,
Who hath his soul and Jesus Christ forgot.
And doth esteem earths empty vanity,
Above that good which Saints in God espy.
I am unlearn'd, and yet have learned how
To crucifie the flesh, yea and to bow
To Jesus Christ, and for his precious sake,
His yoak and burden willingly to take.
And follow him where ever he doth goe,
And him alone determine for to know.
Who for my sake upon the Cross did die,
Him I have learn'd alone to magnifie.
And to exalt him as he's preist and King,
And as my prophet too in every thing.[250]
And this through grace I learned have of late,
To be content what ever be my[h] state.
Some things I must confess I ne'r could learn,
Nor any ways perceive, see or discern.
I never read of *Peters* tripple Crown,
Nor that he ever wore a Popish Gown.
I never learn't that he did *Pope* become,
Or rule o're Kings like to the beast at *Rome*.[251]

I never learn'd that he kept Concubins,
Or ever power had to pardon sins.
I never learn'd he granted dispensations,
To poison Kings, or Rulers of those Nations.
Who were profane or^a turned Hereticks,
Or did refuse the Faith of Catholicks.[252]
I never learn'd he was the Churches head,
Or did forbid^b the Clergy for to wed.
I never read that he had Chests of Gold,
Or that great Benefits by him were sold.
I never read he's call'd his Holiness,
Yet had as much as any Pope I guess.
I never learn'd *Peter* did magnify
Himself above all Gods, or God on high.
Or that upon the neck of Kings he trod,[253]
Or ever he in cloth of Gold was clad.
I never read that he made Laws to burn
Such as were Hereticks, or would not turn
To Jesus Christ, much less to Murder those,
Who did in Truth Idolatry oppose.[254]
I never learn'd, nor could unto this day,
That th' Pope and *Peter* walk'd both in one way:[255]
Yea, or that they in any thing accord
Save only in denying of the Lord.[256]
In that they also greatly differ do,
Of which I think to give a hint or two.
Peter deny'd him, yet did love him dear,
The Pope denys him, and doth hatred bear
To him, and to all those that him do^c love.
Who bear his Image, and are from above.
Peter deny'd him, and did weep amain,
The Pope denys him with the greatest disdain.
Peter deny'd him, yet for him did die,
The Pope in malice him doth crucifie.
Peter deny'd him thrice, and then repented,
The Pope a thousand times, but ne'r relented.
Peter and *John* no mighty Scholars were,
Yet few for knowledg might with them compare.
Poor Fisher-men do find the way to Heaven,
When Scholars go astray, who Arts have seven.[257]
The Learned Schoolmen put our Lord to Death,
And very few of such Christ called hath.
But poor despised persons he doth call,
And passeth by the high-flown Cardinal.
For humane learning, and such kind of Preaching,
Is nothing to th' blessed Spirits teaching.
I learning like, and grant that men may use it,
Yet would I not have them for to abuse it.

Apostate.

Leave off these canting strains, and don't deride
Our holy Father, for I can't abide
To hear such prating Fools,[258] are you so wise,
Dare you the holy Mother Church despise.
'Tis that Religion I like best of all,
The Pope I do adore and Cardinal.
There's Pomp and Riches, and a worldly glory,
What you talk of, is an unpleasant story.
There's pleasure, profit, safety and much ease,
Which doth the flesh as well as spirit please.
Here's Heaven and Earth, what can'st thou more desire,
Or of thy God, or any man require.
Thy way thou hast[a] lost, and *Canaan* wilt not see,
Therefore with speed turn back again[b] with me.

Professor.

Could I no other reason give or urge,
To prove *Romes* Church untrue, I cant but judg.
This which you do[c] speak, doth plainly declare,[d]
For in Christs Church no such vain pomp is there.[e]
No worldly glory doth Christs Church adorn,
For she's afflicted much despis'd and torn.
Her beauty can't with outward eyes be seen,
Her beauty and her glory are within.
When *John* sets forth the antichristian state,
Much outward pomp 'tis true he doth relate.
The Whoor is dek'd with Gold, brave Stones and Pearl,[259]
Who at poor *Sion* doth with envy snearl.
No liberty to th' flesh the Lord doth give,
Saints must alone after the Spirit live.
No serving God and Mammon,[260] Sir tis plain,
To Hell you[f] go except you'r born again.
If you'l be Christs, with speed then turn you must,
To crucifie the flesh with all it's lust.
No cause have I to fear to go astray,
Whilst I walk dayly in the narrow way.[261]
All those who do Gods holy word contemn,
No light nor truth is there at all in them.
Their feet on the dark Mountains soon will fall,[262]
And utter ruin will or'etake them all.
But as for me no cause have I to doubt,[g]
But I shall find this blessed *Canaan* out.
To turn to *Egypt* with you back again,
The thoughts of it my soul doth much disdain.
Dost think I'le leave my *Quales* and *Manna* rare,
For stinking Garlick and for[h] Onyons there.[263]

Apostate.

For all your courage Sir, I do suppose,
You will repent that ever you have chose,
To leave the comforts of a precious World,
And with fond[a] zeal thus blindly to be hurld.
You are a man that might advanced be,
Unto great honour, State, and Dignitie.
Your Father's Master of a good Estate,
And you to[b] are his heir I hear of late.
But if you don't this new Religion leave,
One groat of him you are not like to have.

Professor.

This World in a just ballance oft I try,
And find it lighter far than vanity.[264]
Riches alas! they are but bags of cares,
And honor's nought save fool-bewitching Snares.
Your outward joy will turned be to sadness,
Your pleasure into pain, your wisdom's[c] madness.
You catch at nothing, 'tis at best a bubble,[265]
Which long you cannot keep although you double
Your diligence, and think to hold it fast,
'Twill fly with speed, 'tis but an empty blast:[266]
What frantick fit is this? Will you destroy
Your higher hopes for such a fanci'd joy?[267]
This world's just like th' Strumpet[d] of whom I've read,
Who with sweet fumes inticeth to her bed.[268]
With amorous glance's promises a Bliss,
And hides destruction with a fained Kiss.
She has her tricks, and her insnaring wiles,
But lodges[e] death under deceitful smiles.
She huggs the Soul she hates yea and doth[f] prove,
A very *Judas* where she fains to love.[269]
Take heed therefore, lest you be catch'd i'th' snare,
And by[g] your late repentance much to[h] dear.
These comforts here, which you do precious call,
Each wise man sees they'r vain and sliting[i] all.
To think I should repent, no cause is there,
If things by you rightly considered were.
What *Moses* chose of old the same do I,
All vain allurements I do quite defie.
I knew when first my journy I did take,
I must my fathers house learn to forsake.
In *Abrahams* steps I am resolv'd to go,[270]
What ever I exposed am unto.[271] [j] [k]
What e're I lose, Christ will mak't[l] up to me,
When I of *Canaan* shall possesed be.
I seek no honour here from any one,

True honour comes (dear Sirs)[a] from God alone.
To be an Heir to[b] a great Estate,
Or Son unto some eathly[c] Potentate,
Is nought to what by grace I'm born too.[d]
My portion[e] great I know not how to show.
I'm heir to the[f] mighty King of Heaven,
To me, ere long, sweet *Canaan* will be given.
I do resolve to hold out to the end,
Although I han't one groat nor earthly friend
To favor me: I never will return
Until this glorious *Canaan* I have wone

Apostate.

What ground have you (my friend) for to believe,
If you forsake all things[272] you shall receive.
This land you speak of for your own posession,
Unto your heart 'tis good to put this question.
For divers do unto great things claim,[g]
Yet some oftimes[h] I see, and sure I am,
Unto such lands can no good title[273] show,
Although they strive for them as you may do.
If you should sell what e're you have for this,
And yet at last should also of it miss,
You'l see your self at length then quit[i] undone.
Consider of 't, and back with me return,
For no good title of it can be had,
'Twas this alas which made me sad.[j]
To save my own, I thought 'twas best for me,
Unless of this I could assured be.

Professor.

Don't think you shall my zeal for[k] Heaven cool,
Nor my dear Soul with fancys thus befool.
Rouse up my Soul now in thy own defence,
And shew thy clear, thy[l] precious evidence.
Can any thing be plainer here on earth,
'Twas purchas'd for me by Christ Jesus death.
The father doth this Kingdom own, and he,
For his own child has[m] late adopted me.
And if a child, I also am an heir
And shall with Jesus the[n] like glory share[274]

Apostate.

How do you know you be his child? in this
You may mistake, and so may *Canaan* miss.

Professor.

My late conversion doth most plainly prove,
My inward birth[275] is truly from above.
The Truth and Conscience both agree in one,
I am through grace no Bastar'd, but a Son.
Those whom God doth by his own Spirit lead,
They are his Sons, you in the Scripture read.[276]
Besides all this, since I did first believe,
An earnest of this Land I did receive.
And divers promises also there be,
Which bind it firmly over unto me.
Is not my Title unto heaven good.
When sign'd and seal'd to me by Christ his blood?
You see by these I have a certain ground,
And good assurance for Gods kingdom found.
But you, as it appears, do quite dispair,
Without all hopes of ever coming there;

Apostate.

Nay stay a little, don't affirm that neither,
Why may not I, as soon as you, comª thither.
Though in that way, in which I late did walk,
I was deceiv'd with many other folk;
And thought that Heaven was intail'd to those
Whichᵇ did the Pope and Church of Rome oppose.
Thinking a man a seperate must be,
From that same Church, or else could never see,
Find, nor injoy eternal peace and rest:
And therefore I, like others did protest,
Against that ancient mother Church, whom now:
I am resolv'd to own, yea, and to bow
Down unto,ᶜ with all humble subjection
Thinking 'tis best for safety and protection,
Resolving never more to vex my mind
As I have done, for I shall sooner find
In this smooth way assurance for salvation,
Than if I had kept in my former station.
Hopes I may have, no certain ground I know
The Church affirms we can attain unto.
But promises most clear are made to those,
Who seek for the old way, and with it close:
And that Romes Church can plead antiquity.[277]
No Protestant I'm sure can it deny:
Yea, and must grant, what ever's their profession
That none save *Rome* can prove their true succession
From those brave Churches, which first planted were
By the Apostles, as their *Acts* declare.
And therefore, Youth, you must no longer boast

Of faith and confidence, for you have lost
Your way to Heaven, and must therefore look
Unto that Church which long has been forsook.
From the true Church to rend and schismatize,
Is such an evil in which many lies.[a]
For though Corruption in the Church there be,
Yet all should walk in uniformitie.

Professor.

Sir, I deny your Churches Constitution,
Which makes me loath you, and for your polution,
Corruption, and vile spots, they are so bad,
No Church of Christ the like hath ever had;
Which I resolve to make appear also,[b]
Before I'le leave you, or will let you go.[c]

Apostate.

Romes Church was rightly gather'd that's most clear,
Saint *Paul* himself to this doth witness bear.[278]
Faith and Repentance truly did they own,
And were Baptiz'd also every one.[d]
No Church in constitution right has been,
If that our Church i'th' least doth fail[e] herein.

Professor.

Romes Church I grant was true i'th' Apostles days,
But yours from that doth differ many ways.
Romes Church was very famous heretofore,
But is become th' Scarlet colour'd Whore.[279]
From the true Faith she hath departed quite,
And the true Church was forc't to take her flight.
Into the dark and howling wilderness,
Where she lay hid in sore and great distress,[280]
From the vile Beast, and Dragons furious rage,[281]
And so remain'd until this latter age.
If *Romes* Church now were like unto the old,
Then with the Romanists we all would hold.
But when she is become Christs enemy.
Go[f] *out of Babylon*, doth bid us fly.[282]
If you can prove *Romes* Church has[g] not declin'd,
From that Church-State by *Paul* himself defin'd.
Then you will undertake for to do more
Then any Papist ever did before.
The *Jewish* Church God once did own and love,
But for their sins he did them[h] quite remove.
Out of his[i] sight they'r broken for their sin,
With other Churches which[j] have famous bin.
And yet do keep some outward form and show

Of Worship, and Church-state as *Rome* may do.
Who has in Truth nought left[a] save a bare name,
As hath been clearly prov'd by men of fame.
If you should bring your Visibility
To prove your Church is true, I do reply,
A better argument I need not bring
To prove you[b] false, then that same very thing
For the true Church was[c] hid, did not appear
A thousand two hundred and sixty year.[283]
And then whereas you in the second place
Mention Antiquity, 'tis a clearer[d] case.
Your Church is under age, yea much too young,
Out of the Apostacy alas she sprung.[284]
A basterd Church, base born, mere national,
And therefore that's for you no proof at all.
The fleshly[e] seed 'ith' Church must not be brought,
John Baptist and our Saviour both so taught.
Christs Church is gather'd now[f] by regeneration,
And not as 'was[g] 'ith' former dispensation.[285]
You in a lineal way do go about,
To take in those whom Jesus hath shut out.
The ax is now laid to the root o'th' tree,
And every one true[h] penitent must be.[286]
And must obtain of God true saving grace,
Who in his holy Church would have a place.
Your Church is not so gather'd, therefore I
Deny your Church and it's antiquity;
That[i] Church which is upheld by'th' carnal sword,
And not by the power of Gods holy word.
Is very false,[287] and that *Romes* Church is soe,
Not a few worthy Authors plainly show.
And whereas she much boasts of holiness,
No people doubtless in the world have less.
For *Rome* like to a common stinking[j] shore,
Receives what ev'ry one casts forth o'th door.
She's like a cage of ev'ry hateful bird,
As is recorded in Gods sacred word.[288]
The Councel whih an ancient Author gave,
Let ev'ry soul with special care receive.
"Ye[k] that would holy live, from *Rome* be packing,
"There's all things else, but Godliness is lacking.[289]
She also doth Doctrines of Divels hold,
According as th' Apostle hath[l] foretold.
In charging people to abstain from meat,
Which God alloweth us freely to eat.
And in denying persons for to wed,[290]
Though God allow[m] the undefiled bed.[291]

By means of these most cursed prohibitions,
Your Clergy stinks alive with gross pollutions.
And many of your filthy Popes of Rome,
Have Sodomites and Buggerers become;
Whoredom and Incest[a] they have minc'd so small,
As scarce to count them any sin[b] at all.
Most cursed Stews allowed are by them,
Whom none i'th Popedom dare ith least condemn.
Vile Necromancers many of them were,
Haters of God, no sin (in truth) is there;
But some o'th' Popes of it hath[c] guilty been,
As may upon Record be clearly seen.[292]
Is this your holy Head and reverend Father,
Next unto Christs[d] supream? Is he not rather
A Divel incarnate? the worst of mankind,
Who can in Hell a viler sinner find.
Is *Rome* Christs Church, Christs Spouse, his only Love,
His undefiled one, and spotless dove.[293]
Sir, don't mistake, she is that *Scarlet Whoor*,
Whom *John* characterized heretofore.
Which I shall full evince, and make appear,
If you with patience will but lend an ear.

Apostate.

I fin'd you in reproaches free enough,
But shall expect you so too in your proof.
Those common Epithets of Beast and Whore,
Are daily flung at every bodies door.
But for to warrant your severer doom,
Prove that they properly belong to *Rome*.

Professor.

That truth Gods sacred word doth well explain,
That City which o'er Kings of th'Earth did raign.
Was that same Whore, the spirit clear doth show,
And that *Rome* was that City all men know.
Who then above all others bore the sway,
'Twas *Rome* the Nations fear'd and did obey.[294]
And still you Papists to her Bishop[e] give,
Headship o're all who on the earth do live.
Before him Kings and Emperors must submit,
That so he may the mighty Monarch sit.
Whilst absolute pow'r he claims, and Soveraignty
Above all Princes by his Tyranny.[295]
From whence all persons may conclude it true,
By their first Mark the title is his due.
The second Character of *Babylon*,
Is *Pomp and State wherein she proudly shon,*[f]

That *Rome* has been a rich gay costly Whore,
England once found, I wish she may no more.
Infinite Sums almost she squeez'd from hence,
For pardons, obits,[296] annates, *Peter*-pence.[297]
And through each Land where she her triumph[a] led,
Whole swarms of locusts, Priests and Friars were spread.
These (as the *Janizaries* to the *Turk*)
Were faithful slaves still to promote her work.[298]
Whilst to maintain those drones she swept away,
The fat and wealth of Nations as a[b] prey.
In the third place *she doth mens Souls inslave*,
This mark in *Rome*[c] most evident we have.
With dangerous vows, unwarranted traditions,
Implicit faith and thousand superstitions.
Pretended miracles apparent lies,
Damnable Errors and fond fopperies.
She clogs the Conscience, and to make all well,
Boasts all her dictates are Infallible:
And then (to fill her measure) i'th' last place,
Tis said she would Gods precious *Sion* race.[299] [d]
This can of none but *Rome* be understood,
That drunken whore, who reels in Martyrs blood.[300]
As I more largely now shall make appear,
And then with patience your excuses hear.
Within the compass of six thousand years,
Has been presented to the eyes and ears
Of future[e] ages, the most sad contents
Of bloudy Tragidies, the sad[f] events
Of dreadful wars in several Generations,
The overthrow of many fruitful Nations.
But all comes short of *Romes* most bloudy bill,
Which doth the earth with Sanguine volumes fill.
Jerusalem that City of renown,
Sack't by *Vespatian*, burnt and broken down.[301]
It was indeed a dreadful desolation,
And so have conquerors dealt with many a nation.
All Conquerors ever found a time to cease,
When once they'd[g] conquered, then they were at peace.
They murdered not, but such as would not yield,
To own them for their Lords:[h] and in the fields[i]
They slew them too with weapons in their hand,
For their defence, and always freely[j] stand.[k]
But this vile Strumpits[302] bloud-bedabled hands,
Finds not a period never countermands.
Her cruel rage, her murders find[l] no end,
She slaughters when she pity doth pretend.
Years terminate not her bloud thirsty acts,
She slays without examining their facts.

In times of peace her treacherous hands have shed,
Bloud without measure: she hath murthered
By cursed Masacres her neighbours, when
They thought themselves the most secure men.[a]
One might fill volumes with her bloudy story,
In which she still persists: Makes it her glory
T'invent strange torments to deprive the breath
Of Christians, by a tedious lingring death.
The brutish *Nero* first of Tyrant Kings,
From whose base root nine other Tyrants springs,
Whose most inhuman Acts, not to their glory,
Did leave the world a lamentable story.[303]
And to their lasting and eternal shame,
Did purchase to themselves that hateful name
Of bloudy Monsters in the shape of men,
Whose cruel acts deserve an Iron pen.[304]
That might perpetuate to after-times,
These Heathens cruelty record the crimes.
For which those Christians willingly laid down,
There[b] earthly houses for a heavenly Crown.[305]
Reflect a while Sir! And but cast your[c] eye,
First on those Heathen Emperors cruelty.
Then view the bloudy Papists, and compare
Their cruelties together, and as far
As *Egypts* darkness did exceed our night,[306] [d]
Or midnight differs from the morning light.
So far the Papists cruelty does exceed,
The worst of Heathen Tyrants, and indeed
The worst of Tyrants, since the world began,
Or since dissention fell 'twixt man and man.
If *Cyprians*[307] and *Eusebius*[308] words be true,
These persecuting Emperors yearly slew
Millions of Souls, shedding their guiltless blood,
Which ran like waters from a mighty flood.
So void their hearts were of humane[e] pitty,
They Spar'd no Age, nor Sex, nor Town, nor City.
The things wherein these Christians did offend,
Were only this, they did refuse to bend,
Their Heaven-devoted knees, or fall before
Those Idol Gods, these Emperors did adore.
They did believe one God created all,
They did believe in Christ, and down did fall.
Prostrate upon the earth, and daily bring
Sacrifice only to that Heavenly King.
Their Emperors Gods these Christians did deride,
This was the cause so many millions dyed.
These Emperors thinking themselves ingag'd,

Their Idol[a] to revenge, grew more inrag'd
To see the Christians bouldly to despise,
Their Gods, and honour Christ before their eyes.
They did conclude the nature of th' offence,
Deserv'd no less than death for recompence.
Thus may we plainly see a reason why,
These Heathen Emperors use[b] such cruelty.
'Twas not because they worshipt not aright,
But worshipt not at all, nay, did despight.
Unto these[c] Idols which they Gods did call,
Affirming that they were no Gods at all.
An act not to be born by flesh and bloud,
To have the edicts of their Gods withstood.
Yet in the midst of all those Tyrants rage,
Serious advice a little would asswage
Their hellish fury, and for some time cease,
And give the Christians a breathing space.
And when as those ten Emperors[309] ceast to be,
Then terminate[d] all their cruelty.
Three hundred years did terminate their wrath,[e]
And then the Heathens own'd the Christian faith.
And now there[f] Emperors do as much adore
The God of Heaven and earth, as they before
Had done there[g] Idols, and zealous for the Church,
Gives[h] great donations, makes[i] their Bishops rich.
And now proud *Rome*, since *Constantine* the great,[310]
Thou by degrees has[j] taken up thy seat:
Puft up with riches, swoln with filthy pride,
From Gods pure laws has[k] quickly turn'd aside.
And now such Bishops only dost thou chuse,
As God doth hate and utterly refuse.
Proud sensual, and void of the holy spirit,
Such as the Lord hath said, shall not inherit
Eternal Glory; such thy Bishops be,
Who shoul'd be fil'd with truth and purity.
Shining like lights before the flock, that they
The better might discern the perfect way.
But now instead of such as these, behold
They are presumptious, proud, imperious bold.
Changing the worship that the Lord makes known,
And in its stead will introduce their own.
Yea so presumptious are they in their pride,
As to affirm Gods holy words no guide
For men to walk by; the only rule that they
Do counsel men, nay force[l] them to obey.
Is their traditions which th' affirm to be,
Far more authentick then our Lords decree,
Within his holy Word he us hath given,

For a sure light to guide our steps to Heaven.
And now that Christian,[a] whose more[b] tender heart,
Dares not believe them, neither dare[c] depart
From Gods directions, which in his blest word,
He hath so plainly left upon record.
These are the men this wicked Strumpit hath
So often made the objects of her wrath.
Making the earth to drink the guiltless bloud,
Of such as for Gods holy Word have stood.
Oh! Let the bloud-drunk earth, near[d] cease to cry
Unto the Heaven enthroned Majesty.
'Till God take[e] vengeance as he did on *Cain*,
For all the righteous *Abels* she hath slain.[311]
Not for denying, but honouring the Lord,
Yea, for believing that his sacred word
Is the most perfect, and the truest guide,
The rule by which all doctrins should be tride.
Our blessed Lord bids search them, for saith he,
They are the words that testifie of me.[312]
Lo hears[f] the cause, behold the reason why,
The Whore has acted so much cruelty.
Inhumane murthers doth this Whore invent,
Whereas[g] she daily slays the innocent.
The numbers she hath murdered, doth[h] surmount
The strictest of Arithmeticks account.
What Countrey hath not tasted of the Cup,[313]
That her most bloudy hands hath poured[i] up.
How hath she stir'd up Nations to ingage
Against each other to satisfie her rage.
Where Millions have been brought unto the dust,
Only to satisfie this[j] Strumpits lust;
That she the better might ingrose the power
Of Hell into her hands, and so devour
At her bloud thirsty pleasure, such as she
Could not perswade to love Idolatry.
Perfideous France,[k] whose most inhumane wrath,
Passing the limits of a Christian faith.
Within the space of eight and twenty days,
Thy bloudy hands most treacherously betrays
Ten thousand souls, and to that bloudy score,
Ads quickly after twenty thousand more.[314]
How many murders more that Popish Nation
Have done, the *Romish* Histories make relation;
And yet from cruelty *Rome* has not ceast,
But as her years, her murders have increast:
And swoln[l] to bigger numbers in less space,
As *Bellarmine*[315] affirmeth to her face;
Who thus affirms[m] that from the morning light,

Until the Sable Curtains of the night;
Were closely drawn, her bloudy hands did slay,
A hundred thousand Souls! O let that day
In Characters of bloud recorded be,
That may remain unto eternity.
O let the earth that drinketh in the rain,
That did receive the bloud of all the slain.
Let both the Heavens,[a] and the Earth implore
The God of Heaven to confound the Whore.
O poor *Bohemia*, thou hast had a tast,
When wicked *Julian* laid thy countrey wast.
Burning thy Towns and Villages with fire,
Sparing no[b] young, nor old, nor Son, nor sire.
What multitudes unnumbred were thy slain,
Which in the field unburied did remain.
Thou did'st[c] the wolfish Popes in every age
Contrive thy ruin, many times ingage
Thy neighbour Nations to shed forth thy bloud,
Only because faithful *Bohemia* stood.
For Gods pure worship, *Martin* the sixt excites,
Emperors and[d] Kings, Dukes, Barons, Earls and Knights
With one consent to fall upon that Nation,
On no less terms, then on their own Salvation;
Promising also upon that condition,
To give a full and absolute remission.
Unto the vilest sinner that e'er stood
Upon the earth; that would but shed the blood.
Though but of one *Bohemian*; O rage!
Not to be paralleld in any age.[316]
Except that Monster, who did sore rebuke,
The over charitable Popish Duke
Of *D'Alva*,[e] and would you know his crime,
It was because that he in six years time,
Through too much lenity, caus'd not the earth
To drink more Christians[f] bloud than issued forth
From 18 thousand souls; for this the Duke,
Was thought by Papists worthy of rebuke.
Is eighteen thousand in six years[g] so few,
In the account of your[h] bloud thirsty crue,
Inhumanly to murther, yea indeed,
Because their former numbers did exceed.
But if the Duke of *Alva's* bloudy bill,
Came short in numbers, yet his hand did fill
It up with Torments, so dreadful to rehearse,
As that the very thoughts[i] thereof would pierce
A Marble heart, make infidels relent,
Torments that none but Divels could invent.[317]
But if all this was over little still,

His predecessors added to the bill.
For from the time that hellish Inquisition,
Did from the Devil first receive commision.
As well approv'd History doth relate,
Till thirty years expired had their date.
By cruel torments which they still retain,
Was a hundred and fifty thousand[a] slain.
And yet before they took away their breath,
They for some time did make each day a death.
Depriving them as far as in them lay,
Of all the comfort that either[b] night or day
Affords mankind; for them[c] there was not found,
So much Sun light as to behold the ground
On which they stood: Each day that giveth light,
Was unto them like *Egypts* darkest Night.
In hellish darkness, thus they made them spend
Their weary hours, and kindly in the end
Destroyed them: the company they had
Within those darksome caverns, was their sad
And melancholy thoughts, their sighs and growns,
Their doleful lodgings was[d] upon the stones.
If noysome creatures bred and fostred there,
These[e] noysome creatures their companions were.
What food they eat, was only to secure
Their souls alive, that so they might endure
The several Torments that they did provide,
And so a hundred and[f] fifty thousand di'd,[318]
Beside[g] what di'd by persecuting hands,
Within the *Popes* Confines in several lands.
Thus may I sooner spend my strength and tears,
And tire (if you regard) your eyes and ears.
Then give a full and absolute relation,
Of all the acts of *Romes* abhomination.
Oh! May my native Countrey rather hear
Their bloudy Acts, than in the least part bear
Her burthen, or behold her murdring hand,
Once more spread through the Confines of our land.
But I perceive these truths are dully heard,
And that you little my discourse regard.

Apostate.

Yes, yes, I hear and smile, what Tragedies
You make of lawful just severities.
The Martyrs you applaud were Rebbels too,
And still against authority would goe.
If then they suffer'd, who pray[h] is to blame?

Professor.

That I have shown already to their shame.
And would I[a] have my Countrey men to take
Another taste that may preserve awake
Their drousie Souls, who take a dying nap,
Much like deluded *Sampson* on the lap
Of lustful *Dalela*,[319] whose treacherous breath,
Sends forth the Messenger of *Sampsons* death;[320]
Let not the Strumpits sugred words, perswade
Thee to give credit to her 'thas[b] been her trade,
To promise fairest when she doth intend,
To deal the falsest,[c] she doth betray her friend.
Like wicked *Cain*, first of that sinful race,
That slew his Brother smiling in his face.
From the first time that e're the hellish rage
Of Jesuits appear'd on the stage
To act their parts in *England*, *France* and *Spain*.
And *Italy* her bloudy hands hath[d] slain,
Nine hundred thousand souls or there about,
Ere many years had[e] run their hours out.[321]
Of the *Americans* by *Popish Spain*,
In fifty years was fifteen Millions slain.[322]
The poor religious *Waldenses*, whose eye,
Like the quick sighted *Vulture*, did[f] espy
Rome's[g] filthy whoredomes, and freely[h] disclaim
Her vile Idolitry, and hate the same.
Drunk dreadful draughts of *Rome's*[i] most bloody Cup,
Which She with Helbred fury poured up.
And for no other cause, her bloody hands
She did stretch forth her[j] Hell-inraged bands;
Being sent abroad forthwith, to put to death
Both young & old, each man that draweth breath;
And yet, as if she had not been content,
To Murder Parents with their Innocent,
And harmless Babes, as if their Hellish-breath
Had now been spent with putting souls to death.
Fourscore sweet Babes that never did offend,
Famish'd to Death, their harmless lives did end.[323]
Search, search into the deep, a biss of Hell,
And see if all the Devils can parallel
So vile an Act, O most imperious Treason
Against the King of Kings, and law of Reason.
Are Papists Christians, and are these their Acts
To punish such as ne'r commited Facts.
Are those right actings, fitting Gospel-times,
To lay on Babes the weight of highest Crimes.
Did Christ do thus, or hath he ever given
Them leave to deal so with the Heirs of Heaven.

Those murd'red Souls, under the Altar lie,
Crying, how long Eternal Majesty,
How long wilt be e're thou avenge thy Saints,
And lend thine ear unto their sad complaints.
These *Waldences* being overcome and dead,
A little remnant that escaped fled,
Taught by Dame Natures Moral-Laws,[a] to save
Their much desired lives, within a Cave
Did hide themselves, hoping at last, that they
Taking advantage of another day;
When Golden *Titon*[324] had laid down his head
Upon the Pillows of his[b] Western-Bed:
And *Proserpina*[325] Lady of the Night,
Had drawn her[c] Sable Curtains, then they might
Transport themselves into some other land,
And so escape out of the Hunters hand.
But as the Hounds that hunts[d] the wearied Hart,
Doth[e] ply their steps, and never will depart
The Fields and Meadows, or the silent Wood,
Till they surprise the Beast: ev'n so these blood
Devouring Monsters having found the Cave,
Most barberously did make that place their grave,
Wherein four hundred yielding up their breath,
Were in a barberous manner choak'd to death.
No Nation in the world hath ever seen,
A Foe so dreadful as the Whore hath been.
It is far better to be overcome
By *Turk* or *Heathen*, than by Christian *Rome*.
What part of *Europe* now can make their boast,
And say they have not tasted to their cost
Of *Romish* Mercy, some are yet alive,
Whose Parents felt the Death she did contrive.
O *Germany*! thy poor destress'd Estate
Will speak to future Ages, and relate
Whole Volums of her bloody Murders,[326] and
The murdered Souls of bleeding *Ireland*[327]
Cries[f] night and day for Vengeance, and implore
Gods Heaven enthroned Majesty e'er more,
To put a period to her Hellish power,
That we may overtake her in an hour.
Those dreadful Murders, have the eyes and ears
Of some now living heard and seen the tears
Of Soul afflicted Parents, whose sad eyes
Beheld their Murdred Babes, & heard their cries.
Their Daughters Ravish'd, & when that was done,
Cruelly Murdered, and the hopeful Son
By unheard Torments slain before their eyes,
Whilst they beheld their Childrens miseries:

Their Children Murdred, and their Wives defil'd,
Whose Bodies they ript up being great with child.
And all this while Parents and Husbands were
Forc'd to behold what flesh and blood can't bear
The bare Relation: what Adamant heart
Melts not,[a] when I these dreadful things impart:
Ripping up Child-great-Women[b] was not all,
For that, although inhumane, was but small
Compar'd with others[c] torments they indur'd,
Whose Patience bore what could not else be cur'd.
Tearing out Bowels, boiling of[d] men alive,
These deaths and worse those Monsters did contrive.
We see how they have dealt with every Nation,
And shall we think at last to find compassion.[e]
The pittious cries of Parents, near[f] could move
Them to extend the smallest dram of love.
The tears that ran from dying Infants eyes,
Like plentious showers from the darkned[g] skies:
Whose great abundance might have made a River,
Yet all these floods of brinish tears could nev'r
Enter a Papists heart so hard[h] condenc'd,
So void of pitty, and all humane sence,
To hear the doleful shreaks, and dying groans
Of poor distressed Babes, who makes the[i] moans
To Soul afflicted Parents e're they part,
These are the things delights[j] a Papists heart,
To see the dying gaspes before the death
Of tortured Souls, whose life forsaken breath
Had waited. Oh![k] many a tedious hour past,
When their tormented Souls should breath their last.
Whose dolorous sighings penetrates[l] the skies,
Those objects do delight a Papists eyes.
And can we now at last expect to find,
That *Romes* grown merciful and Papists kind:
No, no, we cannot do't, if we but fix
Out[m] serious thought[n] upon late Sixty six:
When *London* was consum'd, that Famous City,
Its Ruins doth[o] bespeak them void of pitty.
By *Romes* contrivance, was fair *London* burn'd,
Englands Metropolis to ashes turn'd.
Their[p] Merchants of their Riches quite bereft,
To day rich men, to morrow nothing left.
Their Wives and Children harberless became,
Their substance all consumed in the Flame:
To day this Famous City is[q] deck'd in Gold,
To morrow an amazement to behold.
The doleful Shreaks, and lamentable Cries,

The floods of Tears that ran from Weeping eyes
As true resemblances, did represent
The Sorrows that our Neighbours under went.
And can we think that Hell-begotten Rage,
That did provoke so many to ingage
In such an Act, far worse than th' Powder-Treason:[328]
Can we suppose, if we consult with Reason,
The fury of their Hellish Rage expir'd
So soon as e're that Famous Place was Fir'd.
No, no, Good Sir, your Pardon, I presume
Those Hell-ingendred flames that did consume
So fair a City in so short a space.
Hell gave those flames Commission down to raze
Not *London* only, but every Soul that hath
A heart resolv'd to maintain the Faith
Of Jesus. Protestants both great and small,
Rome hath determin'd their eternal Fall.[329]
And those more formal Protestants,[330] whose Zeal
May secretly perswade them to conceal
Their seeming Faith, and feignedly to close
With *Romes* erronious Doctrine, and suppose
Thereby to save their lives; let none believe
Such vain perswasions; many did deceive
Themselves; for *Rome*, that Painted Whore,[a]
Will deal with them as she hath done before,
With such as hoped in the self same kind,
To meet with Mercy, but nought less did find.
Christ never gave unto his Church Commission,
For to make Laws for grievous Persecution.
No outward force were they i'th' least to use,
Much less poor Innocents for to abuse,
By Burning, Starving, Roasting on a Spit,
And tantingly[b] to make a sport of it.
The holy Saints, and People of the Lord,
Their only Weapon was Gods sacred Word.
With that blest Sword always they overcome,
And did refute all Hereticks, but *Rome*
Makes use 'tis plain o'th' Carnal Sword and Fire,
'Tis Blood, 'tis Blood this Locust doth desire.
Death without Mercy, acts of Cruelty,
The Matter must decide continually.
The way they use to turn a Soul from error,
Is the most dreadful flesh amazing terror
Of tormenting[c] Racks, whereon a man must lie
Tortur'd to Death, dying, yet cannot die.
Strange kinds of Instruments, devis'd to tear
The flesh from off the bones, these sometimes were
Her friendly Admonitions, to reclaim

Such whom she doth for Hereticks defame.
What Massacres has[a] she contriv'd by night,
When nature doth to rest each man invite.
When sleep had[b] clos'd their eyes, no thoughts of harms
Did them possess, but in their folded Armes
Their Wives and Children lay, with hopes that they
Through grace might live to see another day.
Then came these murdering Butchers, sent from Hell,
Nothing but Blood would their vile rage repel;
Laying dear Babes and Mothers in their gore
'Till all were dead, they scorn'd to give o're,
If these Church dealings will not work contrition,
She can erect[c] a cursed Inquisition:
A dreadful place of cruelty and blood,
Whose torments scarcely can be understood.
A loathsome Dungeon, and vile stinking Cell,
A place of darkness, representing Hell;
Where nothing is so plentiful as tears,
And bitter Sighs, and yet can find no ears
To hear their cries and lamentable moans,
Nor hearts to pitty them for all their groans,
Where many tedious days and nights they spend,
Not knowing when their sufferings will have end.
If such like arguments (Sir) will confute
A Heretick, the Papist[d] may dispute
With all the world, nay Heathen *Rome* could never
Come nigh a Papist with their best endeavor:
They scorn all *Turks* or *Pagans* for contrival
Of Barbarous Cruelties should be Corrival,
For inhumanities they must defie,
And scorn that Cannibals should them come nigh.
A bloody Papist strives to counterfeit
The Plagues of Hell, as far as man's conceit
Can reach unto, or Devils could invent,
This is a[e] Papists knocking Argument.
Thus, thus is *Rome* drunk with the Martyrs blood
Which has run down like to a mighty flood.
O it is *Rome* that is that Scarlet Whore,
Which thus doth hate and persecute the Poor.
And all which are unto the[f] truth inclin'd,
To serve the Lord with a most perfect mind,
According to the tenor of his Word;
All such she strives to put unto the Sword:
And suffers none to buy, nor sell, nor live,
But such as homage unto her would give.
Upon her head also Saint *John* did see
Was writ the cursed names[g] of Blasphemie;[331]

Setting her self on God's Imperial Throne:
Saying, I am, besides me there is none.
I have the keys of Heaven in my hand,
Both Earth and Hell is at my sole command;
I shut and open unto whom I please,
I torment give to some, to others ease.[332]
Lo, thus God's sacred Word doth point her forth,
This, this is she, there's none in all the earth
That ever did adventure to lay claim
To that presumptuous and blasphemous name,
As King of Heaven, Earth, and Hell, but he,[a]
Therefore *Rome*'s Church must the vile Strumpet be.

Apostate.

Sir, speak no more, forbear your sland'rous lies
The holy Church such murdrous acts defies:
Do not believe all Stories you do hear,
'Tis hard for you to make these things appear.

Professor.

   These things were not (Sir) in a corner done,
Besides, I never yet have heard of one
That is for you, or standeth on your side,
Who by just proof these things ever[b] deni'd;
For they alas notoriously are known,
And many Papists also them do own:
Besides, 'twas late some of these Cruelties,
Murder and Blood, and barbarous Tragedies
Were done, and acted, some alive now be
Who with their eyes these villanies did see.
About th' year (dear Sir) of fifty five
A dreadful massacre did *Rome* contrive
Near unto *France*, i'th' Dukedom of *Savoy*
Were[c] thirty thousand souls she did destroy,
Who were commanded without all delays
Papists to turn, and that within three daies;
Who for refusing, were then presently
Put unto death with barbarous Cruelty.
Some with sharp spears thrust through their[d] privy parts,
Whilst others stabbed were unto their hearts.
Some babes they cut in pieces, some they roasted
And some upon the tops of spears they toasted[e]
Virgins were ravished, Widows and Wives
Then[f] barbarously deprived of their lives:
Some were drove forth on bitter Ice and Snow,
And many knock'd o'th head as they did go;
Thus was[g] those souls brought into misery.
[manicule][h] See it at large in *Moreland*'s History.[333]

Two hundred thousand Protestants or^a more,
Were Massacred by this vile bloody Whore
In *Ireland*; there's many now alive
Who saw what kinds^b of deaths they did contrive,
By which some of their dear relations then
VVere tortured by those most Bloody men.[334]
How can you Sir these things i'th' least deny,
VVhich are so obvious unto ev'ry eye.

Apostate.

Youth, 'tis the Faith of *Roman* Catholicks,
Thus for^c to deal with all vile Hereticks.
Yet 'twas Rebellion too, say what you will,
For which the Church did many thousands kill.
To Magistrates they disobedient were,
And therefore they just punishment did bear.

Professor.

Peter and *John* they Rebels were also,[335]
By that same Argument which use you do.
To Magistrates they did refuse to bend,
VVherein they knew they should the Lord offend.
In civil things they always did submit,
And Preached also, it was^d a thing most fit,
In things which unto man doth^e appertain,
But Christ o're Conscience ought alone to reign.
Ev'n so those^f Martyrs bare^g an upright mind
Unto their Prince, and ever were inclin'd
In all just things obedient for to be:
Yet did stand up for Christ his Soveraignty,
And resolv'd^h in matters of their Faith,
To worship God as holy Scripture saith,
According to that light which he doth give,
Up unto which each Soul on Earth should live.
And though your Church doth put poor men to death,
'Twas from the Devil such curst laws came forth.
The tares with wheat should grow intoⁱ the end,
'Tell God is pleas'd the Reapers for to send.[336]
That 'twas from Satan I don't doubt i'th' least,
For he did give unto this bloody Beast
His Power and Seat, and his Authority,[337]
For to effect all cursed Villany.

Apostate.

They were some evil persons without doubt,
VVho crept^j into the Church, that work'd about
Those Murderous deeds the Church did not allow,
But utterly against them doth Avow.

Professor.

The filthy Pope, and evil Cardinal,
With Bishops, Moncks, and Fryers you so call,
With fiery Jesuits, for[a] to be brief,
In all the[b] murderous Acts these were the chief
Bulls, false Pardons,[c] and cursed dispensations,
From bloody *Rome* has Ruin'd many Nations.
You can't deceive, nor blind[d] the world more,[e]
Times has[f] discovered the Scarlet Whore.
We now know how clearly[g] to bring our charge,
As I could shew, but that I can't inlarge.

Apostate.

I know not how further (Sir) to excuse
The Holy Church, you put me in a muse:
But she's more kind and gentle hear[h] of late,
And doth such cruelties defie and hate.

Professor.

Rome to a Wolf may fitly be compar'd,
Who whilst against his will is quite debarr'd
From seeking of his prey, being ty'd in chains,
Seems very peaceable, though he remains
A Wolf in Nature still, if ever he
At any rate can get his libertie,
Doth straight way run impatient of delay,
And cannot rest until he's got his prey.[338]
So *Rome* seems kind and gentle, until she
Can find again an opportunity,
Which with unwearied pains, and often trial,
She ever seeks, and hardly takes denyal.
Which if she once obtains, she will not stay
From sheding blood a minute of a day.

Apostate.

'Tis a vain thing with you for to contend,
And therefore I had rather make an end:
Tis out of love I speak, to have you leave
Your evil Errors, speedily to cleave
Unto that Church who only can decide
All Controversies, even to divide
The Truth from Error, Light from Darkness so
That every one the ready way may go.
But you seem so resolved in your mind,
That little hopes, alas, of you I find.
But youth consider once again I pray,
The troubles of a now[i] approching day.
For sore amazements will you overtake,

Unless you do your purposes forsake.
If once our Church the day obtains, be sure
Then down you Hereticks must go for ever.[a]
Let former stroaks of Justice take such place,
As for to move you wisely to imbrace
That Councel, which in tender love I give,
That you in safety evermore may live.
Or you'l Repent that ever you begun
These dangerous ways of Heresie to run.
'Tis a dark doleful hazardous[b] path you go,
Recant therefore as many others do.

Professor.

   You may mistake sometimes the waters flow,
Yet on a sudden I observe them low.
A *Hammon* may maliciously devise
Poor *Mordica*, and others to surprise.
Yet may his purposes meet with a blast,
And he himself be hanged too at last.[339]
The flesh withal its lust[c] to mortifie,
Is hard to those that love Iniquity.
The way to Papists wholly is untrod,
And unto all who haters are of God.
The way seems dark to you, untrod, uneven,
Hard 'tis to th' flesh, yet 'tis the way to Heaven.
'Tis dark to you, because that you are blind,
And can't Gods purpose in dark foot-steps mind.
I have[d] a sure hand to lead my trampling places,[e]
To scape the danger of those dangerous spaces.[340]
I shall pass safe, by means of my blest[f] Guide,
Though thousands fall by me on every side.
For to turn back will[g] prove a dolefull fault,
I think upon the Monument of Salt.[341]
I am resolv'd a thousand deaths to dy,
Before I'le ever yield to Popery.

Apostate.

   Thou art too strict, too righteous, and precise,
Thou slights[h] such things which prudent men do prize.
Thou mayst have Christ, pleasures[i] & honours too,
And saved be without half this ado.
There's very few alas are of your mind,
Who unto *Rome* are not at all inclin'd.

Professor.

   You now condemn me for my holy life,
Wherein 'tis true I met with straits and strife.
But when, dear Sir, you come at length to die,

You'l blame your self, and me you'l justifie.
Did ever any on a dying bed,
Lament that they were by Gods spirit led
To crucifie their sins, and undertake
All things to leave for the Lord Jesus sake.
If Righteous ones, alas scarce saved are,
It greatly doth behove me to take care
In holiness to walk, what e're you say,
I from the paths of life will never stray.
The way I know is rough, 'tis hard and strait,
And leads me also through a Thorny Gate,
Whose scratching Pricks are very sharp and fell,
The way to Heaven is by the Gates of Hell.
Your way 'tis true seems very smooth and wide,
Since you from Christ have lately turn'd aside.
My Paths seem long, yours short and very fair,
Free from all Rubs and Snares, yet Sir beware,
The safest path is not always most even,
The way to Hell's like to a seeming Heaven.
Shall Flesh-wantons[a] for a moments pleasure,
Expose themselves to shame, and loss of treasure.
They'l spend their strength, their gold, and Estates[b]
Amongst their sensual Dame-Hellish-Mates.[c]
Shall cursed Pleasures thus be pris'd, and must
The joys above be cheaper than a lust.
The ambitious Gallant, for to hoist his Name
Upon the wings of Honour and of Fame,
How will he venter on the point of Spears,
And face the mouths of Cannons, nought he fears:
With courage stout how will he fight i'th' Flood,
When Brinish Seas are mixt with human blood.
Shall wretched man be at the Devils will,
And dangers run, his last[d] for to fulfil.
And shall not I, when God commands me forth,
Ingage for him with all my might on earth.[e]
Or shall the promis'd Crown of endless life,
Be judg'd a triffle, and not worth a strife.
That which vain man accounts to be most rare,
Is not obtain'd but with much cost and care.
Things of great worth on Earth are got by pains,
And he who venters nought, he[f] nothing gains.[342]
And shall I then be startled with a frown,
When full assured of an Eternal Crown.
The strife which doth an holy life attend,
Will recompenced be I'm sure i'th' end.
I will go on, since Jesus doth invite me,
His strength is mine, and nothing shall affright me.

Apostate.

I do perceive you are resolv'd to run,
In your strict ways until you're quite undone.
Yet hear a little what I have to speak,
And you will find 'tis best for you to take
The Councel which I give; for you'l espy
Great Ruin fall upon you suddenly.
Your father will not own you for his Son,
If in this foolish strictness you'l go on,
His Face expect hereafter not to see,
If this your purpose and your pleasure be.

Professor.

If Father, Mother, and dear Brethren too
Forsake me quite, yet still I well do know
My precious Saviour will my Soul imbrace,[343]
And I shall see sweet smiles from his dear face
My self, and my relations dear[a]
I do deny, such is the love I bear
To my dear Lord, whose Servant now am I,
And do resolve to be until I die:
Come life, come Death, for *Canaan* I'le indeavor,
It is my home, and resting place for ever.
Better it is that earthly friends abuse me,
Then that Christ Jesus should at last[b] refuse me.
I had[c] rather bear my Fathers wrath and ire,
Then to be cast into eternal Fire.

Apostate.

Fie, fie, young-man, forbare and take advice,
Let not hot Zeal thy fancy thus intice,
For to refuse those pleasant things which you
May hear[d] enjoy, as many others do:
'Tis much too soon for thee to mind such things,
For nought but grief and dotage from it springs;
'Twill dull thy wit, and make thee like a droan,
And thou'lt be slighted too by e'ry[e] one.
How mights[f] thou live at ease, and pleasure have,
If once these ways thou wouldst resolve to leave;
And like a Flower, flourish in the Spring,
And with young Gallants mightst rejoyce & sing,
And spend thy days in pleasure sweet and rare:
I prithy youth consider, O take care
To chear thy heart! behold now in thy sight,
What earthly joys most sweetly do invite.

Professor.

Young 'tis[a] true I am, and in my prime,
Therefore resolve for to improve my time:
The flower of my days, dost think I will
Give to the Devil, lust for to fulfil.
Shall Satan have the primest of my days,
And put off Christ with base and vile delays
Until old age, and then at last present
The dregs of time to him; I'le not consent
To such vile thoughts, I will not lend an ear,
I to my Saviour more affection bear.
Since first of the living Spring my soul did drink
All sinful pleasures in my Nose do[b] stink.
More[c] precious Joy I find in my dear Lord,
Then all this world doth, yea, or can afford.
If I am slighted for Christ Jesus sake,
And judg'd a Fool or Droan, yet I can take
All for him, who for me hath undergone
More shame then this before his work was done.
This is my chosing time, I have made choice,
Gods Word I will obey, and hear his voice.
Gods Counsel 'tis that first of all in youth
I should him seek, and cleave unto the Truth.
Your Counsel I abhor, shall lustful fire
Be kindled in my Brest, shall my desire
Run out again to *Egypts* cursed stuff,
I know 'tis nought, of it I have enough.

Apostate.

Alas, the journy's long, you'l wearied be,
And faint before that Kingdom you do see.

Professor.

Nay Sir, be silent, that is false, for I
By Faith most clearly do the Land espie.
But is the Journy long, blame me no more,
Betimes i'th' morning I set out therefore.
Why did'st thou say it was too soon for me
For to set out? If long the Journy be,
I do resolve in youth with speed to strive,
Lest I too late at last should there arrive.
While strength and youth doth[d] last I'l bend my mind
To Travel hard, because I clearly find
Old Age, and weary Limbs, quite out of case
To go a journy, or to run a Race.[344]
Alas, when night is ready to come in,
That's not a[e] time this Journy to begin,
When Sun and Moon, and Stars all darkned be,

And clouds return, that we no light can see.
When rain and tempests doth[a] most sore appear,
And the Keepers of the house all trembling are:
When the strong men themselves are forc'd to bow
And grinders cease also, because that now
They are but few, and ready to fall out,
And those through windows which do look about
Are become dim, nay darkned without light,
And doors to[b] in the street are shut up quite.
When the sound o'th' grinders are low, can't be heard,[c]
He riseth[d] up too at the voice o'th' Bird:
And all the Daughters of sweet Musick rare,
Are brought too low, don't for such Musick care.
And fears increase in[e] thoughts of what's on high,
Fears in the way, and fears for what is nigh.
When flourish shall the Almond Tree also,
And th' Grashopper shall be a burden too.
When loosed is the precious Silver Cord,
And Golden Bowl is brok'n, as we have heard:
When the Pitcher too is at the Fountain[f] broke,
And the Wheel at th' Cistern with a heavy stroke:[345]
When desire fails, and there alas is none,
What will such do who han't this Race begun.
Besides 'tis clear, my days uncertain be,
Old Age alas I may not live to see.
Young men are quickly gon, for I behold
Dayly as young as I are turn'd to th'[g] Mould.
My own experience doth discover this,
My life[h] a bubble and a Vapour is.
The flower which doth spred, and is so gay,
Soon may it fade and wither quite away.[346]
If I therefore have still[i] much work to do,
Or as you say so long away to go.
It doth concern me then, with all my power,
For to improve each day, yea, every hour:
For daies to come I see may not be mine,
My time I'le spend not as thou spendest thine:
My weights I'le cast away this race to run,[347]
Stand still I must not, nor with thee return:
I must provide me oil, get Grace in store,[348]
For e're[j] a-while I shall be seen no more
This side the Grave, I haste therefore to meet
The Glorious Judge at the great Judgment-seat.
I must make haste, be swift, like to the Sun,
Lest that my work's to do when time is done.

Apostate.

To you, young man, I have declared much
Of the sad danger, but your Zeal is such,
Naught what^a I say with you takes any place,
You don't believe me, that's the very case.
But what's the reason, youth, so many folk
Decline those paths in which you now do walk?
Were waies of your strict Holiness so sweet,
They in this sort would never back retreat;
I did resolve with others for to try.
And find you all deceived utterly.
Your whole Religion's naught but meer conceit,
Let none therefore thy soul with fancies cheat.
Since wise men daily do your waies forsake,
Be thou advis'd, and other counsel take.

Professor.

If thousands fall away, it is no more
Than what the Scripture shews was heretofore.
Thousands of old from *Ægypt* did adventer,
And yet but two of them did *Canaan* enter:³⁴⁹
They never had of Christ a saving tast,
Who quite away their seeming hopes do cast:
Their hearts alas are rotten and unsound
Who in Christ Jesus never sweetness found.
But what of this? Shall I my Lord deny
Because that you some Hypocrites espy?
Those who do murmur in the Wilderness,³⁵⁰
The Land of Promise never shall possess.
But if they will the precious Lord revoak,
Shall I from thence resolve to slip the yoak;
Because they don't the glorious Lord believe,^b
Shall *Caleb* think the Land he can't receive;^c
Because so many walk i'th' way to Hell,³⁵¹
Shall I conclude that Heaven don't excel
The vain injoyments of an evil World,
Or shall with fancies thus my soul be hurl'd?
To think, because that Swine the grains do chuse,
And Pearls do tread upon, and them refuse,
There is more worth in those base stinking grains
Than in those true Pearls which the Merchant gains?³⁵²
Because these silly men have lost their way,
Shall I on purpose therefore go astray?^d
Because that *Judas* did for thirty pence
Sell his dear Lord,³⁵³ shall I conclude from thence
Peter a fool, who priz'd his favour^e so,
That for his sake all things did^f undergo.
If fearful Souldiers basely quit the field,

Shall valiant Champions therefore straitway yield
Most cowardly unto their treacherous fo,
Whom they assured were to overthrow.
If Mariners unskill'd in Navigation
Are split on Rocks, shall all then in the Nation
That have that curious Art, resolve therefore
Never to use the Art of Sailing more?
Because the sluggard sees the winds do blow,
The rain descending with cold hail and snow,
He doth give o're, and says[a] no longer will
Remain 'th'[b] field his barren Land to till:[354]
Shall faithful Husband-men from the like ground,
Who have oft-times[c] by good experience found,
Without they sow, no harvest they can[d] have,
Resolve the[e] painful labours quite to leave:
He that won't Plow because o'th snow or rain,
Shall beg at harvest, and shall naught obtain:[355]
So in like sort, to mind my present case,
'Cause persons void of God's true saving grace
Do Postasize[f] as you your self have done,
Must I to th' Devil with you headlong[g] run?
'Cause some Professors secretly do love
Some base corruptions, doth this therefore prove
There's none sincere for God in all the earth,
VVhose souls experience do[h] the second birth.
I for my part through Grace have this to say,
I never shall, nor can I fall away:[356]
All those whom God has unto Jesus given,
They never can be dispossess'd of Heaven;
The Promise of Eternal Life is theirs,
And they like *Isaac*, even so our[i] heirs,[357]
Who could not miss, nor dispossessed be,
Unless God's Word's made a meer Nullitie:[j]
God's Covenant also with Christ doth stand,
Who can supply our wants on ev'ry hand.
Sin shall not reign such is our happy case,
We are not under th' *Law*, but under *Grace*.
This Covenant is not like to the old,
We of a sure[k] person now have hold.
We stand not now as *Adam* did, 'tis plain,
God never will trust that old man again.
Our credit's nothing worth, but[l] our Surety
Is in our room, our wants he must supply:
Besides all this, I'le hint another thing,
Which to my soul doth much refreshment bring:
He that's the Author of my Faith, I spy,
Will finish it himself assuredly.

He that in me has a good work begun,
Will perfect it also e're he has done.
Within God's Saints Eternal Life doth dwell,
This would remove the doubt, considered well.
Those unto whom Eternal Life is given,
How can it be that such should miss of Heaven?
And now to breviate, 'tis my intent,
Sir, if you please, to frame one Argument:
If[a] the new creature in the souls of men
Is of God's Spirit born, I argue then,
The same in nature it be-sure must[b] be,
Which cannot death, or like mutation see,
But that 'tis of God's Spirit born, is clear,
As *John* the Third[358] doth make most plain appear.
The seed also doth[c] in their souls remain,
They cannot sin to death who're born again;
God's fear moreover is so in their heart,
That they from him shall never more depart:
Thus is[d] my standing very firm and sure,
And to the end I know I shall endure:
And as for those who fall away and die,
I shall discover clearly by and by
What kind of men and women they are all
Which will hold forth the cause too of their[e] fall.[359]

Apostate.

Most confident, I do perceive you are
Danted[f] at nothing, yet pray let me hear
Those persons Names which you did lastly[g] meet,
Who finally resolve for to retreat,
And leave those paths which you seem to commend;
Come, speak to this, and we will make an end.

Professor.

Sir, unto me it doth most plain appear
As if they cowards and faint-hearted were:
Under their tongues also close secretly,
Some pleasant morsels I am sure doth[h] lie;
And in them all doth reign some cursed evil,
Which makes them to conform unto the Devil.

Apostate.

As you suppose, but pray, youth, have a care,
For they sincere and sober people are.
And I do question whether yea or nay
Thou dost them know, what further hast to say?

Professor.

I told you, Sir, I knew them very well,
And since you urge me, I resolve to tell
What kind of folk they are, and also shall
Their names discover unto great and small;
Master *fearful* was one that I did see,
With him was goodly *Sensuality*.
With Dame[a] *Misbelief*, and Goodman *Outside*,
Who turn'd from Christ as soon as they were tri'd
With[b] one *Vnbelief*, a very wicked man;
Turn him out of his way, there's no man[c] can:
Besides them,[d] there's one *Earthly heart*
Who loves nothing so well as Plow and Cart:
Also there's *Esau Faint-heart*, most profane,
That[e] sells his Birth-right Pottage to obtain,[360]
With one[f] *Belly-god*, a man that[g] I do find,
Flesh-pots and Onions chiefly he doth[h] mind.
There's Mistress *Discontent* too with the rest,
Who would have naught but what she liketh best.
Master *Hot love soon cold* also was there,
Lastly,[i] for Zeal, with him few could[j] compare.
There's *Ishmael legal heart*,[361] in truth also,
When troubles rise, he strait away[k] doth go
With Master *Balaam*,[362] who doth Christ[l] Jesus leave
The wages of unrighteousness to have:
Some people also I have lately met,
Who were with sin most easily beset:
And divers heavy weights also they[m] bore,
Which wearied them, and made them to give o're.
A Gentleman I also did behold,
Whose Trade was great, & store he had of gold.
He's going back with sorrow I do know,
Because he can't have Christ and th' World too.
One Master *Atheist*, that I think[n] his name
As like your self as if he were the same;
He's fallen back so far, and turn'd aside,
That at Religion he doth much deride:
He thinks Religion's but a foolish thing,
VVhich doth no comfort, nor no profit bring.
This is too true, you also are the man
To clear your self, deny it if you can.
No marvel 'tis you play the Devil's part,
In labouring thus for to deceive my heart,
And blind mine eyes, if that thou knewest how,
Thou'dst make me like thy self, and therefore[o]
I am resolv'd with you[p] for to ingage,
VVho striv'st[q] to stop me in my Pilgrimage:

A foe more vile than you, what soul can meet?
I'le therefore bring you down unto my feet.
Some scores[a] I think to fetch out of God's book,
Though like *Goliah*[363] you do seem to look,
Yet in his Name, whom you so much defie,
I shall prevail against you by and by.
I thought I must confess some years ago,
I should not in the least been stopt by you;
Or that I should have met with opposition
VVith[b] such a foe to add to my affliction.
But since this is my sad unhappy fate,
I'le add a line or two to vindicate
The Dreadful God, so far as lies in me,
I'le vindicate that Glorious Deity;
Who in my soul his Image so has set,
That I his Glorious Being can't forget.
Shall he which form'd both Heaven & the[c] Earth,
From whom I have my precious life and birth
Be trod upon, nay, utterly deni'd?
What soul can such a sinful wretch abide!
VVho strives at once, if that you could it do,
The life of all Religion to o're-throw.
Hast thou ought[d] to speak, and wilt thou enter
On the debate, yea, durst thou adventer[e]
To o'pe thy mouth i'th' least for to defend
Those thoughts of thine, which clearly do desend[f]
From Hell beneath, thou'lt prove thy self thereby
The Devil's Friend, *Jehovah*'s Enemy.

Apostate.

   Thou childish lad, do'st think I am afraid
For to declare my self, or am dismaid
By silly dreams and fancies, which afright
Those simple ones who dare not walk i'th' night;
VVho startle at the[g] shadow which they see,
And think the Devil's near, when 'tis a tree:
And since I do perceive you understand
VVhat my opinion is, I do demand
How you can prove, and fully make appear
There is a God; for none at all I fear.
No God nor Devil I at all believe,
Nor is there any Heaven to receive
The souls of Holy Men when they do die;
Nor is there any Hell of Misery
For sinners after death, as you conceit,
All is naught else save[h] a Religious cheat.

Professor.

Dare you your Maker thus with impudence
Deny, and tread upon: such insolence
VVhat Soul can bear! what Age can shew the like,
VVhere so much light has[a] been! shall Mortals strike
At the Great God, and Glorious Deity!
VVhose dreadful Being and Existency
The Heathens did find out, and greatly fear;
His Godhead did to them most plain appear
By the Creation, Man, as in a Glass
May there behold who his Creator was.
'Tis time to arm my self, and look about,
VVhen by an Atheist I am challeng'd out:
VVhen th'whole of all Religion lies at stake,
'Tis time to rouse, and also for to shake
Off sloth and idleness, and to ingage
VVith such a foe in this my pilgrimage.
If once I should unto an Athiest yield,
And treacherously also acquit the Field:
The strongest hold of Truth betray should I
Into the hands of its worst enemy:
And should unman my self of Christian too,
And my dear soul of reason overthrow.
I should debase my self, should I deny
My Noble Birth from the great Deity.
Man's chiefest glory springs from's Supream Head,
In his descent from him, who made and bred,
And brought him forth, and doth his life maintain,
From hence man doth his greatest[b] honor gain.
'Tis power Divine that man doth greaten thus,
As to make[c] him King of the Universe.
Who e're disowns his blessed Pedigree,
Doth prove himself unnatural for[d] to be.
For man to say he came by hap or chance,
As 'tis a peice of wilful Ignorance.
Himself also he doth depose thereby,
From his own honour and rare dignity.
And vile contempt upon himself doth bring,
As well as durt upon that Essence fling.
Who form'd his Soul, and gave to him his breath,
And made him Ruler here upon the Earth.
But to proceed, and lend my helping hand,
In the defence of Sacred truth to stand,
And vindicate my great Creators cause
By Nature's light, and also by those Laws
Which supernatural are, and most Divine,
Whose light excells, yea, and whose glory[e] shine.[364]

You ask me how I can make it appear,
There is a God, attend and now give ear,
And weigh my arguments and reasons sound,
And let not Satan more your Soul confound,
And Reason quite destroy as he has done,
Least to the Devil you do headlong run.

Apostate.

Before you do proceed, this you must know,
If you a God do think to prove or show,
Besure of this, young man, it must not be
By Scripture proof, for its Authority
I do deny, and cannot it believe,
You never shall that way my heart deceive:
The knowledge which you supernatural call,
Is a mear cheat, I mind it not at all.

Professor.

Though supernatural knowledge you despise,
And count Gods holy Word to be but lies.
I briefly shall stand up in its defence,
And shew you[a] Pride and cursed Insolence.
That all may love Gods Word, prize it, and see
Its worth and weight, and its Authoritie
To be Divine, and by *Jehovah* given
To lead poor Souls in the right way to Heaven.
One thing of you i'th' first place I demand,
Pray let me know, and fully understand
When this supposed Cheat did first commence,
And in what part o'th world bring evidence.
Egypt stands mute, saith it commenc'd not hear,
Nor did the *Jews* invent it, that's as clear.
Ask all the Heathens too in every age,
If their Philosophers brought 't on the Stage.
If you can find it out, pray bring it to light,
Or else confess your darkness worse then night.
'Tis strange that such an universal cheat
Should thus be put upon the VVorld, and yet
No one can shew[b] who did the same devise,
Nor how, nor when the same at first did rise:
Since all the VVorld stands silent, and is mute,
This might a period put to the Dispute.
But secondly, I argue once again,
There's none of them who do so much disdain
The Holy Scriptures, who just proof could bring
To shew i'th' least they were a forged thing:
If none can them disprove, O then say I,
VVhat ground have you the Scripture to deny.

The Scriptures also, I observe, have been
Strangely preserved by a power unseen
In every Age, kept both in word and sense
From secret fraud, and open violence,
Against the num'rous Armies of all those
That were both secret, yea, and open foes.
No wicked and impious[a] men could never[b]
Subvert the Scripture, though they did indeavor:
The beastly Clergy of the Church of *Rome*,
Thorow whose hands, to us, the Scriptures come;[c]
Though guilty of most vile abomination
As ever was committed in a Nation.
Their cursed sins are hateful to relate,
VVhich they committed, and did tolerate:
And that they might more freely do the same,
And to[d] be kept from sad reproach and shame:
They say the Pope himself may change the Laws
Of th' Holy Gospel, as himself sees Cause;
And make the sence of Scriptures to agree
with time and place, as he most fit doth see.
How free those Sacrilegious Monsters were,
Had God admitted to extinguish'd[e] clear
The Sacred Scripture, and put out their light,
And filled the world with eternal[f] night.
But we may see although it made it's way
Thorow those muddy Chanels, yet have they
Been still kept pure, still[g] remain a Law
To keep most men save Bloody Popes in awe.
Now if against so many Enemies,
Who us'd all means that Devils could[h] devise
T' obliterate that Soul-informing Word,
It was preserv'd, and[i] not by human Sword.
How dare you Sir presume for to deny
It's blessed and Divine Authority.
Another ground or reason I shall urge,
Which proves Gods Word Divine as I do judge.
'Tis taken from that influence they have
Upon their hearts whom God intends to save:
It turns them from those cursed ways[j] of sin,
Which once they loved and delighted in.
It brings them out of darkness into light,[365]
Ye,[k] and discovers Jesus to their sight,
Filling their Souls[l] with inward life and peace,
And precious joy, the which shall never cease.
    The glorious Power[366] which God did afford
Always to those who[m] stood up for his Word
Most clearly shews: Methinks to every eye
The Scriptures true, and their Authority

To be Divine, what ever you may say,
I cannot give this Argument away.
How have they been supported in the flames,
Which as it did perpetuate their Names:[367]
So God thereby did stir up ten for one,
To stand up for his Word when they were gone.
Ah! how did they rejoyce Sir in the fire,
Which made their very Enemies admire.
Wouldst thou one instance have, I could give two,
And ten times twenty more if that would do.
But if I should, I'am sure I should transgress,
And over-charge th' Appendix and the Press.
And therefore I will add one reason more
To prove God more[a] Divine, and so give o're.
How has the Scripture made the Atheist quake,
And all his limbs with dreadful horror shake.
When on a death Bed they have come to lie,
Their Conscience waking in their face did fly.
Though in their health they did it much despise,
And did affirm it was made up with lies.
Yet has it made them howl at last and cry,
We are undone to all Eternity.
'Twas like unto the writing on the Wall,
Which did foretell profane *Belshazar*'s fall.[368]
Which was so terrible, yea, and so strange,
It wrought amongst them a most sudden change.
Their Mirth and Jolatry[b] doth now expire,
And the proud King doth[c] earnestly desire
To hear it read, nought then would serve the[d] turn
But an Interpreter: his heart did burn,
His trembling Knees smote one against another,
As if his Joynts were loosed from each other.
Thus those that[e] wont confess *Jehovah*'s Name,
Are forc'd to own him to their utter shame.
And those who will not of Gods Word[f] allow,
Are forc'd by Conscience under it to bow.
These things[g] being weigh'd, make[h] you quite give o're,
Yea, and Gods Word thus to oppose no more.
Now if the Scripture cannot be gain-said,
Methinks each Soul should be exceeding 'fraid
How they contemn that glorious Deity,
Whom they so clearly shew and magnifie.
    But to leave this a little, and descend
To mans own reason which you so commend.
How many Heathens did alone thereby,
Find out (dear Sir) Gods glorious Majesty.[369]
If you your Reason did but exercise,
From Atheism doubtless you soon[i] might rise,

And hate also this Soul destroying evil,
Thus siding with, and yielding to the Devil.[370]

Apostate.

Amongst the Heathens (youth) were men of fame
Who for their skill in Nature had the name
Above all others, which did quite deny
There was a God or such a Deity.

Professor.

  Epicurus,[371] [a] and old *Aristotle*,[372]
With *Theodorus*,[373] *Bion*,[374] and the Rabble,
And such like Atheists I must grant to you
Deny'd there was a God as Stories show.
Philosophy is good, but men abuse it,
VVhen they like those old Heathen Authors[b] use it.
God doth sometimes mens reason[c] darken quite
For not improving of the means of light.
To vile affection, up God[d] doth them give,
Because on earth, like Bruits they seem to live.
But though these natural Sots[e] could not espy[375]
By all their skill th' eternal Deity.
Yet many thousand Heathens I might[f] show,
By Natures light alone did come to know
There was a God, they searched so about
Into Gods works, they found his God-head out.
For when they gave themselves up seriously
To study Natures Book, and come to pry
Into the cause of all thing hear[g] on earth,
And their effects did clearly see the birth
Or first Original of every thing,
From such an Essence to descend or spring.[376]
The very Novices in Dame-Natures[h] School,
May soon convince that man to be a Fool,
Who by the Creatures glory can't discern
The Being of that dreadful Soveraign
Who did them form and make, for every where
His glorious God-head they to all declare.
Had I but time, I could some pages fill,
To shew to you how that mans reason will
Teach him there is a God, for if he mind
The Nature of his Soul, this he might find,
Mans soul is like a spring, or like to fire,
It resteth not aloft, it doth[i] aspire,
And unto *Noah*'s Dove, I'le it compare,
God is the Ark, souls rest alone is[j] there.
The flesh dams up the spring, quenches desire,
Keeps out of th' Ark to whom[k] it would retire:

Since I perceive mans soul doth search about
To find some higher good, and being out;
VVhich doth excel all things which are below,
This doth to us God's glorious being show.[377] [a]
But to conclude this, no man can disown,
God by his judgments daily is made known.
VVhat sad example[b] daily do we hear
Of VVrath and Vengeance almost every where?
Some Drunkards and Blasphemers struck down dead
And others judgments strangely tottered[c]
Some have presum'd th'Holy God to dare,
VVhom he would not one little minute spare.
If this will not convince you of your error,
I fear you will e're long fall under terror;
For if you will not now example[d] take,
God may of you a sad example make.
Your state alas, above all men is sad,
Because of God you once such knowledg had,
And of his waies, which now you loath & hate;
O Sir, consider this your woful state;
And cry to God, if peradventure He
May give you Grace, whereby your soul may see
Your hainous sin, that so you may repent,
And turn to God before your daies are[e] spent.

Apostate.

    I must confess I know not what to say,
If there's a God, then cursed be the day
That ever I was born, for I do know
He never unto me will mercy shew:
I now resolve to open my condition,
Though all's in vain; for there is no contrition
VVill do me good, I utterly am lost;
For I have sinn'd against the Holy Ghost:
I wilfully have sinn'd, and there remains
Nothing for me but everlasting pains.
O that there were no God, for then should I
Be like the Beast when e're I come to die.
For love o'th' VVorld, and for my present ease
I am become like to the troubled Seas.[378]
No rest nor comfort ever shall I find,
Curs'd be the day that ever I declin'd
From those[f] good waies in which dear youth you go,
Or ever I did God or Jesus know:
For if I had not known them, it is clear
My sin would not so hainous now appear:
My Conscience doth prick me to the heart,
I never shall be eased of this smart.

Oh that I were in Hell! for then should I
Soon see the worst of my extremity.
Thou shalt, dear youth, for ever happy be,
For thou art chosen from Eternity
To be an heir of Eternal[a] Bliss;
But I alas am damn'd! what woe like this?
The Devil with his glist'ring golden ball
Has[b] me deceiv'd, and now I see my fall
To be so bad, no tongue can it express,
My woful pain is wholly[c] remediless.
The checks of Conscience I did greatly slight,
And loved darkness greatly, hated light:
Yea, and of good I never lov'd to hear,
Though I of him had hints oft-times most clear;
And now will he my soul to[d] pieces tear,
And make me his Eternal Vengeance bear.
Let all back-sliders of me warning take
Before they fall into the *Stigeon-Lake*;
Yea, and return, & make with God their peace
Before the daies of Grace and Mercy cease;
For mine are past for ever, oh condole
My sad estate, and miserable soul.
My daies will quickly end, and I must lie
Broyling in flames to all Eternity.

FINIS.

Textual variants

5a   The Third Impression, with Additions.] *K103A* insert; The Fourth Impression
      K104; The Fifth Impression *K104A*; The Sixth Impression *K104AB*; The Seventh
      Impression *K105*; The Eighth Impression *K106, K106A*; The Ninth Impression.
      Opie1; The Tenth Impression. *K106B*

5b   By B. K.] By Benjamin Keach. Author of Sion in Distress, or the Groans of the
      Protestant Church. *K106A*; B. Keach *Opie1, K106B, K107*

5c   London ... 1673.] at his Shop at the Stationers Arms in Sweetings Rents, in Corn-
      hill, neer the Royal Exchange. 1674. *K103aA*; 1675. *K103A*; 1676. *K104*; 1678.
      K104A; at his Shop at the Stationers Arms, in the Piazza of the Royal Exchange in
      Cornhill, 1680. *K104AB*; 1683. *K105*; 1684. *K106*; Printed for S. Harris, and are
      to be Sold by Peter Parker, at the Sign of the Legg and Star over-against the Royal-
      Exchange in Cornhill, 1691 *K106A*; by most Book-sellers, 1695. *Opie1*; London,
      Printed and sold by Benj. Harris, at the Golden Boar's-head in Grace-church-street.
      1700. *K106B*; Belfast, Printed by Patrick Neill and Company and sold at his Shop,
      1700. *K107*

6a   Sol enters into] Sprightly Sol enters *K103A, K104, K104A, K104AB, K105, K106,
      K106A, Opie1, K106B, K107*

6b   splendent] splendid *K106A*

6c	quickens] quicken *K104, K104A, K104AB, K105, K106, K106A, Opie1, K106B, K107*
6d	glorious] Natural *K103A, K104, K104A, K104AB, K105, K106, K106A, Opie1, K106B, K107*
6e	*Sol's*] his *K103A, K104, K104A, K104AB, K105, K106, K106A, Opie1, K106B, K107*
6f	garments] Garment *Opie1, K106B*
6g	Nought now save] Nothing but *K103A, K104, K104A, K104AB, K105, K106, K106A, Opie1, K106B, K107*
7a	amongst] among *K107*
7b	ever] *K106* omit
7c	and] or *K106B*
7d	was] were *K104, K104A, K104AB, K105, K106, K106A, Opie1, K106B, K107*
7e	must] *K106* omit
7f	know] learn *Opie1, K106B, K107*
8a	bring is] bring's *K103A, K104, K104A, K104AB, K105, K106, Opie1, K106B, K107*
8b	here] have *K103A, K104, K104A, K104AB, K105, K106, K106A, Opie1, K106B, K107*
8c	have ... horrid] many a bold, and horrid *K103A,K104, K104A, K104AB, K105, K106, K106A, Opie1, K106B, K107*
9a	Pleasures] Pleasure *K104, K104A, K104AB, K105, K106, K106A, Opie1, K107*
9b	th'] that *K106A*
9c	hence] whence *K106A*
9d	Pleasures] Pleasure *K105, K106, K106A, Opie1, K106B, K107*
9e	cry] brings *K106*; *K106A* omit
9f	say] do *K106B*
9g	made] make *K105, K106*
10a	snib] snub *K106A*
10b	Cause] Case *K104*
10c	do or say] do say *K104AB, K105, K106, K106A*
10d	subject] submit *K103A, K104, K104A, K104AB, K105, K106, K106A, Opie1, K106B, K107*
10e	strives] strive *K104AB, K105, K106, K106A*
10f	men] a man *K104AB, K105, K106, K106A, Opie1, K106B, K107*
10g	on] and *K107*
11a	Hant] Hath not *K106B*
11b	Sometimes men stifle] Some men stifle *K104A, Opie1*; Some men so stiffle *K104AB, K105, K106B*; Some men do stifle *K106, K106A, K107*
11c	my] thy *Opie1*
11d	nor] or *Opie1, K106B*
11e	tryst] trust *K103A, K104, K104A, K104AB, K105, K106, K106A, Opie1, K106B, K107*
12a	sear'd] scar'd *K106, K106A*
12b	As] And *K104AB, K105, K106, K106A, Opie1, K106B, K107*
12c	they] thy *K103A, K104, K104A, K104AB, K105, K106, K106A, Opie1, K106B, K107*
12d	cares] care *K103A, K104, K104A, K104AB, K105, K106, Opie1, K106B, K107*

12e   do] *K104, K104A* omit; that *Opie1, K106B, K107*
13a   Whores] Whore *K106B*
13b   nick-names] Nick-name *K106, K106A*
13c   comes] costs *K106A*
13d   do] doth *Opie1*
13e   is] are *K104, K104A, K104AB, K105, K106, K106A, Opie1, K106B, K107*
14a   you] your *K103A, K104, K104A, K104AB, K105, K106, K106A, Opie1, K106B, K107*
14b   i'th'] in *K107*
14c   scar] scare *K103A, K104, K104A, K104AB, K105, K106, K106A, Opie1, K106B, K107*
14d   the] thee *K104, K104 (ESTC R229873), K104AB, K105, K106A, Opie1, K106B, K107*
14e   still] cease *K103A, K104A, K104 (ESTC R229873), K104AB, K105, K106, K106A, Opie1, K106B, K107*
14f   but] *K106A* omit
15a   you ... treat] do you now intreat *K103A, K104, K104 (ESTC R229873), K104A, K104AB, K105, K106, K106A, Opie1, K106B, K107*
15b   I am] I'm *Opie1*
15c   the] *K106A* omit; that *K106B*
15d   it] that *Opie1, K106B*
16a   my] *K104 (ESTC R229873), K104AB, K105, K106, K106A, Opie1, K106B, K107* omit
16b   I] *K105, K106, K106A* omit
16c   shouldst] would *K106A*
16d   so] *K106A* omit
17a   Internal] Eternal *K106A, K106B*
17b   Whilst] While *K104 (ESTC R229873), K104AB, K105, K106, K106A, Opie1, K106B, K107*
17c   Subject] Be subject *K106B*
17d   doth draw] draws *K106B*; should draw *K107*
17e   vile] now *K107*
17f   rightly] rightful *K107*
17g   his dread and] and dread his *K106B*
17h   as soon] sooner far *K106B*
17i   a] *K106, K106A* omit
18a   a] so *K106B*
18b   also turn a deaf ear] so turn a deaf ear *K104 (ESTC R229873), K104A, K104AB, K105, K106A, Opie1*; so turn a deafned ear *K106B*; so oft turn a deaf ear *K107*
18c   thy] the *K104 (ESTC R229873), K104AB, K105, K106, K106A, Opie1, K106B, K107*
18d   ope] open *K106, K106A*; op'n *Opie1, K107*
18e   let's] let'st *K104AB, K105, K106, K106A*
18f   Youths like to] Young-Men like *K106B*
19a   Then ... Doom] *K104 (ESTC R229873), K104AB, K105, K106, K106A, Opie1, K107* omit; Receiv'd his fatal stroke, which was his Doom *K106B*
20a   all] *K104, K104 (ESTC R229873), K104A, K104AB, K105, K106, K106A, Opie1* omit; may *K107*

20b   steal] may steal *K106B*

20c   have often] oft have *Opie1, K106B*

20d   has] hath *K104,K104 (ESTC R229873), K104A, K105, K106, K106A, Opie1, K106B, K107*

20e   pleasures] pleasure *K106B*

20f   pleasures] Pleasure *K106A*

20g   Thou ... end] Thou soure Sawce shalt have before the end *K106B*

20h   save] but *K106B*

20i   draw] drawn *K104 (ESTC R229873), K104AB, K105, K106, K106A, Opie1, K106B, K107*

20j   contrar'wise] otherwise *K106B*

20k   never] ever *K107*

20l   thy] the *K107*

20m   doth] does *K106A*

21a   spy] espy *K104 (ESTC R229873)*

21b   place] set *K107*

21c   Beauty] on Beauty *K107*

21d   nor] or *K107*

21e   Pleasue] other Pleasure *K106B*

21f   striking] trifling *K104, K104 (ESTC R229873), K104A, K104AB, K105, K106, K106A, Opie1, K106B, K107*

21g   hadst] hast K106B

21h   Though] Thou *K103A*

21i   sowr's] soure is *K106B*

21j   Sith ye my Intrests] Sith you my int'rest *K104 (ESTC R229873), Opie1, K107*; Sith you my Intrests *K104AB, K105, K106*; Since you my intrest K106A, K106B

22a   delights] Delight *Opie1*

22b   Pride] bride *K104, K104 (ESTC R229873), K104A, K104AB, K105, K106, K106A, Opie1, K106B, K107*

22c   and also] wantonly *K103A, K104, K104 (ESTC R229873), K104A, K104AB, K105, Opie1, K106B, K107*; won't only *K106, K106A*

22d   fleshly] fleshy *K103A, K104*

22e   should] can *K106B*

22f   with] of *K106B*

22g   now be of a] be of a *Opie1*; be of a deep *K106B*

23a   will] hard *K106B*

23b   assay] Essay *K107*

23c   I] yet *K106B*

23d   o're-come ... infirmity] over-come through humane frailty *K103A, K104, K104 (ESTC R229873), K104A, K104AB, K105, K106, K106A, Opie1, K106B, K107*

23e   filth] filthy *K104, K104 (ESTC R229873), K104A, K104AB, Opie1*; filthiness *K105, K106, K106A*

23f   I do] do I *K104 (ESTC R229873), K104A, K104AB, K105, K106, K106A, Opie1, K106B, K107*

23g   thou ... Cockatrice] Vipers breed and many a Cockatrice *K103A, K104,K104 (ESTC R229873), K104A, K104AB, K105, K106, K106A, Opie1, K106B, K107*

23h   spawn] swawn *K104 (ESTC R229873), K104A*

23i   and ... pain] in everlasting pain *K103A, K104, K104 (ESTC R229873), K104A,*

K104AB, K105, K106, K106A, Opie1, K106B, K107

23j   Oh!] *K106B* omit

23k   also my] my troubled *K103A, K104, K104 (ESTC R229873), K104A, K104AB, K105, K106, K106A, Opie1, K106B, K107*

24a   it is] is most *K103A, K104, k104 (ESTC R229873), K104A, K104AB, K105, K106, K106A, Opie1, K106B, K107*

24b   with him longer] longer with him *K106B*

24c   his] *K106A* omit

24d   doth] does *Opie1, K106B, K107*

24e   its] his *K105, K106, K106A, K107*

24f   If this] And this *K104, K104 (ESTC R229873), K104A, K104AB, K105, K106, K106A, Opie1, K107*; And if't *K106B*

24g   But] And *Opie1, K106B*

24h   stab] stob *K103A, K104, K104A*; stop *K104 (ESTC R229873), K104AB, K105, K106, K106A, Opie1, K106B, K107*

24i   thy] that *Opie1, K106B*

24j   do] *K106B* omit

24k   'tis] is *K103A, K104, K104 (ESTC R229873), K104A, K104AB, K105, K106, K106A, K106B, K107*

25a   has] hath *K106B*

25b   he's full of] his full of *K104 (ESTC R229873), K104A, K105*; his full *K104AB*; he is full of *Opie1*

25c   to] too *K104, K104 (ESTC R229873), K104A, K104AB, K105, K106, K106A, Opie1, K106B, K107*

25d   Resove] Resolve *K104, K104 (ESTC R229873), K104A, K104AB, K105, K106, K106A, Opie1, K106B, K107*

25e   of in your inward part] of in your part *K104 (ESTC R229873), K104AB, K105, Opie1I;* has seiz'd upon your Heart *K106B*

25f   I now will] thy course I'le *K103A, K104, K104 (ESTC R229873), K104A, K104AB, K105, K106, K106A, Opie1, K106B*; my Course I'll *K107*

25g   And ... treasure] To lies and fraud and all unlawful treasure *K103A, K104, K104 (ESTC R229873), K104A, K104AB, K105, K106, K106A, Opie1, K106B, K107*

26a   But contrariwise] Instead of which *K106B*

26b   close] most *K104, K104 (ESTC R229873), K104A, K104AB, K105, K106, K106A, Opie1, K106B, K107*

26c   is] 'tis *K103A, K104, K104 (ESTC R229873), K104A*

26d   thee] *K106* omit

26e   Make-bate] make hate *K106A*

26f   Pleasures] Pleasure *K106B, K107*

26g   thrown] throne *K103A, K104, K104A, K104AB, K105, K106, K106A, Opie1, K106B, K107*

27a   do] doth *Opie1, K106B*

27b   can] can't *K106B*

27c   Tinder] tender *K104 (ESTC R229873), K104A, K104AB, K105, K106, K106A, Opie1, K106B, K107*

27d   knock] stroke *K106B*

27e   you'll] you *K104 (ESTC R229873), K104A, K104AB, K105, K106, K106A, Opie1, K106B, K107*

27f   forth o'th'] out of *K106B*

27g   he's just going now] he is just now going *K106B*

27h   to] for to *K103A, K104, K106, K106A, K107*

28a   the] *K106* omit; a *K106A*

28b   afterwards] afterward *K104 (ESTC R229873), K106, K106A*

28c   were] had *K106B*

28d   loose] lose *K106, K106A, Opie1, K106B, K107*

28e   all] *K106A* omit

28f   do] must *K103A, K104, K104 (ESTC R229873), K104A, K104AB, K105, K106, K106A, Opie1, K106B, K107*

29a   canst thou fly] wilt thou fly *K106, K106A*; wilt thou flee *K107*

29b   when] where *K103A, K104, K104 (ESTC R229873), K104A, K104AB, K105, K106, K106A, Opie1, K107*

29c   strives] strive *K106B*

29d   quite] white *K106A*

29e   one] a one *K106B*

29f   Young-man] Young men *K104 (ESTC R229873), K104AB, K105, K106, K106A, Opie1*

30a   Sun] the Sun *K104AB, K105, K106*

30b   that] which *K106B*

30c   Instruction] Instructions *K106A*

30d   a] the *K106A*

30e   quickly] *K106A* omit

30f   nor] or *K106, K106A, K106B*

30g   with] which *K104, K104 (ESTC R229873), K104A, K104AB, K105, K106, Opie1, K106B, K107*

30h   shews the] sheweth is *K104, K104 (ESTC R229873), K104A, K104AB, K105, K106, Opie1, K106B, K107*; shews is *K106A*

30i   in] into *K107*

31a   My ... now] My pain is wounded, and my wounds do swell *K104A*

31b   very] now *K107*

31c   do] so *K104 (ESTC R229873), K104A, K104AB, K105, K106, K106A, K107*

31d   But] And *K103A, K104, K104 (ESTC R229873), K104A, K104AB, K105, K106, K106A, Opie1, K106B, K107*

31e   gross] cross *K104 (ESTC R229873), Opie1, K106B*

31f   the] thy *K103A, K104, K104 (ESTC R229873), K104A, K104AB, K105, K106, K106A, Opie1, K106B, K107*

31g   of] *K104 (ESTC R229873), K104A* omit

32a   of] or *Opie1, K106B*

32b   swings in] swing in *K104, K104 (ESTC R229873), K104A, K104AB, K106, K106A, Opie1, K106B*; swinge in *K105*; swing on *K107*

33a   Sith] Such *K106A*; Since *K106B*

33b   Thou] And thou *K104 (ESTC R229873), K104A, K104AB, K105, K106, K106A, K106B, K107*

33c   it] Sin *K107*

33d   I'm] I am *K106A*

33e   the] *K106, K106A* omit

34a   may] *Opie1* omit

34b   morsel] Morsels *K107*
34c   storms & with] stormy and *K107*
34d   tempests] tempest *K106, K106A*
35a   must] mud *K104 (ESTC R229873), K104A*
35b   think] do think *K104 (ESTC R229873), K105, K106, K106A, Opie1, K106B, K107*
36a   in you] you in *K106B*
36b   Caitife] Caitist *K103, K103aA*; Caitife *K103A, K104, K104 (ESTC R229873), K104A, K104AB. K105, K106, K106A, Opie1, K106B, K107*
36c   Towards] Toward *K106A, Opie1, K107*
36d   contrar'wise] otherwise *K106B*
36e   God and only you] only God and you *K103A, K104, K104 (ESTC R229873), K104A, K104AB, K105, K106, K106A, Opie1, K106B, K107*
36f   one] not one *K104, K104 (ESTC R229873), K104A, K105, K106, K106A, Opie1, K106B, K107*
37a   yet was he] yet he was *K103A, K104, K104 (ESTC R229873), K104AB, K105, K106A, Opie1, K106B, K107*; yes he was *K106*
37b   an] *K104 (ESTC R229873)* omit
38a   Truth] Truths *K106A*
38b   and inherit] and inherent *K103A, K105, K106, K106A, K106B, K107*; an inherent *K104, K104 (ESTC R229873), K104A, K104AB, Opie1*
38c   fruit] Fruits *Opie1, K107*
38d   exalt'st] extol'st *K106, K106A*
38e   thy] a *K106B*
38f   do come] become *K107*
38g   thinks] think'st *K104 (ESTC R229873), K104A, K104AB, K105, K106, K106A, Opie1, K106B, K107*
39a   Faith] *K106A* omit
39b   Amongst] Among *K106B*
39c   no] nor *K107*
39d   And ... provide] *K106, K106A* omit
39e   Afflictions] Affliction *K104 (ESTC R229873), K104A, K104AB, K105, K106, K106A, K106B, K107*; affliction do *Opie1*
40a   Prayers and Tears] Tears and Pray'rs *K106B*
40b   will fail] they fall *K106B*
40c   contrar'wise] otherwise *K106B*
40d   when Christ] which Christ doth *K104 (ESTC R229873), K104A, K104AB, K105, K106, K106A*; that Christ doth *K106B, K107*; Christ doth *Opie1*
40e   Soul is quite] Soul is quiet *Opie1*; Soul's quiet *K107*
41a   had] have *Opie1*
41b   ye] you *K106B, K107*
41c   from] for *K106A, K107*
42a   hope] Hopes *K106A*
42b   is] are *K105, K106, K106A, Opie1, K106B, K107*
42c   your] forth your *K103A, K104, K104 (ESTC R229873), K104A, K104AB, K105, K106, K106A, Opie1, K106B, K107*
43a   I must declare he is] Must declare he was *Opie1*
43b   to] to do *K107*

43c   filt] filth *K103A*, *K104*, *K104 (ESTC R229873)*, *K104AB*, *K105*, *K106*, *K106A*, *Opie1*, *K106B*, *K107*

43d   predominate] prodominate *K104AB*, *K105*; prenominate *K106*

43e   and] an *K104AB*, *K105*

44a   my] mine *K106B*

44b   Meets] Meet *K107*

44c   gall] *Opie1* omit; Land *K106B*

44d   which] that *K107*

44e   The] This *K106B*

44f   sake] sakes *K104AB*

44g   sear'd] scar'd *K106A*, *K106B*

44h   offend] offends *K106*, *K106A*, *K106B*

44i   truly for] them truly *K104 (ESTC R229873)*, *K104AB*, *K105*, *K106*, *K106A*, *Opie1*, *K106B*, *K107*

45a   which] as *K103A*, *K104*, *K104 (ESTC R229873)*, *K104A*, *K104AB*, *K105*, *K106*, *K106A*, *Opie1*, *K106B*, *K107*

45b   to] for to *K104 (ESTC R229873)*, *K104A*, *K104AB*, *K105*, *K106*, *K106A*, *Opie1*, *K106B*, *K107*

45c   dost] *Opie1* omit

45d   thy] those *K106B*

45e   I am] I'm *K104 (ESTC 229873)*, *K104A*, *K104AB*, *K105*, *K106*, *K106A*, *Opie1*, *K106B*, *K107*

45f   though a] though I a *K104 (ESTC R229873)*, *K104AB*, *K105*, *K106*, *K106A*, *Opie1*, *K106B*, *K107*

45g   not] *K106A* omit

45h   dost] *K106*, *K106A* omit

46a   smallest] least *K106B*

46b   before] besure *K104 (ESTC R229873)*, *K104A*, *K104AB*, *K105*, *K106*, *K106A*, *Opie1*, *K106B*, *K107*

46c   wast] was *K107*

46d   and] the *K106B*

46e   plain] plainly *K106*, *K106A*

46f   oftentimes] utterly *K106A*

46g   me] sets me *K103A*, *K104*, *K104 (ESTC R229873)*, *K104A*, *K104AB*, *K105*, *K106*, *K106A*, *Opie1*, *K106B*, *K107*

46h   th'] thee *K106B*

47a   dreadful] *K106A* omit

47b   go] down *K103A*, *K104*, *K104 (ESTC R229873)*, *K104A*, *K104AB*, *K105*, *K106*, *K106A*, *Opie1*, *K106B*, *K107*

47c   thy] your *K106A*, *K107*; *Opie1* omit

47d   out] out of *K107*

47e   And how] That you *K104 (ESTC R229873)*, *K105*, *K106*, *K106A*, *Opie1*, *K106B*, *K107*

47f   o'th' Haven] o'th' Heaven *Opie1*; of Haven *K106B*

48a   Which you did lose] And vainly lost *K104 (ESTC R229873)*, *K105*, *K106*, *K106A*, *Opie1*, *K106B*, *K107*

48b   And] Thou *K104 (ESTC R229873)*, *K104A*, *K104AB*, *K105*, *K106*, *K106A*, *Opie1*, *K106B*, *K107*

48c thousand] thousandth *K104 (ESTC R229873)*, *K104A*, *K104AB*, *K105*, *K106*, *K106A*, *Opie1*, *K106B*, *K107*

48d tongue] Man *K106A*

48e truly believe] truly do believe *K103A*, *K104 (ESTC R229873)*, *K104A*, *K104AB*, *K105*, *K106*, *K106A*, *Opie1*, *K106B*

48f water] Waters *K106A*

48g may] might *K103A*, *K104 (ESTC R229873)*, *K104A*, *K104AB*, *K105*, *K106*, *K106A*, *Opie1*, *K106B*, *K107*

48h ever must] evermore *K107*

48i than] in *K106B*

49a of thee] *K106B* omit

49b thou] *K106A* omit

49c can] can'st *K104 (ESTC R229873)*, *K104A*, *K104AB*, *K105*, *K106*, *K106A*, *Opie1*, *K106B*, *K107*

49d too in] into *K106A*, *K107*

49e fast too in thy Liver] in thy Liver sure *K106B*

49f smart] smare K103, K103aA; smart *K103A*, *K104*, *K104 (ESTC R229873)*, *K104A*, *K104AB*, *K105*, *K106*, *K106A*, *Opie1*, *K106B*, *K107*

50a or] nor *K106A*

50b must] might *K107*

50c has] hath *K104 (ESTC R229873)*, *K104AB*, *K105*, *K106*, *K106A*, *Opie1*, *K106B*, *K107*

50d whither] whether *K104*, *K104 (ESTC r229873)*, *K104A*, *K104AB*, *K105*, *Opie1*

50e better] bitter *K103A*, *K104*, *K104 (ESTC R229873)*, *K104A*, *K104AB*, *K105*, *K106*, *K106A*, *Opie1*, *K106B*, *K107*

50f Hue] Huy *K104 (ESTC R229873)*, *K104A*, *K104AB*, *K105*

51a hardest rock will] hardest rock would *K106A*; hardned rock will *K106B*

51b grieve] give *K106A*

52a refuge] refuse *K103A*, *K104*, *K104 (ESTC R229873)*, *K104A*, *K104AB*, *K105*, *K106*, *K106A*, *Opie1*, *K106B*, *K107*

52b dead but four days] but four days dead *K106B*

52c then how] how then *Opie1*

52d my] *K106B* omit

52e raise up] raise me up *K103A*, *K104*, *K104 (ESTC R229873)*, *K104A*, *K104AB*, *K105*, *K106*, *Opie1*, *K106A*, *K107*

53a accepted] excepted *Opie1*

53b pour] put *K106B*

53c predominates] prodominates *K105*, *K106*

54a here] her *K103A*, *K104*, *K104 (ESTC R229873)*, *K104A*, *K104AB*, *K105*, *K106*, *K106A*, *Opie1*, *K106B*, *K107*

54b to] unto *K106*, *K106A*

54c a-long-time] of long-time *K103A*, *K104*, *K104 (ESTC R229873)*, *K104A*, *K104AB*, *K105*, *K106*, *K106A*, *Opie1*, *K106B*, *K107*

54d thy] my *K106A*, *K107*

54e thy] with *Opie1*

54f with] thy *Opie1*

54g ne're] e're *K104 (ESTC R229873)*, *K104A*, *K104AB*, *K105*, *K106*, *K106A*, *Opie1*, *K106B*, *K107*

54h   or ever be] nor ever be *K104, K104 (ESTC R229873), K104A, K104AB, K105, K106, K106A, Opie1, K106B*, K107; nor ever could be *K106, K106A*

54i   thee make] make thee *K103A, K104, K104 (ESTC R229873), K104A, K104AB, K105, K106, K106A, Opie1, K106B, K107*

55a   also I] I also *Opie1, K106B, K107*

55b   dost] doth *K106A*

55c   ease] cease *K106A*

55d   pierced] so pierced *K106B*

55e   thy] thine *K106, K106A, K107*

55f   i'th'] in th' *K104 (ESTC R229873), K106, K107*; in the *K106A, Opie1*

56a   Wound] Wounds *K105, K106, K106A, Opie1, K106B, K107*

56b   sent only to] sent unto *K106, K106A* ; only sent to *Opie1, K106B, K107*

56c   Come you not of] Come you not *Opie1*; Come, are you not *K106B*

57a   ope] open *K106, K106A, Opie1, K107*

57b   this] the *K104 (ESTC R229873), K104AB, K105, K106, K106A, Opie1, K106B, K107*

57c   hand] Hands *K106B*

57d   groan] a groan *Opie1, K106B*

57e   which] *Opie1* omit; that *K106B*

57f   make] soon make *K103A, K104, K104 (ESTC R229873), K104A, K104AB, K105, K106, K106A, Opie1, K106B, K107*

57g   gasping] grasping *Opie1*

57h   Whilst] Whiles *K103A, K104, K104 (ESTC R229873), K104A, K104AB, K105, K106*; While *K107*

57i   in] on *K106B*

58a   Before] Because *K104, K104A, K104AB, K105, K106, K106A, Opie1, K106B, K107*

58b   frowns] Frown *Opie1*

58c   to] in *K106B*

58d   adhere] embrace *K107*

58e   embrace] adhere *K107*

58f   Which ... face] Which makes me Blush to view thy heav'nly Face *K106B*

58g   and] to *K106B*

58h   I] it *Opie1, K107*

58i   the] thee *K104 (ESTC R229873), K104A, K104AB, K105, K106, K106A, Opie1, K106B, K107*

59a   up to] upon *Opie1, K107*

59b   dear] my *K106B*

59c   in me put] put in me *Opie1, K106B*

59d   do] *Opie1* omit

59e   I ve] lye *K106B*

59f   Th' fountain] Fountains *K107*

59g   Enter ... unstain'd] *K106B* omit

59h   now do take thee] now thee take *K103A, K104, K104 (ESTC R229873), K104A, K104AB, K105, K106, K106A, Opie1, k106B, K107*

59i   I never will forsake thee] I'le never thee forsake *K103A, K104, K104 (ESTC R229873), K104A, K104AB, K105, K106, K106A, Opie1, K106B, K107*

59j   I'th ... water] In Fire, and in Water *K106B*

59k	Rivers ... swim] *K106B* omit
59l	sit down also] sit also down *K106B*; also sit down *K107*
59m	World, Death, nor Devil ever] World, Death, nor Devil *Opie1*; The World, Death, nor the Devil *K106B*
59n	find is] find's *K103A, K104, K104 (ESTC R229873), K104A, K104AB, K105, K106, K106A, Opie1, K106B, K107*
60a	beyond measure] beyond all measure *K103A, K104, K104 (ESTC R229873), K104A, K104AB, K105, K106, K106A, Opie1, K106B, K107*
60b	What ... mirth] *K106B* omit
60c	joy] joys *K106, K106A*
60d	To] Unto *K104, K104A, K104AB, K105, K106, K106A, K106B, K107*
61a	paths] Path *K106B*
61b	thou] *Opie1* omit
61c	Thou ... forth] *K106B* omit
61d	thy blest] thy best *K104 (ESTC R229873), K106, K106A, K107*; the *Opie1*
61e	Let ... thine] *K106B* omit
61f	remainers] remainders *K104 (ESTC R229873), K106, K106A, Opie1, K106B, K107*
61g	swift-wings] sweet wings *K106, K106A, K107*
61h	breaketh] breaking *K104 (ESTC R229873), K106, K106A, Opie1, K107*
61i	power's] pow'r is *K106B*
61j	Ye] Yea *K104, K104 (ESTC R229873), K104A, K106, K106A, Opie1*
61k	wast] wert *K104 (ESTC R229873), K104A, K104AB, K105, K106, K106A, Opie1, K107*; was *K106B*
61l	lose] loose *K104 (ESTC R229873), K106*
62a	shall] shan't *K106A*
62b	this] my *K107*
62c	its chief light] is chief delight *Opie1*
62d	But ... commend] *K106B* omit
62e	which] who *Opie1*
62f	do] which do *Opie1*
62g	shew] put *K106B*
62h	Judgment] Judgments *K104AB, K105, K106, K106A*
62i	that] *Opie1* omit; now *K106B*
62j	must] *Opie1* omit
62k	speed] spyed *K104 (ESTC R229873), K104A*
62l	receive] perceive *K104AB, K105*
63a	And] He *K104 (ESTC R229873), K106, K106A, Opie1, K106B, K107*
63b	Commands of Christ] Command of Christs *K104 (ESTC R229873), K104A, K106, K106A, K107*; Command of Christ *K104AB, K105, Opie1, K106B*
63c	what e're is his] what-ever is *K106B*
63d	injoyments] enjoyment *Opie1*
63e	wound me again] would make me gain *K104 (ESTC R229873), K104A, K104AB, K105, K106, Opie1, K107*
63f	He uses ... again] *K106B* omit
63g	King] Man *K106A*
63h	he'l give a way] he'll give way *Opie1*; he will give way *K106B*
63i	Fear least] For fear *K106B*

64a   can't] cannot *K104 9ESTC R229873), K106, K106A, K107*
64b   can't steal't] cannot steal *Opie1, K106B*
64c   Devil falls] Devils fall *Opie1, K106B*
64d   his] their *K106B*
64e   But ... wrath] *K106B* omit
64f   repay't upon] repay it on *K106B*
64g   Agents] Agents fell *K103A, K104, K104 (ESTC R229873), K104A, K105, K106, K106A, Opie1, K107*; Agent fell *K104AB*; Hellish Fiends *K106B*
64h   to] *K105, Opie1* omit
65a   cursed] curses *Opie1*
65b   take] takes *K104 (ESTC R229873), K104A, K104AB, K105, K106*
65c   blest] best *K104 (ESTC R229873), K104A, K104AB, K105, K106, K106A, Opie1, K106B, K107*
65d   tear and rend you] rend and tear you *Opie1*; rend and tear thee *K106B*
65e   of] if *K106B*
65f   over-cast] over-cost *K104 (ESTC R229873)*
65g   you will] you'll *K106B*
66a   insnaring] insnared *K106A, K107*
66b   They by] Thereby *Opie1*
66c   they'r] they are *K104, K104 (ESTC R229873), K104A, K104AB, K105, K106, K106A, Opie1, K107*
66d   raz'd] raised *Opie1*
66e   They ... raz'd] *K106B* omit
66f   the Mountains should] Mountains should *K103A, K104, K104 (ESTC R229873), K104A, K104AB, K106, K106A, K107*; Mountains shall *K105, Opie1, K106B*
66g   Yet] Yea *Opie1*
66h   of lasting] of his lasting *K104 (ESTC R229873), K104A, K104AB, K105, K106, K106A, Opie1, K107*
66i   The ... agree] And Truth and Conscience joyntly do agree *K106B*
66j   the] *Opie1* omit
66k   my Heavenly] and my Heav'nly *K104, K104 (ESTC R229873), K104A, K104AB, K105, K106, K106A, Opie1, K106B, K107*
66l   I] I be *K106B*
66m   all] *K106B* omit
66n   Vnless ... repent] Till thou of thy Repentance shalt Repent *K103A, K104, K104 (ESTC R229873), K104A, K104AB, K105, K106, K106A, Opie1, K106B, K107*
67a   still] *K104 (ESTC R229873), K104A, K104AB, K105, K106* omit; thou *K106A, Opie1, K106B, K107*
67b   strength I] strength still *K104 (ESTC R229873)*; strength still I *K104A, K104AB, K105, K106, K106A, Opie1*
67c   mighty] rightly *Opie1, K106B*
67d   my] a *K103A, K104, K104 (ESTC R229873), K104A, K104AB, K105, K106, K106A, Opie1, K106B, K107*
67e   dost on my Arm] on my Arms *Opie1*; wilt on my Arms *K106B*
67f   be forc'd with speed] with speed be forc't *K106B*
67g   thine] thy *K104AB, K105, Opie1, K106B*
67h   will] shill *K104 (ESTC R229873), K104A, K106*; shall *K104AB, K105, K106A, Opie1, K106B, K107*

67i   heart is] Tears is *Opie1*; Tears are *K106B*

67j   Chear] Clear *K104, K104 (ESTC R229873), K104A, K104AB, K106, k106A,*
       Opie1

68a   thou dost do] thou dost *Opie1*; that thou dost *K106B*

68b   *The Young-man experiencing Conversion truly wrought in his Soul, and that he's deliv-*
      ered from the Power of the Tempter, breaks forth into these following Hymns *of Prayer*
      and Praises to God.

A Mystical Hymn of Thanksgiving.

MY Soul mounts up with Eagles wings,
And unto thee, dear God, she sings;
    Since thou art on my side,
My Enemies are forc'd to fly,
As soon as they do thee espy;
    Thy Name be glorify'd.
Thou makest Rich by making Poor,
By Poverty add'st to my Store;
    Such Grace dost thou provide:
Thou wound'st as well as thou mak'st whole,
And heal'st by wounding of the Soul;
    Thy Name be glorify'd.
Thou mak'st men blind by giving sight,
And turn'st [turn'st: turn'd *Opie1, K106B*] their darkness into light:
    These things can't be deny'd.
Thou cloath'st the Soul by making bare,
And giv'st in[in: *K104 (ESTC R229873), K104A, K104AB, K105, K106,*
    K106A, Opie1, K106B, K107 omit] food when none is there;
    Thy Name be glorify'd.
Thou killest by making alive,
By dying do'st the Soul revive,
    VVhich none can do beside:
Thou dost raise up by pulling down,
And by abasing, thou dost crown:
    Thy Name be magnify'd [magnify'd: glorified *K104 (ESTC R229873),*
    K105, K106, K106A, Opie1, K106B].
By making bitter thou mak'st sweet,
And mak'st each crooked thing to meet,
    I'th' Soul which thou has try'd:
The fruitless tree thou mak'st to grow,
And the green tree dost overthrow;
    The [The: Thy *K104 (ESTC R229873), K104A, K105, K106, K106A,*
    Opie1, K106B, K107] Name be glorify'd.
The conquered the conquest gains;
By being beat, the field obtains.
    Which makes me therefore cry,
Lord, while I live upon the Earth,
Since thou hast wrought the second birth,

Thy Name I'le magnify. [Thy ... magnify: Thy Name be Glorify'd *Opie1,
    K106B, K107*]
Thou mak'st men wise by 'coming foolls;
By emptying, thou fill'st their Souls,
    Such Grace dost thou provide:
By making weary, thou giv'st rest,
That which seem'd worst, proves for the best;
    Thy Name be glorifi'd.
Thou art far off, and also neer,
And not confin'd, but ev'ry where.
    And on the clouds dost ride.
O thou art Love, and also Light;
There's none can go out of thy sight;
    Thy Name be magnify'd. [magnify'd: glorify'd *K107*]
Lord, thou art great and also good,
And sit'st upon the [thy K107] mighty flood,
    By whom all hearts are try'd:
Though thou art Three, yet [yet: and *K106B*] art but One,
And comprehended art of none;
    Thy Name be glorify'd.

The Excellency of Peace of Conscience.

MY Conscience is become my Friend,
    And chearfully doth speak to me,
And I will to his motions bend,
    Although that I reproached be:
        I matter not who doth revile,
        Since Conscience in my face doth smile,
My Conscience now doth give me rest,
    My burden's gone, my Soul is free;
Again I would not be opprest
    In the old bands of miserie,
        For Kingdoms, nor for Crowns of Gold,
        Nor any thing which can be told.
My Conscience doth with precious food,
    Feed my poor Soul continually;
Its dainties also are so good,
    All sinful sweets I do [I do: do I *K104 (ESTC R229873), K106, K106A*]
    defy:
        This banquet's lasting, 'twill supply
        My wants, and feast me till I die.
My Conscience doth me chearful make,
    When I am much possest with grief;
And when I suffer for its sake,
    'Twill yield me joy and sweet relief:
        Though troubles rise, and much increase,
        I in my Conscience shall have peace.
When others to the Mountains fly,

And sore amaz'd do trembling stand:
A place of shelter then [then: there *Opie1, K106B, K107*] have I,
  And Conscience will lend me its hand,
    To lock me in the Chambers fast,
    Till th' Indignation's over-past.
At Death, and in the Judgment Day,
  What would men give for such a Friend!
All those which do him disobey,
  They'l it repent I'm sure i' th' end:
    When such are forc'd to howl and cry,
    My Soul shall sing continually.

A Hymn on the Six Principles of Christ's Doctrine.
Heb. 6. 1, 2.

Repentance is wrought in my Soul,
  And Faith for to believe;
Whereby on Jesus I do roul,
  And truly him receive.
As my dread Lord and Sovereign,
  Him always to obey;
And in all [all: *K104 (ESTC R229873), K104A, K106, K106A, Opie1,
  K106B, K107* omit] things o're me to reign,
  And govern night and day.
Christ's Baptisme it [it: *K107* omit] is very sweet,
  With Laying on of Hands:
My Soul is brought to Jesus feet,
  In owning his Commands.
Those Ordinances men oppose,
  And count as carnal things;
I have clos'd with, and tell't to those,
  From them rare comfort springs. [comfort springs: comfort spring *K105*;
    comforts spring *K104 (ESTC R229873), K106, K106A, Opie1, K106B*]
My precious Lord I must obey,
  Though men reproach me still;
I'le do whatever Christ doth say,
  and yield unto his will.
On Christ alone I do rely,
  Though men judge otherwise;
Because I can't God's Truth deny,
  I am reproach'd with lyes.
Let them deride, yet for Christ's sake
  Resolved now am I,
In his own strength the Cross to take,
  Yea, and for him to dy.
Before I'le ever turn my back
  On him whom I do love;
For I do know I shall not lack
  His Presence from above.

For he has Promis'd to the end,
    To me he will be near;
And be to me a faithful Friend,
    Which makes me not to fear.
Whatever Men or Devils do
    In secret place design,
He soon can them quite overthrow,
    And help this Soul of mine.
The Resurrection of the Dead
    I constantly maintain;
When all those which lie buried,
    Shall rise[rise: rise up *K106A*] to life again.
And that the Judgment Day will come,
    When Christ upon the Throne
Shall pass a black Eternal Doom,
    Upon each Wicked one.
But all the Saints then joyfully
    With Bowels he'l embrace,
And Crowns to all Eternity
    Upon their Heads he'l place,
And in the Kingdom shall they reign,
    Prepared long before;
And also shall with Christ remain,
    In bliss for evermore.

A Spiritual Hymn.

The Sun doth now begin to shine,
    And breaketh forth yet more and more,
Mere darkness was that Light of mine,
    Which I commended heretofore.
        I was involved in [in: with *Opie1*] my sin;
        Had day without, but night within.
My former days I did compare,
    Unto the [the: thee *K107*] sweet and lovely Spring;
I thought That time it was as rare,
    As when the chirping Birds do sing:
        But I was blind, I now do see
        There was no Spring nor Light in me.
My Spring it was the Winter-time,
    Yea, [Yea: Yet *K104 (ESTC R229873)*, *K105*, *K106*, *K106A*, *Opie1*,
    K106B, *K107*] like the midst of cold December;
The Sun was gone out of my Clime,
    And also now I do [now I do: I do now *K104 (ESTC R229873)*, *K105*,
    K106, *Opie1*, *K106B*, *K107*; I do *K106A*] remember
        My heart was cold as any stone,
        My leaves were off, and [and: my *K107*] sap was gone.
God is a Sun, a Shield also,
    The Glory of the World is He;

True Light alone from him doth flow,
    And he has now enlightned me:
        The Sun [Sun: Son] doth his sweet beams display,
        Like to the dawning of the day.
How precious is't to see the Sun,
    When in the morning it doth rise,
And shineth in our Horizon,
    To th' clearing of the cloudy Skies! *K104 (ESTC R229873), K104A,*
    K104AB, K105
        The misty Fogs by his strong Light,
        Are vanish'd quite out of our sight.
Thus doth the Lord in my poor heart,
    By his strong beams and glorious rayes,
The light from darkness clearly part,
    And makes in me rare [rare: clear *K107*] shining dayes.
        Though Fogs appear and Clouds do rise,
        He doth expel them from mine eyes.
Were there no glorious Lamp above,
    What dark confusion would be here? [here: *K106B* omit]
If [Opie1 omit] God should quite the Sun remove,
    How would the Seaman [Seaman: Sea-men *Opie1, K106B, K107*] do to
    steer?
        My Soul's the World, and Christ's the Sun,
        If he shines not, I am undone.
In Winter things hang down their head,
    Until Sol's beams do them revive;
So I in sin lay buried,
    Till Jesus Christ made me alive:
        Alas my heart was Ice and Snow,
        Till Sun did shine, and Winds did blow.
Until warm Gales of Heav'nly Wind
    Did sweetly blow, and Sun did dart
Its Light in [in: on *K104AB, K105, K106, K106A, K107*] me, I could not find
    No heat within my inward part;
        Then blow thou Wind, and shine thou Sun,
        To make my Soul a lively one.
In nat'ral men there is a Light,
    VVhich for their sins doth them reprove;
And yet are they but in the night,
    And not renewed from above:
        The Moon is given (it is clear)
        To guide men who in darkness are,
The Sun for brightness doth exceed
    The Stars of Heaven, or the Moon;
Of them there is but little need,
    VVhen Sun doth shine towards high-noon.
        Just so the Gospel doth excel,
        The Law God gave to Israel.

All those who do the Gospel slight,
   And rather have a Legal guide;
The Sun's not risen in their sight,
   And therefore 'tis that they deride
      Those who commend the Gospel-Sun,
      Above the Light in ev'ry one.
Degrees of Light, I do [I do: do they *Opie1, K106B, K107*] perceive
   Some of them weak, and others strong;
That which is saving none receive,
   But those who unto Christ belong:
      Yet doth each Light serve for the end,
      For which to man God did it send.

Divine Breathings.
A Hymn.

Let not the Sun Eclipsed be;
   Nor any dark Cloud interpose
Between thy self (dear Christ) and me,
   Who are [are: art *Opie1, K107*] that blessed Sharon's Rose:
      O let thy face upon me shine,
      Since thou by choice hast made me thine.
Always let me walk in the [thy *Opie1*] Light,
   Till Grace doth me with Glory crown;
Turn not my morning [my mourning *K104AB, K105*; thy mourning *K106*]
  into night,
   Nor ever let my Sun go down:
      O let thy face upon me shine,
      Since by dear purchase I am thine. [thine: always thine *Opie1*]
Let not thick Fogs, O Lord, arise
   From the gross Lump of inward [inward: *Opie1* omit; this dark *K106B*]
  Earth,
To th' hiding of the glorious Skies,
   The thoughts of that's as bad as Death:
      O let thy face upon me shine,
      Since by Adopt'on I am thine.
Lord, let my morning be more bright,
   And my Sun shine to th' perfect day
And let mine eyes have stronger sight,
   That I behold its glory may.
      O let thy face upon [upon: before *K106B*] me shine,
      Since God by Gift has made me thine.
Lord shine and make my heart more soft,
   And temper it, the seal to take;
Make it according as it ought,
   Lord do it for thy own Name's sake:
      O let thy face upon me shine,
      Since by sweet Contract I am thine.
The Light of thy dear Countenance,

It is the thing I only prize;
Let not therefore mine [mine: my *Opie1*] ignorance
   Darken the light of my dim eyes:
     O let thy face upon me shine,
     Since I by Faith am wholly thine.
O be my Strength, my Light, my Guide,
   Alwayes until I come to dy;
And from thy paths ne're let me slide,
   But light me to Eternity:
     O let thy face upon me shine,
     For I my self to thee resign.
There's many, Lord, who daily cry,
   Oh! who [who: whom *K106, K106A*] will shew us any good?
'Tis in thy self, Lord, it doth ly,
   Although by few 'tis understood:
     O let thy face upon me shine,
     For I by Conquest now am thine,
Lord in the Light I thee enjoy,
   And with thy Saints Communion have,
No Devil can that Soul destroy,
   VVhom thou intendest[intendest: intendeth *K104 (ESTC R229873),*
   K104A, Opie1, K106B] for to save:
     O let thy face upon me shine,
     For I can't say, Lord, thou art mine.
Let not the Sun only appear,
   For to enlighten my dark heart;
But to poor Souls both far and near,
   The self-same Glory, Lord, impart:
     O let thy face upon them shine,
     As it doth now, dear God, on mine.
Let Light and Glory so break forth,
   And Darkness fly and quite be gone;
That all thy Saints upon the Earth,
   May in the Truth be joyn'd in one:
     O let thy face so brightly shine,
     As to [to: do *K105, K106*] discover who are thine.
Let Grace and Knowledge now abound,
   And the blest [blest: bright *K107*] Gospel shine so clear,
That it Romes Harlot may confound,
   And Popish darkness quite cashier:
     O let thy face on Sion shine,
     But plague those cursed Foes of thine.
Let France, dark Spain, and Italy,
   Thy Light and Glory, Lord, behold;
To each adjacent Countrey,
   Do thou the Gospel plain unfold:
     O let thy face upon them shine,
     That all these Nations may be thine.

Let Christendom new Christ'ned be,
  And unto thee O let them turn, [turn: tune *Opie1*]
And be Baptiz'ed, O Christ, by thee
    VVith th' Spirit of the [the: thy *K106, K106A*] Holy One:
      O let thy face upon it shine,
      That Christendom may all be thine.
And carry on thy glorious VVork,
  Victoriously in every Land;
Let Tartars and the mighty Turk
    Subject themselves to thy Command:
      O let thy face upon them shine,
      That those blind People may be thine.
And let thy Brightness also go,
  To Asia and to Africa;
Let Egypt and Assyria too,
    Submit unto thy blessed Law:
      O let thy face upon them shine,
      That those dark Regions may be thine.
Nay, precious God, let Light extend
  To China and East-India;
To thee let all the People bend,
    VVho live in wild America:
      O let thy blessed Gospel shine,
      That the blind Heathens may be thine.
Send forth thy Light like to the Morn
  Most swiftly, Lord, O let it fly
From Cancer unto Capricorn;
    That all dark Nations may espy
      Thy glorious face on them to shine,
      And they in Christ for to be thine.
The Fulness of the Gentiles, Lord,
  Bring in with speed, O let them fear
Thy Name in Truth with one accord,
    Live they far off, or live they near:
      O let thy face upon them shine,
      And let us [us: *K104AB, K105* omit] know, Lord, who are thine.
And let also the glorious news
  Of thy Salvat'on, yield relief
Unto the sad distressed Jews,
    Who hardned are in Unbelief:
      O let thy face upon them shine,
      For Abram's sake, that Friend of thine.
O don't forget poor Israel,
  But let thy Light and glorious Rayes
Cause their rare Beauty to excel,
    Beyond what 'twas in former dayes:
      O cause thy face sweetly to shine,
      That Jews and Gentiles may be thine.

O let all Kingdoms now with speed
　And all the Nations under Heaven,
From all grose Darkness quite [quite: now *Opie1*] be freed,
　And Power to thy Saints be given:
　　That they in Glory, Lord, may shine,
　　According to that Word of thine.]
　K103A, K104, K104 (ESTC R229873), K104A, K104AB, K105, K106, K106A, Opie1, K106B, K107 insert

68c　here where I am] where I am *K104*; where I am now *K104 (ESTC R229873), K104A, K104AB, K105, K106, K106A, Opie1, K106B*; where now I am *K107*
68d　disturb'd] disturb *Opie1, K106B*
68e　Would ... remain'd] Ah would to God in Egypt I'd remain'd *K106B*
68f　the] thee *K103A, K104, K104 (ESTC R229873), K104A, K104AB, K105, K106, K106A, Opie1, K107*
69a　of] *K106A* omit
69b　crasy] crafty *K104 (ESTC R229873), K104A, K104AB, K105, K106, K106A, Opie1, K106B, K107*
69c　do] *Opie1* omit
69d　head did] heard dead did *K104 (ESTC R229873)*
69e　that most] thou must *K107*
69f　and] or *K105, K106, K106A*
69g　afterwards] after that *Opie1, K106B*
69h　all] will *K106B*
69i　one that's] that's *K106*; that is *K106A*; none that's *Opie1, K106B, K107*
69j　doth] do *K106, K106A*
69k　or] and *K106B*
69l　pick] pitch *K105, K106*
69m　of] for *K106, K106A*
70a　joys] Joy *Opie1, K106B, K107*
70b　would] will *Opie1, K106B*
70c　with her] *Opie1* omit
70d　To ... are] To court or play thou need'st not fear at all,
　　For all such things they Venial Sins do call. *K106B*
70e　ope] open *K106, K106A, K107*
70f　which] that *Opie1*
70g　hath] has *K107*
70h　thee] the *K106, K106A, Opie1, K107*
70i　believes] believe *K106, K107*
70j　o're] e're *K107*
70k　those] these *K107*
70l　such advantage] such an advantage *K103A, K104, K104 (ESTC R229873), K104A, K104AB, K105, K106, K106A, Opie1, K106B, K107*
70m　I am sure] *Opie1* omit; enough *K106B*
70n　I'd] I'll *Opie1*
70o　Believe] Belye *K104 (ESTC R229873), K104A, K104AB, K105, K106, K106A, Opie1, K106B, K107*
70p　ope] open *K106, K106A, K107*

71a   who are a going] who are going *K104AB, K105, K106*; that are a going *Opie1, K106B*

71b   Cause] 'Cause *K106A*

71c   to] do *K106A*

71d   shall] will *K106, K106A, K107*

71e   also I] I also *K106A*; for which *K106B*

71f   He from whom I most] From whom I once more *K106B*

71g   Contrariwise will] And I'm afraid he'll *K106B*

72a   such a vile] so vile an *K106B*

72b   Church] Churches *K106A*

72c   ye] you *K104 (ESTC R229873), K104AB, K105, K106, K106A, Opie1, K106B, K107*

72d   prevail will] will prevail *K107*

72e   try your skill] him assail *K106B*

72f   of] for *K106B*

72g   to] do *K104 (ESTC R229873), K104AB, K105, K106, K106A, Opie1, K106B, K107*

72h   this] his *K106B*

73a   price] Prize *K104 (ESTC R229873), K104A, K104AB, K105, K106, K106A, Opie1, K106B, K107*

74a   transcendently] transcently *K106B*

74b   thence] *K104 (ESTC R229873), K104A* omit; him *K104AB, K105, K106, K106A, Opie1, K106B, K107*

74c   fruit] fruits *K104, K104 (ESTC R229873), K104A, K104AB, K105, K106, K106A, Opie1, K106B, K107*

74d   real truly] truly real *K107*

74e   hear] here *K104, K104 (ESTC R229873), K104A, K104AB, K105, K106, K106A, Opie1, K106B, K107*

74f   esteemd] esteem *K104, K104 (ESTC R229873), K104A, K105, K106, K106A, Opie1, K107*

74g   within] in *K104 (ESTC R229873), K104AB, K105, K106, K106A, Opie1, K107*

74h   The glory ... Chest] *K106B* omit

75a   of it not be depriv'd] not be depriv'd of it *K106B*

75b   which] that *Opie1, K106B*

75c   ye] you *K104 (ESTC R229873), K105, K106, K106A, Opie1, K106B, K107*

75d   your] you *K104 (ESTC R229873), K104A, K104AB, K105, K106, K106A, Opie1, K106B, K107*

75e   day will] day he will *K104, K104 (ESTC R229873), K104A, K104AB, K105, K106, K106A, Opie1, K106B, K107*

75f   bare] bear *K104, k104 (ESTC R229873), K104A, K104AB, K105, K106, K106A, Opie1, K106B, K107*

75g   Tost'd] Toss'd *K103A, K104, K104 (ESTC R229873), K104A, K104AB, K105, K106, K106A, Opie1, K106B, K107*

75h   am] I'm *K104, K104 (ESTC R229873), K104A, K104AB, K105, K106, K106A, K106B, K107*

75i   satiated] sated *K104*; satiate *K107*

75j   friendship] Comfort *Opie1, K106B, K107*

76a   Storm and Tempest] Storms and Tempests *K103A, K104, K104 (ESTC R229873),*

K104A, K104AB, K105, K106, K106A, Opie1, K106B, K107
76b   Conscience] Consciences K105, K106, K106A
76c   opposition] oppression K106, K106A
76d   Pyrate] Pyrats K104 (ESRTC R229873), K104A, K104AB, K105, K106, K106A,
       Opie1, K106B, K107
76e   cost] cause K105
76f   no] my K106
76g   lose] loose K104 (ESTC R229873), K104AB, K105, K106, K106A, Opie1, K106B,
       K107
76h   there's] there K104 (ESTC R229873), K104AB, K105, K106, K106A, K106B,
       Opie1
77a   shouldst] should K104 (ESTC R229873)
77b   way] right K104, K104 (ESTC R229873), K104A, K104AB, K105, K106, K106A,
       Opie1, K106B, K107
77c   toldst, be] saidst, be Opie1, K106B; toldst me K107
77d   or] and K106A
77e   nature] Natures K104 (ESTC R229873), K104A, K104AB, K105, K106, K106A,
       Opie1, K106B, K107
77f   fearful] dreadful K107
77g   Seeing … mind] Seeing in Writing Christ has left his Mind K106B
77h   can] to K104 (ESTC R229873), K104A, K104AB, K105, K106, K106A, Opie1,
       K106B, K107
77i   have] hath K104 (ESTC R229873), K104A, K104AB, K105, K106, K106A, Opie1,
       K106B, K107
77j   come to] come K104 (ESTC R229873), K104A ; came to K106B
77k   For … have] For you aren't like the Scriptures long to have K106B
77l   dost] doth K106, K106A
77m   wresteth] wrestest K104 (ESTC R229873), K104A, K104AB, K105
77n   has] hath K107
78a   salvation] of salvation K106A
78b   bad] did bid K103A, K104, K104 (ESTC R229873), K104A, K104AB, K105,
       K106, K106A, Opie1, K106B, K107
78c   To] Can K103A, K104, K104 (ESTC RT229873), K104A, K104AB, K105, K106,
       K106A, Opie1, K106B, K107
78d   its] his K106B
78e   bare] bear K104, K104 (ESTC R229873), K104A, K104AB, K105, K105, K106A,
       Opie1, K106B, K107
78f   Husbands] Husband Opie1, K106B
78g   for] of K106B
78h   my] me K104 (ESTC R229873), K104A
79a   or] and K105, K106, K106A
79b   forbid] forget K106A, K107
79c   him do] do him Opie1, K106B, K107
80a   thou hast] th'hast K103A, K104, K104 (ESTC R229873), K104A, K104AB,
       K105, K106, K106A; thou'st Opie1, K106B, K107
80b   again] K105, K106, K106A omit
80c   do] K104 (ESTC R229873), K105, K106, K106A, Opie1, K106B, K107 omit
80d   plainly declare] plainly it declare K103A, K104, k104 (ESTC R229873), K104A,

K104AB, K105, K106, K106A, Opie1, K106B, K107

80e	pomp is there] pomps appear *K103A, K104, K104 (ESTC R229873), K104A,
	K104AB, K105, K106, K106A, Opie1, K106B, K107*

80f	you] ye *K105, K106, K106A*

80g	But ... doubt] I do not fear, nor have I any doubt *K106B*

80h	for] base *K103A, K104, K104 (ESTC R229873), K104A, K104AB, K105, K106,
	K106A, Opie1, K106B, K107*

81a	fond] sound *K104 (ESTC R229873), K104A, K104AB, K105, K106, K106A,
	Opie1, K106B, K107*

81b	to] too *K103A, K104, K104 (ESTC R229873), K104A, K104AB, K105, K106,
	K106A, K106B, K107*

81c	wisdom's] Wisdom *Opie1, K106B, K107*

81d	world's just like th'Strumpet] World the Strumpet's like *K106B*; world's like the
	Strumpet *K107*

81e	lodges] lodgeth *Opie1, K106B, K107*

81f	doth] does *K105, K106, K106A*

81g	by] buy *K104, K104 (ESTC R229873), K104A, K104AB, K105, K106, K106A,
	Opie1, K106B, K107*

81h	to] too *K103A, K104, K104 (ESTC R229873), K104A, K104AB, K105, K106,
	K106A, Opie1, K106B, K107*

81i	sliting] flitting *K103A, K104, K104 (ESTC R229873), K104A, K104AB, K105,
	K106, Opie1, K106B, K107*; fleeting *K106A*

81j	What ... unto] *K106* omit

81k	In ... unto] What-ever I exposed am unto
	In Abraham's steps I am resolv'd to go; *K106A*

81l	mak't] make *Opie1*

82a	Sirs] Sir *K104, K104 (ESTC R229873), K104A, K104AB, K105, K106, K106A,
	Opie1, K106B, K107*

82b	to] unto *K103A, K104, K104 (ESTC R229873), K104A, K104AB, K105, K106,
	K106A, Opie1, K106B, K107*

82c	earthly] *K106, K106A* omit

82d	I'm born too] I am born to *K103A, K104, K104 (ESTC R229873), K104A,
	K104AB, K105, K106, K106A, Opie1, K107*; I'm Born unto *K106B*

82e	portion] Portion's *K105, K106, K106A, K107*

82f	to the] unto the *K104, K104 (ESTC R229873), K104A, K104AB, K105, K106,
	K106A*; unto that *Opie1, K106B, K107*

82g	claim] lay claim *K103A, K104, K104 (ESTC R229873), K104A, K104AB, K105,
	K106, K106A, Opie1, K106B, K107*

82h	oftimes] times *K105, K106, K106A*

82i	quit] quite *K104, K104 (ESTC R229873), K104A, K104AB, K105, K106, K106A,
	Opie1, K106B, K107*

82j	made me sad] once did make Me sad *K103A, K104, K104 (ESTC R229873),
	K104A, K104AB, K105, K106, K106A, Opie1, K106B, K107*

82k	for] from *K106A*

82l	thy] and *K106A, K107*

82m	has] hath *K106A*

82n	the] this *K103A, K104, K104 (ESTC R229873), K104A, K104AB, K105, K106,
	K106A, Opie1, K106B, K107*

83a   com] get *Opie1, K106B, K107*

83b   Which] Who *Opie1, K106B*

83c   unto] unto her *K103A, K104, K104 (ESTC R229873), K104A, K104AB, K105, K106, K106A, Opie1, K106B, K107*

84a   Is … lies] Is a sad thing though many it despise *K103A, K104, K104 (ESTC R229873), K104A, K104AB, K105, K106, K106A, Opie1, K106B, K107*

84b   to make appear also] fully to make appear *K103A, K104, K104 (ESTC R229873),K104A, K104AB, K105, K106, K106A, Opie1, K106B, K107*

84c   or will let you go] if your please to hear *K103A*; if your pleas'd to hear *K104, K104 (ESTC R229873), K104A, K104AB, K105, K106, K106A, Opie1, K107*; if you please to hear *K106B*

84d   also every one] in due form tis known *K103A, K104, K104 (ESTC R229873), K104A, K104AB, K105, K106, K106A, Opie1, K106B, K107*

84e   doth fail] doth fall *K106, K106A*; do fail *K106B*

84f   Go] God *K104 (ESTC R229873), K104AB, K106, K106A, Opie1, K106B, K107*

84g   has] hath *K104 (ESTC R229873), K105, K106, K106A, Opie1, K106B, K107*

84h   them] it *K106B*

84i   his] their *K106B*

84j   which] that *K106B*

85a   nought left] left nought *K107*

85b   you] your's *K107*

85c   was] b'ing *K106B*

85d   clearer] clear *K103A, K104, K104 (ESTC R229873), K104A, K104AB, K105, K106, K106A, Opie1, K106B, K107*

85e   fleshly] fleshy *K106A*

85f   now] *K104, K104 (ESTC R229873), K104A, K104AB, K105, K106, K106A, Opie1, K106B, K107* omit

85g   'was] 'twas *K104 (ESTC R229873), K104A, K104AB, K105, K106, K106A, Opie1, K106B, K107*

85h   true] a true *K106A*

85i   That] The *K106B*

85j   common stinking] stinking common *K104, K104 (ESTC R229873), K104A, K104AB, K105, K106, K106A, Opie1, K106B, K107*

85k   Ye] He *K104 (ESTC R229873), K104A, K104AB, K105, K106, K106A, Opie1, K106B, K107*

85l   Apostle hath] Apostles have *K106B*

85m   allow] allows *K106A*; admits *K106B*

86a   Incest] Incense *K106B*

86b   sin] Sins *K106A*

86c   hath] have *K104, K104 (ESTC R229873), K104A, K104AB, K105, K106, K106A, Opie1, K106B, K107*

86d   Christs] Christ *K104 (ESTC R229873), K104A, K104AB, K105, k106, K106A, Opie1, K106B, K107*

86e   Bishop] Bishops *K104 (ESTC R229873), K104A, K104AB, K105, Opie1, K106B, K107*

86f   she proudly shon] is proudly shown *K106B*

87a   triumph] triumphs *K103A, K104, K104 (ESTC R229873), K104A, K104AB, K105, K106, K106A, Opie1, K106B, K107*

87b as a] for their *K103A, K104, K104 (ESTC R229873), K104A, K104AB, K105, K106, K106A, Opie1, K106B, K107*

87c Rome] Room *K103, K103 Beinecke, K103aA;* Rome *K103A, K104, K104 (ESTC R229873), K104A, K104AB, K105, K106, K106A, Opie1, K106B, K107*

87d race] rase *K104AB, K105, K107*

87e future] futures *Opie1*

87f sad] dire *K104 (ESTC R229873), K104A, K104AB, K105, K106, K106A, Opie1, K106B, K107*

87g they'd] they *Opie1, K107*

87h Lords] Lord *K106B*

87i fields] field *K103A, K104, K104 (ESTC R229873), K104A, K104AB, K105, K106, K106A, Opie1, K106B, K107*

87j freely] ready *K103A, K104, K104 (ESTC R229873), K104A, K104AB, K105, K106, K106A, Opie1, K106B, K107*

87k To give Quarter to those that it demand] *K104 (ESTC R229873), K104A, K104AB, K105, K106, K106A, Opie1, K106B, K107* insert

87l find] know *K104 (ESTC R229873), K104A, K104AB, K105, K106, K106A, Opie1, K106B, K107*

88a secure men] secure of men *K104, K104 (ESTC R229873), K104A, K104AB, K105, K106, Opie1, K106A, K106B, K107*

88b There] Their *K104, K104 (ESTC R229873), K104A, K104AB, K105, K106, K106A, Opie1, K106B, K107*

88c your] an *K106A*

88d night] Light *Opie1, K106B*

88e of humane] of all humane *K103A, K104, K104 (ESTC R229873), K104A, K104AB, K105, K106, K106A, Opie1, K106B, K107*

89a Idol] Idols *K105, K106, K106A, K107*

89b use] us'd *K104AB, K105, K106, K106A, Opie1, K106B, K107*

89c these] those *K106A, Opie1, K106B*

89d terminate] terminated *K103A, K104, K104 (ESTC R229873), K104A, K104AB, K105, K106, K106A, Opie1, K106B, K107*

89e did terminate their wrath] accomplisht their fierce wrath *K103A, K104, K104 (ESTC R229873), K104A, K104AB, K105, K106, K106A, Opie1, K106B, K107*

89f there] their *K104 (ESTC R229873), K104AB, K105, K106, K106A, Opie1, K106B, K107*

89g there] their *K104, K104 (ESTC R229873), K104A, K104AB, K105, K106, K106A, Opie1, K106B, K107*

89h Gives] Give *K104, K104 (ESTC R229873), K104A, K104AB, K105, K106, K106A, Opie1, K106B, K107*

89i makes] make *K103A, K104, K104 (ESTC R229873). K104A, K104AB, K105, K106, K106A, Opie1, K106B, K107*

89j has] hast *K103A, K104, K104 (ESTC R229873), K104A, K104AB, K105, K106, K106A, Opie1, K106B, K107*

89k has] hast *K103A, K104, K104 (ESTC R229873), K104A, K104AB, K105, K106, k106A, K107*

89l force] for *K106A*

90a that Christian] these Christians *K104 (ESTC R229873), K104AB, K105, K106, k106A, Opie1, K106B, K107*

90b more] most *K105, K106, K106A, Opie1, K106B, K107*

90c neither dare] fearing to *K103A, K104, K104 (ESTC R229873), K104A, K104AB, K105, K106, K106A, Opie1, K106B, K107*

90d near] ne're *K104 (ESTC R229873), K104A, K104AB, K105, K106, K106A, Opie1, K106B, K107*

90e take] takes *K106B*

90f hears] here's *K104 (ESTC R229873), K106, K106A, Opie1, K106B, K107*

90g Whereas] VVhereby *K104, K104 (ESTC R229873), K104A, K104AB, K105, K106, K106A, Opie1, K106B, K107*

90h doth] do *K104 (ESTC R229873), K104A, K104AB, K105, K106, K106A, Opie1, K106B, K107*

90i hath poured] have poured *K103A, K104*; have filled *K104 (ESTC R229873), K104A, K104AB, K105, K106, K106A, Opie1, K106B, K107*

90j this] the *K106, K106A, K107*

90k France] frame *K103, K103aA*; France *K103A, K104, K104 (ESTC R229873), K104A, K104AB, K105, K106, K106A, Opie1, K106B, K107*

90l swoln] Sworn *K106A*

90m affirms] attests *K104, K104 (ESTC R229873), K104A, K104AB, K105, K106, k106A, Opie1, K106B, K107*

91a Heavens] Heaven *K107*

91b no] not *K104AB, K105, K106, K106A, Opie1, K106B, K107*; nor *K104 (ESTC R229873)*

91c did'st] found'st *K103A, K104, K104 (ESTC R229873), K104A, K104AB, K105, K106, K106A, Opie1, K106B, K107*

91d and] *K103A, K104, K104 (ESTC R229873), K104A, K104AB, K105, K106, K106A, Opie1, K106B, K107* omit

91e D'Alva] Salva *K103, K103aA*; D'Alva *K103A, K104 (ESTC R229873), K104A, K104AB, K105, K106, K106A, Opie1, K107*; De Alva *K104, K106B*

91f Christians] Christian *K104AB, K105, K106, K106A, K107*

91g years] Year *Opie1*

91h your] you *K106B*

91i thoughts] Thought *Opie1, K106B*

92a Was ... thousand] There was One Hundred Fifty Thousand *K106B*

92b either] the *K107*

92c them] then *K107*

92d was] were *Opie1, K106B*

92e These] Those *K106B*

92f And so a hundred and] And so One Hundred *K106B*; So a hundred and *K107*

92g Beside] Besides *K106B*

92h who pray] pray, who *K106B*

93a would I] I would *K103A, K104, K104 (ESTC R229873), K104A, K104AB, K105, K106, K106A, Opie1, K106B, K107*

93b to give credit to her 'thas] to give credit t'her, that's *K104, K104 (ESTC R229873), K104A, K104AB, Opie1, K106B*; to give credit t'her, it has *K106, K106A*; for to credit her, that's *K107*

93c To deal the falsest] To deal falsest *K103A, K104, K104 (ESTC R229873), K104A, K104AB, K105, K106, K106A, Opie1, K107*; Most false to deal *K106B*

93d hath] hate *K103A*

93e   had] have *K106B*

93f   did] doth *K106B*

93g   Rome's] Rooms *K103*; Rome's *K103 Beinecke, K103aA, K103A, K104, K104A, K104AB, K105, K106, K106A, Opie1, K106B, K107*

93h   and freely] readily *K106B*

93i   Rome's] Rooms *K103*; Rome's *K103 Beinecke, K103aA, K103A, K104, K104A, K104AB, K105, K106, K106A, Opie1, K106B, K107*

93j   did stretch forth her] did stretch forth with *K103A, K104, K104 (ESTC R229873), K104A, K104AB, K105, K106, K106A, Opie1, K107*; stretch'd abroad with *K106B*

94a   Laws] Law *K106, K106A*

94b   his] the *K106B*

94c   her] their *K106B*

94d   Hounds that hunts] Hound that hunts *K104 (ESTC R229873), K104A, K104AB, K105, K106*; Hound hunts *K106A*; Hounds that hunt *Opie1, K106B, K107*

94e   Doth] Do *Opie1, K106B*

94f   Cries] Crie *K103A, k104, K104 (ESTC R229873), K104A, K104AB, K105, K106, K106A, Opie1, K106B, K107*

95a   Melts not] Wont melt *K106B*

95b   Child-great-Women] Children, great-Women *K106A*

95c   others] other *K104, K104 (ESTC R229873), K104A, K104AB, K105, K106, K106A, Opie1, K106B, K107*

95d   of] *K104, K104 (ESTC R229873), K104A, K104AB, K105, K106, k106A, Opie1, K106B, K107* omit

95e   compassion] compassions *K103A, K104*

95f   near] nere *K104, K104 (ESTC R229873), K104A, K104AB, K105, K106, K106A, Opie1, K106B, K107*

95g   darkned] weeping *K106B*

95h   hard] hart *K104AB*

95i   makes the] make their *K103A, K104, K104 (ESTC R229873), K104A, K104AB, K105, K106, K106B, K107*; makes their *K106A*

95j   delights] delight *K103A, K104, K104 (ESTC R229873), K104A, K104AB, K105, K106, Opie1, K106B, K107*

95k   Oh!] *K103A, K104, K104 (ESTC R229873), K104A, K104AB, K105, K106, K106A, Opie1, K106B, K107* omit

95l   penetrates] penetrate *K103A, K104, K104 (ESTC R229873), K104A, K104AB, K105, K106, K106A, Opie1, K106B, K107*

95m   Out] Our *K103 Beinecke, K103aA, K103A, K104, K104 (ESTC R229873), K104A, K104AB, K105, K106, K106A, Opie1, K106B, K107*

95n   thought] thoughts *K105, K106, K106A, K106B, K107*

95o   doth] do *K104 (ESTC R229873), K106, K106A, Opie1, K106B, K107*

95p   Their] The *Opie1, K106B, K107*

95q   City is] City's *K103A, K104, K104 (ESTC R229873), K104A, K104AB, K105, K106, Opie1, K106A, K106B, K107*

96a   Whore] Scarlet Whore *K106B*

96b   tantingly] tauntingly *K103A, K104, K104 (ESTC R229873), K104A, K104AB, K105, K106, K106A, Opie1, K106B, K107*

96c   tormenting] horrid *K104, K104 (ESTC R229873), K104A, K104AB, K105,*

    K106, K106A, Opie1, K106B, K107

97a has] *hath K104 (ESTC R229873), K104AB, K105, K106, K106A, Opie1, K106B,*
   K107

97b had] has *Opie1, K106B, K107*

97c can erect] has erected *K106A*

97d Papist] Papists *K106A*

97e a] the *K105, K106, K106A*

97f the] *K104 (ESTC R229873), K104AB* omit

97g names] name *K103A, K104, K104 (ESTC R229873), K104A, K104AB, K105,*
   K106, K106A, Opie1, K106B, K107

98a he] she *K104, K104 (ESTC R229873), K104A, K104AB, K105, K106, K106A,*
   Opie1, K106B, K107

98b these things ever] ever these things *K106*

98c Were] Where *K103A, K104, K104 (ESTC R229873), K104A, K104AB, K105,*
   K106, K106A, Opie1, K106B, K107

98d their] the *K106B*

98e toasted] tossed *K103 Beinecke, K103aA, 103A, K104, K104 (ESTC R229873),*
   K104A, K104AB, K105, K106, k106A, Opie1, K106B, K107

98f Then] All *K103A, K104, K104 (ESTC R229873), K104A, K104AB, K105, K106,*
   K106A, Opie1, K106B, K107

98g was] were *K104 (ESTC R229873), K104A, K104AB, K105, K106, K106A, Opie1,*
   K106B, K107

98h [manicule]] *K103A, K104, K104 (ESTC R229873), K104A, K104AB, K105,*
   K106, K106A, Opie1, K106B, K107 omit

99a or] and *K106, K106A*

99b kinds] kind *K106B*

99c for] far *K106B*

99d it was] 'twas *K103A, K104, K104 (ESTC R229873), K104A, K104AB, K105,*
   K106, k106A, Opie1, K106B, K107

99e doth] doe *K103A, K104, K104 (ESTC R229873), K104A, K104AB, K105, Opie1*;
   unto man doth] do unto Man *K106, K106A, K106B, K107*

99f those] these *K106B*

99g bare] bear *K106B*

99h And resolv'd] And were resolv'd *K103A, K104, K104 (ESTC R229873), K104A,*
   K104AB, K105, K106, k106A, Opie1, K106B, K107

99i into] unto *K103A, K104, K104 (ESTC R229873), K104A, K104AB, K105, K106,*
   K106A, Opie1, K106B, K107

99j crept] creep *K106, K106A*

100a for] and *K106A*

100b the] these *K103A, K104, K104 (ESTC R229873), K104A, K104AB, K105, K106,*
   K106A, Opie1, K106B, K107

100c Bulls, false Pardons] False Pardons, Bulls *K106B*

100d blind] hoodwink *K103A, K104, K104 (ESTC R229873), K104A, K104AB, K105,*
   K106, K106A, Opie1, K107

100e You ... more] You can't the World deceive nor hoodwink more *K106B*

100f has] have *K103A, K104, K104 (ESTC R229873), K104A, K104AB, K105, K106,*
   K106A, Opie1, K106B, K107

100g now know how clearly] know how clearly now *K106B*; clearly now know how *K107*

100h   hear] grown *K103A, K104, K104 (ESTC R229873), K104A, K104AB, K105, K106A, Opie1, K106B, K107*

100i   now] new *K107*

101a   Then ... ever] You Hereticks must down, and rise no more *K106B*; Longer you hereticks we'll not endure *K107*

101b   hazardous] dangerous *K103A, K104, K104 (ESTC R229873), k104A, K104AB, K105, K106, K106A, Opie1, K106B, K107*

101c   withal its lust] with all its lusts *K104 (ESTC R229873), K104AB, K105, K106, k106A, Opie1, K106B, K107*

101d   I have] I've *K103A, K104, K104 (ESTC R229873), K104A, K104AB, K105, K106, K106A, Opie1*

101e   trampling places] trampling paces *K104 (ESTC R229873), Opie1, K106B, K107*; trembling paces *K105, K106, K106A*

101f   blest] best *K103A, K104, K104 (ESTC R229873), K104A, K104AB, K105, K106, K106A, Opie1, K106B, K107*

101g   will] would *Opie1, K106B*

101h   slights] slight'st *K104, K104 (ESTC R229873), K104A, K104AB, K105, K106, K106A, Opie1, K106B, K107*

101i   pleasures] pleasure *K103A, K104, K104 (ESTC R229873), K104A, K104AB, K105, K106, K106A, Opie1, K106B*

102a   Flesh-wantons] proud Flesh-wantons *K104 (ESTC R229873), K104A, K104AB, K105, K106, K106A, Opie1, K107*

102b   Estates] their Estates *K103A, K104, K104 (ESTC R229873), K104A, K104AB, K105, K106, K106A, Opie1, K107*

102c   Dame-Hellish-Mates] damn'd hellish Mates *K107*

102d   last] lust *K103 Beinecke, K103aA, K103A, K104, K104 (ESTC R229873), K104A, K104AB, K105, K106, K106A, Opie1, K107*

102e   Shall Flesh-wantons ... all my might on earth] *K106B* omit

102f   nought, he] nothing *K103A, K104, K104 (ESTC R229873), K104A, K104AB, K105, K106, K106A, Opie1, K106B, K107*

103a   relations dear] relations all, (though) dear *K103A, K104, K104 (ESTC R229873), K104A, K104AB, K105, K106, K106A, Opie1, K106B, K107*

103b   last] least *K106B*

103c   I had] I'de *K104 (ESTC R229873), K106, K106A, Opie1, K106B, K107*

103d   hear] here *K104, K104 (ESTC R229873), K104A, K104AB, K105, K106, Opie1, K106B, K107*

103e   e'ry] ev'ry *K104 (ESTC R229873), K104A, K105, K106, K106A, Opie1, K106B, K107*

103f   mights] might'st *K104, K104 (ESTC R229873), K104A, K104AB, K105, K106, K106A, Opie1, K106B, K107*

104a   'tis] it is *K104, K104 (ESTC R229873), k104A, K104AB, K105, K106, K106A, Opie1, K106B, K107*

104b   do] did *K106B*

104c   More] Mere *K107*

104d   doth] do *K104 (ESTC R229873), K106A, Opie1, K106B, K107*

104e   a] the *K106A*

105a   doth] do *K104 (ESTC R229873), K104AB, K105, K106, k106A, Opie1, K106B, K107*

105b to] too *K104 (ESTC R229873)*, *K104A*, *K104AB*, *K105*, *K106*, *K106A*, *Opie1*, *K106B*, *K107*

105c When … heard] When the low sound o' th' grinders Scarcely heard *K103A*, *K104*, *K104 (ESTC R229873)*, *k104A*, *K104AB*, *K105*, *K106*, *K106A*, *Opie1*, *K106B*, *K107*

105d riseth] rises *K106A*

105e in] on *K105*, *K106*, *K106A*, *K107*

105f Pitcher … Fountain] weak Pitcher at the Foundtain's K103A, K104, K104 (ESTC R229873), K104A, K104AB, K105, K106, K106A, Opie1, K106B, K107

105g th'] *K106B* omit

105h life] Life's *K106*

105i still] *K105*, *K106*, *K106A* omit

105j e're] o're *K104 (ESTC R229873)*, *K104AB*, *K105*, *Opie1*

106a what] that *K104 (ESTC R229873)*, *K105*, *K106*, *K106A*, *K106B*, *K107*

106b Because … believe] Because so many walk I'th way to Hell *K104AB*, *K105*

106c Because … receive] *K106A* omit

106d To think … astray] *K106B* omit

106e favour] Saviour *Opie1*, *K106B*, *K107*

106f did] hee'd *K104*, *K104 (ESTC R229873)*, *K104A*, *K104AB*, *K105*, *K106*, *K106A*, *Opie1*, *K106B*, *K107*

107a says] say *K106B*

107b 'th'] i'th' *K103A*, *K104*, *K104 (ESTC R229873)*, *K104A*, *K104AB*, *K105*, *K106*, *Opie1*, *K106B*, *K107*

107c oft-times] oftentimes *K106A*

107d they can] can they *K106*, *K106A*

107e the] their *K106A*

107f Do Postasize] Do Posterities *K103*; Do Postasize *K103aA*, *K103A*, *K104*, *K104 (ESTC R229873)*, *K104A*, *K104AB*, *K105*, *K106*, *K106A*, *Opie1*, *K107*; Apostatize *K106B*

107g with you headlong] Headlong with you *K106B*

107h do] *K106B* omit

107i our] are *K103A*, *K104*, *K104 (ESTC R229873)*, *K104A*, *K104AB*, *K105*, *K106*, *K106A*, *Opie1*, *K106B*, *K107*

107j Nullitie] Unlitie *K103*, *K103aA*, *K103A*; Nullitie *K104 (ESTC R229873)*, *K104A*, *K104AB*, *K105*, *K106*, *K106A*, *Opie1*, *K106B*, *K107*

107k sure] surer *K104 (ESTC R229873)*, *K104A*, *K104AB*, *K105*, *K106*, *K106A*, *Opie1*, *K106B*, *K107*

107l but] *K104*, *K104 (ESTC R229873)*, *K104A*, *K104AB*, *K105*, *K106*, *K106A*, *Opie1*, *K106B* omit

108a If] It *K103A*

108b be-sure must] must surely *K106B*

108c also doth] doth also *K106A*

108d is] in *K106A*

108e too of their] of their dire *K106A*

108f Danted] Daunted *K104*, *K104 (ESTC R229873)*, *K104A*, *K104AB*, *K105*, *K106*, *K106A*, *Opie1*, *K106B*, *K107*

108g lastly] lately *K106A*

108h doth] do *K104 (ESTC R229873)*, *K105*, *K106*, *K106A*, *Opie1*, *K106B*, *K107*

109a   Dame] my Dame *K106B*
109b   With] *K104, K104 (ESTC R229873), K104A, K104AB, K105, K106, K106A,*
        Opie1, K106B, K107 omit
109c   man] one *K106B*
109d   them] them also *K103aA, K104 (ESTC R229873), K105, K106, K106A, Opie1,*
        K106B, K107
109e   That] Who *Opie1, K106B*
109f   one] *K103A, K104, K104 (ESTC R229873), K104A, K104AB, K105, K106,*
        K106A, Opie1, K107 omit
109g   that] whom *Opie1, K106B, K107*
109h   chiefly he doth] he doth chiefly *Opie1, K106B, K107*
109i   Lastly] Lately *K103aA, K103A, K104, K104 (ESTC R229873), K104A, K105,*
        K106, K106A, Opie1, K106B, K107
109j   with him few could] few could with him *K106B*
109k   he strait away] then strait away he *K105*
109l   Christ] *K103A, K104, K104 (ESTC R229873), K104A, K104AB, K105, K106,*
        K106A, Opie1, K106B omit
109m   also they] they also *K106B*
109n   think] think's *K104, K104 (ESTC R229873), K104A, K104AB, K105, K106,*
        K106A, Opie1, K106B, K107
109o   therefore] therefore now *K103aA, K103A, K104, K104 (ESTC R229873), K104A,*
        K104AB, K105, K106, Opie1, K106B, K107
109p   you] thee *K104 (ESTC R229873), K104A, K104AB, K105, K106, Opie1, K106B,*
        K107
109q   striv'st] striv'd *K106B*
110a   scores] stones *K103aA, K103A, K104, K104 (ESTC R229873), K104A, K104AB,*
        K105, K106, K106A, Opie1, K106B, K107
110b   With] From *K106B*
110c   the] *K106A* omit
110d   thou ought] thou got ought *K104, K104 (ESTC R229873), K104A, K104AB,*
        K105, K106, K106A, Opie1, K106B, K107
110e   thou adventer] thou to adventure *K104, K104 (ESTC R229873), K104A,*
        K104AB, K105, Opie1, K106B, K107
110f   desend] ascend *K104AB, K105, K106, K106A, K107*
110g   the] a *Opie1, K106B*
110h   save] but *K106B*
111a   has] hath *K104 (ESTC R229873), K106, K106A, Opie1, K106B, K107*
111b   greatest] chiefest *K106B*
111c   make] create *K106B*
111d   for] *K106B* omit
111e   glory] glories *K103A, K104, K104 (ESTC R229873), K104A, K104AB, K105,*
        K106, K106A, Opie1, K106B, K107
112a   you] your *K104 (ESTC R229873), K106, K106A, Opie1, K106B, K107*
112b   shew] see *K106B*
113a   and impious] or malicious *K104, K104 (ESTC R229873), K104A, K104AB, K105,*
        K106, K106A, Opie1, K106B, K107
113b   never] ever *K103A, K104, K104 (ESTC R229873) K104A, K104AB, K105, K106,*
        K106A, Opie1, K106B, K107

113c to us, the Scriptures come] to us the Scripture comes *K104, K104A, K104AB, K105, K106, Opie1*; the Scriptures to us come *K106B*
113d to] so *K104 (ESTC R229873), K104AB, K105, K106, k106A, Opie1, K106B, K107*
113e extinguish'd] extinguish *K106B, K107*
113f with eternal] with an eternal *K104, K104 (ESTC R229873), K104A, K104AB, K105, K106, K106A, Opie1, K106B, K107*
113g still] and still *K103A, K104 (ESTC R229873), K104A, K105, K106, K106A, Opie1, K106B, K107*
113h could] *K103A* omit
113i and] but *Opie1, K107*
113j those cursed ways] that cursed way *K106B*
113k Ye] Yea *K104 (ESTC R229873), K104A, K104AB, K105, K106, K106A, Opie1, K106B, K107*
113l Souls] Soul *K104 (ESTC R229873), K106, K106A*
113m to those who] for those who *K104 (ESTC R229873), K105, K106, K106A*; to those which *K106B*
114a God more] Gods VVords *K103A, K104*; Gods Word *K103aA, K104 (ESTC R229873), K104A, K104AB, K105, K106, K106A, Opie1, K106B, K107*
114b Jolatry] Jo'ity *K103A*; Jollity *K104, K104 (ESTC R229873), K104A, K104AB, K105, K106, K106A, Opie1, K106B, K107*
114c doth] do *K104A, Opie1*; does *K106B*
114d would serve the] will serve the *K106B*; would serve his *K107*
114e that] who *Opie1, K106B*
114f Word] Words *K104*
114g things] *K103A, K104, K104 (ESTC R229873), K104A, K104AB, K105, K106, K106A, Opie1, K106B, K107* omit
114h make] may make *K103A, K104, K104 (ESTC R229873), K104A, K104AB, K105, K106, K106A, Opie1, K106B, K107*
114i soon] *K106B* omit
115a Epicurus] Your Epicurus *K103A, K104, K104 (ESTC R229873), K104A, K104AB, K105, K106, K106A, Opie1, K106B, K107*
115b Heathen Authors] Heathens *K106A*
115c reason] reasons *K104, K104A, K104AB, K105, K106, Opie1, K107*
115d To vile affection, up God] To vile affections, up God *K103A, K104, K104A, K104AB, K105, K106, K106A, Opie1, K107*; And to their vile Affections *K106B*
115e natural Sots] Naturalists *K106A*
115f might] must *K106B*
115g thing hear] thing here K103A; things here *K104, K104A, K104AB, K105, K106, K106A, Opie1, K106B, K107*
115h Dame-Natures] Natures *K103A, K104, K104A, K104AB, K105, K106, K106A, Opie1, K106B, K107*
115i it doth] it does *K106, K106A, K107*; but doth *K106B*
115j is] in *K106B*
115k whom] which *K104, K104A, K104AB, K105, K106, K106A, Opie1, K106B, K107*
116a Since ... show] *K106B* omit
116b example] examples *K104, K104A, K104AB, K105, K106, K106A, Opie1, K106B, K107*

116c   judgments strangely tottered] with strange Judgments tortured *K103A, K104, K104A, K104AB, K105, K106, K106A, Opie1, K106B, K107*

116d   example] fair warning *K106B*

116e   are] be *K106, K106A*

116f   those] these *Opie1, K106B, K107*

117a   of Eternal] of the Eternal *K104, K104A, K104A, K105, K106, K106A, K107*; of that eternal *Opie1, K106B*

117b   Has] Hath *K104AB, K106A, Opie1, K107*

117c   wholly] quite *K103A, K104, k104A, K104AB, K105, K106, K106A, Opie1, K106B, K107*

117d   to] in *K107*

ROBERT WILD, *A PANEGYRIQUE HUMBLY ADDREST TO THE KINGS MOST EXCELLENT MAJESTY* (1673)

Date

A Panegyrique Humbly Addrest to the Kings Most Excellent Majesty was first published in 1673. The meeting of parliament and the King's speech, to which the poem's extended title refers, occurred on 4 and 5 February 1673 respectively.[1] The question of dating is complicated, however, by the lines that refer to actions already carried out by this parliament. The lines concerning supply ('They Thank His *Royal Cares* so much has done, / And *Vote supplies* for what there is to come.')[2] raise particular questions. Supply was first discussed on 7 February, and perhaps at this stage it seemed as if it would be forthcoming with expedience: some of those who had opposed government policy nonetheless proposed a substantial sum. However, it became clear that the granting of supply was going to be dilatory, it being used to extract concessions from Charles. The Supply Bill did not receive its third reading in the Commons until 26 March, when it was passed. By this stage the Declaration of Indulgence had already been withdrawn (on 8 March) and a Test Bill had been passed by the Commons. Given Wild's reference to supply having been voted, it is possible that his poem postdates these latter two events.[3]

Copy Text

A Panegyrique Humbly Addrest to the Kings Most Excellent Majesty: W2144B Robert Wild, *A panegyrique humbly addrest to the Kings most excellent Majesty: on his auspicious meeting his two houses of Parliament, February the 4th. 5th. 1672/3. And his most gratious speech there delivered on that occasion. By R.W.* (London: A.P. for Phillip Brooksby, 1673). 2o.

Variants

A Panegyrique Humbly Addrest to the Kings Most Excellent Majesty: the variant collated is: BL W2144B Robert Wild, *A panegyrique humbly addrest to the*

Kings most excellent Majesty: on his auspicious meeting his two houses of Parliament ... (London: A.P. for Phillip Brooksby, 1673). A variant issue.

Context

On 15 March 1672 Charles II issued a Declaration of Indulgence. This suspended the penal laws against dissent, and allowed for nonconformist ministers and meeting places to be licensed under its terms.[4] (Robert Wild took out a license at his house in Oundle, Northamptonshire.)[5] The Declaration was in part an attempt to obtain the support of Nonconformists for the Third Anglo-Dutch War. The English had promised to ally with the French against the Dutch Republic in the secret Treaty of Dover as early as May 1670 (in which Charles II also promised the future conversion of England to Catholicism, and Louis XIV promised military aid in this endeavour). So incendiary were the terms of this treaty that it was not even known to all of Charles's closest advisors. They were, however, privy to the *traité simulé* dating from December 1670, which left out the most controversial aspects of the secret Treaty of Dover but retained the commitment to war. A public form of the treaty was signed in February 1672, and war on the Dutch was declared on 17 March, although fighting preceded this date. The war was not from the English perspective a success. James, duke of York (1633–1701), Lord High Admiral, had to change ships twice during the battle of Southwold Bay in May 1672 due to extent of the damage inflicted on his vessels by the Dutch. He did not again participate in naval battle. Come 1673, Charles II desperately needed money. He called parliament, and in his opening speech of 5 February he stressed the necessity of supply for war, at the same time as professing his intention to uphold the Declaration of Indulgence. MPs saw things differently. Although many were by no means unsympathetic to dissenters, the Declaration caused them unease for two interlinked reasons. First, Charles had issued the Declaration in an arbitrary way, asserting his prerogative right to suspend in ecclesiastical matters, and thus not going through parliament. Secondly, fears abounded that the Declaration was in fact a measure intended to favour Papists. Charles's parliament soon set about attacking the Declaration, and in the hope of supply Charles abandoned it on 8 March. By the time parliament was adjourned at the end of March a Test Act (primarily aimed at stopping Catholics from taking public office, but also affecting protestant dissenters) had been passed, while a proposed bill for easing protestant dissent had not been completed.[6]

Sources

A Panegyrique Humbly Addrest to the Kings Most Excellent Majesty is in essence a version of Edmund Waller's *A Panegyrick to my Lord Protector* (1655) which was addressed to Oliver Cromwell (1599–1658). Given this, Waller's poem is printed at the first endnote to Wild's poem.[7]

Notes

1. *His Majesties most Gracious Speech ... February 4. and Wednesday February 5* (London: printed by the assigns of John Bill and Christopher Barker, 1673).
2. See R. Wild, *A Panegyrique Humbly Addrest*, below p. 397, n. 21.
3. J. Spurr, *England in the 1670s: 'This Masquerading Age'* (Oxford: Blackwell, 2000), pp. 36–9; 'House of Commons Journal Volume 9: 7 February 1673', *Journal of the House of Commons: volume 9: 1667–1687* (1802), pp. 249–250. URL: http://www.british-history.ac.uk/report.aspx?compid=27344; 'House of Commons Journal Volume 9: 26 March 1673', *Journal of the House of Commons: volume 9: 1667–1687* (1802), pp. 277–278. URL: http://www.british-history.ac.uk/report.aspx?compid=27381.
4. *EHD*, pp. 387–8; F. Bate, *The Declaration of Indulgence 1672: A Study in the Rise of Organised Dissent* (London: University Press of Liverpool, 1908).
5. Bate, *Declaration of Indulgence*, Appendix VII, p. xliii.
6. Spurr, *England in the 1670s*, ch. 1, pp. 33–9; D.L. Smith, *A History of the Modern British Isles: The Double Crown, 1603–1707* (Oxford: Blackwell, 1998), p. 226 (this contains an exceptionally clear account of the different versions of the treaty between England and France).
7. See below p. 391. A modern edition of Waller's poem may be found in R.M. Cummings (ed.), *Seventeenth-Century Poetry: An Annotated Anthology* (Oxford: Blackwell, 2000), pp. 235–40.

A
PANEGYRIQUE
Humbly Addrest to the
Kings Most Excellent Majesty:
ON
His Auspicious Meeting His Two Houses
OF
PARLIAMENT,
February the 4[th.] 5[th.] 1672/3

And His Most Gratious
SPEECH
There Delivered on that Occasion.[1] [2]

By *R.W.*

London, Printed by *A. P.* for *Phillip Brooksby*, next Door to the Ball
in *West Smithfield*, neer the *Hospital-Gate*, 1673. /

A
PANEGYRIQUE
TO
His Sacred Majesty
OF
GREAT BRITTAIN.

GReat *SIR*! When e'r your *Gracious Voyce* we hear
Ravisht we stand, and wish our selves *all Ear*;
Your *Speech*, which equal *Joy* and *Wonder* breeds,
Can be *Excell'd* by nothing but your *Deeds*;
Those Glorious *Deeds* Heaven sent you here to Act,
To Scourge the *Insolent*, and *Good* Protect;
While with a *strong*, and yet a *gentle* hand,
You *Bridle* Nations, and our *Hearts* Command:
Secure us from *Our selves*, and from the *Foe*,
Make us *Unite*, and make us *Conquer* too
Those *Fiercer Factions* which Mens *Souls* did move,
Are by your *Favour* Reconcil'd in Love:
And now our only *Strife* is to Outvye
Each other in the Fruits of *Loyalty*. /
When *Fate* or *Error* had our Age misled,
And o're these Kingdomes black *Confusion* spred,
The only *Cure* which could from Heaven come,
Was so much *pow'r* and *Clemency* in *One*;
The *Genius* of our Nation, with disdain
Beheld those *Puppets* which Usurp'd your Raign;
But long'd, (with their *Strange Madneßes* opprest,)
Upon your *Bosome* its sick *Head* to rest:[3]
So when a *Lyon* shakes his Dreadful Mayn
And angry grows, let *Him* that first took pain
To tame his youth, Approach, the Haughty Beast
Will *bend* to him, but *fright* away the rest.[4]

By *sweet*, yet *secret Politicks* you Raign,
Which *Forraign Statesmen* Pry into in vain;

The Nations Ancient *Honour* you encrease,
And Heal, as well with *Needful Wars*, as *Peace*:[5][6]
Heav'n, that hath plac'd this *Island*, to give Law,
To Ballance *Europe*, and her *States* to Aw;
In this Conjuncture doth on *Brittain* smile,
The *Greatest Soveraign*, and the *Greatest Isle*:
Some think *this Portion* of the VVorld, was Rent
By the rude Ocean, from the *Continent*;[7][8]
But whilst your *Forces* with the *French* Combine,
You make the *Lands* more *Terribly* to *Joyne*.[9]

Fame swifter than your winged *Navy* flies
Through ev'ry Land that near the *Ocean* lies,
Sounding your *Name*, and telling dreadful News
To all that *Pyracy* and *Rapine* use; /
Algiers with trembling Knees for *Peace* does begg,
Undone by 'th Valour of your Noble *Spragg*:[10]
And *greater Pyrates* too, much nearer home,
VVho thought to *graspe* a pow'r great as old *Rome*;
Striving to carry all *Commerce* away,
And make, the *Universe* their *only* Prey:[11]
Are now forc'd to *Disgorge*, and sadly find
Nature has *You, Lord of the Seas* design'd.
VVith such a *Chief*, the meanest Nation, blest,
Might hope to lift her *Head* above the rest:
VVhat may be thought *Impossible* to do
For us, embraced by the *Sea* and *You*:
Lords of the worlds *great wast*, the *Ocean*, we
VVhole *Forrests* send to range upon the Sea:
And ev'ry Coast may *trouble* or *Relieve*,
But none can *visit* us without *your* leave.
Angels and we have this Prerogative,
That none can at our happy Seat Arrive:
Whilst we *discend* at Pleasure to Invade
The *bad* with vengeance, and our *friends* to aid:
Our *little VVorld*, the Image of the great,
Like that amidst the *boundless Ocean* set,
Of her own *growth* hath all that *Nature* craves,
And all that's *rare*, as *Tribute* from the *VVaves*:
As *Ægypt* does not on the *Clouds* rely,
But to her *Nile* owes more than to the *sky*:
So what our *Earth*, and what our *Heav'n* denies,
Our ever constant Friend *the Sea* supplies:
That *friend* whom whilst base *Neighbours* seek to gain, /
Your *Thunder* with their *blood Purples* the Main:
The Tast of *hot Arabian Spice* we know
Free from the *scorching Sun* that makes it grow:
Without the *VVorm*, in *Persian Silks* we shine,

And without *Planting*, drink of ev'ry *Vine*:
To Digg for *VVealth*, we *weary* not our Limbs,
Gold, though the *heaviest* Mettal, hither *Swims*:
Ours is the *Harvest* where the *Indians Mow*,
We *Plow* the Deep, and *Reap* what others *Sow*:
Things of the *Noblest kind* our own Soil breeds,
Stout are our *Men*, and Warlike are our *Steeds*:
Rome, though her Eagle through the world had flown,
Could never make this *Island all* her own:
Here the *Third Edward*, and the *black Prince* too,
Victorious *Henry* flourisht,[12] and now *You*:
For whom, *Proud Dutch*, (reserv'd, like the *Greek* State,
Till *Alexander*[13] came to urge their Fate)
Must make *New Trophies*, which the Couq'ring hands
Of *Mighty York*, or (who in's sted Commands)
The *Matchless Rupert* from the Sea do bring,
To Adorn the *Triumphs* of our Glorious King:
Whilst most *Heroick Montmouth*, to add more,
Transplants the *Laurels* of the *Belgian* Shore.[14]

Yet need your *Foes* not *Dread* (if they'l *Submit*)
Your *Power*, you with such *Sweetness* Temper it:[15]
Prefer'd by *Conquest*, happily o'rethrown,
Falling they'l *Rise*, to be with us made one.[16]
That *Aiery Liberty*, whereof they Boast[17]
Is but a *Spacious Shadow* at the most: /
For they'l find on a *just Account* of things
No *Freedom*, like the *Rule* of Pious *Kings*:[18] [19]
So kind *Dictators* made, when they came Home,
Their *Vanquisht Foes*, Free Citizens of *Rome*,[20]
Less Pleasure take, *brave souls*, in Battails won,
Than in *restoring* those that are *Undone*:
Tygers have *Courage*, and the *rugged* B*are*,
But Man *alone* can, whom he Conquers *spare*;
To *Pardon* willing, and to *Punish* loth,
You strike with *one* Hand, but you Heal with *both*;
Lifting up all that Prostrate lye, you grieve
You cannot make the *Dead* again to Live:
Whilst your Arms make *your Stubborn* Foes to fall,
Your *Gracious Favours* needs must Conquer all.

What you have done *already* is well known,
And we with *humblest Gratitude* must own;
When in your *Royal Robes*, you lately went
To meet your *Kind and Dutious Parliament*,
(That *healing Senate*, which all Storms can Calme,
And cure the Nation with its *Acts* of Balme:)
Blessings and Pray'rs were sent to Heav'n aloud,

By *ev'ry* Member of the Gazeing Croud:
No sooner that *Illustrious body* saw
Their *Dearest Soveraign*, but a *Loveing Awe*
Shines in each Face, and with a *greedy Ear*
Receives those *Oracles* he utter'd there:
Their *Grateful Duties* streight the *Cause* Espouse,
As Highly Just to make our *Lyon* Rouse:
They Thank His *Royal Cares* so much has done,
And *Vote supplies* for what there is to come.[21] /
Ah! *bleßed fruits*! such happy *Union* brings,
The Loyalst Subjects with the best of Kings:
Subjects that to maintain this *needful* Warr,
Freely will *part* with what *he* fain would spare:
Their *publique Purse* they offer – *Let all go*,
Rather then *Truckle* to'th encroaching *Foe*:
When our *Kings Honour*, and our *Countries good*
Is touch'd, we value neither *Coyn* nor *Blood*:
Cursed be he, those *Sacred bonds* that parts,
"*Kings greatest Treasures, are their Subjects*[a] *Hearts:*"[22]
And there your *Majesty* hath such a share,
No *Earthly Monarch* may with you Compare.
But our *Weak Muse* begs Pardon, that she dare
I'th Face of *Dazling Majesty* appear:
She only ment, her *own full Joys* to sing,[23]
Succeeding *Times*, shall *Bays* and *Olive* bring
To Crown your *head*, whilst you in Triumph Ride
O're Vanquisht *Nations*, and the *Sea* beside:
Whilst all the *Neighbouring States* shall unto *You*,
Like *Josephs* Sheaves, pay Reverence, and *Bowe*.[24]

ITER BOREALE.
FINIS. /

Textual variants

159a   Subjects] Subjests *BL W2144B*

BENJAMIN KEACH, *AN ELEGY ON THAT MOST LABORIOUS AND PAINFUL MINISTER OF THE GOSPEL MR JOHN NORCOT* (1676)

Date

First published 1676. John Norcot died on 24 March 1676, and Keach preached his funeral sermon on 28 March.[1] This funeral sermon, *A Summons to the Grave* (1676), which contains a variant of *An Elegy*, was advertised in the catalogue for Trinity Term 1676 (licensed 12 June).[2]

Copy Text

K61 Benjamin Keach, *An elegy on that most laborious and painful minister of the gospel Mr John Norcot, who fell asleep in the Lord the 24th of this instant March 1675/6* (London: Ben. Harris, 1676). Broadside.

Variant.

The variant collated is: K95 Benjamin Keach, *A summons to the grave. Or, The necessity of a timely preparation for death* (London: Ben. Harris, 1676).

Context

John Norcot (d. 1676) was, it seems, that rare thing: a Baptist who had acted as a minister within the national Church during the Interregnum. He was probably minister at Stansted Thele, Hertfordshire (generally known as St Margaret's) from 1657. He thus became one of the small number of Baptists ejected in 1662. During the Restoration he was pastor from 1670 to 1676 to the Particular Baptist congregation that met in Old Gravel-Lane, Wapping, and he published *Baptism Discovered* in 1672, which was republished twice more in the seventeenth century. He wrote an epistle to the reader for Josias Bonham's *The Churches Glory* (1674), as did Benjamin Keach, and upon his death in March 1674 Keach preached his funeral sermon. Other biographical information about Norcot is sparse, and Keach's sermon, in keeping with many other godly sermons, contained little detailed material concerning the deceased.[3] Indeed, in the printed version of the sermon Keach warned that 'we may love Ministers too much, nay, idolize them, esteem them above what is meet, as many in former times have done'.[4]

Keach's elegy was printed both separately as a broadside, and alongside other poems at the beginning of his printed funeral sermon.[5]

Sources

Keach borrows at one point from Francis Quarles's *Emblemes*, first published in 1635.[6] He had previously borrowed heavily from this work in his *War with the Devil*.[7]

Notes

1. B. Keach, *A Summons to the Grave* (London: Ben. Harris, 1676), titlepage, p. 1.
2. E. Arber (ed.), *The Term Catalogues, 1668–1709*, 3 vols (London: Edward Arber, 1903–6), vol. 1, p. 244.
3. G. F. Nuttall, 'Another Baptist Ejection (1662): The Case of John Norcott', in in W. Brackney and P. S. Fiddes (eds), *Pilgrim Pathways: Essays in Baptist History in Honour of B. R. White* (Macon (GA): Mercer University Press, 1999), pp. 185–8; J. Norcott, *Baptism Discovered* (London: s.n., 1672); J. Bonham, *The Churches Glory* (London: the author, 1674), sigs a1r–a7v; Keach, *A Summons*
4. Keach, *A Summons*, sig. A3r.
5. Keach, *A Summons*, sigs b4r–c4v.
6. See Keach, *An Elegy*, below p. 165.
7. For further discussion of Quarles see the Headnote to *War with the Devil*, above p. 3 and the Introduction, above p. xxxi.

AN ELEGY
On the Death of that most Laborious and Painful
Minister of the Gospel
Mr. JOHN NORCOT,
Who fell asleep in the Lord the 24th of this instant
March 1675/6

How doth my troubled Soul amused stand,
On thoughts of God's most sore Chastising hand;
Let Heaven assist my Pen, and help indite
This Mournful Elegy I'm mov'd to write.
My grieved heart knows not what way to take,
Its love to shew and lamentation make.
David for *Jonathan* was sore distrest,[1]
And in like sort has sorrow seiz'd my Brest.
Beloved *John* is gone, dear *Norcot*'s dead;[2]
That *Man of God*, who hath so often fed
Our precious Souls with Manna from above:
Whose powerful preaching did ingage our love
To *Jesus Christ*. O! he had care and skill
To feed poor souls and do his Master's will.
But is he from us also took away,
What, breach still upon breach! Lord *Jesus* stay
Thy hand, such strokes are hardly born,
Here's cause for hundreds to lament and mourn.
The loss is great the Churches do sustain,
Poor sinners too like cause have to complain.
There's few like him surviving to arouse
Their sluggish souls out of their sinful drouse.
They now may sleep secure and not awake.
Until they fall into the *Stygian Lake*.[3]
This Golden Trumpet's stopt, 'twill sound no more,
To warn them of what danger's at their door.
To win sinners to Christ he did not spare
His strength nor time, thought nothing was too dear
To part with all, if any ways he might,

Their Souls turn from false ways unto the right:
Like as a Candle which much light doth give,
Doth waste it self, whilst from it we receive
Much benefit; so did he clearly burn,
To the wasting of himself unto the urn.[4]
This godly Preacher in a little space,
Much work did do, he swiftly run his race;
With's might perform'd what e'r he found to do.
God graciously did bless his work also,
Yea few (I think) have had the like success,
In turning sinners unto righteousness.
O were the worth of this good man but known,
It might produce an universal groan.[5]
Let Brethren dear of different minds lament,
For he for you in prayers much time has spent;
He lov'd you all, though I have cause to fear,
The like affection some did scarcely bear.
'Twould pierce ones heart to think in such a time,
Obedience unto Christ should be a crime;
Or that offence should in the least be took,
'Cause from Gods word he durst not turn nor look.[6]
He would own naught but what *thus saith the Lord*,
Add would not he nor minish from Gods Word.
Come let us live in love, we shall agree,
When at his Port we all arived be,
Let sinners mourn, who shall their loss repair,
Who for their Souls so naturally did care.
Well may ye fear God will proclaim new wars,
When he calls home his choice Embassadors.
What may a *Sodome*[7] look for from above,[8]
When such who stood 'ith gap, God doth remove.
O tremble City, what is God about,
Look for new flames,[9] thy *Lots*[10] are calling out.
And now chastized flock a word or two,
I've double sorrow when I think of you.
When that the Harvest doth for Reapers call.
To lose your Labourer, this wound's not small.[11]
O who shall bear the burthen of the day,
If God doth take the Labourers thus away.
When Pylots die, how shall the Seaman[a] stear,
'Mong'st Rocks and Sands, when stormes also appear.
Have we not cause to think the crafty Fox,
Will out abroad and prey[b] upon the flocks.
And Ravening Wolves[12] also will grow more bold.
And scare some silly Lambs out of the fold;[13]
If God proceed to call the Shepherds home,
O what will of so many flocks become.[14]
'Ith' midst of all, in this doth comfort lie,
The chiefest Shepherd[15] [c] lives when others die.

And he be sure who for the Sheep did bleed,
Will stick to them in times of greatest need.
Come cease your grief, don't you know very well,
The care God has of[a] his own *Israell*.
And its no more which now is come to pass,
Then what by you some time expected was,
And what is done is but our Fathers will.
Therefore be silent, every one be still:
For should we yield to passion I have fears,
We should grieve Christ and wound our Souls with tears.
The narrow Sluces too of dribling eyes,
Would be too streight for those great Springs that rise.
But since our Vessels fills up to the top,
Lets empty them, for every sin a drop.
For it lets wish we were compos'd of Snow,
Instead of Flesh, yea made of Ice, that so
We might in sense of sin and it[b] loathing,
Melt with hot love to Christ, yea thaw to nothing.[16]
And should our sins deprive our Souls of him,
Let tears run from our Eyes till Couches swim.
Yet let's not grudge him that most happy bliss,
Who now in glory with Christ Jesus is.
He did his work apace, his Race is run,
He'as touch'd the Gole yea and the prise hath won.[17]

AN EPITAPH.

A *Sweet and godly Preacher doth lie here,*
Who did his Master Jesus love so dear,
And sinners Souls, that he his strength did spend.
And did thereby ('tis thought) hasten his end,
He brought himself by preaching to the Grave,
The precious souls of sinners for to save.
He lies but here asleep, he is not dead:
To God he lives, to Christ his soul is fled,
And o're[c] while must he awake again,
And evermore with Christ in glory raign.[18] By *B. K.*

London, Printed for *Ben. Harris* at the *Stationers Arms* in
Sweetings Rents near the *Royal Exchange*, 1676. / /

Textual variants

164a   Seaman] Seamen *K95*
164b   prey] play *K95*
164c   Shepherd] Shepherds *K95*
165a   of] on *K95*
165b   it] its *K95*
165c   o're] o're a *K95*

ROBERT WILD, *A EXCLAMATION AGAINST POPERY* (1678) AND *OLIVER CROMWELLS GHOST* (1679) AND *DR. WILD'S POEM. IN NOVA FERT ANIMUS* (1679)

Date

A Exclamation against Popery was first published in 1678. Its extended title refers to a speech given by Charles II to parliament on 9 November, and it was licensed on 14 November.

Oliver Cromwells Ghost is catalogued as having been first published in 1679, although *ODNB* tentatively gives a date of 1678.[1]

Dr. Wild's Poem. In Nova Fert Animus was first published in 1679. The first Exclusion Parliament, to which the poem refers, met on 6 March 1679.

Copy Text

A Exclamation against Popery: W2126A Robert Wild, *A exclamation against popery: or, a broad-side against Rome. Occasioned by His Majestie's last gracious speech, when he was further pleas'd to express his zeal to maintain the truly antient Protestant religion. By R. W. D. D. Licensed, November the 14th. 1678* (London: T. G., 1678). Broadside.

Oliver Cromwells Ghost: W2143 Robert Wild, *Oliver Cromwells ghost: or Old Noll newly revived* (London, 1679). 2o.

Dr. Wild's Poem. In Nova Fert Animus: ESTC R226751 Robert Wild, *Dr. Wild's poem. In nova fert animus, &c. Or, A new song to an old friend from an old poet, upon the hopeful new Parliament* ([London?], [1679?]). Broadside.

Variants

A Exclamation against Popery: the variant collated is: W92 Robert Wild, *An exclamation against popery: or, a broad-side against Rome. Occasioned by His Majestie's last gracious speech, when he was further pleas'd to express his willingness to maintain the truly antient Protestant religion* (London: T.G., 1678).

Oliver Cromwells Ghost: none have been catalogued.

Dr.Wild's Poem. In Nova Fert Animus: the variant collated is: W2145 Robert Wild, *Dr. Wild's poem. In nova fert animus, &c. Or, a new song to an old friend from an old poet, upon the hopeful new Parliament* ([London?], [1679]).

Authorship

All three poems were attributed to Robert Wild. They echo his concerns at a number of points, and as he did not die until July 1679 he could have written them. Richard Greaves, in his *ODNB* article, attributes them to Wild.[2]

Context

In 1678 the pernicious liar Titus Oates (1649–1705) wove a fantastical tale of bloody conspiracy. Oates, who had joined the Roman Catholic Church in March 1677, claimed that in his dealings with other Catholics he had obtained intimate knowledge of a nefarious plot which had English, Scottish, Irish and wider European dimensions. Catholics, particularly Jesuits, were, he said, poised to kill the King. His lies gained credibility in part because the magistrate in front of whom he had given his depositions in September 1678, Sir Edmund Berry Godfrey (1621–78), was murdered in October. Godfrey's death was widely blamed on Catholics. But Oates's tales were not simply believable because of this event. His account of a 'Popish Plot' fed into a strong strain of anti-popery that had developed in England since the Reformation, and it precipitated crisis. Anxieties over the security of Protestantism in the present, alongside concerns that Charles II (1630–85) sought to rule in an arbitrary, 'popish' way, coalesced with fears about the future. James, Duke of York (1633–1701), was a professed Catholic, and because Charles II had no legitimate heirs he was next in line to the throne. Charles II initially sought to quell the fears through his existing parliament. In a speech of 9 November 1678 (the occasion of *A Exclamation Against Popery*) he sought to reassure members that he was 'ready to joyn with ... [them] in all the ways and means that may Establish a firm Security of the Protestant Religion', and to agree to 'reasonable Bills' concerning future reigns.[3] However, tension was ratcheted up in December when Ralph Montagu, former ambassador to France, told the House of Commons how Thomas Osborne, Earl of Danby had previously negotiated for monies from the French in return for the prorogation of parliament, thus demonstrating further how Charles's chief minister had fed the King's popish and arbitrary tendencies. As the crisis escalated, Charles came to be convinced that it was a political necessity to call a new parliament, and the Cavalier parliament, called in 1661, was finally dissolved, and a new parliament (the subject of *Dr. Wild's Poem. In Nova Fert Animus*) met on 6 March 1679. This was the first of the Exclusion parliaments. Over the next two years many in parliament, who came to be called Whigs, sought to exclude the James from the succession. They were resisted in these attempts by others who came to be called Tories.[4]

During this period of crisis political battles were fought not just in court and parliament but out-of-doors. The participation of the broader public in political struggles was nothing new, but, as during the period immediately preceding the outbreak of the civil war, popular politics took on a heightened significance at this time. Also, again as during the years 1640–2, printed polemic was of central importance in driving, and reacting to, politicization. The comparisons were not lost on contemporaries, many of whom thought that they stood on the brink of another civil war.[5] These three poems are all early examples of the kind of political verses that circulated, and one of the poems demonstrates extensively and explicitly how memories of the civil war and Interregnum continued to shape late seventeenth-century political discourse. *Oliver Cromwells Ghost* recalls the dead Lord Protector from hell to survey the nefarious plots of Rome.

Notes
1. *ODNB.*
2. Ibid.
3. *His Majesties most Gracious Speech to both Houses of Parliament, on Saturday 9th of November, 1678* (London: printed by John Bill, Christopher Barker, Thomas Newcomb, and Henry Hills, 1678), p. 4.
4. This paragraph is based on: G. Southcombe and G. Tapsell, *Restoration Politics, Religion and Culture: Britain and Ireland, 1660–1714* (Basingstoke: Palgrave Macmillan, 2010), ch. 3; J. Kenyon, *The Popish Plot* (London: Heinemann, 1972); J. Scott, 'England's Troubles: Exhuming the Popish Plot', in T. Harris, P. Seaward and M. Goldie, *The Politics of Religion in Restoration England* (Oxford: Basil Blackwell, 1990), pp. 107–31; *ODNB*; J. Spurr, *England in the 1670s: 'This Masquerading Age'* (Oxford: Blackwell, 2000), chs 9–10; M. Knights, *Politics and Opinion in Crisis, 1678–81* (Cambridge: Cambridge University Press, 1994); *ODNB*.
5. Southcombe and Tapsell, *Restoration Politics, Religion and Culture*, chs 1, 3, 7.

A
EXCLAMATION
AGAINST
POPERY:
OR
A Broad-Side against ROME.

Occasioned by his *MAJESTIE'S* Last Gracious Speech, when he was
further pleas'd to Express His Zeal[a]
to Maintain the Truly Ancient Protestant Religion.[1]

By R.W. D.D.

LICENSED, November the 14*th*. 1678.

Plot on, Proud *Rome*! and lay thy damn'd Design
As low as Hell, we ll find a Countermine:
Wrack thy curst Parts! and when thy utmost Skill
Has prov'd unable to effect thy Will;
Call thy Black Emissaries, let 'em go
To summon Traytors from the Shades below,
Where Infant *Treason* dates its Monstrous Birth;
Is nurst with Care, and after sent on Earth:
To some curst *Monks*, or wand'ring *Jesuites*[2] Cell;
Where it thrives faster, than it did in Hell!
Call Bloody *Brutus* up, Lean *Cassius* too;[3]
Let *Faux*, and *Catesby* both, be of the Crew! –[4]
Nay, rather than want Help, let your *BULLS* run;[5]
And Damn the *Devil*, if he do not come!
Yet after all your Plots, and Hatchings, we,
(So long as *CHARLES*, and's *Senators*[6] agree)
Will warm our Hands at Bone-fires, Bells shall Ring;[7]
And Traytor's Knells no longer Toll, but Sing.

We doubt not *Rome*, but Maugre all thy Skill,
The Glorious *GOD* of our Religion will,   }
In spite of all thy Art, preserve It still!

And his peculiar Care of It to shew,
Defend in Health, Its Great *DEFENDER* too!

I'th' *Interim*, Do thou new Crimes invent,
And well contrive as Subtle Punishment.
'Tis *Autumn* now with us; and every Tree,
Instead of Fruit, may bend with *Popery*.
'Twould be a Novel, tho no hated Sight,
If every Bough should bear a *Jesuite*!

We'll meet your Plots with Pikes, Daggers with Swords;
And stead of long Cravats, we'll lend you Cords.
Each Stab in Private, we ll with Use return:
And whilst one Hangs, the other he shall Burn;
Till *Tybourn's*[8] long impoverish't *Squire* appear
Gay as the *Idol,* fills the *Porph'ry* Chair.[9]

Yes, Mighty *CHARLES!* at thy Command we'll run
Through Seas of Rebels Blood, to save thy Crown.
Our Wives, Estates, and Children too, shall be
But Whet-stones to our Swords, when drawn for Thee.
We'll Hack and Slash, and Shoot, till *Rome* Condoles;
And Hell it self, is cloy'd with Traytors Souls:
'Till *Godfrey's*[10] wronged Ghost (which still does call
For Shoals of Rebels to attend his Fall)
Cryes out, *Dear* Protestants, *no more pursue*
Their Guilty Blood, my Manes[11] *have their*ª *Due!*

This, Mighty *Monarch*! at thy Beck or Nod,
Shall be effected, as Thou wer't a God;
With so much Readiness, thy Royal Tongue
Shall hardly Speak, e're we Revenge the Wrong
On thy curst Enemies; who whilst they state
Thy Death, shall feel themselves th' intended Fate;
And by a quick Reverse, be forc't to try
The Dire Effects of their own Treachery.

Poor Scarlet *Harlot,*[12] could'st Thou stand in want
Of a Genteel, and Generous Gallant,
Whose Noble Soul to Baseness could not yield;
But wou'd have try'd thy Int'rest in the Field,
We had not thus thy Policies condemn'd;
But thought thee worthy of a Foe, or Friend:
Both which, with equal Estimate thou'lt find,
VVere alwayes valu'd by an *English* Mind.
But Thou of late, so Treacherous do'st grow,
That we should blush, to own thee either now.
Base, and Perfidious too, thou do'st appear;
Sland'rest a *Pope*, and spoyl'st an *Emperor*.

What! is the *Eagle* from the *Mitre* flown?
Is there of *Cæsar* nothing left in *Rome*?
Must that Renowned City, here-to-fore
Fam'd for her Vertues, well as for her Pow'r;
Instead of *Consuls*, Vagabonds imploy?[13]
And suborn *Felons MONARCHS* to Destroy?
Bribe Men (thro VVant made boldly desperate)
To Fire-ball Cities, to their Grov'ling Fate;
Whil'st Hellish *Jesu'ts* Porters Garbs profane;
Assist the Fire, and Bless the growing Flame![14]

Must *Romes* Great *Pope*, whose Piety should run
As an Example, thro all Christendome;
Whose Signal Vertues, Arguments should be
Of his Admir'd Infallability?
Does he hire Ruffains, *Justices* to Kill;
And send the Murd'rers Pardons at his VVill?
Bids them in Hereticks Blood their Hands embrue;
Tells them withal, 'Tis *Meritorious* too! –

If this thy Practice be, false *Rome* Fare wel! –
Go, Teach thy Doctrine to the Damn'd in Hell!
Where, by Black *Lucifer*'s Destructive Pride,
Thou may'st in part thy Future Fate decide:
Whil'st from our City we thy *Imps* remove,
To shake their Heels in some cold Field or Grove.
Since both by Ours, and all Mens just Esteem,
They're fitter to Converse with Beasts, than Men.

FINIS.

LONDON, Printed for *T.G.* 1678.

Textual variants

171a   Zeal] Willingness W92
172a   have their] have had their W92

Oliver Cromwells[1]
GHOST:
OR
OLD NOLL
Newly Revived

Rows'd from Infernal Caverns void of Light,
Where Traytors Souls keep an Eternal Night:
Through the *Earths* friendly Pores at last I come
To view the Fate of mangled *Christendome*.
Treason, and *Blood*, *Ruin*, and U*surpation*,
Deceipt, *Hypocrisie*, and *Devastation*;
Envy, *Ambition*, and *untam'd desire*,
Still to gain more, still to be mounted higher:
Wars, *Janglings*, *Murders*, and a Thousand more
Vices like these, you know were heretofore.
The only grateful Bantlings,[2] which could find,
A kind Reception in my gloomy Mind----
--- But now alas I'm chang'd--- the Pondrous guilt
Of *Treason*, and the *Sacred Blood* I spilt;[3]
Those crouds of *Loyal Subjects* I made groan,
Under pretence of strickt *Religion*,[4]
When I my self, to speak the Truth, had none:
Too weighty for my strugling Soul did grow,
And prest it downwards to the Shades below,
Where it these Twenty Years[5] has Silent lain,
Tormented with Variety of Pain,
Too great for fleshly Mortals to sustain.
   Nor had it budg'd as yet---but that the Fame
Of *Plots*, *Conspiracies*, and *Murders* came
To the Infernal Gates so fast, that I,
For others Good, forgot my Misery:
And whilst the busie *Dæmons* were imploy'd
In culling out a Bloody Regicide,[6]
I bilkt my Keeper, and with wondrous Pain,
Once more I mount my Native Soyl again;

Where to my Grief, more Villanies I view,
Than Heav'd e're Pardon'd, or than Hell e're knew.
Since *Lucifer's* like *Rome's* Destructive Pride,
Both Damn'd himself, and all his Imps beside:
Though old in Artful Wickedness I be,
Yet *Rome*, I now Resign the Wall to thee:
Thou in this single Plot, hast now done more,
Than Mankind, helpt by Hell, could do before.[7]

    What! was thy swell'd Ambition grown so wide,
    That nought but *Kings* could satisfie thy Pride?
Must *Monarchs*, whom the Heav'n it self do's prize,
Now become Morsels for thy gaping Vice.
Methought, though hot with Gluttony thou burn,
A Pious Justice might have serv'd thy turn;
Especially when, (to content you more)
Spitted on's Sword, and Pickled in his Gore;[8]
But now your aim we better understand,
He was the Whet---you gap'd for all the Land.
Strange Cormorant![9] That in her Monstrous Breast,
Could at one Meal three Butcher'd Lands[10] digest.

    Ye *Powers*! I thought my Countries Innocence,
(When in fierce *Whilwinds* you had born me hence)[11]
And by the Pow'r of your most just Command,
Restor'd the Scepter to the Owners hand)[12]
Would have sufficient bin to Wall you free
From the Assaults of such an Enemie.
I little thought, when last I took my leave,
And sadly entred my unwelcome Grave,
That e're the Porphry Idol[13] could command
So great a Friendship in our Native Land;
As by that means to hope to circumvent,
With black Design, both King and Government.

    But yet take heed ye Romish Idiots,
That have a hand in these most Hellish Plots;
Who by your base contrivance, hope to bring
Ruin to Nations, Death unto a King.
Beware, I say, by my Example, do,
For there's a God above do's all things view:
Tho wrapt in Colds[14] amongst the Skies, he dwells,
Yet he discerns you in your closest Cells;
See's your Contrivances, and whilst you poor
Conceipted Traytors think your selves secure,
He your clandestine Plots does plainly view,
And will divulge them, and their Actors too.
Trust my Experience, one, who if you will
Believe, what all the World says of him still,
Had no small share of Pride, Ambition, Wit,
Courage and Conduct too to manage it.

By which I wrought my Curst designs so high,
I could have match'd my *Brewers Family*[15]
With the best Blood in *Brittain*. Right or wrong,
Or Life or Death, attended on my Tongue:
All the three Kingdoms truckled to my Will--
But what of this?---I was a Traytor still.
Nay, so intemperate was my folly grown,
I boldly offer'd at the Sacred Crown;
Which though I mist,---yet by a holy Cheat,
At last I gain'd to fill the tott'ring Seat;[16]
And made Ten thousand Souldiers Arm'd, appear
With Roaring Guns, to plead my Title there.
Not doubting but that happy Seat should be
Transfer'd from me to my Posteritie.[17]
   But all was insignificant, when Death
Unkindly Robb'd me of Beloved Breath:
My Titles all forsook me, and my Race,
Instead of them, inherit my disgrace.

   This is the Fate of Traytors here; but know,
That could you think what they endure below,
I'm sure you would be Loyal; but the Pope
By prating Jesuits, has so rais'd your hope,
That I in vain those Tortures now should tell,
You'l know them when I meet you there---
                              Farewel.[18]

                    R. W. D. D.

Dr. Wild's Poem.
IN NOVA FERT ANIMUS, &c.[1]
OR, A
NEW SONG
TO AN
OLD FRIEND from an OLD POET,
Upon the Hopeful
New Parliament.[2]

WE are All tainted with the *Athenian*-Itch,[3]
News, and new Things do the whole World bewitch.[4]
Who would be Old, or in Old fashions Trade?
Even an Old Whore would fain go for a Maid:
The Modest of both Sexes, buy new Graces,
Of Perriwigs for Pates, and Paint for Faces.
Some wear new Teeth in an old Mouth; and some
Carve a new Nose out of an aged Bum.[5]
Old *Hesiod's*[6] gods Immortal Youth enjoy:
Cupid,[7] though Blind, yet still goes for a Boy;
Under one Hood Hypocrite *Janus* too,
Carries two faces, one Old, th'other New.[8]
Apollo[9] wears no Beard, but still looks young;
Diana,[10] *Pallas,*[11] *Venus,*[12] all the throng
Of Muses Graces, Nymphs, look Brisk and Gay,
Priding themselves in a perpetual *May.*[13]
Whiles doting *Saturn,*[14] *Pluto,*[15] *Proserpin,*[16]
At their own ugly Wrinkles Rage and Grin;
The very Furies in their looks do twine;
Snakes, whose embroydered skyns nenew[a] their shine;[17]
And nothing makes Great *Juno*[18] chase and scold,
But *Joves*[19] new Misses slighting her as Old.
Poets, who others can Immortal make,
When they grow Gray, their Lawrels[20] them forsake;
And seek young Temples, where they may grow Green;
No Palsie-hands may wash in *Hypocrene*;[21]

'Twas not Terse Clarret, Eggs, and Muskadine,
Nor Goblets Crown'd with *Greek* or *Spanish* Wine,
Could make new Flames in Old *Ben Johnsons* Veins,
But his Attempts prov'd lank and languid strains:
His *New Inn* (so he nam'd his youngest Play)
Prov'd a blind Ale-house, cry'd down the first Day:[22]
His own dull Epitaph – *Here lies Ben Johnson*,
(Half drunken too) He Hickcupt – *who was once one*.[23]
Ah! this sad *once one! once* we *Trojans* were;
Oh, better never, if not still we are.[24]
Rhymes, of Old Men, *Iliack* passions[25] be,
When that should downward go, comes up we see,
And are like *Jews*-Ears[26] in an Elder-Tree;
When Spectacles do once bestride the Nose,
The Poet's Gallop turns to stumbling-Prose.
Sir, I am Old, Cold, Mould; and you might hope
To see an *Alderman* dance on a Rope,
A *Judg* to act a Gallant in a Play,
Or an Old *Pluralist* Preach twice a day;
Of a Thin *Taylor* make a Valiant Knight,
Or a *good Subject* of a *Jesuite*;
As an old Bald-pate (such as mine you know)
Should make his Hair, or Wit and Fancy grow
Nor is there need that such a Block as I
Should now be hew'd into a *Mercury*.[27]
When Winter's gone, the Owl his foot may spare,
And to the *Nightingales* resign the Air.
Such is the beautiful new face of things:
By Heavens kind Influences, and the Kings,
Joy should inspire; and all in measures move,
And every Citizen a *Virgil*[28] prove.
Each *Protestant* turn Poet; and who not
Should be suspected guilty of the *Plot*;[29]
If, now the day doth dawn, our Cocks forbear
To clap their Wings and Crow, you well may swear,
It is their want of Loyalty, not Wit,
That makes them sullen, and so silent sit.
Galli of *Gallick* kind[30] – I'le say no more,
But that their Combs are Cut, and they are sore;
Yet to provoke them, my old Cock shall Crow,
That so his Eccho round the Town may go.

Upon the New PARLIAMENT.

My Landlord[31] underprop't his House some years,
Was often warn'd – 'Twould fall about his Ears;
For the main Timber, That above, and under,
By every Blast was apt to rend asunder.
This year He gently took all down, and then
What of the Old prov'd sound, did serve agen.

May all the New be Heart of *English* Oak,[32]
And the whole House stand firm from fatal strok,
And nothing in't, the Founder e're provoke.
My *Grandam*, when her Bees were old and done,
Burnt the old Stock, and a new Hive begun;
And in one year she found a greater store
Of *Wax* and *Honey* then in all before.
Variety and Novelty delights;
Old Shooes and Mouldy Bread are *Gibeonites*.[33]
When Cloaths grow thread-bare, and breeds Vermin too,
To *Long Lane*[34] with them, and put on some new:
When VVine turns Vinegar – All Art is vain,
The VVorld can never make it Wine again.
'Tis time to wean that Child, who bites the Breast;
And Chase those fowls that do befowl their Nest.
When *Nolls* Nose found the Rump began to smell;
He dock't it, and the Nation lik't it well.[35]
Cast the old-mark't and greazy Cards away,
And give's a new Pack, else we will not play;
Nothing but Pork, and Pork, and Pork, to eat!
Good Lanlord give's fresh COMMONS[36] [a] for our Meat.
Trent Council Thirty years lay sows'd in pickle,
Until it prov'd a stinking Conventicle.[37]
And now Old *Rome* plays over her old Tricks,
This *Seventy-nine*, shall pay for *Sixty-six*:[38]
Out of the Fire, like new refined Gold,
How bright new *London* looks above the Old,[39]
All Creatures under Old Corruptions groan,
And for a New Creation make their moan:
The *Phœnix* (of her self grown weary) dyes
Unto succession a burnt-sacrifice.
Old Eagles breed bad Hawks, and they worse Kites,
And they blind Buzzards (as Old *Pliny* Writes),[40]
Deans, Prebends, Chaplains think themselves have wrong,
When *Bishops* live unmercifully long;
And poor *Dissenters* beg they may ascend
Into a Pulpit from the Tables end.[41]
And who hath not by good experience found
Best Crops are gained by new-broken ground,
And the first seed – OATS[42] sifted clean and sound?
      But yet Old Friends, Old Gold, Old King, I praise:[b]
Old *Tyburn*[43] take them who do otherwise:
Heaven Chase the Vultur from our Eagles Nest,
And let no Ravens this *March*-Brood molest?
      So Sings poor Robin[44] *Redbrest.*

FINIS.

Textual variants

179a   renew] nenew *STC R226751*; renew *W2145*
181a   COMMONS] COMMANS *STC R226751*; COMMONS *W2145*
181b   praise] prise *W2145*

BENJAMIN KEACH, *THE GLORIOUS LOVER* (1679)

Date

Entered in the *Stationers' Register* on 20 December 1678 under the title 'The Phoenix of the World, or the Glorious Lover, a divine poem upon the adorable mystery of sinners redemption'.[1] Advertised in the catalogue for Easter Term 1679 (May).[2]

Copy Text

K64 Benjamin Keach, *The glorious lover. A divine poem, upon the adorable mystery of sinners redemption. By B.K. author of War with the Devil* (London: by J. D. for Christopher Hussey, 1679). Octavo.[3]

Variants

The variants collated are: K64A Benjamin Keach, *The glorious lover. A divine poem, upon the adorable mystery of sinners redemption ... The second edition with additions ...* (London: F.L. for Christopher Hussey, 1685); K64B Benjamin Keach, *The glorious lover. A divine poem, upon the adorable mystery of sinners redemption ... The third edition with additions ...* (London: F. L. for Christopher Hussey, 1685); K65 Benjamin Keach, *The glorious lover. A divine poem upon the adorable mystery of sinners redemption ... The fourth edition with additions ...* (London: Christopher Hussey, 1696).

Context

The Glorious Lover was published during the crisis of 1678–81, but it is rarely explicitly engaged with the specific political issues of the time. However, in Keach's condemnation of lustful gallants, and his appropriation of the language and genre of romance to discuss the love of Christ, it is possible to see a critique of the libertine culture which pervaded the court, and was seen to have political implications.[4] But Keach's critique of libertinism was not without its problems. As Southcombe and Tapsell write: 'His poem titillated, and whilst it ultimately contrasted libertinism with the free love given by Christ to the elect, it still tried to arouse the reader with passion for Christ in terms which were not so far removed from the terms it had critiqued.'[5]

Sources

The mystical marriage between the Soul and Christ had a long history as a literary subject. Important early seventeenth-century works engaged with this tradition were Francis Rous's *The Mysticall Marriage* (1631), and Francis Quarles's *Emblemes*, first published in 1635. Most of the images in Quarles's work were drawn from the Jesuit works *Pia Desideria* (1624) and *Typus Mundi* (1628), which were themselves concerned with the relationship between Amor and Anima.[6] The image of Christ as the Bridegroom was, of course, ultimately biblical. And it was one to which Keach was particularly drawn, as he published later: 'THis Metaphor of a *Bridegroom*, as it is exceeding useful, so it is as comfortable and pleasant a Metaphor as most we meet with in the holy Scriptures.'[7]

In *The Glorious Lover* Keach unsurprisingly drew heavily on scripture, and book I contains a retelling in verse of the life of Christ, combining the gospel accounts. The Song of Solomon, to which the image of Christ as bridegroom was often linked, was his main poetic touchstone in representing the wooing of the Soul by Christ and the mystical marriage.[8]

As in *War with the Devil* Keach borrowed from Quarles's *Emblemes* at a number of points.[9] However, the most interesting borrowings from another poet are those taken from Dryden's depictions of councils in hell in his *The State of Innocence* (1677) – itself an adaptation of Milton's *Paradise Lost* in rhyme.[10]

The Glorious Lover also contains versions in verse of lists concerning the attributes of Christ found in Thomas De Laune and Benjamin Keach, *Tropologia* (1681). It is unclear whether Keach was versifying his own unpublished manuscript, composed the versions in verse before the prose ones of *Troplogia*, or worked on both at the same time.[11]

Notes

1. G. E. B. Eyre and C. B. Rivington (eds), *A Transcript of the Registers of the Worshipful Company of Stationers from 1640–1708*, 3 vols. (London: Priv. print, 1913–14), vol. 3, p. 77.
2. E. Arber (ed.), *The Term Catalogues, 1668–1709*, 3 vols (London: Edward Arber, 1903–6), vol. 1, p. 350.
3. This edition was to be sold bound for 18*d*: Arber (ed.), *The Term Catalogues, 1668–1709*, vol. 1, p. 350.
4. On Keach and romance see E. Clarke, *Politics, Religion and the Song of Songs in Seventeenth-Century England* (Basingstoke: Palgrave, 2011), pp. 196–9; S. Achinstein, *Literature and Dissent in Milton's England* (Cambridge: Cambridge University Press,

    2003), pp. 196–9. On Charles II's court culture see M. Jenkinson, *Culture and Politics at the Court of Charles II, 1660–1685* (Woodbridge: Boydell, 2010).

5. G. Southcombe and G. Tapsell, *Restoration Politics, Religion and Culture: Britain and Ireland, 1660–1714* (Basingstoke: Palgrave Macmillan, 2010), p. 158. Achinstein writes of how 'Sexual eroticism may be deployed in the service of evangelical Christianity.' See Achinstein, *Literature and Dissent* p. 199.

6. On Rous and Quarles see Clarke, *Politics, Religion and the Song of Songs*, pp. 52–5, 84–90. On Amor and Anima see B. Westerweel, '"Not Clothed with Engraven Pictures": Emblems and the Authority of the Word', in J. F. van Dijhuizen and R. Todd (eds), *The Reformation Unsettled: British Literature and the Question of Religious Identity, 1560–1660*, p. 123.

7. T. De Laune and B. Keach, *Tropologia* (London: Enoch Prosser, 1681), bk 2, p. 97. For Keach's extensive discussion of the metaphor of the bridegroom see De Laune and Keach, *Tropologia*, bk 2, pp. 97–107.

8. For more on seventeenth-century uses of the Song see Clarke, *Politics, Religion and the Song of Songs*.

9. See B. Keach, *War with the Devil*; B. Keach, *The Glorious Lover*, below e.g. p. 195.

10. See Keach, *The Glorious Lover*, below p. 251.

11. Ibid., below p. 253.

THE
Glorious Lover.

A
DIVINE POEM,
Upon the Adorable Mystery of
Sinners Redemption.

By *B.K.* Author of *War with the Devil.*

Psalm 45.1.
> *My Heart is inditing a good matter.*[1] [a]

LONDON,
Printed by *J.D.*[b] for *Christopher Hussey*, at the *Flower-de-Luce* in
Little Britain. 1679. [c]

The PROEM.

You Gentle Youths, *whose chaster* Breasts *do beat*
With pleasing Raptures, & Love's *generous heat;*
And Virgins kind! *from whose* unguarded *Eyes*
Passion oft steals your hearts by fond[d] *surprize;*
All you who Amorous Stories *gladly hear,*
And feed your wand'ring Fancies by the Ear;
Those treacherous Delights *a while lay by,*
And lend attention to our History:
A History with Love *and* Wonders *fill'd,*
Such as nor Greece *nor* Rome *could ever yield.*
So great the Subject, *lofty the* Design,
Each part is Sacred, *and the whole* Divine.
If you its worth and nature well shall weigh,
'Twill charm your Ear, your best Affections sway,
And in dark Minds spring an Eternal Day. }

My Muse *is rais'd beyond a vulgar flight:*
For Cherubs *boast to sing of what I write.*
I write – But 'tis, alas, with trembling hand:
For who those boundless Depths *can understand?*
Those Mysteries *unvail, which Angels do*
With dread Amaze desire to look into?
     Thou glorious Being! *from whose Bounty flows*
All good that Man, or does, or speaks, or knows;
Whose Altars once mean Turtles *entertain'd,*[2]
And from the mouths of Babes *hast strength ordain'd;*[3]
Purge with thy Beams my over-clouded mind;
Direct my Pen, *my* Intellect *refine,*
That I thy matchless Triumphs may indite,
And live in a due sense of what I write.
    And you, dear Sirs,, that shall vouchsafe to read,
Charity's Mantle o're my failings spread.
High is my Theme, *but weak and short my* Sight;
My Eyes oft dazled with Excess of Light.
Yet something here perhaps may please each Guest;
'Tis Heavenly Manna, *though but homely drest.*
Paul became all to All: *and I would try*[4]
By this Essay of mystick Poesy,
To win their Fancies, whose harmonious Brains
Are better pleas'd with soft and measur'd strains.
A Verse may catch a wandring Soul, that flies
Profounder Tracts, and by a blest Surprize –
Convert Delight into a Sacrifice. –[5]
How many do their precious time *abuse*
On cursed products of a wanton Muse;
On trifling Tables, *and* Romances *vain,*
The poisoned froth of some infected *Brain?*[6]
Which only tend to nourish Rampant Vice,
And to Prophaneness easie Youth entice;
Gilt o're with Wit, black Venom in they take,
And 'midst gay Flowers hug the lurking Snake.
Here's no such danger, but all pure and chast;
A Love most fit by Saints to be[a] *imbrac'd:*
A Love 'bove that of Women: Beauty, *such,*
As none can be enamour'd on too much.
Read then, and learn to love truly by this,
Until thy Soul can sing (Raptur'd in Bliss)}
My Well beloved's mine, and I am his.[7]

BOOK I.

CHAP. I.

The Excellencies and Perfections of the glorious King, the Lord JEHOV AH, discov-
ered: Shewing how he had but one Son, the express Image of the Father, the delight
and joy of his Heart; and of the glorious and eternal Design of this most High and
Everlasting JEHOV AH to dispose of his Son in Marriage, Moreover, how the mat-
ter was propounded by the Father, and whom he had chose to be the intended Spouse,
Shewing also how the Prince readily consented to the Proposal; and of his first grand
and glorious Atchievements in order to the Accomplishment of this happy Design.

IN the fair Regions of approachless Light,[8]
Where unmixt Joys with perfect Love unite;
Where youth n'ere wasts, nor Beauty ever fades,
Where no disease, nor paining-grief, invades;
There reigns, and long hath reign'd, a mighty King,
From whom all Honours, and all Riches spring;
His vast Dominions reach from Pole to Pole,
No Realm nor Nation but he could controul,
So great his Pow'r, there never yet could be,
An absolute Monarch in the World but he.
What e're seem'd good to him, he freely did,
And nothing from his piercing Eye was hid.
To him the mighty *Nimrods*[9] all did Bow,
And none durst boldly question, What dost Thou
Justice and Wisdom waited on his Throne,
And through the World his Clemency was known
His Glory so Illustrious and Bright,
It sparkled[a] forth, and dazled Mortals sight.
Immense his Being; for in every Land
He present was, and by each Soul did stand.
No Spies he needed for Intelligence
In foreign parts, to bring him Tydings thence.
And vain to him was Court-dissemblers Art,
He saw each corner of the subtlest heart,
View'd acts unborn, and plain discoveries wrought
E're labouring Fancy once could mould a Thought
Beheld mens minds clearly, as were their faces,
And uncontain'd, at once did fill all Places;
His awful frown could make the Mountains shake
And Stoutest hearts of Haughty Princes quake.
All things were his, who did them first compose,
And by his wisdom doth them still dispose;
To serve his Friends, and to destroy his Foes.
His Azure Throne with Holiness is spread,
The pure in heart alone his Court may tread;

No vitious Gallant, Proud, Imperious, Vain,
In Court, nor Kingdom will he entertain.
He's th' essence of true Vertue, spotless, pure,
And no ungodly one can he endure.
No wicked person to him dares draw nigh,
Though ne're so Rich, so Mighty, or so High;
'Tis Righteousness his blessed Throne maintains,
Who all Injustice utterly disdains;
Nay, Holiness doth this great Soveraigne cloath,
And such as weare it not, his Soul doth loath.
But above all the Glories which did wait
Upon this High and Peerless Potentate:
His Pity did the most transcendent prove,
Matchless his Power, but greater still his Love;
Such bowels of Compassion ne're were known,
Nor e're such proofs of vast Affection shown;
His kindness beyond all that Pen can write,
Or Heart conceive, or nimblest Brain indite.
This Sovereign Love our wond'rous Subject brings,
Our Hist'ry from those melting Ardours springs.[10]
    For this great King had a most lovely Son,
And had indeed no more save only one,
Who was begotten by him, and brought forth
E're Heav'ns blew curtains did surround the Earth;
Before the World's foundations yet were laid,
Times glass turn'd up, or the Sun's course displaid,
This Prince was brought up with him, and did lye,
In his dear Bosom from Eternity.
He was his only Joy, and hearts delight,
Who ever did behold him in his sight.
And as he made his Father's heart most glad,
He was sole Heir to all the Father had;
Who freely gave all things into his Hand,
And made him Ruler over every Land,
Designing still to raise his Dignity
Above each Earthly Prince, or Monarchy,
And him intitle with a glorious Name,
Which none of all the Heav'nly Host dare claim.
What glory is there in each Seraphim!
Yet must they all do Homage unto him;
The Cherubims likewise must all submit,
And humbly worship at his Royal Feet,
With trembling Reverence; for he doth bear
The express Image of his Father dear;
And his Majestick Glory doth unfold,   }
Too bright for any creature to behold,
Untill transform'd into an Heav'nly mould.
The Lustre of his Face, the loveliness

Of compleat Beauty, and of Holiness.
His Personal Sweetness, and Perfections rare,
No tongue of men, or Angels, can declare:
For, 'tis recorded by unerring Pen,
He fairer was than all the Sons of men.[11]
Which in its proper place will more appear:
But mind at present what doth follow here.

    This mighty King, whose Glories thus did shine,
Had long on foot a very great Design,
Which was, in Marriage to dispose this Son,
The blessedst Work that ever could be done:
This Secret then to him he does disclose,
And whom for him he had already chose,
Tells him the way, and means, whereby to bring
About this strange and most important thing;
What he must do; and all things doth declare:
To which the Son doth lend attentive ear,
Who never did his Father disobey,
Nor him displease, would not in this say nay;
But straight-way shew'd with joy & chearful mind
He was that way himself long time inclin'd:
For with a Heav'nly smile he made reply,
That Creature is the Jewel of mine eye.
Great King of Kings, thy Sacred Sovereign Will
With greatest Joy I'm ready to fullfil.
My heart's inflam'd with love, and will be pain'd
Till she for my imbraces be obtain'd.
With secret transports long have I design'd
That happy Match in my Eternal Mind,
To people with a new and holy Race
Th' Immortal Mansions of this Glorious Place.
Such is the Love which unto her I have,
'Tis strong as Death, and lasts beyond the Grave.
Where e're she be (for well I understand
She's spirited of late to a strange Land)
Winged with Love I le search the World about,
And leave no place unsought to find her out.
If any Foe doth Captive her detain,
I'le be her Rescue, and knock off her Chain:
Or, if half stifled, she in Prison lye,
I'le break the Bars, and give her liberty,
I will refuse no Labour, nor no pain,
Thee (dearest Soul!) into my Arms to gain.
Such was this Prince's love, and now tis fit
We tell you who the object was of it.

Within the Limits of the Holy Land,
Whose Glory once shone forth on every hand;
And near the Borders of rare *Havelah,*
Where Creatures of each kind first breath did draw;
Where *Pison's* streams with *Euphrates* did meet;
Where did abound all Joy and Comfort sweet,
Without the least perplexity or wo;
Where *Bdellium* and the *Onyx Stone* did grow;
Did a most choice and lovely Garden lye,
Renowned much for its antiquity:
For Sacred Story has proclaimd its name,
And rais'd up *Trophies* to its lasting fame.[12]
Within that Garden dwelt in Ancient time
A very lovely Creature in her Prime,[13]
Mirror of Beauty, and the World's chief glory,
Whose rare composure did out-vy all Story:
Fair as the Lilly, e're rude hands have toucht it:
Or snow unfal'n, before the Earth hath smucht it:
The perfectst work which wondring Heav'n could
Of Nature's Volumn, blest Epitome;
Her glorious Beauty, and Admired Worth,
What mortal tongue is able to set forth?
True Vertue was the Object of her will,
There was no stain in her, no Feature ill,
No scarr, nor blemish, seen in any part;
Her Judgment uncorrupt, and pure her Heart;
Her *thoughts* were noble, *words* most wise, not lavish;
Her natural sweetness was enough to ravish
All that beheld her; from her sparkling Eye,
A thousand Charms, a thousand Graces fly:
No evill passion harbour'd in her breast,
Or with bold Mutinies disturb d her rest; }
For what's not borne yet, needs not be represt.
Her Lineage Noble, of such high degree,
None e're could boast a greater Pedigree:
A Dowry too she had, a fair Estate,
Conferr'd upon her at an easy Rate.
In brief, in all Indowments she did shine,
Stampt with his Image, who is all Divine:
But that which most unto her bliss did add,
Was the great Honour which some time she had,
Of the sweet presence of a glorious King,
From whom alone true Happiness doth spring;
He oft declar'd her his grand Favourite,
And that with her was his endear'd delight:
For precious love to her burn'd in his heart,
And nothing thought too dear for to impart,
Or unto her most freely to bestow,
Of all the Treasures he had here below.

This was her state at first, none can gain-say;
But then, mark what befell her on a day.
She did not long in this condition stand,
Before a cursed and most traiterous Band
Of Rebels, who shook off Allegiance,
And 'gainst their Sovereign did bold Arms advance;[14]
Intic'd her to their Party, and destroy'd
All those rare Priviledges she injoy'd.
Which grand offence did so the King displease,
That she his wrath by no means could appease;
Nor had she any Friend to speak a word,
To stay the Tortures of the Flaming Sword.[15]
No purpose 'twas, alas! for her to plead,
Why Sentence should not against her proceed;
Who well knew in her conscience 'twas but right
She should thenceforth be banisht from his sight,
And his most glorious Face behold no more,
As she with joy had seen it heretofore.
The rightful Sentence passed, though severe,
Which might strike dead the trembling Soul to hear,
Exil'd she was from him with fearful Ire,
And laid obnoxious to Eternal fire:
Turn'd out of all her Glory with a curse,
No state of Mortal Creatures could be worse.
And now she's forc'd to wander to and fro,
Finding no rest, nor knowing what to do.
A foreign soile, alas! she must seek out,
And where to hide her self she looks about.
A wretched Fugitive she straight became,
A shame unto her self, to all a shame.
Yet this vile wretched Creature, so forlorn,
The Subject of contempt and general scorn,
She, she's the Object of this Prince's Love,
She 'tis to whom his warm Affections move.
'Twas in her fallen state he cast his eye,
Although he lov'd her from Eternity.
Who wandring thus into a Foreign Land,
Far off of him: he soon did understand
There was no other thing for him to do,
But must a Journy take, and thither go.
If he'l accomplish this his great Design,
Of making Love, a Love that's most divine.
    The Father now doth part whith his dear Son,
Who's all on fire, and zealous to be gone:
And what though it a grievous Journy be,
Its bitterness he is resolv'd to see.
His high Atchievements nothing shall prevent,
His mind and purpose is so fully bent,
That he in his own Kingdom will not stay
One Minute after the appointed Day.

But that you may more fully yet discover
The matchless flames of this most glorious Lover,
Permit us to present unto your view,
The Court he left, the Dungeon he went to.

    The Kingdom, where this High-born Prince did dwell,
All other Countries vastly doth excel,
Its Glory splendid is and infinite,
It cannot be beheld with fleshly sight.
Ten thousand Suns, ten thousand times more bright
Then ours is, could never give such light.[16]
None ever there beheld a Cloud, nor shall;
Nor ever was there any Night at all.
No cold or heat did ever there displease,
No pain nor sorrow there, nor no disease.
No thirst nor hunger there do any know,
Nor any foes to seek their overthrow,
Disturb their peace, or them i'th least annoy;
Nor is there any Devil to destroy.
And if one would that Kingdom search about,
There is no finding of one poor Man out.
No sooner any such do thither get,
But on their Heads a glorious Crown is set.[17]
Congratulating Angels round them wait,
And cloath them all in long white Robes of State.
They live in boundless Bliss, with such content,
It raises Joy unto a Ravishment.
There's Rivers too of Pleasures, fil'd to'th Brim,
In which the Prophets and Apostles swim.[18]
There Beauty fadeth not, nor Strength decayes;
No weary old Age, neither end of Dayes.
Impossible it is for them to dye,
Whose Souls have tasted Immortality.
All there is Love, and Sempiternal Joys,
Whose sweetness neither gluts, nor fullness cloys.[19]
Friends always by; for absence is not known,
Their loss, or departure, none can bemoan.
    Within the confines of this blissful Land
There doth a spacious foursquare City stand,
The noblest Structure 'tis that e're was rais'd,
By men admired, or by Angels prais'd.
The Founder of it was a mighty King;
Yet without hands t'was built, amazing thing!
As for th' Materials, which did it prepare
From a good Author this description hear:
'The Luke-warm Blood of a dear Lamb being spilt,
'To Rubies turn'd, whereof its parts were built,
'And what dropt down in a kind gellied Gore,
'Became rich *Saphire*, and did pave her Floor.

'The Brighter flames that from his *Eyebals* ray'd,
'Grew *Chrysolites*, whereof her walls were made.
'The Milder glances sparkled on the ground,
'And grounsild every Door with *Diamond*:
'But dying, darted upwards, and did fix
'A Battlement of purest *Sardonix*.
'Its Streets with Burnisht *Gold* are paved round,
'Stars lye like *Pebbles* scattered on the ground.
'Pearl mixt with *Onyx*, and the *Jasper* Stone,
'The *Citizens* do always tread upon.[20]
Here he with's Father in great state did sit,
Whilst millions bow'd themselves unto his Feet.
Here 'twas he kept his Court, here was his Throne,
From hence through all the World his Glory shone.
And if ought could unto his Greatness add,
Mark what a rich Retinue there he had.
He Servants kept of very high Degree,
Who did bow down to him continually.
Though they were Nobles all, and far more high
Than proudest of the *Roman* Monarchy;
And mighty great in Power too are they;
For one alone did no less Number slay
Than near two hundred thousand in one night,[21]
Of Valaint Souldiers, trained up to fight.
These Troops still ready stood at his command,
To execute his will in every Land.
Of them he'd an Innumerable Host,
Though some of them in ancient times were lost[22]
Yet the selected number Millions were,
Who still to him do true Allegiance bear:
True Love and Zeal burn'd in their breasts, like fire
To do his Will's their business and desire:
'Tis his great Int'rest which they wholly mind,
Aiding his Friends, whose welfare they design'd:
And likewise evermore to frustrate those,
Who did their Prince's Soveraignty oppose.
Their Nature's quick and clear, as Beams of light
Creatures too pure for Mortals grosser sight.
And if we shall consider well their worth,
Meer Empty Nothings are all Kings 'oth Earth,
When to these Servants they compared be;
So much excells their glorious Dignity.
What of their Sovereign Lord then shall we say,
On whom they do attend both night and day?
When they before his dazling Throne appear,
Their Heav'nly faces straight way cover'd are
As if not able on his Face to look;
Or else with glorious blushings, Heaven-struck.

Such, such his Court, such his Attendants were:
Who could with this great Prince of light compare?
Oh what Celestial Glory didst thou leave,
Almost beyond mans credence to believe!
That thou shouldst thus thy Fathers house forsake,
And such a tedious dismal Journey make!
Could not that charming Melody above,
Allure thy thoughts and, hinder thy remove?
Oh no! there's nothing can retard thy Love.
Hark how the glorious *Seraphims* do sing,
Whose warbling notes do make the Heavens ring!
What Mortals ever did such Musick hear?
Spirits made perfect, are quite ravisht there.
Oh! how they listen whilst the Strains rise higher,
And joyning gladly with th' All-charming Quire,
Sing forth aloud, inspired with his flame,
All Glory, Glory, Glory to his Name.
One strain of this Celestial Harmony,
Could Mortals hear, they soon would thither fly:
They straight would shake off all their carnal shackles
And quit these dull and loathsom Tabernacles;
Like towring Larks, still upwards would they soar,
And ravished, would think of Earth no more:
Or like to herds of Cattel, great and small,
They d leave their feedings, and run thither all.
But yet could not this lovely Paradise,
These Honours, or this Melody intice
The love-sick Prince unto a longer stay,
So much he longed for the Marriage day:
No thing could his Design divert, or move;
So constant was he in his Royal Love.

His Travels next will you be pleas'd to hear
Which raises wonder in me to declare.
Ten thousand millions, and ten thousand more
Of Angel-measur'd Leagues from th'Eastern shore:
Of Dunghil Earth this glorious Prince did come,[23]
Did ever Lover go so far from Home
To seek a Spouse? What brave Heroick Spirit
That e're did love of virtuous Princess merit,
Would not have found his trembling heart to ake
So vast an Enterprize to undertake;
Such dangers to expose himself unto,
Such pleasure, and such glory to fore-go!
But some 'tis like may ask a question here,
Unto what Parts or Region did he steer?
Or whither did he travel, whither go?
A very needful thing for all to know.

Was't to some *Goshen*-Land,[24] of precious Light?
Or in to some *Elysian* Fields,[25] which might
With Boundless Pleasures thither him invite?
Was it a Kingdom somewhat like his own
For Bliss and Glory? or what kind of one
Was this strange Land, to which this Lover went
To find the Soul, forc'd into Banishment?

    Alas! dear Sirs! this may you still amaze,
And to a higher Pitch your wonder raise.
As far as Darkness differs from the Light,
Or dolesom Earth falls short of Heaven so bright;
As Heavens higher are than Earth or Seas,
A thousand times, ten thousand of Degrees;
So far that place where this sweet Prince did dwell
The other (to which he travel'd) did excel.
As that transcends for loveliness most rare:
So this in wickedness exceeds compare.
Egypt was once a dark and dolesom place,
When no one could behold his brother's face.
Though there the sacred stories plainly tel't,
The darkness was so great, it might be felt.[26]
Yet was that but a figure, you must know,
Of the black horror of this Land of Wo,
Whither the wretched wandring Soul was gone,
And whence her Lover now must fetch her home:
It was indeed an howling Wilderness,
A Region of dispair, and all distress:
Where *Dragons, Wolves, Lyons*, and ravenous Beasts
Had their close Dens, and Birds of Prey their Nests.
Besides, throughout the ruinated Land
A Black and fearful King[27] had great Command,
Who had revolted many years before
From his Liege Lord, and to him since has bore
Most cruel spight and curs'd malignity,
Assuming to himself the Soveraignty;
The greatst Usurper that e're being had:
Sylla, nor *Nero*[28] never were so bad.
For 'tis well known he was th'original Syre
Of Tyrants all, and taught them to aspire;
Ambitious through the World to spread his Arms,
He fill'd the Earth with Blood and sad Alarms:
And like a ravenous Lyon rang'd about
To seek his Prey, and find new Conquests out.[29]
Full of State-Policies, and Subtil wiles:
Where's Force attempts in vain, his Fraud beguiles.
Most cruel to those Slaves he can betray,
And yet the Fools, besotted to his sway,
Court their own ruine, and blindly obey.

His Antient Lord he hated most of all,
And such as were his offspring, great and small,
He was resolv'd to be reveng'd upon,
And them for to destroy e're he had done,
From whence his name was call'd *Apollyon*.[30]
A name which doth his Nature full express,
And you of him thereby may[a] further guess.
This greedy *Dragon*, hungry of his prey,
With *wide-stretcht Jawes* stood waiting for the day,
When this dear Prince should come; nay for the hour,
That so he might him instantly devour.[31]
Oh Tyrant Love! dost thou no pity take!
Wilt thou the PHÆNIX[32] of both worlds thus make
A prey to such a Fiend, who by some snare
Hopes to entrap this long expected Heir,
And then to take Possession, and alone
Rule on an undisturbed Hellish Throne?
See how the Troops of his Infernal Power
Combine, this Sacred Person to devour.
Needs must that be a sad and dismal Land,
Where this damn'd Monster hath so great Comand.
What Prince would come from such a Mount of bliss
Unto a Cave, where Poysonous Serpents hiss?
Come from his Father's Bosom where he lay,
To be the *Wolves* and *Dragons* chiefest prey?
To leave his glorious Robes and Cloth of Gold,
And clothed be with Raggs and Garments old!
From ruling men and Devils, now to be
Tempted by both of them, scarce ever free?
To leave a Paradise of all Delight,
And come into a Land as black as night?
A glorious Crown and Kingdom to forsake,
That he his bed might on a Dunghil make?
To leave a sweet and quiet Habitation,
To come into a rude distracted Nation?
Where Wars, Blood, and Miseries abound,
Where neither Truth, nor Faith, nor Peace is found?
To leave his Friends, who loved him most dear,
To dwell with such as mortal hatred bear
To him, and to his blessed Father, and
All such as do for them most faithful stand?
To come so many Millions of long miles
To be involv'd in Troubles and sad Broils?
And all this for a Creature poor and vile,
A Traiterous Vagabond, and in Exile?
Yea, one that still remain'd a stubborn foe,
Hating both him and his blest Father too?
Who ponders all in extasy, can't miss

To cry out, *Oh! what manner of Love is this*?
Sure this is Love that may our Souls amaze,
And to the height our wondring Spirits raise,
In grateful Hymns to celebrate its praise.

CHAP. II.

Shewing what entertainment the Prince of Light met with at his first arrival. How there being no room for him in the Inn, he was forced to lie in the Stable. and make his bed in the Manger. As also how he having laid aside his Glorious and Princely Robes, was not known by the people of that Country; and how he was wronged, and abominably abused by them.

Awake my Muse! I hear the Prince is come;
Go and attend him, view the very Room
Where he at first doth lodg: see how they treat
A King, whose Pow'r is so exceeding great.
Much Rumor of his coming, I am told,
Was spread abroad amongst them there of old,
And many waiting for him, long'd to see
What kind of King and Person he should be.
Oh! what provision now to entertain
Him did they make? my Soul's in grevious pain
To hear of this. Doth not the Trumpet sound,
And Joy and melody sweetly abound
I'th hearts of all, who heard of this good News?
How did they carry't to him, or how use
This lovely One, whom Angels do adore,
And Glorious Seraphims fall down before?
Ah! how methinks should they now look about
Some curious stately Structure to find out,
Some Prince's Palace for his Residence,
Or strong fair Castle for his safe Defence!
Don't people leap for Joy, whil'st Angels sing,
To welcome in their long expected King?
Do not the Conduits through all streets combine
In stead of Water, wholly to run Wine?[33]
Do not great Swarms of people 'bout him fly,
Like to some strange and glorious Prodigy?

What dos't thou say, my Muse, Art wholly mute?
Doth this not with thy present purpose suit?
Ah! yes, it does, but how shal't be exprest?
The grief that seizes on my panting Breast,
My heart into a trembling fit doth fall,
To think how he contemned was of all.
The Savage Monsters did this Prince reject,

And treat him with affronts and disrespect:
When he for them had taken all this pain,
They neither would him know nor entertain:
The very Inn, where first he went to lie,
For to vouchsafe him Lodging did deny.
No Room (alas!) had they; but if 'twere so
He would be there, to th' Stable he must go.
To'th' Stable then goes he contentedly,
Without the least reflection or reply.
The silly Ass, and labouring Ox must be
Companions now to Sacred Royalty;
Expos'd by Greater Brutes, he must (alas)
Take up with the Dull-Oxe, and painful Ass,
Who their great Maker and Preserver was;
And in the Manger's forc'd to make his bed,
Without one Pillow to support his Head.[34]
Let Heav'n astonisht, Earth amazed be
At this ungrateful Inhumanity
Let Seas rise up in heaps, and after quit
Their Course, these Barbarous people to affright.
Oh! what a mighty condescention's here!
What story may with this, *with this*, compare?
Is this the entertainment, they afford!
And this a Palace for so great a Lord!
Is this their kindness to so dear a friend!
Do they him to a filthy Stable send!
Is that a Chamber suiting his Degree!
Or fit the Manger should allotted be,
For him to lay his Glorious Body in,
(Of whom the Prophet saith *he knew no Sin*?)[35]
Whose footstool's Earth, and Heaven is his Throne[36]
What ne're a better Bed for such an one!
That has so vast a Journey undertook,
And for their sakes such Glory too forsook!
Is this great Prince with such mean Lodging pleas'd
So that he may of love-sick pains be eas'd!
O what a Lover's this! Almighty Love!
How potently dost thou affections move!
What shall a Prince be thus ore-come by thee,
And brought into contempt to this degree!
Sure this may melt an heart of hardest Stone,
When tis consider'd well and thought upon.
But no less worthy note is it to hear
The manner how this Soveraign did appear.
Was it in Pomp and[a] outward Splendor bright?
Which doth the sensual heart of man invite,
To cast a view, and deep respect to show,
As unto haughty Monarchs here they do:

Like to a Prince, or like himself, did he
His beams display that every eye might see
In his blest Face most radiant Majesty?
No, no, so far was he from being proud,
That he thought fit his Glories all to shroud;
And, like the Sun,[37] invelop'd in a Cloud,
Did vail his Heav'nly Lustre, would not make
Himself of Reputation, for the sake
Of that poor Soul he came for to seek out:
He saw 'twas good, that he might work about
His blest Design, himself thus to deny,
And shew a pattern of humility.
His glorious Robes he freely did lay off,
Though thereby made th' object of men's scoff,
Who viewing his despised mean condition,
Welcom'd him with contempt, scorn, and derision:
For 'twas 'ith form of a poor servant he
Appear'd to all, the very low'st degree,
Which amongst all the sons of *Adam* are
And doth not this still wondrous Love declare!
The people of that Country too I find
To gross mistakes so readily inclin'd,
They judg'd him a poor Carpenters Son born,
And stigmatiz'd him with it in great scorn.
Nay, some affirm he worked at the Trade,
For which they did him mightily upbraid.
How ever this we must to all proclaim,
He that all Riches had, most poor became;
That so the Soul through his sad poverty
Might be enriched to Eternity.
The *Foxes* of the Earth, and Birds of th' Air
Had more (alas!) than fell unto his share.
In holes the one, in nests the other fed;
But he, (poor he! no where to lay his head.
Not one poor Cottage had this precious King,
Although the rightful Heir of every thing.
The meanest man almost of *Adam's* Race
Seem'd to be in as good, nay better case,
Respecting outward Wealth and Glory here;
Those things no Price in his affections bear.
Silver and Gold the Muckworm Wordling's God
He knew to be but more refined Clods
Of that same Earth, which he himself had made
Ripe by a Sun, scarce fit to be his shade.
No Mony, doubtless, had this Prince at all
In purse or coffer: for, when some did call
For *Cesars* Tribute, then, behold, must he
Dispatch in haste a Servant to the Sea

In an uncertain Fishes mouth to spy
A piece of Coyn (Oh wondrous Treasury!)
With which he straight did *Cæsars* Tribute pay.
(Though small Engagement on the Children lay
Rather than hee'l be disobedient thought,
To raise the Tax, a Miracle is wrought.[38]
 But here tis like some may desire to know
The cause why he abas'd himself so low ?
 The *Answer* to which *Query's* very plain;
His Errand so requir'd, if he'd obtain
The Soul, for whom his Country he did leave,
He of his Glory must himself bereave.
'Twas Love that brought him into this disguise,
To come *incognito* to haughty Eyes,
To lay aside awhile his Robes of State,
And thus in *Pilgrims* weeds upon her wait:
Without this Form assum'd, these Raggs put on,
The mighty Work could never have been done.
She grov'ling lay below, unable quite
Once to aspire unto his Glorious Sight.
Therefore must he a Garb suitable take
To raise her up, and his dear Consort make;
He must descend, that she might mount above,
And joyn in a fit Entercourse of Love.
So the kind Sun beams do the *Dunghil* gild,
That it to Heaven may Exalations yeild,   }
With pregant³ Show'rs to fertilize the Field.

CHAP. III.

*Shewing how upon the arrival of the glorious Prince, the Vice Roy of that Country
contrived in a barbarous maner to take away his Life. And of the horrid Massacre
that fell out upon it in the Town of* Bethlehem. *And how the Prince escaped and fled
nto* Egypt. *Also discovering how the Creature he came; to be a suiter to was prein-
gaged by the black King to the Monster of deformity, a Bastard of his own begetting,
called Lust. And of the great and fearful battel that fell our between the Prince of
Light, and* Apollyon *Prince of Darkness; and how* Apollyon *was over-come and,
after three amazing Incounters, forc'd to fly.*

Though Goodness still's oppos'd by envious Hate
Vertue (like Palms) thrives by th' oppressing weight[39]
Our Princes Welcome is in part exprest,
But what ensues is worse than all the rest.
Of his sad usage further I'le declare,
And the curs'd cruel Foes he met with there.
No sooner flutt'ring Fame the news had told

Of his arrive; and that some Seers of old
(Heralds of Fate) proclaim'd him, on Record
To be a high-born Prince, and mighty Lord:
But presently the Voyce-Roy[a] of that Land
Was fill'd with Indignation on each hand;
Fearing, 'tis like, he might deposed be,
Or much diminisht in his Dignitie;
That this great stranger might assume his Crown,
Or quite eclipse his perishing Renown.
For when the Sun doth rise and shine so clear,
The Moon and Stars do all straight disappear.
Not knowing what strange evils might arise;
He therefore did a bloody Plot devise.
Such was his Rage and undeserved spight,
He needs would butcher this sweet Lamb of Light;
Who though to none he thought one dram of ill,
Yet he resolves[b] his precious Blood to spill;
But failing of one Treacherous Design,
He and his Gang do in a worse combine:
Which was by strict Inquiries for to hear,
When this bright Star did first to men appear?
That so he might exactly know the Day
When he arriv'd, and in a Manger lay.
Which known, to make all sure he straight contrives
To sacrifice a thousand harmless Lives,
And kill the *Males*, yea every one of them
Which had been born in famous *Bethlehem*,
From two years old or under, ever since
The late prediction of this new-born Prince.
Judging this way ('tis like) might be the best
To cut off him, unknown, amongst the rest.
Which horrid Massacre he brought to pass,
And one more bloody sure there never was:
If Circumstances were but weighed well,
Both what they were, and why that day they fell
On the poor Babes; they no compassion have,
But hurle them from the Cradle to the Grave.
The weeping Mothers rais'd a swelling flood
Of their own tears mixt with their Childrens blood;
In every street are heard most dismal Cries,
Bewailing those untimely Obsequies:
As had been prophesied long before,
By *Rachel's* moans, refusing to give o're,
She sighs, and weeps, and has no comfort got,
Because her hopeful Children now are not.[40]
Great was the slaughter, yet their hopes were crost,
The precious Prey these raging Blood-hounds lost:

For th' Prince of Peace had notice of this thing,
And fled to *Egypt* from this wrathful King,
And there remaining, graciously was fed.
Until this Savage Murderer was dead.
And when he heard what had that wretch befel,
He hastned back to'th Land of *Israel*.
But news being brought of *Archilaus's*[41] Raign,
Soon found it needful to remove again.
So being warn'd of God, to *Galilee*[42]
He turn'd aside; and there at present we
Shall leave him, whilst we may more fully hear
The great design of this his coming there.
Some possibly may say, was't not to take
Unto himself a Kingdom, and so make
Himself Renowned, Great and very High,
Above each Prince and Earthly Monarchy?
Was't not to take the Crowns of every King,
And all their Glory to the Dust to bring,
To set their *Diadems* on his own head,
That so the Nations might be better led?
Was't not to take Revenge upon his Foes,
And grind to Powder all that him oppose?
Was it not to commence his glorious Raign,
That so he might the pride of Nations stain?
Herod, tis like, as you before did hear,
Such things might dream, and it might vainly fear:[43]
But wholly groundless: for (alas) he came
Not as a King to punish, but a *Lamb*,
To offer up in sacrifice his Life,
To put an end to all tormenting strife,
And only gain a poor, but long'd-for Wife.
His sole design, I told you, it was Love,
'Twas that alone which brought him from above,
These hardships, and these pains to undergo,
And many more, which yet we have to show:
For these are nothing, in comparison
Of those which must be told e're we have done.

    He in those parts had been but thirty year,
And little had he don that we can hear
About obtaining of the Creatures love,
But gloriously did then the matter move,
Unto the Soul, who little did it mind,
For she (alas) was otherwise inclin'd:
For the Black King that had usurp'd that Land,
An Ill shapt Bastard had, of proud command,
Whom having drest up in much[a] Gallantry,
He did appear so pleasant in her Eye,

That he before had her affections won,
And in her heart established his Throne;
Though he design'd no less than to betray
And murder her in an insidious[a] way:
Of which the silly Soul was not aware,
But fondly blind could not discern the snare.
Too like (alas) to many now a dayes,
Whom fawning words and flattery betrays.
This Imp of Darkness, and first-born of Hell
Transform'd by Witchcraft, and a cursed Spell,
Like a brisk gawdy Gallant now appears,
And still false locks, and borrowed Garments wears:
Then boldly sets upon her, and with strong
And sweet lip'd Rhetorick of a Courtly tongue
Salutes her Ears, and doth each way discover
The Amorous Language of a wanton Lover.
He smiles, he toyes, and now and then lets fly
Imperious glances from his lustful Eye;
Adorns her Orient Neck with Pearly charms,
And with rich Bracelets decks her Ivory Arms:
Boasts the extent of his Imperial Power,
And offers Wealth and worldly pleasure to her.
Jocund he seem'd, and full of sprightly[b] Mirth,[44]
And the poor Soul never inquir'd his Birth.
She lik'd his Face, but dream t not of the Dart
Wherewith he waited to transfix her Heart.
There is no foe to such a Dalilaw,[45]
As pretends love, yet ready is to draw
The Poysonous Spear, and with a treacherous kiss
Bereaves the Soul of everlasting Bliss.
If you would know this treacherous Monster's name
(As you before have heard from whence he came)
'Tis he by whom thousands deceiv'd have bin,
Heav'ns foe, and Satan's cursed Off-spring, SIN.
A violater of all Righteous Laws,
And one that still to all Uncleaness draws;
Author of Whoredomes, Perjuries, Disorders,
Thefts, Rapines, Blood, Idolatries, and Murders.
From whom all Plagues, and all Diseases flow!
And Death it self to him his be'ng doth ow.[46]
This Monster of Pollution, the undone
Poor Soul too long had been enamour'd on;
And by the Craft his Sire *Apollyon* lent,
Doubted not to obtain her full Consent.
But when *Apollyon* saw this Prince of Peace,
His wrathfull spight against him did encrease:
So brave a Rival he could not endure,
But sought all means his Ruine to procure.

Shall I, saith he, thus lose my hop'd-for prey,
See my Designs all blasted in one day,
Which I have carried on from Age to Age,
With deepest Policy, and fiercest Rage?
My utmost Stratagems I first will try,
And rather on the very Spot Ile dye.
Thus Hellishly resolv'd, he does prepare
Straight to commence the bold and Impious War,
And now the sharp Encounter does begin
A Fight so fierce no eye had ever seen,
Nor shall hereafter ere behold agen.
But first be pleas'd to take a prospect here,
Of the two Combatants as they appear:
The first a Person of Celestial Race,
Lovely his shape, ineffable his Face;
The frown with which he struck the trembling Fiend
All smiles of humane Beauty did transcend:
His head's with Glory arm'd, and his strong hand
No power of Earth or Hell can long withstand.
He heads the mighty Hosts in Heav'n above,
And all on Earth, who do *Jehovah* love.
His Camp's so great, they many millions are,
With whom no one for Courage may compare,
They are all chosen men, and cloath'd in white,
Ah! to behold them, what a lovely sight
Is it! And yet more grave and lovely far
To joyn and make one in this Holy War.
The other was a King of Courage bold,
But very grim and ghastly to behold;
Great was his power, yet his garb did show
Sad Symptoms of a former overthrow:
But now recruited with a numerous Train,
Arm'd with dispair, he tempts his fate again.
Under his Banner the black Regiments fight,
And all the Wicked Troops which hate the light:
His Voluntiers are spread from North to South,
And flaming Sulphur belches from his Mouth.
Such was the grand Importance of their sight,
It did all eyes on Earth and Heaven invite
To be spectators, and attention lend:
So much did ne're on any Field[47] depend;
No not *Pharsalia's Plains*, where *Cæsar* fought,
And the Worlds Empire at one conquest caught.[48]
Alas, the Issue of that famous Fray,
May not compare with this more fatal Day.

Should the Black monstrous Tyrant Prince prevail,
The Hearts and hopes of all man-kind must fail:

But above all, she who caus'd their contest
Would be more miserable than all the rest;
Shee, she, poor soul! for ever were undone,
And never would have help from any one;
Twas for Her sake alone the War begun.
     Some fabulous Writers tell a wonderous story,
And give I know not what St. *George* the Glory
Of rescuing bravely a distressed Maid
From a strange *Dragon*, by his Generous aid.
This I am sure our blessed Captain fought
With a fierce *Dragon*, and Salvation wrought
For her, who else had been devoured quite
By that Old *Serpents* subtility and spight.[49]
But now tis time their Combate to display
Behold the Warriers ready in Array.
Apollyon well stor'd with crafty wit
Long time had waited for a season fit,
That so he might some great advantage get.
And knowing, well the Prince of Light had fasted
Ful forty days, then presently he hasted
To give him Battle, and a Challenge makes,
Which no less cheerfully Christ undertakes.
The King of Darkness the first onset gave,
Thinking his foe to startle, or out-brave.
He slung at him a very cruel Dart,
And aym'd to hit him just upon the Heart.
He'd have him doubt or question, if twere so?
Whether he were the Son of God or no?
But the blest Lord did use his Sword so well,
That down the others weapons straight way fell:
It made him reel, and forc'd him back to stand,
And beat his Lance at once out of his hand. [50] [51]
At which this disappointed wrathful King
Doth gnash his threatning teeth, and shews his sting;
Is mad and foams, and fain the Dog would bite:
He swells like to a *Toad*,[52] enough to fright
A mortal man, on him to cast an eye
And then breaks out with sad and hideous cry.

            Apollyon King of Darkness.
    Shall I be foiled thus? or thus give o're,
Whom never any could yet stand before?
Have not the Mighty fallen by my hand,
Enforc'd to yeild to me in every Land?
Whole Kingdoms (*Sir*) have trucled to my pow'r:
If once I'm mov'd, Millions I can devour.
Nay, with one stroke, thou very well dost know,
I all the World at once did overthrow.

My very Name is frightful unto all,
Who trembling fly, if I upon them fall.
My voyce is like unto a mighty Thunder,
And with a word I keep the Nations under.
See how they faint, and shrink, and shreek for fear,
If of my coming once they do but hear:
They quiver all, and like a Leaf do shake,
And dare not stand when I approaches make.
Besides all this, much more I have to boast:
Which of the Champions of thy Earthly Host
Have I not overcome, and put to flight?
None ever able were with me to fight.
Noah that Servant (Holy Just) of thine,
I did o'recome by'th juce of his own Vine[53]
And Righteous *Lot* I next may reckon up,
A Trophy unto my victorious Cup,
Whereby he into Incest fell two Times:[54]
And these thou know'st are no Inferiour Crimes.
Thy *Jacob* too, though he could wrestle well,[55]
Yet by my Arm most grievously he fell:
And so likewise did his most Zealous Mother:
By Lies I made him to supplant his Brother.[56]
Joseph for thee, although he was sincere,
I quickly taught by *Pharoah's Life* to swear.[57]
And *Judah*, from whose Loins thou dost proceed,
I worsted much, do but the Story read.[58]
Moses himself, thy Captain Generall,
By me receiv'd a shrew'd and dismal fall,
Although so meek, when I did him engage,
I mov'd him into passion and great rage,
By which I did so vex his troubl'd mind,
That he could not the Land of Promise find.[59]
Sampson was very strong, I know, yet he
Was overcome by *Dalilah* and me.[60]
And *David*, though a King, and most devout,
Sustained by me almost a total Rout,
Although he slew a *Lyon*, and a *Bear*,
And my *Goliah* likewise would not spare,
But with his sling that Champion did destroy,
Who did the Camp of *Israel* annoy:[61]
For all these mighty Acts, when once I came
To try his strength, I brought him unto shame:
The people numbred, and his God forsaken,
By Adult'ry and Murder over-taken.[62]
And *Solomon*, a mighty King and wise,
Did I by force and subtilety surprize;
I planted for him such a curious Net,
As soon Intangled his unwary feet;

Strange Womens charms withdrew his heart from thee
To doting Lust, and curs'd Idolatrie.[63]
The time would fail me, should I number all
The Noble Worthies, I have caus'd to fall.
Ne're any yet upon the Earth did dwell,
But by my conquering sword they vanquisht fell.
And thinkst thou, Man, that I to thee will yield,
When flusht[a] with Vict'ories, basely quit the Field.
Mistake not thus, Ile have the other blow,
I want no strength nor Courage thou shalt know.

Prince of Light.

Thy pride, *Apollyon*, and thy Hellish Rage,
Long since thy utter Downfal did presage.
Vain are thy Boasts, these Rants no good will doe,
I know thou art a cowardly bragging Foe,
Forbear with Lies my Servants to condemn,
'Twere only *foils*, not *falls*, thou gavest them.
Lurking in Secret, thou didst treacherously
At unawares sometimes upon them fly;
But rallying straight they did renew the Fight,
Quencht all thy Darts, and soon put thee to flight,
And now beyond thy reach, in full renown,
For their[b] reward, enjoy an endless Crown.[64]
And though on some thou hast prevail'd too far,
With me thou art unable to wage War.
'Tis for their sakes that forth my wrath is spread;
Thou *bruisdst[c] their Heels*, but *I will bruise thy Head.*[65]

Apollyon.

Stop there I pray, let's try the other Bout,
And see if thou canst me so quickly rout.
I am resolv'd my utmost force to try,
For all my hopes I find at Stake do ly:
E're I'le be baffled thus, and lose my Prey,
Upon thy back still sharper Strokes I'le lay.

Prince of Light.

What is the Cause thou art so furious now,
And thus on me dost bend thy[d] Brazen brow?
What is thy fear? why dost thou rage? or why
Dost tremble thus, and look so gashfully?
Why doth thy fading Colour come and go?
Speak, Hellish Fiend! what I command thee, do.

Apollyon.

Great Reason's for't; I partly understand

The Cause why thou art come into this Land:
And having found what thy intentions are,
Needs must the same me terrify and scare.
I do perceive what did thee chiefly move
To leave the Glory which thou hadst above;
'T was love that thou didst to a Creature bear,
Which unto me in truth is very dear;
And I will make my glistering Spear to bend,
E're I to thee in this will condescend;
Before I will her lose, I'le tear and roar,
And all Infernal Pow'rs I will Implore,
That I Assistance of them may obtain,
Against a Foe I do so much disdain.

Prince of Light.
But why should this stir up thy hellish rage,
If I in love am moved to engage
The precious Soul, and her betroth to me,
What wrong can that (vile monster) do to thee?
Thy horrid pride hath wrought thy overthrow,
And thou wouldst fain have her be damned too.
But know this Match in Heav'n's made, & thy hand
Can not prevent nor break this Sacred Band.

Apollyon.
She's preingag'd to one, whom I do Love,
And I concern'd am; for 'twas I did move
The question to her, did first the Contract make,
And I'm resolv'd she never shall it break.
The party too is my own offspring dear,[66]
And I to him most true Affections bear;
And reason there is for't, 'twas he alone
Founded my Kingdom, and first rais'd my Throne.
'Tis he who every where doth for me stand,
Yea and maintains my Cause in every Land.
My Subjects he brings in both great and small;
Without his Aid soon would my Kingdom fall.
And if this contract should be broke, I see
But little Service more can he do me.
Blame me not therefore, if I grow inrag'd,
And thus in furious battel am engag'd.

Prince of Light.
Thou canst not hide from me thy curst design,
Most horrid hatred is that love of thine.
Thou seek'st her life, her blood, nought else will do
But her most desperate final overthrow.
I likewise see how the sad game is laid,

How she by treacherous Loves to *Sin's* betraid:
But I that League resolve to break asunder,
Dissolve your Charms, & quickly bring thee under;
Although I know thou art a Son of Thunder.
I'le spoyl all your designs, and make appear
That only I that Soul do love most dear.
I'le spill my dearest blood upon the Ground,
But your Infernal Plots I will confound.
I am her friend, and will so faithful prove,
That all shall say I'm worthy of her love.
My Life is in my hand. I le lay it down
E're she shall miss of the Eternal Crown.[67]
Thou damned art, and wouldst (I fully know)
Bring her into the same eternal wo:
But know, vile Fiend, 'tis more than thou canst do,
Unless thou can'st this day prevail o're me,
Those dreadful Torments she shall never see.

  At this *Apollyon's* parched Lips did quiver,
These words, like darts, struck through his heart and liver,
He gnaw'd his very tongue for pain and wo,
And stampt, and foam'd, and knew not what to do,
Till e're a while, like to a Lyon bold,
Upon his Spear he furiously takes hold,
And doth the second time the Lord engage,
With greater violence and fiercer rage.
As when loud Thunder roars, and rends the Skie,
Or murdering Cannons let their Bullets fly:
So did he cause as 'twere the Earth to quake,
When he at him the second time did make;
And by the force of his permitted power,
Snatches him up, as if he would devour
Him, like the prey which hungry Lyons eat;
But not prevailing, down he did him set
Upon a Pinacle 'oth Temple high,
And then again upon him does let fly:
But finding he no hurt to him could do,
He strives him headlong down from thence to throw
Pretending if he were so great an one,
His foot could not be dasht against a Stone.
But then our Prince did draw his Sword again,
Not doubting in the least he should obtain
Another victory against this foe;
And did indeed give him so great a blow,
That he fell down, being forced to give ore,
And shamefully retreated, as before.[68]

Now would one think the Battel quite were done,
And time for the black Prince away to run:
But he reviv'd, and did fresh Courage take;
As men would do, when all doth ly at stake,
And a third Battel was resolv'd to see,
What ere the fatal Consequence might be.
Apollyon now to his last shift was driven,
Almost of all his Magazine bereaven.
But one poor Weapon more he had to try;
If worsted there, resolved was to fly.
And here indeed God suffer'd him once more
To take him up, as he had done before.
Ah! twas a sight most dismal to behold,
What foe was e're thus impudently bold!
That so was bafled, forced to retreat,
And found his Enemie too wise and great
A thousand times for him, yet would essay
By force of Arms to carry him away.
Don't Heaven and Earth, and all amazed stand
To see the Prince of Light in Satan's hand,
Or rather in his Arms carry'd on high,
As if he would have kill'd him secretly;
But on a mighty Mountain him he set,
Hoping he might some great advantage get;
A cunning Stratagem he did devise,
Thinking thereby our Saviour to surprize,
And him 'orecome by subtile Policy,
And that was to present unto his Eye
The Glory of this World, the only Snare
By which poor Mortals often ruin'd are.
This Hellish Prince is full of Craft and Wiles,
And with's inventions all the World beguiles.
From him the Politick *Achitophel,*[69]
And our more modern famous *Machiavel,*[70]
With other States-men learn't their puzling Arts   }
To plague the World, that Science he imparts,   }
To imbroil Nat'ions, and cheat honest Hearts.   }
Sly Stratagems in War, most wise men know
Have oft prevail'd, where Force no good could do.
The Walls sometimes of Castles down do fall,
When n'ere a Bullet hath been shot at all,
Unless discharged from a Silver Gun;
Thousands (alas!) this way have been undone,
Strong Citties Gates (we know) have open'd been
With Golden Keyes, and Enemies let in,
Which force nor strength could ne're have made to fly,
Nor been broke down by fiercest Battery.
The *Maxime's* true, which frequently we read,

That Policy doth very far exceed
The Strength and pow'r of great & haughty Kings;
And to subjection mighty Nations brings.
But all the Strength, nor Craft, nor power either,
Which Satan hath with all his fiends together,
Could with this Glorious Lord prevail i th least,
Who hath the strength of Heaven to assist,
And was himself Omnipotent in power:
Doth Satan think he can a God devour?
Can fading Glories of vile Earth intice,
Or break his purpose off, when Paradise
Could not upon him any Influence have,
To turn his love from her he came to save?

     How soon deep Policy is overthrown,
And crafty fraud to foolish madness come!
Art thou, *Apollyon*, such a wretched Sot?
Hast thou no other Bait, nor weapon got?
Is this thy wit, and can'st thou do no more
Than give him that which was his own before?
How prodigal thou seem'st? wilt thou bestow
At once on him all Kingdomes here below?
What then will all thy flattered Subjects do?
If thus thou rashly giv'st them all away,
What wilt thou do thy self another day?
What! is poor *Soul* worth more than all the world?
That all thou hast shall thus away be hurld,
Rather then thou of *Soul* would'st be bereav'd?
'Tis time for her to see she ben't deceiv'd.
What! all the Kingdoms of the world! Pray who
Did give them all, or any unto you?
Ah! what a Traytor's here! Is't not a shame
Before thy Soveraign's face to make a Claim
Unto those Kingdoms, where thou hast no right?
Thou know'st they do belong to'th Prince of light.
Thine if thou call'st them, 'tis by Usurpation,
No other right hast thou to any Nation.
     But we discourse too long: behold a sight,
Apollyon rallies all his scattered might.
Now nothing else than a full Conquest will
The haughty Wretch his wild Ambition fill.
How fain would he Majestick Steps have trod,
And worship'd be, nay worship'd by a God?
But the wise *Prince of Light* doth straight advance
To check his bold and vain Extravagance,
Declares his pow'r and shakes the awfull Rod,
Thou shalt not (what?) *tempt* (who?) *the Lord thy God?*
This well-plac'd stroak did Satan quite confound;

He cannot stay, yet's loth to quit the ground.
But seeing that he needs must now be gone;
Looks back, and grins, and howling, thus goes on.[71]

Apollyon.

Although I find thou art for me too strong,
Yet I'le revenged be, for all the wrong
I have sustain'd, either on thee or thine;
For which the powers of Hell shall all combine,
T' engage thee in another sort of Fight,
Although at present I am bafled quite,
Moreover, this I further have to say,
So long as thou dost in this Country stay,
Be sure of troubles thou shalt have thy fill,
I'le sett my Servants on thee, and they will,
By help from me, add sorrows to thy dayes,
Strew all thy Paths with Thorns, and cross thy ways.
I le render thee as odious as I can,
That thou mayst be disown'd by every man.
What I, and all Infernal Powers can do,
To make thee miserable, or o'rethrow
The great Design, which thou art come about,
We are resolved now to work it out.
And though thou thinkst this *Soul* for to obtain,
I tell thee now I have her in my Chain;
And doubt not but I there shall hold her fast,
Till tired out, thy love be over-past.
Nay let me tell thee further in thine Ear,
She unto thee doth perfect hatred bear:
Thee, nor thy Portion doth she like at all,
Although for her thou dost thy self inthrall,
And into Troubles and afflictions bring:
What wise man ever would do such a thing?
What love, where thou no love art like to have,
Tho thou the same a thousand times shouldst Crave?
If this proves not most true, then me you shall
The Father of Lies[72] hereafter Justly call.
Boast not this Conquest, though I go my way,
I'le meet the better Arm'd another day.
A hideous Clap[a] of Thunder then was heard,
And streight the cursed Spirit disappeard.

CHAP. IIII.

Shewing what joy there was in Heaven amongst the Angels, upon the great Victory obtained over the black King. Shewing also how affectionately in a sweet heavenly manner, the Prince of light after this saluted the Soul he came to save, for whose sake he had passed throw[a] *all these sorrows. And how the ungrateful blind & deluded wretch slighted and dispised him in her Heart; choosing rather to bearken to, and side with* Apollyon, *King of Darkness, and to entertain the Monster of pollution, sensual Lusts, than to become a Spouse to so glorious a Prince; pretending she knew him not, neither would she believe he was the son of God, the blessed and eternal Potentate; demanding signs of him. Shewing upon this what strange and wonderful Miracles he wrought amongst the people, who notwithstanding all, went about to kill him. And how he*[b] *was forc'd to fly from one Country to another, to preserve his life. And what hardships and difficulties he passed through, for love he bore to the poor Creature.*

NO sooner had this Overthrow been given,
But Troops of Angels did descend from Heaven,
Unto this Prince with great Congratulation,
Yeilding to him all humble Adoration.
Ah! how the glorious *Seraphims* did sing,
Bringing fresh Bayes of Triumph to their King.[73]
They come to serve him, as was just and right,
Because his En'emy he hath put to flight.
Let Heaven rejoyce, and Earth resound his praise,
For victory or'e him, who did always
Disturb the Earth, and whom none could withstand;
Such was his strength and force in ev'ry Land.
Now might one hope the Prince from trouble's freed
And quickly will in his Affairs succeed,
Wherein he hath such great obstructions met,
Since first his feet upon the Earth were set,
Kindly he now doth the poor *Soul* salute,
And with such fervency begins his suit;
And in such sort he did himself declare
That none in Woing could with him compare.
No Orator on Earth like him could speak,
So powerfully, and sweet enough to break
And melt a breast of Steel, or heart of Stone,
If well his words be weigh'd and thought upon.
He to this purpose doth salute her Ears
Some times with sighs, sometimes with bitter tears.

Prince of Light.

Look unto me, dear Soul! behold 'tis I,
Who lov'd thee deeply from Eternity;
Who at at thy doors do stand, oh let me in,

And do not harken to that Monster, *SIN*.
Refuse me not, because my thoughts descend
Below themselves, so far to recommend
My dearest Love to thee; although that I
No Beauty can at all in thee espy:
I love not as your Earthly Lovers doe;
'Tis Beauty that engages them to woo,
Or the great Portion, or the Vertuous mind:
There's none of these in thee that I can find.[74]
Yet my Affections burn, and Love's so much,
No mortal ever did experience such.
Why dost thou frown? Ah doth thy hardned Brow,
Not made at first to wrinkle, wrinkle now?
I am a Person of no mean Degree,
Although my heart is fixt and set on thee.
My Father, who hath sent me, is most high;
He rules above, and all beneath the Sky.
All Kingdoms of this World they are his own,
Whether inhabited, or yet unknown.
To this great Monarch (*Soul*) I am most dear,
What ere he has is mine, I am his Heir,
His choice Delight, his Joy, and only Son,
Moreover, He and I am only one.
My Father is in me, in him am I,
And was with him from all Eternity.
There's many Mansions in his House,[75] and there
Of all Delight thou shalt enjoy thy share.
I'le raise thee unto Honour and Renown,
And arch thy Temples with a radiant Crown:
In Robes of State I'le clothe thee every day,
All glorious within shall thy Array
Be wrought of finest needle-work so bright,
As shall transcend and dazle mortals sight.[76]
Then clear thine Eyes, and purifie thy Mind,
Accept my Love, and to thy self be kind,
All these Advantages thou sure shalt find.
But oh! such stubborn dulness who can bear?
This *Soul* seem'd not to mind, or lend an Eare
To any thing the Lord did thus declare;
But lay like one a sleep or rather dead,
Being by other Lovers falsely led.
She rather entertains him with a scoff,
And frames Slight Answers for to put him off;
Would not believe he was of such descent;
His sighs, nor Tears, could move her to relent,
But joyns in League with other bitter Foes,
Who did contemptuously his Grace oppose.
Signes they demand, and tokens to be given,

To make it known that he was sent from Heaven.
He graciously to this did condescend,
That from Reproach he might himself defend,
To manifest he no Deceiver was,
Strange things in sight of all he brought to pass:
The Miracles he wrought did all amaze,
And highest wonder in the People raise.
The Lame and Impotent he made to walk,
The Blind he caus'd to see, the Dumb to talk;
Nay, such as were born blind, he made to see;
Which never any did, nor could, but he.[77]
His Love was such, he daily went about
To find the Sick, and the Distressed out.
All kind of sad Diseases he did heal;
No Friend like him unto the Common-weal.
The *Feaver*,[78] *Phrensy*, and the *Leprosy*,[79]
Were all remov'd by him most speedily;
Yea, *Bloody-fluxes* too by him were cur'd,
When all the Doctors could no help afford:
Though all they had were on *Physicians* spent,
Yet whole by him they all were *gratis* sent.[80]
'Twas meer Compassion, Bowels,[81] and sweet Love,
And not Reward, did this *Physician* move.
By these bless'd deeds he soon obtain'd a Name,
And all the Country *Eccho'd* with his Fame,
So that vast multitudes did daily croud
After Him, and implore his Help aloud.
Poor wretches who with *Devils* were possest;
And sorely griev'd, could see no hopes of rest,
Were all deliver'd by his mighty Hand.[82]
Such Pow'r had he Hell's power to Command,
That if he said, *Satan, come out*, straight-way
He forced was this Prince for to obey.
Thus as with smallest touch he heal'd their Evils,
He with a word *cast out* the foulest *Devils*.[83]
Nay, more than this, that he might quite remove
All doubts from her he did so dearly love,
That she might know he power had to save,
He *rais'd the dead to Life*, though in the Grave
The Corps had buried been full four days;
This very thing must needs his Glory raise.[84]
He still went on, and more strange things did do,
Though very few to him did kindness show.
Is it not plain he can do what he list,
Who holds the mighty Winds as in his fist?
He that gave bounds unto the Sea and Land,
What is not in his Power to command?
He that doth suck the Clouds out of the Seas,

And makes them fall again where e're he please;
He that doth brake th' amazing Thunder Crack,
And bid the raging frightful Seas go back;
That doth the dreadful angry Ocean still,
And call Heavn's Meteors to obey his Will;
That counts the Sands, and doth the Stars survey,
And Hills and Mountains in a Ballance weigh;
No other Name for him can be Assign'd,
But God most high, *Jehovah* unconfin'd.[85]
The precious Name, which to this Prince is given,
Shews who he is, he's call'd *The Lord from Heaven.*
Another Title doth the same express
He is *Jehovah, our Righteousness.*
Do not his Works, and his most glorious Name,
His blessed Nature unto all proclaim?
Shall not the Soul this gracious Lord receive?
Who worketh Wonders, that she may believe.
Sure if the Soul did doubt of his descent,
She now has cause with sorrow to repent.
The vilest *Atheist* it might satisfie,
Touching his glorious Birth and Dignity;
But not withstanding this those Evil men
In most base sort did this great Prince contemn:
Him impiously they grand Impostor[a] call,
And with foul Blasphemies upon him fall.
Though in his life there was no stain nor spot,
Yet they would needs his Conversation blot:
Behold, said they, *a person gluttonous!*
You seldom read of any charged thus.
But that's not all, *Drunkenness* next did they
Unto the charge of this Just Person lay.
They did him often a *Wine-bibber* call,[86]
That odious they might render him to all.
His holy Doctrine too they did despise,
And horrid things on that Account devise,
As if he taught all men to violate
God's holy Law, and thereby tolerate
All kind of sin, pollution, and offence;
Though of the Law he had such reverence,
As none had more, and daily shew'd his Love
Unto the same, in striving to remove
Those false and evil Glosses, whereby they
Its purer spiritual part had thrown away.
His Company and Country they upbraid,
Yea, and the Education which he had.
But that which may all persons most amaze,
Was those Reports which they of him did raise,
As if that he some curs'd Familiar had.

They cry, *he hath a Devil, and is mad:*[87]
When he the unclean spirits does cast out,
By th' Prince of Devils he brings it about;
Those strange and wondrous things we see are done,
Are all perform'd by *Belzebub* alone.[88]
Thus did *Apollyon* shew his hellish spight,
And them to coyn Black-slanders still invite,
Against this glorious Prince of Peace and Light.
But though they did blaspheme, and him disdain;
He bore it all, reviling not again;
But still retains his kindness, hopes to find
The Soul hereafter in a better mind.
For now he saw she was of sense bereav'd,
And by the Devil grievously deceiv'd.
But oh! consider what a Lover's here,
Who all these oft-repeated wrongs would bear,
And not be gone in fury and disdain,
Leaving her subject to Eternal pain.
To suffer thus in's Person, and his Name,
And undergo all this Reproach and Shame,
And yet continue constant in his Love,
This from her breast might sure all scruple move;
Nor was this all, for still he's tost about,
And Malice daily finds new projects out,
How to torment and grieve his tender heart,
Yet nothing could from her his kindness part.
They now with slie temptations on him set,
To draw him in, and some Advantage get.
This with kind Anger curdled[a] his blest Blood,
To see how stoutly they withstood their good.
It fill'd his Heart with sorrow, made him grieve,
They so hard-hearted were not to believe;
Tho he most mighty works among them wrought,
Yet to ensnare him they occasions sought.
Their tempting him, I find did grieve him more,
Than all the vile Affronts he met before.[89]
      Here might I stop, to reason with the *Jews*,
Who him deny, and slight the Gospel news.
May not his Miracles convince you quite,
He was the true Messias, *Prince of Light*;
How dare you to deny matter of Fact,
That he those great and mighty things did act?
For they were not in private Corners done,
But before all, in open face 'oth Sun.
Your Fathers might with ease laid o'pe the cheat,
Shame the Imposture, and the plot defeat,
If any grounds they had for to decry,
The Man himself, or his strange works deny.

Besides (you know) *Josephus* he doth own,
There was at that same time such a blest One,
And for him had so great a veneration,
That thus I find of him he makes Relation:
In the time of Tiberius's *Reign* (saith he)
One JESUS liv'd, a Man (if 't lawful be
To call him so) for He strange things did do,
Yea mighty Miracles[90] – This Records show.
But you perhaps in your forefathers stead,
Are apt to think he by the Devil did
Those great and wondrous things of which we read.
Now this is so absurd, ridiculous,
And vain, 'tis strange men should be cheated thus.
Can any think the God o'th Universe
Would be unfaithful, as to change the course
Of Nature, meerly to assert a Lye?
What Odium here is thrown on's Majesty!
Could Satan all these real Wonders do,
He all Religion quickly might o're-throw:
The foulest Errors make the world believe;
And him for the true God men would receive.
This is to set the Devil in God's place,
And bring the Holy One into Disgrace;
T' ascribe his glorious Attributes to one
That fain would be exalted in the Throne.[91]
What Help or Touchstone then can Mortals have,
Their precious Souls from Satan's wiles to save,
If real Miracles perform he can?
This too would show God mindless were of Man:
And *Moses* who in *Egypt* Wonders wrought,
Might into Shame and great contempt be brought;
If this once granted be, which you would have,
Moses of old your Fathers might deceive.
Why might not he by th' Devil's power do
Those mighty Miracles, which Scriptures Show
He wrought in *Egypt*, and at the Red-Sea?[92]
Against your Law 'twould be as strong a plea,
And thus both Testaments 'twould throw away.
To the Magicians could the Devil have given
Such power as *Moses* had receiv'd from Heaven,
He would such equal works have made appear;
None should have cry'd, *The finger of God is here.*[93]
But now as *Moses* did this way confute
His faithless foes, who did with him dispute,
By greater deeds, and all their Arts o're-throw,
The self-same thing did *JESUS* also do.
The Strongest Arguments he then did use,
For to convince the unbelieving *Jews*,

Were the great Signs & wonders which he wrought,
And did this way refell what e're they thought,
Against his Person, or his Doctrine either,
And they thereby were silenc'd all together:
My works, saith he, *to me do witness give,*
And for their sake you ought me to believe.
For if that I such mighty works do'nt do,
As none e're did or can pretend unto,
Believe me not: but if they witness give,
How unexcusable then will they you leave?
He also had a witness from Great *John,*
Besides his works which were divinely done;
And God himself from Heaven witness bore,
So great a witness ne're was heard before.
The written Word likewise this Truth did tell,
If they the same would have consider'd well:
And therefore *search the Scriptures,* Sirs, saith he,
For they are those which testifie of me.[94]
Thus every way you see the proofs are plain,
He was the true Messias you have slain,
Therefore repent you unbelieving *Jews*;
With fained scandals longer don't abuse
Your blessed Lord, nor's Gospel more refuse.
The dangerous troubles of the *Prince of Light,*
The scandals that he met with, and the spight;
The hatred by that *Soul* unto him shown,
Whom he design'd the Consort of his Throne;
Her weak pretences for this causeless scorn,
And with what wond'rous patience it was born!
How she receiv'd him with a scornful Brow,
We have in part set forth, and also how
By mighty Signs and Wonders he did prove
Both his divine Ascent, and matchless Love.

　　But now the *Reader* with attentive Ear,
And longing mind, desires, 'tis like, to hear
How the poor blinded *Soul* behav'd her now:
Does she not straight unto his Scepter bow?[95]
Doth she not yield, and readily consent
To close with him, and heartily repent
She ever did his precious Love abuse,
And such a Proffer wilfully refuse?
He ample proof and witness now hath given,
That he was sent down to her out of Heaven;
His Noble Birth, and Sovereign Dignity
Sure now she can't, nay dares not to deny:
What can she further say, I pray what more
Hath she to urge, to keep him out o'th Door?[96]
Or, has he left her, and will come no more?

What Prince would ever put up so much wrong,
Or wait upon a stubborn Soul so long?
Or who would ever make another tryal,
That has so often had such flat denyal?
Ah, no! he can't, his Love's so great and strong,
He hopes still to obtain her Love e're long.
See how with tears and sighs, and melting heart,
He woos, intreats, and doth his Love impart,
As one resolv'd he'l no denial have:
True Lovers press their suit ev'n to the Grave.

Prince of Light.

    Tis not Ungratefulness which yet can[a] change
My purpose, or my heart from thee estrange.
My strong Affections on thee are so fixt,
That nought has them remov'd, or come betwixt
My Soul and thine; but had I lov'd thy face,
And that alone, my kindness had giv'n place,
My slighted suit should long e're this have ended,
And never more on thee had I attended.
Or, did I love thee for thine Heav'nly Eye,
I then might court Angelick Majesty:
Or, if the smoothness of thy Whiter Brow
Could charm mine eyes, or mine affections bow
To outward Objects, pollisht Marble might
Have given as much content, as much delight.
No, no, 'tis neither brow, nor lip, nor eye,
Nor any outward thing I can espy,
That has or could surprize my tender heart:
I know thy Nature, who, and what thou art.
Nor is it Vertue in a homely Case;
Wherein lies hid much rich and precious grace,
Together rarely mixt, whose worth doth make
Me love the Casket for the Jewels sake:
'Tis none of this! My eye doth pierce within,
But nothing there can I behold but Sin.[97]
The reason of my Passion wholly lies
Within my Self, from whence it first did rise.
And though thou canst not it at present see,
Thou shalt, if thou wilt hearken unto me.
O come, poor Soul! and give me but thy heart,
And unto thee choice Love I will impart.
I come to call thee, and do call again:
O shall I not of thee my Suit obtain!
Dost not perceive what I for thee endure?
And may not all this thy Love to me procure?
    The Soul seem'd not at all to mind this Friend,
Nor would she yet to him attention lend:

She could not in him any beauty see,
Nor^a did she know her own sad misery.
She bid him then depart, and said to all,
He had no form nor comeliness. And shall
I 'gainst my fancy foolishly admire,
Where I no beauty see to tempt desire?[98]
      Whilst he was thus extending forth his Love,
And studying all obstructions to remove,
That so he might the Souls affections get,
Behold, his Enemies with malice set
Themselves against him with such horrid rage,
It seems no less than's ruin to presage.
Ah! for this Prince methinks my heart doth ake,
To see what head against him they do make.
But that which doth the greatest trouble bring,
Is to see th'Soul combine against the King.
Did ever creature deal thus by a Lover,
Or ever such inhumaneness discover?
What hurt did this dear Prince unto her do,
That she would seek his utter overthrow?
Is this to recompence his fervent Love?
What will she now a Traitor to him prove?
If she his Love will not accept, must she
Expose him thus to shame and misery?
Is love to Sin, and filthy Lust so sweet,
That *Jesus* must be trodden under feet?
Because he would that Contract break asunder,
This surely is Earth's shame and Heavens wonder.
What? he that went about still doing good,
And in the gap of danger always stood
Them to Defend from Ruin, ah! shall he
The object of their Rage and Malice be?
He that to them no harm did do or think,
And yet must he this bitter potion drink?
Ah, precious Lord! how doth my spirit grieve,
To think what wrong from them thou didst receive:
So strange their malice, and so fierce their spight,
That if God's Word did not the same recite,
Who there unto would any Credence give,
Or the Relation of their Deeds believe?
But, *how was he expos'd, what did they do?*
'Tis that (say some) that we would have you show.
Their hearts were fill'd with wrath, & up they rise,
And thrust him out o'th City: then devise
To get him up to th'brow of a great Hill,
And cast him headlong down, from thence they will
Break all his bones, and kill him out o'th way;
This they designed Holy Authors say.

Not that their Cruelty performed was,
For through the midst of them he free did pass.[99]
His Pow'r Divine did his Protector stand,
And rescued him from all this treacherous Band.
Again, as he stood tendering his Love,
Striving their vain Objections to remove,
That so they might not all be ruin'd quite,
And blind-fold led to shades of endless night.
The common Rabble in a Tumult got,
Threaten to kill him on the very spot;
With hearts more hard than stone, up stones they take,
And throwing, vow they'l his Sepulcre make:
By which cruel show'r of Flints he now must die,
Unless through them he's able to 'scape[a] by;
Which by his mighty Power indeed he did,
And carefully from them himself he hid:
And yet all this was on no other ground,
But because he their wisdom did confound:
'Cause he stood up the Truth to testifie,
And witness to his own Divinity:[100]
Because he said, he was sent down from Heaven,[101]
From Place to Place this Prince was daily driven.
No sooner were his feet out of one snare,
But ten i'th room thereof devised were.
Of killing him in *Jury*[102] was a talk,
To *Galilee* therefore he thought fit to walk:[103]
But staid not long, for to *Jerusalem*
He quickly went to shew himself to them:
And though he knew his Life they daily sought,
Yet in the Temple openly he taught,
And did again his Suit of Love renew,
Yet would the *Soul* no kindness to him shew.
Long had he not been here, but presently
The *Scribes* and *Pharisees* did him espy,
And straight agreed their Officers to send,
Him without any cause to apprehend:
But when they came, and did him see and hear,
Poor Souls! they all most strangely smitten were
With awful Reverence, and trembling fear!
Untoucht, they leave him, and return again
To tell their Masters, Violence was vain;
They highly spake in his just Commendation,
And told his Wonders, worthy Admiration.
Have you not brought him then? the Scribes do cry:
No Sirs, (alas) we see no reason why;
We never saw, nor heard the like: Who can
Lay hands on such a blest and God-like Man?[104]
         Thus did the Prince escape their Rage that day,
But other Snares *Apollyon* still did lay.

CHAP. V.

Shewing how the people of that Land in a base manner used John *the beloved servant of* Jesus, *the Prince of Light, who (for his Master's sake) was barbarously murthered; And how narrowly the Prince himself escaped. As also shewing how he again and again tendered his indeared love to the* Soul, *and how unkindly she denied his Suit. Moreover, how* Vicinius – *(a Neighbor) hearing of this great News, enquired of* Theologus *concerning the Creature this Prince in such a manner had set his affections upon. The miserable and deplorable condition of the* Soul *discovered and laid open, being infected with a loathsome Disease full of Vlcers and Running sores from head to foot, naked, wounded, and in her blood, her eyes also being put out; and this the Prince knew before he came from Heaven, his own Country: shewing, that as she was in her fallen state, she was the object of his love and desire.*

BEfore this Prince did in that Land appear,
His servant came his way for to prepare.
Such an Ambassadour he was indeed,
That we of him in Sacred Story read;
That of all those that born of Women are,
None was so great, nor with him might compare.[105]
Yet was the King of that same Land so bold,
As on this gracious Person to lay hold,
And into a vile Prison cast is he,
For witnessing against Iniquity.
Herod would marry one most near of Kin,
But *John* affirms that 'tis an horrid sin,
For him to have his Brother *Philip's* Wife:
And for asserting this, he lost his Life.
To please a wanton Harlots Dancing pride,
The Prophet's head from's body they divide.[106]
This doubtless did his Master greatly grieve,
To see they should him thus of *John* bereave;
His servant *John*, whom all the people own
To be a Prophet, yea a mighty one;
Though the chief work that he was sent about,
Was to describe and point this Saviour out.
He faithful was, and show'd his constant Love,
Told them his Prince descended from above:
So Great, in pow'r, the Latchets of his shoes
He was not worthy to unty, or loose.[107]
The loss of such a Servant needs must be
Great ground of sorrow. But, alas! If we
With care do mind what after came to pass,
We shall conclude with him much worse it was
For *Herod* now, like to his Predecessor,[108]
Proceeds from sin to sin, until no lesser
A Crime he does attempt, than for to kill
The *Prince of Light himself;* Thereby to fill

His measure up, as some before had done,
For seeking the dear Life of this Just one.
But of this Plot he had such Information,
As quite defeated their black Combination.[109]
Ah! to and fro, how was he daily hurld,
Whilst he abode in this ungrateful World.
His persecutions were so great, that He
Was often forced for his Life to flee,
To flit from Town to Town, from place to place;
For, Blood-hound like, they did him daily chase.
From *Jury*[110] to *Samaria* he did go,
And down from thence to *Galilee* below.[111]
From *Nazareth* he fled to *Capernaum*,[112]
And long he staid not when he thither came:
For he was tost about continually,
And found no Harbor nor security.
Sometimes quite beyond *Jordan* he would get,
Yet even there with dangers was beset.
Small Rest, alas, he had in full three years,
His days were fill'd with sorrow, sighs and tears,
Oft may we read he wept, but never find
He laught, or was to merriment inclin'd.
The Prophet said, *with grief he was acquainted,*[113]
When long before he forth his Person pointed.
And few there were did him at all regard,
So blinded were their Eys, their Hearts so hard.[114]
He was despis'd almost by every one,
Rejected scornfully and trod upon.
And the poor *Soul,* for Love of whom he came,
Expos'd him daily to the greatest shame
No countenance would she to him afford,
Although so high a Prince, so great a Lord.
She bid him hold his peace, his Suit desist,
And all's indearing proffers did resist.
No more would she vouchsafe his face to see,
But hid her self from him continually.
Far from his presence with delight she rouls
In filthy Puddles, and in Loathsom holes:
Nay, did combine with his most Cruel Foes,
To lay upon him stripes and bitter Blows;
To break his heart with often saying Nay;
Or by surprize him bloodily to slay.

Object.
But some may ask, *Why th' people of that Land*
Did rise against him thus on every hand?
Why should they manifest such causeless hate,
When he'd not injure them at any rate,

But sought their peace and everlasting good?
'Tis pity such a Prince should be withstood.

Answ.

One Reason, Sirs, of this their baneful spight,
Was meerly 'cause he was *the Prince of Light*.
'Twas from that bitter enmity you read
Between the Serpent's and the Woman's seed.[115]
Another cause of the Contempt they show,
Is 'cause they neither him, nor's Father know.
But that which most of all their Hatred breeds,
Is his reproving of their Evil deeds:
Because he did expose each horrid Sin,
Yea, and ript up their filthiness within:
Through each Religious Mask, and trim disguise,
Their canker'd Breasts lay open to his Eys.
He knew their Hearts, & them he would not spare,
And thence to him such Malice they did bear.
But 'twas *Apollyon*, (whose deceit and Lies
Abroad amongst the people did devise)   }
Most of these Troubles which on him did rise.
No stone that Monster left unturn'd, that he
Might bring this Soveraign Prince to misery,
Though all in vain: For he miscounts his sum,
Alas! the fatal hour's not yet come.
Christ still persists the stubborn Soul to woo,
Intreats her, not her self thus to undo.
He is not gone, behold, he's at her door,
And patiently Admission doth implore.
He knocks, he calls, and doth his Suit renew,
Until the Heavens his gracious Head bedew,
Until his Locks with drops o'th Night are wet,
And yet from her can no kind Answer get.[116]
Oh! hark I pray unto his melting words,
Enough to pierce ones heart, like sharpest swords.[117]

Prince of Light.

Soul! Harken to me or thou art undone,
I cannot leave thee thus, nor yet be gone,
I see thy state; thy state I pity too,
Thy treacherous Lovers seek thine overthrow.
It is in vain for me to ask thy Love,
Until thou breakst with them, and dost remove
Thy Heart from those that thy Affections have,
Who to vile Lusts thy Faculties inslave.
What dost thou think I can have in mine Eye?
What self-advantage will accrew thereby?
What gain I, if thou grantest my request?

All that I beg's thy greatest Interest.
I ever happy was, and so shall be,
Although at present thus distrest for Thee.
How can'st thou, cruel *Soul*, thus let me stand,
Barr'd out of Doors, whilst others do command
The choicest Room within thy yielding Breast,
Lodgings too good for such destructive Guests.
Believe me, poisonous Toads and Serpents[118] lurk
Within thine Arms, which will thy ruin work:
Those Lovers which thou keep'st so close within
Are Murderers. Trust not that Monster *SIN*,
Nor any of his Hellish Company;
For though no harm thou dost at present spy,
But wantonly presum'st to sport and play,
And canst not see the fatal snares they lay:
Soul! o'pe the Door, and I'le discover all
The secret Plots, devised for thy fall;
Or, push the Window back, let in some light,
And I will shew thee a most dismal sight:
Thy self I'le shew thee, which couldst thou behold,
Thou'dst see thou art undone, betray'd and sold
To slavery, from whence there's no Redemption,
Torments, from wch ther's not the least exemption,
Then wake, look now, behold thy wretched plight,
Or straight thour't seized with eternal Night.
　　　The *Soul* is deaf, or certainly she's dead,
Or by some pow'rful Magick Charms misled:
For she no Answer in the least doth give:
Sad 'tis with them whom Satan doth deceive.
　　　How blind are Creatures in their natural state?
Oh! how insensible and desperate!
They sleep securely, and will never hear,
Till direful Thunder bore their stupid Ear:
Boldly they frollick on Hell's smoaky Brink,
And never on its gaping dangers think,
Till swallow'd down, to endless flames they sink.

But silence now! Here comes a Reverend Friend,
A Servant to the Prince, pray, Sirs, attend:
He's sent about the Business that's depending,
Oh! that it might obtain an happy ending:
He is a man his Master loves most dear,
And he to him doth like Affection bear:
His int'rest he will now be sure t' improve,
That all obstructions he may quite remove,
Which in the way of the poor Soul doth lie,
For whose sad state, lo! tears stand in his Eye:
His Heart is full, his Spirit greatly griev'd,

To think how she by crafty Sin's deceiv'd,
And seeing what his glorious Master bears,
His Soul's almost dissolved into Tears.

Theologue.

I from the Great and mighty Prince am sent,
To see, vile Soul! If thou wilt yet repent,
And o'pe thy Eyes to view what thou hast done.
In piercing the dear heart of such an one,
As is that Soveraign Lord thou dost abuse,
And all his offers shamefully refuse.
Two things consider throughly: first of all,
Thy sad and wretched state under the Fall,
Which thou receivedst many years ago,
When *Eden's* Groves bewail'd thine overthrow.
Ah! Didst thou know thy lost undone Condition,
Sure it must move thee unto great Contrition;
'Twould make thee roar, and mightily condole
Thy woful state, O! thou condemned Soul!
    The second thing is this, O! mind with speed,
The worth of him whose Soul for thee doth bleed!
Didst thou but know his Dignity and Birth,
Soon wouldst thou say, *none's like him upon Earth.*
Nor is this all: for further I declare
No other help thou hast, far off, or near,
'Tis he who is thy choice and only Friend;
Reject him still, and sad will be thine end.
Shall he such grief and sorrow undergo?
And unto him wilt thou no kindness show?
Would he thy guilty Soul from Treason free,
By making of a marriage-League with thee?
Shall not his Love, nor thy distressed Case,
Court thee in prudence to his safe Embrace?
Will nothing work upon thee to Relent,
Nor be a means to bring thee to Repent?
I pray thee, Soul! these things lay to thy heart,
And unto me thy true Resolve impart.

Soul.

What mean you thus to vex and grieve my mind?
My Heart's to other Lovers more inclin'd.
It lies not in your power, to command
Against my will: and well I understand
What's best for me; I am for present ease:
He suits not my Conditions, doth not please
My curious fancy; I le content mine Eye.
Will you the liberty of Choice deny?[119]
You must indeed have some mysterious Arts,

To change the secret sympathies of Hearts:
If that you ever make me to comply,
So as to loath the Jewel of mine Eye.
What! force Affection? who can violate
The Law of Nature? weigh my present state:
Can Earth forget her burthen, and ascend?
Or yet, can Flames aspiring downward bend?
For if Fire should descend, and Earth aspire;
Earth were no longer Earth, nor Fire, Fire.
Even so, dear Sir! I find it is with me;
Consenting, I no more my self shall be.
As Love is free, so are its bonds as strong
As Death; to break them is a grievous wrong.
Can the kind Heavens do a damage greater,
Than to destroy and ruin their poor Creature?
Or, shall I think the Righteous God will fill me
With such strange Joys, which if enjoy'd, will kil me?
Can I believe things 'bove my sense and reason?
And ignorant be when guilty of high Treason?
How can I think my self a Criminal.
When of the fact I nothing know at all?
My present state is good, I know no cause
To blame my self for breach of unknown Laws.
Why shall injurious Friends such things alot,
To have me place my Heart where I love not,
And break the League with those I love so dear?
These hardships are too great for me to bear.
Those Joys therefore in which I have delighted,
Shall not for fancied sweetness e're[a] be slighted.
He whom you call *The glorious Prince of Light*,
Is not a person lovely in my sight;
He's not so modish, pleasant, Debonair,
As those brisk Gallants, whom my Fancy share.
I must have other Eys wherewith to see,
Before he can be countenanc'd by me.[120]

    This said, away the foolish Soul doth fly;
Will hear no more, but with a scornful Eye
Neglects her Bliss, & Deaths dark paths doth trace.
Rather than saving Truths of Life imbrace.
Who being gone, a Neighbour does appear,
That would be glad fully her Case to hear;
And that he clearly might have it exprest,
He thus himself *to Theologue* Addrest.

Vicinus.[121]

    Grave Sir! Since in your Reverend face I read
All works which do from Curtesy proceed,

I am emboldened to desire of you
Some satisfaction in a point or two.
I late have heard some Rumours of such News,
As puts my wondring spirits to a muse:
'Tis of a Prince unparallel'd for Love,
That took a Journey down from Heav'n above
To seek himself a Spouse; and as I hear
She unto him will no Affection bear,
Though for Descent, Riches and Beauty too,
Never the like did mortal Creatures know.
This Soul-amazing, Sense-bereaving story,
Has fill'd my ravisht Ears: What matchless Glory
Is his, whose Love is far beyond Expression?
And what Creature is this must have possession
Of such a glorious Heart? Sure she's no less
Than one of High Descent, some Emperess,
Or Virgin Queen at least, whose Beauty's rare,
Mixt with choice Vertue, both beyond compare:
The total sum doubtless of every Grace,
Makes a composure in her Heav'nly Face;
And there all true Perfection is united,
To make one Phœnix, that has thus invited
This mighty Prince to do her so much Honour,
As seek her Love and set his Heart upon her,
To sue so earnestly, and undertake
Mighty Atchievements only for her sake;
For to encounter with a wrathful Foe,
That sought an universal overthrow
Of mortal Creatures, and in every Land
Subjected all unto his proud Command.
The strangeness of it sets me all on fire,
And kindles in my heart a strange desire,
Impatient of delay, till you discover
The Creature that has got so rare a Lover.

Theologue.

To put a period to thy Admiration,
Come let thy Wonder-smitten Cogitation;
Now give attention, and I soon will show
The truth of what thou dost desire to know.
The Creature whom this mighty Prince doth grace
With Love, lives very near unto this place.
We all do her as our next Neighbour own;
Much is she talkt of, yet but seldom known,
You sure have heard before, she was by Birth
Of high descent, the splendor of the Earth,
Unblemisht Beauty, neither spot nor stain,
Whilst in her Virgin state she did remain.

To speak her pedigree, in Truth she springs
From no less Root than from the King of Kings:
Whom Scriptures call *The Father of all Spirits*;[122]
And none but he that Blessed Name inherits.
From him she did at first derive her Name,
And Heaven and Earth eccho'd her glorious Fame:
Fair *Cynthia*,[123] Illustrious Queen of Night,
With all her borrowed Rays, ne're shone so bright.
The King's true Image in her face did shine.
No Glory like to Glory that's Divine.
But that which doth the greatest Wonder raise,
And may the quick'st profoundest Wits amaze,
Is the sad change, and miserable state
She's in, since first she did degenerate;
Her Lustre tarnisht, and her Beauty faded,
Filth and Corruption every part invaded:
Oh! it was then on her this Prince did look,
When of her God and guide she was forsook:
For though she was indeed thus nobly born,
Her Blood is tainted, and her state forlorn.
She that in splendor once appear'd so bright,
Is now deform'd, and blacker than the Night.
Foul putrifaction doth her Beauty cover,
She's full of Ulcers, and defil'd all over,
Th' infection, spreads it self in every part,
Her eyes, her hands, her head, but most her heart;
Her feet, whose loyal steps she once divided
To follow the great God, have so backslided,
That they most swiftly from him run astray
In every sinful and forbidden way.
Her Arms are filled with unchast Embraces,
She's stain'd her Beauty, and lost all her Graces.
Her Breath once sweeter than *Arabian* Spices,
Whose rare Perfumes make Houses Paradises,
Offensive is to all that come but near her,
Her Tongue is so unclean, God loaths to hear her.
Which was her Glory in her youthful days,
When she with joy sung forth his blessed Praise.
But that which may found stranger in thine Ear,
And seem indeed too hard for Love to bear,
Is her Adult'ries, her unchast delights
Her Amorous Kisses, wherewith she invites
Her wanton Lovers; nothing else can prove
So much distastful to unspotted Love;
As when the Embers of Lusts raging fires
Burn in the Bosom of unchast desires.[124]

Vicinus.
But stay, Dear Sir! What Lover is't would kiss
A Creature loathsom, and so vile as this?
And how came she into so sad a Case,
That once adorned was with so much Grace?

Theologue.
If you kind Neighbour, please to lend an Ear,
These things in order I will fully clear.
Her Lovers are more loathsom far than she,
With whom she's joyned in Affinity.
From them she took the foul disease at first,
And ever since remains vile and accurst.
The Serpent did beguile her with such fruit,
As did her Vitals poison, and pollute.
Not that the fruit in 'moral sense was evil;
But 'cause she took it, tempted by the Devil,
After on pain of Death it was forbid:
Ah! t'was from hence it so much mischief did.[125]
Besides, she's guilty of another Deed,
She's made a League with one that did proceed
From Hell's black Region, where her wanton Eye
Could see no Object but Deformity;
A Contract she has made, I say, with one,
Begot by proud, but curs'd *Apollyon*;
Monstrous by Nature, and as vile by Name,
Ah! she has chosen him unto her shame:
His nature's poisonous, his very Breath
Is so infectious, that it threatens Death
To every one to whom he is united;
Yet with this Monster is her heart delighted:
Who to my Prince is a most desperate Foe,
And to speak plain, the cause of all his woe.
Since first the *Soul* was with base Lust acquainted,
From Top to Toe all over is the tainted.
She that was once so rare a comely Creature,
Sin has not left her now one lovely Feature.
The Splendid Beauty of the whole Creation,
Is thus become a meer Abomination.
For since her self to Lust she prostituted,
Her inward Faculties are so polluted,
That she's become unto *Jehovah*'s Eye,
The truest pourtraict of Deformity.
She that sometimes no Evil understood,
Is now become an Enemy to Good:
For this vile Monster by *Apollyon*'s pow'r,
Did not only corrupt the Soul all ov'r,
But very cruel they did further prove,

Whilst they pretended kindnesses and Love;
For they most wickedly put out her Eyes,
She might not see her own Deformities:
And being thus both blinded, and defil'd,
Was also rob'd, and treacherously spoil'd
Of all the Jewels which her Soveraign gave her,
Whilst she remained in his Love and favour;
Of all her goodly Vestments they bereft her,
And stript her naked, she had nothing left her.
Nothing to hide her shameful nakedness,
But filthy Rags, how loathsom you may guess.
Besides all this, they wounded her full sore,
And left her sadly weltring in her Gore,
Expecting Death each moment she did lie,
A loathsom spectacle to passers by,
Unhelpt, unpitied too by every Eye. }
Each humane Soul that is not born again,
In this sad state doth certainly remain.[126]
The rich, the poor, the wise, the old, the young,
Though ne'r so high, so beautiful and strong
They seem, or think themselves, in truth they are
In as bad Case as we've described here.

Vicinus.
    Sir! You have fully answer'd my Desire;
Yet let me be so bold as to inquire
One passage more, since happily I see
You can inform all such as ign'rant be
Of these weighty Affairs; blest be the Lord
That so much Wisdom doth to you afford.
O! that there were more of you in our Land,
That to the Truth might always faithful stand.
But tell me, if it mayn't too tedious prove,
Whether this Prince that manifests such Love, }
Knew her sad state when he came from above?
Did he her filthy bad Condition know
Before he came from Heaven, or did show
That precious kindness which his Breast retain'd
Unto her, even after she was stain'd?
May be his Eye upon the Soul was plac'd,
Before God's Image in her was defac'd:
And as consider'd so, then doubtless he
Might find some Cause to her so kind to be.
But, if as she did in pollution lie,
And so consider'd, he did cast his Eye
Upon the Creature; then I must declare
It may astonish all that of it hear.

Theologue.

The Question you propound is very good;
And would t' were throughly weigh'd and understood.
The Answer's easy; But I greatly fear
Some mind it not enough, who chosen are.
Before the World was made he fully knew
Ev'n what below would afterwards insue:
He knew the Creature, *Man*, would sin and fall,
And in sad misery himself inthral.
The time therefore when first he cast an Eye
To be her Suiter, (our Security)
It was not when she did her Grace inherit,
Then one would think she might his favour merit;
'Twas not when she was in prosperity,
But when she in her Blood and filth did lie.
Her time of sorrow, was his time of Love,
Her misery did bring him from above.
Whilst she in actual bold Rebellion lives,
His Grace and offer'd Pardon then he gives.[127]

Vicinus.

Sir! You have said enough, I am amaz'd,
Strange wonderment within my Spirit's rais'd.
The nature of his Love who can conceive?
Such Love as this no mortal Creatures have.
I pray go on, and further now let's know
Concerning her estate, her Bliss, or Woe.

Theologue.

You'l find it worse and worse; and what's behind
Will strange Impressions make upon your Mind:
For now you'l hear what Justice has to say,
What horrid Crimes he to her charge will lay.
And though she seems undaunted without fear,
Once more I'e[a] try if she will lend an Ear.

CHAP. VI.

Shewing how Theologue, *the Prince's Spokesman, indeavour'd to obtain the love of this poor Creature for his blessed Master, by whom the aggravation of the Creatures sin and misery is layed open; the Soul is in debt ten thousand Talents, worse than nothing. Moreover, shewing how the Creature was guilty of high Treason against the Soveraign Lord* Jehovah; *is also Arraigned and condemned to be burned alive. A Dialogue or discourse between the Divine Attributes: Justice cryes for Execution, to have the fatal blow struck; Mercy steps in. Justice must be satisfied. Goodness and Mercy will not lose their Glory, being alike esteemed by God. Divine Wisdom recon-*

ciles all the other Attributes, and makes them meet together in a sweet harmony: the
Soul being condemned to die, the Prince sees no other way to obtain her for his own,
but by satisfying Justice, and becoming Surety, and yielding himself up to die for her.

Theologue.

HOW is it Soul! art minded yet to leave
Thy Lusts, and Lovers, and to Jesus cleave?
Dost not perceive the sad state thou art in
By curs'd *Apollyon*, and his off-spring, *SIN?*
Wilt thou for evermore thy self destroy,
And not accept of Health? wilt not enjoy
One who in value doth all Worlds excel?
Wilt thou refuse in Paradise to dwell?
Dost see thy state, thy bloody state? oh speak!
My bleeding heart for thee doth greatly ake.

Soul.

You had my Answer plain enough before:
Forbear, I pray, and trouble me no more.
I do'nt believe what you have said is true;
Such pains I never felt, nor sickness knew:
But if my state were worse than yet I see,
I will not have you thus to trouble me.
I have all things which naturally delights me,
And from them you shall not deter, nor fright me;
You know the Proverb used in our Land,
Each Tub shall upon its own Bottom stand.[128]

Theologue. [a]

Soul, b'not[b] so rash, be more considerate;
Ponder on things before it be too late.
Sith what I said before no good can do,
More of thy wretchedness I now will show;
And if that fails, then afterwards I'le leave thee,
And o're into the hands of Justice give thee.
    First, from God's Word I have Authority
To lay before thee thy great poverty.
Thy Soveraign Lord most highly is distasted
For all the precious Treasure thou hast wasted.
First, of his Glory thou hast him bereav'd,
And to rebel against him been deceiv'd.
Next, thy whole self to him 'tis thou dost owe,
Yea all thou either art, hast, or canst do,
Which thou hast not regarded hitherto:
But to thy self, and not to him dost live,
Who did thy self at first unto thee give,
And from whom thou dost ev'ry thing receive.
Thy knowledge, judgment, and thy memory,

Th' excellent nature of each Faculty,
Should all have to, and for him, been laid out,
As being all his Goods; *Soul!* look about,
For time, for Health, and for the day of Grace;
Thou must be brought before the Judge's Face:
And for thy[a] Riches, and all things thou hast,
Which thou Imbezel'st, and dost vainly wast,
A strict Account must at the Bar of Heaven
By thee in a short time be surely given.
Ten thousand Talents doth thy God demand;
Which thou canst neither pay, nor yet withstand
His dire proceedings, 'cause he is most Just,[129]
And thou but sinful Ashes and vile Dust.[130]
Thou wilt be seiz'd, and in a Prison laid,
Till the last Mite be satisfi'd and paid.
Canst thou, poor Soul! dost think quit the old score,
When thou contractst new debts still more & more?
Would not a Friend that's able to defray
All thy vast Debts, and a full Ransom pay
To thy just Creditor, most welcom be,
If such an one could be found out for thee?
But things yet worse, I fear, there are behind,
The truth of which most certainly thoul't find.

      Hark, trembling Soul! thou to the Bar art cited,
And for high Treason there dost stand Indicted,
Committed by thee 'twas in antient time,
When thou didst dwell in *Eden*, in thy prime:
When thou hadst flourisht there but a short season,
Thou didst contract that guilt of horrid Treason
Against thy Soveraign, in whose Princely Eye
Was Grace and favour mixt with Majesty:
Gracious to pardon many great Offences,
And yet severe to punish Insolences.
But thou both Grace and Justice didst despise,
And in thy Heart didst evil things surmise
Against thy Soveraign Lord, and secretly
Join'st with his Foes in close Conspiracy.
'Twas with the King of Darkness thou didst close,
Obeyd'st his will, and didst thy God oppose.
A dreadful Sentence then against thee past,
Which ne're by humane Art could be reverst.
Thy Sentence was in Prison long to lie,
And for thy fact at last Condemn'd to die.
And Death on thee did seize the self-same time,
When thou commitst that high and fearful Crime;
The sad effects of it I this Day see,
Thou still ly'st dead in thine Iniquity.
Ah! I may preach untill my heart doth ake,

And it on thee will no Impression make.
Thou art depriv'd of Life and Light of God,
And long hast thou in this estate abode.
But a worse Death doth in thy Sentence lie,
(Though very few on it will cast an Eye)
Condemn'd to suffer everlasting pains,
And on thee then were fastned heavy Chains.
And though thy Execution be delay'd,
Yet 'tis by means of Jesus only stay'd.
His precious Grace preserves thee from that fire,
Whose torments once begun, shall ne'r expire.
That Soul-amazing Sentence who can bear
The thoughts of it, and not let fall a tear?
What Malefactors are Condemn'd to die,
But on the sense of Death's approaching nigh,   }
Contracts not horrour on their Souls thereby?
What then to suffer Death for evermore,
Where Torments ne're abate, nor will be o're?
To be a thousand tedious Ages Rackt,
Not Dead, yet always in the dying Act.
A fiery Furnace with a sevenfold heat
We read of,[131] yet its flames were not so great,
But that they soon would languish and grow cold,
Whereas these Tortures, still increasing, hold.
If e're thou shouldst be cast into that place,
Before thou dost take hold of Love and Grace,
There's this will then thy sorrows aggravate,
None will thee pity in that wretched state.
Never was Malefactor in distress,
But met with pity either more or less;
And though it do not take away the grief,
Yet where there's pity, there's some small Relief.
But if thou dost this fearful Sentence bear,
There's none to pity, none to shed a tear.
O think of this, alas! thy wretched Eyes
Are blinded now, thou basely dost despise
The best of Comfort, Joy and Consolation,
For love to Sin, horrid Abomination!
Thou swell'st in pride, unmindful of thine end,
And seest no need of comfort[a] from a Friend:
But what wouldst thou for such a Friend then give,
And for those Comforts thou mayst now receive?
Dost not thou tremble at this frightful news?
Tremble at least at that which next ensues.
Three things there are, three Circumstances great,
Which much thy final woe will aggravate:
Which severally unto thee I'le relate,
That thou mayst think upon thy future state.

First, from thy high Descent thy birth did crown
Thee with the greatest Honour and Renown,
That ever any had upon the Earth,
Thou being own'd a Soveraign Queen by Birth.
Yet that which did so much advance thy fame,
Was not alone the Honour of thy Name,
As the rare properties of thy sweet Nature,
A most transcendent and accomplisht Creature;
An Heav'n-composed frame, as if thou'dst bin
Deriv'd from some Celestial *Seraphim*.
When great Jehovah's fruitful Word had made
The whole Creation, touching thee, he said,
This Creature shall alone our Image bear,
Whom all things else shall reverence and fear;[132]
Our Sacred Portraiture we solely place,
In this sweet Creatures Heaven-erected face.
And when he sent his first-begotten down,
No other form or Image must he own.
The Angels Nature wholly he refuses,
And rather Humane Soul and flesh he chuses.[133]
Alas! there's not a greater aggravation,
Than for a person of the highest station
To be thrown down into the deep'st Abyss
Of woe and sorrow! oh! how sad is this?
Thy self caus'd change a miserable Creature,
Will surely make thy Torments far the greater.
    The second Circumstance of Aggravation,
Is worthy of thy serious observation.
And that I may more fully make it known,
Under two Heads I'le briefly lay it down.
First, from the timely notice that was given,
By thy most Soveraign Lord, the King of Heaven,
When with his glorious Image he had grac'd thee,
And in fair *Eden*'s fruitful Garden plac'd thee;
Ordain'd thee Mistress of that famous Bower,
Where thou mightst see his Glory every hour;
Granting whatever might accommodate
Thy pure perfect spotless Virgin state;
Excepting one reserved Fruit alone,
Which did indeed of Right belong to none
But to himself; that hidden Mysterie,
Which in the midst of Paradise did lie;
To know what Evil was as well as Good,
Which never could by men been understood,
But by an Art of the most horrid Evil,
And hearkning to, and siding with the Devil;
The dire effects to thee were told most plain,
The danger and the loss thou shouldst sustain;

The loss[a] of Life, the loss of *Eden*'s Glory,
The loss of God; a lamentable Story.
Warning was giv'n, God strictly did require,
On pain of Death, thou shouldst not once desire,
Nor tast, nor touch, nor cast a longing Eye
Upon this fatal Fruit, which certainly
Would straight procure thy final overthrow:
This timely notice shall augment thy Woe.
Fore-warn'd, fore-arm'd, you know we use to say:
Thou wast fore-warn'd, and yet didst go astray.
Contemptuous Soul! alas, how couldst thou think
The mighty God would at Rebellion wink?
Though he is said to wink at Ignorance,
Presumption is a different Circumstance.
Thou knew'st[b] before-hand if thou didst trangress,
Assured Death would follow, and no less;
The Lord had said it, he that gave us breath,
Said, *thou shouldst die*, & yet thou feardst not Death.
This is the height, as well as spring of Evil,
To doubt and mistrust God, yet trust the Devil.
Against God's sacred Truth to shut ones Eyes,
And credit blindfold th' Father of all Lies.
Ah Soul! 'twas listning to a wanton lust,
That was the cause thou didst at first distrust
The glorious Lord, and falsely to surmise,
He was unwilling that thou shouldst be wise;
Afraid that thou shouldst know as much as He,
And grow a Rival to his Deity.
This blasphemous Conceit the Devil first,
In thine already wicked fancy nurst:
"'Tis (saith this Prince of Darkness) God's intent
"In this unjust Restraint, but to prevent
"Thy being like himself: for he doth know
"If once thou taste this Fruit, it will be so.
"Do thou but try, and taste, and presentlie
"Thou'lt find thy dim, dark Eye shall open'd be.
"This hidden Secret will be understood,
"And thou'lt know Evil, as thou now know Good
"*You shall become as Gods:* and I pray when
"'Tis so, what fear you? who can punish then?
"Your wisdom may the threatned Death evade,
"And with an equal pow'r Heav'ns pow'r upbraid
Thus spake the Tempter, and thou straight didst yield,
And treacherously to him didst quit the field.
Forthwith the fatal Fruit with impious hand,
Thou pluckst, and eatst, against thy God's command,
Branding thy self, and thy posterity,
With Treasons Guilt and endless misery.[134]

And here, vile Soul! I cannot chuse but tell
Thee one thing more that will increase thy Hell,
The Devil had no power to compell
Thee to have tasted this his poisonous Feast,
But wilfully thou hast God's Law transgrest:
For though thou hadst a pow'rful Sword to weild,
Tempted to Lust, thou cowardly didst yield:
Thou to thy self dost thy destruction owe,
And this doth greatly aggravate thy woe.
If want of strength or weapons, if oppression
Do force a Man to give up his possession,
He is excus'd, and his unhappy fall
Condol'd, lamented, and bewail'd of all.
But he deserveth neither love nor pity,
That unconstrain'd surrenders up a City;
When he has pow'r to make strong opposition,
Furnisht with Arms and warlike Ammunition,
Yet at one slender Summons yields his Fort;
The mis'ries he sustains in such a sort,
Reflect upon himself, and do redouble
His conscious Anguish, self-accusing Trouble.
Just as the Southern Sun with burning beams,
Reflecting^a from a Wall with fierce extreams,
Above its natural strength or wonted course,
Scorches and burns with a far greater force:
So do those Flames, first kindled with desire,
Grow dangerous, and prove the stronger fire.
The wounds receiv'd from self-confounding Arms,
Have ever done poor Souls the greatest harms.
    There's yet another Circumstance behind,
That aggravates thy smart, which, prethee mind.
When once thy fearful Torments are begun,
Thy fatal Glass will never cease to run;
Years fill'd with months, and months with weeks retire,
Weeks fill'd with days, & days with hours expire;
And hours in nimble minutes swiftly fly
Unto their End. But in Eternity
There is no End, nor will thy woes diminish,
Although years, moneths, weeks, and hours finish.
The toilsome Day when once it does expire,
All Creatures here to pleasing rest retire,
Slaves, Bondmen, Prisoners, Captives, all have ease,
No Drudgery so great, but then doth cease,
Each bustling Day ends in a Night of peace.
But thou must look to be with pains opprest,
Where mid-day torments find no night of Rest.
Death puts a period to the greatest grief,
I'th silent Grave the weary find relief:

But wish't-for Death from thee shall fly away,
Eternity's a never-ending Day.
Where th' angry mouth of Justice loud doth cry,
Here must thou *ever, ever, ever* lie.
How miserable! ah how sad's thine end!
When thou in vain shalt court Death for thy friend.
Men now do fly from Death, whilst Death pursues,
But then shall seek to Death, who will refuse
At their Request such favour to afford,
As frees them from that Breath giv'n by the Lord.
Death knows no pity: Nay, observe it well,
'Tis Death that opens wide the Gates of Hell,
Where thou must be tormented with the Devils,
As the just punishment of all thy evils.
Distressed Soul! oh unto what shall I
Compare thy easeless, endless misery!
In various Volumes of the World's Records,
Strange Tortures we may find exprest by words,
But Oh! so great, so sore is thy distress,
As flesh can't bear't, so words can't it express.
Devils rejoyce, and welcom in the Day
That crown'd their Conquests with so rich a prey.
To see thee thus quite buried in thy spoils,
Bereft of Earthly joys, and Heav'nly smiles;
And I do fear th'incensed God above
With direful Wrath will quickly thee remove
Into that place – , But hark! methinks I hear
Some dreadful noise – see how the Mountains tear,
And rending Hills, do into pieces fly,
Whilst Thunder bellows through the troubled sky:
The Stars and Planets in confusion hurl'd,
Have banisht Natures order from the World.
See how the melting Orbs of Heaven sweat,
Like Parchment parch'd, & shrivel'd up with heat,[135]
Swift Lightning flashes through the Air appear,
And now, O hark! the dreadful Trump I hear,
It sounds exceeding loud, enough to make
The Dead from their deep silent Graves awake,[136]   }
And stoutest Sinners stubborn hearts to quake.
Ah! 'tis Mount *Sinai*,[137] God himself is come
Now to convince thee of thy final Doom.
The Law and Justice will thee now Arraign:
Poor Soul! for thee my Soul's in bitter pain.
From them be sure no Mercy thou wilt meet,
Although thou shouldst turn Suppli'nt at their feet.
Their method is so rigid, so severe,
The Guilty by no means they ever spare.
Awake, awake, poor soul! and look about,

Jehovah doth command the Sinner out,
And active Justice having seiz'd her fast
Doth hale her to the Judgment-seat in hast.

Justice.

Most Soveraign Lord! who daresi'th least gainsay
What thou commandst? thy Word I must obey.
Lo! here I bring this wretched Prisoner forth
Unto thy Bar, who mad'st both Heaven and Earth,
See! with what dread the trembling wretch doth stand,
To know thy Sacred Pleasure & Command.

Jehovah.

Justice, what is her Fact? her Crimes declare:
I patiently will now the matter hear.

Justice.

Then will I legally, my Lord, proceed,
And presently her black Indictment reade.
Come forth thou Conscious wretch, and hear thy Crimes,
In wicked deeds thou didst begin betimes,
By th' name of *Soul*, thou standst indicted here,
Being without true Grace and godly fear,
Most treacherously in *Eden* long ago,
Didst then and there, with God's most horrid Foe,
Conspire against his Soveraign Majesty,
To the dethroning of him privily,
Then setst thou up a Traitor in his place,
And traiterously his Image didst deface,
And ever since hast in Rebellion stood,
Pursuing Evil, and forsaking Good.
For Treason, Murder, Theft, thou standst Indicted:
These Crimes were all in thy first fact united.
Nay, more then this, yet worser is thy Cause,
Thou art Arraign'd for breach of all those Laws,
Which in thy Nature God at first ingrav'd,
The same thou hast in every point deprav'd.
This Royal Law much hast thou violated,
And every Day thy Crimes are aggravated.
That Spirit's still in thee which was at first,
When God did thee out of his Garden thrust;
Thou sid'st with Satan, and dost him obey,
Not minding what, or God, or good men say.
All Evil Rebels in thy House remain,
And nobly there thou dost them entertain,
Whilst God thou hat'st, his proffer'd Love refuse,
And precious Patience daily dost abuse.
Therefore, my Lord! she worthy is of Death,
As ever any that on Earth drew Breath.

Jehovah.
Soul! What dost say, hold up thy guilty head,
Thou unto this Indictment now must plead:
Guilty, or not Guilty, I charge thee, speak;
Lest Justice doth severer Courses take.

Soul.
I dare not say I am not Guilty, Lord,
Of some of these foul Crimes which I have heard
Read in my Charge, 'tis vain for to deny,
My Conscience makes me *Guilty, Guilty*, cry.
Thy Law is broke, which doth all Lust forbid,
My Sin I know from thee cannot be hid.
Although methinks Justice seems too severe,
For the whole Charge hee'l scarcely make appear.

Jehovah.
Art guilty of that first and hainous Crime,
Which was committed, Soul, in Ancient time,
By him who was thy Representative,
From whom thy evil Nature didst derive?[138]
If guilty of that one horrid Offence,
'Tis easie for thee to perceive from thence
Thou art under my Just and fearful Curse,
Condemned by thy God, what can be worse?

Soul.
To *Adam*'s Sin, Lord, I must guilty plead,
Nay, and to many an actual Evil Deed.

Divine Justice.
The Prisoner does confess her vile offence,
And now there needs no further Evidence.
Shall Execution, Lord, on her be done?
How canst thou bear such a Rebellious one?
Lord, let me straightway strike the fatal blow,
Let her with vengeance to Hell-torments go.
She's guilty, even by her own Confession,
Of heaping up Transgression on Transgression.
She's in my Debt, she cannot it disown,
And I demand my Right, Come, pay it down.
Ten thousand Talents;[139] *Soul*, thou owest me,
Which must be paid, and that full speedily.

Soul.
That I am in thy Debt I don't gainsay,
But I have not one farthing now to pay.
Some pity show, I for forbearance cry,
Since thy Demands I cannot satisfy.

Justice.

Full satisfaction 'tis that I must have,
In vain from me you compositions crave;
My Name is *Justice*, and my Nature so,
I never did, nor can I mercy show.

Soul.

If there's no mercy, then my state is sad,
And never was there any News so bad
For *Adam*'s seed, who under Sin do lie,
All then must perish to Eternity.

Theologue.

That God is gracious, Soul, is not deny'd,
Yet Justice will also be satisfy'd.
Consider if thou canst the matter reach;
One Attribute God never will impeach
To magnify another, He's so Just,
As to take vengeance on each Sin and Lust;
Each Attribute know thou assuredly
Must meet together in sweet Harmony.

Soul.

What will thy Wrath, O *Justice*! then appease?
Upon what terms wilt thou afford some ease
To me, after this terrifying News?
Vouchsafe to tell the means that I must use,
To satisfie a Judge that's so severe,
And will not of sweet Acts of pardon hear.

Justice.

There's nothing can appease me, that is less
Than a compleat and perfect Righteousness;
Like that thou hadst whilst thou in *Eden* stood:
Nothing, save this, will do thee any good.
What e're is due to me of the old score,
Must be paid down, or never any more
Will the great God with thee concerned be
On gracious terms of Peace and Amitie;
A Sacrifice can only make thy peace,
That, that alone, will cause my wrath to cease.

Soul.

If that be all, I'le get a Sacrifice;
Let me consider, what shall I devise?
A thousand Rams, and Rivers of sweet Oil,
I'le offer up but for one gracious Smile;
With fat of firstling Lambs I'le Heaven invoke,
And purest Incense up like Clouds shall smoke;

Each Morn I le sacrifice whole Hecatombs,[140]
With Frankincense, and sweet *Arabian* Gums.
If these, O Lord! I offer up to thee;
May they atone for mine Iniquity?

Justice.

Oh no! give o're those trifling low designs;
The Eastern Spices and the Western mines
United, are too mean an Offering
To satisfy this great incensed King.
In such poor offerings God does take no pleasure;
Couldst thou therefore procure all *Europes* Treasure;
Nay, all the Wealth that in the World has bin,
'Tould[a] not his wrath appease for one small sin.
Shouldst thou thy dearest Son or Daughter take
For Sacrifice, 'twould no Atonement make:
The fruit of thine own Body were in vain
For thy Soul's sin a pardon to obtain.
No friend or Brother can'st thou now find out
To pay thy Ransom, or release thee out,
Their[b] Riches never can be help for thee,
Nor once redeem thy Soul from misery.
Nay, couldst thou yet ascend to Heaven above,
And holy Angels with compassion move
For to engage for thee, and signify
That in thy stead, and for thy sake they'd die,
It would not do; for in them's no such worth
As to remove thy guilt, appease God's wrath.
Their Glory's great, as holy Scriptures show;
Yet all they have and are to God they owe.
They cannot help thee in thy great distress,
Nor satisfy the Law thou dost transgress.
In brief, look where thou wilt; no Balsam's found
In any Creature for to cure thy wound.
No Surety can'st thou get; then come away,
Eternal Torments must thy Reckoning pay.

Soul.

Hold, hold, thou art too hasty and severe,
To one word more I pray thee lend an Ear.
I will amend my life, if this be so.
The Promise runs to such as truly do
Their Evil courses leave; I hope hereby
Thou wilt some pity show, not let me die.

Divine Justice.

Fond Soul! though such thy promises Indeed
So often broke, deserve but little heed;

Yet grant thou shouldst henceforth with strictest care
Endeavour thine offences to repair,
Couldst thou so live, as never to sin more,
Will this, dost think, pay off thy former score?
Can thine imperfect Righteousness to come,
Discharge of by-past ills, so vast a sum?
When even that which thou callst Righteousness
It self wants pardon, and must Guilt confess.
When thy Bond's su'd, thou dost thy self forget,
To offer menstruous Rags to pay thy Debt;[141]
For what is past, not future, I demand,
And thou shalt feel the rigors of my hand.

Soul.

Lord! then I'm drown'd in an Abyss of fears,
If hearty Sighs, nor penitential Tears
Can wash me clean, nor yet relieve my wo:
My case is desp'rate, what shall Mortals do?

Divine Justice.

If thou with Tears couldst the vast Ocean fill,
Or grieve till thou thy self with sorrows kill,
And make ten thousand Rivers with thy blood,
'Twould not contribute the least dram of Good.
Nay, couldst thou live, and never more offend,
Yet for old sins to Hell I must thee send,
To th'place of Execution thou must go:
Lord, shall I strike, O shall I strike the blow?[142]
Lo, here the Soul, condemned wretch doth stand;
My Ax is up, if thou but giv'st command,
I presently will cut her down with Ire,
Fit fewel for an Everlasting fire.

Divine Mercy.

Stay, Justice! hold, forbear to strike; shall I
My Glory lose to all Eternity?
Though thou art just, as just as God can be,
Yet something Mortals still expect from me.
'Tis gracious Love and pity I afford,
In me shines forth the Glory of the Lord:
In me God doth (O Justice) take delight,
Though thou art pleasant also in his sight.
How shall we both then meet in Harmony,
And shine in splendor³ to Eternity?

Divine Wisdom.

I have found out the way, which will you both
With equal Majesty and Glory cloath.

God is as just as Justice doth require,
And yet as kind as Mercy can desire.
Here is a glorious Prince come from above,
Who all obstructions quickly will remove,
Which in the way of the poor Soul doth lie,
And you appease, and jointly satisfy;
To save her now from the infernal pit,
I have a Ransom found, a Ransom fit,

Divine Justice.
I cannot hold,[143] – I'le strike the fatal Blow:
Hell she deserves; with vengeance let her go
Unto the place appointed for all them
Who do God's holy Laws and Grace contemn.

Jesus Prince of Light.
O who is this? What Traitor's at the Bar,
That is condemn'd, and Justice wo'nt defer
The Execution? speak, hold up thy head;
Hast any thing to say? What canst thou plead?
Methinks, methinks, I should this Creature know:
Ah! *Soul,* is't thee? What shall I for thee do?
I told thee what thy state would be i'th end,
When first my Love to thee I did commend.
Soul! Speak, 'tis I, why dost thou not look up?
I'm sorely griev'd to think upon the Cup
That is prepar'd for thee; What dost thou say?[144]
Shall I step in, that *Justice* may delay
To strike the stroke, for then too late 'twill be
To show my Love and pity unto thee?
Hast any kindness for me in thine Heart?
I doubt that still thou the same Creature art
Thou wast before? and hast no love at all:
Why speakst then not? shall vengeance on thee fall?
Ah! how can I see Execution done,
And Tears not from mine Eyes like Rivers run?

Divine Justice.
Lord, be n't concern'd, she is thy bitter Foe;
Oh let me therefore freely strike the blow.
There's nought in her but Sin, and poisonous Evil;
To God a Foe, and Friend unto the Devil.

JESVS.
I know not how to let this stroke be given,
For I am come on purpose down from Heaven
To make Atonement, and to satisfy
For all her sins and foul Iniquity.
Though she to me doth no affection bear,
Yet her I pity, and do love most dear.

Justice.

Blest *J E S V S!* hold, 'tis my just Master's sense,
Abused Mercy must have recompence.
There is no other way but she must die,
Unless thou wilt be her Securitie:
If in her stead thy life thou wilt give up,
Then mayst thou save her from this bitter Cup.
The price which thou on that account wilt pay,
Will make a Compensation, and defray
All her vast debts, yea[a] plenarily
God's wrath appease, and Justice satisfy.
What must be done? Who is't the stroke must bear?
Is't not most fit such[b] should who guilty are?
I cannot hold my hand, nor longer stay,
Law must be satisfy'd, what dost thou say,
Thou wretched Soul? behold the knife and spear!
Can'st thou dost think, God's fearful vengeance bear?
Now, *Soul!* look to thy self, this Spear I'le run
Into thy Bowels, ere I it return.

JESVS.

Stay Justice, stay, withold thy furious Dart,
And, let its glitt'ring point first pierce my Heart.
Her guilty state aloud calls for relief,
It wounds my Soul and fills my Heart with grief.
My Bowels yearn, my inward parts do move,
Now, now's the time to show her my great Love.
Let Law and Justice be suffic'd in me,
'Tis I will die, to set the Sinner free.
Behold me, *Soul!* my life shall go for thine,
I will redeem thee with this Blood of mine,
Although most Precious, Sacred, and Divine.[145]

CHAP. VII.

Shewing what Consultations there were amongst the infernal Spirits to bring Jesus, *Prince of Light, under the power of Death; a Council called in Hell: the Princes of the fallen Angels in a deep combination against him, for fear their Kingdom should fall, and the poor Creature be delivered. The grand Counsel of Old Satan is taken. He enters into* Judas. *Judas's sin discovered. Jesus is apprehended. A terrible battel, or Christ's Agony before his Passion. Sin and Wrath combine together: shewing the Prince's Conquests over them both. Seven aggravations of Christ's sorrows in the Garden; and a Dialogue between the Devil, King of Darkness, and Death, the King of Terrors.*

HEre let's a while reflect with careful heed;
What! doth the guiltless for the guilty bleed?
This may astonish all, here's Love indeed!

Do Mortals ever greater love extend,
Then to lay down their lives for a dear Friend?
But for a Prince, a mighty Prince to die,
Not for a Friend, but for an Enemy,
Convicted and condemn'd for horrid Treason,
Thus to step in at that most Critick season,
When just the fatal blow was to be given,
This Love's above our Reach, higher than Heaven,
Deeper than Ocean Seas, so Infinite,
As well deserves our wonder day and night.
What? Was the Father free his Son to give,
His dear and only Son, that she might live?
And doth the Son i'th midst of Enemies
Yield up himself to be a Sacrifice?
Yet who can be so bold to lay their Hands
Upon this Prince, that Heaven & Earth commands?
How shall this thing be now accomplished?
And by what means shall his dear Blood be shed?
Let's now inquire who is't that will consent
To be the grand and chiefest Instrument
To execute this precious spotless Lamb,
Who for this purpose down from Heav'n came?
Has he on Earth any such spightful Foe,
As dare's attempt this 'mazing thing to do?
      You heard before he daily was beset,
And with what Enemies he often met,
But now his hour is drawing very near.
Great Consultations 'mongst his Foes there were,
How they might take his blessed Life away,
Who seem'd himself impatient of delay.
He long'd until his work were finished,
Which could not be until his blood were shed:
And though he had most raging Enemies,
Yet knew they not what project to devise
To bring this bloody traiterous deed to pass,
Which long before by them designed was:
Until *Apollyon* finding by his Art
The dire Intentions harbour'd in their Heart,   }
Doth rouse them up, and first the matter start
To the Infernal powers, to wake them al
A second time upon this Prince to fall.
Then *Belzebub, Satan,* and *Lucifer,*
Consult afresh how to renew the War,
And to this purpose wee'l suppose they spake:

                    Apollyon.
      Shake off your fears, and speedily let's make

The strongest Head that possibly we can
Against this strong, this Devil-amazing man.
Now, now's the day, let's bring him to Death's sting,
And then with shouts of Triumph we may sing:
For over Death 'tis we the power have,
And we may sure secure him in the Grave.
'Tis he alone who frights us in our station,
And puts us all into great Consternation.
Our Kingdom by this means is like to fall,
And we thereby be ruin'd great and small.
I have engag'd him once, but could not stand,
I know his strength, he has a pow'rful Hand.

Belzebub.

    My Sentence is for War;[146] this Enterprize
Well managed, will make our Kingdom rise,
And re-inthrone us in our Antient Skies,
To a great Height and flourish, as before:
When he is down, we'l let him rise no more.
Can we but once deprive him of his Life,
'Twill put an end to all our fears and strife.

Lucifer.

    Dominions, Pow'rs, and Principalities[147]
You all in danger are, awake and rise
From off your Seats, and lazy Beds of Down:
Sleep you secure, or, fear not the dread frown
Of him who cast you down, and joys to see
Your abject state confess his Victory?[148]
Shall all our brave infernal Regiments yield,
And basely quit the even yet doubtful Field?
What? by one man shall such a pow'rful Host
Be overcome, and all at once be lost?
Come, shew your valour, I'le command the Van,
Tho we're to engage with one that's more than Man,
Yet fear him not; why doth each spirits hand
Shake thus? why do you all amazed stand?
Has none found out a way to make him yield,
And either by fraud or force to quit the Field?
    At this old *Satan* rose from off his Seat,
Ready to burst with Rage and Malice great,
And cast a terrible look (if minded well)
Enough to fright all th' Devils out of Hell.

Satan.

    You mighty Lords of the Infernal Lake,
Hark unto me, who for our Empires sake
Have now devis'd a Stratagem, that may

(If I mistake not) prove the only way
To bring about the Ruin of our Foe,
Whom I both hate and dread, as you well know.
There is his Servant *Judas*, he's our Friend,
And into him forthwith will I descend,
Who by my strong persuasions soon will do
That which may make for's Master's overthrow.
He will betray him to our Servants hand,
Who will secure him safe at your Command,
And put him unto Death, who when destroy'd,
We never any more shall be annoy'd.
        They all agreed to what old *Satan* said,
Combining jointly to assist and aid
Him in this great, though cursed enterprise,
And bid him make what hast he could devise.
Delays are dangerous, Devils well know that:
But why need they Grim *Satan* instigate?
He needs not be provoked to make haste,
When 'tis to injure *Souls*; or them to waste;
Or wreek his Malice, Rage, and Hellish spight
On the sweet person of the *Prince of Light*.
For now, alas! is come the dismal hour,
The time of Darkness. And Hell's direful pow'r
No sooner spoke, but *Satan* flew away,
Winged with spight, impatient of delay.
He takes possession of poor *Judas* heart,
And unto him in secret doth impart
The grand Design of this *Cabal* of Hell;[149]
Who presently *consents*, and likes it well.
Away he goes, resolv'd the work to do:
A work, Lord, did I say? *sad work!* Oh who
Could think that a *Disciple* could do this,
Betray his Lord with a false treach'rous kiss?[150]
Perfidious wretch! what villany is here?
Who can conceive the Crime? or who declare
The horrid nature of this vile offence?
Transcending all degrees of insolence.
No treacherous Act like it was done on Earth,
Since Man first from *enliv'ned Clay*[151] took breath.
Where was thy Conscience, wretch, it did not fly
Into thy face for this Impiety?
Were all his wondrous works out of thy mind,
His tender Love and pity to mankind?
Betray the Son of Man! Can this be so?
What hadst thou in thine Eye? what made thee do
This horrid deed? Was't mony did thee move
To forfeit thy *Allegiance*, and thy love?
'Twas from that filthy Root, *Root of all Evil.*[152]

Base sordid *Gain*, thou soldst Christ to the Devil;
(That is to those vile men he did employ
To perpetrate this cursed Tragedy.)
This shew'd thy malice, and how thou didst hate him;
But tell us, *Judas!* at what *price didst* rate him?
What price didst set upon his blessed Head?
Are *Thirty pence* enough? What, valued
At this low price? – Is Jesus worth no more?
Such a *sad Bargain* ne're was made before.[153]
A Box of *Ointment*'s worth, in thy esteem,
Three hundred pence;[154] and dost thou value him
Not to amount in worth 'bove the Tenth part?
Thou shew'st how blind, and how deceiv'd thou art?
He whose most precious personage out-shines
The fading Lustre of all *Ophirs* Mines.[155]
And carries sweeter Odours in his Breast,
Than all the *Spices* that perfume the East;
He that's *Omnipotencies* choice delight,
Whom trembling Angels *worship* day and night;
He that the Saints above all Worlds do prize,
In whom all worth and true enjoyment lies;
Shall he be sold at such a rate? O fie!
Thou wilt repent it to Eternitie,
That thou didst ever such a Bargain make:
What? Thirty Bits of cursed Silver take
For th' *Pearl of matchless price*;[156] thou sordid Sot!
Wilt thou be trading, when thou knowest not
What 'tis thou sell'st? Fool, 'tis a *precious stone*,
The *Indian* Quarries yield not such an one,
Worth more than Heaven & Earth. But it is gone?
So rich a *Jewel* lost?[157] – Go howl and cry;
Thou'lt *hang* thy self;[158] next in Hell-torments fry.
And who can pity thee? I prethee who
To such a Traytor will compassion show?
Now 'tis too late thou dost begin to mourn;
Better (vile) wretch) thou never hadst been born.
    Under incensed wrath, ah! now he lies,
Where flames torment, and Conscience terrifies.
Be not offended, Sirs, I judg him not;
But his own *Master*'s words can't be forgot,
Who speaking of his sad and sinful fall,
Doth him the *Son* of black *perdition* call,
And says that *he is lost*.[159] Christ is the Judge,
And to repeat his Sentence who can grudge?
But to proceed – how can my spirits hold?
I need Relief, my heart (alas) grows cold,
Whilst I with wonder look on what's behind,
Soul-melting pity overwhelms my mind.

Who can of such heart-breaking sufferings hear,
And not dissolve each Eye into a Tear?
But, ah! methinks something doth intervene,
The thought of which puts me to as much pain,
As doth the sad, but useful contemplation
Of his unhappy happy bloody passion.
Then let's retreat, and to the *Garden*[160] go,
For in that place began his grievous woe:
Before he doth with th' *King of Terrors*[161] fight,
Another King sets on him full of spight,
Whose powr's great, by cursed usurpation,
He domineers and rules o're every Nation;
He brings the Mighty down unto his feet,
And makes them all with rigour to submit:
The good, the bad, the wise, the old, the young,
The rich, the poor, the beautiful, and strong,
All that live, or e're liv'd, have worsted bin
By this proud lofty one, whose name is *SIN*.
A Bastard Devil of most monstrous Birth,
Begot in Hell, by Satan first brought forth;
Already you have of his Malice heard,
And how in wrath he never Mortal spar'd.
A *crafty Foe*, who oftner steers his course
In all his wars, by *fraud* than open *force*:
'Tis he that keeps the Soul in Iron Chains,
And robs her of all Sense; lest those great pains
She otherwise might feel, should make her cry
To be deliver'd from his slavery;
Unless our *Jesus* doth this Foe destroy,
The *Soul* he loves he never can enjoy.
He had with him before oft a hard Duel,
And worsted him, escaping all his cruel
Attaques, but *rallying* now with other Foes
He joyns, to lay on more impetuous blows.
Well may we dread here an amazing Fight,
For lo! with him confederate in our sight
The *Wrath of God*, most fearful to behold:
Both these sad Enemies, with courage bold,
Are making all the Head that e're they can
Against this blessed Prince, *the Son of Man*.
Oh! let our Souls be arm'd with courage bold,
Whilst we this furious Battel do behold.
Before the Fight begins, do you not hear
How he doth cry unto his Father dear;
O let this Cup from me, Lord, *pass away*,
If it be possible;[162] Let it, I pray,
Pass from me, that of it I may not drink.
Until this time he never seem'd to shrink

From any pain, conflict, or suffering;
This Combat is, alas, a different thing,
From what before he ever met withal;
From hence he did unto his Father call
Once and again, repeating of his cry,
It'h sense of what was now approaching nigh.
Some may at this 'tis likely much admire,
That our dear Saviour should so loud desire
To be deliver'd from that bitter Cup,
Which was *prepared* for him to drink up.
It did not rise for his *unwillingness*;
But from the pain, the anguish, and distress
'Twould bring him to: this *humane Nature's* weak
From thence he might such supplications make.
Ah! wrath *Divine*, what humane Soul can bear?
But of *Divinity* he hath his share,
Which doth again his fainting spirit chear.
And such support he needs – Cast but an Eye,
See how the Combatants with fury fly
Upon each other; What a Battel's here,
Enough to melt our Souls into a tear.
Lo! the first blow that *Sin and Wrath* doth give,
It is the worst he ever did receive.
Behold! how frightfully grim Wrath[a] doth frown;
Nay, more, the *Prince* seems by their strength *cast down*.
Now *Sin & Wrath* upon him both do lie,
Which makes him groan, and bitterly to cry,
With panting breast, and half-expiring Breath,
My Soul is sorrowful, ev'n unto Death.[163]
        Can the great *Prince* of Earth and Heaven feel
Such heavy strokes, as thus to make him reel?
The dismal weight of Sin this doth declare;
None but a *JESVS* could it fully bear.
Happy are we, as the blest Prophet said,
Our Help was *upon One that's mighty laid*.[164]
Could man or Angel ev'r have born all this,
And not have been cast down to th' deepst Abyss?
Nay of this mighty One, Saint *Mark* hath rais'd
Our wonder higher, *He was sore amaz'd*:
Nay more than this, *he fell upon the Ground*:[165]
No Soul before such anguish ever found,
To see the Lord of Life brought to the Earth,
Under the pressure of God's heavy Wrath;
And that he suffer'd all this in our stead,
May make our Souls to stand astonished;
Especially, if to these Trials we
Shall add his great and bloody *Agony*,
Wherein the *sweat* fell from him as he stood,

In Crimson dy, like trickling *drops of blood*.[166]
Ah! precious Lord! this work was very sore;
But still thy Love, and its blest Vertue's more;
Through all these Toils thou graspst at Victory,
And *Captive lead'st* at last *Captivity*.[167]
If^a *Sin* that day had not receiv'd a fall,
Grim *Death* and *Hell* had quickly swallow'd all
The race of *Man*; we all had been undone,
No help,^b no hope, no life for any one;
Sin was condemn'd, it had a fatal blow,
That now to *Saints* it little hurt can do.

　　But to proceed, here I shall^c now relate
Some things which very much do aggravate
The sufferings which Christ in's Soul indur'd,
When he this Conquest for our Souls procur'd;
No greater sorrows did he ever know,
Than those which then his Soul did undergo.[168]

Several Circumstances which demonstrate the *Greatness* of our *Saviours sufferings* in his Soul in the Garden.

First.

　　They did not seize him with the least *surprize*,
From thence oft-times doth great Amazement rise
Unto poor Mortals: we are not aware
Oft-times what's nigh, know nothing of the^d snare.
But thus 'twas not with the blest Prince of Light;
What can be hid from Great *Jehovah's* sight?
He knew full well what would upon him fall;
Yet when it came, so great, surpassing all
Were th' Griefs he felt, he in amaze doth call
Unto his Father dear most earnestly,
If 'twere his will to let that Cup pass by.[169]

Secondly.

It was the very thing he *came to do*,
And yet cry'd out in such sad sort; O who
Can then conceive what he did undergo?
He *freely* did his precious Life give up;
And yet he's ready to *refuse* the Cup.
He takes it (as it were) into his hand
Most willingly, but presently doth stand
Pausing a while: then puts it to his Lip,
And after he had took one *bitter sip*,
Looks up to Heav'n, and cryes, O may it be
Thy will, dear God, this Cup might pass from me.

Thirdly.

He knew unless he drank it up, that we
Must perish All to all Eternitie;
And that his coming would prove all in vain,
If he refused for us to be slain;
And yet with sighs and groans how did he cry,
In sense of wrath, and that extremity,
Which he beheld would quickly overtake him,
When once his blessed Father did forsake him![170]

Fourthly.

The *Angels* which did there to him appear,
Demonstrate plain how great his sorrows were:
For like as one distressed, makes complaint,
Quite tired out, and all his spirits faint,
Needs to be strengthned by some faithful Friend:
So God to him did Holy Angels send,
For to *relieve* and comfort him that Day,
When *Sin* and *Wrath* so heavy on him lay.[171]

Fifthly.

But what's Assistance from an Heavenly Host,
To the great Power of the Holy Ghost!
Some little measure of the Spirit hath
Caused blest Saints to triumph over Death.
How have they sung with flames about their Ears,
Contemning pains, regardless of all fears?[172]
This *Spirit* rested on him *bodily*,
Without measure;[173] and yet how doth he cry!
As scarce well knowing which way to bear up,
Whilst he partakes of this most painful Cup.
This greatly doth his suff'rings amplify
To humane sense, if weighed seriously.

Sixthly.

O Lord! what means these melting sighs and Tears?
Why is thy Soul amaz'd, why fill'd with Fears?
Ah! 'tis enough to break our hearts to think
Upon that bitter potion thou didst drink;
Thou knewst thy sorrows would be quickly o're,
And then thou shouldst ne'r sigh nor suffer more;
'Twas from *thy worth*, both *Wrath* and *Justice* cryes,
We are *appeas'd* with this thy *Sacrifice*.
Might not the shortness of this Conflict yield
Thee some Relief? Besides thou knew'st the Field
Thou shouldst obtain, the Conquest was thine *own*,
And quickly too the Conflict would be gone.
I'th midst of Wars, or anguish, Men indure,

If any can them certainly assure,
That in short time their Troubles will be over,
They straight rouse up their spirits to recover,
And patiently resolve to bear the smart,
For this is like a Cordial to the Heart.
All this thou knew'st, and more abundantly;
Yet *Sins* dire weight so heavily did lie,
That with strong groans & horror thou didst cry.
The Torments, Lord! of Hell took hold on thee,
Our Souls from that devouring Wrath to free.

      But why didst thou into a Garden go
Thus to encounter with the hellish Foe?
Was it because *there* first began our woe?
Or, was it, Lord, to have us call to mind
When we in *Walks and Gardens* pleasures find,
What thou didst for us in a *Garden* bear,
To take our Hearts from flitting *pleasures* here?

      But stop, my Muse! look back, and let us see
What did succeed *Judas* his Treachery.
O mind, what Joy's amongst th' Infernal Crew,
In hopes of what is likely to ensue.
Hark how those *Scrietchowls* cry, but with small reason,
As will be manifested in its season.
   It was decreed the Glorious Prince should die,
Already you have heard the reason why.
And though the first contrivance was *Divine*,
Yet *Hell* hereby had also a design
Of horrid mischief; and for that intent
They first prompt on the cursed Instrument.
For having try'd their utmost strength before
In open force, they will engage no more
In that vain way; but now resolve to try
What may be done by Hellish policy.
This Project taking[a] hitherto so well
New *Summons* straight are issued out in Hell
To all *Infernal Spirits* to make speed,
And push on boldly the last cursed Deed;
Fearing this *Prince* would prove a mortal Foe,
Their Hellish Kingdom utterly o'rethrow,
And bring them to deserved punishment,
(For *old* and latter Treasons they invent)
Where they perpetual Tortures shall sustain.
They feard also that he would again
Restore that poor *condemn'd* degenerate
Forsaken Wretch, unto her first Estate,
Which she by Lust had lost; nay, furthermore,
Make her more *famous* than she was before.
Which to prevent, they all consult the way,

How him to *Death* with speed they may betray,
From's Heavn'ly Kingdom to be banisht quite,
And ever kept under the shades o'th Night.
Various their *treacherous* Consultations be,
Yet all on Death do mutually agree.
Apollyon pusht it on with raging haste;
But *Satan*, cry'd, Forbear, drive not too fast,
Such mighty matters call for Consultation;
We strike uncertain, when we strike in passion.
Thus black-mouth'd Envy op'd his snaky Jaws,
To have them conduct well their Hellish cause:
Ere further you proceed in this design,
Pray take, saith he, these transient thoughts of mine.

    The hearts o'th *Jews* must first prepared be
With Pride, Revenge, and strongest Enmity;
And we must think upon some Friends that will
Forswear themselves, our pleasures to fulfil;
Such Witnesses our crazy Cause will need,
And such must we provide too with all speed.
For well we know his Innocence is such,
With the least stain Truth could it never touch;
Therefore those Crimes he wants in verity,
Malice must raise, and Perjuries supply;
And that they may pass current when he's try'd,
A Council we must pick, fit to decide
The matter right or wrong on our side.
Besides, 'tis fit e're we the work begin,
We should the King of Terrors summon in.
If his Commission will not reach so far,
In vain, alas, is all our present stir.
His Pow'r is great, but don't you understand,
He has refus'd to be at our Command,
Not once, but many times? this makes me quake:
We are undone, should he refuse to take
Part now with us in this Extremity,
When all we have and are at stake doth lie.

    To this Advice the Devils all consent,
And call for Tyrant *Death,* who doth present
His gastly face, and boldly do's demand,
What 'twas they would have him to take in hand?
Then soon *Apollyon,* King of Darkness, breaks
Silence, and to this purpose gravely speaks.

Apollyon.

    Dread King of Terrors, if thou stepst not in,
Down goes our Hell-bred Monarchy of Sin.
We now can walk the spacious Earth about,
And have we Friend or Foe, we find him out.

Where e're we see a person that's upright,
We seek his ruin with the greatest spight.
When we by fraud or craft can't him intice
To yield to Pride, or Lust, or any Vice,
But that he'l watch us with a wary Eye,
And persevere in all true Piety;
Then on him do we bring outward distress,
To make him lose, or leave his Holiness.
Our Kingdom by this practice is made strong,
Potent and large, and so has prosper'd long.
But now thy help we need, for much we fear
The downfal of our Kingdom draweth near.
Upon the Earth there now appears in sight
A mighty Foe, one call'd *The Prince of Light*.
And for what end should he from Heaven come,
If not to execute on us that Doom
Which Heav'n long since decreed? To end which strife,
We are resolv'd to take away his Life.
Already he's betray'd; if things hit right,
And then we'l yield him up unto thy Might.
For thy Assistance, *Death*, we do implore,
Else to these mischiefs this will happen more,
That Creature we so long have captivated,
Will in her Pomp again be re-instated.
The thoughts of which there's none of us can bear,
Speak, speak, pale Monarch! for we long to hear
What's thy Advice? Thou mighty art in pow'r,
And canst, we know, whole Nations soon devour.

The King of Terrors.

   Great *Prince of Darkness*, you must understand
We are not wholly at your proud Command.
For there's a mighty Pow'r in Heaven high,
Which you are subject to as well as I:
'Tis true, from him I cannot say at all
That I derive my strange Original;
Yet by his pleasure am circumscrib'd,
And 'gainst his will cannot be forc'd nor brib'd.
Wherefore, if he this *Prince of Light* protect,
In vain at him shall I my shafts direct.
Besides, in this Exploit methinks I find
Some strange foreboding ills possess my mind,
As if engaging thus against your Foe,
I should but hasten mine own overthrow.
Take mine Advice then, meddle not at all;
Better sit still, you know, than rise to fall.
'Tis true indeed, as you have well observ'd,
Your threatned Judgment has been long deferr'd:

But if your Execution-Day be come,
You can't escape, but must abide your Doom.

Prince of Darkness.

Thou pale-fac'd Traytor! shan't we have thy Aid?
Then all our Hellish Projects are betray'd.
How oft have we stood by thee; sent thee forth
To do our will and pleasure on the Earth?
The first that ever thou hadst in thy hand,
Committed was by me, at my Command;
I caused *Cain* to slay his godly^a Brother;[174]
And so taught thee how to bereave the Mother
Of her most dear, of her most hopeful Son;
And shall not now my will in this be done?
'Twas I which did thy being to thee give:
How many Subjects dost each day receive
From me and mine? who do in every Land
Promote thy State, and lend their helping-Hand.
Therefore consent, and show thy angry Brow,
And make this Conqueror to thy Scepter bow,
Yielding himself to thee, strike him with speed,
And pierce his very Heart until it bleed.
Then some dark Cave near the Earths Centre find,
Where Light ne're pierc'd, nor *Phœbus*[175] ever shin'd,
There, there, the vanquisht Foe do thou retain
Close Prisn'er with an Adamantine Chain.
When e're thou strik'st, be sure strike home thy blow,
Lest he revive and work our overthrow.
Be bold, attempt, and let thy pow'r be known,
The Glory of this Deed shall be thine own.

King of Terrors.

I must confess I have been often sent
By Hellish means unto the Innocent.
To satisfy your Envy, Pride, and Lust,
Some thousands I have turn'd into the Dust.
Yet never did I strike, but on Condition,
As Heaven did permit, in my Commission.
And though by *Thee*, and by that Monster, *Sin*,
The Child of Hell, I first of all came in;
Yet am I not subservient still to thee,
But bounded by *Jehovah*'s own Decree:
For had I wholly been at thy Command,
Poor *Job* had fell before thy pow'rful hand.[176]
Where my dread *Sovereign Lord* do's give me charge,
To stay my hand (though my Commission's large)
I must forbear; But if he once permit,
The Just, and the Unjust, alike I hit.

Apollyon King of Darkness.

Wilt thou eclipse my Glory and Renown?
Destroy my Pow'r, and tread my Kingdom down?
Fy *Death*! for shame forbear thy Insolence,
And do'nt dispute the Mandates of thy Prince.
Strike! I conjure thee; do not vainly think
'Twill be thy Int'rest from this work to shrink.
That hand, that powerful hand[a] that conquers me,
If he prevail, at last will vanquish thee.
Though now on Earth thou dost in triumph dwell,
If he o'recome, he'l cast thee down to Hell.
Thou from thy Monarchy shalt then be driven,
And shalt abide in no place under Heaven.
Thou that hast been a Conqueror heretofore,
Shalt conquer'd be, and never conquer more.
Ah! lend thy Hand, shew forth thy mighty pow'rs,
'Tis for thy Int'rest, *Death*, as well as ours.
If Arguments and Reason may convince
Thee; try thy weapons on this dangerous Prince.

King of Terrors.

Say, say no more. If you find things agree
In order to his downfall, I will be
His Executioner, do you not fear,
I tremble at the thoughts of what I hear.

Damned Spirits.

Bravely resolv'd! At last they all Reply'd,
Swelling in Wrath, in Malice, Envy, Pride,
Wee'l now proceed, and craftily prepare
All things in readiness to end this War.

Apollyon.

Though *Judas* has a party for our turn,
Yet we have more to do e're we adjourn.
If we should bring this Enterprise to pass,
Yet when all's done, I shall be where I was.
We must seek out some persons to defame
His so much honour'd and unblemish'd Name.
He's Just and Virtuous, and esteem'd so high,
Who dares charge him with th' least Impurity?

Satan.

At this an envious Devil strait jump in;
I'le lead the people on, let me begin;
I'le stir them up to Envy more and more,
Such Envy that he shall not stand before.

Belial.
These are but sparkles from an hasty Fire,
Which will for want of fuel soon expire.
His Glory still encreases, ours decays.
Words without Actions are but faint delays.
The rarest Wit amongst us must look out,
With wariness to bring this thing about.
I'le tell you what I newly have contriv'd:
Let my Lord *Lucifer*, the King of Pride,
Make one amongst their Rulers in the Seat
Of seeming Justice; Tell them they are Great
And Prudent men, yeaᵃ Learned ones likewise,
And in their Breasts alone true Wisdom lies.
Yea, tell them that the Soveraign Lord of Heaven
To them the name of Gods on Earth hath given;[177]
Tell them both God and men have thought it fit,
That they like Gods should in this Grandeur sit;
And, answerable to this lofty station,
The people have them in great veneration.
Thus, when h' has put their Honours in a Heat,
And swell'd them up with Pride and self-conceit,
Tell them 'tis much below their high Degree,
That such a low inferiour Man as he
Should be their Prince, or over them bear sway,
Who rather ought their Greatness to obey.
Then, when the uncontrouled breath of Fame
Has spread abroad the Glory of his Name,
And fill'd each Eye and Ear with Admiration,
Giving to him Applause and Veneration,
Then let our envious Friend once more take's place,
And sit as pale as Death in every Face;
And let him tell them, if they do not take
Some speedy course, their Honours lie at stake;
He grows so famous in the peoples Eyes,
They shortly will their Soveraignty despise.

Satan.
Nay, I can tell them yet another thing,
The people seek by force to make him King.
Which if the Roman Pow'r should understand,
They'd quickly come and take away their Land;
This sure will work, or other ways I'le find,
Good Mariners can sail with every wind.

Thus these Infernals seeking to prevent
Their future, but deserved punishment,
Far swifter than the lofty Eagle flies,

Did set upon their Hellish enterprize.
The King of Pride threw forth his poisonous Darts,
Which did not miss to pierce the yielding Hearts
Of those that sat at Stern, who should delight
To do the thing that's equal, just, and right:
But disregarding great *Jehovah's* Laws,
They sought (poor Souls) for popular Applause,
Puft up with Pride, and swoln with vain Ambition
(That Tympany of th' Soul) They had suspition
That if the Prince of Light were once affected,
They by the people soon should be rejected.
For first they saw[a] his Miracles were great,
His Vertues, rendred him still more compleat,
And made him so illustriously to[b] shine,
He gain'd the Appellation of *Divine.*
Nay, furthermore, they heard how some did sing,
*Hosanna in the Highest to the King
Of Israel!* the fragrant Flower of *Jess,*
The Root of *David,*[178] Oh! who can express
The depth of Envy which in them did burn,
With raging flames, almost at every turn?
Close Consultation in their Courts appears,
And i'th mean while strange Rumors fill their Ears.
The Miracles which he before had wrought
Into the minds of people fresh are brought,
Those wond'rous things did much encrease the strife:
He rais'd, said some, the Dead again to Life:
Gave sight unto the Blind, who from their Birth
Had never seen the Light that guilds the Earth:
The Dumb, the Deaf, the Lepers, and the Lame,
In all Distempers, whosoever came,
Had perfect Cure in every Disease;
Nay, he could hush the Winds, and calm the Seas;[179]
Could dispossess the black Infernal Rout,
And cast whole Legions of fierce Devils out.[180]
Of five mean Barly loavs, and two small Fishes,
He made above five thousand plenteous Dishes.[181]
Thus many talkt what he before had done,
Grieving to think what now was coming on.
His gracious words, and vertuous Life commended
Him to the Multitude, but much offended
Th' inraged Rulers; yet his Innocence
Was still so sure a Guard and strong defence,
That they could not their wicked ends obtain.
Yet from their malice would they not refrain.
How often did they in clandestine way
Endeavour their blood-thirsty hands to lay
Upon this Sacred Prince? yet still through fear

The people would rise up, they did forbear.
Sometimes they thought to trap him in his words,
That Law & Justice then might draw their Swords.
And cut him off. And then again devise
Another course, charg'd him with Blasphemies
Against the God of Heaven, by which way
They surely thought they might his Life betray.
But never could they over him get pow'r
Untill his time were come: Now, now's their hour.
The work must needs^a be carried on with speed,
When Heaven and Hell about it are agreed.
Though different ends in these great Agents are,
Yet in the thing they both consenting were,
That Christ should be of his dear Life depriv'd.
Though Hell alone the guilty Act contriv'd,
Yet God indeed from all Eternitie,
Knowing what rage and curs'd malignity
Would be in their base Hearts, resolved then
He would permit and suffer these vile men,
To bring his Purpose and Decree to pass,
Which for our Good, and his own Glory was.

CHAP. VIII.

Shewing how the Lord Jesus died in the Sinner's stead. Such was his love, and yet the Soul an Enemy at that time to him, and hated him. A full discovery of Christ's bloody Passion, enough to make a heart of stone to melt. The Prince gives up the ghost. Death *the King of Terrors, insults over* Jesus, *Prince of Light.* Death *is threatned with* Death: *shewing also what fear there was amongst the Devils, lest the Prince should rise again, and overcome* Death. *A second Council held in Hell: the Devils, tremble.* Death *subdued. Heathen Oracles cease. The Devil's destroyed upon the Prince's resurrection, and put to open shame. Joy in Heaven. Angels sing. Saints rejoyce. The end of the First Part.*

BUT to proceed, Will you lift up your Eyes,
And view the Rage of Hellish Enemies?
The final troubles of the Prince of Light
Are coming on; Behold a frightful sight!
A multitude with Clubs, and Swords, and Spears
About his Sacred Person now appears.¹⁸²
This wretched Rabble's come on a design,
Which wounds and breaks this stony heart of mine
To think upon't; behold, they are conducted
By the grand Traitor, and by him instructed
How to proceed on this great Enterprise,
Which he by Hellish power did devise.

Arm'd, as you heard, they seiz'd on him, as if
He had indeed been some notorious Thief.
Fond men! If you this Prince's Nature knew,
Your Weapons are too many, or too few.
As Man, so meek, you need no rescue fear;
As God, so strong, he can in pieces tear
A thousand Troops that should approach him near,
Of which a present Instance did appear.
Some little rays of his dread Deitie
He caused to break forth, and suddenly
They stagger'd, and fell backwards on the ground,[183]
That they might see he quickly could confound
Them utterly, and lay them at his feet,
But that he saw it better to submit
Unto his Father's will, and take the Cup
Which was prepared for him to drink up.[184]
But they recov'ring strength, got up again,
Regardless of all dread, and now amain
Resume their purpose, and with wicked hands
Take hold of him, who Heav'n & Earth Commands.
He's taken Prisoner, and strongly bound,
Who in one moments time could quite confound
The Universe, and all that him offend
Down to Hell's bottom quick with vengeance send.
Yet like a Lamb he's to the slaughter led,
And, as a Malefactor, suffered.
    Most dreadful sorrows did his Soul indure
That peace and Joy for her he might procure;
To bring his purpose to an happy end,
He manifests himself indeed a Friend,
A bounteous Friend, who thinks his Life not dear,
But freely lays it down, doth freely bear
The stroke of Justice, that he might recover
Her forfeit Life again. Oh! Sacred Lover!
Oh! Matchless Love and Grace! Let every Eye
Open its Sluces, draw its Fountains dry.
If he for us such bitter sorrows felt,
Then let the thoughts of his strong Passion melt
Our sin-congealed hearts, our hearts of stone.
    What was the reason why this Sacred One
Did bear all this? Were not our sins the cause?
He suffers, but 'twas we had broke the Laws.
Is he betray'd to Death? Weep o're his Herse,
Who only di'd our Death for to reverse.
    You sin-sick Souls,[185] think on his bloody Passion,
And then take up this bitter Lamentation:
Dear God! I sin'd, and did a Saviour need,
And must the Lord of Life and Glory bleed!

Ah! must his dear and precious blood be spilt,
To free me from my vile and horrid Guilt?
Didst thou, sweet Lord, my heavy burthen bear?
And shall not I lament, nor shed a Tear?
Shall not my hard and flinty heart dissolve,
To think how nought but thy own blood could salve
My fester'd wounds? What heart is so condens'd,
That cannot by these thoughts be influenc'd
And mov'd unto remorse and great Contrition,
I'th sense of the Lord Jesus's Crucifixion?
     They hal'd him (bound) unto the High Priests Hall,
Where Priests and Council did for witness call.
They search'd about for such, but none could find,
Who did agree together in one mind.
They us'd him like a Thief, put him to shame.
Who bore it with great patience, like a Lamb.
They blindfold him in a disgraceful sort,
And ignominiously made him their sport.
They smote him on the face, pluckt off his hair,
And bid him prophesy then who they were
That did him strike, that so they might thereby
His Office of a Prophet[186] vilifie.
His own dear Servants in this dismal Day
Did him forsake, and from him fly away.
They, they in whom his Soul took sweet delight,
His cursed Foes did so amaze and fright,
That they disown'd him too, and left him all
To stand alone, or otherwise to fall.
Yea, *Peter*, who would have his Lord confide
In him above the rest, stoutly deny'd
He ever knew him, nay, and furthermore,
To put it out of doubt, he curst and swore.
Ah! What is man when God withdraws his hand?
A *Peter* then one moment cannot stand.
This doubtless did add grief unto his Heart,
To see his own Disciples to depart,
And leave him thus in his Adversitie,
When in their stead it was he came to die.[187]
     He after this bore much, rebuke and shame,
Scoffs, blows, reproaches, stripes, oh who can name
The many Cruelties he underwent
Before his painful Death, and not lament?
They cru'lly smite him on his precious Cheeks,
Which he with patience bears, and never seeks
To free himself from this their Insolence,
Although he knew his spotless Innocence
O gracious Lord! how, how wast thou abus'd,
Unjustly judg'd, and falsely too accus'd?

Accus'd as guilty of some grievous fact,
Who thoughtst no Evil, none didst ever act?
No stain nor spot of sin was found in thee,
Though thus thou suffer'st for Iniquity.
The Injuries which thou that Night did'st bear,
How great, my God! how numberless they were?
     When he had past away that tedious Night,
Early next morning they with Hellish spight,
Like some great Malefactor, him present
To *Pontius Pilate*: where with innocent
And pleasant Countenance he then did stand,
To know what 'twas of him they did demand.
Then with an humble Silence held his peace,
Which made the fury of his Foes increase.
Next was he unto wicked *Herod* sent,
Who at his presence seemed much content,
Hoping he might some Miracle behold,
Because he had been of strange Wonders told.
But he that knew the secrets of all Hearts,
Who tries the Reins and views the inward parts,
Knew well his curious, but presumptuous mind,
Was only unto wickedness inclin'd.
Christ Answer'd not when he lookt for Replies.
Which made King *Herod* and his men despise
Our precious Lord, the Prince of Peace, whilst he
Became the pattern of Humilitie.
Thus Sinners contradict, and dare reprove
The Lord of Life, who quickly could remove
The lofty from their Seats, and them confound,
But nought but Love and Mercy doth abound.
This was the Day of his Humiliation,
He's first abas'd, then comes his Exaltation.
But, oh! that ever men should be so vile,
To smite those Lips that never utter'd guile!
He at whose great Command the Seas were still,
Is now commanded by each Tyrant's will.
He's sent to *Herod*, then sent back again
Unto the Judgment-Seat; But oh! what pain
Did he indure there by most wicked men,
What Heart can think, what Tongue express, what Pen
Can set it forth? Their sacrilegious Hands
Bound him about with strong and cruel bands:
They mock'd and did deride him shamefully,
And then aloud set up a cursed Cry,
Hold, hold him fast, deliver Barabbas,
Who a notorious Malefactor was,
A *Barabbas* is now prefer'd before
Him, whom the glorious Angels do adore.

A Murderer shall spared, saved be,
When *JESUS* shall be hanged on a Tree.
With torturing whips they scourged him most sore,
Until his flesh was dy'd with Purple Gore.
O dreadful dismal Cup! what heart can think
On what he underwent, and's flesh not shrink?
The Blood that once run through his sacred Veins,
Is now let out by Soul-tormenting pains,
And all the blushing Pavement gilds, not stains.
Ah! don't you see how it fell trickling down.
Yet unto him was no compassion shown.
The Blood that issued forth from every wound,
Descends in pearly drops unto the ground.
Oh Earth! that didst receive that holy Blood,
Nor fruitful *Nile*, nor *Tagus* golden Flood
Could ever yield like Vertue, or such good,
Ne're such a stream did water thee before,
Nor shall again refresh thee any more.[188]
    Nor were these cruel barb'rous scourgings all
That he endur'd in that remorsless Hall,
For after this they clothed him in scorn
With Purple, when his flesh was lasht and torn,
And in derision of his Princely State,
Their impious hands a Crown of thorns did plate,
Pressing it on his gracious Head with pain,
Till Sacred Drops did issue forth again
In ruful sort, as they had done before,
Spreading his precious Neck and Face all o're.
Thus like a Lamb amongst those Wolves he stood,
From head to foot besprinkled o're with blood.
His Kingly Office[189] further to debase,
'Stead of the Scepter due to *Judah's* Race,
They put a Reed in's hand, then kneel before him,
And in Derision feignedly adore him.
Thus, thus did they the Sacred Prince abuse,
Crying in scorn – *All hail, King of the Jews:*[190]
Then in Disdain they spit in's his lovely Face.
Could Devils offer God a worse Disgrace?
Oh depth of Love alone, that knows no bounds,
To suffer such dire stripes, such mocks & wounds!
'Twas we that sin'd, 'twas thou that sufferst[a] shame,
To free us from the guilt. Oh let thy Name
Thy Sacred Name for ever honour'd be,
Who thus wast us'd, to set poor Sinners free.
But yet, alas! these sufferings were not all,
More bitter things did unto him befall.
Off next they took the Robe, his own put on,[191]
And now as if their malice fresh begun,

Not satisfy'd their God for to deride,
They loud cry'd out, *Let him be Crucify'd.*[192]
His Blood they thirst for. *Pilate* gives consent,
Though Conscience told him he was Innocent,
And had deserved neither Death nor Bands,
Yet up he gives him to the Rabbles hands.
He knew of malice they had brought him thither,
Yet he and they at last combine together
'T imbrew their guilty hands in guiltless Blood,
Who never did them harm, but always good.
Rather than *Pilate* will displease the *Jews,*
Hee'l stifle Conscience, utterly refuse
All Admonitions; though his bosom Friend
A timely warning unto him did send,
Uses Intreaties, urges Arguments,[193]
But nothing would prevail, nothing prevents
Their wicked purpose.[194] Sentence being past,
Unto his Execution now they hast.
Though he was wounded very much before,
His flesh, his Virgin flesh, with stripes made sore,
Yet they upon his Martyr'd shoulders lay
His heavy Cross, till fainting by the way
By reason of th' intolerable pain
His bleeding wounds procured, they constrain
A Country-man of *Cyrene*[195] (who did pass
Along that way) to bear his pond'rous Cross.
And coming up to dismal *Golgotha,*[196]
Without remorse of Conscience, dread, or awe,
They still persist in putting him to Death,
A Death the worst that e're stopt humane Breath;
The *cruel Death o th Cross,* matchless for pain,
And by God's Curse most liable to shame.
To cause the Just to die was crueltie,
But Crucifixion's more than 'tis to die.
Prodigious Rage! strange metamorphos'd mind!
What? kill the Lord, who was to you so kind!
What was his Crime? what his so great offence?
That not contented to remove him hence
By violent Death, but you must look about
Whereby to find exquisite torments out?
The vilest wretch that ever did draw breath,
Or in the strictest sense deserved Death,
Could never meet with more severitie
From barb'rous Foes and brutish Tyranny.
He meets with no compassion, every heart,
And every hand is set to throw a Dart.
So far from shame in this their villany,
They chuse for time to act the Tragedy,

Their chiefest Feast, when to *Jerusalem*
From every part thousands of people came;
Then, then they chose this cursed work to do.
That he the greater shame might undergo.
When *Priest* and *Pilate* finisht had their Court.
Dear *Jesus* must be fetcht to make them sport.[197]
And now behold (if yet thy delug'd Eyes
Can stay to see so sad a Sacrifice)
Behold him lift up on the cursed Tree.
Expos'd to Torture, Death, and Infamy.
His Arms spread wide, as ready to imbrace
His bitter'st Foes, if they'd accept his Grace,
Quite through each hand & foot sharp nails they drive,
And fix him there to wait for Death alive,
Hanging betwixt two Thieves.[198] *Numbred among*
Transgressors[199] by the giddy partial Throng:
For passers-by did rail on him with scorn,
Wagging their heads,[200] who ought rather to mourn.
With taunts and scoffs the vulgar him abuse.
Prompted by the *Chief Priest*, and barb'rous *Jews*.[201]
And when he thirsts through his excessive pains,
Behold what favour at their hands he gains;
All they afford to quench his drought withal,
Was Vinegar, mixed with bitter Gall.[202]
Was ever such a perfect hatred known?
No Dram of pity, but all malice shown.
He that for them had Water turn'd to Wine,[203]
And shown his Pow'r and Charity Divine,
Nor Wine, nor Water now could be allow'd
T' asswage his thirst from this ungrateful Croud:
But into's tender side they thrust a Spear,
From whence there came both *blood & water* clear.[204]
Thus hand, and foot, and head, and every part,
They pierce and wound, for to encrease his smart.
Ah! see that stream wch from his Heart-blood flows,
The precious Balm and Cure of all our woes!
Each pious Soul, which truly doth believe,
Its Soveraign Vertue freely may receive.
One drop of that most Sacred Blood is worth
Ten thousand Thrones & Kingdoms of the Earth.
When you by Sin do see your selves undone,
Think on that Blood which from his Side did run.
Those cordial Drops apply'd unto thy heart,
Will heal thy Soul, and cleanse thy inward part.
Ah! canst thou of Christ's dismal passion hear,
And not dissolve thy Soul into a Tear?
    But to return – There's something, still behind,
Which makes strange meltings in my grieved mind,

That's worse than all the rest, oh hear his moan,
And how his poor distressed Soul doth groan!
His Father hides his face, that gracious Eye
Casts forth an angry frown, which made him cry
(After he had these bitter torments felt
From cruel hands, and found his Soul to melt,
His spirits fail, and wounded heart to break)
Why, why, my God? Oh why dost thou forsake
Me in this needful hour?[205] Hard is the case
When thou, my God, from me shalt hide thy face.
My Servants who forsook me, are but Dust,
Poor flesh and blood, alas! what stay, what trust
Is there in man? the best of men are frail;
Such as confide in them, their strength will fail.
But, ah! My Trust, my Hope, my Confidence,
Thou, thou that art my Rock and safe Defence,
Even thou, my God! O thou, O thou hast left me,
And this at last has of all Peace bereft me.
Whilst Souls can see their Interest in their God,
They can bear up under the sharpest Rod:
But when thy face is hid, as 'tis from me,
They sink, they die, they die Eternally.[206]
        Thus, thus the *Prince of Peace* in sore distress,
His bitter moan doth unto God express.
Great depths of sorrow did oppress his Soul,
When his sad portion thus he did condole.
He saw himself forsaken and forlorn,
When in our stead this anguish great was born.
That which was due for our Iniquity,
Did heavy on our gracious Saviour lie.
For Justice spar'd not, but laid on her Hand,
Whilst in the room and stead he seeks to stand
Of the poor *Soul*, he came from Heaven to save;
Justice, alas! will the last farthing have.[207]
The torments Saints have born's another thing
From what befel their Soveraign Lord & King.
His Spirit's gracious, great, magnanimous,
Yet ne're was any Soul distressed thus.
That much renowned holy Martyr, *Stephen*,
He had so glorious a prospect from Heaven,
As fill'd his Soul brim-full of Consolation,
And by that means with joy he bore his passion.[208]
        Should I attempt to walk the spacious Field
Of instances, how many would it yield,
Where flames of Fire were like to Beds of Roses,
Through Heav'nly Rays, wch gloriously composes
Their spirits so, that they in Triumph sing,
When half-consum'd in Fire, they felt no sting.

God smiles, and Heav'n appears so clear & bright
All fears and terrors were extinguisht quite.
But he who for our sakes his Life laid down,
Is forc'd to bear his Father's angry frown,
And in our stead he felt his Indignation,
The bitterest part of all his bitter Passion.
How heavy is that stroke, how sharp that Rod,
That's lifted up by men, laid on by God?
When Heav'n and Earth, and Hell do all agree
To lay on stripes with greatst severitie?
That grief, that pain, that anguish must be sore;
And yet all this for us blest *Jesus* bore.

  Who that beholds Heav'ns glorious lamp of Light
When in his strength, obscur'd from our sight
By the dark body of the pale-fac'd Moon,
Making black shades of Night appear at Noon,
But would conclude from thence the Sun were gone,
And had forsaken quite our Horizon?
And yet we know he's but eclips'd a while,
And soon will lend the World another smile,
Disperse those shades that counterfeited Night,
And fill the Earth again with splendor bright.
Lo, thus our Sun in his Celestial Sphear
Is near his setting, yet but lend your Ear
Unto the Voice, th'amazing Voice of Heaven,
You'l find an universal notice given
Unto the world when this bright Sun went down,
Heav'ns lightfoot Herauld quickly makes it known.
Christ lies a^a bleeding, nailed on the Tree,
And now the universal World shall see
Heaven act a part in this black Tragedy.   }

  The Worlds great Eye, the natural Sun, whose Rays
Each day throughout the Universe displays,
From East to West, from North to South, his face
Visiting and refreshing every place,
No sooner doth he spy the Prince near dead,
But straightaway^b he withdraws his blushing Head.
That horrid sight bright *Sol* abhor'd to see,
And hides his face from Noon till after Three.
At Three Christ's matchless Torments made him cry,
Eli, Eli, Lama sabachthani.
Then was the Temple Vail rent quite asunder,
The earth did shake, the rocks did roar like thunder,
The Clouds grew thick, and such as scatter'd were,
Conjoin'd to darken all the Hemisphear.
Thus for three hours Darkness great remain'd,
All hearts now tremble, every spirit's pain'd.[209]

Th' Astronomers, who starry motions trace,
And read Earth's wonders in Heav'ns various face,
(*Eusebius*,[210] and other Authors write)
Were much amaz'd at that unusual sight;
Their Learning could no natural Causes spy,
Nor give a Reason of that Prodigie.
The Moon being then *at full*, just opposite,
Could not in Natures course eclipse *Sol's* Light.
'Twas supernatural what he suffered,
And that was it which fill'd them all with dread.
Some smote their breasts, whilst others in confusion
Drew from the premises this just Conclusion,
Either the God of Nature suffers now
(When Sol in Sables muffles thus his brow)
Or the whole frame o'th World in a short space,
Will be dissolv'd and end its painful Race.[211]
These dreadful things which then did come to pass,
Do fully prove He the Messiah was,
And many when they saw those Wonders done,
Cry'd out indeed he was God's only Son.
Had not this obvious been to every sight
A real thing, with what great ease then might
The Foes of Christ and Christianity,
Detected all as horrid Forgery?
But matt'r of Fact being so very clear,
The *Jews* and *Heathens* thereby silenc'd were.

    Thus he yields up at last his painful breath,
And for a while lay conquered by Death.
Conquer'd, said I! forbear my lavish Muse,
Recall that word, and be not so profuse.
What, shall we say. The Lord of Life is dead?
'Tis but a slumber, he's not conquered.
He only for a while Retreat hath made,   }
To bring his Foes into an Ambuscade,   }
And soon will rise more gloriously Array'd.   }
Thus did the Glory of the World lay down
His precious Life, to purchase a rich Crown
Of Life[212] and Glory for his Spouse, whom he
Found under Wrath, condemn'd eternally,
Who had receiv'd that Sentence full of Ire,
Goe, go thou Wretch into eternal Fire.
But he has bail'd her from Hell's gaping Jaws,
And satisfy'd Justice's strictest Laws
By this his Death, where he in her stead stood,
And ransom'd her even with his dearest Blood.

    But hark, my Muse! What Triumph dost thou hear?
What Voice is that hoarse sounding in mine Ear?

'Tis *Death*, doubtless 'tis *Death* that ghastly King,
Who over *Christ* doth now insulting sing;
Now he has got him down, I prethee hear
How he o're him doth vaunt and domineer.

The *King of Terror*'s boasting Triumph over *Christ* whilst he lay in the Grave.

King of Terrors.

  What am I? or from whence? For though I be,
Yet know I not my self; nor why to me
The mightiest Monarchs bend. I rule, I raign,
And am the High and Lofty's Soveraign.
All tremble at the thoughts of my grim face,
They look, they run, yet cannot find a place
To hide themselves. My Powr's very great,
Yet know I not who set me in this Seat.
There's none that live, have liv'd, or ever may,
But I o're them an awful Scepter sway.
But, oh! what kind of subject have I here?
A Subject, t' whom no Monarch is a Peer;
Ah! how I smile to fee't; I'le never fear
Being worsted now. Alas! dost thou submit?
Art thou likewise brought down unto my feet?
Who's able my dread Power to withstand;
Since thou canst not escape my pow'rful hand?
Now I have seiz'd thee, be assur'd that I
Will keep thee down, for ever thou shalt lie
In the dark Regions of eternal Night.
Lo! here, proud Mortals, an amasing sight!
What can't I do, since he that made the Day,
By my strong hand is turned into clay?
If thou can'st not thy self from me deliver,
The hope of Creature-man is gone for ever.
None out of these close Regions can repair,
Nor re-salute again the ambient Air,
I never did so great a Conquest gain,
O what a mighty Monarch I have slain!
Now, now let me be crown'd victoriously!
For what is done, which none could do but I.
Who dares my Triumphs lessen or defer,
Since I am now a perfect Conquerour?
Here, here, Great Prince, with me in this dark Cell
My Captive thou with other Kings shalt dwell.

Prince of Light.

  Thou proud Imperious Tyrant, prethee hear:
Don't boast too soon, nor vainly domineer.
A feeble Warriour may the Field obtain,

When his strong Foe is willing to be slain.
My Life, *proud Death*, thou didst not take away
By any strength of thine: for I did lay
It freely down, as God did me command,
This made me yield my self into thy hand.

King of Terrors.

I'le not contend, let that be so or not,
I have thee safe in my Dominions got;
And e're thou do return, I'le make thee know
What pow'r I have, what 'tis that I can do.
My Prisoner thou art, and here shalt lie
In these dark Cells unto Eternitie,
Whilst worms on thy most lovely flesh are fed,
And with Corruption thou art covered.

Prince of Light.

Stay, stay, pale *Death*, that thou canst nev'r do,
For I must not the least Corruption know.

King of Terrors.

Strange speech! who's this? or how can this thing be?
What's in the Grave shall not Corruption see?
Though with rich Spices thou imbalm'd dost lie,
Old hoary Time shall make thee putrify.
Kings fortifi'd by Lead and Searcloth's[213] aid,
In precious heaps of fragrant Odours laid,
To stench and rottenness I soon betray'd.
None ever into these low Vaults do come,
Who can escape that sad and dismal doom,
Of being turned into Dust, – I will
Thy mouth with filthy putrefaction fill.
The holiest man I e're depriv'd of breath,
I turned into loathsom stinking Earth.
And dost thou think thou shalt escape this fate?
No, thou must share of all my Subjects state.

Prince of Light.

Is't fit I should be threatned thus by thee?
Shall Death prevail and triumph over me?
Dost know, grim Tyrant, who 'tis thou treadst down?
I am thy lawful Prince, and thou shalt own
My Sovereignty; thou must, O *Death*, submit,
And yield thy self, as conquer'd at my feet.
On me thou shalt not have thy proud desire;
No sooner shall three Days and Nights expire,
But I will make thy bonds and chains to fly,
And thereby spoil thy Principality.
But for thy insolence this thou shalt gain,

To be thy self, o're-thrown, vanquisht and slain.
The tidings which I bring will make thee quake,
For I resolve on thee Revenge to take.
O Death, I'le be thy Death,[214] 'tis even so,
Thy utter ruin, and great overthrow
Is near at hand; I'le rouse up from the Grave,
And make the stone to fly that's on the Cave.
Let Hell and Devils all combine to do
What's in their pow'r to save thee from this blow,
I mind it not; I'le tear and rend them all,
And cause them with great vengeance down to fall.
Captivity a Captive[215] I will take,
And him a slave and Captive ever make.

     The Devils fearing what would come to pass,
Great consternation straight amongst them was.
Their Chief amaz'd, with envious horror cryes,
And to the rest with hast himself applies.

               Lucifer.
    Dominions, Pow'rs of the Infernal Host!
Awake, attempt with speed, or all is lost.[216]
Death's like to lose our great and hop'd for prey,
Secure him fast, more Chains upon him lay.
Hark! are there not strange tremblings under ground
Mixt with a cry, enough for to confound
All the whole Host of this amased Lake,
Fear seizes me, I quiver, oh, I quake.
What shall we do? make speed, let him not rise.
Help, *Satan!* help, canst thou no way devise
To hold him under ground? now, now, or never,
If he awake, we are undone for ever.
Should he the cords of *Death* to pieces burst,
Our latter ills will far exceed the first.

     Thus see how all the hellish Fiends do stand
Agast, amaz'd, each holding up his hand;
Bewailing their sad fates, their hearts grow cold,
With thoughts of what they fear'd they should behold,
When[a] was the Resurrection from the Dead
Of him who for poor Mortals suffered.
Belzebub he cryes out to *Abaddon,*
Ah! what a day is this! all will be gone.
Satan doth gnash his teeth, perplext in mind,
Because they could no more Inventions find
Their Kingdom to support, cryes out, alas,
We never were before in such a case!

Apollyon.
Ah! what a dismal day, Great Lords, is here!
The Grave doth o'pe, that sight doth just appear
Of which you talk, of which you stand in fear.
Now all our hopes, and expectation's gone.
Ah! who is it has rould away the stone?[217]
All proves in vain that ever we have done.
We must our selves in Chains of darkness lie,
And be tormented to Eternitie.

Now from the Earth fresh Light doth gild the skies
Thick darkness vanishes; awake, arise,
Ye Mortals, and with joy open your Eyes;
Behold the morning of that long'd for Day;
The Grave doth o'pe, whilst Devils fly away
To hide themselves, but cannot find a place,
For Vengeance hastens after them apace.
The first Day of the week[218] is now come in,
The Glorious Prince has made an end of *Sin.*
See how he rouses up from the dark Grave,
The Soul from thence, from Sin and Hell to save.
Ah! how the damned Spirits cry and houl,
Their fearful fall with anguish to condole.
Hell's Principalities are spoiled quite,
And all infernal Pow'rs put to flight.
See what an open shew is made of them,
And how great *JESVS* doth their Pride contemn.
See how he doth triumph over them all,
He's on his back who gave the Soul its fall.
See *Death's* by *Death* destroy'd, a wond'rous sight,
Which doth the hearts of Angels much delight.
They pry into, and wonder at this thing,
Accomplisht thus by our victorious King.
How like a sneaking, conquer'd, spoiled Foe,
That's quite o'recome and brought to utter woe,
Doth Satan look. Ah, see the fatal Rout,
And how the Prince doth drag these Dogs about,
He makes a show of them; Come, take a view
O'th conquer'd, bloody, baffled Hellish Crew.
What a victorious Conqueror is here?
What Victor may with this great Prince compare?
All Warriours you admir'd heretofore,
Let them not be so much as thought on more.
CHRIST JESUS he is risen from the Dead,
Sin, Wrath, Death, Hell, Devils, and all are fled.
This glorious Conquest o're th' infernal crew,

Is yet more plain by that which doth insue.
Some passages from ancient Records[a] show
The truth of this their final overthrow.
Upon this rising of the *Prince of Light*,
The *Heathen Oracles* were silenc'd quite.
Although their Priests and Prophets cry and call,
Henceforth they'r dumb, and answer not at all.
Which Accident and unexpected change
Amaz'd them all; 'twas so prodigious strange,
It made them look about to find the cause
Of such their silence and surprising pause.
Surely, saith *Plutarch, they are either dead,*
Or else Wise men are risen in their stead,
Which in these days diviner Secrets know,
That Oracles before were wont to show.[219]
Yet he knew better things, and did deny
That Spirits either could wax old, or die.
Some higher Reason therefore must find out
E're he resolve this sense-confounding doubt.
Had he convers'd with *John,* he might have known
By whom, and how those Gods were overthrown.
Christ was reveal'd (saith he) *unto this End,*
That he the works of every Hellish Fiend
Might bring to nought, destroy and ruine quite,
Confining them to their eternal Night.
That this is truth, from Authors of their own
Might be made good, and evidently shown;
Sharp *Juvenal*(*) to speak it out is pleas'd,
All Oracles at Delphos *now are ceas'd.*[220]

And lofty *Lucan* long since did complain
That they their Deities invok'd in vain,
The Gods (saith he,†) *by whom this Empire stood*
But with one instance more I may conclude,
Though I indeed might urge a multitude;
'Tis that which *Plutarch* doth affirm, and I
Esteem above what e're Antiquity
Hath left recorded, or most curious Eyes
Can view in best approved Histories,
Relating to the matter we have stated,

*   *Sat. 6. Cessant*[a] *oracula Delphis*
†   *Excessere omnes Adytis Arisq; relictis*
    Dii, quibus Imperium hoc steterat, &c.
    Are from their empty Temples now remov'd.
    Their Altars too they have abandon'd quite,
    And left the places of their old delight.[221]

Which follows thus, as 'tis by him related.
About the period of *Tiberius*'s Raign
(Who at *Christ*'s Death was *Rome*'s proud Sovereign)
Strange hideous Cries, shriekings and howlings be
Heard with amazement, in the *Grecian* Sea,
Complaining that their great God *Pan* was fled.
From whence great Consternations followed.
No sooner did the louder Trump of Fame
This news of their great *Pans* Retreat proclaim,
But it was brought unto the Emperours Ears,
And unto him a certain Truth appears.
Who being startled at the strange Relation,
Falls with his Wisemen into Consultation,
Who sought by Magick to resolve the doubt:
Which all their Art and Skill could not find out.[222]
Yet Christians in those days could quickly spy
The way to open the whole Mysterie.
Comparing times, they found this strange Relation
Did just fall out upon Christ's Death and Passion;
And then concluded straightway by the Fall
Of their great *Pan*, which signifieth *All*;
All Spirits by *Christ's Death* were so afflicted,
Their utter Ruin thereby was predicted.
Yea others of their own Records, still do
Confirm the truth of this their overthrow.[223]
How one of them constrain'd sometime before
By God himself, their fall did thus deplore:
"*An Hebrew Child that shall be born, will be*
"*The final downfal of our Dignity.*
"*All our usurpt Dominions by that Child*
"*Shall come to nought, and utterly be spoil'd.*
"*He strikes us dumb, and nonplus's our Art,*
"*Henceforth in vain no further Questions start,*
"*But sad and silent from our Shrines depart.*[224]
Thus God doth force Devils sometimes to speak,
That which doth much against their Int'rest make.
      But stay, my Muse; the Cherubs chant again,
O listen to this more melodious strain.
The glorious Angels do[a] sweet Triumphs sing,
Upon the Conquests of our Heav'nly King;
They clap their wings, and leap for joy to see
This total Rout and happy Victorie.
Shall Heav'n rejoyce, and more concerned Earth
Not sing aloud *Jehovah*'s praises[b] forth?
O happy Day, blest hour, the best of all
Poor Mortals ever saw since *Adam*'s fall;
Christ of a truth is risen from the Grave,
No Pow'rs of Hell could keep him in the Cave.

Yet are there some in these last evil days
Deny that he from Death himself did raise.
The *Jews* also, with their Forefathers, say,
'T was a Deceit; for he was stoln away
Whilst drousy Soldiers fell into a sleep,
Who the Sepulchre had a charge to keep.
A thing themselves, no doubt, could not believe,
But was forg'd by the Devil, to deceive
And blind mens Eyes, who wanted that inspection
They might have had touching his Resurrection.
'Twas the last game the Devil could devise,
To hinder Christ's most glorious Enterprise.
They knew that if his Resurrection were
Received for a truth, no hope was there,
But all that they had done, it tumble must:
So the last Evil would exceed the first.
But if they had believ'd it, certainly
The Souldiers had with great'st severity
Been punished, for being so remiss,
About a thing so weighty as was this.
Besides, were they asleep, how could they tell
What things there came to pass, or what befell?
Or, if awake, why did they not prevent
Those men who came with such a strong intent?
And can one think, if the Disciples durst
Attempt that thing, they should have stript him first?[225]
Would they not take the body in the cloaths,
Lest e're they'd done, the Sould'ers should have rose,
And caught them doing it? and then be sure
Great sufferings for it they must endure.
Nay, had these men been guilty of such evils,
They'd been no better than seducing Devils,
The worst of Mortals: and how was it then
That God should own and witness to such men,
By aiding them? Would[a] Heavens Pow'r have gone
To prove a Cheat, when Miracles were done?
Again, they were of such Integrity,
As none could brand with the least infamy.
And they 'ith face of Foes, without least dread
Declare that he was risen from the Dead;
That they convers'd with him full forty days,
Whilst he instructed them in all his ways,
Before he did ascend.[226] And then agen,
In *Galilee* at once five hundred men
Saw him with joy, and in their witness gave,
That he indeed was risen from the Grave.[227]
      Here stop again, my Pen, Time calls away,
Upon this *Theme* thou must no longer stay;

Leave them to perish, let them fall and die,
That this blest Resurrection do deny.
Shall God, his Saints, and Angels, witness bear
Unto this thing, and yet shall Mortals dare
To call the same in question, or deny
What is confirm'd by such Authority?
No, firm as Earth, or Heav'ns more stable poles,
Let this great Truth be fixt in pious Souls.
Without it Faith's a Fancy, and the best
Of men more wretched than the vilest Beast.

    But now, awake my Muse, no longer slumber,
The Day doth dawn, and joys which none can number
Are rushing in upon the *Prince of Light*;
This sorrow's gone, nought now but Glory bright
Shines forth in him; now is he rais'd on high,
Far out o'th reach of all malignity.
Nor men nor Devils can annoy him more,
He's safely landed on the long'd-for shore.
Go Turtles, go, whilst thousand Joys betide[228]
The glorious Bridegroom and his purchas'd Bride.
That Sun is risen who will ne're go down,
Who will his Spouse with light of Glory crown.
But where's the Soul! O where, alas, is she,
For whom he dy'd and hung upon the Tree?
What greeting? O what Joy, when they do meet,
There will abound! the thoughts thereof are sweet.
He that was Dead is come to Life again,
And ever shall in bliss Eternal raign.
Thrice happy is that Soul which he hath chose
To be his Love, his Dove,[229] his *Sharon*'s Rose.[230]
But where is she, and what is her Estate?
For nothing of her we have heard of late.
Doth she not wait? doth she not long to see
His lovely Face, and to embraced be
In his dear Arms? O do'nt she greatly crave
One sight of him, *one* visit more to have?
Doth not her Soul dissolve then into tears,
With thoughts of him who freed her from all fears?
Read the next Part, and you will quickly find
The Fruit of Sin, and nature of the mind
That is corrupt, and fill'd with carnal Love,
How nothing can those vile Affections move;
Oh how unkind to Christ do Sinners prove!
             The End of the First Book.[a]

BOOK II.

The Glorious Lover,
A Divine POEM.

CHAP. I.

Shewing how Christ renews his Suit again and again, which is done either by the ministration of the Gospel, or by his various Providences, and yet the Soul refuses to receive him.

THUS have you heard a Sacred Story told,
Fill'd full of Wonders, Wonders, which unfold
Such depths of Wisdom, depths of Grace and Love.
Which none can comprehend, it is above
The reach of men; no knowledge is so high
That can conceive of it; nay, Angels pry
Into this thing, this Myst'ry is so deep,
It all the glorious *Seraphims* doth keep
In holy admiration, they'r amaz'd
To see how all the Attributes are rais'd
In equal Glory, and do sweetly shine
In their own proper Sphere, alike divine.
Here by diviner Art you all may find
What was in our great God's eternal mind,
Before the Earth's foundation long was laid,
Or e're bright *Sol* his glorious beams display'd,
Respecting Man, whom he foresaw would fall,
And bring his Soul thereby into sad thral:
Here may you with much ease and joy espy
The great result of the blest Trinity.
In that eternal Council held above,
About the Soul, the object of Christ's Love.
Here also, here's a proof of true affection,
And how to love from hence let's take direction.
Who ever had or shew'd such love as he,
Who for his Love was nailed to the Tree?
        But, hark! some do enquire, they long to hear
What is become of th' *Soul* he loves so dear?
Lo, from the Grave he's come, he looks about,
He searches every place to find her out.
What is she fled! and where? in what strange Isle
Of clouds and darkness lurks she all this while?
Good *Reader*, urge me not, I'le let thee hear
That which may melt thy Soul into a tear.
Excuse my Pen for what its lines shall speak.
Such Marble hearts as cannot melt, must break.
To leave off here, I'm sure it is not fit,

Nor would I write what you would have unwrit.
But since it doth upon the Soul reflect,
It matters not how much we do detect
The folly which doth in the Sinner lie,
When Soveraign Grace exalted is thereby.
My Heart and Pen seem both to be at strife,
To paint unkindness forth unto the life.
Wilt Thou, who dost the *Muses* aid, afford
Divine assistance, that each pow'rful word
May rend a heart at least, and every line
Turn Kingdoms and whole Nations into brine
Of their own tears? teach me, O Lord, the skil
T' extract the spirit of grief, O let my Quil,
Like *Moses* Rod, make Adamants to fly,
That tears may gush like Rivers from each eye.[231]
How can it once be thought that such a Friend,
Who loveth thus, doth thus his love commend,
And in such sort so strangely condescend,
Should when all's done by her contemned be,
Though he's most high, and she of base degree?
The grand design, the end and reason why
This Prince from Heaven came, was scourg'd, did die,
Was to redeem the *Soul*, and so endeavour
To get her love, and marry her for ever,
As is before declar'd, But will you hear
How things are carry'd, how they manag'd are?
The time is come, you'l find, by what ensues
That this great Lord his Suit a-fresh renews.
When Sacred Love runs thus with greatest force,
What pity is't ought should disturb its course?
How can the *Soul* refuse to entertain
A Lover, which for her with shame was slain?
But stop again, my *Muse*, thou must give o're,
The Prince is come, lo he is at her door.[232]

Jesus *Prince of Light.*
  Most precious Soul! I now am come again,
Behold 'tis I, who for thee have been slain.
How is't with thee, hast thou not heard the news,
What for thy sake I suffer'd by the *Jews?*
That through a Sea of blood, and sorrows great,
I now am come with bowels to intreat
Thee to embrace the offer I present.
And, first of all, with tears do thou repent
That ever thou hast entertained Sin,
That has to me so very bitter bin.

Soul.

Repent! This is a melancholly strain;
It suits with such whose lives are fill'd with pain,
And guilty are of some notorious crime,
Whose glass is near run out, whose precious time
Draws to an end; 'tis good for such indeed
To look about them, and repent with speed:
But thus 'tis not with me, I know no sorrow
I'le wave that work, I'le wave it till to morrow,
To morrow, I mean, till some fitter season:
I see no cause, alas, I know no reason
To hark to thoughts that may disturb my peace,
When joys abound, and sweat delights increase.
Repent! of what strange kind of voice shall I
Amazed stand, yet can no danger 'spy.[233]

JESUS.

No reason why! Ah Soul, art still so blind,
Wounded from head to foot, and canst thou find
No ground of grief, no cause to lay to heart
Thy horrid guilt, nor yet the bitter smart
Which I indur'd for thee, to prevent
Severer Wrath, severer punishment,
And dost not savour this sweet word, *Repent?*
'Tis well there's room, a call, a season fit,
There's thousand Souls who are denied it.[234]
Dar'st, dar'st adventure still to live in Sin?
What, crucifie thy dying Lord agin!
Were not my pangs sufficient? must I bleed
Afresh? O must thy sinful pleasures feed
Upon my torments? and augment the story
Of the sad passion of the Lord of Glory?
Is there no pity in thee? what, no remorse
Within thy breast? Seek, seek a firm divorce
Betwixt thy self and Sin; do thy endeavour
To break that league, depart, depart for ever.
Did I not suffer to dissolve the knot
Between thee and all Lust? and wilt thou not
Regard me now, but entertain my Foe?
What, cruel unto me, and thy self too!
I prethee, *Soul,* be think thy self, and yield,
And let thy Lovers for my sake be kill'd;
Ah, let them die, who if they live, will be
Thy death at last, who have bin death to me.

Soul.

Those joys are sweet which do delight my heart;
Ah! how can I and sinful Objects part?

Must gainful Lusts, and those which honour's yield,
At once be put to th' Sword? And those be kill'd
Which so much pleasure unto me afford?
How can it be? alas, it is too hard:
The thoughts of it's a perfect death to me;
Lord, say no more, I cannot yield to thee.

Jesus.

    Ah! Didst thou know, poor *Soul*, what 'tis to sin,
And how my Soul for it has tortur'd bin,
Thou wouldst revenged be on it, I'm sure,
And a divorcement speedily procure.
Or, didst thou know what grief it is to me
To be contemned and despis'd by thee;
Such churlish Answers wouldst thou not return
To him, whose soul in fervent love do's burn
To thee, poor wretch, and only for thy good,
'Tis that I seek, and sought with tears of blood.
Once more I ask thy love, I cannot leave thee,
Until my everlasting Arms receive thee.

Soul.

    If I may have those pleasures which delight me,
Whose amorous glances sweetly do invite me
To love them dear, who stollen have my heart,
I am contented thou shouldst have some part
Of my affection: Worldly joy is sweet,
And I resolve to take[a] some part of it.

Jesus.

    Ungrateful Soul! did I not wholly give
My self for thee? and shall I now receive
A piece of thine, nay but a little part,
That have deserved more than a whole heart:
'Tis all the heart, or none; do'st think it fit
Sin and the Devil should have part of it?
Would any Lover such strange love receive,
To be contented that his Spouse should have,
Some other Suiters, and to them should cleave?
What sayst, deceived Soul? why standst thou mute?
Disclose thy inward thoughts, and grant my Suit.
O speak! or, if thy doubtful mind be bent
To silence, let that silence be consent.
If thou wilt grant me that whole heart of thine;
We'l exchange hearts, I'le give thee all of mine.

    She look'd about, she mus'd, she paus'd a while,
Whilst he on her cast forth an Heav'nly smile;
Sweet rays of Glory glanced from his Eye,

Enough to ravish all the standers-by;
So great a lustre from his garments shone,
It dazl'd all weak eyes to look upon.
Like as the Sun his glorious beams displays,
Dispersing every way his sparkling rays,
When in his strength & splendor bright doth shine,
So glister'd forth his Glory all Divine.[235]
Ne're such a beauty carnal eyes beheld.
Ah! one sweet sight of him has wholly fill'd
The greatest Soul that liv'd, and there is still
Enough in him millions of Hearts to fill.
And none but Him alone can satisfie
The Soul of Man, the Soul-enlightned eye.
But stay and hear the Answer which is given
By the deceived Soul. O let the Heaven
And Earth astonish'd stand, whilst stubborn she
Deny'd his Suit, will not persuaded be
To o'pe her door, who longs to enter in,
To fill her Soul with joy, destroy her sin.

      Soul.
    Strange 'tis to me such beauty should be there!
What, so amazing glorious, none so fair!
When I no loveliness in him can see.
The World, and outward pleasures, seem to me
More rare and spriteful, far the better choice;
Such things I like: but for this Lover's voice,
His Face and Favour I ca'nt so esteem,
Nor can I leave all things for love of him.
Therefore be gone, and cease thy suit; for I
Have fixt my mind elswhere, my heart and eye
Is set on that which outward eyes can see.
Lord, let me not be troubl'd more with thee.

    O stay, my Muse! reach me an Iron Pen,
T engrave this on the marble hearts of men.
Let Sinners look within, then let them read
Themselves ungrateful, blind, and dark indeed.
Would not each Soul conclude this Creature were
Besides her self, or else deserv'd to bear
The great'st contempt, and pity'd be by none,
That bids such a dear Lover to be gone?
How oft has he by precious motives try'd
The Soul from sin and evil to divide,
And make her too obdurat heart relent,
And take such ways as Wisdom do's invent?
His Passions, Sighs and Tears are ready still,
As the officious agents of his Will,

To work her to a sence of her estate:
But she's (alas) so dark and desperate,
That his sweet voice, of so divine a strain,
So moving, mov'd her, but seems all in vain.
He sighs for her, he knows her sad distress,
He asks her love, but still without success.
Ah Sinners! view your rocky hearts, and then
Smite on your breasts, lament, and read agen.
The glorious Lord his love's so strange, so great,
He knows not how not how to think of a retreat.
His soul is griev'd, yet takes not her denial,
But makes a new Essay, another Trial.

Jesus.
Did, did I love thee from Eternity?
And my celestial Kingdom leave for thee?
Did I Man's humane nature freely take?
Did I my bed in a poor Manger make?[236]
Did I engage the cruel'st of all Foes?
Did I from men and Devils meet with blows?
Did I such kind of tortures undergoe
Which men nor Angels can't conceive or know?
Did Wrath pursue, and Justice fall on me?
And did I bear it all for love to thee?
Ah! did I sweat great drops of Sacred Blood,
Until the ground was sprinkled where I stood?[237]
And were my feet and hands nail'd to the Tree,
Whilst my dear Father hid his Face from me?
Have I with joy, delight, and chearful heart
Indur'd all this excessive pain and smart,
And out of precious love to thee I bore?
And must I still be kept out of thy door?
    Shall, shall I leave thee then, and take my flight
Into some foreign Land, and let the Night
Of dismal darkness be thy lot for ever,
Where direful Wrath all graceless souls do sever
From all sweet shines of my Eternal Face,
That thou mayst there bewail with shame thy case?
When shades of frightful darkness thee do cover,
Thou wilt condole the loss of such a Lover;
Must I be gone, must I my farewel take
And leave thee to thy self? my heart doth ake
To think upon thy state, when I do leave thee;
Far rather would I have these Arms receive thee.
What, slight a Saviour thus, a Friend indeed,
An early Friend, a Friend, who chose to bleed
For thee, and in thy stead, that so thereby
He might enjoy thee to Eternitie!

Farewel, false Soul, I bid thee now adieu;
Take what will follow, dread what will insue.
Grief, sorrows, sickness and a troubled mind,
Will thee pursue, until thou com'st to find
A changed heart; and vengeance do's allot
Ruin to those thou lov'st, who love thee not.
I'le kill them all who have insnar'd thy heart,
Before from thee for ever I depart.
Ah! how my Soul with a tempestuous tide
Of tears is overwhelm'd, whilst I'm deny'd
My Suit by thee! my passions overflow
To see thee slight me, and my passion too;
What, tread me underfoot! whilst vanity,
And worldly joys, are Jewels in thine eye!
As if best good, and sweet'st content lay hid
In that gay fruit, which is alone forbid.
　　　He woo's, the Soul says no; he still replies;
He sweetly sues, she wickedly denies,
He woos afresh, she answers with disdain,
I cannot love, but he intreats again.
At last he leaves her, and his Suit adjourns;
He views the Soul, and griev'd, away returns;
He bids farewel, and yet he bids it so,
As if he knew not how to take her No.
He bids farewel, but 'tis as if delay
Did promise better farewels, than his stay.
He now withdraws, but 'tis with a design
His absence might her heart the more incline
To th' love and liking of him, or to see
What by some other means perform'd may be.
As Lovers often times by rules of Art
Devise new ways to gain upon the heart
Of such they love, to bring them to* their bow;
Like things sometimes doth *Jesus* also do.
T' incline the Sinners heart, he hides his face,
And brings them into a distressed case.
He lays them on sick beds, for to discover
The worth and need of such a Sacred Lover.[238]
Poor Sinners, ponder well what you do read,
And mind those thoughts which woo you to take heed
How you neglect & slight the day of Grace,
Or to base lusts and vain delights give place.
Now sickness comes, & Death begins to fright her,
And 'tis no marvel if the Lord do slight her.
Her drousy Conscience also now awakes;
Alas, she startl'd much, she weeps, she quakes,
She crys out for a Christ, but non's in sight,
And all her other Lovers fail her quite.

She yields, she loves, but with a servile heart,
When other Lovers slight her and depart.
She loves thee not, Lord Christ, for what thou art,
But what thou hast: and should she spared be,
She'd shew her love to Sin, more than to thee.

No sooner the sad Soul her state laments,
But bowels mov'd in *Jesus*, he relents.
In her afflictions, he's afflicted too,
And can't be long e're he'l compassions[a] shew.
He sent relief, he eas'd her of her pain,
And rais'd her up to former health again.
But as 'twas hinted, so it came to pass,
The wretched Soul proves vile as ere she was.
Affliction will not bring to *Jesus*'s feet,
Unless great Pow'r do go along with it.
The Soul's like *Phar'oh*; crys when smitten sore;
Then, then for Christ, and O 'twill sin no more!
But when rais'd up, and has sweet health restor'd,
It cleavs to Sin afresh, forgets the Lord.[239]
But the affections of the Prince of Peace
Abated not, but rather did increase.
His love and patience both alike shine forth,
To 'stonishment of all who live on Earth.
And that he might obtain the Soul at last,
His Servants call'd and sent away in hast
To recommend his love, and in his stead
To o'pe those precious Glories, which lie hid
To her and to all those who carnal be:
Alas! they ca'nt behold, they cannot see
Those high perfections which in *Jesus* are,
Nor can they think his beauty is so rare,
Exceeding all conception, all compare.

Dear Reader, prethee mark what here insues
Mind, mind the Arguments this man dos use
To move the Soul to tears of true contrition,
Fetch'd from Christ's love, and from her lost condition.

Theologue.
By *Jesus* sent! by such a Prince as he!
Ah! 'tis a work too great, too high for me.
What glory, Lord, hast thou conferr'd on those
Thou do'st imploy, thy secrets to disclose!
What! be a Spokesman for a Prince so great,
To represent his Love, and to entreat
Poor Sinners in his stead, to entertain
His Sacred Person! Lord, I'le try again
(Since thou command'st me forth) what may be done;
Thou bidst me go, my duty is to run.

Did *Abraham*'s Servant readily comply
With his Command with great'st fidelity?[240]
And shall I be unfaithful unto thee?
No, Lord, I will not; do but strengthen me,
Prosper my way, and let me have success,
That I with him thy Sacred Name may bless;
And how shall I, poor nothing I, rejoice
To see the Soul, thy Spouse, thy Father's choice.
What next thy love's so sweet, Lord, unto me,
Than to bring in poor Sinners unto thee?

CHAP. II.

Shewing the evil of Sin, and how compar'd.

HAIL, precious Soul! once glorious, noble born,
But now debas'd, defil'd, in garments torn;
Nay, naked quite, yet mindst it not at all;
Thy wounds do stink, and Vipers in them crawl.
So many sins of which thou guilty art,
So many Serpents cleave[a] unto thy heart.
What's Sin? is't not a frightful Cockatrice?
No Serpent like the Serpent called *Vice*.[241]
And dost thou love to play with such a thing?
Ah fool! take heed, view, view its poisonous sting.
Brute Beasts by Nature's instinct are aware
Of the gilt bait and sence-beguiling snare,
Though it seems ne'r so sweet, or ne'r so fair,
And art thou such a fool to hug a Snake,
And in thy breast such great provision make,
That it may harbour there both day and night?
Ah! Couldst thou see, or hadst a little sight,
'Twould soon appear a very loath'd delight.
No evil like the evil called Sin,
Which thou dost love, which thou tak'st pleasure in.
      For what is Sin, is't not a deadly evil,
The filthy spawn and off-spring of the Devil?
And is thy mind on folly wholly bent?
What, love the Devils odious excrement!
Shall that which is the superfluity
Of naughtiness, be lovely in thine Eye?
What, dost thou value Christ, and all he hath
Not worth vain joys and pleasures on the Earth?
Has he so much esteemed thee? and must
Thou value him less than a cursed Lust?
Dost thou more good in that foul Brat espy,
Than is in all the glorious Trinitie?

That which men judge is best, they strive to chuse,
Things of the smallest value they refuse.
O wretched Soul! what thoughts dost thou retain
Of thy dear Lord and blessed Soveraign?[242]
Come, view thy choice, see how deprav'd thou art
In judgment, will, affection, thy whole heart
Is so corrupt, defiled, and impure,
Thou canst not Christ, nor Godliness indure.

     Again, what's Sin? is't not a trait'rous Foe,
A Traytor unto God, and Rebel too?
It first of all against him took up Arms,
And made his Angels fall by its false charms.
Nought is so contrary to God as that,
Nor more the perfect object of his hate.
The Devil was God's Creature, good at first;
'Twas sin that made him hateful and accurst.
Sin ne'r was good, its essence is impure;
Evil at first, so now, so will indure.
And darest thou, O Soul, conceal this Foe?
Nay, hide him in thy house, and also show
Such deared love to him, as to delight
In his base company both day and night?
Nay, sport and play, and merry be with him,
What Gods dos hate and loath, dost thou esteem?
Dost not, O Soul, deserve for this to die?
What greater crime, what greater enmity
Canst thou be guilty of, or canst thou show,
Than thus to harbour God's most traitrous Foe?
The chiefest room he can always command,
Whilst my dear Master at thy door must stand,
And can't one look, nor one sweet smile obtain,
Who is thy Saviour, and thy Soveraign.

     What's Sin? a thing that's worser than the Devil.
Sin made him so, sin is a thing so evil,
'Tis worse than Hell, it dug that horrid pit,
'Tis sin that casts all Sinners into it.
No lake of Fire, no *Tophet*[243] had there bin
For souls of Men nor Devils, but through sin:
'Tis that which lays them there heap upon heap,
Sin was the cause 'twas made so large and deep.
Sin is the fuel that augments Hell-fire;
Wer't not for sin, Hell-flames would soon expire.
And wilt thou dandle sin still on thy knee?
Wilt make a mock of it? wilt jolly be?
Wilt sin and say, alas! I am in sport?
Ah! see thy folly, ere thou pay'st dear for 't.

Is sin God's foe? and is it so to thee?
Then part with sin, break that affinitie:
Dissolve the knot with speed, do thy endeavour;
Which will destroy thee otherwise for ever.

Nay, what is Sin? it is a Leprosy:
When Scripture so compares it, may not I
Call it a sickness, or a loathsom sore,
That quite covers the Soul, and spreads all o're,
Like to an Ulcer, or infectious Biles,
That do corrupt, that poisons and defiles[244]
The Soul afflicted, and all others too
That dwell with him, or have with him to do?
Oh how do men fly from the Pestilence?
And wilt not thou learn wisdom Soul, from thence?
Sin is a plague that kills eternally
All souls of men, unless they swiftly fly
To *Jesus Christ*, no Med'cine will do good,
Nor heal this plague, but this Physicians Blood.
What blindness is there then in thy base heart?
'Tis not the plague, th' Physician must depart:
Thou shutst the door, wilt not let him come in
Whose purpose is to heal the plague of sin.[245]

Nay, what is sin? 'tis poison in a Cup,
That's gilt without, and men do drink it up
Most earnestly, with joy, and much delight,
Being pleasant to the carnal appetite.
Sin's sweet to him whose soul is out of taste,
But long alas, its sweetness will not last.
Sin's sweet to th' flesh that dos it dearly love,
But to the Spirit it dos poison prove,
Hast, hast thou suck'd this deadly poison in,
And dost not see thy vital parts begin
To swell? art poison'd, *Soul*, look, look about
To get an *Antidote* to work it out,
Before it is too late. The poison's strong,
Don't stay a day, twelve hours is too long.
One dram of Grace mixt with repenting tears,
The grace of perfect love, that casts out fears,
Mixt with that Faith, which kills all unbelief,
Took down with speed, will ease thee of thy grief,
Will purge thy soul, and work by vomit well,
And all vile dregs of venom 'twil expel.
Unless thou vomit up each dreg, be sure
No hope of life; one sin will Death procure
Unto thy soul. Repentance is not right,
Till sin, nay, every sin's forsaken quite.

Not only left, but, as a poisonous Cup,
They greatly loath what e're they vomit up.
No evil like the evil called Sin,
Which thou dost love, which thou tak'st pleasure in.
     Again, what's sin? it is an horrid Thief,
Or a Deceiver; nay, it is the chief
Or grandest Cheater too that e're was known,
He has rob'd thousands; nay, there is but one
That lives, or e're has liv'd, but rob'd have bin
By this great Thief, by this Deceiver, *SIN.*
No petty Padder, his ambitious Eye
Doth search about, he subtilly does spy
Into the place where all the Jewels lie.
The first he seizes is the Jewel *Time.*
He likely robs each Soul of all their prime
And chiefest days, which mercy doth afford,
Which should be dedicated to the Lord.
And more then this, not one good thing they have,
But them of it does this curst Thief deceive.
Sweet Gospel Grace, nay and the Gospel too,
And all that glory which they also do
Confer on us, Souls are deceiv'd hereby,
And yet they know it not, they don't espy
The way it works, it's done so secretly.
Sin robs the soul of its sweet Jewel *Peace,*
And in its room do's *grief* and *anguish* place.
Who ever doth this grievous loss sustain,
Can't have it made up unto him again
By Treasures of all Kingdoms here on Earth,
No valuing it, no knowing of its worth.
Another thing this Thief has in his Eye,
And lays his Fingers on, then by and by
Doth bear away, it is the Jewel, *Soul,*
A loss which mortals ever shall condole.
For had a man ten thousand worlds to lose:
The loss of them far better had he chose,
Than lose his soul, why would you think it strange?
What shall a man for's soul give in exchange?
There's one rich Jewel more, and 'tis the chief
That is aim'd at by Satan and this Thief,
Ah! 'tis a thing more worth than all the rest:
How, how can then the value be exprest?
It is a precious Stone that shines so bright,
It doth the heart of the great God delight.
He loves it dear, 'tis that his eye's upon,
And nought he prizes like this precious Stone.
This Stone, poor Soul, he offers unto thee,
What sayst thou to't, canst thou no beauty see,

No worth in that which God accounts so rare?
Strange 'tis! shall I the cause of it declare?
Sin blinds thine eyes, and dos beguile thee so,
Thou for a Pebble[a] lets this Jewel go.
This stone (know thou) is the *Pearl* of great price,
Let not this base Deceiver thee entice
To slight dear *JESUS:* wilt be such a fool,
To lose thy *time*, thy *Christ, peace*, and thy *Soul?*
Be thou more wise, and more considerate,
Thou dost, alas, thy pleasures over-rate.
Let's go to[b] th' ballance, prethee, Soul, let's weigh
The Pearl of price; make hast, and quickly lay
Into the scales, the flesh, and loads of pleasure;
For honour, all the acts of mighty *Cesar*,[246]
And cast whole mines in too, whole mines of treasure!
Add world to world, then heap a thousand more,
And throw them in, if thou canst find such store;
And see which ballance of them is too light;
Lo it is done, and thine's such under-weight,
It seems as if thy scale was empty quite.
Let's take the Pearl out, and then lets put in
An airy bubble; now let's weigh again.
See, see, fond Soul, thy scale aloft dos fly,
There's nothing in't, 'tis less than vanity.[247]
What folly was't to make the first compare?
What weigh the world with Christ! no need is there
To run that parallel, thou now mayst find
Thy self deceiv'd, thou labour'st for the wind.
For sin's compos'd of nought save subtil wiles,
It fawn's and flatters, and betrays by smiles.
It's like a Panther, or a Crocodil,
It seems to love, and promises no ill;
It hides its sting, seems harmless, as the Dove,
It hugs the Soul, it hates, when vow's tru'st love.
It plays the Tyrant most by gilded pills,
It secretly insnares the Soul it kills.[248]
Sin's promises they all deceitful be,
Does promise wealth, but pay us poverty:
Does promise honour, but dos pay us shame;
And quite bereaves a man of his good name.
Does promise pleasure, but does pay us sorrow;
Does promise Life to day, pays Death to morrow.
No evil like to th' evil called Sin,
Which thou dost love, which thou tak'st pleasure in.
    Again, what's Sin? a second *Dalilah*,
Which in the bosom lies, does tempt and draw
The Soul to yield unto its cursed ways,
And resteth not until it quite betrays

It's Life into the proud *Philistines* hands,
Who take and bind it with base churlish bands,
Nay, and most cruelly puts out its eyes,
Makes it grind in their Mill.[249] Devils devise
All this, and more then this, when they do get
The poor deluded Soul into their net.

    Lastly, what's Sin? read thou the former Part
Of this small Book, O view the bitter smart
Thy Saviour bore, it pierc'd his very heart.
Think thou upon his bloudy Agony,
'Tis that opes best its hellish mysterie,
And shews the venom which in it dos lie.[250]
No evil like the evil called Sin,
Which thou dost love, and tak'st such pleasure in.
Had evil man's fool-hardiness extended
No further than himself, and there had ended,
'Twere not so much, but O! I do espy
Another is much injured thereby,
Ten thousand times more excellent in worth:
For the great God, who form'd the Heav'n & Earth,
Doth look upon himself as wrong'd thereby,
For he that sins, doth little less than fly
I'th very face of his blest Majesty.
And when the Son of Glory hither came,
O how was he exposed unto shame!
It brought his Sacred Person in disgrace,
When Sinners vile spat in his Heavn'ly face.
They taunt him with base terms; and being bound
They scourged him; he bled: but the worst wound
Was in his Soul, occasioned by Sin;
And thou thereby woundst him most sore agin.
O wilt thou paddle in the pure stream
Of precious Bloud! contemn it! O extream[251]
And hideous Monster! dost thou hug the Knife
Which wounded him, yea took away his Life,
And will let out thy blood, though now it be
Delighted in, and loved much by thee?

    Of Wonders strange, and Prodigies that are
Amazing unto all who of them hear,
None can come nigh, or be compar'd to this,
A Prodigie of Prodigies it is.
Of Love and Lover, ne'r the like was known,
Nor was the like Ingratitude e're shown.
The one doth love beyond all admiration,
And suffer'd things beyond humane relation.
And he a King, but she a filthy brute,
A beggar vile, and yet denies his Suit!

Question.

From whence is it? O why will she not close
With this great Lord? how can she still oppose
His Oft-repeated proffers? how, not yet!
Yield unto him? pray what's the cause of it?

Answer.

'Tis not in her own power to dispose
Her self in marriage: also here are those
Who dwell with her, and her Relations be,
Who spoil the match, or the affinitie,
Which otherwise in all appearance might
Be throughly made with *Jesus* Prince of Light.
Two proud Relations loftily stand off,
Who urge her to reject him with a scoff.
The one is *Will*, a very churlish piece,
Who all along for *Sin* and *Satan* is.
The other's *Judgment*, once most grave and wise,
But now with *Will* both cursed Enemies;
To God and Christ true Piety oppose,
And lead the Soul with evil ways to close.
'Tis they who must dispose of her, if she
E're yield to Christ his dearest Spouse to be.[252]
But Sin has so by craft corrupted them,
And drawn them to its party, they contemn
This glorious Lover, and will not consent
The Soul should yield to him, or should repent,
And so break off with other Lovers, who
She yet doth love, and loth is to for-go.
Besides them, in her house doth also dwell
An Enemy call'd *Old-man*,[253] known full well
To be a grand and horrid Instrument,
To keep the Soul from granting her consent.
O! he's the cause of all the inward strife,
And hates the thoughts she should become his Wife.
And will prevent it, if he can find out
Meet ways and means to bring the same about.
Nay such a Foe this *Old-man* is indeed,
That till he's slain by th' *Spirit*, or does bleed,
Or weakned in his power, ne'r will she
With the Lord Christ firmly united be.
Slight wounds wo'nt do, he must be slain out-right,
Such is his rage, his subtilty and spite
Against this happy match; till he's near dead,
It cannot be in truth accomplished.
Therefore expect to hear of his black doom,

Before the sweet espousal Day doth come.
   There's also yet another Inmate, I
Perceive dwells in her house (which by and by
You'l hear much of) who all her secrets knows,
And can her very inward thoughts disclose,
His name is *Conscience*, whose Power's so great,
That in her house he hath a Regal Seat.
These three Allies by *Old-man* so corrupted,
Have all along the business interrupted,
They naturally are opposite to Grace,[254]
And are far more inclined to give place
To sensual Objects, and the Prince o'th Night,
And so betray the Soul, for want of light,
Into their hands, of whom you heard before,
Who secretly design for ever-more
To take away her life, and quite undo her,
Whilst flatteringly they promise peace unto her;
The Soul's deprav'd and captivated so,
It chuses *Evil*, and lets *Jesus* go,
The chiefest good, and takes the chiefest evil,
Being by nature acted by the Devil.
This well consider'd, may the cause discover
Why she denies to entertain this Lover.
The Soul is dead, and cannot see, nor hear,
'Tis sensless as a stone, a stone can bear
The greatest weight,[a] and neither break, nor melt:
Souls dead to God, ne'r love-sick passions felt
Unto this day; nor can they love, until
They are convinc'd of sin and all the ill   }
They have committed 'gainst his holy Will.
Being sensible hereof, then with strong cryes
They fly to God for salve to o'pe their Eys;
The Eys affect the Heart, when thou canst see
Christ will be dear, and not till then to thee.
The Conscience first is always wrought upon,
Which never is effectually done,
But by the Spirits Pow'r and operation,
Which sets it equally against transgression.
But lest I should be tedious, I'le forbear,
Craving attention to what follows here.

CHAP. III.

Shewing Christ's Heavenly and admirable Beauty, Riches, Bounty, Power, and Wisdom.

Theologue.

Wilt thou be cruel to so dear a Friend?
Upon thy self 'twill fall, poor Soul, ith'end.
Did not *Rebecka* yiel'd, and chuse to go
With *Abram's* servant? and wilt thou say no?
What was an *Isaac* unto him, whom I
Desire thee to fix thy tender Eye
Upon? was *Isaac* fair and wealthy too?
Or was he great?[255] Ah Soul! will such things do?
If beauty, wealth, or honour thou dost prize,
I do present one now before thine Eys,
That is the Object, this alone is he;
None, none like him did ever mortals see.
He is all fair, in him's not one ill feature,
Ten thousand times more fair than any Creature
That lives, or ever lived on the Earth,
His Beauty so amazingly shines forth;
Angelick Nature is enamor'd so,
They love him dearly, and admire him too.
His Head is like unto the purest Gold,[256]
His curled Tresses lovely to behold,
And such a brightness sparkles from his Eys,
As when *Aurora*[257] gilds the Morning skies.
And though so bright, yet lovely like the Doves,[258]
Charming all hearts, where rests diviner Loves,
Look on his beauteous Cheeks, and thou'lt espy
The Rose of *Sharon*[259] deckt in Royaltie.
His smiling Lips, his speech, and words so sweet,
That all delights and joy in them do meet;
Which tends at once to ravish ear and sight,
And to a kiss all heavenly Souls invite.[260]
The Image of his Father's in his face;
His inward parts excel, he's full of grace.
If Heaven and Earth can make a rare Complexion,
Without a spot, or the least imperfection,
Here, here it is, it in this Prince doth shine,
He's altogether lovely, all Divine.[261]
    1. His Beauty is so much desirable,
No Souls that see it any ways are able
For to withstand the influ'nce of the same;
They'r so enamour'd with it, they proclaim
There's none like him in Earth, nor Heav'n above;
It draws their hearts, and makes them fall in love

Immediately, so that they cannot stay
From following him one minute of a day.
The Flock is left, the Herd, and fishing Net,
As soon as e're the Soul its Eye doth set
Upon his face, or of it takes a view,
They'l cleave to him, whatever doth insue.

2. Christ is the Spring, or the Original
Of earthly beauty, and Celestial.
That Beauty which in glorious Angels shine,
Or is in Creatures natural, or Divine,
It flows from him: O it is he doth grace
The mind with glorious Beauty, as the face.

3. Christ's Beauty's chast, most pure, and without snares,
Not like to other's, which oft unawares,
Like *Josephs*,²⁶² most treacherously betrays
Poor wanton Souls, and leads them to the pit,
Before they are aware, or think of it!
Here may'st thou look, and love, and take thy fill,
(Yea every one who hath a heart, a will)
Whose sweetness ne'r will glut, surfeit, or kill.

4. His Beauty's real, 'tis no glistering paint;
That suits vain Sinners, this affects the Saint.
The painted face pleases the carnal Eye,
But none but Saints through faith can this espy
That's a vain show, but this a precious thing,
In sight of which Celestial joy doth spring.

5. This Beauty fills, and fully satisfies
The hearts of all who have enlightned Eyes.
He that sees Christ, doth say, Lord, now I have
What e're I long'd to see, no more I crave,
I have enough, my heart and I are fill'd,
Which was not so before, whilst I beheld
Things with a sensual heart and outward eye.
There's nothing here, save Christ, can satisfie
That precious Soul, which lieth in thy breast,
Reject him, and ne'r look for peace nor rest.

6. Christ's Beauty s hidden, 'tis so mystical
No glimmerings of it can appear at all
To carnal Souls. This is the cause why he
Is thus deny'd, and slighted still by thee.

7. There's one thing more which I'le to thee impart,
Touching Christ's Beauty, by diviner Art,
He doth transmit his beauty unto those
Who are deform'd, as soon as e're they close
With him in truth, in a contract of love,
He all their homely features doth remove.
Oh! he can make those lovely, very fair,
Who ne'r so filthy, ne'r so ugly are.

8. This Beauty fadeth not, 'twill not decay.
'Twill be as rare to morrow as to day.
Not like to that, which as a fading flower,
Ev'n now shines bright, but wither'd in an hour.[263]

Riches of Christ.[264]

Or, is thy heart on Riches set? know then,
Christ is more rich than all the sons of Men.
The Father hath to him all fulness given
In Earth beneath, and all that is in Heaven.[265]
All Kingdoms of the world they are his own,
Whether inhabited, or yet unknown.
He's heir of all things, and the time is near[266]
When he will make his Right most plain appear.
All Potentates his Tenants are at will,
And such who wast his goods, or govern ill,
Account must give to him, and then will find
What 'tis to bear to him a treach'rous mind.
    Christ's glorious Riches are discovered
Yet further unto thee; for all are fed
By him alone that on the Earth e're liv'd,
Both food and clothes they all from him receiv'd,
And still receive; 'tis at his proper charge
They are maintain'd, as might be shew'n[a] at large.
I'le only give a hint or two at things,
His Treasures far surmount all Earthly Kings.
He has paid all the debts of every one
That clos'd with him. O do but think upon
This very thing, and wisely then account
To what a sum this payment will amount:
Suppose each Soul ten thousand Talents were[267]
In debt to God: some little time we'l spare
To cast it up. 'tis done, and lo 'tis found
Eighteen hundred sev'nty five thousand pound.
And less than that what sinners ow'd that's clear'd,
As often-times, I doubt not, you have hear'd.
What did they altogether, think you, owe?
Who's able to account it? who can show
The quantity of that great debt, which he
Paid at one single payment on the Tree?
The quality too of his Riches are
So great in worth, O so transcendent rare, }
Their Nature Men nor Angels can declare.
No other Coin would with God's Justice go,
To satisfie for debts which Sinners owe.
Nay the whole World, nor yet ten thousand more,
Could not discount one farthing of that score,
But had Christ's worth and Riches only bin

Sufficient to discharge from debts of Sin,
And had he not more Treasure to bestow
On such who do believe, or truly do
Cleave unto him, it might be thought to be
A lessening of his vast Treasurie.
But 'tis not so; for he enriches all,
Who are discharged from sin's bitter thral.
None comes to him, nor ever came, but they
Receive, besides such sums that very day
They are espous'd, that holy Truth relates,
They'r made more rich than earthly Potentates.
A golden Chain about their necks he places,
And them with Rings and precious Jewels, graces.
And clothes them also in rich Robes of state,[268]
Whose sparkling glory far exceeds the plate
Of beaten Gold; nay *Ophir*'s Treasury,[269]
And all the Wealth which in both *Indies* lie,
Must not compared be; alas, they can't
Equal in worth the Robes of one poor Saint.
He Heirs also doth make them every one
Of a most glorious Kingdom, and a Crown
He doth assure them that they shall obtain,[270]
And when they come to age, for ever raign
With him triumphantly, and tread down those
Who were their Enemies, or did oppose
Their rising up to such great Dignity.
Or treated them on Earth with cruelty.
He's rich in every thing, no good is found,
No wealth nor worth, but all in Christ abound.
Few in all kind of Riches do exceed:
But there's in him whatever Sinners need.
Cast but a look, O view this Treasury,[271]
Riches of Life, Love, Pardon, all dos lie,
Laid up in Christ, in him tis hid, for those
Who do with him in true affection close.
These Riches do enrich the Soul of Man,
Which earthly Riches never did, nor can.
Nay prethee hark to me, I'le tell thee more,
Although Christ has paid off our former score,
He han't consum'd one farthing of his store.
Though he has made some millions rich and high,
He hath with him such a redundancy
Of glorious Riches, that let come who will,
Their Treasuries with substance he can fill.
The Sun is not more full of precious Light,
Whose sparkling rays do dazle mortals sight;
Nor is the great, the vast and mighty Sea
More fill'd with water than (in truth) is he

With Grace and Riches, yea of every kind:
Which if thou close with him, and dost not find
To be a truth (Soul) then let me obtain
Reproach from all, yea an eternal shame.
Christ's Riches are so great, St. *Paul* knew well
No tongue could set them forth, no Angels tell
Th' nature of them, they unsearchable be;[272]
Men may find out the bottom of the Sea,
As soon as they can learn or comprehend
How rich Christ is, who is thy dearest Friend.
Nay, more than this his Riches are so stable,
Moths can't corrupt them, nor can Thieves be able
To rob us of them. Nay, yet further-more,
He that hath them, what e're comes, can't be poor.
His Riches can't be spent, his Treasury
Cannot exhausted be, nor yet drawn dry.
These Riches will rejoyce thee, make thee glad,
Revive thy heart; and God will never add
Sorrow with them whilst thou dost live on earth;
They'l quiet thee, and fill thy Soul with mirth,
They'l be a breast of such sweet Consolation,
That when all other dwellers in the Nation
Shall be perplext through loss of earthly gain,
Thou shalt be satisfied, and remain
In perfect peace, nought shall distress thy mind,
When they shall nought, save horrid anguish find.
Though Gold and Silver will not satisfie
The Soul of Man, yet this I do espy,
The loss of them, and other earthly things,
It grief and sorrow to the Spirit brings.
And so uncertain are things of the world,
Though here to night, e're morning all are hurl'd
Away from him who now possession hath,
Like to a bubble are all things on Earth.[273]
He that on worldly Riches sets his mind,
Strives to take hold on shadows, and the wind.
But if Christ's Riches once thou dost obtain,
The loss of them thou never shalt sustain,
Nor will they leave thee when thou com'st to die,
But cleave unto, and thee accompanie
Beyond the Grave, ev'n to Eternitie.
What dost thou say? canst make a better choice
Than close with Christ? O hearken to his voice,
And don't with stand the proffer made to thee,
If any good thou dost in Riches see.[274]

Christ's Bounty.

What sayest thou? what hast thou in thine eye?
Will not Christ's Riches move thee? then I'le try
To gain thee by some other property.
He's bountiful, and of a generous heart,
Most free and noble, ready to impart
What e're he hath unto the Soul he loves.
O see how his Heroick Spirit moves
In him, whose generous, whose bounteous hand,
Holds forth to thee what e're thou canst demand.
'Tis thine for asking; do but speak the word,
Thou hast it done. O! none like this dear Lord.
Some mens great Riches seem to overflow,
Who do a base ignoble Spirit show.
They treasure up their bags, lay heap on heap,
Yet with a narrow covetous spir't keep
All from the poor: Nay their own Wives can get
But now and then a little in a fit;
In a good mood sometimes perchance they'l be
Kind unto them, though but unfreely free.
But Christ's rich Bounty does to all extend,
He stretches forth his hand to Foe and Friend.
Refined Gold, Eye-salve, and Rayments white,
Ev'n all choice things for profit and delight;
Sweet Frankincense, Spicknard, Calamas fine,
Myrrh, Saffron, with all choice of spiced Wine,[275]
He freely gives to all: O come who will,
He'l bid you welcome, and your Treasures fill.
O what doth he then to his Friends impart,
Unto his Spouse, the Soul who has his heart?
Come, eat, O Friends, and drink abundantly,
Beloved ones, 'twas for your sakes that I
This Banquet made. There's nought (says[a] he) too good
For those that I have purchas'd with my blood.
Take Grace and Glory; all I have I give you,
And to my self I will e're long receive you.
Ask, that your joy may now be full: for I
Can't any thing that's good your souls deny.

The Soveraign Power and Dignity of Christ.

What can I now do more, if still thou art
Resolved to deny *Jesus* thy heart?
If Beauty will not move thee to incline
To close with him, who longs till he is thine:
Strange! Beauty oft prevails great Conquests gains;
Like to a mighty Victor, binds in chains

Those wch would not by other means e're yield.
Such is the nature of his pow'rful Shield,[276]
Triumphantly it has obtain'd the Field.
No standing out against its piercing Darts,
It hath a secret way to wound those hearts,
Whose constitution leads them naturally
To steer that course, and on it cast an Eye
To search the sweet, which Fancy says doth lye
Hid in the same. For human Beauty's vain,[277]
Which some have sacrific'd their lives, to gain.
But Christ's sweet Beauty is a real thing,
And doth substantial joys and pleasures bring;
Such pleasures also which will still abide
For evermore, like Rivers by thy side.
Shall Beauty which is spotless,[278] without stain,
Nor Riches neither, sweet Imbraces gain;
Nor generous Bounty, win thy purer love?
Then let Ambition thy affections move.
Is Greatness barren quite of solid joys?
Are all her Merchandize but empty toys?
If it be earthly, 'tis an Airy thing,
Though 'twere to be a Spouse unto a King.
But let it not be so look'd on by thee
To be espous'd to that great Majestie,
From whom alone true Honour dos descend,
This Greatness lasting perfect, ne'r will end.
Come, *Soul*, let us most seriously now pry
Into Christ's Pow'r and regal Soveraignty,
And next let me his glorious Pow'r show
By which he works, and all great things can do.
Some have a Pow'r whereby they can command,
But to accomplish things do want a hand:
But Christ in both excels, 'tis he alone
Hath regal Pow'r; and what he will have done
He can effect i'th twinkling of an eye,
Though all combine against him far and nigh.
He's over Angels, (as thou heardst before)
They gladly him do rev'rence, and adore.
The Head o'th Church makes Laws, and governs it,
According as he sees 'tis best and fit.[279]
His regal Pow'r also doth descend,
And over all the Devils doth extend.
The Keys of Hell and Death to him are given;[280]
'Tis he alone can shut and open Heaven.
Power to Rule, to command, to forbid,
To punish, or deliver, they'r all hid
In him alone; 'tis he can bind or loose;
To damn or save, 'tis all as he doth chuse.

He's King of Kings, all mighty men below
To him their Princely Crowns & Kingdoms owe.
Yea such an universal Monarch's he,
Commands the mighty Winds, and stils the Sea.
'Twas by his hand the glorious Heav'ns were made,
And wondrous Earth's foundations first were laid.
The Sun, the Moon, and Stars receiv'd their light
From him at first, to rule both Day and Night.
His Power's absolute without controle,
He governs all the World from Pole to Pole.
His Soveraign Pow'r was not gain'd by fight,
Or Usurpation, but a lawful Right;
As he is God, 'tis his essentially,
Born Heir of it from all Eternity.
And as he's Mediator,[281] th' God of Heaven
This glorious Power unto him has given.
His Pow'rs Infinite, it hath no bound,
No ends, or limits of it can be found.
He made the World, which by him doth subsist,
Nay he can make ten thousand if he list.
He can do more than we can think or know,
Can kill, and make alive, save, or o'rethrow.
The Conquests he has gain'd, demonstrate
The matchless Pow'r of this dread Potentate.
Sin is ore-come, the Devil's forc'd to fly,
Nay, h' hath obtain'd a perfect Victory
O're Death, o're Hell, o're Wrath, & o're the Grave,
And from them all he able is to save.
If thou wilt but consent, grant his request,
Thou never more by Foes shalt be distrest.
Ah Soul! is't not a very glorious thing,
Daily to be thus courted by a King,
And such a King? shall *Jesus* woo[a] in vain?
Shall such a Prince not thy sweet love obtain?[282]

The Wisdome of Christ.

What say'st to Wisdom, from whose Odour Springs
That wch makes glorious inferiour Men, as Kings:
This spreads the sweet perfume of *Solomon's* fame;
'Twas this that rais'd his most illustrious Name.
The noise of Wisdome made so great report,
'T was heard as far as *Sheba's* Princely Court.
It made the Lady's Charriot-wheels to run
Most swift, like to the new-rais'd Eastern Sun,
Mounting aloft, and vanquishing black Clouds:
She hasts away, and through obstructions crouds;
Defying danger, she's resolv'd to see
What Fame reports touching this Prodigie.

The emulous Queen's arriv'd, she stands amaz'd,
She listens,ª wonders, and be'ng over-daz'd
With this great Beam, she breaks forth, could not hold
But must express, that what to her was told
In her own Country, was in no wise nigh
Half what she found did in his Wisdom lie.[283]
What's Riches, Bounty, Honour, Beauty rare,
Unless true Wisdom also do dwell there?
If Wisdom may a person recommend,
Christ is all Wisdom. Shall I now descend
Into particulars? wilt lend an Ear
Whilst I endeavour to make it more clear?
Alas, I stand amaz'd! Can Infinite
Perfections be exprest? what shall I write?
He's wise, all-wise, only wise; shall I speak?
Wisdom it self i'th' abstract. Can I take
Upon me then to ope this Mystery,
When in him doth all depths of Wisdom lie.
The Wisemans wisdome, if't compar'd might be,
Was like a drop of Water to the Sea;
Nay, far a greater disproportion's there,
Should we Christ's wisdom once with his compare.
'Twas he which did to *Solomon* impart
That wisdom, and that understanding heart.
'Tis he which makes all good men grave and wise,
To hate all evil, and true Vertue prize.
He to our Fathers doth right knowledg give,
And 'tis by him all pious Judges live.
Th' infinite wisdome of th' Eternal One
Shines forth in him, nay, 'tis in him alone
All is laid up; he is God's Treasury,
Where Wisdom and true Knowledg both do lie.
He knows all things and persons here below;
Nay, perfectly does he the Father know,
And all Decrees and Counsels, which of old
Have been, and their events he can unfold.
He knows each glorious purpose, and design,
In him alone do all Perfections shine.
The frames the thoughts, the ways, the fears, the wants,
Temptations, burdens & the grief of Saints
Most perfectly he knows, and quickly can
Save and defend from th' greatest rage of Man.
For Counsel and wise conduct he exceeds,
And in the midst of paths of Judgment leads.
The crafty Counsel♭ of *Achitophel*[284]
He can defeat, though laid as deep as Hell.
He over-turns the wisdome of the wise,
Confounds their plots, and shews what folly lies

In their grand Councils, making them to know
Their purposes can't stand, if he says no.
He orders things, that no design shall take
Further than 'twill for his own Glory make.
None like to Christ, he is without compare,
He's wise as well as wealthy, great and fair.
What's thy opinion, Soul, canst not espy
All Glory hid in his blest Majesty?
What hinders then but that without delay
Triumph may celebrate th' espousal day?

CHAP. IV.

Shewing how the Conscience of the Sinner comes to be effectually awakened; together with the effects thereof.

THIS being said with bowels of Affection,
Tho often mixt[a] with gall of sharp detection,
Her former stubbornness being all laid o'pe,
Yet this, nor that, nor nothing, gave much hope
He should prevail, which put him in a maze,
And did his voice and spirits higher raise.
He still went on with sweet commiseration,
Yet was his pity mixt with some small passion,
And to this purpose did this good man speak,
Not knowing how his last farewel to take.

Theologue.
Poor stupified Soul! Alas! alas!
What is the cause? whence doth it come to pass
Thou art so sensless? why dost thou despise
All those Soul-melting tears, those sighs and crys?
What, is thy heart more harder than the Rocks,
That thou canst bear these oft repeated knocks,
And never break at all? O strange! O strange!
Thy heart, poor Soul, is t harder than a stone,
That feeble drops of water fall upon,
And makes impression. What, shall stones relent,
And yield themselves, and as it were consent
These frequent droppings should impression make;
And showers move thee not? Awake, awake,
Before the dreadful Message I impart,
Shall rouse thy hard and sin-congealed heart.
Thy night comes on, thy Sun's a going down,
Thy seeming favourites begin to frown.
So all thy pleasures with their wanton charms
Are flying from thee Death spreads forth his Arms,

To take thee hence unto another place:
Canst thou poor wretch, this ghastly King imbrace?
What will become of all thy wealth and pleasure?
Behold (alas) Death's come to make a seisure
Upon thy poor deceived Soul this night!
Then all thy joys, and empty vain delight
Will vanish like the smoke, and thou shalt be
Cast into Prison for Eternitie,
Where thou shalt evermore bewail thy loss,
In changing Gold for that, that's worse than dross.[285]
Shall Beauty, Wealth, or Honour make thee yield?
Much more that Wisdom wherewith Christ is fill'd.
Shall Love and Patience be so ill rewarded
By thee, by whom he should be most regarded?
And sensual Objects harbour'd in thy heart?
Then wilt thou hear what further I'le impart?
Soul, now thou must be anathematiz'd,
And when Christ comes, how wilt thou be surpriz'd?
For those that love not *Jesus*, are accurst,
And when he doth appear, for ever must
That fearful doom and sentence then receive.
O may the thoughts of this cause thee to cleave
To him with speed, before this day is gone.
I'le now break off, adieu, this think upon:
Poor drousy wretch, let sin no more deceive thee,
Give me thine Answer now before I leave thee.
O may these Soul-confounding terrors break,
Thy stony-heart, and make thy Conscience speak!

     Eternal God, do thou thy Spirit send,
'Tis he which must the Soul in pieces rend.
The work's too hard for weakness. Alas! I
Shall not prevail, if help thou dost deny.
Speak to her heart, set home the Word with Pow'r.
Shall this be the good day, the happy hour?
Her Conscience touch, O wound her, let her see
What 'tis to be a Captive unto thee.
Open her Eyes, blest Spirit, thou canst do it.
Sad is her state; O come, and let her know it.
Let not my pains nor labour quite be lost:
For dear she has my Master, *Jesus*, cost.
Thou canst effectually change her bad mind,
Which unto sensual Objects is inclin'd.
O shed and scatter precious Love abroad,
And unto her some of that grace afford.
Moral persuasions barely ne're will bring
The Soul to love and like our Heav'nly King.
But I'le return and speak yet one word more
Unto her Conscience, e're I do give o're.

Speak *Conscience,* if alive! thou us'd to keep
A faithful watch: what[a] art thou now asleep?
Hath she not slighted Christ, like unto those
That him reject, and cleave unto his Foes?
What dost thou say? speak, I adjure thee, rouse!
Conscience, I speak to thee, shake off thy drouse;
Gripe this deluded Soul, who puts her trust
In those that seek her Life, 'tis thou that must
Stop her vain course: what, shall the Sinner die
When *Conscience,* God's Vicegerent, is so nigh,
And gives not one sad sigh, nor groan, nor cry?
Strange! what's befallen thee? art lost, or fled,
Who shouldst the tidings bring that all are dead?
Like *Job's* last Messenger, thou shouldst declare,
How all the faculties corrupted are.[286]
Wilt thou betray that trust repos'd in thee,
And lose thy regal Right and Soveraignty?
Wilt thou connive and wink at such a crime,
Or fault which she commits? O no, 'tis time
Now to awake, and fiercely her reprove.
What, hate that Prince whom she pretends to love?
Immediately the Spirit Sweetly Spake,
And touch'd her heart, and Conscience did awake.

Conscience.

What Soul-amazing voice is this I hear?
What Heav'n-rending Thunder fills mine Ear?
Awake, why do I sleep? can Conscience nod,
That keeps a watch betwixt the Soul and God?
If so, yet when Heav'ns voice cryes out amain,
That will awake and make me rouse again.
I have most basely (Sir) corrupted bin,
By *Satan* and that poisonous Evil, *SIN.*
A Register I kept, but then alas
It has so fallen out, so come to pass,
That I unfaithful was: for always when
I should have set down scores, I set down ten;
Nay, to their party so entic'd have bin,
That I have often winked at her sin.
And when my Office was for to accuse,
'Twas to wrong ends, her Light I did abuse.
My faults I see, I'le watch that no offence
May pass the Soul without intelligence.
Sir, Strange it is, it puts me in a muse,
As one amaz'd to see the Soul refuse
To hearken to your voice, which constantly,
Like pointed Darts, against her breast doth fly.
I'le take up Arms, and fight for *Jesus* now,

And make her bend to him, if I know how.
I now declare my self, though for a season
I silence kept, to hear what Goodman *Reason*
Could find to say, whereby he might excuse her,
But he's most blind, and surely doth abuse her.
I know her byass'd Judgment will conjecture
She's not oblig'd to hearken to that Lecture
She lately heard, although it was Divine.
Her will and judgment doth with Hell combine
To work her ruin; do you what you can,
Till Judgments rectifi'd, and the Old man
Be put to death, she'l be rebellious still,
Yield to her lusts, and please her vicious will.

Theologue.

    Doth *Conscience* yield? Blest day! I'le try again,
With hope of a full Conquest to obtain.
Good service may'st thou do, act well thy part:
Whilst the great King doth thus besiege the heart;
Keep thou a narrow watch, look well about,
Observe who doth come in, and who goes out.
In one thing am I glad, I know from hence
I shall by thee have true intelligence.
How things are manag'd in her house always;
Thou know'st her thought,[a] hearst all the words she says.

Apollyan Prince of Darkness.

    Apollyon, that degraded Seraphim,
And Grand-sire of that Hell-bred Monster, *Sin*,
No sooner did of these late tidings hear,
How Conscience was awakened, but in fear
Presently calls a Council to advise
Which way they might the Soul by craft surprize
And hinder her from being crowned Queen.
Which to prevent, successful have we been,
Saith he, till now, but I am in great doubt
Much longer we shall hardly hold it out.
The Preacher doth his business follow so,
I am afraid of some great overthrow.

Satan.

    Dread Prince! fear not, we yet possession have,
And want no skill. Can't subtilty deceive?
Can't strength subdue? besides, she's in our chain;
Though one links broke, we'l fasten it again.
And if grave Judgment will with us abide,
Conscience will not be able to decide
The diff'rences, nor right dicision make;

No matter then which side the fool doth take.
But since, my Lord, I see what grieves your mind,
No safety shall these Gospel-Preachers find:
Our Vassals we'l prepare with Hellish rage,
Them to extirpate, and drive off the stage.

Lucifer.
          I do approve of that last Counsel given;
Let not a place nor corner under Heaven
Be found for those our int'rest dare oppose,
Or once attempt to move the Soul to close
With him whom we account our mortal Foe,
Satan, for this I bless and thank thee too.
The brave design which we have now in hand,
Will soon effect this thing in every Land.
That Enterprise let us pursue with care,
But mind as well how things more inward are.
To Judgment look, lest he from us should run;
If once his Eyes are ope, we're all undone.

Soul.
          Lord, what sad gripes and lashes do I feel?
My courage fails, and resolutions reel.
Strange thoughts disturb my mind, no rest, alas,
Can heart or eyes obtain; whole nights do pass,
Whole weeks and months, and nought can I possess
But horror great, sad grief, and weariness.
What's my condition now? who'le shew to me
My present state and future misery?
Hark, what's within, a very frightful noise,
It mars my hopes, imbitters all my joys.
My morn's ore-cast, my fair day proveth foul,
My Conscience terrifies, and makes me howl:
Lash after lash, and blows succeeding blows,   }
He's void of mercy, and no pity shows,
Here ends my joy, and here begins my woes.
O how my mind is hurried to and fro!
I know not where to fix, nor what to do.
My unresolv'd resolves do greatly vary,
This way one while, and then the quite contrary.
Who is't will counsel give? to whom must I
Go for some ease in this perplexity?
My Conscience says I wickedly have acted,
Not breaking the vile contract I've contracted
With those sweet Lovers which my sensual heart
So long a time has lov'd, how shall we part?
Must I be forc'd, by Conscience to imbrace
One whom I cannot love? 'tis a hard case

Yet have I cause to love him dearly too,
But how shall I for him let others go?

Depraved Judgment.

    Poor silly Soul! and is thy choice so hard?
In two extreams can thy weak thoughts reward
Two so unequal, with the like respect?
Know'st thou not which to slight, which to affect?
Submit to me, tis Judgment must advise,
In this great case take heed and be thou wise.
Fix where thou wilt, thy doubt-depending cause
Can ne'r expect a Verdict 'twixt two Laws
Which differ, and are opposit in kind,
Yet a fit medium I'le attempt to find[287]
To ease thy sad, and sore perplexed mind.
Divert those thoughts by some rare Speculations,
And vanquish all these dolesome cogitations.
Look, look abroad, and view the world, pray mark
The Wise and Prudent, and the Courtly Spark.[288]
Will they direct thee so, such counsel give
That thou an Hermits life on Earth shouldst live?
What, marry one that in possession hath
Not one small house, or foot of Land on Earth,
When Wealth, and Honour, Dignity and Power
Are offer'd to thee, as a present Dower?
Thou may'st be deckt with Bracelets rich and rare
And live on Earth free from perplexing care;
If thou dost look about and take advice,
And suffer Men nor Conscience to entice,
Or thee allure, such a choice to make,
Those joys to leave, and utterly forsake,
Which most men do, nay all accounted wise
Pursue amain, esteem, and highly prize:
But if thou hast a thought to change thy state.
Be wise and stay, don't holy Writ relate,
He that believes, doth not make hast:[289] O why
Shouldst thou have thoughts to mind it presently?
Come, pause a while, be not so hot, alas
By inconsiderateness it comes to pass,
So many Souls are spoil'd and ruined,
Be wary then, not rashly be misled.
    Nay, furthermore, I'le speak to thee again,
Thou mayst love him, and yet mayst thou retain
Respect and love to other objects too.
Love thy God well, but why shouldst thou let go
This world, with all the precious joys therein?
But don't mistake, thou must leave off thy sin,
For Holiness I must tell thee is right,

And very pleasant in *Jehovah*'s sight:
But know, O Soul, yet over and above,
Thy Sovereign Lord and Prince hath set his love
So much upon thee, that his gracious Eye
Will overlook thy smaller vanitie.
Ne'r doubt but thou shalt have his favour still,
Though in some things thou satisfie thy will.
Dost think that he who came down from above,
And dy'd for thee, will ever quite remove
His dear affection from thee, or e're hate,
And leave the Soul he bought at such a rate?
It is enough, and happy wilt thou be,
If thou escap'st all gross impurity.[290]

Thus the base heart be'ng inflam'd by the Devil,
Vndoes the Soul. No Enemy's more evil
Than that curst Foe we harbour in our breast,
Which all enlighten'd ones have oft exprest.
Corrupted Judgment blindly would inform her,
Christ having dy'd, her sins can never harm her.
Alas, saith Reason, do not all men sin?
Nay, more than this, the very best have bin
To blame in many things, and yet esteem'd
As righteous ones, and as the Lord's redeem'd
If famous Men of old offenders were,
What needst thou be so nice, what needst thou fear?
The glorious King is filled with compassion,
Besides he sees in thee great reformation:
Thy love to sinful lusts is but in part
To what it was, and thou must know thou art
Plac'd in this world, and therefore must comply
In some respects with smaller vanity.
When Reason *to the vicious* Will *gives ear,*
How can the Vnderstanding then be clear?
When vile Affection thus corrupteth Reason,
All works and thoughts are turn'd to perfect Treason.
O see how blind poor Souls by Nature are,
How vain their thoughts, how ready to insnare
Themselves are they with false Imaginations,
With earthly toys and idle speculations.
To learn and understand all humane Arts
Most apt they are, they'l magnifie their parts;
How very quick and dext'rous are they when
They talk of things that appertain to men?
But things of God are quite above their sphere,
*Can't them*ᵃ *discern, nor do they love to hear*
Of God, or Christ, they count that man a fool
That daily goes to learn at Jesus's School.

Vnto the blindness of the natural mind
Add this besides, most evident you'l find
It doth resist the Truth, 'twill not receive it;
Nay 'tis incredulous, 'twill not believe it.
Apt to believe false tales, and stories vain;
Nay, like to Eve, 'twill quickly entertain
Suggestions of the cursed Prince o'th Night,
But what God says, seems evil in their sight.
Nay, more than all, this treach'rous faculty   }
Is so deprav'd, St. Paul doth plain descry
Much enmity to God therein to lie.
Vnto God's Law it will not subject be;[291]
For in the mind is great malignity.
But I must not the Reader *here detain;*
Because that our old Friend is come again.

CHAP. V.

Shewing how the Judgment of the Soul comes to be enlightened, and the effects thereof.

Theologue.

My patience's not yet tyr'd, my bowels move,
With bended knees shall I now gain thy love
To *Jesus Christ?* how shall I leave thee quite,
When I behold such terrors, which afright
My trembling Soul? wch soon will thee o're-take,
Unless thou dost with speed this Contract make.
Thy Judgment 'tis which I would fain convince.
Thy danger's great, I do perceive from thence:
When *Conscience* had almost (in truth) persuaded
Thee to repent, it was straightway invaded
By thy blind Understanding, and dark mind,
From whence thou art to evil still inclin'd.
Thou ofen-times hadst listen'd unto me,
And left thy sin: but they deceived thee,
And chang'd thy thoughts (as *Conscience* doth relate)
Till thy condition's grown most desperate.
Wilt thou once dare to harbour such a thought;
Because with bloud thy Soul by Christ was bought,
Thou mayest sin, and take thy pleasure here,
And prize the world as equal, nay, more dear
To thee than him? How canst thou be so dark
This to imagine, Soul? I prethee hark;
Did he not bleed, and die upon the Tree   }
Thee to redeem from all iniquitie,
And that to him thou shouldst espoused be?

Should a great Prince love a poor Virgin so,
As for her sake ten thousand sorrows know,
And be content at last when all is done,
Another should enjoy her for his own?
        Oh! ope thine eyes, imbrace the chiefest Good;
Let him be dear to thee, who with his Bloud
Hath thee redeem'd from Sin, the chiefest ill,
Be not unto thy self so cruel still,
And void of Reason, foolishly to chuse
The greatest Evil and chief'st Good refuse.
The good in Christ with every state agrees,
It suits the Soul when troubles on it seize.
When thou art sick, he'l thy Physician be,[292]
He all distempers cures. Nay, it is He,
And he alone, that heals the precious Soul,
And with a word can make the Body whole.
Art dark? O, he can straight way make thee see;
Nay, if born blind, he can give eyes to thee.
If thou art weary, he alone's thy rest.
Or, art thou sad, and grievously deprest?
He is thy comfort, and thy joy will be,
Like to the deep and overflowing Sea.
If thou an hungry art, he is thy food.
O tast and see, and thou wilt find him good.
The Fatling's slain, and all things ready are;
Thou'rt welcome too; O come, and do not spare,
But freely eat, and drink his spiced Wine,
Wch will make glad that drooping heart of thine,
The Father calls, the Spirit says, O come;
And Christ doth say, here's in my heart yet room,
O Sinner! come to me: hark, he doth cry,
O come to me, poor Soul, why wilt thou die?
Art thou in Prison, he will ope the door,
He'l pay thy debts, and wipe off all thy score.
If thou a Widow or an Orphan be,
Husband and Father both he'l be to thee:
A Husband that does live, yea, live for ever:
Match here, poor Soul, where Death can part you never.
Or, art thou weak, & canst not go alone?
He is thy strength, O thou mayst lean upon
His mighty Arm; for that is thy support.
Art thou beleaguer'd? he's thy Royal Fort.
In times of danger and of trouble great,
Unto his holy Name do thou retreat:
Which is a Tower strong to all that fly
With care and speed from all iniquity.[293]
Under his wings he'l hide his purchas'd One,
Till these calamities are past and gone.

Or, art thou dying, and dost fear the grave?
He is thy life, from Death he will thee save;
They cannot die, who such a Husband have.
Or, art a Sinner? he's thy Righteousness;
He's more than I can any ways express.
The good in Christ is so exceeding sweet,
None understand until they tast of it.
He is a Good which none can comprehend,
He is a Good which doth all others send;
The chiefest Good, good of himself alone,
When carnal joys and pleasures all are gone.
That's not the good that fills not the desire,
That can't be chief, if there be yet a higher.
God is so good, noughts good if him we want;
Small things, with him, will satisfie a Saint.
He is so good, that nought can bitter make him,
Unto that Soul, who chearfully does take him,
And his sweet love and precious grace enjoys;
Yet this rare Good ne'r gluts, nor sweetness cloys.
The best of earthly sweets, which fools do prize,
By sin and sickness doth much bitter rise.
They loath them straight, and can't abide to hear
Of that which lately they esteem'd so dear.
That, that's the Good on which thou shouldst depend,
That is desired for no other end
Than for it self! O tast of him, and try,
And thou'lt be filled to Eternity.
That's not the Good which suddenly doth leave us,
That's not the Good of which Death can bereave us,
Christ is a Good that's lasting, and abides;
All other Good, alas, will fail besides.
Make him thy choice, dear Soul, O do but try
How sweet it is in *Jesu's* Arms to lie.
Make him thy joy, and thou'lt see cause to sing,
Whatever days or change may on thee bring.

Soul.

Sad times, alas! here is a sudden change;
Nought can I hear of now but rumors strange,
Of Wars and Tumults, with perplexity,
Which do encrease and swell most vehemently
Within the regions of my inward man,
Which causes tears, and makes my face look wan.
Cross workings in me clearly I discover,
I am distrest about this glorious Lover.
The counsel which my heart did lately give
I cannot take, I dare not it receive.
Great slaughters there will be in my small Isle,

For without bloud be sure this fearful broil
Will never cease; which side now shall I take?
I tremble much, yea all my bones do shake.
Some of my sins which I have loved dear,
Are forc'd to fly, and others can't appear,
Lest *Conscience* should upon them fall: for he
Crys out, Kill all, let not one spared be.
Nay, *Judgment* too is all-most at a stand,
Which doth amuse me much o'th other hand.
Yet *Will* and *Old-man*,[294] are resolv'dly bent
To hinder me from granting my consent.
Yet it I could but have some glimm'ring sight
Of this great Prince, I know not but it might
Work strange effects in me: for I do find
My Eyes are out, my Understanding blind.
Lord, pity me: for I a wretch have bin,
To slight thee thus, and love my cursed sin.
        Thus whilst God's Word was preacht, and she also
Began to cry, I did observe, and lo,
A Friend was sent from the blest Prince of Light,
The glory of whose Face did shine so bright,
That none were able to behold, for he
Seem'd not infer'our to the Majesty
Of the great God, and his eternal Son:
For they in Essence are all three but one.
His Power's great, and Glory is his merit;
His nature's like his Name (*most holy Spirit.*)
Who to the Soul did presently draw near,
And toucht her heart, and then unstopt her ear;
And from him shone such glorious rays of light,
Some scales flew off, and she recover'd sight.
Which straitway did her judgment rectifie,
Who to this purpose did himself apply
Unto the Soul whom he had led astray.
I must confess my faults to thee this day.[295]

Judgment.

        For want of light false judgment I have given,
And treacherously conspired against Heaven;
And 'gainst thy life and happiness have I
Been drawn into a vile conspiracy
Of th' highest nature: for I did consent
With thy base Foes, who hellishly are bent,
To tear thee into pieces,[296] quite undo thee,
Whilst smilingly they proffer pleasures to thee.
And now though not t' extenuate my sin,
I'le tell thee how I have been drawn in.
Thy heart's corrupted, and from it proceeds

The cursed *Old-man*, with his evil deeds.
They with *Apollyon* jointly did unite
To draw a Curtain 'twixt me and the light
And thus though I sometimes was half inclin'd
To judge for God, they basely kept me blind.
They've me corrupted with thy wilful *Will*.
Who, I do fear, remains most stubborn still:
Which if 't be so, and he's not made to bend,
Conclude the match thou canst not with thy friend
And I, poor I, can't make him condescend:
Some higher Power 'tis must make him yield,
Or he'l stand out and never quit the Field.
For he's a churlish piece, and thou wilt find
To what is evil, he is most enclin'd:
But hath no will at all to what is right,
A very Traytor to the Prince of Light.
But as for me, my thoughts are clearly now
Thou oughtst forthwith to yield, and meekly bow
To the great King, thy mighty Lord and Lover.
And more then this to thee I must discover;
Now, now I know thy Soveraign Lord will pry
Into thy very heart, his piercing Eye
Will find that Soul amongst the Company
Who wants the Wedding-garment, and will sever
That unprepared man in Wrath for ever
From his sweet presence: *Soul*, his Word doth shew
Nothing will serve but *universal* new.
He is a *jealous God*,[297] will not endure
To see thee only counterfeited pure;
O now I see he will not take a part,
But claims both ears, eyes, hands, yea, the whole heart.
Now, now I see 'tis pure simplicity
That is alone accepted in his Eye.
That sin which has been like to a right hand,
For profit sweet, thou must at his command
Cut straight-way off. Nay, Soul, look thou about;
For Right-eye sins must all be pulled out.[298]
Though they for pleasure have to thee bin dear,
Yet must they have no room, nor favour here.
Of every sin thou must thy self deny;
One sin will damn thee to Eternity,
If thou to it dost any love retain.
Nay, hark to me, Soul, listen once again;
The Law must also unto thee be dead,[299]
And thou to it, or never canst thou wed
With Jesus Christ. If thy first Husband live,
Who to another Husband can thee give?
The smallest sin thou ever didst commit,

The Law's so strict, it damns the Soul for it.
Let this divorce thee from it, 'tis severe,
No life nor help (alas) canst thou have there.
And therefore unto Jesus come with speed,
For such a Bridegroom 'tis which thou dost need.
And th' glory of the blessed Bridal-state,
Will far exceed the greatest Potentate.
What's he? Ah Soul! what grace and favor's this?
Where dwels that Queen, nay where that Emperess,
Whose splendent glory can e're equal thine,
When thou canst say, I'm his, and he is mine?[300]

A Consultation held between the Prince and Powers of Darkness, hearing how the Judgment was rectified, and the understanding of the Soul somewhat enlightened.

Apollyon.

Most mighty Pow'rs, who once from Heav'n fell,
To raise this Throne and Monarchy in Hell;[301]
Do not despair, rouse up, all is not gone,
The Conqueror han't yet the Conquest won.
Tis far below your noble extract thus
To stand amaz'd; is there no pow'r in us,
For to revive our scattered force? let's try
What may be done, we can at last but fly.
Ne'r let us yield that she should raised be
To such a height, to such great Soveraigntie.
What, she, whose birth and pedigree was mean
To what our's was, shall she be crowned Queen,
Whilst we are made the Objects of her scorn,
Hated of God and Man? This can't be born.
What, shall eternal Arms embrace the Soul,
Whilst we in chains of Darkness do condole
Our former loss? in spite of Heaven let's try
Yet once again to spoil th' Affinity.

Satan.

Bravely resolv'd! and if in Hell there are
A legion of such Spirits, never fear
But we the Conquest yet o're Heaven shall gain,
And all the hopes and pride of Mortals stain.
We venture very little, yet shall win
All at one blow, if we prevail again.
And there's great hopes methinks; for ev'n success
Makes foes secure, and makes our danger less.[302]
Lo! don't you see how the fond Soul doth lie
Ope to our Arms in great security?
And though some ground is lost, yet seek about,
View well our force within, and that without.

We in her house have a strong party yet,
Who in our bands keep her unwary feet.
Let's make a search, and now more careful be,
For sad it is the wretch such light should see,
Without all doubt there has been some neglects,
Which has produce'd such undesir'd effects.
Could none keep out the light? or has her heart,
Always so true to us, play'd a false part?
Sure *Will* and *Old-man* both do stand and pause,
Or some grand Foe hath quite betray'd our cause.
We must be-stir us, and give new directions,
And by all means keep fast the Souls affections.
Affection's still by *Old-man* is directed;
And *Will* to us does yet stand well affected.
Let us pursue our present enterprize,
With all the craft and pow'r we can devise.
Our Prince, I see, is very much offended,
And thus in short the Consultation ended.
    Apollyon with whole troops of hellish Fiends
Immediately into the Soul descends,
To raise sad storms and tempests in her breast,
Who being curst, hates any should be blest.
And that he might the better have his ends
Accomplished, he thus bespeaks his Friends:
The Flesh with all its lusts, to whom he said,
Old-man, my grand Ally, I am afraid
Thy[a] tottering Kingdom has not long to stand,
If to my aid thou dost not lend thy hand.
Tis thou (old Friend) that must my cause maintain,
Or otherwise thou wilt thy self be slain.
Hark! dost not hear that flesh-amazing cry,
"Kill the *Old-man*, O kill, O crucifie[303]
"The Old-man with his deeds,[304] rise up and slay,
"Let not that Foe survive another day?
"'t is that cursed *Old man* works our bane,
"Then let him die, let the *Old-man* be slain.
Bestir thy self, and try thy utmost skill,
Undoubtedly thou must be kill'd, or kill.
'Tis not a time to pause, or slack thy hand,
Negligence will not with thy int'rest stand.
Tell, tell the Soul, in vain thou dost deny
Thy self of that which satisfies the Eye;
Adorn thy self with Pearl, be deckt with Gold,[305]
Such pleasant things are lovely to behold;
Avoid all those penurious Nicities,
That makes thee hateful in thy Neighbour's eyes;
Delight[b] thy self in that the world 'counts brave,
And let thy senses have what e're they crave.

Say to the Soul, let not thine Ears and Eyes
Be satisfy'd alone, but please likewise
Thy Appetite, grant all the Soul desires.
And if it chance to kindle lustful fires,
Tel her the earth was fil'd with boundless treasures
That she thereby might take her fill of pleasures.
And for that end the senses are united
In one fair body, there to be delighted.
And tell her, if she do restrain one sense
Of what it craves, she offers violence
Unto her self, and doth her self deny
Of the best good, and chief'st felicity.

The Old-man's Reply.

This Hellish Lecture past, the *Old-man* breaks
His Silence; and, half Angry, thus he speaks:
Renowned Father! let thy Servant borrow
A word or two to mitigate my sorrow.
This Counsel might have done some time ago,
But now enlightned[a] Judgment lets her know
All these are painted pleasures, and their date
Ends with her life: dread Prince! it is too late
To mind this Counsel, she will not receive it,
Her understanding now will not believe it.
I by thy Aid have oft endeavoured
In fitter times such kind of things to spread
Before her eyes; but now of late we find
There is an alteration in her mind.
Could you have took the Gospel quite away,
'T would not have been as 'tis, you do delay.

Apollyon.

No more of that – *Old-man*, take my direction
Improve thy int'rest now with her *affection*.
I know *Affection* still's inclin'd to love
That which the Understanding doth reprove.
This being so, if we improve our skill,
And can but keep firm unto us the *Will*,
If he's not over-powr'd, thou maist gain,
Thy former strength, and long thou mayest reign,
For *Conscience* thou may'st once again hereby
Lull fast asleep, and then also her Eye
Will grow so weak, her light diminished,
That *Judgment* by *Affection* shall be led.
And if thou canst but once this way persuade her,
Will and *Affection* quickly will invade her
To please her senses; and for those intents
Affection may use weighty Arguments;

And thus being overcome, she will be more
Intangled in our fetters than before.
Lusts of the eyes, and *pride of life*,[306] these be
My Agents both, they are employ'd by me.
Old-man, therefore proceed, the Intrest's mine;
But be victorious, and the Conquest's thine.
Once lose the day, and thou be sure must die.
Which being lost, thou'lt suffer more than I.

Old-man.

   Most dread *Apollyon*! thou must understand,
As I have ever been at thy command,
And am thy Servant, so I will remain;
And fight until I slay, or else am slain.
Yet let me lodge this secret in thy breast,
Canst thou be ignorant, how she's possest
With such a Soul-convincing beam of light,
That I do seem a Monster in her sight.
I shall not overcome her now, unless
I do appear to her in some new dress.
Time was indeed when I have been respected,
But now, alas, I greatly am suspected
Of being thy great favourite; nay, she
Affirms that I am wholly led by thee.
These things consider'd, I must be advis'd,
Fear lest I should be unawares surpriz'd.

Apollyon.

   Thou hit'st the case, and I agree thereto;
Thou shalt be clothed new from top to toe:[a]
And I'le transform my shape, and will appear,
For thy assistance; haste, and nothing fear.
With specious shews of love, do thou pretend,
Thou com'st to reason with her as a Friend,
Not meaning to perswade her to remove,
Or to withdraw in any case her love
From her great Soveraign, whom thou maist confess
Can only her advance to happiness;
Yet tell her she's too strict, she's too precise,[307]
She'l never hold it; bid her to be wise:
Soft pace goes far; an over-heated zeal
Ruins the Soul, and spoils the Common-weal.
Go bid her carry't in her Princes sight
With Saint-like sweetness; bid her to delight
In his presence, and there demurely stand,
But when she's absent, let both heart and hand
Be still delighted, as they were before,
With sense-deluding Objects. Furthermore,

Tell her he's not so strict as to debar
Her of these joys below, for her's they are:
Of which *Paul* rightly speaks, this is the sum,
All things are yours, both present and to come;[308]
Thus we'l combine, and all our pow'rs unite,
And in this mode and curious dress incite
Th' enlighten'd Soul to play the Hypocrite.[309]

    The flesh being thus with th' pow'rs of Hell agreed,
The inward Foe bestirs himself with speed;
Vile Traytor like, a *Panther* doth become,
To work about the Soul's eternal doom.
A cruel Serpent, in a Saint-like guize,
The better to trapan the long'd-for prize.
As *Balaam*, once, and *Balak*, so do they
Seek to find out some curst insidious way,
The poor unwary Soul for to betray
To the last Death's dark and eternal shade.
Balaam advises *Balak* to invade
God's Heritage, 'twas by the beauteous train
Of *Moabite* Damsels, who he thought might gain
The *Israelites* affections, and there by
Make them offend against the Majesty
Of God All-mighty, by whose powerful hand
Jacob prevails, and *Moab* could no wise stand.[310]
Ah! see how the wise Fowler lays his snare
To catch the poor enlighten'd Soul. Beware,
And do not close thy new-inlighten'd Eyes;
Under the Golden clew the *Panther* lies.
The Eye-intangled Creature stands to gaze
Upon the lovely *Panther* in a maze,
Till the deluded Beast doth by his stay
Unwillingly become the *Panther's* prey.
Just as you see sometimes the nimble fly,
Dancing about the flame, advance so nigh,
Until it's taken and doth burn its wings.
Thus from it self its own destruction springs,
Or like two Men, who running in a Race,
With hopes the Golden Diadem shall grace
The Victor's Temples, in the way doth lie
A Golden Ball, one of them casts his Eye
Upon the same, makes but a little stay
To take it up, the other hasts away,
And never turns aside to fix his Eyes
On this or that, but runs and wins the prize:
The other he the Ball espies, is loth
To let it lie: in hopes to get them both,
He loses both: for when he comes to try,

Doth find the Golden Ball deceiv'd his Eye;
For when he thought to lay it up in store,
Finds it an Earthly Ball, but gilded o're.
O! then he grieves, but then it is too late,
His Eye's the cause of his unhappy fate.
A fit resemblance: for thus stands the case
With every Soul. This mortal life's the Race.[311]
A blessed Kingdom crowns the Victor's brow
With endless glory, but whilst here below
We're tempt by Earthly pleasures, that's the Ball;
Satan's the Sophister, who lets it fall.
Now look about thee, Soul, thy time's at hand,
Thine Enemies approach, nay, lo they stand
Ready prepared, and resolv'd to try
Both strength and craft to get the Victory.
Thy precious Lord is the eternal Prize.
Mind well thy Mark, take heed of wanton Eyes,
If Pleasures thou, or Honours, shouldst espy,
Stop not to gaze, run swift, and pass them by;
Take no regard unto that painted Ball,
Which Satan, to deceive thee has let fall.
The *Old-man*'s near (the flesh) in a new dress,
And whose with him? Ah! thou mayst eas'ly guess.
'Tis to deceive thee he appears so trim,
And thou mayst see the *Devil* plain in him.
The pow'rs of Hell in thee will try their skill
For to insnare *Affections*, and the *Will*;
Nay, *Satan* has got them to take his side;
Thus treacherously thy heart they do divide.
    Thus though the Soul obtains inlightned Eyes,
Whilst thicker darkness vanishes and flies,
Yet is she vex'd with sore perplexities
'Twixt two extreams and two contrary Laws,
Judgment is led by one, *Affection* draws
The other way; she can't tell which to please:
She knows what's best, but strong temptations seize
Upon her so, that she's at a great stand,
This way she goes, then to the other hand.
Her faculties fall out, they disagree.
O look, methinks I in the Soul do see
Four mighty Warriours draw into the Field
To try their Valour, and refuse to yield
Unto each other: here's two against two:
Judgment with *Conscience* are united[a] so,
That *Will* and the *Affections* do resolve
The trembling Soul in Wars still to involve.
Will rouses up, refuses to give way,

That his great opposites should have the day;
Apollyon also with him doth take part,
To hold his own, and to beguile her heart.
They meet, they strike, & blows exchange for blows,
Darts are let fly, they with each other close.
The conflict's sharp, 'tis very hard to know
Which will the other beat and overthrow.
Will's hard put to't, nay, had lost the day quite,
But that more Traytors join'd him in the Fight.
Th' *Old-man* rouses with rebellious flesh,
And these domestick Wars renew afresh.
They fight about the *Soul*, would know who must
Have th' *heart* and its *affections, Christ*, or *Lust*.
Satan by inward motions straight reply'd,
My sentence is, we'l equally divide,
And give alike, both can't have the whole heart;
Christ take a piece, and I the other part.
He'd have the question by the Sword decided,
Knowing the Soul lies dead whilst 'tis divided.³¹²
　　　Thus 'tis with many. Ah! look well within,
Judgment convinc'd may be, yet may thy sin
In thy *affections* live, and also thou
Mayst not to th' pow'r of Grace and *Jesus* bow.
Thou mayst have light, and speak as *Balaam* did,
Whose Eyes *Jehovah* so far opened,
That he cry'd out, *O happy Israel!*
How goodly are the Tents where thou dost dwell!
He (like to many Preachers) did commend
God's holy ways, and wish'd that his last end
Might be like his, who righteously doth live,
And his whole heart doth unto *Jesus* give.
He to this purpose spake, yet ne'r-the-less,
*Lov'd best the wages of unrighteousness.*³¹³
The Understanding may much light receive,
And yet may not the Soul rightly believe,
Nor be espous'd to *Christ*, may not rely
On him alone in true simplicitie.
But to proceed; with careful Eye let's view
What follows here, what 'tis doth next ensue.
As Combatants sometimes a Parly beat
After some sharp Encounter, or retreat.
And with each other do expostulate
About their rising, or their sinking fate.
Even so likewise do these strong inward Foes,
They pause as 'twere, parly, then fall to blows.

Old-man.

The *Old-man* moves, and presently he meets
With the poor Soul, and thus *Affection* greets:
Thou for my Int'rest ever yet hast been,
And sweet (says he) Ah! sweet's a bosom sin;
Thou never yet deny'dst to yield subjection
Unto my will; and now, indear'd *Affection,*
Our Master, great *Apollyon,* doth command
That we unite our force, and faithful stand
Against our Foes, thy int'rest is invaded,
Thou seest by whom, thou knowst who are inraged:
Hold fast thine own, ne'r let those Objects go
Thou lov'st so dear, 'twill be thy overthrow;
And thereby too the Soul will unawares
Be much involv'd in more vexatious cares;
And those delights which thou wert wont to have
Will be obscured in the darksom Cave
Of black Oblivion, buried out of sight,
Should once the Soul close with this *Prince of Light.*
Not that we think thou canst 'ith' least approve
Of this where by she should withdraw her love
Quite from those things which we esteem so dear;
For Heart and Will some ways do yet adhere
Unto our Int'rest; yet basely misled
She is, e're since she's been enlightened.
We are content she should cry up the choice
She thinks to make, let her in that rejoice;
Yet there's a secret we would fain reveal,
She's blinded by her over-fervent zeal.
It is enough since she has made such vows
To love him so, as to become his Spouse,
Why should she not have yet sweet sensual pleasures,
To please the flesh, to whom the greatest treasures
Of right belongs that ever were possest?
How can her glory better be exprest
Than to imbrace what is so freely given,
Joys here below as well as bliss in Heaven?
Let her not fear to spend her days in mirth,
That's Heir of Heaven, and Lady of the Earth.
This think upon, and secretly impart
So sweet a Message to the yielding heart.
Affection hears, and willingly consented,
And strives with this to make the Soul contented,
Nay, with it too, the Soul began to close,
Until poor *Conscience* did them both oppose.
Affection, Will, and *Conscience* talk a while;
Apollyon straight starts up, and with a smile
Salutes them all, seeming as if he were
One unconcern'd with any matters there:
Who well observing how these three contended,

Begs leave to speak a word, as he pretended,
In favour to them all, desiring he
Might at this time their Moderator be.
At this they seem'd to pause, and stand all mute,
At length the Soul, but faintly, grants his Suit:
The Devil having thus obtain'd his end,
Salutes the Soul, *Fair Virgin*, I commend
Thy happy choice, almost, if not quite made,
Yet, if all matters were but wisely weigh'd,
Thou'lt find *Affection*[a] has advis'd thee right;
And 't can't be safe such Counsel now to slight.
The greatest honours oft, for want of care
In just improvements, have been made a snare.
What bount'ous Heav'n & Earth affords, refuse not;
Be not so nice; ye 'buse the things you use not.
What, is thy Soveraign willing to receive thee
Into Celestial Joys, yet quite bereave thee
Of present sweetness? Tush! this cannot be;
He will sure ne'r such wrong do unto thee.
Reflect not what thy former state hath been,
But what 'tis now, *a Saint*, more than a Queen.
Things present, and to come, nay, all are thine;
Come, merry be, drink of the choicst Wine.
Thine honour's great, and let thy joys abound;
Chant to the Viol, hear the Organ sound;
Let the melodious Lute and Harp invite thee,
And each transcendent joy on Earth delight thee.
A sweet is (What?) a thing reproacht, call'd *Sin*;
It in the bosom lies, has harbour'd bin
By chiefest Saints: O then, do not deny
The present good, that's pleasant to the Eye.
But it thou fearst thou shouldst thy Lord offend;
Observe this Rule, which I shall next commend:
Let all thy words be pleasant, smooth, and sweet,
When him thou dost in daily Duties meet.
Seem to be chast, and let no Saints espy
The smallest sign of Immoralitie.
Be grave in speech, and lowly when thou meetst them
And call them thy *dear Brethren*, when thou greetst them.
And if thy Soveraign seek to have thy heart,
Let him have some, yet must the World have part.
Call him *thy Friend, thy Saviour*, own him so;
And to poor Saints thou must some kindness show,
Or else thy covetousness they will espy,
And thou'lt be charg'd, *with what?* Idolatry.
Thus mayst thou keep his love; but when thou go's
Amongst thy old acquaintance, (yet his Foes)
Let them know nothing, let no sentence fall

Which may discover this to them at all.
Thus having spoken briefly, be thou wise,
And with thy Friends, my Agents, now advise.
Thus ends the *Old-man* and *Apollyon*'s suit;
And the poor *Soul* in this assault stood mute,
Not well discerning who these thoughts did dart
Into her yielding and divided heart.
Nor hath she got that grave and good inspection
What's best to do, and where to take direction,
But goes to th' *Flesh*, with that doth she consult,
Which quickly brings her to a sad result.
I hitherto, saith she, have been deprest;
What shall I do, how may I be at rest?

The Flesh, or corrupt Affection.

What's the reversion of a Prince's State,
When't must be purchas'd at so dear a rate?
'Tis but arriving at a seeming pitch
Of Honour, and to be conceited Rich.
If there's no way to get this promis'd Crown,
But to incur the world'ds vile scoff and frown,
With loss of life, and all we call our own;
'Twould folly be to seek for such a prize:
For what we have is pleasant in our Eyes.
A real thing, and present, as 'tis dear,
To part with it, is more than flesh can bear.
But by the way, mind what our Friends propound;
A *Medium* to enjoy them both, is found;
Wherefore 'tis best in this perplexing case,
For to unite, that Counsel let's imbrace.

Soul.

Hast thou forgot, or knowst thou not, mine eyes
Have been enlight'ned? let us first advise
With *Judgment*, lest this over-rash conclusion
Turn all our Consultations to confusion.
It would be well could we (I must confess)
Those sinful sweets and present joys possess,
Without the loss of those transcendant pleasures
That's in *Jehova*'s unconfined Treasures.
But what if *Judgment* says it must not be,
Nor *Truth* nor *Conscience* with us will agree?
If so, what shall I do, what shall I choose?
Whilst I secure one, I both may loose.

The flesh, or corrupt Affection's Reply.

One word I'le briefly drop, and speak no more.
Thou'st put thy case to *Conscience* heretofore,

And what redress pray had you, what didst gain?
Did he not gripe thee sorely for thy pain?
Wilt thou neglect so sweet advice as this?
Judgment and *Conscience* both may judg amiss.
But if thou lik'st it, and canst be contented,
By knawing *Conscience* still to be tormented,
Then I'le be silent, and improve thy skill,
Yet will I love and like where I did still.
Hadst thou been counsel'd to forsake the Lord,
Would I, do'st think, have spoken the least word,
Once to dissuade thee from so just a thing?
Nay. *Soul*, thou oughtst, nay must respect this King:
But whilst he's absent, whilst he dwells on high,
Thou hast no other Object for thine Eye
Then these –
Consult with *Conscience*, now do what you please,
But as for me I am for present ease.

CHAP. VI.

Shewing the policy of Satan in keeping the Soul from a full closing with Christ. Also the nature of a bosom sin.

No sooner was this sharp Encounter over,
But in a little time you might discover
The Soul half vanquish'd by her weak opposing,
Sometimes resisting, and then faintly closing.
Sometimes you'l see her just as 'twere consenting,
And presently you'l find her much lamenting,
Beset on every side with troops of fears;
Which makes her to bedew her cheeks with tears,
Complains to *Conscience*, hoping for relief,
Till *Conscience* checks her, and renews her grief.
Sometimes she's drawn to fix her tender Eye
Upon the Gospel's pure Simplicitie.
Her love-sick thoughts at fits seem to aspire,
As if she could pass through hot flames of fire,
And say with *Peter*, Though all should deny
Thee, my blest Lord, yet so will never I.[314]
But when the Soul once comes to see the Cross,
Its courage fails, O! 'tis at a great loss.
When she perceives she and her lusts must part
O that sticks close, go's to the very heart.
The thoughts of that is hard; 'tis *Self-denial*
That puts the Soul upon the deepest tryal.
Some ready are to make a large profession
In hopes of somewhat, perhaps the possession

Of Heav'n at last; but straight sounds in their Ear,
Deny thy self; come, part with all that's dear
For Jesus sake. Ah! this they cannot bear.
The Young-man ran, he seem'd to be in haste,
But news of this, did all his courage blast.[315]
The gate is strait; O! 'tis no easie thing
To for-go all in love to this blest' King.
The way is narrow which leads unto life,
'Tis *Self-denial*, that begets the strife.[316]
'Twixt Flesh and Spirit there's a constant War,[317]
They opposite, and quite contraries are.
As Fire and Water, Light and Darkness be,
Such diff'ring Natures never can agree,
So between these is like antipathie.
The flesh is like the Young-man, give's attention
To what the Preacher says, until he mention
His bosom-sin, the Lust he so much loves;
This makes him face about, and back removes.
He goes away, yet lov'd to hear Christ preach
Up Legal works; but when he came to reach
His *Dalilah*,[318] that blow so griev'd his heart,
That Christ and he immediately must part.
His great possessions could not give to th' poor,
Though he had th' promise of abundance more
Treasures above; but being not content
To pay that price for Heaven, away he went.
How loth's the *Flesh* to yield, that *Grace* may win
The happy Conquest of a Bosom-sin?
How will it plead, how wittily debate,
Excuse, or argue, to extenuate
The Crime? at length it yields, fore'd to give way.
But first cry's out, O give me leave to stay
A year, a month, a week, at least one day:
But when it sees it cannot that obtain,
The loser looks, and pleads yet once again:
Ah! let my fond, my fainting, breaking heart
Hug it the other time, before we part.
Much like *Rebeckah's* Friends, the flesh appears;
It parts with sin, but 'tis with floods of tears.[319]
Each has his Darling, his beloved sin,
Whilst unconverted, much delighted in.
Give me, say some, but leave to heap up Treasure,
And I'le abandon all forbidden pleasure.
Others again there be that only prize
The popular applause of being wise,
A name of being learn'd, judicious, grave,
Able Divines, 'tis this too many crave.
Some boast their natural and acquired parts,

Which take the ears of some, seduce the hearts
Of many simple Souls who go astray;
While others are for feasting day by day.
There's some delight in drinking choice of Wine,
Whilst others are to Gaming more inclin'd.
That sin that finds more favour than the rest,
That is thy darling sin, thou knowst it best.
O search thy bosom well, pry, pry within,
Till thou findst out thy own beloved sin,
That gives thee kisses, that's the lust that slays thee
O that's the cursed *Judas* which betrays thee.
Ah! see how blind, how foolish Sinners are;
Like to rebellious *Saul*, they'l *Agag* spare,[320]
They entertain this Lust close in their heart,
And are indeed as loth with it to part,
As with a Hand or Eye; and therefore she
Crys out with *Sampson*, O this pleases me.[321]
Ah! I will freely part with all the rest,
Might I but hug this Darling in my breast.
Souls once convicted, quickly do begin
To hate, detest, and leave all grosser sin;
Sins visible unto the natural Eye,
Such which are of the black and deepest die,
They are possest with such a dread and fear,
They'l not touch them, nor venture to come near
These foul defilements – nay, such spots disdain;   }
Then presently conclude they'r born again,
And shall be sav'd, though bosom lusts remain.
And if at any time some beams of light
Discover secret Sin, or Conscience smite,
Or touch the *Dalilah*, they then begin
To think of making covers for such sin,
(Which in the secret of the bosom lies)
With the fair Mantle of Infirmities.
But if at any time the searching Word,
Which cuts and trys like a two-edged Sword,
Pierces the heart, and will divide asunder
The soul and spirit,[322] and e're long bring under
These Soul-deluding Covers, and espies
Those secret Lusts which in each corner lies;
And doth unmask those evils, and disclose,
The Soul's hypocrisie, yea and expose
It's nakedness to view, unto its shame:
Now, now the Flesh begins to change the name
Of every Lust that lies so closely hidden,
Soul, touch not, saith the Lord, 'tis Fruit forbidden.
O! saith the Flesh, 'tis pleasant in mine eyes;
Yea, says the Tempter, Soul, 'twill make thee wise,

Taste, it is sweet, the liberty is thine;
And Wisdom is a Vertue most divine.
And Vertue, saith the flesh, will make thee shine.[323]
Christ he prohibits Souls from taking pleasure
In laying up their bags of Earthly Treasure;[324]
For these things have in them a secret Art,
To steal away th' affections of the Heart:
Christ tells the Soul, Our Heavenly Father knows
What 'tis we want, and so much he allows
Which he sees best, which we contentedly
Should take from him, who will our wants supply,
And no good thing from us will he deny.
But hark! What saith the Flesh? O Soul, saith she,
In this give ear and harken unto me:
'Tis not unlawful here to lay up Treasure.
Provided thou therein tak'st no great pleasure.
The World thou seest disdains those wch are poor;
And if thou'rt Rich, thou'lt be ador'd the more.
Nay, if thou once arrivest at the pitch
Of being by the World accounted Rich,
Thy words will far the greater influence have,
And may'st thereby perchance more rich ones save.
Besides all this, when Rich, thou mayest feed
With thy abundance such who suffer need.
And this also will take thee off from care,
Which is to some a most perplexing snare,
And thou for God may'st the more hours spare.
If thou art poor, and of strict conversation,
That will not be a fit Accommodation
To draw men by; for some thereby are frighted,
Who might by temporizing be invited.
Accommodate thy self to all, *become.*
All things to all men, that thou mayst gain some.[325]
These subtil Covers doth the Flesh devise,
To hide those sins which in the bosom lies;
And by this crafty course perhaps a while
The poor unwary Soul it may beguile.
And if *Apollyon* sees the Creature yield
In this respect, he's Victor in the Field,
He glory's in the Conquest he has gain'd,
As if a Diadem he had obtain'd.
      But now, behold, here comes her former Friend,
Christ's precious Love this once to recommend.
True Ministers are filled with compassion,
As their long patience's worth all commendation.
The preciousness now of the Soul you'l hear,
And how things go within he will declare.
He'l call her *Conscience* to examination,

For *Conscience* 'tis must give a full Relation
Of all false Covers – Nay, and will reveal
Those secret Lusts the Flesh seems to conceal.

Theologue.
   Conscience, thou knowst, and privy art to all
The secret strivings, and the words let fall
To bring the Soul to join in bonds of love
With Jesus Christ, and finally remove
Her heart from sin, yea from the smallest evil;
One sin belov'd will send her to the Devil.
Speak therefore now, her inward parts reveal:
What faith hath she, what love, and O what zeal,
What indignation, care, and what desire?
Is she inflamed, is she all on fire
In love to him, who out of love did die,
Her to espouse, and save Eternally?

Conscience.
   She loves, (*but who?*) she sighs, Sir, shall I speak?
She's doubtful still, she knows not which to take.
Some kind of love, some faint desires do rise
Within her breast, but then the Enemies
Immediately such great disturbance cause,
That she's amaz'd, and put into a pause.
Although she dos love Christ, I must confess,
Some secret sin is favour'd ner'theless.
She wants some glorious Rays, her eyes are dim,
She never yet had a true sight of him.
I must speak all, e'en the whole truth impart;
Alas! she has new Objects in her heart.
Her love is treach'rous, her affections burn
Chiefly to self, loves Christ to serve her turn.
And such a Legalist she's become now,
To her own drag she blindfoldly do's vow
To offer Incense, in her seeming grace
She glory's much, nay, sets it in the place
Of Jesus Christ, and on that Idol pores;
This is the Object now she most adores.[326]

Theologue.
   Wilt thou expose thy self to scoff and shame.
And bring a blot for ever on thy name?
A Monster (thou) in Nature wilt appear,
To all who of thy faults and folly hear.
Canst be so vile, so impudent, and base?
Disloyal Soul! how canst thou still give place
To *Jesus's* Foes, and up an Idol set?

What, offer sacrifice to thy own Net?[327]
I stand amaz'd! what guilt is on thy head?
Remember that black Bill, what crimes are spread
Before thine Eyes already. But, now, further,
I am to charge thee with another Murther,
Committed on a spotless Man; nay, worse,
Thou letst him be betrayed to the Curse
Of a most shameful Death; nay, what exceeds,
His hands, feet, sides die, and his Soul still bleeds;
And what is worst of all, he is God's Son,
On whom this bloody Tragedy was done;
Thy Friend (O Soul) who came down from above,
To sue to thee for kindnesses and love.
And yet doth he, whose blood thy hands have shed,
Sue unto thee, nay his deep wounds do plead
For mercy, and he's able to forgive:
He's God as well as Man; dead, yet doth live.
What Object is't thou hast got in thine eye?[328]
Dost think the Law can help thee? make hast, fly;
For 'tis by that thou stand'st condemn'd to die.
Seek a Divorcement: stand'st thou still in doubt
'Twixt Law & Grace? strange! canst thou not find out
What *Judgment* told thee? sure thou knowest better:
It is severe, O! 'tis a killing Letter.
'Tis time to leave that Husband, and for-go
All hopes from him, who seeks thy overthrow.
Christ has fulfill'd it, he alone has life;
And if thou once art his espoused Wife,
Thou wilt receive a full discharge from all
Those Debts, those Deaths, and dangers wch inthral
The Souls of those, whose blind deceived breast
Seeks to self-righteousness for peace and rest.
Thou canst not (Soul) become a Virgin Spouse,
Until thou art divorced from all vows
To that, nay to Relations, though they're dear
Must thou the lesser love, and kindness bear.
Thy Fathers house, and all, thou must forsake,
If thou this happy contract e're dost make.[329]
Yield thy whole heart to Christ, bend to his feet
In pure simplicity; there's ground for it:
For he that lay within a Virgins Womb,
And who was buried in a Virgin-Tomb;
He that alone did lead a Virgin-Life,
Must have a chast and holy Virgin-Wife.[330]
Needst thou more motives still? what shall I say,
What shall I speak to move thee? I will lay
The nature of the Soul unto thy view:
Wouldst know its worth? read then what dos ensue,

First.

'Tis capable, such is its nature, State,
On Great *Jehovah's* Pow'r to contemplate:
It searches, prys and nicely looks about
On Nature's frame, and finds the former out.
David's amaz'd when he doth cast his Eye
On all the glorious things beneath the skie,
He looked up and down, above, and under,
And stood astonish'd, seeing cause of Wonder;
And then reflecting his own frame, did see
Nature's great Volume, blest *Epitome*.
Fearfully am I made: how canst tell?
His Answer is, *My Soul knows it full well*.[331]
We should have known no more of Earth, or Heav'n
Than the brute beasts, had not *Jehovah* given
This precious Soul to us: O then be wise,
And it secure as the chiefest Prize.

Secondly.

Nay more then this, the Scripture makes relation
'Tis capable of glorious Inspiration.
There is in Man a Soul, a Spirit do's live
And move in him, to which the Lord doth give
By Inspiration, Wisdom, Knowledg, Fear,
That fools know more than the Philosopher.
The Soul's God's Candle, a light of acceptation,
But from himself must come its Information.
Shall not this Candle (pray you) lighted be?
O let God's Spirit (Soul) inlighten thee.

Thirdly.

Nay, once again, it's Nature to declare,
'Twill sweet Impressions take, God's Image bear.
It bore it once, O then, how did it shine!
A glorious shadow of him, who's Divine:
But now 'tis blurr'd, and soil'd by filthy dust;
O 'tis defac'd and spoil'd by means of Lust.
But he who stamp'd it there at first, can make
It once again a new Impression take:
He can wash off the soil, refine the Ore,
And make it shine fairer than heretofore.
O what a glorious thing! how rare 'twill be,
When God renews his Image once in thee?
Lose not the Soul, (the wax) for nought can bear
This Image then, nor can that loss repair.

Fourthly.

The Soul's a glorious Piece, wherein doth lie
So great an Excellence, as doth out-vy

All outward Glory: for 'tis only she
That's capable of so great Dignitie
To be espoused to the Glorious Three.
Strange condescention! an amazing thing!
What joy and ravishment from hence may spring
Up unto thee, when into't thou dost pry;
Will the high God take sweet complacency
In such a one? What, doth he please to chuse
Thee for his dear Consort, make thee his Spouse?
May'st thou in Christ's dear Arms and Bosom lie?
Ah! is the Soul the Jewel of his Eye?
Can any joy and sweetness be like this?
Can worldly Comforts raise thee to such bliss?
What, is thy Soul capable of such Union;
And doth there flow from thence such rare Communion?
Admire it! is not one kiss worth more,
Than all the Riches of the Eastern shore?
O! lose not then thy Soul! Ah! who would miss
Of this sweet Union and Eternal Bliss?

Fifthly.

It's nature, worth, and rare transcendency,
Appears in that great incongruity,
And weakness of all Creatures to suffice it;
And from this ground great cause hast thou to prize it.
Nothing but God himself can satisfie
That precious Soul, which in thy breast do's lie.
The Univers's too little, th' whole Creation
Will not appease its longing expectation.
How vast's the Deeps? how lofty the desires
Of Man's poor Soul, above all bounds aspires,
It seeks, it prys, and views all kind of Treasure,
And still it craves, its wishes know no measure.
It walks again, it rambles, O it flies,
And ransacks all the secret Treasuries
Of Art and Nature, hurried, nay 'tis driven
To and fro, being restless, till to Heaven
It casts a look, and *Jesus* does espy,
And then full soon with greatest joy doth cry,
O there's the Pearl! I must have him, or die.
Thou must expect no peace, there's nought can still it,
Nor give it rest till God himself do's fill it,
Hark to its sighs, do not befool and cheat it,
Nor of its wishings baffle and defeat it:
For nothing but that God that made it, can
Suffice the Soul, the precious Soul of Man.[332]

Sixthly.

What thinkst thou of that price, that price of blood
Which Christ laid down? does it not cry aloud?
O precious is the Soul! it cost full dear:
Doth not this noise sound always in thine Ear?

Seventhly.

Don't *Satan*'s rage, his enmity, and wrath
Against the Soul, shew forth its precious worth?
Take pleasures here, and Coffers fill with Coin,
The Shop with Wares, & Cellars with rich Wine:
Let him but have the Soul, he does not care,
Take what you please besides, and do not spare.
He rages when one Soul escapes his paws;
Ah! that's the Prize his black and bloody jaws
Are open for. These *Demons* grin, and swell
With venom great, and Councils hold in Hell,
(As hath been hinted) that by craft they may
Catch the poor Soul, and this Pearl bear away,
That, that's the Morsel, that's their only prey.

Eighthly.

Its blest Infusion, and God's constant care
For food and Ornaments which he does spare,
For to adorn her on th' espousal day,
Fully declares this Truth, therefore we may
Amazed stand, and wondring all ways[a] cry,
O precious Soul! thy worth and exc'llency
Is very great, who can it comprehend?
It's that which does oft-times to Christ ascend
In strong desires, and longings: O! 'twill pry
Into all places for his Company.
She in his sight rejoyces, and is glad;
But when once gone, she sighs, she mourns, is sad.
All other joy's but meer perplexity;
Without his love, 'twill swoun'd away, nay die.
Nothing but Grace, Heaven's off-spring, can revive it;
And nought but sighs of *Jesus* can enlive it.
These things considered, may make thee see
Its worth, nay more, how also 'tis with thee.

Ninthly.

How shall we prize the Soul? what rate shall we
Upon her set? O what against her weigh?
Come, bring the ballance, and now let us try
What further worth or preciousness doth lie
In the fair Soul: 'tis done, all Golden Ore
Of both the *Indies* are ith' scales, yet more

We still do want, more Riches pray put in,
All precious Stones and Pearls; now weigh agin.
Alas the ballance flies, here yet wants weight,
The Soul out-vies them all: Lord, here's a sight
Th' whole world at once is in, yet 'tis too light.
Add world to world, and heap ten thousand more,
Were there so many, could you find such store,[333]
Yet would the Soul in worth exceed them far.
Nay, I might multiply, and yet not err.
Oh! then take heed thou dost not chaffer so,
To get the World, and in exchange let go
This precious Soul: nor let it be thought strange,
What shall a Man for's Soul give in exchange?

Tenthly.

She is Immortal, O she cannot die;
Though 'twas not so from all Eternity.
She was created, but in such a state,
Man can't her kill, nor her annihilate.
Her Beings such, her Life shall still remain
(Although the body die) in bliss or pain.
Then hast thou not good ground to watch & ward
With wary eye, and set a constant guard
Upon the portals of the treach'rous heart,
Lest of this Jewel thou deceived art?
What Man to gain a shilling, would let go
A Pearl of such great price and value?[334] who
Would think that Men, accounted grave and wise,
For toys and trifles should their Souls despise?[335]
Many, I fear there be, who day by day,
To gain a Groat, unjustly, giv't away;
Whilst others prostitute it to their lust:
Nay, do by it, as by a bone or crust
That's cast unto the Dog for him to knaw.
This Dog's the Devil, whose wide stretcht-out jaw
Stand gaping for't: his Eyes are upon all,
Knowing when e're they sin, they let it fall.
O then take heed, and if this Dog should fawn,
Or wag his Tail, let not so sweet a pawn
Of future Glory be contemn'd or lost,
Think, think from whence it came, & what it cost.

CHAP. VII.

Christ's Love Epitomiz'd, the Old-man wounded, Will made willing: shewing also the nature of the Soul's Espousal to Christ.

IF all that hath been said yet will not move thee
To close with Christ, I once again will prove thee,
By making of a brief or short collection
Of his sweet Love and wonderful Affection;
And then I trust thou wilt with sacred Vows
Contract thy self to him, become his Spouse,
Whose left hand's full of Treasure, in his right
Are Honours great, and Pleasures infinite.
     A Prince (you know) dispos'd to make Election
Of a Consort, before he'l place Affection,
Will first enquire if she Virgin be
In Person, Parts, Estate, or Pedigree
Equal unto himself: but if in case
She be of low descent, of Parents base,
Compar'd with his; or not so noble born,
Or has debas'd her self, or is forlorn;
He thinks it is below him once to place,
Or fix his love on her, he fears disgrace:
But if the Lady chance to equalize him,
She's not so much oblig'd to love or prize him
'Yond common bounds, because, saith she, I am
No whit inferiour unto him; my name
Records the noble stock from whence I came.
But if a Prince should chance to set his love
Upon a person that has nought to move
So great a Lord to make that choice, then she
Amazed, yields with all humilitie;
Can do no less than humbly give consent,
Yield up her self with great astonishment:
But she who doth reject such love, is acted
Like one bereav'd of sense, nay quite distracted.
Misguided Soul! and is not this the case?
What worth's in thee to him? O! vile, and base!
Instead of love, deservest to be hated,
Since from thy God thou hast degenerated,
And yet the blessed *Jesus* don't despise thee,
But from thy loathsom dunghil fain would raise thee.
But to proceed, I now will give to thee
Of Christ's sweet Love a short *Epitome*.
     1. 'Tis a first-love, as soon as he past-by,[336]
And saw thee in thy blood, he cast his Eye
Whilst thou in that sad gore didst weltring lie.
Nay, unto thee most precious love he had

Before the fabrick of this World mas made.

    2. It is attracting Love, its nature's such,
'Tis like the Loadstone; hadst thou once a touch,
'T would make thy Iron-heart with speed to move,
Nay, cleave to him in bonds of purest Love.

    3. 'Tis a free Love,[337] there's nought at all in thee
Which can deserve his favour, yet does he
Not grutch thee his dear Love, although so great,
The glorious King of Kings does oft intreat
Those Souls to his imbraces, who contemn
His proffer'd grace, and still love shews to them.

    4. 'Tis 'bounding Love, like *Nilus*, overflows
All banks and bounds, his Grace no limit knows.

    5. 'Tis a delighting Love, there's nought more sweet,
She found it so who washt his precious feet.[338]
He takes delight and sweet complacency
In those he loves, his heart affects his Eye.
He resteth in his love; and who can turn
His heart away, or damp those flames that burn
In his dear breast? none ever lov'd as he,
Who for his Spouse was nailed to the Tree.

    6. It is a Victor's Love, he'l wound and kill
All Enemies who do oppose his will;
Where he lays Siege, he'l make the Soul to yield,
By love he overcomes and wins the Field;
His Captive (Soul) thou certainly must be:
His love is such, 'twill have the Victorie.

    7. It is abiding and Eternal Love,[339]
'Twill last as long as he, nought can remove
His love from such on whom he casts his Eye,
And for whose sake alone he chose to die.
The love which did appear to Saints of old,
Did graciously this glorious Truth unfold.
I with an ever lasting Love, saith he,
Have set my heart upon (or loved) *thee*,[340] }
And therefore I have drawn thee unto me.
Know he who thus doth his sweet love commend
To his dear Saints, loves them unto the end.

    8. 'Tis a great Love, most powerful and strong,
Hence 'tis he thinks each hour and minute long,
Till he imbrace thee in his Sacred Arms, }
Where he'l secure thee from all the[a] harms
And dangers great, by Men or hellish charms.
Fathers, although they love their Children dear,
Yet never did from them such love appear.
David lov'd *Absolom*, yet gives consent,
Nay he himself decrees his banishment.[341]
A Mother may forget her sucking Child,

As some have done, although of nature mild,
Yet forc'd by famine, cruelly have shed
Their Childrens bloud, and of their flesh have fed:
But Ah! his Love's so free, so strong, so great,
He gives his bloud to drink, his flesh for meat
Unto the Soul; and those who it receive,
Shall never die, and none but such can live.
          9. His Love is matchless, 'tis without compare,[342]
Who neither flesh, nor bloud, nor life did spare.
The love of Women, which the World esteems
Most strong in sweet affection, their love seems
An empty shadow, and not worth regard,
When with his Sacred Love it is compar'd.
The Husbands, Wives, and Fathers may abound,
Yet no such love as Christ's was ever found.
Abraham and *Isaac* both lov'd their Wives,
Yet neither of them sacrific'd their lives.
Jonathan's love to *David* did exceed
The love of Women, 'twas a Love indeed![343]
But what was *Jonathan*'s great love to this?
Ah! less than nothing, when compar'd to his.
Christ's love exceeds all natural Love as far
As bright *Aurora* doth the smallest Star.
But Oh! in vain do we compare his Love
With any thing below, no, 'tis above
Comparison, 'tis so immense, so great,
We cannot find it out, though Man's conceit
Is larger than expression, though profound,
Yet Man's conception never yet could sound
The depth of Love's unfathomable bliss,
So great, so deep, so bottomless it is.
Betwixt his Love and ours, the disproportion
Is like one drop of Water to the Ocean.
Or as the smallest dust that's fiercely driven,
To the whole Globe; or like as Earth's to Heaven
The Sun for clearness with his splendent face,
The Moon for swiftness in her Zodiack Race;
The Sands for number and the Heaven[a] for height
The Seas for depth, the ponderous earth for weight
Yet with more certainty, and with less doubt
Be weigh'd and measur'd, than Christ's love found out.
O depth! O heigth! O breadth! O wonderous length
Of this great Love![344] O uncompared strength
Of true affections! Love that is Divine!
What's natural love; Lord, when compar'd to thine?
Such a redundancy of Love is found,
Whoever dives into these depths is drown'd.
Ten thousand Seas, ten thousand times told o're,

Add to these Seas ten times as many more,
Let all these Seas become one deep Abyss,
They'd all come short in depth compar'd to this.
The Moral, Natural, nor the Spiritual Man,
With all their Understanding, never can
Find out the Nature of Christ's Love! alas,
It doth all Knowledg 'nfinitely surpass.
O may these *Depths & Heights* have pow'r to move
On thee, till thou art swallowed up in Love.
That, that which cannot comprehended be
By Men nor Angels, may comprehend thee;
And thou being fill'd with it, may'st sweetly lie
In depths of Love unto Eternitie.[345]

    The Spir't with this let fly a piercing Dart,
Which wounded dreadfully her stubborn heart,
It pierc'd to[a] th' very quick and made her smart.
Now, now she mourns, Ah! how she weeps, she crys,
And water runs like fountains from her Eys.
Now her whole Souls dissolved into tears[346]
By Love-sick passions; yet she's fill'd with fears,
Lest Christ should now with angry frown deny
To give her one sweet aspect of his Eye:
Because his love she had so long refus'd,
And wondrous patience shamefully abus'd.
Oh! now she spends whole days & nights in prayer,
She sighs and grieves, but can't see Christ appear.
The panting Hart ne'r long'd for Water-brooks
More than does she for some reviving looks
From the great Prince, the God of Love & Grace;[347]
But he at present seems to hide his face.

    But stop, my Muse, hark how the Winds do roar,
All storms i'th Soul alas; are not yet o're.
No sooner did the *Old-man* cast his Eyes,
And view'd this change but in great wrath did rise
For to renew the War, he joins afresh
With scatter'd force of *Will* and *Lusts*[b] *of th'flesh*,[348]
To make what strength they can, with hellish spite.
The Devil's with these conquer'd pow'rs unite,
Arm'd with despair, and like to Lamps, wch make
The greatest blaze at going out, they take
Their blunt and broken Weapons in their hand,
Resolving, Christ in her shall not command;
Nor she desert their cause, nor break her Vows
With *Sin* and *Self*, and so become *Christ's* Spouse.
But now, I find in vain they do resist:
True Grace is come, the *Spirit* doth assist.
Sin, World, the *Flesh*, nor *Devil*, can long stand

Before the *Spirits* strong and pow'rful hand.
See how the *Spirit* now doth search about
To find each *Sin*, and cursed *Darling* out.
Did you never behold in what dread sort
The wide-mouth'd Canon plays upon the Fort,
And how by whole-sail[a] it doth batter down
The shattered walls of a besieged Town?
Even so the *Spirit* with his powerful Sword
Makes glorious slaughter, will no Truce afford,
Kills all before him, will no Quarter give,
Nor will he suffer any Lust to live.[349]
The Strong-man, *(Satan)* quakes; good reason why;
A stronger's come, a stronger he doth spy
Is enter'd in – O therefore he's much pain'd;
All, all is gone, and he himself is chain'd.
The *Old-man* trembling, likewise thinks to fly
Into some lurking-corner, secretly
To hide himself: but th' Spirit's piercing Sight
Discovers him, and now with heavenly might
Laid on such strokes, and gave him such a wound,
Wch with dire vengance brought him to the ground.
Now the *Affection's* chang'd, and *Will* doth yield,
Being willing made, says *Grace* shall have the Field.
O happy season! and thrice long'd-for hour!
This is the day of God's most mighty Power
Upon the Soul. But hark, methinks I hear
Most bitter sighs and groans sound in mine Ear.
The Soul's afflicted! it is she doth mourn,
To think what sorrows for her Christ hath born.
She hates, nay loaths her self to th' very dust,
And seeks to mortifie each former Lust.
And something more doth still perplex her mind,
Him whom she dearly loves, she cannot find.
Her heart I fear will quickly burst asunder,
If any long time she should be prest under
This heavy weight: no grief like hers, is there: }
Who can (alas) a wounded Spirit bear? }
She's almost swallow'd up in deep despair. }
You next shall hear if you attention lend
How she bewails the absence of her Friend.

Soul.

Ah me! I faint, my Spirits quite decay,
And yet I cannot die: O who can stay
My sinking Soul, whilst I these sorrows feel?
My feeble knees under their burden reel.
Infernal deeps, black gulphs, where horror lies,
Open their ghastly mouths before mine Eys.

O wretched Soul! curs'd Sin! I might have been
The Lamb's fair Bride,[350] and a Celestial Queen,
Had I imbrac'd my Lord, my King, my Love,
(Who was more faithful than the Turtle Dove.)
O had I then received him in mine Arms,
He would have sav'd me from eternal harms.
But now I fear those happy days are past,
And I poor wretch shall into Hell be cast,
Bound up in fetters, and eternal chains
Of burning Wrath, and everlasting pains.
O sinful Soul! I who have lightly set
By the blest Prince, who would have paid my debt
O he that would have freely quit my score,
Ah! Now I fear I shall ne're see him more.
Could I but once more hear his Sacred Voice,
I would make him my joy, and only choice.
But's Wooing-time I fear is[a] out of date,
Now I repent, but dread it is too late.
I melt, Lord, into tears, whilst thou the Sun
Of precious Light, art hid, where shall I run
For Light and comfort in this dolesom hour,
Whilst I lie drenched in this brinish shower?
More would she speak, but her great passion stops
Her mournful speech, whilst her eys flood-gates opes,
Smote with despair, so faint, she scarce appears
To breath or live, but by her sighs and tears.
       A Friend amidst this passion straight arriv'd,
Whose shining beams and lustre much reviv'd
The troubl'd Soul on every side, that she
Cry'd out, O heavenly Spirit, it is thee,
Who with Diviner and mysterious Art
Did such illustrious beams of Glory dart,
Which did not only tend to joy and peace,
But much inflam'd her heart, made love increase,
And lo, before her Eys she doth behold
The *Prince* to stand, whose Glory to unfold
Is 'bove the reach of Man, or Seraphim;
And thus had she a blessed sight of him.
Like as the Sun breaks forth beneath a Cloud,
Whose conqu'ring light cast off each envious shroud,
And round about his beauteous beams displays,
Making her Earth like Heav'n with his bright rays.
This glorious Aspect of his lovely Eye,
Which she through Faith beheld, did by and by
With such transports, or Raptures, on her seize,
And from her former sorrows gave her ease:
Yet could she not be fully satisfy'd,

Until the Marriage-knot was firmly ty'd
A Promise she endeavours to procure,
To make Christ's Love and Pardon to her sure.
She to this purpose does her self address
To him she loves, with sweet composedness
Of heart and mind; tho thinking what she'd bin,
She's under fears, and oft distrest agin;
Much questioning (for want of Faith) how he
Could e're forget past wrongs and injurie.

Soul.

   Life of my life! alas, Lord, what am I?
A wretched Creature; who deserves to die
A thousand deaths, nay, and a thousand more,
For wounding thee within, without, all o're,
In every part: O this doth make me mourn,
It melts my heart to think what thou hast born
For a vile worm. But wilt thou view the wound
That's made in me? Lord, I am drench'd & drown'd
In bloud, and brinish tears, my wasting breath,
And sighing Soul, will period soon in Death,
Unless thou seal, and dost confirm to me
Thy Love by promises; O! shall I see
Thy hand stretch'd out? or shall I hear thee say,
Come, come to me, poor Soul, O come away?
'Tis thou that wilt not bruise the broken reed,
Hurt not my sores, nor crush the wounds that bleed.[351]
O let my chilled Soul feel the warm fires[352]
Of thy sweet Voice, that my dissolv'd desires
May turn a soveraign Balsam, to make whole
Those wounds my sins have made in thy dear Soul.[353]
Ah! wilt thou let me swoun'd away and die,
Whilst thou standst looking on? Lord, cast an eye
On me, for whom thou on the Cross didst bleed;
Some comfort, Lord, now in my greatest need:
No Corrosives, some Cordial Spir'ts, or I
For ever perish must; Lord, hear my cry.

Jesus.

   Afflicted Soul! the purchase of my Bloud,
Come, hear, come hear a consolating Word.
Shall I who have through sore Afflictions past
For love of thee, refuse thee now at last?
No, no! I cannot, Soul, I cannot bear
Such piercing moans that wounds my tender Ear
Now will I magnifie my Pow'r and rise
To scatter thy malicious Enemies;
I'le thee enlighten with my glorious Rays,

And make thee happy, happy all thy days.
Who will betroth, or give this Soul to me?
Let's Celebrate with great'st Solemnity,
And glorious Triump, the espousal Day:
Come, come, my Dear, let us no longer stay.

The Father.

'Tis in my Pow'r, 'tis I, I give her thee,
As th' fruit of my own Choice, Love and Decree.

CHAP. VIII.

The mutual and blessed Contract between Christ and the Sinner.

Jesus.

GIVE me thy heart then, Soul, I do betroth
Thee unto me, that no approaching Wrath
May any ways be hurtful unto thee,
In Righteousness I thee betroth to me.
In Judgment also thou betrothed art,
And all I have to thee I do impart
In faithfulness and tender mercy, so
That thou thy Lord, thy Friend, & God shall[a] know.
I do betroth thee unto me for ever,
And neither Death, Nor Earth, nor Hell shall sever
Thy Soul from me. If thou will pay thy vows,
I will be thine, and thou shalt be my Spouse.
I take thee now for better, and for worse:
Give me thy hand, let's jointly both of us
With mutual love tie the conjugal Knot,
Which, on my part shall never be forgot.
My Covenant with thee is seal'd by bloud,
'Tis firmer than the Oath at *Noah*'s Flood.[354]
Into my folded Arms, I now do take thee,
And promise that I never will forsake thee.
Thy sins are cast behind my back, and I
Will cover each future infirmitie

The Sinners closing with Christ.

Soul.

Upon my bended knees I do this day
Accept of thee, my Lord, my Life, my Way
By whom alone poor Sinners have access
Unto the Father; nay, and do confess,
Declare, pronounce i'th' sight of God, that I
Do enter now with all simplicity
Into a Contract with thee, make my Vows

That I will be to thee a faithful Spouse.
O blessed *Jesus,* I'm as one undone,
A naked, vile, loathsom and guilty one,
Unworthy far to wash the very feet
Of th' Servants of my Lord, O how is it
That thou, the glorious Prince, shouldst ever chuse
Such an unworthy Worm to be thy Spouse.
O what's thy Love! O Grace, beyond expression.
Doth the great God on me place his affection?
But sith 'tis so, this I engage to do,
I'le leave all for thy sake, and with thee go.[355]
And in all things own thee alone as Head,
And Husband dear, by whom I will be led,
And in all states and times will thee obey,
What ever comes, unto my dying-day.
I take thee as my Prophet, Priest, and King:[356]
And my own worthiness in every thing
I do renounce, and further vow that I
Upon thy Bloud and Righteousness will lie,
On that, and that alone, will I depend
By Faith always until my life shall end.
I covenant with thee, and so I take thee,
And whatsoe'r falls out, I'le ne'r forsake thee,
But run all hazards in this dolesom day,
And never from thy holy ways will stray.
All this and more I promise shall be done,
But in thy strength, Lord, in thy strength alone.
    Th' Solemnity thus ended, presently
The glorious Prince, the Bridgeroom, casts his Eye
Upon the Soul, and bound up all her sores,
Nay healed them, and cancelld all her scores:
But be'ng her self defil'd, she soon espy'd
A precious Fountain flowing from his side,
A Fountain for uncleanness to wash in
In which she bath'd, and wash'd away her sin.[357]
Then gloriously by him she was array'd
With Robes imbroid'red, very richly laid
With Gold and Diamonds, that she did seem
Like an adorned Heav'nly Seraphim.
One Vesture was especially most rare,
Without a seam, much like what he did wear;
It is the Wedding Robe, both clean and white,
Whose lustre far exceeds the Morning-light,
And other garments also, which she wore,
Curiously wrought with Silk, and spangl'd o're
With stars of Gold, of Pearl, of precious Stone,
Enough to dazle all to look upon:
Which be'ng made up of every precious Grace,
Did cause a splendent Beauty in her Face,

That whilst he did behold her, could discry
His Father's Image clearly in her Eye,[358]
Which did so please him, that he now admires,
And after this her Beauty much desires.
O see the change, she which was once so foul,
Is now become a sweet and lovely Soul.
Her beauty far excels what it had been
In ancient days, no mortal Eye hath seen
So sweet a Creature, no such Virgin Queen,
Yet all her Beauty now's but spots and stains,
To what it will be when her Saviour raigns.
O hear the melody! Angels rejoice,
Whilst she triumphs in this most happy choice.
Who would not then all Earthly Glories slight,
To gain a minutes taste of such delight?
     No sooner did *Apollyon* cast his Eyes
On what was done, but furiously did rise
To damp her joy, or cause her much to cease,
And by some stratagams to spoil her peace.
He first stirs up the *Old-man*'s broken force
For to estrange her: if he can't divorce
Her from her Friend, yet raises inward strife,
How to deprive her of those joys of life,
Which do abound in Lovers every way,
Betwixt th' espousal and the Marriage-day.
A thousand tricks contriv'd before had he
How to delay or spoil th' Affinitie.
But if he can't rob us of inward joy,
Our name, or goods, or life he will destroy.
For failing in the first, he stirs up Foes
To lay upon her persecuting blows.
He that will follow Christ, must look each day
To have his worldly comforts took away.[359]
Besides, the *Old-man* being not yet slain,
Great troubles in her mind there rose again.
But her dear Friend so faithful is, that he
Will never leave her in Adversitie.
And to the end her joy may more abound,
A way by him immediately is found
To free her from the *Old-man*'s hellish spite,
He must be crucify'd;[360] but first they cite
Him to the Bar to hear what he can say,
Why now his life should not be took away.
But hear, before that's done, how the blest Lover
Doth his dread threats and awful frowns discover
Against the Foes of her he loves so well,
Whoe're they be, Men, Lusts, or Fiends of Hell.
He reads his great Commission, lets them know
He in a moment can them overthrow.

The dread Power and awful frowns of Jesus Prince of Peace over his Saints Enemies.

When Man transgress'd 'twas I, Eternal I,
Gave forth the Sentence, *Thou shalt surely die.*
'Twas I that curs'd the Serpent,[361] who remains
Unto this day, and shall in lasting Chains.[362]
When *Cain* did shed his righteous Brother's bloud,
I sentenc'd *Cain;*[363] 'twas I that brought the Flood
Upon the Earth. By me the World was drowned[364]
Proud *Babels* Language was by me confounded.[365]
I am *Jehovah's* everlasting Word,
Who in my hand do bear th' two-edg'd Sword.[366]
'Twas I, and only I that did Command
The dismal darkness in the *Egyptians* Land.[367]
'Twas at my Word the Seas divide in twain,
And made an even passage through the Main.
At my Command *Pharaoh* and all his Host
Were utterly within the Red-Sea lost,[368]
'Twas I that made *Belshazzers* joints to quake,
And all his Nobles tremble when I spake.[369]
'Twas I that made the *Persian* Monarchs great,
And threw them with the *Grecians* from their Seat.[370]
I say the Word, and Nations are distress'd,
I spake[a] again, and the whole World's at rest.
Let all Men stand in fear and dread of me,
I was the first, and I the last will be.
All knees shall bow to me when I reprove,
And at my Voice the Mountains shall remove.[371]
The Earth shall be dissolved at my Threat,
And Elements[b] shall melt with fervent heat.[372]
My Word confines the Earth, the Seas, the Wind,
I am the great *Jehovah* unconfin'd.
'Tis I divide between the joints and Marrow;[373]
No place so close, no cranny is so narrow,
But, like the Sun's bright beams, I enter in,
Discovering to each heart, the darling Sin
That lodges in the Soul. 'Tis I alone,
Who by my piercings make them sigh and groan
If from true sense and sorrow they complain.
I graciously bind up those wounds again.[374]
'Tis I that save the humble and contrite,
And do condemn the formal Hypocrite.
My circuit's large, I coast the World about,
No place, nor secret, but I find it out.
All Nations of the World I rule at pleasure,
To my Dominion's neither bound nor measure.
Therefore, dear Soul, chear up, and do not fear,

I'le confound all thy Foes both far and near.
And now I do command to bring to th' Bar
That inward[a] Foe, *Old-man*, I wo'nt defer
His Tryal longer, his Indictments read,
And he had leave and liberty to plead,
And on his Trial he deny'd the Fact,
But *Conscience* swears she took him in the act,
And other witness too; but to be brief,
All prove him the Soul's Foe, nay and the chief
And only cause of all the horrid Treason
Acted against the Lord unto this season.
He was deny'd to speak, the Proofs being clear,
You shall therefore his fatal Sentence hear;
Come thou base Traytor, impure Mass of Sin;
That, Villain-like, dost seek revenge agin
Upon the Soul, and striv'st to raise up strife,
Nay thirsts again to take away her life;
Hear, hear thy Sentence, *Old-man*, thou must die,
I can no pity shew, nor mind thy cry:
Thy Age! away, 'tis pity thou hast bin
Spared so long, when guilty of such Sin.
Soul, thou must see to bring him in subjection,
With every evil lust, and vile affection.
This heap of Sin thou must strive to destroy,
That so thou maist all perfect peace enjoy:
Under the strictest bonds let him abide,
Till he is slain, or throughly crucity'd.
        The *Old-man* being sentenc'd, and confin'd,
The Soul is consolated in her mind.
Affection, Judgment, Will, do all rejoyce,
And are united now: O happy choice!
Ah! she admires the excellence and worth
Of her Beloved, that she sets him forth,
As one that's ravish'd in the contemplation
Of his great Glory and her exaltation,
In this her sacred choice: and this so raises
Her ravish'd senses, that Angelick praises
She thinks too low, O now she doth discover,
And not till now th' affections of a Lover.
There's nothing now so tedious as delay,
Betwixt the 'spousal and the Marriage-day,
Her former joys in which she much delighted,
She treads them under-foot, they are quite slighted,
Nay altogether loathsom in her Eye,
Compared with his sacred Company.
Unto the place where he appoints to meet her,
Thither she runs with speed, there's nothing sweeter.
Nay there is nothing sweet, nothing is dear

Or pleasant to her, if he be not there.
O! saith the Love-sick Soul, in such a case
May I but have one kiss,[375] one sweet Imbrace,
O how would it rejoyce this heart of mine!
His Love is better than the choisest Wine.[376]
His Name is like an Ointment poured forth,[377]
And no such Odour e're enrich'd the Earth.
The Eastern Gums, *Arabian* Spices rare,
Do not perfume, not so enrich the Air,
As the Eternal and renowned Fame
Of his most precious and most glorious Name!
Perfumes my Soul, it elevates my voice,
Whilst gladness fills my heart: O happy choice!
My sacred Friend, my Life, my Lord, and King,
Doth me into his secret Chambers bring;[378]
Although ten thousand fall on either hand,
My Soul in safety evermore shall stand.
Tell me, my Lord, tell me, my dearest Love,
Where thou dost feed, whither the Flocks remove,
And where they rest at Noon in soultry gleams,[379]
Bring me into those Shades, where silver streams
Of living Waters flow, most calm and still,
There, there I'le shelter, there I'le drink my fill.
The Fountains ope, O see it runs most clear,[380]
Green Pastures by; a lodg is also near,[381]   }
To hide in safety, and to save from fear
Of scorching heat; under this shade I'le rest,
My Love shall be inclosed in my breast.[382]
My heart shall be his lodging-place for ever,
Nothing shal me from my Beloved sever.
The terrors of the Night[383] shall never harm me,
He saves from heat, in Frost,[a] his love doth warm me
You Virgins who yet never felt the smart
Of Love's soul-piercing and heart-wounding Dart.
If all these sacred Raptures you admire,
Know, Virgins, know that this Celestial Fire
That's kindled in my breast, comes from above,
And sets my Soul into this flame of Love
O he that has endured so much pain
To gain my Love, is worthy to obtain
Ten thousand times more love than his poor spouse
Is able to bestow: yet shall my Vows
Be daily paid to him, in whose sweet breast
My love-sick Soul shall find eternal rest.
Know, know I ne'r obtain'd true peace, before
My soul cast anchor on this sacred shore.
All earthly pleasures are but seeming mirth,
His presence is a Heaven upon Earth.

How heavy, O how bitter was the Cross
Once unto me? to think upon the loss
Of temporal comforts, made me to complain
But now I find such losses are my gain.
Terrestrial joys,ª as dross to me appear;
My joy's in Heaven, O my treasure's there.
Had I all Riches of both th' *India's* shore
At my command, ten thousandᵇ times told o're,
My soul would loath them, they should be abhor'd
Being worse than dung, compared to my Lord.³⁸⁴
O may these Sun-beams never cease to shine,
By which I see that my Beloved's mine.
He is my flesh and bone, therefore will I
Rejoyce the more in this Affinity.
He is my All, my soul's to him united,
As *Jonathan's* to *David*, who delighted
So much in him that in his greatest trouble
Dear *Jonathan* did his affections double;
When *David* was in great distress and fear,
Then did his love and loyalty appear.³⁸⁵³⁸⁶
So when my dear Beloved is distrest,
My love to him shall chiefly be exprest.
But why, said I, distrest? What, can my Lord,
Who hath consuming power in his Word,
Be touch'd by Mortals? what, can he be harm'd,
Who with all strength of Heaven and Earth is arm'd?
No, no; I must recall that lavish strain:
No hand can touch him, he cannot sustain
The smallest injury from th' greatest Pow'r;
For in a breath he can his Foes devour.
    But now, methinks, I presently espy
Upon the Earth the Apple of his Eye;
Which are his servants, nay his members dear,
Which wicked men do oft oppress; O there
My Lord's distrest; for if his Children smart,
O that doth pierce and wound his tender heart.
If cold or nakedness afflicts their souls,
He sympathizes, and their state condoles.
If sick they be, or if by cruel hands
They are in Prison cast, and under bands,
And there with hunger and with thirst opprest,
He feels their grief, he is in them distrest.
What wrong soever they on Earth receive,
'Tis done to him, for which my soul doth grieve
To see th' afflictions of his servants here;
This is the fruit true loyal Love does bear.³⁸⁷
Her sorrows are his woes; for they alone,
Being his members, are my flesh and bone.

And all make but one Body, he's the Head,
From whence all flows, 'tis he alone has shed
His love abroad, in this my love-sick heart,
Whereby I feel when any members smart.
My bowels move and tender heart does bleed,
VVhich makes me for his sake supply their need
Thus for my Christ, and for his Children's sake
I'le suffer any thing; yea I do take
My life, and goods, and all into my hands,
To be disposed of as he commands
But know for certain evermore that I
      For aid and help on him alone rely.
These pleasant Fruits, O these delight the King
And hereby 'tis that we do honour bring
Unto his Name; all souls of the new birth,
Who are sincere, this precious fruit bring forth.
Let not these things seem strange, because so few
Do bear such Fruit, believe the Maxim's true,
That as the Sun doth by its warm reflection
Upon the Earth, produce a resurrection
Of all those Seeds, which in the Earth do lie,
Hid for a time in dark obscurity:
Ev'n so the Sun of Righteousness doth shine
Into this cold and barren heart of mine;
The precious seeds that have been scattered there
Take root and blossom, nay their branches bear
Sweet fruit, being the product of those Rays,
Which that bright Sun into my soul displays.
'Tis precious and most lovely in his Eye,
Both for its Beauty and Veracity.
You Virgins all who are by Love invited
Into his Gardens where he is delighted
With all his pleasant Fruits,[388] come, come and see,
How choice, fair, sweet, and beautiful they be:
One cluster here's presented to thy view,
That thou mayst see, and then believe 'tis true.
These be the Fruits which I shall now express
Love, Joy, and Peace, Long suffering, Holiness,
Faith, Goodness, Temperance, and Charity,
These are the products of th' Affinity
That's made between me and my dearest Friend;
Nay, more than these, Eternal life i'th' end.
But if (through sin) thou canst not cast thine Eye
On these rare Fruits, then know assuredly
When th' Vintage comes, and thou beginst to crave
For one small taste, one taste then canst not have
The fruitful Soul it is the King will crown
With th' Diadem of Glory and Renown.

O let these things the Soul's affections raise,
In grateful Songs to celebrate the Praise
Of great *Jehovah*, who is King of Kings,
Whose glorious Praise the heav'nly Quire sings;
Then let us sing on Earth a Song like this,
My well beloved's mine, and I am his.[389]

An Hymn of Praise to the Sacred Bridegroom.[390]

PRaise in the Highest, Joy betide
  The sacred Bridgegroom, and his Bride,
   Who doth in splendor^a shine:
Let Heaven above be fill'd with songs,
  In Earth beneath let all Mens Tongues
   Sing forth his Praise Divine.

  If sullen Man refuse to speak,
Let Rocks and Stones their silence break;
   For Heaven and Earth combine
To tie that sacred Bridal Knot,
O let it never be forgot,
   The Contract is Divine.

  You holy Seraphims above,
Who do admire Jesus's Love,
   O hast away and come,
With Men on Earth your joys divide;
Earth ne'r produc'd so fair a Bride,
   Nor Heaven a Bridegroom.

Another.

  'Tis not the gracious lofty strain;
Nor record of great Hector's[391] *glory,*
Nor all the conquering mighty Train,
Whose Acts have left the World a story;
Nor yet great Cesar's[392] *swelling fame,*
Who only look'd, and overcame.

  Nor one, nor all those Worthy Nine,[393]
Nor Alexander's[394] *great Renown,*
Whose deeds were thought almost Divine,
When Vic'tries did his Temples crown,
   But 'tis the Lord, that Holy One,
   Whose Praises I will sing alone.

  My Heart and Tongue shall both rejoyce,
Whilst Angels all in Consort sing
Aloud with a melodious voice
The praises of sweet Zion's *King.*

O'tis his praise, that Holy One,
I am resolv'd to sing alone.

My Heart indites whilst I proclaim
The Praises of the God of Wonder,
My lips still magnifie his Name,
Whose Voice is like a mighty Thunder:
  I'le praise his Name, and him alone,
  Who is the glorious Three in One.

Whose feet are like to burning Brass,
Whose Eyes like to a flaming Fire,
Who bringeth mighty things to pass,
'Tis him I dread, and do admire:
  I'le magnifie his Name alone,
  Who is the glorious Three in One.

My Heart and Pen shall both express,
The Praises of great Juda's Lion,
The sweet and fragrant Flower of Jess,
The holy Lamb, the King of Zion.
  To him that sitteth on the Throne,
  Be everlasting praise alone.

Whose Head is whiter than the Snow
That's driven by the Eastern Wind,
Whose Visage like a flame doth show,
Confining all, yet unconfin'd:
  Forever prais'd be Him alone,
  Who is the glorious Three in One.

I'le praise his Name, who hath reveal'd
To me his everlasting Love,
Who with his stripes my Soul hath heal'd,
Whose Foot-stool's here, his Throne above,[395]
  Let Trumps of Praise be loudly blown,
  To magnifie his Name alone.

This sacred Subject of my Verse,
Though I poor silly Mortal should
Neglect his Praises to rehearse,
The ragged Rocks and Mountains would
  Make his deserved Praises known.
  Who is the glorious Three in One.

You twinkling Stars that Day and Night;
Do your appointed Circuit run,
Sweet Cynthia[396] in her monthly flight,
Also the bright and flaming Sun,

Throughout the Universe make known
The Praises of the Holy One.

   Let every Saint on Earth rejoyce
Whom Christ hath chosen, let him sing,
Whilst I to him lift up my Voice
To sound the praises of my King:
      For He it is, and He alone,
      Hath made me his Beloved one.

FINIS.

Textual variants

187a   Psalm ... matter] The Second Edition with Additions; and Illustrated with Copper
       Cuts, relating to the chief passages in the Book.
       O thou that wert the King of Heav'n and Earth
       How poorly wert thou attended at thy Birth!
       A Manger was thy Cradle, and a Stable
       Thy privy Chamber, Mary's knees thy Table:
       Thieves were thy Courtiers, and the Cross thy Throne.
       Thy diet gall, a wreath of Thorns thy Crown.
       All this the King of Glory endur'd and more,
       To make us Kings that were but Slaves before.
       John 3.16. *For God so loved the World, that he gave his only begotten Son, that whoso-*
       ever believeth in him should not perish, but have everlasting life.
       John 25. 13. *Greater Love hath no man than this, that a man lay down his life for his*
       Friends. K64A; The Third Edition with Additions ... *K64B*; The Fourth Edition
       with Additions... *K65*
187b   by J.D.] by F.L. *K64A, K64B; K65* omit
187c   1679] 1685 *K64A, K64B*; 1696 *K65*
187d   fond] found *K64A, K64B*
188a   be] *K64A, K64B* omit
189a   sparkled] sparked *K65*
198a   may] my *K64*; may *K64B, K65*
200a   and] end *K64B*
202a   pregant] pregnant *K64B. K65*
203a   Voyce-Roy] Vice-Roy *K64B, K65*
203b   resolves] resolve *K65*
204a   much] a much *K64*; much *K65*
205a   an insidious] a perfidious *K64B, K65*
205b   sprightly] spightly *K64B*; spritely *K65*
209a   flusht] flesht *K64B*
209b   their] thy *K64B, K65*
209c   bruisdst] bruis'd *K64B, K65*
209d   thy] thus *K64B, K65*
210a   Clap] Clapy *K64, K64A*; Clap *K64B, K65*
215a   throw] through *K64B, K65*

215b   he] we *K65*
218a   Impostor] imposture *K64B, K65*
219a   curdled] curled *K64*; curdled *K65*
222a   can] *K65* omit
223a   Nor] No *K65*
224a   'scape] escape *K65*
230a   e're] ne're *K64B, K65*
235a   I'e] I'le *K64B*, I'll *K65*
236a   Theologue] *K64B, K65* omit
236b   b'not] ben't *K65*
237a   thy] the *K65*
238a   comfort] comforts *K64B, K65*
240a   loss] lose *K65*
240b   knew'st] know'st *K65*
241a   Reflecting] Reflection *K64B, K65*
246a   'Tould] 'Twould *K64B, K65*
246b   Their] There *K64B*
247a   splendor] spendor *K64, K64A*; splendor *K64B, K65*
249a   yea] yea and *K64A*
249b   such] they *K65*
255a   Wrath] Death *K64B, K65*
256a   If] *K64B, K65* omit
256b   help] helps *K65*
256c   shall] shalt *K64B*
256d   the] *K64B* omit
258a   taking] taken *K65*
261a   godly] goodly *K65*
262a   hand] *K65* omit
263a   yea] yet *K65*
264a   saw] say *K64B, K65*
264b   to] *K65* omit
265a   needs] now *K64B, K65*
269a   sufferst] suffer'dst *K65*
273a   a] *K65* omit
273b   straightaway] straightway *K65*
277a   When] Which *K64B, K65*
279a   Records] Record *K65*
279b   Cessant] Cessent *K64B, K65*
280a   do] do so *K64B, K65*
280b   praises] praises prrises *K65*
281a   Would] Could *K64B, K65*
282a   The ... Book.] *K64B, K65* omit
286a   take] make *K65*
289a   to] *K64B* omit
290a   compassions] compassion *K65*
291a   cleave] clave *K65*
295a   Pebble] Pepple *K64*; Pebble *K65*
295b   to] *K64B, K65* omit

298a weight] weigh *K64B*
301a shew'n] shew'd *K64B*
304a says] say *K65*
306a woo] who *K64B*
307a listens] lessens *K64*; lessons *K64B*; listens *K65*
307b Counsel] Council *K64B*, *K65*
308a mixt] mix *K64B*
310a what] why *K65*
311a thought] thoughts *K65*
314a them] then *K64B*, *K65*
321a Thy] My *K65*
321b Delight] Delights *K64B*
322a enlightned] enlighted *K64*, *K64A*; enlightned *K64B*, *K65*
323a toe] to *K64*; toe *K65*
325a united] untied *K64B*, *K65*
328a Affection] Affections *K64B*, *K65*
331a blest] best *K64B*, *K65*
338a all ways] always *K64B*, *K65*
341a the] *K65* omit
342a Heaven] Heavens *K65*
343a pierc'd to] piercing *K64B*, *K65*
343b Lusts] Lust *K65*
344a whole-sail] whole-sale *K65*
345a is] it is *K64B*, *K65*
347a shall] shalt *K64B*, *K65*
350a spake] speak *K64B*, *K65*
350b Elements] Element *K65*
351a inward] inwarded *K65*
352a Frost] Frosts *K64B*, *K65*
353a joys] Joy *K65*
353b thousand] thousands *K64B*
355a splendor] spendor *K64*, *K64A*; splendor *K64B*, *K65*

MARTIN MASON, 'IN MEMORIAM JOHANNIS PEROTTI' (1682)

Date

First published in 1682. The poem is dated at its end 'The 27*th*. of the 8*th*. Month, 1676' (i.e. 27 October).[1] Perrot died between 30 August and 7 September 1665, and thus Mason's sonnet appears to have been composed a considerable amount of time after his death.[2]

Copy Text

P1637 J[ohn] P[errot], *The vision of John Perrot wherein is contained the future state of Europe* (London, s.n.: 1682), sig. A1v. Quarto.

Variants

None have been catalogued.

Context

The Quaker John Perrot (d. 1665) entered Rome in 1658 with the intention of converting the Pope. He was quickly imprisoned and then committed to the 'Pazzarella' or 'Prison of Madmen'. He was only released in 1661.[3] It was while in Rome that he composed a letter which contained the seeds of schism. He wrote to Friends that 'if any ffriend be moved of the Lord god to pray in the Congregation of god fallne downe with his face to the ground, without takeing of[f] the hatt, or the shoes, let him do so in the feare & name of the Lord'.[4] This defence of men keeping their hats on during prayer threatened conventional Quaker behaviour, and incensed many Friends – most notably George Fox. Matters worsened upon Perrot's return to England. His charismatic preaching and conduct won him supporters but also strengthened the fears of those Friends who saw him as a new James Naylor (the Quaker who had ridden into Bristol in 1656 in symbolic recreation of Christ's entry to Jerusalem, and whose actions had helped to cement the Quakers' public image as dangerously subversive). Schism became inevitable, and he was denounced by leading Quakers. Denunciations from within the movement did not, of course, preclude him from suffering persecution as a Quaker, and he was imprisoned under the terms of the Quaker Act in June 1662. Although he was soon freed, he had to exile himself. He landed in Barbados in October 1662, journeyed to Maryland and Virginia in 1663, and then went back to Barbados in 1664 where he was, rather improbably, made a captain. More improbably still, he was employed as a court clerk in Barbados and Jamaica, and took money to administer oaths (despite the fact that all oath-taking was descried by Quakers). The dispute he had instigated with Fox rumbled on into the year following his death in 1665.[5]

Martin Mason viewed the question of whether or not hats were worn during prayer as a matter of indifference, and he clearly saw Perrot as a committed and talented man.[6] Mason's sonnet makes reference to both Perrot's stoical endurance of physical suffering in Rome and his inspirational writings. The poem prefaces Perrot's *The Vision of John Perrot* (1682) in which Perrot, writing from Jamaica, had prophesied the oncoming destruction of the present state of Europe at the Lord's hand and had specifically foretold the shape of events in Greece, France, Germany, Italy, Spain and England.

Notes

1. J. Perrot, *A Vision of John Perroti* (London: s.n., 1682), sig. A1v.
2 *ODNB.*
3. See the Headnote to *A Sea of the Seed's Sufferings* and the references cited there, Volume 1 above p. 29.
4. Quoted in K. L. Carroll, *John Perrot: Early Quaker Schismatic* (London: Friends' Historical Society, 1971), pp. 44–5.
5. Smith, 'John Perrot'; Carroll, *John Perrot*; W.C. Braithwaite, *The Second Period of Quakerism*, 2nd edn prepared by H. J. Cadbury (York: William Sessions Limited in association with the Joseph Rowntree Charitable Trust, 1979), pp. 228–50.
6. *ODNB.*

In Memoriam *Johannis Perotti*.

SWeet was thy Voice,[1] *and Ravishing thy Strain,*
Thy Silver Trumpet[2] *Sounded not in Vain:*
In Vain did Sions *Enemies, we see,*
Labour, by Cruelties, to Conquer Thee:
Patience and Holy Zeal did Overcome
The Cruelties of Antichristian-Rome:
Thy Sufferings there for Truth, what Tongue can tell?
The Zeal God gave thee, few do parallel.[3]
In Shilohs[4] *Holy Ink thy Learned Pen*
Was dipt, which Ravished the Sons of Men:
Where thy Fair Fabrick's Fall'n, if ere I come,
I'll drop some Tears upon thy Honoured Tomb:
Thou Heaven-Born Seed,[5] *Blest let thy Memory be,*[6]
The Love of Men and Angels Honour Thee.

NOTES

Keach, *War with the Devil*

1. *The* Naturalists ... *abide the Spring-time of the year*: The comparison between youth and spring, said to begin when the sun entered the constellation of Aries, was a poetic commonplace with an antecedent in, for example, Ovid: Ovid, *Metamorphoses*, XV, ll. 201–5 (ed. Miller, rev. Goold, pp. 378–9): 'For in early spring it is tender and full of fresh life, just like a little child; at that time the herbage is young, swelling with life, but as yet without strength and solidity, and fills the farmers with joyful expectation. Then all things are in bloom and the fertile fields run riot with their bright-coloured flowers; but as yet there is no strength in the green foliage'. It becomes clear that Keach's Youth is on the cusp of manhood; correspondingly, he is depicted in the frontispiece which appeared in some editions as a sixteen year old: see S. Achinstein, *Literature and Dissent in Milton's England* (Cambridge: Cambridge University Press, 2003), p. 20.

2. *But I will suck the sweetness of it out*: cp. Bunyan on the soul of 'sinners' and the 'unsanctified': J. Bunyan, *The Greatness of the Soul* (London: Ben. Alsop, 1683), p. 27: 'They can relish and tast that which delighteth them; yea they can find Soul-delight in an Alehouse, a Whore-house, a Play-house. Ai, they find pleasure in the vilest things, in the things most offensive to God, and that are most destructive to themselves ... Nor is the Word barren as to this; *They feed on ashes, they spend their money for that which is not Bread*, yea they eat and suck *sweetness* out of sin, *They eat up the sin of my people as they eat Bread*'. Keach returned to the image: B. Keach, *A Summons to the Grave* (London: Ben Harris, 1676), p. 4: 'if wicked men have a sight of the shortness of their lives, it hath not this effect upon their hearts; they many times the more pursue their lusts: they endeavor to get as much pleasure as they can, and to gratifie their covetous, ambitious, and carnal appetites, and suck out what sweetness they can out out of this perishing world; they resolve to have it as sweet as outward enjoyments can make it; they know no higher or better good then what is earthly and sensual'.

3. *fear me*: frighten me.

4. *At Cards & Dice, and such brave Games I'le play*: on Restoration gambling and some of its social meanings see J. E. Evans, '"A Sceane of Uttmost Vanity": The Spectacle of Gambling in Late Stuart Culture', *Studies in Eighteenth-Century Culture*, 31 (2002), pp. 1–20.

5. *Courtier*: Charles II's court developed a reputation for lasciviousness and libertinism. The best guide to court culture and its political meanings is M. Jenkinson, *Culture and Politics at the Court of Charles II, 1660–1685* (Woodbridge: Boydell Press, 2010).

6. *Goloshoos*: overshoes. Keach's Youth might have been misguided in thinking them stylish: see G. Etherege, *The Man of Mode*, in D. Womersley (ed.), *Restoration Drama: An*

Anthology (Oxford: Blackwell, 2000), I.i.570–7, p. 296 and n.: 'Why hang an Estate, marry *Emilia* out of hand, and provoke your Father to do what he threatens; 'tis but despising a Coach, humbling your self to a pair of Goloshoes, being out of countenance when you meet your Friends, pointed at and pityed wherever you go by all the Amorous Fops that know you, and your fame will be immortal'.

7.   *Where Bulls & Bears they bait*: Pepys describes going to the Beargarden in Southwark to see bull baiting on 14 August 1666: 'where I have not been I think of many years, and saw some good sport of the bull's tossing of the dogs – one into the very boxes. But it is a very rude and nasty pleasure'. See Pepys, *Diary*, vol. 7, pp. 245–6.

8.   *Cocks do fight*: Pepys describes a cock-fight in Shoe Lane on 21 December 1663. His account points to the broad social composition of the gathered crowd and the gambling practices – including the heavy losses incurred by some. See Pepys, *Diary*, vol. 4, pp. 427–8.

9.   *I do resort ... also love*: cp. F. Quarles, *Emblemes* (Cambridge: Francis Eglesfeild, 1643), bk 2, p. 78: 'And that fond soul which wasts his idle dayes / In loose delights, and sports about the blaze / Of *Cupids* candle'.

10. *And court fair Ladies ... comes all my choice and felicity*: A sexually libertine lifestyle became fashionable for young men in the Restoration: see F. Dabhoiwala, 'The Construction of Honour, Reputation and Status in Late Seventeenth- and Early Eighteenth-Century England', *Transactions of the Royal Historical Society*, 6th ser., 6 (1996), pp. 205–7. Libertinism was a central preoccupation of much Restoration culture. See W. L. Chernaik, *Sexual Freedom in Restoration Literature* (Cambridge: Cambridge University Press, 1995); G. Southcombe and G. Tapsell, *Restoration Politics, Religion and Culture: Britain and Ireland, 1660–1714* (Basingstoke: Palgrave Macmillan, 2010), pp. 150–7.

11. *My Lust I'le satisfie, and have my Will*: Libertinism could be philosophically grounded in a partial reading of Hobbes. Here echoes of Hobbes's redefinition of the Will might be detected. See T. Hobbes, *Leviathan*, ed. R. Tuck, rev. edn (Cambridge: Cambridge University Press, 1996), pp. 44–5: 'In Deliberation, the last Appetite, or Aversion, immediately adhaering to the action, or to the omission thereof, is that wee call the WILL ... By this it is manifest, that not onely actions that have their beginning from Covetousnesse, Ambition, Lust, or other Appetites to the thing propounded; but also those that have their beginning from Aversion, or Feare of those consequences that follow the omission, are *voluntary actions*'.

12. *O're this inferiour Court placed am I*: cp. Augustine quoted in Quarles, *Emblemes*, bk 2, p. 115: '*Go up my soul into the tribunall of thy Conscience; There set thy guiltie self before thy self*'.

13. *Those I I condemn who vile and guilty are*: cp. Quarles, *Emblemes*, bk 3, p. 165 (Sin is speaking in an allegorical courtroom scene): 'I'm too vile and base / To tread upon the earth, much more to lift / Mine eyes to Heav'n: I need no other shrift / Then mine own conscience'.

14. *And bring ... cursed Vanity*: cp. Quarles, *Emblemes*, bk 3, p. 166 (Sin is speaking in an allegorical courtroom scene): '[I am] now a poore accurst / Convicted catiff, and degen'rous creature, / Here trembling at thy bar'.

15. *My Name is* Conscience ... *Cleer immediatelie*: cp. J. Milton, *Paradise Lost*, ed. A. Fowler, 2nd edn (London and New York: Longman, 1998), III, ll. 194–7: 'And I will place within them as a guide / My umpire conscience, whom if they will hear, / Light after light well used they shall attain, / And to the end persisting, safe arrive'.

16. *To the brave Boys, who toss the Pot about*: heavy drinkers. Toss-pot also plays a minor role in B. Keach, *The Travels of True Godliness*, 3rd edn (London: John Dunton, 1684).

17. *I have ... quit the field*: cf. Quarles's repentant speaker: see Quarles, *Emblemes*, bk 3, p. 149: 'I've done, I've done; these trembling hands have thrown / Their daring weapons down: the day's thine own: / Forbear to strike where thou hast won the field; / The palm, the palm is thine: I yield, I yield'.

18. *snib*: rebuke.

19. *Unless your Light ... disturbance you will see*: unless you are a hardened sinner, you will continue to feel the pangs of your conscience when you sin. Extensive discussion of the different meanings of biblical images of light is found in: T. De Laune and B. Keach, *Tropologia* (London: Enoch Prosser, 1681), bk 1, pp. 82–6 (p. 86 mispaginated as p. 76), 106–8. The following is significant here: 'With respect to *Equality*, for the Sun *rises on the Evil and the Good*, (affording its light without distinction to all things sublunary) *Matth* 5. 45. which nevertheless *blind men*, and such as *Sleep* by day, do not enjoy: So Christ illuminates every man that cometh into the World, (that is, he affords the means of illumination,) 1 John 1. 9. Yet unbelievers, who are blinded by the *Devil*, and such as give themselves the liberty to sleep securely in sin (and that by their proper, fault and particular vice) John 3. 19. and 2 Cor. 4. 4. Do not enjoy that saving light or illumination': De Laune and Keach, *Tropologia*, bk 1, p. 84.

20. *That will be better ... or what else thou hast*: Keach may have had in mind a number of Biblical passages. See e.g. Psalm 119:72; Proverbs 16:16; Ezekiel 7:19; James 5:3; 1 Peter 1:17–19.

21. *Spark*: a stylish fop.

22. Tyburn: London's main place of execution.

23. *The Husband-man the Land-mark can't remove*: see Deuteronomy 27:17. The landmark is a boundary.

24. *Country Clown*: a stock character in Restoration literature, with a long pedigree. The clown's lack of sophistication was met with the condescension of city dwellers. See A. Fox, *Oral and Literate Culture in England, 1500–1700* (Oxford: Oxford University Press, 2000), pp. 105–6.

25. *Phanaticks*: a common term of abuse for dissenters.

26. *There's very few ... judg'd not fit to live*: those nonconformists of whom Keach approved, and who were given abusive names by others. A number of religious labels started as terms of abuse, e.g. Puritan and Anabaptist.

27. *That most of all mankind i'th' broad-way go*: see Matthew 7:13 (Geneva).

28. Stygian *Lake*: a synecdoche for the underworld. Keach uses it again in his *An Elegy on the Death of ... Mr. John Norcot*: see above p. 163.

29. *the cursed Serpent so*: see Genesis 3:14.

30. *As I enlightned ... to my steps*: cp. Quarles, *Emblemes*, bk 4, p. 194: 'Where shall I seek a Guide? where shall I meet / Some lucky hand to lead my trembling paces? / What trusty Lantern will direct my feet / To scape the danger of these dang'rous places?'

31. *Could Cain or Judas get out of my reach*: a reference to the pangs of conscience felt by Cain for the murder of his brother Abel, and Judas for betraying Christ.

32. *'Tis time enough ... chiefest treasures*: cp. Quarles, *Emblemes*, bk 2, p. 82: 'What mean dull souls, in this high measure / To haberdash / In earths base wares, whose greatest treasure / Is drosse and trash? / The height of whose inchaunting pleasure / Is but a flash?'

33. *But wo to you ... his Light to Darkness turn*: cp. De Laune and Keach, *Tropologia*, bk 1, p. 108: 'as the mystery of *Regeneration* and the restoring of man to Eternal Salvation

is expressed by *light*, so by opposition *darkness* denotes a state of corruption, sin, and *damnation*.'

34. *legal Light*: Keach retained a belief that God's moral law was binding for all, despite justification being by faith alone, as worked out within a Calvinist schema. On this aspect of Keach's theology see J. W. Arnold, 'The Reformed Theology of Benjamin Keach (1640–1704)' (PhD dissertation, University of Oxford, 2009), ch. 5.

35. What thy hand finds to do, do with thy pow'r: see Ecclesiastes 9:10 ('pow'r' suggests that Keach is drawing on the Geneva Bible translation at this point).

36. *whither shall I fly*: see Psalm 139:7.

37. *though Conscience ... it leads astray*: that the individual's conscience could be misguided was accepted across the religious spectrum, though of course the Youth's claims are misplaced and may be simple sophistry. Cp. e.g. R. Baxter, *The Saints Everlasting Rest* (London: Thomas Underhil and Francis Tyton, 1650), p. 117: 'O what a potent instrument for Satan is a misguided Conscience! It will make a man kill his dearest friend, yea, father or mother, yea, the holiest Saint, and think he doth God service by it'.

38. For all things there's a time under the Sun: see Ecclesiastes 3:1.

39. *Don't God ... Remember thy Creator therefore now*: see Ecclesiastes 12:1.

40. *first ripe Fruit of old, God did desire*: see Exodus 22:29.

41. *Did not* Jehovah ... *subject be*: cp. Quarles, *Emblemes*, bk 5, p. 310: 'He whom thy hands did form of dust, / And gave him breath upon condition, / To love his great Creatour, must / He now be thine by composition?'.

42. *And fly from sin and youthful Vanity*: see Ecclesiastes 11:10.

43. *Nor never knock hereafter at thy door*: Truth's characteristic reliance on images from the Song of Solomon (see below n. 45) suggests that Keach is referring to Song of Solomon 5:2 here, where the male figure, typically interpreted as Christ, knocks on his beloved's door. But cp. also Revelation 3:20.

44. *The Blackamoor ... hard to be forsak'n*: see Jeremiah 13:23 (Geneva). Keach made use of this passage again in his *Travels of True Godliness*, p. 60: 'evil Habits are not easily changed, the Blackamore may as soon change his skin, or the Leopard his spots, as you may learn to do well, and open to me when you have been a long time accustomed to do evil'.

45. *With Myrrh ... and* Saffron: cp. Song of Solomon 4:13–14.

46. *yet nothing will ... drops of the long night*: cp. Song of Solomon 5:2.

47. *For none ... no Tongue declare*: cp. Quarles, *Emblemes*, bk 5, p. 289: 'HOw shall my tongue expresse that hallow'd fire / Which Heav'n hath kindled in my ravisht heart? / What Muse shall I invoke, that will inspire / My lowly quill to act a loftie part!'

48. Summum bonum: the highest good.

49. *Such is ... perfect rest*: cp. Quarles, *Emblemes*, bk 5, p. 250: 'Tell him, O tell him, how my panting breast / Is scorch'd with flames, and how my soul is pin'd; / Tell him, O tell him, how I he opprest / With the full torments of a troubled mind'.

50. *'Tis not in Honour, that is vanity*: see Ecclesiastes 6:2.

51. *Belshazzar ... final Doom*: Daniel 5 contains the biblical account of Belshazzar, king of Babylon. Belshazzar defiles vessels taken from the temple in Jerusalem, but is then terrified by the 'fingers of a man's hand' writing on the wall. Eventually Daniel is asked to interpret the words, and he does so: Daniel 5:26–28. Belshazzar is killed that night.

52. *For man in Honour ... so ends his race*: cp. Quarles, *Emblemes*, bk 3, p. 145: 'beasts draw the self-same breath, / Wax old alike, and die the self-same death'.

53. *Where's* Nimrod *now, that mighty Man of old*: see Genesis 10:8–10. A large extra-biblical tradition concerning Nimrod as the first king and tyrant developed. On the seventeenth-

century uses of Nimrod, including those of Bunyan and Milton, see C. Hill, *The English Bible and the Seventeenth-Century Revolution*, pbk edn (London: Penguin, 1994), pp. 217–22.

54. *Head of Gold*: tyrannical king of Babylon, Nebuchadnezzar. See Daniel 2:38.

55. *Of* Alexander ... *to Conquer*: Alexander the Great (356–323 BC) was apocryphally said, following his extensive triumphs, to have wept that there were no more worlds to conquer. This claim was commonplace by the time Keach wrote.

56. *Riches, O young man ... away with Eagles wings*: see Proverbs 23:5.

57. *When riches thou dost heap, thou heap'st up sorrow*: see Psalm 39:6.

58. *Riches and Wealth ... gone to morrow*: cp. Peter Chrysologus quoted in Quarles, *Emblemes*, bk 2, p. 79: '*Vexation and anguish accompany riches and honour: The pomp of the world and the favour of the people are but smoke, and a blast suddenly vanishing: which, if they commonly please, commonly bring repentance, and for a minute of joy, they bring an age of sorrow*'. Cp. St Bernard quoted in Quarles, *Emblemes*, bk 1, p. 43: '*O you Sonnes of* Adam, *you covetous generation, what have ye to do with earthly riches, which are neither true, nor yours. Gold and silver are reall earth, red and white, which the onely errour of man makes, or rather reputes, pretious: In short, if they be yours carry them with you*'.

59. Job: Job suffered terrible afflictions at the hands of Satan, with God's assent. His story is found in the eponymous book of the Bible. For an extensive meditation upon it, by a very different nonconformist, see J. Perrot, *A Sea of the Seed's Sufferings*, Volume 1 above pp. 29–67.

60. *With this sweet meat ... i'th'end*: cp. Quarles, *Emblemes*, bk 1, p. 14: 'The dainties here, / Are least what they appear; / Though sweet in hopes, yet in fruition sowre'; Quarles, *Emblemes*, bk 1, p. 30: 'sweet tasts have sowre closes'.

61. *What's outward Beauty save an evil snare*: cp. St Ambrose quoted in Quarles, *Emblemes*, bk 3, p. 163: '*The reward of honours, the height of power, the delicacie of diet, and the beautie of a harlot are the snares of the devil*'.

62. *curled Locks*: cp. Quarles, *Emblemes*, bk 2, p. 97: 'Where be those killing eyes, that so controul'd / The world? And locks, that did infold / Like knots of flaming wire, like curles of burnisht gold?'

63. *spotted Face*: there was a vogue for beauty spots in Restoration England. Others also moralized about these fashions: see e.g. E.S., 'On Painted and Black-Spotted Faces', in Miso-Spilus, *A Wonder of Wonders* (London: Richard Royston, 1662), sig. A4r, quoted in W. Pritchard, 'Masks and Faces: Female Legibility in the Restoration Era', *Eighteenth-Century Life*, 24:3 (2000), p. 43: 'spotted faces have but spotted souls'.

64. *Let Swine take Husks*: a reference to the prodigal son who, having left his father and frittered away his living, underwent tribulation before his return to his father: Luke 15:16: 'And he would fain have filled his belly with the husks that the swine did eat: and no man gave unto him'.

65. *Come, look ... empty toyes*: cp. Quarles, *Emblemes*, bk 2, p. 94: 'We'll look to Heav'n, and trust to higher joyes; / Let swine love husks, and children whine for toyes'.

66. *empty toyes*: cp. Quarles, *Emblemes*, bk 5, p. 261: 'Thus finding all the worlds delights to be / But empty toyes, good God, she points alone to thee'.

67. Come taste ... *best enjoyments naught*: cp. Augustine quoted in Quarles, *Emblemes*, bk 5, p. 291: '*O fountain of life, and vein of living waters, when shall I leave this forsaken, impassible, and dry earth, and tast the waters of thy sweetnesse, that I may behold thy virtue, and thy glory, and slake my thirst with the streams of thy mercy; Lord, I thirst: Thou art the spring of life, satisfie me*'.

68. Right hand pleasures for evermore: see Psalm 16:11.

69. *fleshly mind*: cp. Colossians 2:18.
70. *Your sin will now be of a scarlet-dye*: Isaiah 1:18 contains the reference to sin as scarlet but also maintains the possibility of redemption.
71. *And many stripes ... perfectly do know*: see Luke 12:47.
72. *Oh! tremble Soul, and dread thy present case*: cp. Psalm 119:120.
73. *Soul, thou art ... putrifying sin*: cp. Quarles, *Emblemes*, bk 3, p. 149, quoted below n. 158.
74. *In God no Interest ... fearful thing*: In these two images of the Youth's relationship to God (his being an 'enemy' and his lack of 'Interest') Keach paves the way for his subsequent creative use of two analogies for Christ's role in salvation: mediator and surety. The importance of these analogies to Keach, his particular use of them, and the sources for his thought are expertly illuminated in Arnold, 'Reformed Theology', ch. 5, to which this note is heavily indebted. The image of God and postlapsarian humankind as enemies without the intervention of Christ is biblical. See e.g. Romans 5:10.
75. *full of bowels*: a reference to the merciful giving of grace. See De Laune and Keach, *Tropologia*, bk 1, p. 47: '[*Bowels*] are attributed to God, by which his Mercy and most ardent love is expressed, Esa. 63. 15. *Where is thy zeal and thy strength, the sounding of thy* Bowels, *and of thy Mercies towards me?* Jer. 31. 20. My Bowels are troubled for him (that is, for *Ephraim*) Luke 1. 78. *Through the* Bowels *of the Mercy of our God, whereby the day-spring from on high hath visited us*'. Cp. also Philippians 2:1–2.
76. *He's full ... Justice magnifie*: cp. Quarles, *Emblemes*, bk 3, p. 166 (Jesus is speaking in an allegorical courtroom scene): 'Stay, Justice, hold; / My bowels yearn, my fainting bloud growes cold'.
77. *consuming fire*: see Hebrews 12:29; De Laune and Keach, *Tropologia*, bk 2, p. 65: 'WE meet with many Metaphors in the Sacred Scriptures, which set forth the Terribleness of an angry God to impenitent Sinners, but none more dismal nor terrible than this: *For our God is a consuming Fire.* ... Amongst the Metaphors taken from Elementary Things, we find that God is called *Fire*, yea, a *consuming Fire, Deut.* 4. 24. & 9. 3. & 32. 22. *Isa.* 10. 17. & 66. 15, 16. *Ezek.* 21. 31, &c. Which denotes his Wrath against Sin and wicked Men, in whose Power it is to consume those miserable Persons against whom it burns, as Fire does Stubble, or other combustible Materials. See *Psal.* 18. 8'. See also De Laune and Keach, *Tropologia*, bk 2, pp. 65–9.
78. *Those who are whole ... came to save*: see Matthew 9:12; Mark 2:17; Luke 5:31.
79. *sin-sick-Soul*: cp. J. Bunyan, *Come & Welcome Jesus Christ* (London: B. Harris, 1678), p. 210: 'And if Satan meets thee, and asketh, Whether goest thou? Tell him, Thou art Maimed, and art going to the Lord Jesus. If he objects thine own Unworthiness, Tell him; That even as the Sick seeketh the Physitian, and as he that hath broken Bones, seeks him that can Set them: So thou art going to Jesus Christ for Cure and Healing, for thy Sin-sick-Soul'.
80. *old-man*: cp. De Laune and Keach, *Tropologia*, bk 2, p. 182: 'Before a Man can put on the Lord Jesus Christ, and be cloathed with the Garment of Holiness, he must put off the abominable filthy Cloaks, and Covers of Wickedness, he must be stript of his filthy Rags, that he may be cloathed with the Spirit and Graces of Christ, *Put off the former Conversation, the Old Man, and put on the New Man, which after God is created in Righteousness and true Holiness*'. The italicized words are based on Ephesians 4:22, 24.
81. *Lust forced is in corners now to fly*: cp. Quarles, *Emblemes*, bk 5, p. 302: 'corner-haunting Lust'.
82. Honour, Pleasure, Wealth, and things: cp. R. Baxter, *A Christian Directory* (London: Nevill Simmons, 1673), pt 1, p. 115: '*so when the bait of* pleasure, *and honour, and wealth*

is presented by the Devil, to the fornicator, gamester, proud or covetous, they shall not see what the Devil is doing now, and what a game he is playing for their souls! They shall not perceive the connexion that there is between the pleasure and the sin, and the sin and the threatning, and the threatning and the judgement, and the judgement and the everlasting punishment'.

83. Make-bate: sower of discord.

84. *Playes they Act*: Following the Restoration, the theatres re-opened and women were officially allowed to act on stage for the first time. See S. J. Owen (ed.), *A Companion to Restoration Drama* (Oxford: Blackwell Publishers, 2001).

85. *Uicinus*: neigbour (Lat. vicinus).

86. *God may wash thy Soul in Christ his blood*: cp. Revelation 1:5. Cp. Quarles, *Emblemes*, bk 3, p. 138 (Jesus is speaking): ''T is either thou-must bleed, sick soul, or I: / My bloud's a cordiall. He that sucks my veins, / Shall cleanse his own, and conquer greater pains / Then these: cheer up; this precious bloud of mine / Shall cure thy grief; my heart shall bleed for thine: / Believe, and view me with a faithfull eye, / Thy soul shall neither languish, bleed, nor die'.

87. *Of th' hideous howlings ... devouring fire dwell*: cp. Matthew 13:42.

88. *lowest Hell*: cp. Deuteronomy 32:22; Psalm 86:13.

89. *All Fornicators, Drunkards ... the self-same curse*: cp. Revelation 21:8; 1 Corinthians 6:9–10.

90. *Hypocrisie*: Keach was later to preach specifically on the dangers of hypocrisy: see B. Keach, *The Counterfeit Christian* (London: printed and are sold by John Pike ... and by the author ... , 1691).

91. *tries the reins, and searches every heart*: see Jeremiah 17:10.

92. *Tophet*: in this instance, hell. See Isaiah 30:33.

93. *And God also put out your Candle-light*: see Proverbs 24:20; Job 21:17.

94. *And give you up unto a heart of stone*: cf. Ezekiel 36:26.

95. *Man's Life a bubble*: the *homo bulla* trope. See also note to J. Perrot, *A Sea of the Seed's Sufferings*, Volume 1, p. 287, n. 8.

96. *Your own Experience ... and do's decay*: cp. Quarles, *Emblemes*, bk 2, p. 78: 'See, how his wings are sing'd in Cyprian fire, / Whose flames consume with youth, in age expire: / The world's a bubble; all the pleasures in it, / Like morning vapours, vanish in a minit: / The vapours vanish, and the bubble's broke; / A slave to pleasure is a slave to smoke'. Cp. Quarles, *Emblemes*, bk 5, p. 273 (mispaginated as p. 261): 'Life is a bubble, blown with whining breaths'.

97. *The Meadow's ... all to Hay*: cp. Quarles, *Emblemes*, bk 3, p. 177: 'And what's a Life? the flourishing array / Of the proud Summer meadow, which today / Wears her green plush, and is tomorrow hay'.

98. *a vapour is ... gone most speedily*: cp. T. De Laune and B. Keach, *Troposchemalogia* (London: the author, 1682), bk 4, p. 397: '*David* desired a Measure of his Days, that he might know how frail he was. Some do not measure their Days by the King's Standard; they measure their Days by the Life of their Progenitors. My Father and my Grand-father, saith one, lived so long, and why may not I live as long as they did? Others measure their Days by their present Health and Strength; Others by the sound and healthy Constitution of their Bodies. Now these Things are not a fit nor lawful Measure of your Days, but rather those Things of which you have heard, *viz*. The Weaver's-Shuttle, the morning Dew, the Flower of the Field, the early Cloud, the Shadow and Vapor that flieth away'. De Laune and Keach, *Troposchemalogia*, bk 4, pp. 393–6, identifies the biblical

passages from which these images of transience are drawn; they are as follows: James 4:14 (vapour); Job 14:2 (shadow); Job 14:2 and Isaiah 40:6 (flower); Job 7:6 (weaver's shuttle); Job 9:26 (ship). For Jonah's gourd see Jonah 4:6–10.

99. *My Soul ... my Duty find*: cp. Quarles, *Emblemes*, bk 3, p. 137 (the Soul is responding to Jesus's question 'Who art thou?'): 'Oh, a deeply wounded breast / That's heavy laden, and would fain have rest'.

100. *Professor*: Watson comments that 'professor' was 'a word of considerable abuse in Puritan literature'. See J. R. Watson, *The English Hymn: A Critical and Historical Study* (Oxford: Clarendon Press, 1997), p. 113. Certainly, the *false* professor was vigorously attacked: see e.g. a work published in the same year as Keach's, J. Bunyan, *The Barren Fig-Tree: Or, the Doom and Downfall of the Fruitless Professor* (London: Jonathan Robinson, 1673). See also the comments of Richard Greaves: R. L. Greaves, *Glimpses of Glory: John Bunyan and English Dissent* (Stanford, CA: Stanford University Press, 2002), pp. 304–9.

101. *born again*: see John 3:3. As Arnold writes, for Keach, the application of the covenant of grace to individuals 'not only happened in time, but it happened individually within the life of each member of the elect. Agreeing with Samuel Petto, Keach argued that although all of the fœderal conditions of the *Covenant of Grace* had been fulfilled by Christ, the individual member of the elect could not partake of the promises of the covenant until Christ's merits had been applied to the individual'. See Arnold, 'Reformed Theology', pp. 161–2.

102. *When it is common Grace ... true Regeneration*: Keach later wrote: 'All generally grant that legal Convictions, and the Operation of common Grace through the Workings of natural Conscience, have some considerable Power in them to reform the Life of a wicked Person'. But:

   • *Morality, external Gifts and common Grace, are but like a vain Paint, a mere empty and artificial Garnish.*

   • They make a fair show in the Flesh, they pride it in themselves, and Men praise and admire them, but what doth all this signify? they are still under a diabolical Power and Influence, and *twofold more the Children of the Devil than they were before:* Nay, as I shall hereafter shew, rather seven times worse than when they were openly wicked and prophane.

   See Keach, *The Counterfeit Christian*, pp. 4, 15. For Keach, common grace was distinct from special grace (here 'the Grace that's supernatural'), which was only given to the Elect. Some could thus seem godly through the exercise of common grace but ultimately remain unsaved. See Arnold, 'Reformed Theology', pp. 199–203.

103. *narrow passage enter*: see Matthew 7:13–14.

104. *I doubt*: I do not doubt.

105. *The Pharisee ... was the Publican*: see Luke 18:10–14. In this parable both the publican and the Pharisee pray at the temple, but only the publican goes away 'justified'. This is because he was humble and acknowledged his sin while the Pharisee arrogantly gloried in the outward shows of his religiosity.

106. *King Pharaoh, Esau, yea, and Judas too*: key scriptural examples of those who were reprobate, and whose signs of repentance were therefore misleading.

107. *Esau it appears ... born again*: cp. Romans 9:13; Hebrews 12:16–17. Esau, the son of Isaac, was much discussed as an example of one of the reprobate whose signs of repentance were thus misleading. Esau sold his birthright for pottage to his brother Jacob, and was also duped out of the blessing due to him as the firstborn (see Genesis 25:23–34,

27:6–40). For a survey of seventeenth-century writing on Esau, including the exposition of his example within Calvinist theology, see Hill, *English Bible*, pp. 203–15. John Owen and Bunyan both 'stressed the uselessness of Esau's repentance': Hill, *English Bible*, pp. 212–3, at p. 213. Calvin, in his commentary on the verse from Romans quoted above (which includes discussion of its source in Malachi 1:2–3), wrote: 'The spiritual condition of Jacob was witnessed to by his dominion, and that of Esau by his bondage. Jacob also obtained this favour through the kindness of God, and not by his own merit. This declaration of the prophet, therefore, shows why the Lord conferred the birthright on Jacob. It is taken from Mal. I, where the Lord declares His kindness to the Jews, before reproaching them for their ingratitude. "I have loved you", He says. He then adds the source from which His love sprang. "Was not Esau Jacob's brother?" as if to say, "What privilege had he, that I should prefer him to his brother? None at all. Their right was equal, except that the younger ought by the law of nature to have been subject to the older. Yet I chose Jacob and rejected Esau, induced to this course by my mercy alone, and not by any worthiness in his works. ... "': J. Calvin, *The Epistles of Paul the Apostle to the Romans and to the Thessalonians*, ed. D. W. Torrance and T. F. Torrance, trans. R. Mackenzie (Edinburgh: Oliver and Boyd, 1960), pp. 201–2.

108. *When* Pharaoh ... *wicked be*: the Pharaoh's contrition in the face of the plague of hail (referenced here) was soon replaced by his return to sin once the plague had ended. See Exodus 9:22–35.

109. Saul: king of Israel who was rejected by God. See 1 Samuel 15.

110. *From outward ... he has done*: cp. Proverbs 30:12; Matthew 23:27 (Geneva).

111. *The Swine ... manifest it will*: see 2 Peter 2:22; Luke 11:39. See also Proverbs 26:11; Matthew 23:25–26.

112. Except your Righteousness ... *in God's Kingdom dwell*: see Matthew 5:20.

113. *Old* Herod ... *against him sought*: on Herod and the beheading of John the Baptist see Matthew 14:1–12; Mark 6:14–29. The deriding of Jesus by Herod and his 'Men of War' is recounted in Luke 23:7–11.

114. *cursed Caitife*: in Quarles, *Emblemes*, bk 3, p. 165, Sin describes himself as 'now a poore accurst / Convicted catiff'.

115. Simon *the Sorceror ... inward vile*: Simon Magus was apparently converted by Philip the evangelist. But he provoked Peter's anger by attempting to buy the power of the apostles to pass on the Holy Ghost through the laying on of hands. Peter rebukes him, saying 'For I perceive that thou art in the gall of bitterness, and in the bond of iniquity': see Acts 8:9–24.

116. *Like a Sepulchre painted, inward vile*: see Matthew 23:27.

117. *There is ... only is effectual*: Calvinism distinguished between the outward and the inward (effectual) calling. See J. Calvin, *Institutes of the Christian Religion*, ed. J. T. McNeill, trans. F. L. Battles, 2 vols (Philadelphia, PA: Westminster Press, 1960), 3.24.8: 'The statement of Christ "Many are called but few are chosen" [Matt. 22:14] is, in this manner, very badly understood. Nothing will be ambiguous if we hold fast to what ought to be clear from the foregoing: that there are two kinds of call. There is the general call, by which God invites all equally to himself through the outward preaching of the word – even those to whom he holds it out as a savor of death [cf. II Cor. 2:16], and as the occasion for severer condemnation. The other kind of call is special, which he deigns for the most part to give to the believers alone, while by the inward illumination of his Spirit he causes the preached Word to dwell in their hearts. Yet sometimes he also causes

those whom he illumines only for a time to partake of it; then he justly forsakes them on account of their ungratefulness and strikes them with even greater blindness'.

118. *Faith of Credence*: a faith based simply on belief. Cp. Keach, *The Counterfeit Christian*, p. 29: ' ... whatsoever Men may act or do from those common Operations of the Spirit, or by the Power of natural Conscience, under the external Preaching of the Word, or means of the Rod or Afflictions, by the Assistance or Help of which I doubt not he may become another Man, a great Professor, pray, hear the Word, have a sort of Faith, *viz.* that of Credence, be baptized, and so become a Church-Member, yea, a Preacher, and may be in the Sight of Men of a blameless Life and Conversation, and yet never changed in Heart, or regenerated by the effectual and special Operations of Christ's Spirit, nor have Union with Christ'.

119. *Some* Jews *believ'd ... not freed*: see John 8:30–59, esp. 8:44.

120. *Gall of bitterness*: said by Peter of Simon Magus. See Acts 8:23, quoted above n. 115.

121. *The stony ... soon 'twas gone*: a reference to the parable of the sower Matthew 13:3–23; Mark 4:3–20; Luke 8:5–15. See in particular Matthew 13:20–21 (Geneva).

122. *The* Devils do believe *... tremble also*: see James 2:19.

123. *'Tis easie ... for to apply*: cp. Quarles, *Emblemes*, bk 5, pp. 309–11.

124. *Historical*: Calvin drew attention to those who had a simple faith in gospel history but who remained unsaved. See e.g. Calvin, *Institutes*, 3.2.9: 'Of course, most people believe that there is a God, and they consider that the gospel history and the remaining parts of the Scripture are true. Such a judgment is on a par with the judgments we ordinarily make concerning those things which are either narrated as having once taken place, or which we have seen as eyewitnesses'. Cp. also B. Keach, *A Golden Mine Opened* (London: printed and sold by the author ... and William Marshall, 1694), p. 326: 'They may know the True Church, and also know what is required of Persons in order to their becoming Members thereof, namely, Repentance, Faith and Baptism: Nay, and they may have some kind of Repentance; *Judas* repented: Also they may believe; *Simon* believed: They may have a common Faith, the Faith of Credence, or an Historical Faith; believe the Report of the Gospel and Revelation of Christ, and the Sum of the Christian Religion; nay, believe or receive the Word with some sort of Joy, *Mat.* 13. 20'.

125. *'will never grow ... you may be sure*: see Matthew 13:23; Mark 4:20; Luke 8:15.

126. *Christ thou exalt'st ... Prophet too in every thing*: the three offices of Christ: priest, king and prophet. For relevant discussion see De Laune and Keach, *Tropologia*, bk 2, pp. 142–161; Calvin, *Institutes*, 2.15.

127. *Men by its fruits ... same do also show*: the works of the elect, while not efficacious, are said to be signs of salvation.

128. *They with the Flock ... left hand*: see Matthew 25:31–46.

129. *The foolish Virgins ... saving Grace provide*: see Matthew 25:1–13.

130. Ye wicked ... workers of Iniquity: see Luke 13:27.

131. *Some Pray in Form, and other Pray by Art*: While nonconformists rejected the forms of prayer found in the Book of Common Prayer, Keach's later defence of hymn-singing led him into a careful clarification of what 'forms' could be acceptable: see B. Keach, *The Breach Repaired* (London: the Author, 1691), p. 161: 'The Prayers that a Minister makes in the publick Congregation may, and oft do, contain many Scripture-Expressions, (may be half his Prayer may be such) and who shall say he doth not pray spiritually? Nay, moreover, and that Prayer some will tell you is a Form to others, which he that is the Mouth puts up, and many times I have heard some good and godly Christians speak softly over the same words in the Congregation. Now since all Forms are cried down by you, sure

this must needs be a sad Crime, or a carnal and formal Practice. There is nothing, I tell you again, without its Form: Is not the reading of God's Word a formal thing? and yet dare you say that is no Duty to be performed in the Church? If a formal thing, then, by your arguing, say I, 'tis no Duty to read the Scripture in private neither. Now because all legal Forms are gone, must all Gospel and Spiritual Forms go too?'

132. *They Sin i'th' day ... filth away*: cp. Augustine quoted in Quarles, *Emblemes*, p. 115: '*In vain is that washing, where the next sinne defileth: He hath ill repented whose sinnes are repeated*'.

133. *The Young-man ... true Christianity*: see Matthew 19:16–22; Mark 10:17–22. The young man enquires of Christ how to 'have eternal life'. Christ tells him to 'keep the commandments'. The young man says 'All these things have I kept from my youth up: what lack I yet?' Christ then tells him to 'sell that thou hast, and give to the poor'. On hearing this the young man 'went away sorrowful: for he had great possessions'. Quotations are from Matthew's account.

134. *Have you no Dalila ... in your bosom ly*: Delilah inveigled the secret of Samson's strength from him, and thus caused his capture by the Philistines: see Judges 16:4–20.

135. *bankerout*: bankruptcy.

136. *Thy Hope ... its ebb*: cp. Job 8:13–14 (Geneva). AV contains the phrase 'spider's web'.

137. *Thy spots ... hath chose*: see Deuteronomy 32:5.

138. *Precise*: the godly had been called Precisians from an early stage because of their precise adherence to what they saw as the practical and theoretical consequences of their religious beliefs.

139. *When Hypocrites ... purpose for their sake*: cp. Isaiah 33:14.

140. *one dram of saving Grace*: cp. J. Bunyan, *A Treatise of the Fear of God* (London: N. Ponder, 1679), p. 235: 'Hypocrite, God hath not intrusted thee with the least dram of his saving grace, nor will he, because thou art an Hypocrite'.

141. *on false bottoms he has built 'tis clear*: cp. Matthew 7:24–27 and Luke 6:46–49, in which the significance of acting upon Christ's words is stressed by analogy to the man who built his house on rock in contrast to the man who built on weak foundations.

142. *The Plague ... cause him to reel*: in this shift to a medical metaphor Keach is referring to the 'treatment' of plague by the lancing of buboes: see P. Slack, *The Impact of Plague in Tudor and Stuart England* (London and Boston: Routledge & Kegan Paul, 1985), p. 32.

143. *His Sword ... like thee offend*: cp. Psalm 7:11–12.

144. *And from his Presence, Youth, thou canst not fly*: Psalm 139.

145. *Dost think ... inward thoughts espy*: for a further relevant discussion of the anthropomorphic image of the eyes of God, see De Laune and Keach, *Tropologia*, bk 1, pp. 43–4.

146. *Thy secret Lust ... come to light*: cp. Mark 4:22 (Geneva); Luke 8:17 (Geneva).

147. *Then my black Bill ... bring a Charge*: the legal language deployed by Conscience may suggest a specific reference to the Bill as a Chancery procedure. The procedures of Chancery (a court of conscience) allowed the full rehearsal of the case against the accused.

148. *And am by Satan ... into th' right again*: on the fallibility of conscience see above n. 37.

149. *Go, go, ye Cursed*: cp. Matthew 25:41.

150. *scalding Sulphur dost roul*: cp. Revelation 21:8.

151. *And how you ... lead your feet aright*: cp. Quarles's description of God: see Quarles, *Emblemes*, bk 4, p. 194: 'Great God, that art the flowing Spring of Light, / Enrich mine eyes with thy refulgent Ray: / Thou art my Path; direct my steps aright; / I have no other Light, no other Way: / I'll trust my God, and him alone pursue; / His Law shall be my Path; his Heav'nly Light my Clue'.

152. *Thou might'st, hadst thou improv'd the means of Grace*: cp. De Laune and Keach, *Tropologia*, bk 2, p. 250: 'Improve the Means of Grace God is pleased to afford thee, attend upon the Ministry of the Word'.

153. *Beheld with Saints God's reconciled face*: cp. Romans 5:10; De Laune and Keach, *Tropologia*, bk 1, pp. 43 (on the face of God): 'Sometimes the *Grace*, Favour, and Mercy of God is exprest by it, as *Dan.* 9.17. *Psal.* 13. 2. *Ezek.* 39. 24. *Psal.* 31. 20. *Psal.* 17. 2. 2 *Chron.* 29. 12. *Num.* 6. 25, 26. *Psal.* 4. 7, *and* 31. 17. *and* 67. 1, 2, 3. *Psal.* 80. 4, 8, 20. 'Tis said of men to seek the *Face* of God, that is his *Grace* and favour by Prayer, *Psal.* 27: 8. 2 *Chron.* 7. 14, 17. *Esa.* 18. 3. *&c.*'

154. *With those ... to all Eternitie*: see Revelation 7:9–10.

155. *Vessels of Wrath*: see Romans 9:22.

156. *In Hell ... doleful place*: cp. J. Milton, *Paradise Lost*, I, ll. 60–74: 'The dismal situation waste and wild, / A dungeon horrible, on all sides round / As one great furnace flamed, yet from those flames / No light, but rather darkness visible / Served only to discover sights of woe, / Regions of sorrow, doleful shades, where peace / And rest can never dwell, hope never comes / That comes to all; but torture without end / Still urges, and a fiery deluge, fed / With ever-burning sulphur unconsumed: / Such place eternal justice had prepared / For those rebellious, here their prison ordained / In utter darkness, and their portion set / As far removed from God and light of heaven / As from the centre thrice to the utmost pole'.

157. *Didst thou but hear ... and quake*: cp. Psalm 119:120.

158. *Dost know ... 'tis venomous*: cp. Quarles, *Emblemes*, bk 3, p. 149: 'O my ragged wound / Is deep and desp'rate, it is drench'd and drown'd / In blood and briny tears: It doth begin / To stink without, and putrifie within'.

159. *wound receive ... venomous*: cp. Psalm 38:5.

160. *The sting ... mortal wound*: cp. Proverbs 7:23. Proverbs 7 is concerned with a harlot's temptation of a young man; it is thus particularly relevant here, given Keach's concentration on the Youth's lust.

161. *And since ... Soul thou art*: Keach held that Christ had died for the elect only. He had no truck with hypothetical universalism. On Keach's understanding of limited atonement see Arnold, 'Reformed Theology', pp. 189–92.

162. *Yet by the Law ... Soul thou art*: cp. the allegorical courtroom scene involving Jesus, Justice and Sinner in Quarles, *Emblemes*, bk 3, pp. 165–6.

163. *sweet-pleasing evil*: cf. M. de Montaigne, *Essays*, trans. J. Florio (London: Edward Blount and William Barret, 1613), p. 410: 'this sweete pleasing passion, which tickleth us with selfe-joying pleasure'.

164. *And thou false ... am ruined by thee*: cp. Quarles, *Emblemes*, bk 2, p. 81: 'Thou ask'st the Conscience what she ails, / And swear'st to ease her; / There's none can want where thou supply'st: / There's none can give where thou deny'st. / Alas, fond world thou boasts; false world thou ly'st'.

165. *with* Hue and Cry: by calling out for aid in capturing the perpetrator of a crime.

166. *O whither ... present ev'ry where*: a version of Quarles, *Emblemes*, bk 3, pp. 173–4:

> Whither shall I fly? what path untrod
> Shall I seek out to scape the flaming rod
> Of my offended, of my angry God?
>
> Where shall I sojourn? what kind sea will hide
> My head from Thunder? where shall I abide,
> Untill his flames be quench'd or laid aside?

What, if my feet should take their hasty flight,
And seek protection in the shades of night?
Alas, no shades can blind the God of Light.

What, if my soul should take the wings of day,
And find some desart; if the spring away,
The wings of vengeance clip as fast as they.

What if some solid rock should entertain
My frighted soul? Can solid rocks restrain
The stroke of Justice, and not cleave in twain?

Nor Sea, nor Shade, nor Shield, nor Rock, nor Cave,
Nor silent Desarts, nor the sullen Grave,
Where flame-ey'd fury means to smite, can save.

The Seas will part; Graves open; Rocks will split;
The Shield will cleave; the frighted Shadows slit;
Where Justice aims, her fiery darts must hit.

No, no, if stern-brow'd vengeance means to thunder,
There is no place above, beneath, nor under,
So close, but will unlock, or rive in sunder.

'T is vain to flee; 't is neither here nor there
Can scape that hand untill that hand forbear;
Ah me! where is he not, that's every where?

167. *Oh* Truth! ... *God's heavy hand*: cp. Quarles, *Emblemes*, bk 3, p. 174: 'Thou art my God; by thee I fall or stand; / Thy Grace hath giv'n me courage to withstand / All tortures, but my conscience and thy hand'.
168. *Physitian*: on Christ as physician see De Laune and Keach, *Tropologia*, bk 2, p. 112–19.
169. *Will Tears ... all afford*: cp. Psalm 39:12.
170. *Will Tears ... of the Word*: Keach was later to write about the inefficacy of outward shows of devotion. See Keach, *The Counterfeit Christian*, p. 11: 'And evident it is, that this sweeping or external cleansing with the Broom of outward Reformation, or the Garnish of moral Righteousness, common Gifts and Graces of the Spirit, Prayer, hearing the Word, partaking of the Sacraments, and doing many good Works, cannot secure the Soul against Satan's Attempts, in order to his taking up his Habitation in such Persons Hearts'.
171. *Rivers of Oyl, much Gold, or Earthly Wealth*: cp. Micah 6:7.
172. *Epidemical*: cp. Quarles on original sin (Jesus is speaking): ''T is Epidemicall: / Thy bloud's infected, and th' infection sprang / From a bad liver': Quarles, *Emblemes*, p. 138.
173. *By Law nor Levite*: through Old Testament law nor priests.
174. *Common-shore*: common sewer.
175. *call thee home*: cp. Luke 15:6.
176. *Alas! on me ... can't revive*: cp. Quarles, *Emblemes*, bk 4, p. 217:

Thus like a lump of the corrupted Masse,
I lie secure, long lost, before I was:
And like a block, beneath whose burden lies
That undiscover'd worm that never dies,
I have no will to rouze, I have no power to rise.

> Can stinking *Lazarus* compound, or strive
> With deaths entangling fetters, and revive?

Lazarus was raised from the dead by Christ: see John 11:1–46.

177. *And raise ... set thy feet*: see Psalm 40:2.

178. *The good* Samaritan ... *Soul of thine*: see Luke 10:30–37. Here the Samaritan is interpreted as a type of Christ.

179. *Cry ... saving Grace*: Keach personifies the differences between true saving grace and common grace, see above n. 102.

180. *'Tis she must ... out of Captivitie*: Keach is referencing the robe of righteousness, which is given to the elect to wear through no merit of their own. Cp. Keach, *A Golden Mine*, p. 425: 'Are you poor, and naked, and have nothing to cover your Nakedness but filthy Rags? Well, be it so, yet this Salvation brings to you a rich and glorious Robe, *viz.* Christ's Righteousness, nay change of Raiment; Salvation it self is called a Garment, and it is by this Salvation also you have the Robe of Sanctification and Grace wherewith you are clothed'.

181. *like* Jacob, *wilt prevail at last*: a reference to Jacob's wrestling with God: see Genesis 32:24–29. In Keach's schema Jacob and the Youth both prevail only because they are given strength by God.

182. *As thou polluted in thy blood dost lie*: cp. Ezekiel 16:6.

183. *Is there no Balm in* Gilead, *is there none*: see Jeremiah 8:22.

184. *Why were thy sides pierced ... i'th' highest degree*: Keach sets out in poetic terms the penal substitutionary theory which governed his understanding of salvation. Christ was substituted for the elect to make satisfaction to God on their behalf. See Arnold, 'Reformed Theology', ch. 6.

185. *Lord ... Ravens when they cry*: cp. Psalm 147:9.

186. *Oh! come ... now I do knock*: cp. Quarles, *Emblemes*, bk 5, pp. 265–7 (p. 265 mispaginated as p. 253).

187. *Was I not sent ... further don't proceed*: both Jews and Gentiles were saved by Christ. See e.g. B. Keach, *Christ Alone the Way to Heaven* (London: printed and sold by Benja. Harris, 1698), p. 44: '*It is by the blood of Jesus, through him by one Spirit we have both (that is* Jews *and* Gentiles,) *access unto the Father*'. Keach compresses Ephesians 2:11–18.

188. *O Son of David ... what is't thou dost desire*: cp. the dialogue between Jesus and the Soul in Quarles, *Emblemes*, bk 3, pp. 137–8.

189. *My bowels yearn*: the same phrase is used by Jesus in Quarles's imagining of a dialogue between Jesus, Justice and a Sinner: Quarles, *Emblemes*, bk 3, p. 166, quoted above n. 76.

190. *The Earth's a blast, and all this World's a bubble*: found almost verbatim in Quarles, *Emblemes*, bk 4, p. 213.

191. *My gasping Soul's dissolv'd into tears*: found almost verbatim in Quarles, *Emblemes*, bk 4, p. 229.

192. *Lord, I believe, O help my unbelief*: cp. Quarles, *Emblemes*, bk 3, p. 137: 'Lord, I believe; Lord, help my unbelief'.

193. *Over* Jerusalem *thou didst lament*: Christ's lament over Jerusalem is found in Luke 13:34–35 and in Matthew 23:37–9.

194. *On such a Worm as I*: cp. Psalm 22:6.

195. *whose wounded breast ... fain have rest*: cp. Quarles, *Emblemes*, bk 3, p. 137: 'Oh, a deeply wounded breast / That 's heavy laden, and would fain have rest'.

196. Canst thou ... forgiven are: cp. Quarles, *Emblemes*, bk 3, p. 138: "T is either thou must bleed, sick soul, or I: / My bloud's a cordiall. He that sucks my veins, / Shall cleanse his own, and conquer greater pains / Then these: cheer up; this precious bloud of mine / Shall cure thy grief; my heart shall bleed for thine: / Believe, and view me with a faithfull eye, / Thy soul shall neither languish, bleed, nor die.

197. Enter the Royal Fort ... treasure is above: cp. Quarles, *Emblemes*, bk 4, p. 197: 'But when I come to Thee, my God, that art / The royall Myne of everlasting treasure, / The reall Honour of my better part, / And living Fountain of eternall pleasure, / How nervelesse are my limbs! how faint and slow! / I have nor wings to fly, nor legs to go'.

198. Chear up ... Soul of thine: cp. Quarles, *Emblemes*, bk 3, p. 138, quoted above n. 196.

199. Rivers of Pleasures ... brim: cp. Psalm 36:8.

200. *My frozen Soul ... dissolv'd the rock*: cp. Quarles, *Emblemes*, bk 5, p. 265 (mispaginated as p. 253): 'LOrd, has the feeble voyce of flesh and bloud / The pow'r to work thine ears into a floud / Of melted mercy? or the strength t'unlock / The gates of Heav'n, and to dissolve a rock / Of marble clouds into a morning show'r?'; 'O can my frozen gutters choose but run, / That feel the warmth of such a glorious Sun?'

201. *What heart ... Earth's pleasures empty toys*: cp. Quarles, *Emblemes*, bk 5, p. 261, quoted above n. 96.

202. *Such is ... sorrow into mirth*: cp. Quarles on 'The royall Of-spring of a second Birth': 'A shrine of Grace, a little throne of Glory: / A Heav'n-born Of-spring of a new-born birth; / An earthly Heav'n; an ounce of Heav'nly earth': Quarles, *Emblemes*, bk 2, p. 122.

203. *Ah happy I ... dissolv'd*: cp. Quarles, *Emblemes*, bk 2, p. 122: 'O then it lives; O then it lives involv'd / In secret raptures; pants to be dissolv'd'.

204. *see him face to face*: cp. 1 Corinthians 13:12.

205. *Thou'st brought ... set my feet*: cp. Isaiah 2:3.

206. *Thou hast ... restored sight*: cp. Isaiah 42:16; 1 Peter 2:9. See also the mission given by Christ to Paul in Acts 26:18. The restoration of Paul's sight, following the blindness brought about by the vision of Christ during his conversion, is also relevant: see Acts 9:17–18, 22:11–13. Finally, Mark 8:22–26 recounts Jesus's healing of a blind man in Bethsaida who 'was restored, and saw every man clearly'. Other New Testament accounts of Christ healing the blind are to be found in Matthew 20:30–34; Mark 10:46–52; Luke 18:35–43; John 9.

207. *Nay, hast my Soul sav'd ... Name of thine*: cp. Quarles, *Emblemes*, bk 1, pp. 1: 'ROwze thee, my soul; and drein thee from the dregs / Of vulgar thoughts: Skrue up the heightned pegs / Of thy sublime Theorboe foure notes higher, / And higher yet; that so, the shrill-mouth'd Quire / Of swift-wing'd Seraphims may come and joyn, / And make thy consort more than halfe divine'.

208. *Let not ... be brought*: cp. Quarles, *Emblemes*, bk 1, p. 1: 'Let not the frailtie of thy flesh disturb / Thy new-concluded peace; Let Reason curb / Thy hot-mouth'd Passion; and let heav'ns fire season / The fresh Conceits of thy corrected Reason'.

209. *Nay, hast my Soul sav'd ... for evermore*: In addition to the specific borrowings noted above (n. 207), the whole of this passage may be usefully compared to the invocation at the beginning of book 1 of Quarles's *Emblemes*. See Quarles, *Emblemes*, bk 1, p. 1–2.

210. *What Melody ... humble thankfulness*: cp. Quarles, *Emblemes*, bk 4, p. 234: 'O how mine eyes now ravish'd at the sight / Of my bright Sun shot flames of equall fire! / Ah! how my soul dissolv'd with ov'r-delight, / To re-enjoy the Crown of chast desire! / How sov'reigne joy depos'd and dispossest / Rebellious grief! And how my ravish'd breast – / But who can presle those heights, that cannot be exprest?'

211. *Though of Deceivers ... Ignorant as they*: Keach's characterisation of the Deceivers, as those who 'cry up [Light] in all' suggests that he has the Quakers in mind. He lambasts them for their perceived failure to give due attention and respect to scripture. This was a typical Baptist criticism of Quakerism. Cp. B. Keach, *The Grand Impostor* (London: B. Harris, 1675), pp. 290–1: 'You by your speeches would insinuate, / Believing what the Scripture doth relate / Is inconsistent with true Holiness, / And none so Holy as the Scriptureless, / So subtily suggest into mens mind, / That cleaving to the Scriptures makes men blind: / Fitly comporting with that *Romish* Notion, / Where is most Ignorance, there's most Devotion. / Thus Ignorance we see advanced high, / Scripture's thrown down; O great Impiety! / If Scriptures make men wise unto *Salvation*, / Then Quakers Doctrine is abomination. / What, do we think, because the God of heaven / To *Israel* his written Laws had given; / By reading which they plainly understood / What God esteemed evil, what was good; / That Heathens therefore better might fulfill / Without the written Laws, his Holy will'. On the Quaker-Baptist conflict over the issue of scripture see T. L. Underwood, *Primitivism, Radicalism, and the Lamb's War: The Baptist-Quaker Conflict in Seventeenth-Century England* (Oxford: Oxford University Press, 1997), ch. 2. Underwood notes a later use by Keach of a version of this passage's claims about foreign heathens: see B. Keach, *The Progress of Sin* (London: John Dunton, 1684), pp. 247–8, quotation at p. 248 (partially quoted in Underwood, *Primitivism, Radicalism, and the Lamb's War*, p. 113): [A '*Stranger*' is speaking before a Judge] 'Yea my Lord, the Heavens and Earth by the *Light* of mine own natural Conscience teach me that there is a *God*; and many other good things; as not to *lye, steal, swear, bear false Witness against my Neighbour*, &c. because I would not have him to do so by me; but as for him you call *Christ*, none of us, who are called *Pagans*, ever heard of him, therefore we know not that it is a *Sin* not to believe in him'.

212. *Since he hath found Earth's best injoyments vain*: cp. Quarles, *Emblemes*, bk 4, p. 206: 'Thus worthlesse, vain, and void / Of comfort, are the fruits of earths imployment; / Which ere they be enjoy'd / Distract us, and destroy us in th' enjoyment; / These be the pleasures that are priz'd / When Heav'ns cheap pen'worth stands despis'd'.

213. *He uses me ... Christ's Glory he should stain*: The Youth's resolve to defend tender conscience, detailed in these lines through the voice of Conscience, is a classic nonconformist defence of remaining strong in the face of persecution and denying the authority of the state Church. Compromising conscience in the Restoration ultimately meant compromising 'Christ's Glory'. See G.S. de Krey, 'The First Restoration Crisis: Conscience and Coercion in London, 1667–1673', *Albion*, 25:4 (1993), pp. 565–80; G.S. de Krey, 'Rethinking the Restoration: Dissenting Cases for Conscience, 1667–1672', *Historical Journal*, 38:1 (1995), pp. 53–83.

214. *vengeance is mine ... of thine*: cf. Romans 12:19.

215. *Yet I'le return ... ere't be long*: cp. 1 Peter 5:8.

216. *Father of Lyes*: see John 8:44.

217. *Thy head is broke*: cp. Genesis 3:15 (Geneva).

218. *But I have so much craft and subtilty*: cp. 2 Corinthians 11:3; Genesis 3:1.

219. *That the young Saint will an old Devil be*: Burrow, in his article on the proverb and its use, comments that "'young saint, old devil" seems to have acquired a certain notoriety in the medieval and Renaissance periods. Quite frequently pious writers cite the proverb as expressing a dangerous, even diabolical error'. See J. A. Burrow, '"Young Saint, Old Devil": Reflections on a Medieval Proverb', *Review of English Studies*, n.s, 30:120 (1979), p. 385–96, quotation at p. 386.

220. *'Cause thou ... happy state*: cp. Milton, *Paradise Lost*, I, ll. 141–2: 'Though all our glory extinct, and happy state / Here swallowed up in endless misery'.

221. *With malice ... wicked spite*: cp. Milton, *Paradise Lost*, II, ll. 380–6: 'for whence / But from the author of all ill could spring / So deep a malice, to confound the race / Of mankind in one root, and earth with hell / To mingle and involve, done all to spite / The great creator? But their spite still serves / His glory to augment'.

222. *My standing's firm ... strong hand*: cp. 1 Peter 5:4; John 10:16; John 10:27–28.

223. *Upon ... can be raz'd*: cp. De Laune and Keach, *Tropologia*, bk 2, p. 171: 'The Lord Jesus hath the Stability of a Rock in him. He is the *Rock of Ages*; the *same yesterday, to day, and for ever*; He grows not weak; as his Years, so his Strength decays not'. The marginal note to Isaiah 26:4 in AV records that the Hebrew for 'everlasting strength' is the Rock of Ages.

224. *And my foundation ... Mercy cease*: see Isaiah 54:10.

225. *The Head ... Monster were*: cp. e.g. 1 Corinthians 12:12; Ephesians 4:15–16. Cp. Keach, *A Golden Mine*, p. 228: 'By this Spiritual Union with Christ, we partake of his Blessed Image or Divine Nature: So that the Head and Members are of one kind, and not like *Nebuchadnezzar's Image, a Head of Gold*, and a *Belly and Thighs of Brass*, and *Legs of Iron*, and *Feet* and *Toes*, part of *Iron* and part of *Clay:* This would be to make the Mystical Body of Christ a Monster, an Immortal Head, an Incorruptible Head, and a Mortal Body and Members, that may corrupt, putrify and become loathsom. No, this cannot be; such as is the Head (as to Nature and Quality) such is the Body, and every Member in particular, a living Head and living Members; a Head of pure Gold, and Members of pure Gold; also a Head that cannot die, and therefore the Members cannot die'.

226. *A threefold Cord can't easily broken be*: see Ecclesiastes 4:12 (Geneva).

227. *HOw many ... n'er have seen*: Keach figures the journey to salvation as the journey of the Israelites from Egypt through the Red Sea and the wilderness to Canaan. Cp. De Laune and Keach, *Tropologia*, bk 2, p. 168: 'Christ, the spiritual Way, leads from Sin to Grace, out of Satan's Kingdom to his own Kingdom, from *Egypt* to *Canaan*'.

228. *When others ... honour and renown*: a reference to those nonconformists of whom Keach approved: those who were imprisoned, and whose conscience would not let them take an easy way to liberty. See also above n. 213.

229. *Thou hast ... cares and fears*: cp. the attitude of the rich man, Luke 12:19–21.

230. *Thy Seed establish'd too shall be on Earth*: probably a reference to the seed of the serpent (Satan): Genesis 3:15.

231. *Thoughts of Religion ... most do so*: the Devil's arguments are a caricature of the arguments of 'Freethinkers', on which see J. A. I. Champion, *The Pillars of Priestcraft Shaken: The Church of England and its Enemies, 1660–1730* (Cambridge: Cambridge University Press, 1992).

232. *Come eat and drink, tomorrow thou must die*: cf. 1 Corinthians 15:32–3; Isaiah 22:13.

233. *For a small ... hate and oppose*: Although the sale of indulgences was stopped by the Council of Trent, references to the practice persisted within anti-popish rhetoric. Keach also caricatures papal dispensations here.

234. *Beads*: the rosary.

235. *Shew how ... Charitie*: the Devil points to the divisions between Christians in England, and in particular their failure to treat each other with charity. They prefer instead to ignore Christ's injunction that we love our neighbours as ourselves, favouring either angry disputation or, in the case of some Anglicans, actual persecution. Given its publication date of 1673, *War with the Devil* probably appeared

after the revocation of the second Declaration of Indulgence and the passing of the Test Act in March 1673: see J. Spurr, *England in the 1670s: 'This Masquerading Age'* (Oxford: Blackwell, 2000), pp. 37–9.

236. *For Moses ... never can be told*: cp. Hebrews 11:24–27.

237. *If thou ... bags of mony*: cp. e.g. Deuteronomy 8:7–8.

238. *In that same ... day and night*: Keach obliquely refers to the immorality of Charles II's court, which the Apostate shares.

239. *Sir, Storm ... toss'd about*: while Keach's description of Paul is primarily metaphorical, his language draws on the biblical account of Paul 'being exceedingly tossed with a tempest': Acts 27:18.

240. *Getting the Crown which ne'r away shall fade*: see above n. 222.

241. *The storms ... Righteous to undo*: the extended maritime metaphor used by both the Apostate and the Youth bears some comparison with Quarles, *Emblemes*, bk 3, pp. 169–71. Quarles writes of a stormy sea journey, and ends by calling upon God to aid the hapless sailor. Obviously the Apostate's sense that he has reached a safe port after a tempestuous voyage is, unlike the Youth's, false.

242. *My portion's great*: cp. e.g. Psalm 16:5; Psalm 73:26. Keach later drew attention to these scriptural references in *Tropologia*, at the beginning of the section on 'God a Portion': De Laune and Keach, *Tropologia*, bk 2, p. 6–9.

243. *The Heathens ... best felicity*: see above n. 211.

244. *This writings firm ... curst desire*: cp. Revelation 12:9.

245. *holy Church*: the Roman Catholic Church, which asserted the authoritative status of the Vulgate Bible.

246. *They are unlearn'd ... and Authority*: here Keach makes a point about the Holy Spirit being the true guide for each individual believer, and as such he denigrates Catholic clericalism. On this role (of the Holy Spirit as teacher) see De Laune and Keach, *Tropologia*, bk 3, pp. 323–5, esp. p. 324: 'So the Holy Ghost teacheth Sinners the Knowledg of the Scriptures: for as the Spirit gave them forth so he is the best Interpreter of them: *Then opened be their Understandings, that they might understand the Scriptures. He shall teach you all things, and shall bring my Words to your Remembrance; he shall take of mine and shew it unto you* &c. that is, he shall open and explain my Word and Doctrine to you. How ignorant are some Men of the Scriptures, and of those glorious Mysteries contained therein? notwithstanding all their humane Learning (or that Knowledg they have of Hebrew, Greek, and Latine) for want of the Spirit's Teaching'.

247. *They are unlearn'd ... notorious Whore*: the Youth, caricaturing as he goes, lists a number of what he sees as Catholic false beliefs: justification by works, clericalism, transubstantiation, communion in one kind for the laity, purgatory, the papacy. The final charge suggests that the Catholic 'claim' that the Church has two heads means that the church's role as the bride of Christ alone is sullied. Hence the Catholic Church is referred to as a whore, with the inevitable inference that it is the whore of Babylon.

248. *That man's unlearn'd ... nature he is in*: cp. De Laune and Keach, *Tropologia*, bk 3, p. 324: 'The Holy Ghost teacheth and instructeth poor Sinners gradually, first the *a, b, c,* of Religion, *viz.* the Knowledg of Sin, and their lost and undone Condition thereby; the Vanities of this World, together with the necessity of a Saviour'. Keach also references catechisms. He was a major catechist himself: see Arnold, 'Reformed Theology', ch. 3. On catechisms generally see I. M. Green, *The Christian's ABC: Catechisms and Catechizing in England c. 1530–1740* (Oxford: Clarendon Press, 1996).

249. *That man's unlearn'd ... become a fool*: cp. 1 Corinthians 3:18.

250. *preist and King ... every thing*: see above n. 126.

251. *Or rule over Kings like to the beast at* Rome: a comparison between the Pope and the beast of Revelation.

252. *I never learn'd ... Faith of Catholicks*: the most famous Catholic defence of resistance and tyrannicide was Juan de Mariana's (1536–1623/4) *De rege et regis institutione* (1598). Despite its controversial status among Catholics, and the rejection of resistance by the majority of the English Catholic community, it was still seen by hostile Protestants as emblematic of Catholic thinking. On Mariana see *ODR*.

253. *Or that that upon the neck of Kings he trod*: cf. Joshua 10:24.

254. *I never read ... Idolatry oppose*: the Youth is referring to Catholic persecution of Protestants in general. However in an English context such a statement resonated with the records of the Marian burnings, which had been kept alive in the English imagination, particularly by John Foxe: see J. Miller, *Popery and Politics in England, 1660–88* (Cambridge: Cambridge Univeristy Press, 1973), ch. 4.

255. *I never read ... both in one way*: the Youth compares the Pope with the apostle Peter, to whom Catholics claimed the popes were successors. He draws on a full array of antipopish rhetoric, on which see Miller, *Popery and Politics;* J. Scott, 'England's Troubles: Exhuming the Popish Plot', in T. Harris, P. Seaward and M. Goldie (eds), *The Politics of Religion in Restoration England* (Oxford: Basil Blackwell, 1990), pp. 107–31.

256. *Save only in denying of the Lord*: Peter denied Christ three times, as Chist foretold he would at the Last Supper. Accounts of the denials can be found in Matthew 26:69–75; Mark 14:66–72; Luke 22:54–62; John 18:16–18, 25–27.

257. Peter *and* John ... *Arts have seven*: the pointed comparison between the book-learning of scholars and the humble origins of the apostles was a commonplace in nonconformist literature. 'Arts have seven' is a reference to the seven forms of learning which made up the liberal arts (arranged as an initial trivium of grammar, rhetoric and logic, and a further quadrivium of arithmetic, geometry, astronomy and music).

258. *prating Fools*: cf. Proverbs 10:8. Here, as elsewhere, the Apostate wrests a scriptural phrase from its original context. His use of this term is of course tinged with a particular irony.

259. *When* John ... *and Pearl*: see Revelation 17:4.

260. *No serving God and Mammon*: see Matthew 6:24; Luke 16:13.

261. *narrow way*: see above n. 103.

262. *Their feet on the dark Mountains soon will fall*: see Jeremiah 13:16.

263. *Dost think ... Onyons there*: cf. the misguided attitude of the children of Israel: Numbers 11:5–6. In addition to manna God sends them quails: see Numbers 11:31–32. Keach's use of this imagery might seem at first strange, in that the Israelites are given quails as a result of their lusting after flesh, but they are also punished for this lusting. However, see also Psalm 105:40 which does not focus on their punishment.

264. *This World ... far than vanity*: cp. Psalm 62:9. Also see Quarles on this verse: Quarles, *Emblemes*, bk 1, pp. 17–19.

265. *'tis at best a bubble*: cp. Quarles, *Emblemes*, bk 1, p. 17: 'Lord, what a world is this, which day and night, / Men seek with so much toyl, with so much trouble? / Which weigh'd in equall scales is found so light, / So poorly over-balanc'd with a bubble?'

266. *empty blast*: see above n. 58.

267. *What frantick fit ... fanci'd joy*: cp. Quarles, *Emblemes*, bk 1, p. 17: 'Good God! that frantick mortals should destroy / Their higher hopes, and place their idle joy / Upon such airy trash, upon so light a toy!'

268. *This world's ... to her bed*: cp. Quarles, *Emblemes*, bk 1, p. 18: 'The world's a craftie Strumpet, most affecting / And closely following those that most reject her'.

269. *With amorous glance's ... fains to love*: cp. Quarles, *Emblemes*, bk 1, p. 18: 'O what a Crocodilian world is this, / Compos'd of treacheries, and ensnaring wiles! / She cloaths destruction in a formall kisse, / And lodges death in her deceitfull smiles; / She hugs the soul she hates; and there does prove / The veriest tyrant where she vowes to love, / And is a Serpent most, when most she seems a Dove'.

270. *In* Abrahams *steps I am resolv'd to go*: cp. Romans 4:12.

271. *What* Moses *chose ... exposed am unto*: Keeble comments: 'This is the tenacity required of the saint: he must be not merely bold in undertaking his pilgrimage and watchful in pursuing it but also resolutely determined to complete it'. See N.H. Keeble, *The Literary Culture of Nonconformity in Later Seventeenth-Century England* (Leicester: Leicester University Press, 1987), p. 275.

272. *forsake all things*: cf. Luke 14:33.

273. *good title*: the Apostate refers metaphorically to legal title to land (evidence of the right of possession).

274. *The father ... glory share*: cp. Romans 8:15–17.

275. *inward birth*: see above n. 117.

276. *Those whom God ... Scripture read*: see Romans 8:14.

277. *And that Romes Church can plead antiquity*: the antiquity of the Roman Catholic Church, and the question 'where was your church before Luther?', were two of the biggest polemical weapons in the Roman Catholic armoury: see A. Milton, *Catholic and Reformed: The Roman and Protestant Churches in English Protestant Thought, 1600–1640* (Cambridge: Cambridge University Press, 1995), ch. 6.

278. Romes *Church ... witness bear*: alongside Paul's letter to the Romans, see also Acts 23:11.

279. *But is become th' Scarlet colour'd Whore*: see Revelation 17:4.

280. *Into the dark ... great distress*: see Revelation 12:6. For Keach's choice of language cp. Deuteronomy 32:9–10.

281. *From the vile Beast, and Dragons furious rage*: this continues the reading of the period of Roman Catholic historical dominance through the lens of Revelation. During his career Keach developed an elaborate eschatology, including lengthy exegesis of the precise terms of Revelation: see Arnold, 'Reformed Theology', ch. 7.

282. Go out of Babylon, *doth bid us fly*: cp. Revelation 18:4 (Geneva); Jeremiah 51:6.

283. *A thousand two hunred and sixty year*: the period of 1,260 years is taken from a prophetic interpretation of Revelation 12:6. The woman represents the true Church. The claim that a prophetic day was equal to an actual year was commonplace: see Arnold, 'Reformed Theology', p. 227. It is unclear here as to when precisely Keach believed this 1,260 years to have commenced. Most commentators placed commencement between the deaths of Julian the Apostate (363) and Valentinian (455) (although there was variation in the dating of Julian the Apostate's death in early modern texts): see Arnold, 'Reformed Theology', p. 228.

284. *Out of the Apostacy alas she sprung*: cp. Keach's later more detailed comment in prose on when the Roman Church apostasized from the true church: B. Keach, *Antichrist Stormed* (London: Nath. Crouch, 1689), sig. A2v: ' ... *we conclude that the six first Seals spoken of, Rev. 6. open things that were to come to pass in the World, from the time that* John *received his Revelations until the years* 311 *or* 320, *or thereabouts, which produced,* (1.) *That fearful Apostacy from the Apostolical Faith, and true Christianity of the Gospel Church'*.

285. John Bapist ... *former dispensation*: cp. e.g. John the Baptist in Matthew 3:8–9; Luke 3:8; John the Baptist in John 1:17; Titus 3:5.
286. *The ax ... must be*: a further reference to John the Baptist: see Matthew 3:10; Luke 3:9.
287. *That Church ... Is very false*: cp. 2 Corinthians 10:4.
288. *She's like ... Gods sacred word*: see Revelation 18:2.
289. *The Councel ... Godliness is lacking*: a translation of the final lines of the Carmelite, Baptista Mantuanus's (1448–1516) *In Romam bellis tumultuantem*: 'Vivere qui sancte cupitis discedite, Romae / omnia cum liceant, non licet esse bonum': quoted in Lee Piepho, 'Mantuan's Eclogues in the English Reformation', *Sixteenth Century Journal*, 25:3 (1994), p. 624 n. 6. The lines were cited in numerous anti-Catholic texts in the sixteenth and seventeenth centuries. For more on how Mantuanus's other works were used in the English Reformation to bolster the Protestant cause see Piepho, 'Matuan's Eclogues', pp. 623–32.
290. *She also ... for to wed*: see 1 Timothy 4:1–3.
291. *Though God allow the undefiled bed*: see Hebrews 13:4.
292. *And many ... clearly seen*: cp. the statement of the General Baptist Thomas Grantham: T. Grantham, *The Baptist against the Papist* (London: s.n., 1663), p. 55: 'For I find it laid to the charge of divers Popes, that they were Drunken-Whoremongers, Theeves, given more to War, than Christ, rooted in all unspeakable sin; furious men, prophane Scoffers of Christ; Incestuous persons, Murderers, Poysoners of their own Parents and Kindred; open Sodomites or Buggerers; Blasphemers, incorrigible Hereticks, Enchanters; callers upon the Devil to help them to play at Dice; Drinkers of the Devil's Health, and Traitors to Princes. These things are so notorious and evidently true of the Popes of *Rome*, as that the Papists do not deny them'.
293. *Is Rome ... spotless dove*: the disparity between Rome and the true church is shown in this rhetorical question, which draws on the Song of Solomon for images taken to represent the true church. For more on this see above n. 43.
294. *That truth ... did obey*: it was indeed commonplace to identify Rome as the specific referent of Revelation 17:18: 'And the woman which thou sawest is that great city, which reigneth over the kings of the earth'.
295. *Before him ... his Tyranny*: the Pope had most recently exercised his claimed power over temporal monarchs in *Regnans in Excelsis* (1570), which pronounced the excommunication and deposition of Elizabeth I.
296. *obits*: an obit was an endowed regular service in commemoration of a dead person.
297. *annates,* Peter-*pence*: annates were monies due to the papacy upon its provision of clergy to certain benefices, or, in the case of bishops, sees; Peter's Pence was a tax on the laity which was delivered to Rome. On the eve of the Reformation fewer than £200 a year was collected in Peter's Pence. See A.G. Dickens, *The English Reformation*, 2nd edn (London: Batsford, 1989), p. 64; R. Hoyle, 'War and Public Finance', in D. MacCulloch (ed.), *The Reign of Henry VIII: Politics, Policy and Piety* (Basingstoke: Macmillan, 1995), p. 79.
298. *These ... slaves still to promote her work*: the Janissaries were elite troops in the Ottoman army, drawn from the children of subjected people and thus 'slave warriors': see G. Parker, *The Military Revolution: Military Innovation and the Rise of the West, 1500–1800*, 2nd edn (Cambridge: Cambridge University Press, 1996), p. 125.
299. race: raze.
300. *That drunken ... Martyrs blood*: see Revelation 17:6.
301. Jerusalem ... *burnt and broken down*: Jerusalem was sacked in 70 during the reign of Vespasian (9–79).
302. *vile Strumpits*: cp. the marginal note to Revelation 18:7 (Geneva).

303. *The brutish Nero ... lamentable story*: the Emperor Nero (37–68) had infamously blamed the Christians for the fire in Rome in 64, and was thus held responsible for the persecution that followed. For early modern England, John Foxe's *Acts and Monuments* detailed the first ten persecutions of the primitive church, as referred to here by Keach. The various early texts of Foxe are now available in accurate and searchable forms at http://www.hrionline.ac.uk/johnfoxe/index.html [accessed 16 November 2010].

304. *Iron pen*: cp. Job 19:22–24.

305. *There earthly houses for a heavenly Crown*: cp. 2 Corinthians 5:1. For passages relating to the winning of 'a heavenly Crown' in the face of earthly tribulation see e.g. 1 Corinthians 9:25; 2 Timothy 4:7–8; James 1:12; Revelation 2:10.

306. *As* Egypts darkness did exceed *our night*: see Exodus 10:21–23.

307. Cyprians: St Cyprian (*c.* 200–258) lived through persecution during the reign of Decius (249–51) before being banished by Valerian in 257 and executed in 258. His writings contained much on the history of the church, although unsurprisingly they were also often used by the enemies of nonconformity. See *OCTCL*; J. Spurr, "'A Special Kindness for Dead Bishops": The Church, History, and Testimony in Seventeenth-Century Protestantism', *Huntington Library Quarterly*, 68:1 & 2 (2005), p. 323.

308. Eusebius: Eusebius's (*c.* 260–*c.* 340) most famous and pertinent work was his *Eccelesiastical History*, which was available in the Restoration in English translation and in abridged form.

309. *ten Emperors*: the emperors of the ten persecutions of the primitive church were classically listed as follows: Nero (37–68), Domitian (51–96), Trajan (53–117), Marcus Aurelius (121–80), Severus (145–211), Maximinus (*c.* 173–238), Decius (*c.* 201–51), Valerian (*c.* 200–after 260), Aurelian (*c.* 215–75), Diocletian (244–311) and Maximian (*c.* 250–310). See Augustine, *City of God*, XVIII.52 (although Augustine remains sceptical about such precise enumeration of persecutions).

310. Constantine *the great*: Constantine I (*c.* 272/3–337).

311. *Oh! Let ... hath slain*: see Genesis 4:8–15.

312. *Our blessed Lord ... testifie of me*: see John 5:39.

313. *What Countrey hath not tasted of the Cup*: see Revelation 17:4.

314. *Within the space ... twenty thousand more*: a reference to the St Bartholomew's Day Massacre of 1572 and its aftermath, although Keach would later, following Pierre du Moulin, put the figure killed at more than 80,000: B. Keach, *Sion in Distress* (London: Enoch Prosser, 1681), p. 61.

315. Bellarmine: Cardinal Roberto Bellarmino (1542–1621), Catholic controversialist.

316. *O poor* Bohemia ... *in any age*: the Bohemian Hussites were held up by Protestant martyrologists as exempla of the true church before the sixteenth century. On 17 March 1420 Pope Martin V (1368–1431) (Keach mistakenly writes '*Martin* the sixt') started a crusade to 'destroy all Wycliffites, Hussites, and other heretics in Bohemia'. 'Julian' is Cardinal Giuliano Cesarini (1398–1444), who went into Bohemia with the invading army of Friedrich, Margrave of Brandenburg, in 1431. See 'Hussite Wars (1420–36)', *ODR*. Foxe writes of Cesarini, alongside a marginal note which reads 'The cruell slaughter done by the Cardinall', that: 'the Cardinall entred into Boheme with an huge army, & destroyed many of the protestantes townes, killing men, women, and children, sparing neither olde nor yong: notwithstanding, this his tiranny was exercised in the vttermost borders of Boheme, for his captaines feared to enter farre into the land'. See *Foxe's Book of Martyrs Variorum Edition Online*, http://www.hrionline.ac.uk/johnfoxe/main/5_1583_0656.jsp [accessed 16 November 2010].

317. *Except that Monster ... Divels could invent*: Ferdinando Álvarez de Toledo, third Duke of
Alva (1507–82) was deployed by Philip II to the Netherlands in 1567 and subsequently
became Governor-General. It was intended that he should suppress any remnants of
revolt and Protestantism. The infamous Council of Troubles or Council of Blood was
erected, and, presided over by Alva, tried 12,302 and executed or banished 1,105 of
those believed to be enemies of Spain. The Netherlands went into full revolt in 1572, and
Alva was replaced by Don Luis Requesens in 1573. See 'Alba or Alva', 'Council of Blood',
in *ODR*: J. I. Israel, *The Dutch Republic: Its Rise, Greatness, and Fall, 1477–1806*, pbk
edn (Oxford: Clarendon Press, 1998), pp. 155–183. The six years of persecution under
Alva became an often repeated part of protestant martyrology and anti-popish polemic.
The claim that Alva oversaw the deaths of around 18,000 was a commonplace: cp. e.g.
N. Billingsley, *Brachyy-martyrologia* (London: Tho. Johnson, 1657), pp. 86–7: 'He on
a time (at his own Table sate) / Boasted his diligence t'eradicate / Heret'cal weeds: for
that besides the slain / During the war in six years space, a train / Of more then eighteen
thousand persons were / By him deliv'red to the hangmans care'.
318. *For from the time ... hundred and fifty thousand di'd*: unsurprisingly the Inquisition was
attacked as an instrument of popish tyranny: cp. e.g. P. Du Moulin, *The Accomplishment
of the Prophecies* (Oxford: by Joseph Barnes and are to be sold by John Barnes dwelling
neere Holborne Conduit, 1613), p. 247: 'The punishments of the Inquisition surpasse
all crueltie. The bull of *Phalaris* is nothing in respect of this. A man is carried to prison
not knowing wherefore: after he hath beene cubd up in solitarinesse, and never seene one
glympse of light for a whole yeare together, at last there coms one unto him, and questions with him about certaine interrogatories; if hee say that he is a good Catholike, and
doe renounce his former heresie, hee shall haue this favour to die a more gentle death'.
319. *Much like deluded ... lustful* Dalela: cp. Quarles, *Emblemes*, bk 2, p. 70: 'Take heed thou
trust not the deceitfull lap / Of wanton *Dalilah*; The world's a trap'.
320. *Much like deluded ... Sampsons death*: see Judges 16:15–21. Cp. J. Milton, *Samson Ago-
nistes*, in *CSP*, p. 376, ll. 532–39: 'Then swoll'n with pride into the snare I fell / Of
fair fallacious looks, venereal trains, / Softened with pleasure and voluptuous life; / At
length to lay my head and hallowed pledge / Of all my strength in the lascivious lap / Of
a deceitful concubine who shore me / Like a tame wether, all my precious fleece, / Then
turned me out ridiculous, despoiled, / Shaven, and disarmed among my enemies'.
321. *From the first time ... run their hours out*: the Society of Jesus (Jesuits) was a religious order
founded originally by ten men (including Ignatius Loyola) and given papal sanction in the
bull *Regimini militantis ecclesiae* in 1540. Their declared aim of proselytising in foreign
lands, their later role as a force of the Counter Reformation, the express political radicalism
of some members (see e.g. n. 252 on Mariana above), and their emphasis on ultramon-
tane authority, led inevitably to them being seen as particularly potent and dangerous. See
ODR; Miller, *Popery and Politics*, pp. 29–30. Claims about Jesuit cruelty were rife.
322. *Of the Americans ... fifteen Millions slain*: Keach's polemic is, needless to say, anti-popish
in its portayal of events. The sixteenth-century Spanish conquest in the New World did,
however, wreak demographic havoc, mainly as a result of the spread of European disease
(in New Spain the indigenous population diminished from *c.* 10,000,000 in 1519 to
fewer than 1,000,000 in 1600). See R.P.-C. Hsia. *The World of Catholic Renewal 1540–
1770*, 2nd edn (Cambridge: Cambridge University Press, 2005), pp. 187–96; D.A.
Brading, 'Europe and a World Expanded', in E. Cameron (ed.), *The Sixteenth Century*
(Oxford: Oxford University Press, 2006), ch. 6.

323. *The poor religious* Waldenses ... *lives did end*: the Waldensians were a heretical group originating in the twelfth century, who later Protestants saw (among other groups) as keepers of the true church in the time of papal oppression. See P. Biller, 'Goodbye to Waldensianism?', *Past and Present*, 192:1 (2006), pp. 3–33; E. Cameron, *Waldenses: Rejections of Holy Church in Medieval Europe* (Oxford: Blackwell, 2000), Epilogue. The atrocities which Keach recounts here were detailed elsewhere in different forms. Given his later reference to the work (see below n. 333) it is possible that in his telling of the first atrocity Keach was drawing on S. Morland, *The History of the Evangelical Churches of the Valleys of Piemont* (London: Adoniram Byfield, 1658), bk 2, p. 194: ' ... I shall content my self to begin onely with the Year of our Lord 1400. wherein the Inhabitants of the Valley of *Pragela* were set upon by their Popish Neighbours about the time called *Christmas*, and that in so violent and furious a manner, that those poor Creatures were forced to fly in all haste with their Wives and little one in their arms, to one of the highest Mountains thereabouts ... In this their flight, a very great number of them were overtaken by their Pursuers, whose *Feet were swifter to shed Bloud*, than the Feet of the others to fly, and so were most barbarously murdered. The residue being overtaken by the Night, wandered up & down in the Snow, till such time as their Joints were frozen and become stiff by the extremity of cold, in so much that there were found the next Morning, lying on the Snow, no less than fourscore small Children, and most of their Mothers by them, all frozen to Death, a most miserable Spectacle to behold'.For the second atrocity cp. e.g. S. Clarke, *A General Martyrologie* (London: Thomas Underhill and John Rothwell, 1660), p. 113:

> *Anno* 1488. Pope *Innocent* the eight sent *Albert de capitaneis*, Arch-Deacon of *Cremona* against these *Waldenses*, who craved aid of the Kings Lieutenant of *Dauphine*, against them. This Lieutenant for his service levied troops of men, and at the Arch-Deacons request, led them against the *Waldenses* in the valley of *Loyse*, and to colour his proceedings with a pretence of justice, he took a Counsellour of the Court along with him. But when they came to the valley, they found no inhabitants, for they were all retired into their Caves in the high mountains, having carried their little children, and all their provision of food with them. Then did this cruel Lieutenant cause much wood to be laid to the mouths of the caves, and set it on fire, so that some were choaked with smoak, others burnt with the fire, others cast themselves headlong from the rocks, and were broken in pieces; and if any stirred out, they were presently slain by the souldiers.
>
> In this Persecution, there were found within the Caves four hundred infants stifled in their cradles, or in the arms of their dead mothers: and in all, there perished above three thousand men and women at that time, so that there were no inhabitants left in all that valley ...

324. Titon: used as a term for the sun god. See R. Kirby and J. Bishop, *The Marrow of Astrology* (London: for the authors, 1687), bk 1, p. 50.

325. Proserpina: used as a name for the moon. Kirby and Bishop, *Marrow of Astrology*, bk 1, p. 67.

326. O Germany ... *bloody Murders*: the persecutions of Protestants in Germany were frequently detailed cp. e.g. Billingsley, *Brachyy-martyrologia*, pp. 82–4, 91–6.

327. *bleeding* Ireland: there were manifold printed accounts of atrocities committed by Catholics on Protestants following the outbreak of the Irish rebellion in October 1641. The rebellion was the central subject of one sixth of all pamphlets published from November 1641 to the start of the English Civil War in August 1642: J. Morrill, 'The Causes and

Course of the British Civil Wars', in N.H. Keeble (ed.), *The Cambridge Companion to Writing of the English Revolution* (Cambridge: Cambridge University Press, 2001), pp. 21–2.

328. *Powder-Treason*: the Gunpowder Plot of 1605.

329. *No, no, we cannot … eternal Fall*: on the Great Fire of London, and the claims that it was a Catholic plot, see *Upon the Rebuilding of the City* above, Volume 1 p. 240.

330. *those more formal Protestants*: most prominently Anglicans.

331. *Upon her head … of Blasphemie*: see Revelation 17:3.

332. *I have the keys … others ease*: see the words of Christ to Peter in Matthew 16:19. In Keach's view the words had been used corruptly by the Catholic Church, which claimed the Pope as Peter's successor.

333. *About th' year … Moreland's History*: a reference to the massacre of the Waldensians in Piedmont in 1655, subject of a famous sonnet by Milton. The massacre of Waldensians in Alpine villages by the troops of Charles Emmanuel II, Duke of Savoy began on 24 April 1655. These events, when retold in horrific detail, sent shockwaves through the European Protestant community, and elicited a diplomatic response from Oliver Cromwell. As part of this response Sir Samuel Morland (1625–95) was appointed Commissioner-Extraordinary and despatched to the Duke of Savoy. Following his return to England, by late 1655 Morland published a lengthy, illustrated *History of the Evangelical Churches of the Valleys of Piemont* in 1658. See *CSP*, pp. 341–3; G. Campbell and T.N. Corns, *John Milton: Life, Work, and Thought* (Oxford: Oxford University Press, 2008), pp. 258–60; *ODNB*. The material relating to the 1655 massacre to which Keach points his reader may be found in *History of the Evangelical Churches of the Valleys of Piemont*, esp. bk II, ch. 6.

334. *Two hundred thousand … Bloody men*: see above n. 327. The figures given for the numbers of Protestants killed in the Irish rebellion varied, but 200,000 was commonly suggested.

335. *Peter and John they Rebels were also*: see Acts 4; 5:17–42.

336. *The tares … for to send*: see Matthew 13:24–30.

337. *For he did give … Authority*: see Revelation 13:4.

338. *Rome to a Wolf … he's got his prey*: it is relevant to this construction of Rome as a wolf that the coat of arms of the founding Jesuit Ignatius Loyola bore two wolves: *CSP*, p. 252 n.

339. *A Hammon … too at last*: in the book of Esther Haman was promoted by King Ahasuerus, but the Jewish Mordecai did not bow down to him or show him due 'reverence'. As a result Haman resolved to 'destroy all the Jews', and had a specific gallows prepared for Mordecai. But at a banquet Queen Esther told the King that Haman was an 'enemy'. The King left the banquet, but returned to find that Haman, who had been asking the Queen for his life, had 'fallen upon the bed whereon Esther was'. The King saw this as lustful assault, asking 'Will he force the queen also before me in the house?' Haman was hanged on the gallows intended for Mordecai. See Esther 2–7. Cp. the treatment of this in Quarles, *Emblemes*, bk 4, pp. 209–10.

340. *Hard 'tis … dangerous spaces*: cp. Quarles, *Emblemes*, bk 4, pp. 193–4: 'and he that goes unguided wanders: / Her way is dark, her path untrod, unev'n; / So hard's the way from earth; so hard's the way to Heav'n. / This gvring lab'rinth is betrench'd about / On either hand with streams of sulph'rous fire, / Streams closely sliding, erring in and out, / But seeming pleasant to the fond descrier; / Where if his footsteps trust their own invention, / He falls without redresse, and sinks beyond dimension. / Where shall I seek a Guide? where shall I meet / Some lucky hand to lead my trembling paces? / What trusty Lantern will direct my feet / To scape the danger of these dang'rous places? / What hopes have I to passe without a Guide? / Where one gets safely through, a thousand fall beside'.

341. *For to turn back ... Monument of Salt*: cp. Quarles, *Emblemes*, bk 4, p. 194: 'My backward eyes should nev'r commit that fault, / Whose lasting guilt should build a Monument of Salt'. The reference is to Lot's wife becoming a pillar of salt: Genesis 19:26.

342. *The way I know ... he nothing gains*: this is, for the most part, a version of Quarles, *Emblemes*, bk 2, pp. 105–6.

343. *If Father ... Soul imbrace*: see Psalm 27:10.

344. *run a Race*: see 1 Corinthians 9:24; Hebrews 12:1 quoted below n. 347.

345. *When Sun ... heavy stroke*: a version of Ecclesiastes 12:2–6.

346. *My life a bubble ... quite away*: see the similar phrasing and note on it above p. 30, n. 95.

347. *My weights I'le cast away this race to run*: see Hebrews 12:1.

348. *I must provide me oil, get Grace in store*: most obviously a reference to the parable of the ten virgins in Matthew 25:1–13, but see also De Laune and Keach, *Tropologia*, bk 2, p. 172 (on Christ as a rock, and oil being said to come from rocks): 'Christ affords us Store of precious Oil; the Spirit is so called, with which the Godly are all more or less anointed: *We have received an Unction from the Holy One*. No Oil like that which comes from this Rock'.

349. *And yet but two of them did Canaan enter*: Caleb and Joshua: see Numbers 14:30.

350. *Those who do murmur in the Wilderness*: a reference to the behaviour of the Israelites in the wilderness, and God's denial of Canaan to them as a result: see Numbers 14.

351. *Shall Caleb ... way to Hell*: Caleb was one of the two to enter Canaan: see Numbers 14:24: 'But my servant Caleb, because he had another spirit with him, and hath followed me fully, him will I bring into the land whereinto he went; and his seed shall possess it'.

352. *To think ... Merchant gains*: see Matthew 7:6; Matthew 13:45–46.

353. *Judas ... his dear Lord*: see Matthew 26:15.

354. *Because the sluggard ... to till*: see Proverbs 20:4.

355. *He that ... naught obtain*: see Proverbs 20:4.

356. *nor can I fall away*: Keach succinctly encapsulates the Calvinist position on the perseverance of the saints.

357. *The Promise ... even so our heirs*: cp. Galatians 4:28.

358. John *the Third*: John 3.

359. *All those whom God ... cause too of their fall*: on Keach's theology, as expressed in this lines, see above n. 34.

360. Esau Faint-heart ... *Pottage to obtain*: see above n. 107.

361. Ishmael legal heart: God covenanted with Isaac not Ishmael (Abraham's son with the bondwoman Hagar). See Galatians 4:30. The phrase 'legal heart' refers to one who claims to adhere to the dictates of the law, and who believes that to be sufficient: see above n. 34.

362. *With Master* Balaam: Balaam was called upon by Balak to curse the people of God, but due to God's intervention he was unable to complete this task: see Numbers 22–24. Keach's specific point is neatly encapsulated in De Laune and Keach, *Tropologia*, bk 3, p. 32: 'There is also as the effects of this Reconciliation, Peace and sweet Harmony in the Soul between all the Faculties; they do not fight as formerly one against another, the Conscience drawing one way & the will another, the Will opposing that which Conscience would have done, the Judgment may be convinced in some measure as *Balaams* was, who cryed out that Gods wayes were best, *how Goodly are thy tents O Jacob, and thy tabernacles O Israel*, and yet the Affections may be for sin, and love the wages of unrighteousness'. The scriptural quotation is from Numbers 24:5.

363. Goliah: Goliath, Philistine giant slain by David: see 1 Samuel 17. It may be significant here that 'when the Philisitine looked about, and saw David, he disdained him: for he was but a youth, and ruddy, and of a fair countenance': see 1 Samuel 17:42.

364. *By Nature's ... glory shine*: Keach returns here to an attack on deist and atheist arguments, based upon a particular notion of rationality which questioned the authority of revelation. See above n. 34, and J. Spurr, '"Rational Religion" in Restoration England', *Journal of the History of Ideas*, 49:4 (1988), pp. 563–85.

365. *It brings them out of darkness into light*: see above n. 33.

366. *Power*: cp. 2 Samuel 22:3, 51; Psalm 18:2; Psalm 61:3; Psalm 144:2; Proverbs 18:10.

367. *How have ... their Names*: Keach returns to the theme of martyrdom: see above p. 99.

368. Belshazar's *fall*: see above n. 51.

369. *How many ... glorious Majesty*: cp. n. 91 above.

370. *If you ... yielding to the Devil*: this nonconformist defence of a particular concept of reason leading away from atheism is further explored in Spurr, '"Rational Religion"'.

371. Epicurus: Epicurus (341–271 BC), Greek originator of Epicureanism.

372. Aristotle: Aristotle (384–322 BC) in his *Metaphysics* did hold that there was an 'unmoved mover', but this was so far removed from Keach's conception of God that he had no problem with labelling him an atheist.

373. Theodorus: Theodorus the Atheist (*c.* 340–250 BC).

374. Bion: Bion the Borysthenite (*c.* 325–*c.* 246 BC), Greek philosopher, not of any one school but nearest in his work to the Cynics. See *OCTCL*. Bion was reputed to have been, through the influence of Theodorus, an atheist for some time at least, see e.g. R. Baxter, *The Reasons of the Christian Religion* (London: Fran. Titon, 1667), p. 134.

375. *Because on earth ... Sots could not espy*: cp. Jude 1:10; 2 Peter 2:12.

376. *Yet many ... descend or spring*: Keach returns again to what it was possible for heathens without revelation to know: see above p. 62.

377. *And unto* Noah's *Dove ... being show*: cp. Genesis 8:6–12.

378. *I am become like to the troubled Seas*: cp. Isaiah 57:20.

Wild, *A Panegyrique Humbly Addrest to the Kings ... Majesty ... Delivered*

1. *A Panegyrique ... that Occasion*: Wild's poem borrows so heavily from Edmund Waller's panegyric addressed to Oliver Cromwell that it is necessary to reproduce it in its entirety: see Headnote. The copy text is W507 E. Waller, *A Panegyrick to my Lord Protector* (London: printed by Thomas Newcomb, 1655).

> *A*
> PANEGYRICK
> TO MY
> Lord Protector.

WHILE with a strong, and yet a gentle Hand
    You bridle Faction, and our Hearts command;
Protect us from our Selves, and from the Foe;
Make us United, and make us Conquer too;
    Let partial Spirits still aloud complain,
Think themselves injur'd that they cannot Raign,
And own no Liberty, but where they may
Without controule upon their Fellows prey.

Above the Waves as *Neptune* shew'd his Face
To chide the Winds, and save the *Trojan* Race;
So has your Highness rais'd above the rest
Storms of Ambition tossing us represt:
    Your drooping Country torn with Civill Hate,
Restor'd by you, is made a glorious State;
The seat of Empire, where the *Irish* come,
And the unwilling *Scotch* to fetch their doome.
The Sea's our own, and now all Nations greet
With bending Sayles each Vessel of our Fleet;
Your Power extends as farr as Winds can blowe,
Or swelling Sayles upon the Globe may goe.
    Heav'n, that has plac'd this Island to give Lawe,
To balance *Europe*, and her States to awe,
In this Conjunction does on *Brittain* smile,
The greatest Leader, and the greatest Ile;
Whether this portion of the World were rent
By the rude Ocean from the Continent,
Or thus Created, it was sure design'd
To be the Sacred Refuge of Mankind.
Hither th'oppressed shall henceforth resort,
Justice to crave, and Succour at your Court;
And then your Highness, not for ours alone,
But for the Worlds Protector shall be known:
Fame, swifter then your winged Navie, flyes
    Through every Land that near the Ocean lyes,
Sounding your Name, and telling dreadfull newes
To all that Piracy and Rapine use:
With such a Chief the meanest Nation blest,
Might hope to lift her Head above the rest;
What may be thought impossible to doe
For us embraced by the Sea and You?
    Lords of the Worlds great Waste, the Ocean, wee
    Whole Forrests send to Raigne upon the Sea,
And ev'ry Coast may trouble or relieve,
But none can visit us without your leave;
Angels and we have this Prerogative,
That none can at our happy Seat arrive,
While we descend at pleasure to invade
The Bad with vengeance, or the good to aide:
Our little World, the Image of the Great,
Like that amidst the boundless Ocean set,
Of her own Growth has all that Nature craves,
And all that's Rare as Tribute from the Waves;
As *Egypt* does not on the Clouds rely,
But to her *Nyle* owes more, then to the Sky;
So what our Earth, and what our Heav'n denies,
Our ever constant Friend, the Sea, supplies;

The taste of hot *Arabia*'s Spice we know,
Free from the scorching Sun that makes it grow;
Without the Worm in *Persian* Silks we shine,
And without Planting Drink of every Vine;
　To digg for Wealth we weary not our Limbs,
Gold, though the heavy'st Metall, hither swims;
Ours is the Harvest where the *Indians* mowe,
We plough the Deep, and reap what others Sowe.
Things of the noblest kinde our own soyle breeds,
Stout are our men, and Warlike are our Steeds;
Rome, though her Eagle through the world had flown,
Could never make this Island all her own;
Here the third *Edward*, and the black Prince too,
France conqu'ring *Henry* flourisht, and now You
For whom we stay'd, as did the *Grecian* State,
Till *Alexander* came to urge their Fate:
　When for more Worlds the *Macedonian* cry'de,
He wist not *Thetis* in her Lapp did hide
Another yet, a world reserv'd for you
To make more great, then that he did subdue:
He safely might old Troops to Battail leade
Against th'unwarlike *Persian*, and the *Mede*,
Whose hastie flight did, from a bloodless Field,
More Spoyle then Honor to the Victor yield;
　A race unconquer'd, by their Clyme made bold,
The *Calidonians* arm'd with want and cold,
Have, by a fate indulgent to your Fame,
Bin, from all Ages, kept, for you to tame,
Whom the old *Roman* wall so ill confin'd,
With a new chain of Garisons you bind,
Here forraign Gold no more shall make them come,
Our *English* Iron holds them fast at home;
They, that henceforth must be content to know,
No warmer Region then their Hills of Snow,
May blame the Sun, but must extoll your Grace,
Which in our Senate has allow'd them place;
Preferr'd by Conquest, happily o'rethrowne,
Falling they rise, to be with us made one;
So kinde Dictators made, when they came home,
Their vanquish'd Foes, free Citizens of *Rome*.
　Like favor find the *Irish*, with like Fate
　Advanc'd to be a portion of our State;
While by your Valour, and your Courteous mind
Nations divided by the Sea are joyn'd.
　Holland, to gain your Friendship, is content
To be our Out-guard on the Continent;
Shee from her fellow-Provinces would goe,
Rather then hazard to have you her Foe:

In our late Fight when Cannons did diffuse
Preventing posts, the terror and the newes
Our neighbor-Princes trembled at their rore,
But our Conjunction makes them tremble more.
    Your never-fayling Sword made War to cease,
And now you heale us with the arts of Peace,
Our minds with bounty, and with awe engage,
Invite affection, and restrain our rage:
Less pleasure take, brave minds in battails won,
Then in restoring such as are undon,
Tygers have courage, and the rugged Bear,
But man alone can, whom he conquers, spare.
To pardon willing, and to punish loath,
You strike with one hand, but you heal with both,
Lifting up all that prostrate lie, you grieve
You cannot make the dead again to live:
When Fate, or Error had our Age mis-led,
And o'r these Nations such confusion spred,
The onely cure which could from Heav'n come down,
Was so much Power and Clemency in one.
    One, whose Extraction from an ancient Line,
Gives hope again that well-born Men may shine,
The meanest in your Nature milde and good,
The noble rest secured in your Blood.
Oft have we wonder'd how you hid in Peace
A minde proportion'd to such things as these?
How such a Ruling-spirit you could restrain?
And practice first over your self to raign?
Your private Life did a just pattern give
How Fathers, Husbands, pious Sons, should live,
Born to command, your Princely vertues slept
    Like humble *David*'s, while the Flock he kept;
But when your troubled Countrey call'd you forth,
Your flaming Courage, and your Matchless worth
Dazeling the eyes of all that did pretend
To fierce Contention, gave a prosp'rous end:
Still as you rise, the State exalted too,
Finds no distemper, while 'tis chang'd by you.
Chang'd like the Worlds great Scene, when without noise,
The rising Sun Nights vulgar Lights destroyes.
    Had you some Ages past, this Race of glory
Run, with amazement, we should read your story;
But living Virtue, all atchievements past,
Meets Envy still to grapple with at last.
This *Cesar* found, and that ungrateful Age
Which losing him, fell back to blood and rage:
Mistaken *Brutus* thought to break their yoke,
But cut the Bond of Union with that stroke.

That Sun once set, a thousand meaner Stars,
Gave a dim light to Violence and Wars,
To such a Tempest, as now threatens all,
Did not your mighty Arm prevent the fall.

    If *Romes* great Senate could not weild that Sword,
Which of the Conquer'd world had made them Lord,
What hope had ours, while yet their power was new,
To rule victorious Armies but by you?
You that had taught them to subdue their Foes,
Could Order teach, and their high Spirits compose,
To every Duty could their Minds engage,
Provoke their Courage, and command their Rage.
So when a Lyon shakes his dreadfull Mayn,
And angry growes, if he that first took pain
To tame his youth, approach the haughty Beast,
He bends to him, but frights away the rest.
As the vex'd World to finde repose at last
It self into *Augustus* arms did cast;
So *England* now does with like toyle opprest,
Her weary Head upon your Bosome rest.

    Then let the Muses with such Notes as these
Instruct us what belongs unto our peace;
Your Battails they hereafter shall indite,
And draw the Image of our *Mars* in fight:
Tell of Towns storm'd, of Armies over-run,
And mighty Kingdomes by your Conduct won;
How while you thunder'd, Clouds of Dust did choak
Contending Troops, and Seas lay hid in smoak:
Illustrious acts high Raptures doe infuse,
And every Conqueror creates a Muse.

    Here in low Strains your milder Deeds we sing,
But there (my Lord) we'll Bayes and Olive bring
To Crown your Head, while you in Triumph ride
O're vanquish'd Nations, and the Sea beside;
While all your Neighbor-Princes unto you
Like *Joseph*'s Sheaves pay rev'rence and bow.
      FINIS.

2.   *His Auspicious ... that Occasion*: the eleventh session of the Cavalier parliament met on 4 February 1673, and on 5 February the King addressed it concerning supply for the Third Anglo-Dutch War and his intention that the Declaration of Indulgence should remain in place. See Headnote.

3.   *Those* Fiercer ... Head *to rest*: the civil wars and Interregnum are figured as a sickness cured by the return of Charles II. Wild had previously extensively used the metaphor of the sick England in his most famous poem, *Iter Boreale*, which contained a detailed account of the collapse of the interregnal regimes and looked forward to the return of the King: see above Volume 1, p. 1.

4. *When* Fate ... *away the rest*: Wild appropriates and reorders a series of images which Waller used to praise Cromwell for bringing peace and asserting his authority.
5. *By* sweet ... *as* Peace: a public version of the treaty with France was released in February 1672, and war was declared on the Dutch in March. See Headnote.
6. *And Heal, as well with* Needful Wars, *as* Peace: cf. Waller, *A Panegyrick*: 'Your never-fayling Sword made War to cease, / And now you heale us with the arts of Peace'. Cp. *His Majesties most Gracious Speech ... February 4. and Wednesday February 5* (London: printed by the assigns of John Bill and Christopher Barker, 1673), p. 3: '*Since you were last here, I have been forced to a most important, necessary, and expensive War*'.
7. *Some think* ... Continent: Early modern antiquaries, for example John Twyne (*c.* 1505–81) and William Camden (1551–1623), had posited that at one stage Britain had been connected by land to the continent. Twyne wrote of how this land had been eroded away by the surrounding seas. See W. Poole, *The World Makers: Scientists of the Restoration and the Search for the Origins of the Earth* (Peter Lang: Witney, 2010), p. 86.
8. *By the rude Ocean, from the* Continent: Wild tellingly omits lines from Waller's poem which praise Cromwellian Britain as a haven from oppression. Cf. Waller, *A Panegyrick*: 'Or thus Created, it was sure design'd / To be the Sacred Refuge of Mankind. / Hither th'oppressed shall henceforth resort, / Justice to crave, and Succour at your Court; / And then your Highness, not for ours alone, / But for the Worlds Protector shall be known'.
9. *But whilst* ... *to* Joyne: on the various versions of the Anglo-French treaty see Headnote.
10. Algiers ... *Noble* Spragg: Sir Edward Spragge (*c.* 1629–73) was admiral during the triumph over the Algerine fleet at Bugia Bay in May 1671. Peace terms were agreed with Algiers later that year. See *ODNB*; *Articles of Peace and Commerce* (London: printed by the assigns of John Bill, & Christopher Barker, 1672).
11. *And* greater Pyrates ... Universe *their* only *Prey*: the Dutch. The claim that the Dutch aimed at universal dominion was widely made. However by this stage popular hostility was starting to gather around fears that the French were seeking such power, and the clearly satirical intent of Wild's poem means that its anti-Dutch language cannot be simply interpreted. See S. Pincus, 'From Butterboxes to Wooden Shoes: The Shift in English Popular Sentiment from Anti-Dutch to Anti-French in the 1670s', *Historical Journal*, 38:2 (1995), pp. 333–61.
12. Third Edward ... Henry *flourisht*: Edward III (1312–77); Edward, Prince of Wales, the Black Prince (1330–76); Henry V (1386–1422). Wild omits Waller's epithet for Henry, '*France* conqu'ring'. Ostensibly this change allows for the fact that at the time Wild was writing, England and France were in league against the Dutch. But Wild's audience would obviously have remained aware that the greatest victories of those named were against the French, and as before Wild's satirical intent makes his anti-Dutch language difficult to interpret.
13. Alexander: Alexander the Great (356–323 BC).
14. Mighty York ... Belgian *Shore*: James, Duke of York (1633–1701) was Lord High Admiral, and was personally involved in the Third Anglo–Dutch War at the battle of Southwold Bay in May 1672. However, in the course of the battle he had to change ships twice due to the damage inflicted on his vessels by the Dutch. He did not participate in another naval battle, and Rupert, Prince of the Rhine (1619–82) instead commanded the fleet. In 1672 Charles II's illegitimate son, James Scott, Duke of Monmouth (1649–85), was put in charge of British troops dispatched to aid Louis XIV in war with the Dutch. See *ODNB*.

15. *For whom ... Sweetness Temper it*: These lines are for the most part Wild's addition to Waller, and are specifically focused on the Third Anglo-Dutch War. See Headnote.

16. *Prefer'd ... made one*: Wild turns Waller's lines concerning the situation of the Scots in the 1650s into a couplet which looks forward to the condition which the compliant, vanquished Dutch might enjoy.

17. *That* Aiery Liberty, *whereof they Boast*: the Dutch Republic was (in)famous for its religious toleration.

18. *That* Aiery Liberty ... *Pious* Kings: these lines are a notable addition to Waller's.

19. *No* Freedom, *like the* Rule *of Pious* Kings: the position of the comma in this line is significant. It allows the reading that 'Pious *Kings*' (ie. Charles II (1630–85) and Louis XIV (1638–1715)) in actuality provide 'No *Freedom*' at all. I am grateful to Tom Freeman for this point. See further below n. 20.

20. *So kind* Dictators ... *of* Rome: Timothy Raylor explains in relation to Waller's poem that he here 'invokes the policy of 'donating' (the aptness of the term is arguable) *ius Latii*, a limited form of Roman citizenship, to the citizens of incorporated territories – a policy for which the Consul Camillus (five times dictator: hence Waller's "kind dictators") had argued in Livy's *History* (VIII. xiii. 11–18; cf. VIII. xxi), and whose arguments were quoted approvingly by Machiavelli (*Discourses*, II. xxiii).' See T. Raylor, 'Waller's Machiavellian Cromwell: The Imperial Argument of *A Panegyrick to my Lord Protector*', *Review of English Studies*, 56:225 (2005), p. 405. However, what in Waller's poem is praise for Cromwell's policy in classical terms, in Wild's takes on an anti-popish edge. To be a citizen of Rome in the context of Wild's poem has an inevitable religious implication: the freedom offered by 'Pious *Kings*' is in fact the spurious liberty of popery.

21. *They Thank ... to come*: see the discussion of dating above, Headnote.

22. *Kings greatest Treasures, are their Subjects Hearts*: cp. James VI and I, 'A Speach to the Lords and Commons ... Wednesday XXI. of March. Anno 1609 [ie. 1610]', in his *The Workes* (London: printed by Robert Barker and John Bill, 1616), p. 540: 'for the hearts and riches of the people, are the Kings greatest treasure'.

23. *Whilst your Arms ... to sing*: These lines are Wild's addition to Waller, and for the most part concentrate on the parliament that met in February 1673. See Headnote.

24. *Like* Josephs *Sheaves, pay Reverence, and* Bowe: see Genesis 37:7.

Keach, *An Elegy on the Death of that most Laborious ... John Norcot*

1. *David for* Jonathon *was sore distrest*: the intense friendship of David and Jonathan, son of Saul, is recounted in 1 Samuel 18–20, 23. See also 2 Samuel 1:25–6.

2. *Beloved* John *is gone, dear* Norcot's *dead*: John Norcot (d. 1676), the subject of the elegy. See Headnote.

3. *There's few ... Stygian Lake*: cp. Conscience's words in *War with the Devil*, above p. 13: 'What though they will of me no warning take, / 'Till they drop down into the *Stygian* Lake?'

4. *Like as a Candle ... the urn*: cp. Matthew 5:15 and Luke 11:36.

5. *O were ... universal groan*: cp. R. Wild, *On the Death of Mr Calamy*, Volume 1, p. 185: 'For had this Prophet's Funeral been known, / It must have had an Universal Groan'.

6. *'Twould pierce ... nor look*: As a nonconformist, Norcot was subject to the legal strictures on dissent. Norcot was one of the few Baptists who held a living in the national Church in the 1650s. He was ejected from it in 1662. See G. F. Nuttall, 'Another Baptist Ejection (1662): The Case of John Norcott', in W. Brackney and P. S. Fiddes (eds), *Pilgrim*

Pathways: Essays in Baptist History in Honour of B. R. White (Macon (GA): Mercer University Press, 1999), pp. 185–8; Headnote.

7. Sodome: London is figured as the famously corrupt biblical city Sodom: see Genesis 19:1–26; Jude 1:7.

8. *Well may ... above*: cp. 'An Achrostick upon his Dear Deceased Friend Mr. Vavasor Powell', Volume 1, p. 249: 'Slighted Ambassadors, when called home, / Often bespeaks great evils for to come'; 2 Corinthians 5:20.

9. *Look for new flames*: The Great Fire had torn through London in 1666, see Volume 1, p. 240.

10. Lots: The righteous Lot was allowed to escape the destruction of Sodom: see Genesis 19:12–26 and 2 Peter 2:6–8.

11. *When that Harvest ... wound's not small*: Keach's point is apocalyptic. See Christ's explanation of the parable of the tares: Matthew 13:39. Cp. Revelation 14:15.

12. *Ravening Wolves*: See Matthew 7:15.

13. *Have we ... Lambs out of the fold*: Keach's point is broadly anti-popish, although it may also apply to persecutory Anglicans. The coat of arms of the founding Jesuit Ignatius Loyola bore two wolves: *CSP*, p. 252 n.

14. *When Pylots die ... flocks become*: Keach's lines bear some comparison with J. Milton, *Lycidas*, in *CSP*, pp. 250–2, ll. 108–131: 'Last came, and last did go, / The pilot of the Galilean lake, / Two massy keys he bore of metals twain, / (The golden opes, the iron shuts amain) / He shook his mitred locks, and stern bespake, / How well could I have spared for thee, young swain, / Enow of such as for their bellies' sake, / Creep and intrude, and climb into the fold? / Of other care they little reckoning make, / Than how to scramble at the shearers' feast, / And shove away the worthy bidden guest; / Blind mouths! that scarce themselves know how to hold / A sheep-hook, or have learned aught else the least / That to the faithful herdman's art belongs! / What recks it them? What need they? They are sped; / And when they list, their lean and flashy songs / Grate on their scrannel pipes of wretched straw, / The hungry sheep look up, and are not fed, / But swoll'n with wind, and the rank mist they draw, / Rot inwardly, and foul contagion spread: / Besides what the grim wolf with privy paw / Daily devours apace, and nothing said, / But that two-handed engine at the door, / Stands ready to smite once, and smite no more.'

15. *chiefest Shepherd*: Christ.

16. *The narrow Sluces ...thaw to nothing*: a version of F. Quarles, *Emblemes* (London: I.W. and F.E., 1669), bk 3, VIII, pp. 157–8: 'These narrow sluces of my dribling eyes / Are much too streight for those quick springs that rise / And hourly fill my Temples to the top; / I cannot shed for ev'ry sin a drop: / Great builder of mankind, why hast thou sent, / Such swelling floods, and made so smal a vent? / O that this flesh had been compos'd of snow, / Instead of earth; and bones of ice, that so, / Feeling the fervor of my sin; and loathing / The fire I feel, I might be thaw'd to nothing!'

17. *He did ... prise hath won*: see 1 Corinthians 9:24.

18. He lies but here asleep ... raign: cp. 1 Corinthians 15:20. Figuring death as sleep was commonplace in epitaphs: see P. Sherlock, *Monuments and Memory in Early Modern England* (Aldershot: Ashgate, 2008), p. 74.

Wild, *An Exclamation against Popery*

1. *Occasioned by ... Protestant Religion*: In his speech of 9 November 1678, Charles II told his parliament 'that I do as much study your Preservation too, as I can possibly; and that I am as ready to joyn with you in all the ways and means that may Establish a firm Security of the Protestant Religion, as your own hearts can wish.' Furthermore, he told them 'That whatsoever reasonable Bills you shall present to be Passed into Laws, to make you Safe in the Reign of any Successor (so as they tend not to Impeach the Right of Succession, nor the Descent of the Crown in the true Line, and so as they restrain not My Power, nor the Just Rights of any Protestant Successor) shall find from Me a ready Concurrence.' See *His Majesties most Gracious Speech to both Houses of Parliament, on Saturday 9ᵗʰ of November, 1678* (London: printed by John Bill, Christopher Barker, Thomas Newcomb, and Henry Hills, 1678), p. 4; Headnote.
2. Jesuites: the Society of Jesus (Jesuits) was a particular focus of animosity during the Exclusion Crisis, and was the key player in the tale of conspiracy woven by Titus Oates. See J. Kenyon, *The Popish Plot* (London: Heinemann, 1972), pp. 54–8; Headnote.
3. *Call Bloody* Brutus *up, Lean* Cassius *too*: Marcus Junius Brutus (*c*. 85–42 BC) and Gaius Cassius Longinus, conspirators against Julius Caesar. Cp. Shakespeare, *Julius Caesar*, I.ii.193: 'Yond Cassius has a lean and hungry look'.
4. *Let* Faux, *and* Catesby *both, be of the Crew!* –: Guy Fawkes (bap. 1570, d. 1606) and Robert Catesby (*c*. 1572–1605), infamous Roman Catholic conspirators in the Gunpowder Plot of November 1605.
5. BULLS *run*: a pun on papal bulls.
6. Senators: In keeping with the poem's later distinction between the glories of classical Rome and contemporary papist corruption, parliament is figured positively as the Roman senate.
7. *Will warm our Hands at Bone-fires, Bells shall Ring*: traditional modes of celebration. This line may also specifically refer to the pope-burning processions, held on 17 November (Elizabeth I's accession day), which punctuated the period: see O. Johnson, 'Pope-Burning Pageants: Performing the Exclusion Crisis', *Theatre Survey*, 37:1 (1996), pp. 35–57.
8. Tybourn's: Tyburn, London's main place of execution.
9. *Gay as the* Idol, *fills the* Porph'ry *Chair*: the idol is the pope. It was claimed that incoming popes were tested to ensure their sex. They were seated on a porphyry chair, and a cardinal, putting his hand through a hole in the base of the chair, would grasp the pope's testicles. Two porphyry chairs did form part of papal ceremonial, but the sex-test was a fabrication. It was linked to the myth that there had been a female pope, Pope Joan, and was seen as a ceremony instituted to avoid the possibility of another woman ascending to the papal throne. See E. Duffy, *Saints and Sinners: A History of the Popes*, 3rd edn (New Haven and London: Yale University Press, 2006), pp. 157–8.
10. Godfrey's: Sir Edmund Berry Godfrey (1621–78), magistrate who heard Titus Oates' depositions concerning the Popish Plot in September 1678, and who was killed in mysterious circumstances in October. His death was blamed on Catholics. See *ODNB*; Headnote.
11. Manes: ghost 'demanding to be propitiated.' See *OED*.
12. *Scarlet* Harlot: the whore of Babylon: a typical way of referring to the Church of Rome. See Revelation 17:4–5.

13. *What! is the* Eagle ...*Vagabonds imploy*: A comparison between the ancient Rome of Caesar (symbolized by the eagle) and its current corrupted state under the Pope. See also above n. 3.
14. *Bribe Men ... growing Flame*: the Great Fire of 1666 was widely blamed on Catholics Volume 1, p. 240. Plans for another fire were said to be part of the Popish Plot. See Kenyon, *Popish Plot*, p. 57.

Wild, *Oliver Cromwells ghost: or Old Noll newly Revived*

1. *Oliver Cromwells*: Oliver Cromwell (1599–1658), Lord Protector (1653–58). See Headnote.
2. *Bantlings*: small children, *OED*.
3. *Of* Treason, *and the* Sacred Blood *I* spilt: a reference to the execution of Charles I on 30 January 1649, and the key role which Cromwell played in its accomplishment.
4. *Those crouds ... strickt* Religion: Despite the religious toleration of the Cromwellian era (which itself was considered contemptible by many), it was a period that was remembered by many for its 'strickt *Religion*', and the attempts made to further the reformation of manners and impose morality on a recalcitrant populace. Such attempts were not successful, but remained burned into English memories. See e.g. D. Hirst, 'The Failure of Godly Rule in the English Republic', *Past & Present*, 132 (1991), pp. 33–66.
5. *Twenty Years*: Oliver Cromwell died on 3 September 1658.
6. *Bloody Regicide*: most likely another of those involved in the trial and execution of Charles I.
7. *Thou in ... could do before*: the Popish Plot. See Headnote.
8. *A Pious Justice ... in his Gore*: the magistrate Sir Edmund Berry Godfrey (1621–78), before whom Titus Oates had sworn depositions concerning the Popish Plot, was found dead on 17 October 1678. See above p. 168.
9. *Strange Cormorant*: the cormorant was considered voracious. Satan sits 'like a cormorant' on the tree of life in *Paradise Lost*: J. Milton, *Paradise Lost*, ed. A. Fowler, 2nd edn (London and New York: Longman, 1998), IV, ll. 195–6.
10. *three Butcher'd Lands*: England, Scotland and Ireland.
11. *When in fierce* Whilwinds *you had born me hence*: On 2 September, the day before Cromwell died, there was a great storm. This storm was linked to Cromwell's death in both hostile and elegiac texts. See e.g. the imagined dialogue between Charles I and Oliver Cromwell in the hostile *The Court Career* ([London]: s.n., 1659), p. 3:
     Charles. H*OW now NOLL! what wind blew you thither?*
     Noll. The fiercest and furiousest *Whirlwind* that ever breathed on the *middle Region*.
     References to the storm in elegiac verse may be found in E. Waller, 'Upon the Late Storme and Death of his Highnesse', in *Three Poems Upon the Death of his Late Highness* (London: printed by William Wilson, 1659), pp. 30–2; A. Marvell, 'A Poem Upon the Death of his Late Highness the Lord Protector', in *Poems*, pp. 306–7, ll. 113–22. See also the idiosyncratic G. Wither, *Salt Upon Salt* (London: L. Chapman, 1659). There are also numerous, potentially relevant, scriptural references to whirlwinds. Cp. e.g. Proverbs 10:25; Jeremiah 23:19.
12. *And by the Pow'r ... Owners hand*: the Restoration of Charles II in 1660, which is looked forward to in Wild's most famous poem, *Iter Boreale*, see Volume 1, p. 1.
13. *Porphry Idol*: the Pope. See n. 9 to *A Exclamation against Popery*, above p. 399.
14. *Colds*: presumably 'clouds'.

15. Brewers Family: Cromwell's great grandfather, Morgan Williams, had been a brewer in Putney, and Cromwell was regularly depicted in hostile literature as a brewer: see L. L. Knoppers, '"Sing Old Noll the Brewer": Royalist Satire and Social Inversion, 1648–1660', *The Seventeenth Century*, 15:1 (2000), pp. 32–51; *ODNB*.

16. *Nay, so intemperate ... tott'ring Seat*: Cromwell, seen as ambitious and proud, was widely thought to have aimed at the Crown, but 'mist'. In fact the reasons for his refusal of the crown were more complex. He did, as is intimated here, 'become king in all but name.' See Morrill, 'Oliver Cromwell'; B. Worden, 'Oliver Cromwell and the Sin of Achan', in D. Beales and G. Best (eds), *History, Society and the Churches: Essays in Honour of Owen Chadwick* (Cambridge: Cambridge University Press, 1985), pp. 125–45.

17. *Not doubting ... my Posteritie*: It was widely thought in the late seventeenth century that Cromwell had nominated his eldest living son Richard to follow him as Lord Protector, and that he had thus established a hereditary succession. This belief informs the poem at this point: Cromwell's ghost, king-like, claims that when living he expected his 'Posteritie' to rule after him. However, it now seems very unclear that Oliver did, in fact, nominate Richard. See J. Fitzgibbons, '"Not in Any Doubtfull Dispute"? Reassessing the Nomination of Richard Cromwell', *Historical Research*, 83:220 (2010), pp. 281–300.

18. *Farewel*: The reader might, due to the climactic progress of the rhyme scheme, legitimately expect the final words to be 'in hell'.

Wild, *Dr. Wild's Poem. In Nova Fert Animus*

1. IN NOVA FERT ANIMUS, *&c.*: see Ovid, *Metamorphoses*, I, ll. 1–2 (ed. Miller, rev. Goold, p. 2–3): 'In nova fert animus mutatas dicere formas corpora' ('My mind is bent to tell of bodies changed into new forms'). In the early seventeenth century George Sandys translated the line (quoted here from a late seventeenth-century edition): 'OF Bodies chang'd to other shapes I sing.' See G. Sandys, *Ovid's Metamorphosis Englished* (London: G. Sawbridge, A. Roper, T. Basset, J. Wright, and R. Chiswell, 1678), p. 1.

2. *New Parliament*: The first Exclusion Parliament met on 6 March 1679. See Headnote.

3. Athenian-*Itch*: see Acts 17:21. The phrase 'Athenian itch' had a pre-history in Presbyterian discourse, see e.g. T. Manton, *A Practical Commentary, or An Exposition with Notes on the Epistle of Jude* (London: Luke Fawn, 1658), p. 249: 'That it is a spiritual disease, *a Surfet of Manna*, when men must still be fed with *new things;* no truths are *too plain* for our *mouths,* or *too stale* for your *ears;* the itch of novelty puts men upon *ungrounded subtleties,* and that maketh way for *errour,* or *hardness of heart,* though you hear nothing but what you are acquainted with be content; they were carnal people that complained they had nothing but the *old Burden,* Jer. 23. 33, 34. Take heed of the *Athenian itch,* many times it argueth *guilt'*; T. Hall, *A Practical and Polemical Commentary, or, Exposition Upon the Third and Fourth Chapters of the Latter Epistle of Saint Paul to Timothy* (London: John Starkey, 1658), p. 354: 'There is an Athenian Itch when men are all for *Noveltie,* They must have *Novum aut nihil.* Ordinary Truths will not down with them, they must have New-notions which are extraordinary'; S. Clarke, *A Collection of the Lives of Ten Eminent Divines* (London: William Miller, 1662) p. 59 (on John Cotton (1585–1652)): 'And afterwards being again called to preach in the same place (as one Oration of *Pericles* left his hearers with an Appetite after another) so the memory of his former accurate Exercises, filled the Colleges, especially the young Students, with a fresh expectation of such Elegancies of Learning, as made them flock to the Sermon with

an *Athenian* Itch after some new thing, as to the ornaments of *Rhetorick,* and abstruser notions of *Philosophy.'*

4. *News, and new Things so the whole World bewitch*: this line was to be frequently used by the publisher John Dunton (1659–1732). It is relevant that Dunton's most significant publication was called the *Athenian Mercury*. See J. P. Hunter, '"News, and New Things": Contemporaneity and the Early English Novel', *Critical Inquiry*, 14:3 (1988), p. 493; *ODNB*.

5. *Carve a new Nose out of an aged Bum*: Techniques using grafts from other body parts were developed to replace damaged noses (in this context perhaps particularly noses damaged as a result of sexual disease). Cp. S. Butler, *Hudibras The First and Second Parts* (London: John Martyn and Henry Herringman, 1674), p. 18: 'So learned *Taliacotius* from / The brawny part of Porter's Bum, / Cut supplemental Noses, which / Would last as long as Parent breech'. '*Taliacotius*' was Gaspare Tagiacozzi (1545–99) of Bologna, who published on rhinoplasty techniques in the late sixteenth century. See S. L. Gilman, *Making the Body Beautiful: A Cultural History of Aesthetic Surgery* (Princeton (NJ): Princeton University Press, 2000), pp. 66–7.

6. Hesiod's: Hesiod (lived *c.* 700 BC), Greek poet, whose *Theogony* was concerned with the Greek gods.

7. Cupid: god of love, represented as a boy.

8. *Under ... one Old, th'other New*: Janus was the Roman god of doorways, represented with two faces.

9. Apollo: son of Zeus and Leto, represented as a young male.

10. Diana: huntress and goddess of wildlife.

11. Pallas: Pallas Athena, goddess of wisdom.

12. Venus: goddess of love.

13. May: the association of spring with youth was commonplace. See e.g. B. Keach *War with the Devil*, above p. 6.

14. Saturn: father of Jupiter.

15. Pluto: god of the underworld.

16. Proserpin: equivalent of Persephone, bride of Pluto and daughter of Demeter.

17. *The very Furies ... their shine*: the Furies, who meted out punishments for various crimes, were represented with snakes coiled around them.

18. Juno: goddess associated, among other things, with marriage. Juno was the wife of Jove.

19. Joves: Jove, chief Roman god.

20. *Lawrels*: the laurel wreath was awarded for poetic prowess.

21. Hypocrene: Hippocrene, fountain on Mount Helicon, associated with the Muses. Drinking from the fountain was meant to provide poetic inspiration.

22. *No Palsie-hands ... first Day*: The poet and playwright Ben Jonson (1572–1637) had a stroke in late 1627 or 1628, and suffered by this stage from a 'palsy'. His play *The New Inn* (performed by the King's Men in Blackfriars in 1629; published 1631) was by his own account not a success. In 'The Dedication, To the Reader' Jonson wrote: 'if thou canst but spell and join my sense, there is more hope of thee than of a hundred fastidious impertinents who were there present the first day, yet never made piece of their prospect the right way. 'What did they come for, then?' thou wilt ask me. I will as punctually answer: "To see, and to be seen. To make a general muster of themselves in their clothes of credit, and possess the stage against the play. To dislike all, but mark nothing. And by their confidence of rising between the acts, in oblique lines, make affidavit to the whole house of their not understanding one scene.'" Hattaway has argued that these lines

contain the source for the reference to *The New Inn's* failure in 'In Nova Fert Animus'. B. Jonson, *The New Inn*, ed. M. Hattaway (Manchester: Manchester University Press, 2001), pp. 1–9, 48–9; *ODNB*.

23. *His own ... who was once one*: cp. *Poor Robin's Jests* (London: Francis Kirkman and Richard Head, 1667), pp. 75–6:

> *BEn Johnson* having over-night taken a Cup too much of the juice of the Grape, the next morning his head aking he wore a Cap, and meeting with Master *Drayton* his fellow-Poet, told him he thought he should dye, and therefore desired him for the love that had been betwixt them, to prefix these two lines upon his Grave, for his Epitaph:

> *Here lies Ben Johnson*
> *That was once one.*

> That shall I do Brother *Ben* (said Master *Drayton)* and for the love I always bore to your Muse, I shall add two more of my own, which shall be these.

> *Who whilst he lived in his bravery*
> *Was exceeding full of Knavery.*

> A separate tradition was transmitted through manuscript, in which Jonson's companion was Shakespeare. See *Shakespeare's Poems*, ed. K. Duncan-Jones and H. R. Woudhuysen (London: Arden Shakespeare, 2007), pp. 446–7 (which also contains a discussion of the manuscripts in which the text is found, and a list of variants):

> Master Ben Jonson and Master William Shakespeare being merry at a tavern, Master Jonson having begun this for his epitaph:

> Here lies Ben Jonson
> That was once one

> he gives it to Master Shakespeare to make up who presently writes:

> Who while he lived was a slow thing,
> And now, being dead, is no thing.

> It is not possible to establish which tradition is being drawn upon in 'In Nova Fert Animus', although the final line of the poem might suggest some connection with the 'poor Robin' tradition.

24. *once we* Trojans *were ... we are*: A reference to the myth that Britain was founded by Brutus, descendant of the famous Trojan Aeneas, and thus that the British were once Trojans.

25. Iliack *passions*: 'painful affection (frequently fatal), due to intestinal obstruction': see *OED*, 'ileus, *n.*', 1. The metaphor clearly follows on from the previous reference to Trojans, and the meaning of Iliac as pertaining to Troy.

26. Jews-*Ears*: type of fungus.

27. *Nor is ... Mercury*: a play on the proverb 'every block will not make a Mercury'. This derives from the practice of making statues of gods out of wood and the recognition that not all pieces of wood could or should be sculpted into the swift, intelligent Mercury. The proverb is thus used to make the claim that not all are naturally equipped to fulfil prestigious roles. For discussion see Erasmus, *Adages*, II. 5. 47.

28. Virgil: Virgil (70–19 BC), revered Roman poet.

29. Plot: the Popish Plot: see Headnote.

30. Galli *of* Gallick *kind*: i.e. the silent cockerels (Lat. Galli) are French (Gallick) (the cock-erel also being a symbol of France). Anti-French feeling was high at this time, with the French monarchy being seen as the quintessence of arbitrary and popish power. Fears of the ways in which relations with France had corrupted politics at the highest level in England were intensified by the revelations of Ralph Montagu, former ambassador to France. In December 1678, Montagu told the House of Commons how Thomas Osborne, earl of Danby had negotiated for monies from the French in return for the prorogation of parliament. See *ODNB*.

31. *Landlord*: cp. Robert Wild's reference to Charles II as 'Landlord' in *Iter Boreale*, Volume 1, p. 7.

32. English *Oak*: here symbolizing the patriotism of the new parliament (in the face of French encroachments), the oak was particularly associated with Charles II following his much publicized adventure in the Boscobel Oak. Thus, in a move typical of Robert Wild's verse, the new parliament's loyalty to the King is protested within a framework which is deeply critical of previous government actions. Cp. the references in Robert Wild's *The Loyal Nonconformist* and *An Ingenious Contention*.

33. *Old Shooes and Mouldy Bread are* Gibeonites: See Joshua 9:4–5. The Gibeonites deceived the Israelites into making a league with them.

34. Long Lane: '*Long Lane*, so called for its length, coming out of *Aldersgate street* against *Barbican*, and falleth into *West Smithfield*. A Place also of Note for the sale of Apparel, Linnen, and Upholsters Goods, both Second-hand and New, but chiefly for Old': J. Stow, *A Survey of the Cities of London and Westminster ... Very Much Enlarged ... by John Strype*, 2 vols (London: A. Churchill, J. Knapton, R. Knaplock, J. Walthoe, E. Horne, B. Tooke, D. Midwinter, B. Cowse, R. Robinson, and T. Ward, 1720), vol. 1, bk 3, p. 122.

35. *When* Nolls *Nose ... it well*: Oliver Cromwell (1599–1658) (Noll) forcibly dissolved the Rump parliament in April 1653. For further scatological puns on the Rump see R. Wild, *Iter Boreale*, Volume 1, pp. 1–16.

36. *COMMONS*: a pun on the House of Commons and victuals.

37. Trent ... *Conventicle*: the Council of Trent, which did much to define Counter Reforma-tion Catholicism, opened in 1545 and was closed in 1563.

38. Sixty-six: the Great Fire of 1666 was widely blamed on Catholics. See Volume 1, p. 240.

39. *Out of the Fire ... above the Old*: on the rebuilding of London after the Great Fire see Volume 1, p. 240.

40. *Old Eagles ... Old* Pliny *Writes*: book 10 of Pliny the Elder's *Natural History* concerns birds.

41. *Deans, Prebends, Chaplains ... Tables end*: the poem here turns to religious matters. First, by satirising those lower down the Church hierarchy who are impeded from preferment by long-lived bishops, and secondly by pointing to the plight of nonconformists barred from preaching. The exclusion crisis was to see the reawakening of calls for toleration and/or comprehension in parliament. See H. Horwitz, 'Protestant Reconciliation in the Exclusion Crisis', *Journal of Ecclesiastical History*, 15:2 (1964), pp. 201–17.

42. *OATS*: a pun on Titus Oates (1649–1705). See Headnote.

43. Tyburn: London's main site of execution.

44. poor Robin: Poor Robin was the penname of William Winstanley (d. 1698). However it was not only used by him, and was at times associated with Robert Wild. See *ODNB*; and e.g. Y.Z. *An Answer to the Author of Humble Thanks* (London: J. Edwin, 1672); *A Dialogue between Death and Doctor Robert Wyld* (London: s.n., 1679).

Keach, *The Glorious Lover*

1. My Heart is inditing a good matter: the full verse reads: Psalm 45:1.
2. Whose Altars once mean *Turtles* entertain'd: cp. Psalm 84:3 (Douai-Rheims). Rather than the Douai-Rheims it is likely that Keach drew on an unidentified source.
3. And from the mouths of *Babes* hast strength ordain'd: see Psalm 8:2.
4. Paul *became all to All*: and I would try: see 1 Corinthians 9:22.
5. A Verse ... a Sacrifice: Sharon Achinstein notes the echo of George Herbert's 'Perirrhanterium' ('A verse may find him, who a sermon flies, / And turn delight into a sacrifice.'): see S. Achinstein, *Literature and Dissent in Milton's England* (Cambridge: Cambridge University Press, 2003), p.198; G. Herbert, 'Perirrhanterium', in G. Herbert, *The Complete English Poems*, ed. J. Tobin, rev. edn (London: Penguin, 2004), p. 6, ll. 5–6.
6. All you ... *infected* Brain: Elizabeth Clarke notes that: 'Keach is deliberately addressing himself to romance readers of both sexes – "all you who amorous Stories gladly hear" – despite thundering with the conventional denouncement of romances as "the poisoned froth of some infected brain"': E. Clarke, *Politics, Religion and the Song of Songs in Seventeenth-Century England* (Basinstoke: Palgrave, 2011), p. 196.
7. My Well beloved's mine, and I am his: see Song of Solomon 2:16 (Geneva).
8. *IN the fair Regions of approachless Light*: cp. E. Benlowes, *Theophila* (London: printed by R.N., sold by Henry Selle ... and Humphrey Moseley ..., 1652), p. 110: 'ARCHES-SENCE! THOU, Self-full! Self-Infinite! / Residing in approachlesse LIGHT! / In the INCOMPREHENSIBILITIES of HEIGHT!'
9. Nimrods: Nimrod, 'the mighty hunter before the Lord' of Genesis 10:8–10, was the archetypal earthly tyrant.
10. *IN the fair ... melting Ardours springs*: Keach contrasts the absolute monarchy of God with earthly monarchies, their corrupt courts and reliance on espionage; he hints particularly at the court of Charles II. On these two latter themes see M. Jenkinson, *Culture and Politics at the Court of Charles II, 1660–1685* (Woodbridge: Boydell, 2010); A. Marshall, *Intelligence and Espionage in the Reign of Charles II, 1660–85* (Cambridge: Cambridge University Press, 1994).
11. He fairer was than all the Sons of men: a version of Psalm 45:2.
12. *Within the Limits ... lasting fame*: Keach describes Eden. See Genesis 2:10–14.
13. *A very lovely Creature in her Prime*: Despite the Edenic setting this 'Creature' is not Eve but the Soul. As Elizabeth Clarke writes, initially with reference to the illustration at the front of the text: 'The girl on the front cover is not Eve: the text spells out that she is alone in Paradise except for a divine Lover. She suffers Eve's fate of a fall which entails transportation to a "strange land", although characteristically for Keach this is described in warlike terms as seduction by armed rebels, despite the snake on the front cover of *The Glorious Lover*.' See Clarke, *Politics, Religion and the Song of Songs*, p. 196.
14. *Before a cursed ... bold Arms advance*: the rebel angels, most famously represented in Milton's *Paradise Lost*.
15. *Flaming Sword*: see Genesis 3:24.
16. *It cannot be beheld ... such light*: see S. Pordage, *Mundorum Explicatio* (London: Lodowick Lloyd, 1661), p. 303: 'Ten thousand Suns, ten thousand times more bright / Than ours, would not have paralell'd this Light: / Need must it dazling be; what mortal eye / Can view the Splendors of *Aeternity*?' Cp. also Benlowes, *Theophila*, p. 87: '*Thou, CROWN of BLISSE, whose Footstool's Earth, whose* Throne / *Outshines ten thousand Suns in One, / Who art the Radical LIFE of all true JOY alone!*'

17. *But on their Heads a glorious Crown is set*: see the discussion of the meaning of the crown in T. De Laune and B. Keach, *Tropologia* (London: Enoch Prosser, 1681), bk 1, p. 180: 'It denotes heavenly *Reward* or Eternal Life, 1 *Cor.* 9. 25. 2 *Tim* 2. 5. *and* 4. 8. *Jam.* 1. 12. 1 *Pet.* 5. 4. *Rev.* 2. 10. *and* 3. 11. &c.'

18. *There's Rivers ... Prophets and Apostles swim*: see W. S., *The Poems of Ben Johnson, Junior* (London: Tho. Passenger, 1672), p. 57: 'Rivers of heavenly *wine* full to the brim, / Wherein the *Prophets* and *Apostles* swim'; B. Keach, *War with the Devil*, above p. 59.

19. *All there ... nor fullness cloys*: see F. Quarles, *Emblemes* (London: I. W. and F. E., 1669), bk 5, XIV, p. 302: 'But simple Love, and sempiternal Joyes / Whose sweetness neither gluts nor fulness cloyes'.

20. *'The Luke-warm Blood ... tread upon*: see Quarles, *Emblemes,* bk 5, XIV, pp. 301–2: 'The luke warm bloud of this dear Lamb being spilt; / To rubies turn'd whereof her posts were built; / And what dropp'd down in a kind gelid gore, / Did turn rich Saphyres, and did pave her floor: / The brighter flames, that from his eye-balls ray'd, / Grew Chrysolites, whereof her walls were made: / The milder glances sparkled on the ground, / And groundsild every door wth Diamond; / But dying, darted upwards, and did fix / A battlement of purest Sardonix. / Her streets with burnish'd gold are paved round, / Stars lie like pebbles scatt'red on the ground: / Pearl mixt with Onyx, and the Jasper stone, / Made gravell'd cause-wayes to be trampled on.'

21. *For one alone ... one night*: see 2 Kings 19:35: See also De Laune and Keach, *Tropologia*, bk 2, p. 31: 'God can command Millions of Angels to destroy his and his Peoples Enemies: One of which, in one Night, slew 185000 *Assyrians*'.

22. *Though some of them in ancient times were lost*: see above n. 14.

23. *Ten thousand millions ... glorious Prince did come*: see Quarles, *Emblemes*, bk 5, XIV, p. 301: 'Ten thousand millions, and ten thousand more / Of Angel-measured leagues, from th'Eastern shore / Of dungeon earth this glorious Palace stands'.

24. Goshen-*Land*: the land in Egypt in which the Israelites dwelt. It remained light during the plague of darkness: see Exodus 10:23.

25. Elysian *Fields*: in Greek mythology, paradise for the notably heroic or good.

26. Egypt *was once a dark ... be felt*: see Exodus 10:21.

27. *A Black and fearful King*: Apollyon, who at this stage seems to be a representation of Satan.

28. *Sylla, nor Nero*: the Roman general Sulla (*c.* 138–78 BC) and the Emperor Nero (AD 37–68) were infamously tyrannical.

29. *And like a ravenous Lyon ... new Conquests out*: cp. 1 Peter 5:8.

30. Apollyon: see Revelation 9:11.

31. *This greedy Dragon ... him instantly devour*: for the identification of Satan as the dragon see Revelation 12.

32. *PHÆNIX*: the phoenix, which died every five hundred years only for a new bird to rise from out of its ashes, was often used as a symbol of Christ.

33. *Do not the Conduits ... run Wine*: in contradistinction to Christ's reception, the fountains did run with wine when Charles II returned in 1660: *Diary of John Evelyn*, ed. E. S. De Beer, 6 vols (Oxford: Clarendon Press, 1955), III, p. 246.

34. *The very Inn ... support his Head*: see Luke 2:7.

35. *Of whom the Prophet saith* he knew no Sin: see 2 Corinthians 5:21.

36. *Whose footstool's Earth, and Heaven is his Throne*: see Isaiah 66:1 and Acts 7:49.

37. *like the Sun*: on the representation of Christ as the sun see De Laune and Keach, *Tropologia*, bk 2, pp. 214–20.

38. *for, when ...a Miracle is wrought*: see Matthew 17:24–7.
39. *Vertue (like Palms) thrives by th' oppressing weight*: a common simile. See Psalm 92:12.
40. *As had been prophesied ... hopeful Children now are not*: see Jeremiah 31:15 and Matthew 2:17–18.
41. *Archilaus's*: Herod's son: see Matthew 2:22.
42. *No sooner flutt'ring ... to* Galilee : the visit of the magi, the massacre of the innocents on Herod's orders, the flight of the holy family into Egypt and their subsequent settling in Galilee are recounted in Matthew 2.
43. Herod ... *vainly fear*: see Matthew 2:1–18.
44. *This Imp of Darkness ... sprightly Mirth*: Sin adopts the form of a Restoration gallant, a courtly libertine.
45. Dalilaw: Delilah, who was loved by Samson and betrayed him to the Philistines: see Judges 16:4–20.
46. *Heav'ns foe ... doth ow*: Keach represents Sin as taking a male form, in contrast to Milton's female Sin, although Sin remains in Keach's poem the progenitor of Death. For Milton's allegory of Sin and Death see J. Milton, *Paradise Lost*, ed. A. Fowler, 2nd edn (London and New York: Longman, 1998), II, ll. 648–884.
47. *Field*: battlefield.
48. *No not* Pharsalia's Plains ... *conquest caught*: Julius Caesar was victorious over Pompey in Pharsalia in 48 BC. The battle of Pharsalus was versified by Lucan in book 7 of his *Pharsalia*.
49. *Some fabulous Writers ... Old* Serpents *subtility and spight*: There had been many retellings of the legend of St George and the dragon by the time Keach was writing. He compares his scepticism over its veracity with assuredness in Christ's triumph over Satan, identified as the dragon and the serpent. See Revelation 12:9 and Genesis 3:1. In contrast to Keach's approach, previous authors had associated St George's dragon with Satan. See e.g Spenser, *Faerie Queene*, I.xi.
50. *fasted ... out of his hand*: Keach turns Christ's temptation in the wilderness into a military contest. For the Gospel accounts of the Christ's temptation see Matthew 4:1–11; Mark 1:12–13; Luke 4:1–13.
51. *And knowing, well ... out of his hand*: see Matthew 4:1–4 and Luke 4:1–4.
52. Toad: cp. Milton, *Paradise Lost*, IV, ll. 799–800: 'him [Satan] there they found / Squat like a toad, close at the ear of Eve'.
53. Noah ... *own Vine*: see Genesis 9:20–27 for the drunkenness of Noah.
54. *And Righteous* Lot ... *Incest fell two Times*: Lot's daughters made their father drunk and he impregnated them: see Genesis 19:30–38.
55. *Thy* Jacob *too, though he could wrestle well*: a reference to Jacob's wrestling with God: see Genesis 32:24–30.
56. *Yet by my Arm ... supplant his Brother*: Esau, son of Isaac, was duped out of the blessing due to him as the firstborn by his brother Jacob and his mother Rebekah: see Genesis 27:6–40.
57. Joseph ... *by* Pharaoh's Life *to swear*: see Genesis 42:15–16. As the note on Genesis 42:15 in the Geneva Bible explains: 'The Egyptians, which were idolaters, used to sweare by their kings life: but God forbiddeth to sweare by any but him: yet Joseph dwelling among the wicked smelleth of their corruptions.'
58. *And* Judah ... *Story read*: see Genesis 38.
59. Moses *himself ... could not the Land of Promise find*: see Numbers 20:7–12.
60. Sampson ... *overcome by* Dalilah *and me*: see Judges 13–16.

61. David ... *Camp of* Israel *annoy*: see 1 Samuel 17.
62. *For all these ... Adult'ry and Murder over-taken*: David's adultery with Bathsheba, and his part in the death of her husband Uriah, are recounted in 2 Samuel 11. Following Uriah's death and a period of mourning, Bathsheba became David's wife: 'But the thing that David had done displeased the Lord': 2 Samuel 11:27.
63. *And* Solomon ... *curs'd Idolatrie*: see 1 Kings 11.
64. *For their reward, enjoy an endless Crown*: on the meaning of 'Crown' in this context see De Laune and Keach, *Tropologia*, bk 1, p. 180: 'It denotes heavenly *Reward* or Eternal Life, 1 *Cor*.9. 25. 2 *Tim* 2. 5. *and* 4.8. *Jam*. 1. 12. 1 *Pet*. 5.4. *Rev*. 2. 10. *and* 3. 11. &c..'
65. *Thou* bruisdst their Heels, *but* I will bruise thy Head: see Genesis 3:15.
66. *my own offspring dear*: Sin. See above n. 46.
67. *Eternal Crown*: see above n. 17.
68. *But not prevailing ... retreated, as before*: see Matthew 4:5–7; Luke 4:9–12. Keach follows Matthew's ordering of the temptations, in which Christ is placed on the pinnacle before the mountain.
69. Achitophel: Achitophel was counsellor to Absalom, David's son. Absalom rebelled against David. See 2 Samuel 13–18. The rebellion of Absalom, and the role played by Achitophel were the subjects of the John Dryden's famous anti-Whig poem *Absalom and Achitophel* (1681).
70. Machiavel: Niccolò Machiavelli (1469–1527). While Machiavelli was interpreted subtly by some Restoration readers, his name remained a watchword for deviousness and amoral political calculation.
71. *Now would one ... and howling, thus goes on*: an extensive retelling of the temptation of Christ on the mountain recounted in Matthew 4:8–11; Luke 4:5–8. Keach follows Matthew's ordering of the temptations, with the temptation on the pinnacle preceding the temptation on the mountain. However, the words of Christ recorded by Keach towards the end of this section, 'Thou shalt not tempt the Lord thy God' (Matthew 4:7; Luke 4:12), are Jesus's response to the temptation on the pinnacle, and as such come later in Luke's narrative than Matthew's.
72. *Father of Lies*: see John 8:44.
73. *NO sooner ... Triumph to their King*: see Matthew 4:11.
74. *Look unto... that I can find*: in line with Calvinist thought, Keach's Christ stresses the total depravity of humankind.
75. *There's many Mansions in his House*: see John 14:2.
76. *In Robes ... dazle mortals sight*: Keach refers to the robe of righteousness, which is given to the elect to wear through no merit of their own. See Isaiah 61:10.
77. *The Miracles ... nor could, but he*: see Matthew 15:30–31.
78. *Feaver*: see Matthew 8:14–15; Mark 1:30–31; Luke 4:38–39; John 4:46–53.
79. *Leprosy*: see Matthew 8:2–4; Mark 1:40–44; Luke 5:12–14.
80. *Yea*, Bloody-fluxes ... gratis *sent*: see Mark 5:25–34 and Luke 8:43–48.
81. *Bowels*: See De Laune and Keach, *Tropologia*, bk 1, p. 47: '[*Bowels*] are attributed to God, by which his Mercy and most ardent love is expressed, Esa. 63. 15. *Where is thy zeal and thy strength, the sounding of thy* Bowels, *and of thy Mercies towards me?* Jer. 31. 20. My Bowels are troubled for him (that is, for *Ephraim*) Luke 1. 78. *Through the Bowels of the Mercy of our God, whereby the day-spring from on high hath visited us.'*
82. *By these bless'd deeds ... mighty Hand*: cp. Matthew 4:23–25.
83. *That if he said ... cast out the foulest Devils*: see Luke 4:33–37.

84. *He* rais'd the dead ... *Glory raise*: Christ raised Lazarus from the dead after four days: see John 11:1–45.
85. *Who holds ...* Jehovah *unconfin'd*: see Proverbs 30:4 and Isaiah 40:12.
86. *Though in his life ...* Wine-bibber *call*: see Matthew 11:19 and Luke 7:34.
87. he hath a Devil, and is mad: see John 10:20.
88. *By th' Prince of Devils ...* Belzebub *alone*: see Matthew 12:24; Mark 3:22.
89. *Yet to ensnare him ... met before*: see e.g. Matthew 16:1–4; Matthew 19:3–9; and, in particular, Matthew 22:15–40.
90. *Besides (you know) ...* mighty Miracles: the Jewish historian Falvius Josephus (AD 37– after 93) wrote of Jesus. See *The Works of Josephus with Great Diligence Revised and Amended According to the Excellent French Translation of Monsieur Arnauld D'Andilly* (London: Abel Roper, 1676), p. 480: 'At that time was *JESUS*, a wise man, if it be lawful to call him a man. For he was the performer of divers admirable works, and the instructer of those who willingly entertain the truth; and he drew unto him divers Jews and Greeks to be his followers. This was CHRIST, who being accused by the Princes of our Nation before *Pilate*, and afterwards condemned to the Cross by him; yet did not those who followed him from the beginning, forbear to love him for the Ignominy of his death. For he appeared alive to them the third day after, according as the Divine Prophets had before testified the same, and divers other wonderful things of him: And from that time forward the Race of the Christians, who have derived their name from him, hath never ceased.'
91. *But you perhaps ...exalted in the Throne*: Keach draws a distinction between miracles that are outside nature, and thus could only be the work of God, and what the devil has the power to do. The demonologists, in general, asserted a distinction between *mira*, acts that appeared extraordinary but which could nonetheless be performed within nature, and *miracula*, miracles that broke natural laws. While the devil was said to be able to possess remarkable natural knowledge, and thus to be able to perform *mira*, only God could perform *miracula*. See S. Clark, *Thinking with Demons: The Idea of Witchcraft in Early Modern Europe* (Oxford: Oxford University Press, 1997), ch. 10.
92. *And* Moses ... *Red-Sea*: see Exodus 7–14.
93. *To the Magicians ...* God is here: see Exodus 8:16–19.
94. *The Strongest Arguments...* testifie of me: see John 5 and John 10:22–42.
95. *Does she not straight unto his Scepter bow*: In slanderous political verse, Charles II's sceptre was often related to his penis. This line might thus be seen as part of the poem's appropriation and radical redescription of libertine discourse. See R. Weil, 'Sometimes a Scepter is Only a Scepter: Pornography and Politics in Restoration England', in L. Hunt (ed.), *The Invention of Pornography: Obscentiy and the Origins of Modernity, 1500–1800* (New York: Zone Books, 1996), pp. 125–56.
96. *Hath she to urge, to keep him out o'th Door*: cp. Song of Solomon 5:2–6 and Revelation 3:20.
97. *Nor is it Vertue ... but Sin:* see above n. 49.
98. He had no form ... *to tempt desire*: see Isaiah 53:2.
99. *Their hearts ...free did pass*: see Luke 4:28–30.
100. *Again, as he stood ... own Divinity*: see John 8:12–59 and John 10:22–39.
101. *Because he said, he was sent down from Heaven*: see John 6:38.
102. Jury: Jewry: Judea.
103. *Of killing him ... fit to walk*: see John 7:1.
104. *But staid ... God-like Man*: see John 7:10–46.

105. *BEfore this Prince ... might compare*: see Matthew 11:10–11 and Luke 7:27–28.
106. *Yet was the King ... they divide*: In the biblical accounts, Herod was upbraided by John the Baptist for marrying Herodias, the wife of his brother Philip. John the Baptist was put to death at the request of Herodias's daughter after she danced for Herod. See Mark 6:14–28 and Matthew 14:3–11.
107. *Though the chief work... or loose*: see Mark 1:7; Luke 3:16; John 1:27.
108. *For Herod now, like to his Predecessor*: the Herod referred to here, Herod Antipas, was the son of Herod the Great (73–4 BC), who was responsible for the massacre of the innocents: see above p. 407, n. 42.
109. *For Herod ... black Combination*: see Luke 13:31–33.
110. Jury: Jewry: Judea.
111. *From Jury ... to Galilee below*: see John 4:3–4.
112. *From Nazareth he fled to Capernaum*: see Matthew 4:13.
113. with grief he was acquainted: see Isaiah 53:3.
114. *So blinded were their Eys, their hearts so hard*: see John 12:40 and Isaiah 6:10.
115. *'Twas from ... Woman's seed*: see Genesis 3:15.
116. *He is not gone ... Answer get*: see Song of Solomon 5:2–6.
117. *Oh! hark ... sharpest swords*: cp. Hebrews 4:12.
118. *Toads and Serpents*: related to the demonic: see above n. 31.
119. *Will you the liberty of Choice deny*: the Soul's is a peculiarly libertine understanding of liberty.
120. *He whom ... countenanc'd by me*: George Southcombe and Grant Tapsell comment that 'The libertine "Gallants", the men of mode, usurp the position that should be held by Christ': G. Southcombe and G. Tapsell, *Restoration Politics, Religion and Culture: Britain and Ireland, 1660–1714* (Basingstoke: Palgrave Macmillan, 2010), p. 158.
121. Vicinus: Latin: neighbour.
122. The Father of all Spirits: see Hebrews 12:9.
123. Cynthia: goddess of the moon, often used in representations of the Virgin Queen, Elizabeth I.
124. *Her Lustre tarnisht ... unchast desires*: Keach represents the fallen state of the Soul through images of physical decay, and emphasises her sexual laciviousness.
125. *From them ... much mischief did*: For the Calvinist Keach, post-lapsarian humanity possessed a totally 'vile and accurst' nature. For discussion of the place of original sin in Keach's thought, see see J. W. Arnold, 'The Reformed Theology of Benjamin Keach (1640–1704)' (PhD dissertation, University of Oxford, 2009), pp. 196–8.
126. *Each humane Soul ... certainly remain*: In Keach's Calvinist theology, all those who are not recipients of freely given, unearned grace remain in the fallen state graphically represented in the previous lines.
127. *The Question ... Pardon then he gives*: Although established outside of time, Keach believed that the Covenant made by the Son with the Father on behalf of the elect came into effect following the Fall (which was foreseen) and the breaking of the Covenant of Works. Keach thus held an infralapsarian view, whereby the elect were picked from amongst a *fallen* humanity. See Arnold, 'Reformed Theology', chs 5 and 6, esp. pp. 148–9, 192–5. In the poem's terms, Christ chooses to give his love to the Soul in her fallen state, not before she had fallen. Christ's love for the Soul is thus wholly unmerited.
128. Each Tub shall upon its own Bottom stand: a proverb arrogantly, and misguidedly, asserting the independence of the Soul.

129. *Ten thousand Talents ... most Just*: In the parable of Matthew 18:23–35, a servant is initially forgiven a debt of ten thousand talents by a king. However, when the same servant insists on payment from another (who is also unable to pay) the king 'delivered him to the tormentors, till he should pay all that was due unto him.' Christ explains 'So likewise shall my heavenly Father do also unto you, if ye from your hearts forgive not every one his brother their trespasses.' See also De Laune and Keach, *Tropologia*, bk 2, pp. 102–3: 'Sinners were miserably indebted to the Law and Justice, owed ten thousand Talents, but had not a Farthing to pay; liable every day to Arrests, and to be sent to the dark Shades of eternal Night, or Prison of utter Darkness, under the Wrath of the incensed Majesty, having whole Mountains of Sin and Guilt lying upon them, running every day into new Scores, adding Sin to Sin, one heavy Debt upon another. O how great is the Guilt of sinful Man! and how unable to satisfy Divine Justice! How then shall these Debts be paid, all these Sins expiated, and the Guilt taken away? Justice calls for full Payment; it's Language is, Pay, or perish: yet we cannot make the least Reparation, nor right God for the Wrong we have done him, by offending the Eyes of his Glory. But now by a Marriage-Covenant with Jesus Christ, all is at once discharged, and the Sinner acquitted; there being Riches and Worth enough in him, who hath fully satisfied the Demands of Law and Justice; and by Union with him the Sinner comes to be interested into all.'
130. *Ashes and vile Dust*: cp. Job 30:19.
131. *A fiery Furnace ... read of*: see Daniel 3:19–20.
132. *This Creature ... reverence and fear*: see Genesis 1:26.
133. *And when he ... flesh he chuses*: see Hebrews 2:16.
134. *The second Circumstance ... endless misery*: the biblical account of the creation of Adam and Eve and the Fall is contained within Genesis 1–3. For Keach's theology of original sin see above n. 125. For the controversy over the Fall in the seventeenth century see W. Poole, *Milton and the Idea of the Fall* (Cambridge: Cambridge University Press, 2005).
135. *See how ... shrivel'd up with heat*: cp. Revelation 6:13–14.
136. *the dreadful Trump... Graves awake*: cp. 1 Corinthians 15:52.
137. *Mount* Sinai: on which the Ten Commandments were given to Moses. Cp. Exodus 20:18.
138. *Art guilty ...evil Nature didst derive*: For Keach, Adam represented all of humanity when he made the Covenant of Works with God. His sin was thus imputed to them. See Arnold, 'Reformed Theology', pp. 166–7.
139. *Ten thousand Talents*: see above n. 129.
140. *Hecatombs*: public sacrifices of one hundred oxen.
141. *When even ... pay thy Debt*: see Isaiah 64:6. 'Filthy rags' was frequently translated as 'menstruous rags'.
142. *Lord, shall I strike, O shall I strike the blow*: The character of Justice in Quarles's allegorical courtroom scene asks twice 'Lord shall I strike the blow?' and once 'Shall I yet strike the blow?' See Quarles, *Emblemes*, bk 3, X, pp. 166.
143. *I cannot hold*: a phrase used by Quarles's Justice: see Quarles, *Emblemes*, bk 3, X, pp. 166.
144. Soul! *Speak ... What dost thou say*: cp. Quarles, *Emblemes*, bk 3, X, pp. 165: '*Jes.* What sayst thou sinner? hast thou ought to plead, / That sentence should not passe? hold up thy head, / And shew thy brazen, thy rebellious face.'
145. *Stay Justice ... Precious, Sacred, and Divine*: cp. Quarles, *Emblemes*, bk 3, X, pp. 166: '*Jes.* Stay, Justice, hold; / My bowels yearn, my fainting bloud growes cold, / To view the trembling wretch; Methinks, I spie / My fathers image in the pris'ners eye. / *Just.* I cannot hold. *Jes.* Then turn thy thirsty blade / Into my sides: let there the wound be made:

/ Chear up, dear soul; redeem thy life with mine: / My soul shall smart; my heart shall
bleed for thine.'

146. *My Sentence is for War*: cp. Moloch: 'My sentence is for War; that open too': J. Dryden,
The State of Innocence (London: Henry Herringman, 1677), p. 4.

147. *Dominions, Pow'rs, and Principalities*: angelic orders: see Colossians 1:16.

148. *Dominions, Pow'rs ... Victory*: cp. Lucifer: 'Dominions, Pow'rs, ye Chiefs of Heav'n's
bright Host, / (Of Heav'n, once yours; but now, in Battel, lost) / Wake from your slumber: Are your Beds of Down? / Sleep you so easie there? or fear the frown / Of him who
threw you thence, and joys to see / Your abject state confess his Victory?': Dryden, *The
State of Innocence*, pp. 2–3.

149. *He takes posession ... Cabal of Hell*: see John 13:2.

150. *Betray his Lord with a false treach'rous kiss*: see Matthew 26:48–49 and 14:44–45.

151. enliv'ned Clay: see e.g. Isaiah 64:8 and Romans 9:21.

152. *'Twas from that filthy Root,* Root of all Evil: see 1 Timothy 6:10.

153. *Was't mony ... made before*: see Matthew 26:14–16.

154. *A Box ...* Three hundred pence: see John 12:4–6.

155. *He whose ...* Ophirs *Mines*: see Isaiah 13:12.

156. Pearl of matchless price: cp. Matthew 13:45–46.

157. *The* Indian *Quarries ...* Jewel *Lost*: cp. De Laune and Keach, *Tropologia*, bk 2, p.188:
'Christ is of an inestimable value, may well be called the Pearl of great Price. The Worth
& Excellency of Christ far exceeds the Riches of both *Indies*. He is the rarest Jewel the
Father hath in Heaven and Earth, more precious unto Believers than Rubies, and all that
can be desired cannot be compared unto Him'.

158. *Go howl ... Thou'lt* hang *thy self*: see Matthew 27:3–5.

159. *But his own ...*he is lost: see John 17:12.

160. Garden: the Garden of Gethsemane.

161. King of Terrors: death. For the specific phrase see Job 18:14.

162. O let this Cup... be possible: see Matthew 26:39.

163. My Soul is sorrowful, ev'n unto Death: see Matthew 26:38.

164. *Our Help was* upon One that's mighty laid: see Psalm 89:19.

165. *Nay of this ...* he fell upon the Ground: see Mark 14:33–35.

166. *Shall add ...* drops of blood: see Luke 22:44.

167. *And* Captive lead'st *at last* Captivity: see Psalm 68:18 and Ephesians 4:8.

168. *Then let's retreat ... his Soul did undergo*: The ultimate sources for this passage are the
synoptic accounts of Christ in the Garden of Gethsemane: Matthew 26:36–46; Mark
14:32–42; Luke 22:39–46.

169. If 'twere his will to let that Cup pass by: see Matthew 26:39.

170. *And yet ... Father did forsake him*: cp. Christ's words on the cross: 'My God, my God, why
hast thou forsaken me?: Matthew 27:46; Mark 15:34.

171. *The* Angels *... heavy on him lay*: see Luke 22:43.

172. *Some little ... regardless of all fears*: Keach refers to the deaths of martyrs by burning.

173. *This* Spirit ... Without measure: see Luke 3:22.

174. *I caused* Cain *to slay his godly Brother*: see Genesis 4:1–8.

175. Phœbus: sun god.

176. *Poor* Job *had fell before thy pow'rful hand*: God allowed Satan to cause Job great sufferings,
but did not permit him to kill him.

177. *Yea, tell ... hath given*: cp. Psalm 82:6–7. See also James VI and I, 'A Speach to the Lords
and Commons ... Wednesday XXI. of March. Anno 1609 [ie. 1610]', in his *The Workes*

(London: printed by Robert Barker and John Bill, 1616), p. 529: 'For Kings are not onely GODS Lieutenants upon earth, and sit upon GODS throne, but even by GOD himselfe they are called Gods.'

178. *Nay, furthermore ... Root of* David: see Matthew 21:9; Mark 11:10.

179. *Nay, he could hush the winds and calm the Seas*: see Matthew 8:26; Mark 4:39.

180. *The Miracles which... fierce Devils out*: see above p. 408, n. 83.

181. *Of five mean ... plenteous Dishes*: see John 6:5–14.

182. *A multitude ... now appears*: see Matthew 26:47; Mark 14:43.

183. *Of which ... on the ground*: see John 18:6.

184. *But that ... drink up*: see John 18:11.

185. *sin-sick Souls*: see Keach, *War with the Devil*, above p. 370, n. 79.

186. *Office of a Prophet*: one of Christ's three offices (the other two being priest and king). For relevant discussion see De Laune and Keach, *Tropologia*, bk 2, pp. 142–161; J. Calvin, *Institutes of the Christian Religion*, ed. J. T. McNeill, trans. F. L. Battles, 2 vols (Philadelphia, PA: Westminster Press, 1960), 2.15.

187. *They hal'd ... came to die*: see Matthew 26:57–75; Mark 14:46–72; Luke 22:54–65; John 18:12–27.

188. *When he had past ... refresh thee any more*: see Matthew 27:1–2, 11–26; Mark 15:1–15; Luke 23:1–25; John 18:28–40; 19:1. Herod's role is recounted only in Luke.

189. Kingly Office: one of Christ's three offices, see above n. 186.

190. All hail, King of the Jews: see Matthew 27:29; Mark 15:18; John 19:3.

191. *Nor were these ... Robe, his own put on*: see Matthew 27:27–31; Mark 15:16–20; John 19:2–3.

192. Let him be Crucify'd: see Matthew 27:23.

193. *though his bosom friend ... urges Arguments*: see Matthew 27:19.

194. *They loud ... wicked purpose*: see Matthew 27:19–26; Mark 15:12–15; Luke 23:21–25; John 19:4–16.

195. *A Country-man of* Cyrene: Simon of Cyrene.

196. *Sentence being past ... dismal* Golgotha: see Matthew 27:32–33; Mark 15:21–22.

197. *When Priest ... make them sport*: cp. Samson (often seen as a type of Christ) Judges 16:25. Cp. also R. Wild, *The Tragedy of Christopher Love*, above Volume 1, p. 23: 'The *Philistins* are set in their High Court, / And *Love*, like *Sampsons*, fetch'd to make them sport'.

198. *Hanging betwixt two Thieves*: see Matthew 27:38; Mark 15:27; Luke 23:33; John 19:18.

199. Numbred ... Transgressors: see Mark 15:28.

200. Wagging their heads: see Matthew 27:39; Mark 15:29.

201. *For passers-by ... barb'rous* Jews: see Matthew 27:39–43; Mark 15:29–32.

202. *And when he thirsts ... bitter Gall*: see Matthew 27:34.

203. *He that for them had Water turn'd to Wine*: see John 2:1–11.

204. *But into's tender side ... blood & water clear*: see John 19:34.

205. *Why, why ... in this needful hour*: cp. Matthew 27:46 and Mark 15:34.

206. *But when ... die Eternally*: cp. Psalm 104:29.

207. *last farthing have*: see above p. 411, n. 129.

208. *That much renowned ... passion*: see Acts 7:55–60.

209. *The Worlds great Eye ... every spirit's pain'd*: see Matthew 27:45–54; Mark 15:33–38; Luke 23:44–45.

210. Eusebius: The *Chronicon* of Eusebius (*c*. 260–*c*. 340) refers to the second century Greek writer Phlegon of Tralles recording an eclipse. This was often referenced in the early modern period. See e.g. Vives' comment in *St. Augustine, Of the Citie of God with Learned*

Comments of Io. Lod. Vives, trans. J[ohn]. H[ealey]. (London: printed by George Eld, 1610), bk 18, ch. 54, p. 749: 'So saith *Eusebius,* alledging heathen testimonies of that memorable eclips of the Sunne, as namely out of *Phlegon,* a writer of the Olympiads: who saith that in the fourth yeare of the two hundered and two Olympiade (the eighteenth of *Tyberius* his reigne) the greatest eclips befell, that ever was. It was midnight-darke at noone-day, the starres were all visible, and an earth-quake shooke downe many houses in Nice a city of Bythinia.'

211. Either the God of Nature ... end its painful Race: the italicized words are Dionysius the Areopagite's.

212. *Crown / of Life*: cp. Revelation 2:10.

213. Searcloth's: waxed winding sheet: see 'cerecloth, *n.*', 1, *OED*.

214. O Death, I'le be thy Death: see Hosea 13:14 (Geneva).

215. Captivity a Captive: see Psalm 68:18; Ephesians 4:8.

216. *Dominions, Pow'rs ... all is lost*: see above n. 148.

217. *Ah! what ... rould away the stone*: see Matthew 28:2; Mark 16:4; Luke 24:2.

218. *The first Day of the week*: see Mark 16:9; John 20:1.

219. Surely, ... wont to show: Plutarch's 'On the Cessation of Oracles' (*De defectu oraculorum*), which discusses the decline in numbers of oracles, forms part of his *Moralia*.

220. *Sharp* Juvenal ... now are ceas'd: see Juvenal, *Satires*, 6 ('Delphis oracula cessant').

221. *And lofty* Lucan... old delight: in fact this is Virgil, *Aeneid*, 2.351–2: 'Excessere omnes, adytis arisque relictis, / di, quibus imperium hoc steterat'.

222. *'Tis that which* Plutarch... *not find out*: see Plutarch, *De defectu oraculorum*, 419.

223. *The glorious Conquest ... this their overthrow*: for relevant discussion see C. A. Patrides, 'The Cessation of the Oracles: The History of a Legend', *Modern Language Review*, 60:4 (1965), pp. 500–7.

224. An Hebrew Child ... Shrines depart: an answer given by the Oracle at Delphos to Augustus, and recorded in various versions throughout the early modern period. See e.g. Browne, *Pseudodoxia Epidemica* (London: E. Dod, 1646), p. 362: 'An Hebrew child, a God all gods excelling, / To hell againe commands me from this dwelling. / Our Altars leave in silence, and no more / A resolution 'ere from hence implore.'

225. *And can one ... stript him first*: Christ's 'linen clothes' were left in the sepulchre: see John 20:5–7.

226. *That they convers'd ... ascend*: see Acts 1:2–3.

227. *And then ... risen from the Grave*: see 1 Corinthians 15:6.

228. *Go Turtles, go, whilst thousand Joys betide*: cp. Song of Solomon 2:12.

229. *his Love, his Dove*: see Song of Solomon 2:14, 5:2, 6:9.

230. *Sharon's Rose*: see Song of Solomon 2:1.

231. *Like* Moses Rod ... *each eye*: see Exodus 17:5–6.

232. *lo he is at her door*: see Song of Solomon 5:2–6.

233. *Repent! ... no danger 'spy*: cp. Keach, *War with the Devil*, above p. 17.

234. *And dost not ... who are denied it*: Under Calvinism true repentance was not open to all; only the elect were effectually called. See J. Calvin, *Institutes of the Christian Religion*, ed. J. T. McNeill, trans. F. L. Battles, 2 vols (Philadelphia: Westminster Press, 1960), 3.24.8: 'The statement of Christ "Many are called but few are chosen" [Matt. 22:14] is, in this manner, very badly understood. Nothing will be ambiguous if we hold fast to what ought to be clear from the foregoing: that there are two kinds of call. There is the general call, by which God invites all equally to himself through the outward preaching of the word – even those to whom he holds it out as a savor of death [cf. II Cor. 2:16], and as

the occasion for severer condemnation. The other kind of call is special, which he deigns
for the most part to give to the believers alone, while by the inward illumination of his
Spirit he causes the preached Word to dwell in their hearts. Yet sometimes he also causes
those whom he illumines only for a time to partake of it; then he justly forsakes them on
account of their ungratefulness and strikes them with even greater blindness.'

235. *She look'd about ... Glory all Divine*: cp. De Laune and Keach, *Tropologia*, bk 2, p. 216:
'The Saints adore and worship him, as it is their Duty, because he is God; and were there
ten thousand Suns, the Saints would love and admire Christ ten thousand times more
than them all. He doth so attract and ravish their Hearts, by the beaming forth of the
Rays of his Love on them, that they open when he visits them, and shut when he withdraws, drooping and languishing in his absence, and will not be kissed by any Lips, nor
embraced by any Arms but his.'

236. *Did I my bed in a poor Manger make*: see Luke 2:7; above p. 200.

237. *Ah! did I sweat ... where I stood*: see Luke 22:44; above p. 271.

238. *He lays them ... Sacred Lover*: see Matthew 9:12–13.

239. *The Soul's like* Phar'oh *... forgets the Lord*: The Pharaoh admitted his sin when afflicted by
the plagues of hail and locusts, but when the plagues had been lifted he returned to sin.
See Exodus 9:27–35; Exodus 10:16–20.

240. *Did* Abraham's *Servant ... great'st fidelity*: see Genesis 24.

241. *HAIL, precious* Soul *... Serpent called* Vice: cp. Isaiah 59:2–6 and Psalm 38:5:.

242. *Shall that ... blessed Soveraign*: a version of lines in Keach, *War with the Devil*, above
p. 18.

243. *Tophet*: in this instance, hell. See Isaiah 30:33.

244. *it is a Leprosy ... poisons and defiles*: see De Laune and Keach, *Tropologia*, bk 2, p. 268: 'Sin
is of a rotting, stinking, and putrifying Nature, compared to a Leprosy, and filthy Sores';
the marginal note references Isaiah 1:5–7.

245. *Sin is a plague ... plague of sin*: in addition to Matthew 9:12–13, on Christ as physician
see De Laune and Keach, *Tropologia*, bk 2, p. 112–19.

246. *Cesar*: Julius Caesar (100–44 BC).

247. *Let's go ... than vanity*: see Quarles, *Emblemes*, bk 1, IV, p. 17:

> PSALM 62. 9.
> *To be laid in the ballance, it is altogether lighter than vanity.*

>   1
> PUt in another weight: 'Tis yet too light:
> And yet. Fond *Cupid,* put another in;
> And yet another: Still there's under weight:
> Put in another hundred: Put again;
> Add world to world; then heap a thousand more
> To that, then to renew thy wasted store,
> Take up more worlds on trust, to draw thy ballance lower.

>   2
> Put in the flesh with all her loads of pleasure;
> Put in great Mammon's endless inventory;
> Put in the Ponderous acts of Mighty *Cæsar:*
> Put in the greater weight of *Swedens* glory;
> Adde *Scipio's* gauntlet; put in *Plato's* gown:

Put *Circes* charmes, put in the triple crown.
Thy ballance will not draw; thy ballance will not down.

3

Lord what a world is this, which day and night,
Men seek with so much toil, with so much trouble?
Which weigh'd in equal scales is found so light,
So poorly over-ballanc'd with a bubble?
Good God! That frantick mortals should destroy
Their higher hopes, and place their idle joy
Upon such airy trash, upon so light a toy!

248. *For sin's compos'd ... the Soul it kills*: see Quarles, *Emblemes*, bk 1, p. 18: 'O what a Croc-
    odilian world is this, / Compos'd of treacheries, and ensnaring wiles! / She clothes
    destruction in a formal kiss, / And lodges death in her deceitful smiles; / She hugs the
    soul she hates; and there does prove / The veryest tyrant, where she vows to love, / And
    is a Serpent most, when most she seems a Dove.'
249. *a second Dalilah ... in their Mill*: sin is likened to Delilah who betrayed Samson to the
    Philistines: see Judges 16:4–20.
250. *Lastly ... in it dos lie*: see above p. 222.
251. *Had evil man's ... O extream*: see Quarles, *Emblemes*, bk 3, II, p. 134: 'Had rebell-man's
    fool-hardiness extended / No farther, than himself, and there had ended, / It had been
    just; but thus enrag'd to fly / Upon the eternal eyes of Majesty, / And drag the Son of
    Glory from the brest / Of his indulgent Father; to arrest / His great and sacred Person:
    in disgrace, / To spit and spaul upon his Sun-bright-face; / To taunt him with base terms;
    and being bound, / To scourge his soft, his trembling sides; to wound / His head with
    thorns; his heart with humane fears; / His hands with nails, and pale flank with spears: /
    And then to paddle in the purer stream / Of his spilt blood, is more, than most extream'.
252. *Two proud Relations ... Spouse to be*: see De Laune and Keach, *Tropologia*, bk 3, p. 65:
    'That Heart is not savingly wrought upon, where one Lust is spared, and left untouched,
    or when it reacheth not to the changing the evil Qualities of every Faculty. The Word
    must not reach the Conscience only, but the Judgment, Will, and Affections also.'
253. *Old-man*: see Ephesians 4:22–24.
254. *They naturally are opposite to Grace*: a consequence of the Fall.
255. *WILT thou ... was he great*: Abraham's servant was sent to find a wife for Isaac, and
    returned with Rebekah: see Genesis 24.
256. *His Head is like unto the purest Gold*: see Song of Solomon 5:11.
257. *Aurora*: goddess of dawn.
258. *And such a brightness ... Doves*: see Song of Solomon 5:12.
259. *The Rose of Sharon*: see Song of Solomon 2:1.
260. *And to a kiss a heavenly Souls invite*: see Song of Solomon 1:2.
261. *That is the Object ... all Divine*: a version of these lines is found in De Laune and Keach,
    Tropologia, bk 3, pp. 16–17.
262. *Josephs*: see De Laune and Keach, *Tropologia*, bk 3, p. 16: '*Joseph* was a beautiful Person,
    but it was attended with a Snare'. Joseph was placed in a literal pit by his brothers: Gen-
    esis 37:24.
263. *1. His Beauty is ... wither'd in an hour*: a ten-point list particularizing Christ's beauty,
    which contains these eight points and also gives some scriptural references, is to be found
    in De Laune and Keach, *Tropologia*, bk 3, p. 16.

264. Riches of Christ: near the beginning of a section on the riches of Christ, De Laune and Keach cite the following key passages of scripture: Ephesians 1:7; Romans 2:4; Ephesians 1:18; Ephesians 3:16. See De Laune and Keach, *Tropologia*, bk 3, p. 18.
265. *The Father ... all that is in Heaven*: see John 16:15.
266. *He's heir of all things, and the time is near*: see Hebrews 1:2.
267. *Suppose each Soul ten thousand Talents were*: see above p. 411, n. 129.
268. *Robes of state*: see above n. 76.
269. *Ophir's Treasury*: see above n. 155.
270. *Of a most glorious ... shall obtain*: see Revelation 2:10.
271. *Treasury*: see Colossians 2:3.
272. *St. Paul knew well ... unsearchable be*: see Romans 11:33 and Ephesians 3:8.
273. *Like to a bubble are all things on Earth*: one of Keach's favourite similes.
274. *Riches of Christ ... Riches see*: see De Laune and Keach, *Tropologia*, bk 3, pp. 18–19, for a congruent examination of the riches of Christ in prose, containing scriptural citations (including those cited at n. 264 above).
275. *Ev'n all choice ... spiced Wine*: see Song of Solomon 4:14.
276. *Such is the nature of his pow'rful Shield*: see De Laune and Keach, *Tropologia*, bk 1, p. 71: 'When a [*Shield* or *Target*] is ascribed to God, it is to be understood of his propitious Favour and Mercy to men through Christ, becoming their defence, protection and security – warding (as a Sheild does blows) all assaults and violences of the Enemy, and converting all into Good for his people. *Gen.* 15. 1. *Deut.* 33.29. *Psal.* 3. 3, 4. *Psal.* 18. 2. 3. *Psal.* 28. 6, 7. *Psal.* 84. 11, 12. *Psal.* 5. 12. *For thou, O Lord, wilt bless the Righteous: With favour wilt thou compaß them as with a Shield.*'
277. *For human ... vain*: Proverbs 31:30.
278. *Beauty which is spotless*: see Hebrews 9:14 and 1 Peter 1:19.
279. *The Head ... best and fit*: Keach is perhaps implicitly critical here of the Royal supremacy as having usurped the rightful position of Christ as Head of the Church.
280. *The Keys of Hell and Death to him are given*: see Revelation 1:18.
281. *Mediator*: alongside 'surety', 'mediator' was the analogy used most creatively by Keach in discussing Christ's role in salvation. The importance of these analogies to Keach, his particular use of them, and the sources for his thought are expertly illuminated in Arnold, 'Reformed Theology', ch. 5.
282. *The Soveraign ... love obtain*: see De Laune and Keach, *Tropologia*, bk 3, pp. 20–1, for a congruent examination of Christ's power, containing scriptural citations.
283. *This spreads ... Wisdom lie*: see 1 Kings 10:1–7 and 2 Chronicles 9:1–6.
284. *Achitophel*: see above n. 69.
285. *Where thou ... worse than dross*: cp. e.g. Lamentations 4:1.
286. *Like Job's last Messenger ... corrupted are*: see Job 1:18–19.
287. *Fix where ... I'le attempt to find*: Depraved Judgment preaches a perverted notion of the Aristotelian mean. While for Aristotle virtue was the mean between two vices, here Depraved Judgment seeks to find a mean between the Soul's wholly unequal earthly and divine lovers.
288. *Courtly Spark*: the corruption of the Soul is linked specifically to the advice of a 'Courtly Spark'. Charles II's court was famed for its libertinism. See also above n. 44.
289. He that believes, doth not make hast: see Isaiah 28:16.
290. *Nay, furthermore ... gross impurity*: Depraved Judgment fails to recognize that as sanctification follows justification, holy living was a sign of election. The kind of partial

adherence to moral living vindicated by Depraved Judgment is thus based on corrupt reasoning, and a failure to understand Calvinist theology as espoused by Keach. See Arnold, 'Reformed Theology', pp. 203–5, 213.

291. *St. Paul ... subject be*: see Romans 8:7.

292. *Physician be*: see above n. 245.

293. *he's thy Royal Fort ... all iniquity*: see Psalms 18:2, 31:3, 71:3, 91:2, 144:2.

294. *Old-man*: see above n. 253.

295. *Thus whilst God's Word... this day*: on the role of the Holy Spirit in Keach's thought see Arnold, 'Reformed Theology', pp. 115–20, 158–60, 203–5.

296. *To tear thee into pieces*: cp. Psalm 7:2.

297. *jealous God*: see e.g. Exodus 20:5.

298. *That sin ... pulled out*: see Matthew 5:29–30.

299. *The Law must also unto thee be dead*: see De Laune and Keach, *Tropologia*, bk : 'Paul asserts himself to *be Dead to the Law*, Gal. 2. 19. that is, the accusation or curse of it, for he could not by that be Justified, nor did he depend upon works but upon free Grace, and so was Dead as to that hope, (viz. of a legal Justification) as a Dead man has not the power of operation, See *Rom.* 7.4.10.'

300. *When thou can'st say, I am his, and he is mine*: see Song of Solomon 2:16.

301. *Most mighty Pow'rs ... Monarchy in Hell*: cf. Lucifer: 'Most high and mighty Lords, who better fell / From Heav'n, to rise States-General of Hell': Dryden, *State of Innocence*, p. 4. In Dryden's work Hell is a republic on the Dutch model; in Keach's poem it is a monarchy.

302. *Bravely resolv'd ... our danger less*: cp. Satan: 'I agree, / With this brave Vote; and if in Hell there be / Ten more such Spirits, Heav'n is our own again: / We venture nothing, and may all obtain. / Yet who can hope but well, since ev'n Success / Makes Foes secure, and makes our danger less': Dryden, *State of Innocence*, p. 4.

303. *Kill the Old-man, O kill, O crucifie*: see Romans 6:6.

304. *The Old-man with his deeds*: see Colossians 3:9.

305. *Adorn thy self with Pearl, be deckt with Gold*: cp. the description of the Whore of Babylon: Revelation 17:4.

306. *Lusts of the eyes, and pride of life*: see 1 John 2:16.

307. *Yet tell her she's too strict, she's too precise*: cp. the words of the Apostate in Keach, *War with the Devil*, above p. 101. The godly had been called Precisians from an early stage because of their precise adherence to what they saw as the practical and theoretical consequences of their religious beliefs.

308. *All things are yours, both present and to come*: see 1 Corinthians 3:22.

309. *Hypocrite*: Keach was often exercised by the dangers of hypocrisy. See Keach, *War with the Devil*, above p. 47; B. Keach, *The Counterfeit Christian* (London: printed and are sold by John Pike ... and by the author ..., 1691).

310. *As Balaam ... no wise stand*: see Revelation 2:14; Numbers 22–25, esp. 25:1.

311. *This mortal Life's the Race*: see 1 Corinthians 9:24.

312. *My sentence ... 'tis divided*: Satan offers a version of the judgment of Solomon, but whereas Solomon's judgment was intended to identify the true mother of the child, Satan's is intended to destroy the Soul. See 1 Kings 3:16–28.

313. *Thou have light... wages of unrighteousness*: see De Laune and Keach, *Tropologia*, bk 3, p. 32: 'There is also as the effects of this Reconciliation, Peace and sweet Harmony in the Soul between all the Faculties; they do not fight as formerly one against another, the Conscience drawing one way & the will another, the Will opposing that which Con-

science would have done, the Judgment may be convinced in some measure as *Balaams* was, who cryed out that Gods wayes were best, *how Goodly are thy tents O Jacob, and thy tabernacles O Israel*, and yet the Affections may be for sin, and love the wages of unrighteousness.' The italicized quotation is from Numbers 24:5. See also 2 Peter 2:15.

314. *And say with* Peter ... *never I*: see Matthew 26:35; Mark 14:31. Peter then denied Christ three times.

315. *The Young-man ... courage blast*: see Matthew 19:16–24.

316. *The gate is strait ... begets the strife*: see Matthew 7:13–14.

317. *'Twixt Flesh and Spirit there's a constant War*: see Galatians 5:17 and Romans 8:1–13.

318. Dalilah: see above n. 249.

319. *Much like* Rebeckah's *Friends ... floods of tears*: see Genesis 24:50–61, in which, while her family seek to delay her leaving, Rebekah departs to become Isaac's wife (see above n. 255). The chapter heading of the Geneva Bible refers to Rebekah's family members of Genesis 24:50 as her 'friends'. The flesh is likened to Rebekah's friends because, although it will depart from sin, it does so only haltingly, with sadness.

320. *Like to rebellious* Saul, *they'll* Agag *spare*: see 1 Samuel 15:9.

321. *Crys out with* Sampson*, pleases me*: see Samson's reaction to the Philistine woman of Timnath: Judges 14:3.

322. *But if ... soul and spirit*: see Hebrews 4:12.

323. *Soul, touch not ... thee shine*: cp. above p. 240, n. 134.

324. *Christ he prohibits ... Earthly Treasure*: see Matthew 6:19.

325. All things to all men, that thou mayst gain some: a perversion of Paul's meaning in 1 Corinthians 9:22.

326. *And such a Legalist ... most adores*: the Soul makes the mistake of reveling in following the dictates of the Law rather than recognizing that salvation is through Christ alone. Indeed, the Soul becomes an idolator as a result of her legalism. Her vow to offer incense smacks of popery. See also n. 129 above.

327. *What, offer sacrifice to thy own Net*: see Habakkuk 1:16.

328. *What Object is't thou hast got in thine eye*: see Matthew 7:3–5 and Luke 6:41–43.

329. *To that, nay ... contract e're dost make*: see Matthew 19:29; Mark 10:29–30; Luke 18:29–30.

330. *Must have a chaste and holy Virgin-Wife*: see 2 Corinthians 11:2.

331. David*'s amaz'd ... it full well*: see Psalm 139:14.

332. *It seeks ... Soul of Man*: cp. Quarles, *Emblemes*, bk 5, IV, p. 261: 'Ev'n so my soul, being hurried here and there, / By ev'ry object that presents delight, / Fain would be setled, but she knows not where; / She likes at morning what she loaths at night, / She bows to honour; then she lends an eare. / To that sweet Swan-like voice of dying pleasure, / Then tumbles in the scatter'd heaps of treasure; / Now flatter'd with false hope; now foyl'd with fear: / Thus finding all the worlds delights to be / But empty toyes, good God, she points alone to thee.'

333. *Th' whole world ... such store*: cp. Quarles, *Emblemes*, bk 1, IV, p. 17: PUt in another weight: 'Tis yet too light: / And yet. Fond *Cupid*, put another in; / And yet another: Still there's under weight: / Put in another hundred: Put again; / Add world to world; then heap a thousand more / To that, then to renew thy wasted store, / Take up more worlds on trust, to draw thy ballance lower.'

334. *A Pearl of such great price and value*: see above n. 157.

335. *For toys and trifles should their Souls despise*: cp. Quarles, *Emblemes*, bk 5, IV, p. 261, quoted above n. 332.

336. *'Tis a first-love, as soon as he past-by*: see 1 John 4:19.
337. *'Tis a free Love ... shews to them*: see Hosea 14:4.
338. *She found it so who washt his precious feet*: see Luke 7:37–50.
339. *It is abiding and Eternal Love*: see John 13:1.
340. *I with ... (or loved) thee*: see Jeremiah 31:3.
341. *David lov'd Absalom, yet ... banishment*: see 2 Samuel 13:37–39, 14:1–21.
342. *His Love is matchless, 'tis without compare*: see Ephesians 3:17–19.
343. *Jonathan's love to David ... Love indeed*: see 1 Samuel 18:1, 18:3; 2 Samuel 1:26.
344. *O depth ... great Love*: see Ephesians 3:18.
345. *His Love is matchless ... Love unto Eternitie*: see De Laune and Keach, *Tropologia*, bk 3, pp. 17–18, for a congruent examination of Christ's love in prose, containing scriptural citations (including those cited at n. 264 above).
346. *Now her whole Souls dissolved into tears*: cp. Quarles, *Emblemes*, bk 4, XI, p. 229: 'Ev'n so my gasping soul, dissolv'd in tears, / Doth search for thee, my God'.
347. *The panting Hart ...God of Love & Grace*: see Psalm 42:1.
348. *Lusts of th' flesh*: cp. 2 Peter 2:18.
349. *But now, I find ... Lust to live*: The Holy Spirit played a key role in Keach's conception of the Covenant of Grace. As a result of Christ's sacrifice the Elect were filled with the Holy Spirit, and this 'in-dwelling of the Holy Spirit ... served as the instrument by which the Elect became "the Lord's People"'. See Arnold, 'Reformed Theology', pp. 158–60, at p. 159. Arnold quotes B. Keach, *The Display of Glorious Grace* (London: printed by S. Bridge, and sold by Mary Fabian ... Joseph Collier ... and William Marshall, 1698), p. 245.
350. *Lamb's fair Bride*: see Revelation 21:9.
351. *But wilt ... wounds that bleed*: cp. Quarles, *Emblemes*, bk 3, VI, pp. 149–50: 'These treach'rous hands that were so vainly bold / To try a thriveless combat, and to hold / Self-wounding weapons up, are now extended / For mercy from thy hand; that knee that bended / Upon her gardless guard doth now repent / Upon his naked floor; See both are bent, / And sue for pity: O my ragged wound / Is deep and desp'rate, it is drench'd and drown'd / In bloud and briny tears: It doth begin / To stink without and putrefie within / Let that victorious hand that now appears / Just in my blood, prove gracious to my tears: / Thou great preserver of presumptuous man. / What shall I do? what satisfaction can / Poor dust a ashes make? O if that bloud / That yet remains unshed were half as good / As bloud of oxen; if my death might be / An offering to attone my God and me; / I would disdain injurious life, and stand / A suiter to be wounded from thy hand. / But may thy wrongs be measur'd by the span / Of life? or balanc'd with the bloud of man? / No, no, eternal sin expects for guerdon, / Eternal penance, or eternal pardon: / Lay down thy weapons, turn thy wrath away, / And pardon him that hath no price to pay; / Enlarge that soul, which base presumption binds; / Thy justice cannot loose what mercy finds: / O thou that wilt not bruise the broken reed, / Rub not my sores, nor prick the wounds that bleed.'
352. *O let my chilled Soul feel the warm fires*: cp. Quarles, *Emblemes*, bk 4, I, p. 190: 'Sometimes a sudden flash of sacred heat / Warms my chill soul'.
353. *Of thy sweet Voice ... dear Soul*: see Quarles, *Emblemes*, bk 5, V, p. 266: 'Of thy sweet voice, and my dissolv'd desires / Shall turn a sov'reign balsome, to make whole / Those wounds my sins inflicted on thy soul.'
354. *'Tis firmer than the oath at Noah's Flood*: see Genesis 8:21, 9:8–17; Isaiah 54:9.
355. *I'le leave all for thy sake, and with thee go*: see above n. 77.

356. *Prophet, Priest and King*: see above n. 186.
357. *A precious Fountain ... wash'd away her sin*: for the image of Christ as a fountain see De Laune and Keach, *Tropologia*, bk 2, pp. 173–7 (p. 177 is mispaginated as p. 185).
358. *Then gloriously ... in her Eye*: see above n. 16.
359. *For failing ... worldly comforts took away*: Keach refers to the persecution of the godly throughout history, but also alludes specifically to the position of Restoration nonconformists.
360. *He must be crucify'd*: see above n. 192.
361. *When Man transgress'd ... curs'd the Serpent*: see Genesis 2–3, see also above p. 240, n. 134.
362. *who remains ... in lasting Chains*: see Revelation 20:2.
363. *When Cain ... sentenc'd Cain*: see Genesis 4:11–15.
364. *By me the World was drowned*: see Genesis 7–8.
365. *Proud Babels language was by me confounded*: see Genesis 11:1–9
366. *I am ... two-edg'd Sword*: see above n. 322.
367. *'Twas I ... Egyptians Land*: see Exodus 10:21–3.
368. *At my Command ... Red-Sea lost*: see Exodus 14:15–31.
369. *Belshazzers ... tremble when I spake*: see Daniel 5:6, 9.
370. *'Twas I ... Grecians from their Seat*: Keach considered the Persian and the Greek monarchies to be two of the four (the second and third respectively) monarchies that would fall before the coming of the fifth monarchy of Christ. As noted here, they had already fallen. See Arnold, 'Reformed Theology', p. 235.
371. *And at my Voice the mountains shall remove*: see Job 9:5.
372. *The Earth shall be dissolved... fervent heat*: see 2 Peter 3:10.
373. *'Tis I divide between the joints and Marrow*: see above n. 117.
374. *'Tis I alone ... bind up these wounds again*: see Job 5:17–18.
375. *May I but have one kiss*: for a discussion of 'The Kisses of Christ's Mouth' see De Laune and Keach, *Tropologia*, bk 3, pp. 41–4.
376. *May I ...choisest Wine*: see Song of Solomon 1:2.
377. *His Name is like an Ointment poured forth*: see Song of Solomon 1:3.
378. *My sacred Friend ... secret Chambers bring*: see Song of Solomon 1:4.
379. *Tell me ... soultry gleams*: see Song of Solomon 1:7.
380. *Bring me ... runs most clear*: see Song of Solomon 4:15.
381. *a lodg is also near*: see Song of Solomon 7:11.
382. *My Love shall be inclosed in my breast*: see Song of Solomon 1:13.
383. *terrors of the Night*: see Psalm 91:5.
384. *Had I all Riches ... compared to my Lord*: cp. Philippians 3:8.
385. *He is my ... loyalty appear*: Sharon Achinstein comments that: 'Here the allegory no longer identifies the soul as female. To become "all" is to divest of a particular gender marking and to assume another': Achinstein, *Literature and Dissent*, p. 199.
386. *As Jonathan's to David ... loyalty appear*: see 1 Samuel 20, 23:16–18.
387. *If cold ... Love does bear*: Again Keach refers in general to the sufferings of the godly, but alludes in particular to the position of Restoration nonconformists. See also 2 Corinthians 11:27–28.
388. *Into his Gardens ... pleasant Fruits*: see Song of Solomon 4:13, 16.
389. My well beloved's mine and I am his: see Song of Solomon 2:16 (Geneva).
390. *An Hymn of Praise to the Sacred Bridegroom*: on Christ as bridegroom see Headnote.
391. *Hector's*: Hector, Trojan hero, killed by Achilles.

392. *Cesar's*: Julius Caesar.
393. Nor one, nor all those Worthy Nine: the Nine Worthies were Hector, Alexander the Great, Julius Caesar, Joshua, David, Judas Maccabaeus, Arthur, Charlemagne and Godefroi de Bouillon.
394. *Alexander's*: Alexander the Great (356–323 BC).
395. Whose Foot-stool's here, his Throne above: see Isaiah 66:1; Acts 7:49.
396. *Cynthia*: goddess of the moon.

Mason, *In Memoriam Johannis Perrotti*

1. SWeet was thy Voice: see Song of Solomon 2:14.
2. Silver Trumpet: see Numbers 10:1–2.
3. Patience ... few do parallel: In 1657 Perrot had set out with the aim of converting the Pope (as well as the Sultan in the Ottman Empire). He arrived in Rome in 1658, where he was imprisoned and then committed to the 'Pazzarella' or 'Prison of Madmen'. There he underwent considerable physical suffering until his release mid-way through 1661. See the Headnote to J. Perrot, *A Sea of the Seed's Sufferings*, above Volume 1, p. 29 and the references cited therein.
4. *Shilohs*: Perrot used 'Shiloh (Genesis 49:10) as a name for the Messiah, present in nature, vertuous and emanating, the power which transforms nature and man': N. Smith, 'Exporting Enthusiasm: John Perrot and the Quaker Epic', in T. Healy and J. Sawday (eds), *Literature and the English Civil War* (Cambridge: Cambridge University Press, 1990), p. 258. See also the references in Perrot, *A Sea of the Seed's Sufferings*, Volume 1, p. 43.
5. Heaven-Born Seed: 'Seed' was used widely and variously within Quaker discourse. Here it refers to Perrot himself, and recalls the title of his *A Sea of the Seed's Sufferings*. On the various meanings of the term, and the ways in which they could overlap, see further the note to Perrot, *A Sea of the Seed's Sufferings*, Volume 1, p. 287, n. 2.
6. Blest let thy Memory be: see Proverbs 10:7.